COMMERCIAL LAW IN
THE SOUTH PACIFIC

This book provides a detailed examination of the core areas of commercial law in common law jurisdictions across a range of South Pacific countries: Cook Islands, Fiji Islands, Kiribati, Marshall Islands, Niue, Nauru, Samoa, Solomon Islands, Tonga, Tuvalu and Vanuatu.

Commerce is an area of central importance to the South Pacific region. Although the countries in question are small it is widely acknowledged that their need to promote and develop commercial enterprise is crucial for their future sustainability. With a focus on case law and legislative provisions in individual jurisdictions, it sets out the framework of legal principles that regulate commercial activity within the South Pacific region, highlighting the common patterns and principal differences between countries of the region. It includes a discussion of PACER Plus, post-Cotonou discussions and the EU-OACPS Partnership Agreement as well as key amendments and challenges to commercial law in the region. It explores the legal structures of commerce, control and management of commercial entities, banking and transactions and termination. Importantly, the book has two new chapters, on digital currency and e-commerce in the South Pacific, reflecting the increasing use of technology in financial and commercial transactions.

Offering a detailed analysis of the legal principles that regulate commercial activity within the South Pacific region, this book will be a useful resource for students, academics and practitioners working on commercial law in the South Pacific region.

Professor Mohammed L. Ahmadu is Vice Chancellor at Rayhaan University, Birnin Kebbi. As Professor of Law with research interests in information technology, commercial, corporate and human rights laws, amongst others, he is widely published locally and internationally, and has engaged in numerous international consultancies. He had also served as Professor of Law and Director of the Institute of Justice and Applied Legal Studies and earlier as Assistant to the Head of School at the University of the South Pacific (USP), School of Law in Oceania. During his time at USP, he wrote the first edition to *Commercial Law and Practice in the South Pacific* with the late Professor Robert A. Hughes. He also held the position of Pro Vice Chancellor, Emalus Campus, USP.

Dr Bridget Fa'amatuainu is a Law academic in the School of Law at Auckland University of Technology (AUT), who completed a PhD under the supervision of a leading torts lawyer and theorist of private law. Bridget is committed to engaging in critical legal, queer and feminist scholarship to elevate the voice and lived experiences of gender diverse communities, seeking to unravel and transform laws. Bridget's research and supervision interests include law reform with an emphasis on pacific (e.g. Talanoa) and indigenous research methodology and theory in gender and equity legal research, private law and decolonial legal pedagogy.

Routledge Research in International Commercial Law

COMMERCIAL LAW IN THE SOUTH PACIFIC

Mohammed L. Ahmadu and
Bridget Fa'amatuainu

LONDON AND NEW YORK

Designed cover image: Zolnierek / Getty Images

First published 2025
by Routledge
4 Park Square, Milton Park, Abingdon, Oxon OX14 4RN

and by Routledge
605 Third Avenue, New York, NY 10158

Routledge is an imprint of the Taylor & Francis Group, an informa business

British Library Cataloguing-in-Publication Data
A catalogue record for this book is available from the British Library

ISBN: 978-1-032-54912-5 (hbk)
ISBN: 978-1-032-54913-2 (pbk)
ISBN: 978-1-003-42806-0 (ebk)

DOI: 10.4324/9781003428060

Typeset in Times New Roman
by Deanta Global Publishing Services, Chennai, India

CONTENTS

ACKNOWLEDGMENTS

The pursuit of the second edition came about during the global COVID-19 pandemic, much inspired by a genuine commitment and enjoyment of private law in the South Pacific region, after close to 20 years since the first edition was published in 2005, with the late Professor Robert A Hughes.

We acknowledge the support of our Series Editors and Editorial Assistants (EA) at Routledge, initially Siobhán Poole and her EA, Sanjo Joseph Puthumana, and more recently, Nicola Sharpe and her EA, Diksha Bhugra, for without their continued guidance and oversight, the second edition would not have been completed. We also acknowledge all the people behind the scenes, the copy-editors, the printers and the typesetters for their hard work on this project.

Lastly, we dedicate this edition to our families and friends for their patience and understanding throughout this project.

ABBREVIATIONS

FLR	Fiji Law Reports
CI	Cook Islands
F	Fiji
FSM	Federated States of Micronesia
JSPL	Journal of South Pacific Law (electronic)
K	Kiribati
MI	Marshall Islands
N	Nauru
Ni	Niue
S	Samoa
SI	Solomon Islands
SILR	Solomon Islands Law Report
T	Tonga
Tu	Tuvalu
V	Vanuatu
WSLR	Western Samoan Law Report

TABLE OF CASES

TABLE OF LEGISLATION

Solomon Islands

Tuvalu

European and International Legislation

Directives

Treaties and Conventions

PART A

The legal structures of commerce

Introduction

In Part A of the book we will examine some of the most common legal structures that are available for the conduct of commercial enterprises and for the carrying on of business. Commerce and business are two terms that overlap considerably. We will use them interchangeably in this book. Some might dispute the merit of doing so, but we see no particular point in indulging in fine distinctions between the two terms within this book.

Much commercial and business activity is carried on by individuals who are sole traders. The same is probably as true in the South Pacific as it is in more economically developed regions, although it is to be noted that the peoples of the South Pacific, as is well established, are generally more disposed than elsewhere to community-based activity. However, it is sometimes said that real commerce begins where two or more people get together in order to combine their resources and increase their investment power by establishing some kind of common enterprise for the conduct of their business. There is strength in numbers and there are also increased profits on combined investment power.

Some of what we will be examining in this book is of as much relevance to sole traders as it is to the combined commercial endeavours of groups of individuals. In this Part we will not be paying much attention to sole traders as commercial actors. Sole traders engage in commerce through entering into contracts of various kinds, just as do large corporations and commercial trusts. What we will do is focus on some of the major legal structures that exist as the basis for the carrying on of commercial activities. In some cases, for example with respect to companies, the structure involves the creation of what is in law a new individual or a new

DOI: 10.4324/9781003428060-1

sole trader, viz the company itself. But companies also have features that compel us to recognise that they are associational structures, much as are partnerships. Trusts also in a sense involve, or can involve, an individual carrying on business on behalf of a trust, viz the trustee. But in such a case there will usually be other interests involved and these are the beneficiaries under the trust.

Thus, in this Part we will pay no more attention to the single trader than to simply acknowledge that it is one basis for carrying on business. We will look at partnerships in Chapters 1 and 2. In Chapters 3 and 4 we will look at the legal nature of trusts, particularly those used for carrying on business. In Chapters 5 and 6 we will examine the legal structure and methods of the creation of companies. Other associations such as cooperatives, friendly societies, banks and credit unions and registered associations will provide the focus for Chapter 7.

Before proceeding further, let us look at some of the issues that arise in respect of the making of choices between these various legal structures for the conduct of commerce.

The structure of commerce or business

Promoters of new commercial ventures are presented with many options as to how they might legally structure the operation of their proposed commercial enterprise. It is a relatively basic principle of law that a person can select whatever structure or combination of structures they like. That is the case even though one structure might have very different taxation and different consequences from another. In relation to taxation, there are different taxation regimes in relation to companies, trusts and partnerships. Opting for one structure will thus affect the taxation obligations both of the individual parties or investors and of the entity as a whole.

By 'other consequences' we refer to the likes of liabilities in relation to third parties as well as internal relationships. Liabilities and rights in respect of third parties are dealt with in different ways depending on whether a trust, a company or a partnership is involved. Legal managerial responsibilities will be different depending on whether it is a trustee managing a commercial trust or a board of directors managing a company. We will look at these issues later on. The different legal structures available have various advantages and disadvantages. Much depends upon factors such as the number of interested parties, the taxation benefits and the size of the operation, the involvement of the parties, management relations and the type of investment involved. In fact, it has become increasingly common to adopt a combination of different structures in a single business, as will be seen from the following discussion.

Even though there are significant differences there is still scope for choice. In respect of partnerships, there are some limitations. As we will see, partnerships of a certain size must be registered as companies. They cannot carry on business otherwise. But aside from this, generally the law respects the choice of structure made by the promoter of the business venture. In other words, in most cases, the choice of which structure to adopt is left to the promoters of the venture themselves.

However, whether the parties have in fact chosen one structure as opposed to others is not something that depends solely on the words of choice which are used. That is a matter for the courts to decide. In some cases, as with companies, cooperatives and limited liability partnerships, there are specific legal processes that must be followed in order to set up the relevant entity. In respect of trusts, joint ventures and partnerships, generally there is not. In those contexts, the parties might think they are setting out to adopt one kind of structure and actually create something of quite different legal effect.

It is a matter for the courts to determine the legal effect of the arrangement that the parties have made and to construe the negotiations and agreements of the parties accordingly. The fact that they have called their arrangement a partnership, a joint venture, a trust or something else is one factor only. It is by no means conclusive. The legal effect of what has been agreed is to be decided by the courts largely as a matter of construction.

A trust is one possible structure, as noted above. Trusts are creatures of equity rather than commercial law, although, as noted above, it is clear that, historically, trust law has made significant contributions to the law of associations, including partnership and corporations law. The parties might opt for a trust where one person holds property on behalf of the others with a power of trustee to carry on the business. The trustee might be one or more of the investing parties, some independent trustee or in fact a company. In the case of a company, it might be independently owned, or it might be one in which the investors, promoters or their relations have a shareholding or other investment interest. It could be that the trustee is a completely independent company which carries on the business of a professional trustee, or it could be a professional management company. In order to carry on business, the trustee must in the trust instrument be provided with a power to carry on business. Traditionally, as we will see, trusts were not regarded as vehicles for commercial enterprise; in fact, commercial activities were discouraged by the courts. Thus, for example, the courts prohibited the trustee from carrying on business in the absence of an explicit power to do so. Nevertheless, they were, and now frequently are, used to provide the basis for business operations.

Under a trust arrangement, the trustee holds the outward interest in the initial and accumulated property of the venture. However, the trustee is compelled to hold and deal with the trust property exclusively for the benefit of the beneficiaries. These are the persons who are regarded by the equity courts as the true 'owners' of the trust property.[1] There are, however, many different types of trust. Under some trusts, for example discretionary trusts, the interests of the beneficiaries may not be immediately vested. The entitlement of the beneficiaries to capital or income, or both, is dependent on the trustee exercising their discretion in favour of

---

1 Whether the interest of beneficiaries can be approximated to those of owners in equity is a moot point. Much depends on the type of trust involved.

some or all of the beneficiaries before they can be said to have a determinate interest. Thus, the idea that the trust beneficiaries have ownership of the trust property in equity is perhaps not as straightforward as might be thought.

Basically, however, it is the trustee or trustees of the particular trust who operate the business venture. Generally, it is not for the beneficiaries to direct the trustee as to how the business is to be carried on. The trustee is obliged to act exclusively in the interests of the beneficiaries. However, the trustee, at the same time, is required to exercise independence of judgment in determining what those best interests might be. A trustee would be in breach of trust if he or she fettered or restricted this capacity for independent judgment. The trustee is not an agent of the beneficiaries at all.

The trustee, like many other types of manager, is a fiduciary as against the beneficiaries. Indeed, the trustee falls into the highest category of fiduciary, in the sense that the trustee is required to act exclusively in the interests of the beneficiary. Partners are, as we shall see, fiduciaries of one another but they are *also* principals and agents of one another. Furthermore, as we noted above, a trust is not, unlike a partnership, a form of association at all. The beneficiaries are not legally associated with one another as are partners in a partnership. Certainly, they are related because they all have interests in the same trust institution. But being related or having common rights does not necessarily mean that there is an association in the legal sense.

Significantly, it is the trustee who carries on the business of the trust on behalf of the beneficiaries. As noted already, the beneficiaries are not participatory *members* of the trust because one can only be a member of an association. People will inevitably use membership notions to describe a trust, and we admit that there are areas of some obscurity here. It is the large public unit trust which perhaps places this notion under stress. In many respects, the position of an investor in this entity is indistinguishable in fact from the position of an investor in a large corporation. One is no less associated than the other. But in principle, beneficiaries are not members and do not have membership rights.

Given that the trustee operates the trust and the trust business, it is the trustee who enters into transactions with third parties in respect of trust transactions. It is the trustee who incurs debts and liabilities. The 'trust' does not exist as a juristic entity at all even though it might be common enough to call the trust by some name. It is the trustee who is personally liable for such debts and liabilities even though it might be clear that they were incurred on behalf of the trust rather than in the capacity of a private individual. The creditor or third party does not have to, and indeed cannot, sue the trust or the beneficiaries.

The other major choice is that of an incorporated company or some other corporate form. Companies are one form of corporation, along with cooperatives, friendly societies and the like. There are various types of company: one example is the proprietary company, in which membership is defined by the holding of shares. Such companies have the advantage of limited liability, which serves to protect directors and members or shareholders against personal liability in respect of the claims of creditors and other third parties against the company. Neither a trustee nor the partners in a partnership have this protection. This in itself might be a factor that motivates the promoters of the venture towards the incorporation of a company to run the business, especially where the proposed business involves some high degree of risk. The amount to which the member is liable to contribute is limited to the amount that remains unpaid in respect of the allotment price for the shares. Other types of company include companies limited by guarantee and no-liability companies. However, the proprietary company is the main type of company used for engaging in commercial activity. Such companies may be private or public depending on the scale of their operation.

Companies, like partnerships, are legal forms of association. However, they have a special legal status, in that when they are incorporated by a process of registration, as is required under the Companies Acts of the region, they acquire a separate legal personality which is independent of their members and the directors who control them. They are legally persons, such that it is the company that must sue or be sued concerning company matters, and it is the company itself and not the shareholders or the directors that acquires legal rights and duties in respect of matters pertaining to the company proper. The members cannot generally assert the rights of the company. That is a matter for the company itself, although in practice it is controlled by a board of directors or various other agents and organs as part of its internal management. Furthermore, as we shall see, there are occasions when the company interest or identity must be assimilated with the interest or identity of those who control it; for example, when questions of company responsibility or liability come into play.

In terms of the range of interests that fall under a company, it is clear that companies can be the vehicles for relatively small operations with a small-scale business and with few shareholders and investors. However, they can be extremely large international multi-billion-dollar operations. We normally assume that trusts are entities that relate to small-scale affairs, but whilst this might be true of family deeds of settlement of the 19th century, the assumption no longer holds sway. Trusts are frequently used for very large-scale business operations and investments. The units held by their beneficiaries are often listed on the stock exchanges. They compete intensively with companies for a share of the public investment markets around the globe.

In respect of partnerships, the usual expectation is that they relate to a relatively small association in terms of number of members. Certainly, there are some private companies with the mere minimum of two members. However, in general, the expectation is that a partnership will always be confined to a relatively small membership base. We will see in this Part that under certain circumstances an association with more than a prescribed minimum number of members must be incorporated under the provisions of the Companies Acts. If the members of the association proceed to carry on business, then they commit a breach of the Companies Acts and the association could well be regarded as a form of illegal association.

Leaving that issue aside, the selection of a partnership versus a company is a matter of choice for those promoting or setting up the arrangement in the first place. The relative advantages of each have to be considered. The limited liability of a company and the separate juristic identity achieved on incorporation is a considerable advantage of the company structure. Partnerships and trusts, as we shall see, do not give rise to any separate legal identity. They remain aggregations of the individual partners who are members of them. Each of the partners is a fiduciary and an agent of each of the other partners. The trustee is a fiduciary of the beneficiaries. Both structures give rise to expectations of a high degree of trust and confidence between the parties.[2]

Whilst a company has the advantage of limited liability and separate legal identity, as well as a relatively streamlined administrative and management structure, a partnership or a trust might be much more appropriate in some circumstances. This might be the case where the members of the association are members of a family or are relatively well known to each other. Likewise, it will be appropriate where the operation is a small one. In some instances, particular businesses cannot be incorporated at all. Professions – law, medicine, accounting and others – have long shied away from allowing their professionals to incorporate, although this is no longer entirely the case. It was a policy founded in the nature of the professional relationship with clients and between members of the profession themselves. The corporate form has often been perceived as remote from the essential types of relationship involved here.

There have been changes here, given that many such professional firms are now very large in terms of membership, and the nature of professional practice, including relationships with clients, has been undergoing transformation. Professional services are now seen as just one range of services that are available to the market and the consuming public. In jurisdictions such as the United Kingdom, Canada, Australia and New Zealand, the partnership legislation has been amended to provide for limited partnerships which have some of the benefits of incorporation. These partnerships have been extended to professional partnerships of the types mentioned. Because a limited partnership is not a legal entity capable of holding and conveying title to real property, it is often the case that provision is made in the Limited Partnerships Act for a general partner to conduct and manage the business of the limited partnership, including acquiring and conveying real property on its behalf.[3]

Singularity of the business to be conducted is not an issue in respect of any of the business structures we will discuss. Companies, many other corporate forms,

---

2 For an exposition of the relative values of the various commercial structures, see the judgment of King CJ of the Supreme Court of the Federated States of Micronesia in *Mid-Pac Construction Co Inc v Senda* [1990] FMSC 23; 4 FSM Intrm 376 (Pon. 1990) (14 December 1990) 23.

3 See *Kucor Construction & Developments & Associates v Canada Life Assurance Co* (1998) 167 DLR (4th) 272 (Ont CA) at 287.

trusts and partnerships can carry on several different businesses under the one roof, so to speak. For partnerships, it was common in the past for professional partnerships, such as those in law and accounting, to be confined to the carrying on of a single or single type of business. This is a matter of complying with requirements from the professional bodies rather than anything arising out of partnership law. However, even here some countries have developed notions of partnerships between different professions or disciplines and thus multi-disciplinary professional partnerships have emerged.[4]

Whether such a development is likely or desirable for the South Pacific countries is reasonably unclear. Partnerships have long been regarded as the primary vehicle of small business operations and thus their role in developed as also in developing economies is seen as a vital one. Large international partnerships are making their mark, although sometimes this gives rise to confusion on conflict-of-laws issues, as is illustrated in the Vanuatu case of *Hill v KPMG*,[5] where there was an element of indeterminacy as to the proper forum for a large international accounting firm with offices in several countries.

Combinations of structures

Aside from selecting just one structure, it is possible that entrepreneurs might seek to combine several of them. Some instances of this have already been indicated. A company might be a trustee of a trust. That company on behalf of the trust might enter into partnership with other companies or corporate entities as well as natural individuals. Companies can be beneficiaries of trusts. Trusts can be created over the shares or debentures of particular investors in companies. Individuals might form a partnership and then arrange for a company to run the partnership business under a licence or some such arrangement, or otherwise manage it. Partnerships can be intermingled with joint ventures.

The choice of a particular structure can sometimes have an undesirable effect on the rights of creditors to recover their debts. One common form is where a trust is created with a limited liability company as the trustee. Companies of this kind can have a very limited paid-up share capital. Limited liability means that the liability of the shareholders in the company is limited to the amount unpaid on their shares. In respect of trust debts, the creditors have rights of recovery against the trustee personally. Under some circumstances where the trustee fails to pay, the creditors have subrogation rights against either the trust assets or the beneficiaries personally. Subrogation gives them the right to the trustee's own right of indemnity, but only so far as those rights of indemnity still actually exist. It appears that

---

4 See Gallagher, H, 'United we stand ... multi-disciplinary partnerships' (1995) 69 LIJ No 1, January, pp 10–11.
5 [2000] VUSC 54; Civil Case 105 of 1997 (18 October 2000).

the trustee's rights of indemnity can be excluded by the trust deed.[6] A combination of both factors – a trustee company with little capital, as well as a trust with an appropriate exclusion clause – could produce a situation where creditors of the business entity are precluded from all rights of recourse in respect of their debts. As Ford comments, this serves as a limitation of the rights of recovery of creditors, which is far more radical in its implications than the principle of limited liability of a company.

These are a few of the possible permutations. Some might approximate contrivances for taxation or estate-duty purposes. Others might have greater legitimacy. The result of the complexity that occurs here is that it will be difficult to disentangle the arrangements that have been established in order to work out the rights and liabilities of those involved. To take one point of illustration, it could be that something that was once intended as a partnership was in fact run through the medium of a company or perhaps a trust. The court will have to decide what the overall effect of this is and which body of law, partnership, company or trust law should apply in order to sort out the rights of the parties in the event that the operation malfunctions in some way.

Let us look at one example. In the decision of the High Court of Ireland in *Morgan v Murray and Milton*,[7] there was just such a problem of disentangling a partnership from a company that had run the partnership business. The plaintiff – one of the partners – brought an action under the Companies Act 1963 but also brought a partnership action seeking an injunction against the other parties to prevent them from offloading assets of the partnership. It was alleged that the partnership was set up before the company and continued to subsist despite the company becoming the medium to carry on the business. The defendants, the two other partners, denied that there was a separate partnership. They also sought to rely to some extent on s 1(2) of the Partnership Act 1890 (Ireland), which states that 'the relation between members of any company or association which is registered as a company … is not a partnership within the meaning of this Act'.

The plaintiff's claim was struck out on the basis that the court found that the company was intended to be the entire medium of the relationship between the three 'partners'. There was no other relationship between the three 'partners' that could be held to constitute a partnership. His Honour gave apparent approval in part to the comments of Murphy J in *Crindle Investments v Wymes*, where it was held that "the undertaking was conceived and consciously promoted in the form of a company incorporated under the Companies Act 1963, and it was the requirements of that legislation which governed the relationship between the parties".[8]

---

6 See *MacLean v Burns Philp Trustee Company Ltd* [1985] 2 NSWLR 623; *Helvetic Investment Corp Pty Ltd v Knight* (1982) 7 ACLR 225.

7 [1999] IEHC 65.

8 [1998] 4 IR 567 at 576.

1

PARTNERSHIP

1.1 Legal partnerships

Although a statutory legal definition of partnership is frequently referred to as 'the firm' (most notably in section 4 of the Partnership Act 1975 (Vanuatu)) or by some registered business name, there is no separate legal personality involved. The relations between partners are essentially dealt with under the law of agency. As we will see in due course, the relationship is expected to be one of the highest confidence and trust between the partners.

There is evidence of the existence of partnerships in a sophisticated form in older cultures such as that of Babylon.[1] Roman law treated several possible forms of partnership under the general heading of *societas*.[2] They were all forms of contract created by consent or agreement. No particular form such as writing was then required in order to create a partnership.[3] This remains a common feature in most contemporary legal systems, presumably as this facilitates the formation of commercial enterprises.[4] The law of partnerships in the South Pacific countries closely follows that of other common law countries. The Partnership Acts in the

---

1 Johns, CHW, *Babylonian and Assyrian Laws*, 1904, New York, Kessinger Publishing, pp 287, 290, 291.
2 Pothier, RJ, *Pandectae Justinianeae*, LXVII, Tit II. See also the Catholic Encyclopedia, at: www .newadvent.org/cathen/1150aa.htm.
3 They were perfected by consent alone – *qui nudo consensu perficiuntur*, in *Pandectae, ibid. The Commentaries of Gains*, III, 1874, Cambridge, pp 135–36, quoted in the Catholic Encyclopedia, *ibid*.
4 Except those acquired from France, Holland and Spain. See Burge, W, *Commentaries on Colonial and Foreign Laws*, 1907, London, at: www.newadvent.org/catnen/11509a.htm, pp 1, 7, 8.

DOI: 10.4324/9781003428060-2

South Pacific countries are taken from the UK Partnership Act 1890 with little variation or adaptation.

Unlike companies and other corporations, on formation of a partnership no separate legal identity is brought into being. A partnership is usually not incorporated.[5] It is, in effect, an aggregation of the partners as individuals. Although a partnership is frequently referred to as 'the firm' or by some registered business name, there is no separate legal personality involved. It is the partners together who own the partnership business and who incur liabilities in respect of its operation.

The relations between partners are essentially dealt with under the law of agency. As we will see in due course, the relationship is expected to be one of the highest confidence and trust between the partners. Throughout the term of the partnership, and within the scope of the partnership, each partner is 'virtually both a principal and an agent'.[6] The sense of this is that, as a principal, each partner binds himself or herself, whilst, as an agent, he or she binds all partners in transactions which take place within the scope of authority of the partnership. If, for example, a partner buys property or sells partnership property, normally that transaction will bind the other partners and the transacting partner as members of the partnership. The proviso is that the transaction has to be within the course and scope of the business of the firm.

According to Lindley, '[the] terms partnership and partner are evidently derived from *to part* in the sense of to divide amongst or share'.[7] Perhaps this would be better expressed in the sense of taking part or participating in a common enterprise, because essentially that is what a partnership involves in so far as partners are members of an association. The word 'co-partnership' was once employed in English law to refer to co-ownership of property, but this is now redundant.

A partnership is one type of legal association of persons, as indeed are companies and cooperatives. A partnership is an association that is established to engage in commercial activity. The legal sense of the term 'partnership' is employed just for this purpose, viz engaging in business or commerce. The terms 'partnership' and 'association' might be employed for other non-commercial purposes, but in partnership law they have this sense and no other.

The commercial element of a partnership is that there is some degree of expectation that the parties have joined into association for the purpose of making a profit. It does not particularly matter what activities are to be undertaken to earn, or attempt to earn, that profit, although where the purposes are illegal the validity of the partnership could be affected. The commercial focus does not have to relate to buying or selling. It can just as readily be for professional services, such as those conducted by dentists, architects, lawyers or medical practitioners. Whatever the

---

5 That remains generally true in the South Pacific, although see further below.
6 *Cox v Hickman* (1860) 8 HLC 312 at 313.
7 Lindley, R, *The Law of Partnership*, 13th edn, 1971, London, Sweet and Maxwell, p 10 or 13.

particular type of activity involved, it does not really matter whether a profit is actually made at any time. In fact, there might be a partnership which continually makes a loss.

Partnerships are sometimes known by the names of the partners themselves. On the other hand, there might be a firm name. The name can be established by agreement or can be acquired by usage. Registration of the business name is generally necessary to comply with Business Names legislation applicable in the South Pacific countries.[8] Whilst partnerships are regarded fundamentally as aggregations of individual partners without attributing any juridical status to the partnership or group as such, the legislation conventionally has permitted partners to sue and be sued in the name of the partnership. This is largely a matter of procedural and administrative convenience. It does not amount to a conferral of corporate status on the partnership as an 'entity', although sometimes it has been contended that it does.

The Partnerships legislation employs the term 'firm' in relation to a partnership. This is, of course, conventional terminology for a commercial association. Section 4 of the Partnership Act of Vanuatu defines a 'firm' in this context in the following way:

4 Persons who have entered into partnership with one another are for the purposes of this Part called collectively a firm, and the name is called the firm-name.[9]

As to the question of liability between partners, s 9 of the same Act provides that the liability is effectively joint liability with the other partners:

9 Every partner in a firm is liable jointly with the other partners for all debts and obligations of the firm incurred while he is a partner; and after his death his estate is also severally liable in a due course of administration for such debts and obligations, so far as they remain unsatisfied, but subject to the prior payment of his separate debts.[10]

Section 10 of same Act provides:

10 Where by any wrongful act or omission of any partner acting in the ordinary course of the business of the firm, or with authority of his co-partners, loss or

---

8 See fn 9 below.

9 Registration of Business Names Act: s 2 (F), (N), (SI), (K); s 7 (CI), (Ni), (Tu); s 4 Partnership Act (UK) (SI), (K), (T).

10 Section 9 (N), (S), (V); s 12 (Tu), (Ni), (CI); s 12 Partnership Act 1890 (UK) (K), (T), (SI); see *African Pacific (Singapore) Ltd v Kalnpel* [2015] VUSC 84; CC 27 of 2013 (3 July 2015) – ss 9 and 12 of the Partnership Act are applicable in this case.

injury is caused to any person not being a partner in the firm, or any penalty is incurred the firm is liable therefor to the same extent as the partner so acting or omitting to act.[11]

Section 12 of that Act goes on:

> 12 Every partner is liable jointly with his co-partners and also severally for everything for which the firm while he is a partner therein becomes liable under either of Section 10 and 11.[12]

Although a partnership is not a juristic entity, and does not have legal personality as such, it can be assimilated to a legal person for some purposes. For example, on the basis of the above and other provisions in the Partnership Act of Vanuatu,[13] the Supreme Court of Vanuatu held in *McCormack v Barret and Sinclair*[14] that a partnership clearly fell within the provisions of the High Court (Civil Procedure) Rules 1964, Ord 33 r 5. That rule provided:

> 5 If any party to a cause or matter be a body corporate or a joint-stock company, whether incorporated or not, or any other body or persons, empowered by law to sue or be sued whether in its own name or in the name of any officer or other person, any opposite party may apply for an order allowing him to deliver interrogatories to any member or officer of such corporation, company, or body, and an order may be made accordingly.

In the state of Truk, in the Federated States of Micronesia, it has been held that a partnership with power to sue in the name of the association could be regarded as a citizen of the state for certain purposes. However, this would not extend to the likes of a joint venture without the powers to sue or be sued in the name of the

---

11 Section 10 (N), (S), (V); s 13 (Tu), (Ni), also see Partnership Application Act 1994 (CI); s 13 Partnership Act 1890 (UK) (SI), (K), (T).
12 Section 12 (N), (S), (V); s 15 (Ni), also see Partnership Application Act 1994 (CI), (Tu); s 15 Partnership Act 1890 (UK) (SI), (K), (T).
13 Which are common to other South Pacific jurisdictions.
14 [1998] VUSC 63; on appeal [1999] VUCA 11. See also the decision of the Ontario Court of Appeal in *Kucor Construction & Developments & Associates v Canada Life Assurance Co* (1998) 167 DLR (4th) 272 (Ont CA) at 289–90, which agreed with this view, citing the Ontario equivalent of the above provision. Recently, in the matter of fraudulent misrepresentation, Porter QC DCJ relied on [1999] VUCA 11 in *Wylie v Orchard (No 2)* [2020] QDC 315 at 156, arguing that fraud resulted in the total absence of consideration, in that 'there was the taking of something without something in return. In every case, a proprietary remedy was appropriate'. In Vanuatu, however, recent cases do not refer to this case for contractual matters but rather issues concerning witness evidence submitted in Court (*Mafe v Komi* [2020] VUSC 59; Civil Appeal Case 814 of 2019 (28 April 2020)).

association and without limited liability of the individual members of the association, even though its principal place of business is in the state.[15]

For conflict of laws purposes, the partnership will sometimes be viewed as if it were one individual entity rather than an aggregation of individuals, as is normally the case. Benson J of the Federated States of Micronesia in *International Trading Corp v Hitec and Toe Joint Venture* said:

> The general rule in the United States is that the citizenship of the members of a partnership or joint venture is examined to determine whether diversity of citizenship exists. The rule has been questioned in some cases in which the association has significant aspects which make it more akin to corporations than an association of individuals. Examples of aspects which the courts have found significant are the power to sue and to be sued in the name of the association, and the limited liability of the individual members of the association.[16]

Expressions such as 'partnership' and 'firm' tend to be used interchangeably. 'Firm' appears originally to have signified the collective aspects of the partnership.[17] However, given the feature we have just mentioned, the collective aspects of a partnership are an uncertain point of reference. On the other hand, civil law systems have been happy enough to accord even the unincorporated partnership some kind of collective existence. In common legal systems, all of the property of the firm, including stock in trade, is owned by the partners jointly. For the most part, it is the partners individually who are bearers of rights and duties concerning partnership matters. It is to be noted, however, that the Business Names legislation accords certain rights to a firm to sue and be sued in its own name. This will be discussed later on.

In a partnership it is usually expected that each of the partners contributes something of value to the partnership capital to enable the business enterprise to be carried on. However, the contribution of one of the partners could be in terms of monetary contributions alone and the other or others in terms of skill alone. The

---

15 *International Trading Corp v Hitec Corp* 4 FSM Intrm. 1, 2–3 (Truk 1989); *International Trading Corp v Hitec and Toe Joint Venture* [1989] FMSC. In FSM, this case has been most applicable in matters concerning joint ventures and diversity jurisdiction: *Geoffrey Hughes (Export) Pty Ltd v America Ducksan Co Ltd* [2004] FMSC 18; 12 FSM Intrm. 413 (Chk. 2004) (2 April 2004); *FSM Development Bank v Ehsa* [2013] FMSC 18; 18 FSM Intrm. 608 (Pon. 2013) (19 March 2013).

16 *Ibid.*

17 See Lindley, *op cit* fn 7. The idea of indigenous communities establishing unincorporated partnerships with implications for deep sea mining in the Oceanic region and opportunities with the developer company to own shares in parent companies rather than acquiring an equity stake for developer companies was explored in: Anthony Kung, Sarah Holcombe, Joel Hamago & Deanna Kemp (2022) 'Indigenous co-ownership of mining projects: a preliminary framework for the critical examination of equity participation', *Journal of Energy & Natural Resources Law*, 40:4, 416, DOI: 10.1080/02646811.2022.2029184

partnership agreement (and it is conventional, though not essential, to have a written one) will normally allocate the relative values to be accorded to the partners' contributions in whatever form.

As just noted, a partnership is an association for the carrying on of business. This commercial character is retained in the statutory definition of a partnership, which we will examine in a moment. Partnerships are created by contract and hence are consensual creations. They generally give rise to relationships between the partners that are, from the point of view of the law, fiduciary in nature. Hence there are special legal duties imposed on the partners. We will examine this more fully later on. However, partnership relations are not entirely distinguished by this special type of relationship. In fact, they apply to persons who manage companies and trusts, as well as a variety of other types of enterprise. For example, a joint venture,[18] which is not a partnership, can still give rise to fiduciary relationships, but the relationships are different in their nature and scope from those in respect of a partnership. In *Schipp v Cameron* it was said:

> In the absence of a finding that a joint venture constituted a partnership in the eyes of the law, any fiduciary relationship which may arise out of the joint venture agreement is limited to a certain extent. It will not circumscribe a fiduciary in a joint venture relationship in all areas of commercial activity in which that participant might be involved: *Hospital Products Ltd v United States Surgical Corp* at 97, 102 and 123; *Pacific Coal Pty Ltd v Idemitsu (Qld) Pty Ltd*. In general, participants in a joint venture are free to pursue their own interests and to compete in areas outside the scope of the venture. ... The scope and content of the fiduciary duties arising out of a non-partnership joint venture are to be determined by the terms of the agreement and/or the nature of the relationship between the parties. Clauses in the joint venture agreement are the principal source of any fiduciary obligations which may exist between the participants in the joint venture. Contractual and fiduciary relationships between the same parties may co-exist, provided that there is no inconsistency between the two sets of obligations.[19]

The legal definition of a partnership appears in the respective Partnership Acts[20] that apply in the South Pacific jurisdictions (see below). We should note, perhaps, that the legal relationship between partners is a formal one, which the law puts in terms of the language of rights, duties, liabilities and powers. However, the law has never been able to retreat entirely into an empty formalism when considering

---

18 Joint ventures are discussed further below.
19 [1998] NSWSC 997, paras 729 (as per Einstein J).
20 Partnership Acts: s 1 (V); s 2 (N), (F); s 4 (CI), (Ni), (S), (Tu); s 135 (MI); s 1 Partnership Act 1890 (UK) (K), (T), (SI).

the nature of the relationships between particular partners. It has very often had to determine whether a partnership or some other relationship is brought into being by looking closely at the substance of the transactions and negotiations which have taken place in the formation of the partnership.[21]

1.1.1 Partnerships and other commercial associations and entities

As will already be apparent, a partnership is not the only vehicle that the law provides for the carrying on business as some kind of joint enterprise. Leaving aside sole traders, the law provides a choice between various institutions, some of which are associations and some of which are not. A trust can be the vehicle for either investment or the carrying on of business. A trust is not an association but an arrangement for the holding of property.

The beneficiaries under a trust are not, according to James LJ in the leading authority of *Smith v Anderson*,[22] persons who are members of any association at all. Amongst associations there are companies, friendly societies, clubs, cooperatives, joint ventures and partnerships. Many of these have the legal status of incorporation. Partnerships and joint ventures are not usually incorporated, but there are exceptions to this.[23] Joint ventures are not incorporated at all. Clubs need not be incorporated, but where the club engages in a particular business activity – for example, so-called registered clubs in Australia and New Zealand where liquor is consumed and gambling takes place – registration is required under special legislation. In respect of partnerships, the law permits partnerships to sue and be sued in their own registered business name, but this does not make the partnership an incorporated entity or a juristic person. The unincorporated nature of a partnership remains and influences the nature of the legal relationships involved in a partnership. In particular it determines how the 'partnership' (i.e. the partners) relate to the outside world, particularly to the third parties with whom they deal. Each partner is treated, in effect, as both the principal and the agent of every other partner as regards the partnership business. In one sense the absence of corporate status for partnerships deprives them of commercial advantages as against corporations because they lack the corporate veil which often protects interests in the venture from liability to outsiders.

Just as equity and particularly the law of trusts contributed, especially in the 19th century, to the development of the limited liability company, so also has equity contributed over a long period of time to the articulation of the nature of a

---

21 See e.g. the comments of Teague J in *Hanlon v Brookes* [1996] ATPR 41–523 at pp 42715 ff, also finding that a clear obligations falls on the partners owing a fiduciary duty to each other to disclose all information regarding the property or transaction, and to maintain proper accounting records in fulfilment of their fiduciary duty; and *Johnson v Sneddon and Others* [1999] VSC 243.

22 (1880) 15 ChD 725, and see below.

23 See below.

partnership, and particularly to the nature of the relationship which exists between partners. The partnership as an association was recognised by the common law, but equity added considerably to our current understanding of the association. Partnerships are now to some extent regulated by legislation. Yet the role both of the common law and of equity is explicitly preserved. For example, s 46 of the Partnership Act of Fiji provides:

> 46 The rules of equity and of common law applicable to partnership shall continue in force except in so far as they are inconsistent with the express provisions of this Act.[24]

1.1.2 Limited liability partnerships

Legislation has been introduced in many jurisdictions to allow partnerships to acquire some of the features of limited liability companies; in particular the benefits of incorporation and the application of the limited liability principle itself. These entities are called limited liability partnerships.[25] Limited liability partnerships are a newer form of business entity with unlimited capacity.[26] However, at the same time, the members of a limited liability partnership can define by agreement between themselves the substantive relationship between them, just as partners do in a normal partnership. A limited liability partnership is a separate legal entity 'owned' by the members themselves. The limited liability partnership is able to continue in existence independent of underlying changes in membership which occur from time to time. Legislation has not yet been introduced in the South Pacific jurisdictions to permit the registration of limited liability partnerships. However, there is provision for the creation of entities called 'international partnerships' or 'limited partnerships' or 'limited liability partnerships' in some jurisdictions.[27]

1.1.3 International partnerships or limited partnerships

Two South Pacific countries have introduced legislation allowing the incorporation of partnerships called variously 'international partnerships' and 'limited partnerships'. The purpose of this legislation is to facilitate the creation of venture capital partnerships with international participants. Similar legislation exists in

---

24 Partnership Acts 1910 (Cap 248): s 46 (F); s 3 (S), (Ni), (Tu), (CI); s 45 (N), (V), last updated on 1 December 2017; s 46 Partnership Act 1890 (UK) (K), (SI), (T).

25 See e.g. in the United Kingdom at the present time ss 1, 2, 5 Limited Liability Partnerships Act 2000; Limited Liability Partnerships Regulations 2001; Limited Liability Partnerships (Fees) (No 2) Regulations 2001.

26 See e.g. s 1 Limited Liability Partnerships Act 2000 (UK).

27 Samoa's Trustee Companies Act 2017 and Tax Information Exchange Act 2012 recognise LLPs.

some South Pacific countries with respect to international trusts and companies.[28] Such partnerships enjoy certain exemptions from taxation and other benefits and are seen as a means of attracting investment into the smaller economies of the countries concerned. For example, the International Partnership and Limited Partnerships Act 1998[29] of Samoa permits the formation of international or limited partnerships. For the purposes of the Act, a partnership means, subject to certain exemptions, a partnership, joint venture, syndicate or association entered into for the purpose of carrying on a business or a single transaction with a view to a profit and evidenced by an instrument.[30] An international partnership is defined in s 8 as:

a partnership that is registered under this Act and in respect of which –

(a) all of the partners are at all times non-resident; and

(b) the partnership or limited partnership does not carry on business or engage in a trade in Samoa; and

(c) one of the partners of the international partnership or one of the general partners of the limited partnership is either:

(i) an international company;

(ii) a foreign company;

(iii) a trustee company

Section 16 of that Act provides for the constitution of a limited partnership. It must consist of one or more persons, called general partners, who shall, in the event that the assets of the firm are inadequate, be liable for all its debts and obligations, along with one or more persons called limited partners. These limited partners must, at the time of entering into the partnership, contribute capital or property valued at a stated amount. They are not liable for the debts or obligations of the firm, except as provided in the partnership agreement or as provided in ss 19 and 26 of the Act. A general partner may also take an interest in the same firm as a limited partner. A general partner must at all times act in good faith in the interests of the firm.

A body corporate with or without limited liability and a partnership may be either a general or a limited partner. All of the property of a firm held by or on behalf of any one or more of its general partners or the firm name is deemed to be held by the general partners jointly and severally, upon trust as an asset of the firm in accordance with the terms of the partnership agreement. Section 16(5) provides

---

28 International Companies Act 1981–82; International Trusts Act 1984 (CI); International Business Companies Act 1994 (Ni); International Companies Act 1988 (S); International Companies Act 1992 (V).

29 See also the International Partnership Act 1984 (CI).

30 Section 2 International Partnership and Limited Partnerships Act 1998 (S). This relies on a more general definition of a partnership whilst also including other entities.

that any debt or obligation incurred by a general partner in the course or conduct of the business of a firm shall be a debt or obligation of that firm.

Specific privileges and exemptions are set out in Part V of the legislation. These mainly include exemptions from taxation stamp duties and similar imposts, and exemption from the filing of returns.

1.1.4 Partnership law in the South Pacific

The South Pacific countries have generally adopted legislation based on the Partnership Act 1890 of the United Kingdom as providing the major source of partnership law within their jurisdictions. The common law and doctrines of equity are generally imported as part of the original received law within the countries concerned at the end of colonial rule and on the attaining of independence. Sometimes this has been modified in various ways, but not generally so in the area of partnership law.

However, in partnership law generally, much has been left to the supposed agreement by the parties to form the partnership. Considerable freedom has been accorded to them to determine their own arrangement, and the courts will enforce those terms where possible. The same assumptions are largely found in the Partnership Acts, where very often provisions are said to apply only if the agreement does not provide otherwise. As was said in *Maillie v Swanney & Ors*:[31]

> [The] Partnership Act 1890 recognises throughout the scope for parties to regulate their relationships and interests by agreement. Business activities and the approaches individuals adopt to the conduct of business are almost infinitely variable and the 19th century Parliament, with commendable restraint, avoided prescription in many situations where there might have been a temptation to impose restrictive or regulatory solutions. In such a context there is a risk of error if one attempts to develop an over-rationalised analysis of the provisions of the Act.

Fiji has enacted the Partnership Act Cap 248. This Act is largely a direct copy of the original UK legislation. In Nauru the Partnership Act (UK) is specifically excluded by operation of the Customs and Adopted Laws Act 1972, s 6 and First Schedule, cl (1). However, Nauru has its own Partnership Act (No 22/76). Vanuatu has its own partnership legislation based largely on the UK model: the Partnership Act Cap 92.

The Solomon Islands has no Partnership Act of its own, which raises the question of application of the English Act of the 19th century. Current authority

---

31 [2000] SLT 464, Penrose L.

might suggest that if, say, the United Kingdom Companies Act does not apply,[32] then neither does the Partnership Act. The latter, however, is in most respects merely a consolidating statute. It does not appear to be restricted to regulating conduct or conditions peculiar to persons, activities or institutions in the United Kingdom.[33] It cannot be denied that the general principles of partnership and particularly the doctrines of equity were absorbed as part of the law of England prior to independence.

None of this should imply that the Partnership Acts of the respective jurisdictions are the sole sources of partnership law as such. Partnerships for specific business purposes are often dealt with in other legislation. For example, in Vanuatu the Foreign Investment Act No 25 of 2019 (as amended) purports to regulate the right of Vanuatu citizens to enter into joint ventures, partnerships and other associations with foreign investors, and their composition.[34] In Samoa the International Banking Act 2005 prohibits a partnership and indeed anything other than a company from eligibility to hold a licence under the Act.[35] There are numerous other specific provisions of this nature. Notwithstanding these, the primary concern of this book will be with the provisions of the Partnership Acts.

1.2 The institutional and contract theories of partnership

It was noted above that a partnership at law is a special type of association, viz one which involves two or more persons carrying on business activity. Furthermore, it is generally conceived as an aggregation of individuals rather than a unified or singular legal entity, such as is a company or a corporation. As we will see in due course, there are some limitations to this second notion because sometimes the courts have felt compelled to treat a partnership for some purposes as if it were a singular entity.

One issue in partnership law, which will be dealt with more fully later on, is just how the law approaches the nature of a partnership. There are legal definitions provided by the statutes, which we will look at in a moment. However, there are also some more fundamental questions as to the nature of a partnership. There is a dispute about how they are to be conceived in legal theory, and there are two dominant views which are not compatible with each other. They affect the approach to certain questions about the nature of the relationship once it has been created, and also affect how the law is to approach questions of rights and duties of the partners.

The more traditional view is that a partnership is an institution of the law (the institutional theory). A partnership is thought to have certain fundamental,

---

32 See *Indian Printing and Publishing v Police* [1932] 2 FLR 142.

33 *R v Ngena* [1983] SILR1.

34 See s 1A (1)–(3).

35 Repealed the Off-shore Banking Act 1988 (SI).

defining features without which any association could not be a partnership. It is thought that we need to maintain this approach in order to be able to distinguish conceptually between what is a legal partnership and what is not. A joint venture is not a partnership because there are certain conceptual criteria involved to enable the courts to distinguish between the two. But that is only part of the story. The institutional view is that there are fundamental or essential aspects of the partnership as an institution. If those features are removed, the institution cannot survive as a partnership. Fundamental obligations of partners in terms of their relationship in a partnership institution, for example, cannot be excluded. There are certain rights and obligations which they must have as a result of their becoming partners. These are implied by the nature of the institution.

The other view is called the contract or contractarian view. It is more recent and emphasises the consensual creation of the partnership. The view is influenced by Law and Economics thinking, and perhaps other anti-essentialist and even anti-positivist views of law. The view here, to put it simply, is that if the partnership arises by consent or agreement between the partners then the agreement itself determines what the rights, duties and liabilities of the partners are. One does not posit some institutional archetype of a partnership and then impute fundamental rights and obligations to the participant parties.

1.2.1 Statutory definition of partnership

A partnership is defined in the Partnership Acts of the various South Pacific countries. For example, s 1 of the Partnership Act Cap 92 of Vanuatu adopts a provision common throughout the region. It defines a partnership in the following terms:

> 1 Partnership is the relation which subsists between persons carrying on a business (which expression shall include every trade, occupation or profession) in common with a view of profit, but the relationship between members of any company or association which is: –
>
> (a) registered as a company under the Companies Act Cap 191 or any other Act for the time being in force relating to the registration of joint stock companies;
> (b) formed or incorporated by or in pursuance of any Act of the Parliament of the Republic of Vanuatu

is not a partnership within the meaning of this part.[36]

---

36 Partnership Acts: s 1 (V); s 2 (N), (F); s 4 (CI), (Ni), (S), (Tu); s 135 (MI); s 1 Partnership Act 1890 (UK) (K), (T), (SI).

The exception in respect of registered or incorporated companies is to be noted. Entities such as trusts are not within the definition. Some associations which would otherwise be partnerships must be incorporated as companies. Associations, the number of members of which exceeds a prescribed minimum, must be incorporated, otherwise the association will be an illegal one.[37]

The ways in which partnership is approached for the purposes of the Partnership Acts and those for other purposes, for example taxation legislation, differ on some fine details. The purpose of income tax legislation is to set out a regime for the collection and payment of taxation. Different regimes exist for companies as opposed to trusts and partnerships. It is a common approach to the taxation of partnerships that the partnership will be treated as if it were an independent entity, especially for the purposes of calculation and collection of income tax. This, however, does not affect the general law position which holds that partnerships are, except in the case of limited or incorporation partnerships, merely aggregations of individual partners without any separate legal identity. It can be noted, however, that these regimes also vary somewhat from one jurisdiction to another.

In the Australian authority of *South Sydney District Rugby League Football Club Ltd v News Ltd* it was said:

> The definition of a partnership for the purposes of general law and that used for taxation purposes often varies. The latter usually includes any arrangement whereby income is received by an association of two or more persons jointly. But something more is required by the common law definition of a partnership and that adopted by the Partnership Acts of the various jurisdictions. ... Sometimes the income tax legislation creates the impression that a partnership is to be treated as an incorporated entity but the courts have shied away from treating it as such so as to maintain its common law sense as a mere aggregate of the individual partners[38]

---

37 See the Introduction, where the relevant provision in the Kiribati legislation is quoted. One can compare a civil law conception partnership with that under the Vanuatu definition above. For example, that in the Quebec Civil Code also regards companies as partnerships, although with legal personality: "2186 A contract of partnership is a contract by which the parties, in a spirit of cooperation, agree to carry on an activity, including the operation of an enterprise, to contribute thereto by combining property, knowledge or activities and to share any resulting pecuniary profits. A contract of association is a contract by which the parties agree to pursue a common goal other than the making of pecuniary profits to be shared between the members of the association".

38 [2000] FCA 1541, *News Ltd v South Sydney District Rugby League Football Club Ltd* [2003] HCA 45; (2003) 215 CLR 563 (13 August 2003). See also *Henderson v Federal Commissioner of Taxation* (1970) 119 CLR 612 at para 6, cited recently in *The Buddhist Society of Western Australia Inc v Commissioner of Taxation* (No 2) [2021] FCA 1363 at para 29, 30; *Rose v FCT* (1951) 84 CLR at 124, cited recently in *Jamsek v ZG Operations Australia Pty Ltd* (No 3) [2023] FCAFC 48 at para 42.

1.2.2 Elements of the legal definition

A partnership is formed when an entity that complies with all of the elements of the statutory definition comes into existence. However, it should be noted that, on the traditional analysis, what comes into existence is something more than a mere contract, association or agreement. The relationship between the partners is a special one, involving mutuality and interdependence. It is also one where the parties are deemed to be fiduciaries of one another. As it was put by Bacon, VC in *Helmore v Smith:*

> Each member of a partnership owes fiduciary obligations to act in the joint interests of the partners in relation to the conduct of the business of the partnership and in respect of its assets.[39]

The parties to the arrangement may have called it something else. Often it will be called a joint venture. However, the term 'joint venture' is often used just as a general term to describe any undertaking that has some component of a commonality about it.[40] Some things called joint ventures can in fact be partnerships. Others involve arrangements that do not amount to partnerships but are very similar to them, whilst yet others are more remote still from the nature of partnership. The first two will involve fiduciary relationships between the parties at all times, whilst the third might or might not involve a fiduciary relationship.

A partnership is an intentional relationship that is brought about by agreement. In other words, it is consensual in nature, being largely the product of some agreement between two or more parties. In general, the law acknowledges the intention of the parties to create their own legal relations and will enforce the obligations that are created on the basis that they are the product of consent. In this area the law does not provide standard terms of relationship which the parties then assume apply in their case, although, as we will see, there are some standard terms which can apply to partnerships. Very often the bringing into existence of a partnership involves the execution of a formal agreement embodying the agreed terms of the partnership. However, there might be no formal agreement at all. The status of any agreement reached prior to the execution of a formal agreement will depend on the intentions of the parties.

Applying the reasoning of Brooking J in *Toyota Motor Corp Australia Limited v Ken Morgan Motors Pty Ltd,*[41] it is a common enough assumption that the parties are not to be taken as intending that a partnership agreement should come into existence until, in a given situation, they (or their attorney) have executed a document dealing with 'matters which are ordinarily agreed upon in transactions

---

39 (1886) 35 Ch D 436
40 See further below.
41 [1994] 2 VR 106 at 130–34, 201.

of the class in question'. However, this is not always reliable. The parties in a specific case might well have concluded a partnership agreement without purporting to formalise that relationship. They might have embarked on a partnership venture even though they thought it was something other than a partnership and in total ignorance of what the legal requirements for a partnership might be. Similarly, a partnership agreement might exist orally or otherwise without the parties ever turning their mind to formalising the arrangement.

The courts themselves have the role of determining finally whether the legal requirements for a partnership are made out. The parties could still be part of some legal relationship other than a partnership, such as that of co-owners.[42] Issues as to formation of partnership, especially in the public investment context, can give rise to some complicated legal issues, particularly in situations where it is alleged that a partnership is dissolved and a new one created each time there is a new investor or change of investor in the partnership.[43] Factual determinations by the courts in the midst of complicated and conflicting evidence are of considerable importance.

The basic import of the statutory definition is that a partnership is the relation which exists between persons carrying on business in common with a view to profit. Whether a partnership exists in conformity with the elements of that definition is a matter of fact. The definition postulates three necessary criteria. These are:

(1) the carrying on of business;
(2) the requirement that the business be carried on in common; and
(3) the requirement that the business be carried on with a view to profit.

1.2.3 Definitional elements

Whether a partnership exists in any given case depends largely on the intentions of the parties and the nature of the contract that they have made.[44] The Partnership Acts lay down certain rules that are intended to give guidance in determining whether a partnership exists in a given case. We will look at these below. The statutory definition of a partnership, as indicated above, mentions certain key elements. The court must be satisfied that each of these is established in any given case. As noted above, they must be found to exist as a matter of fact.

---

42 See *Henderson, Russell Fraser v Amadio Pty Ltd* (No 2) [1996] FCA 79; 62 FCR 221, cited the case of *Everet v Williams* (1725), involving a dispute between two highwaymen, also referred to in the case of *Burrows v Rhodes* [1899] 1 QB 816.

43 See also *Banfield v Wells-Eicke* [1970] VR 481; *Carlton Cricket & Football Social Club v Joseph* [1970] VR 487.

44 *Sutton and Co v Grey* [1894] 1 QB 285; *Re Hulton; Hulton v Lister* (1890) 62 LT 200.

1.2.4 Carrying on business

Since 2006, 'business' is now defined in several of the South Pacific Partnership Acts.[45] In other jurisdictions, there have been amendments to the legislation to provide a definition of sorts. For example, s IB of the Partnership Act (NSW) defines business as including any trade, occupation or profession. The definition is, in any event, inclusive rather than exhaustive. It is clear that receipt of a share of profits is *prima facie* evidence that a partnership exists,[46] but the sharing of gross returns is not, even if they are traced to some joint or common right with other parties.[47]

It is not necessary that every partner must work in the partnership business to be involved in carrying on such a business. It is always possible that there are one or more dormant or sleeping partners. In *Pooley v Driver*[48] Lord Jessel MR said:

> You can have, undoubtedly, according to English law, a dormant person who puts nothing in – neither capital, nor skill, nor anything else. In fact, those who are familiar with partnership know it is by no means uncommon to give a share to the widow or relative of some form of partner who contributes nothing at all, neither name, nor skill, nor anything else. Therefore it is not quite accurate, as Chancellor Kent puts it, that they must contribute labour or skill or money or some or all of them.

The United Kingdom Partnership Act 1890 contains a provision that the regional statutes now have: s 45 deems the expression 'business' to include 'every trade, occupation or profession'.

However, if this were not the case, some assistance regarding the nature of business can be gleaned from the taxation cases. This is because the receipts and expenditure from the carrying on of a business are brought to account as taxable income or deductible expenditure, respectively, under the relevant legislation. Whilst it might not be possible to enumerate fully all of the facts or circumstances that would amount to the carrying on of a business or which are determinative

---

45 See Partnership Acts: s 2(b) (F); s 2(c) (V); s 3 (N) includes 'business' and 'business name', Partnership Act 2018 repealed Partnership Act 1976; s 7(1) (Ni), repealed in 2020 by s 85 Partnership Law Act 2019 (NZ); s 2 (Tu), Cap 40.36, revised in 2008; s 1 Revised Partnership Act 2005 (MI), repealed the Partnership Act 1990; s 2 (S) Partnership Act, revised in 2008–22, includes the definition of 'business' amongst others; s 2(3) Partnership Act 1890 (UK) (K), (T), (SI).

46 See Partnership Acts: s 2(b) (F); s 2(c) (V); s 3(4) (N); s 5(c) (Ni); s 5(4) (Tu); s 136(d) Corporations and Partnership Act (MI); s 5(c) (S) Partnership Act; s 2(3) Partnership Act 1890 (UK) (K), (T), (SI),

47 Partnership Act (NSW): s 2 (F); s 5(3) (Tu); s 5(b) (Ni), (CI); s 136(c) (MI); s 3(3) (N); s 7 (S); s 2(b) (V); s 2(2) Partnership Act 1890 (UK) (SI), (K), (T).

48 Pooley v Driver (1876) 5 Ch D 458 at 473. See also *Ward v Newalls Insulation Co Ltd* [1998] EWCA 422 at para 12.

of a business being in existence,[49] some general indicia can be stipulated. These include the following:

- the repetition or frequency of certain similar activities by the same person or persons,[50] although under certain circumstances a business might be carried on in respect of an isolated transaction;[51]
- the existence of system and organisation in respect of the activities;[52]
- scale or size of the operation;[53]
- intention to make profits as a result of the activity, although no actual profit needs to be made;[54]
- conformity of the activity with established business methods or models or adoption by the parties of those methods or models.[55]

Perhaps none of these indicia alone would suffice. The courts tend to make an assessment of the activity based on the presence of several of them.

1.2.5 In common

The business must be carried on 'in common'. Whether an enterprise is conducted in common has been thought to be evidenced by a relationship of agency and the existence of mutual rights and obligations inherent in such an agency relationship. The requirement is not that the partners carry on a business in some sense. They must carry it on in common. It is in fact usually this element that distinguishes a partnership from a joint venture, where the element of agreed commonality is missing even though the parties might be carrying on a business and deriving some mutual benefit from the arrangement.

It would seem that inferences can be made from the existence of valuable rights held by the parties in such a way as to constitute partnership property and therefore also to give grounds for inferring the existence of a partnership.[56] Lord Wensleydale stressed the need for an agency relationship in *Cox and Another v Hickman*:

---

49 *London Australia Investment Ltd v Federal Commissioner of Taxation* (1977) 7 ATR 757 at 771.
50 *Hope v Bathurst City Council* (1980) 12 ATR 231.
51 *Jones v Leeming* [1930] 1 KB 279; *Federal Commissioner of Taxation v Whitford's Beach Pty Ltd* (1982) 150 CLR 355.
52 *Ferguson v FCT* (1979) 9 ATR 873.
53 *Federal Commissioner of Taxation v Whitford's Beach Pty Ltd* (1982) 150 CLR 355.
54 *IRC v Incorporated Council of Law Reporting* (1889) 22 QBD 279; *Graham v CIR* [1961] NZLR 994, 998.8 AITR 309.
55 *IRC v Livingstone* (1927) 11 TC 538 at 542.
56 See *Kelly v Kelly* (1990) 92 ALR 74 at 78, *per* Mason CJ, Deane, Dawson, Toohey and Gaudron JJ, citing *Ambler v Bolton* (1872) LR 14 Eq 427; *O'Brien v Komesaroff* [1982] HCA 33; 150 CLR 310.

A man who allows another to carry on trade, whether in his own name or not, to buy and sell, and to pay over all the profits to him, is undoubtedly the principal, and the person so employed is the agent, and the principal is liable for the agent's contracts in the course of his employment. So if two or more agree that they should carry on a trade, and share the profits of it, each is a principal, and each is an agent for the other, and each is bound by the other's contract in carrying on the trade, as much as a single principal would be by the act of an agent, who was to give the whole of the profits to his employer. Hence it becomes a test of the liability of one for the contract of another, that he is to receive the whole or a part of the profits arising from that contract by virtue of the agreement made at the time of the employment. I believe this is the true principle of partnership liability.[57]

Likewise, Griffith CJ said in *Lang v James Morrison & Co Ltd*:

Now, in order to establish that there was a partnership it is necessary to prove that JW McFarland carried on the business of Thomas McFarland & Co on behalf of himself, Lang and Keates, in this sense, that he was their agent in what he did under the contract with the plaintiffs – not that they would get the benefit, but that he was their agent.[58]

In *Duke Group Ltd (in liq) v PilmerI*, it was said, approving the above statements:

In order to meet this criterion, it is not necessary that each of the alleged partners should take an active part in the direction and management of the firm. The business may well be carried on by or *on behalf of* the partners by someone else. The person carrying on the business must be doing so as agent for all the other persons who are said to be partners.[59]

However, agency can be rather a vague term that is used in many different senses in law. It is clear enough that more than mere agency is required in this context: it is agency of a specific sort, or with particular features. There must be mutuality of rights and obligations between the parties in order that there be a partnership. It is to be remembered that partnerships and companies, unlike trusts, are associations and this requires the element of mutuality. In this regard, James L said in *Smith v Anderson:*

---

57 (1860) 8 HLC 268 at 312–13; (1860) 11 ER 431 at 449.
58 (1911) 13 CLR 1 at 11; [1911] HCA 49.
59 See *Duke Group Ltd (in liq) v Pilmer* [1999] SASC 97; 73 SASR 64.

Persons who have no mutual rights and obligations do not, according to my view, constitute an association because they happen to have a common interest or several interests in something which is to be divided between them.[60]

Perhaps, then, the best way to put it is that a certain sort of agency is required. In fact, the joint need for agency and mutuality are reflected in ss 6 and 7 of the Partnership Act of Fiji, for example. But there, of course, they are stated as being the consequences of entering into a partnership. In *Fliway-AFA International Pty Ltd v Australian Trade Commission*[61] one of the parties to an agreement was a freight forwarder in Australia. This party entered into certain reciprocal arrangements with freight forwarders located overseas. The arrangements usually involved profit-sharing. There was some mutuality between them, in that they were to refer work to each other and provide each other with certain information. Nonetheless there was no partnership in this case, because there was no evidence of any of the overseas freight forwarders having entered into any obligation binding upon the respective parties as principals. Furthermore, there was nothing in the nature of a fiduciary relationship. They were in fact merely co-venturers or joint venturers.

1.2.6 Partnership and joint venture

The existence or absence of some degree of commonness – i.e. mutuality and agency between the 'partners' – is the factor that differentiates a partnership from a joint venture. In a joint venture the participants are involved in some joint enterprise or commercial undertaking. However, it takes effect without the element of carrying on business together or in common.

The difference between the two is a very fine one. Whether one or the other exists will depend usually on interpretation of complicated factual situations by the court. However, the legal consequences can be very important because matters such as the rights to property and profits, the rights to dissolution of the arrangement and so on might be very different if the relevant Partnership Act applies. Both arrangements can in fact give rise to fiduciary relations between the parties involved, so it would be incorrect to say that a partnership involves some close element of trust or confidence, whereas a joint venture does not. It is also incorrect to say that a partnership involves mutual agency relations and a joint venture does not.

Sometimes a joint venture might be part of a process which leads to the final formation of a partnership, and sometimes joint ventures are formed deliberately

---

60 (1880) 15 Ch D 247 at 275.
61 (1992) FCA 905; 39 FCR 446.

with no partnership ever intended. In *United Dominions Corp Ltd v Brian Pty Ltd* the High Court of Australia said:

> The term 'joint venture' is not a technical one with a settled common law meaning. As a matter of ordinary language, it connotes an association of persons for the purposes of a particular trading, commercial, mining or other financial undertaking or endeavour with a view to mutual profit, with each participant usually (but not necessarily) contributing money, property or skill. Such a joint venture (or under Scots law 'adventure') will often be a partnership.
>
> The term is, however, apposite to refer to a joint undertaking or activity carried out through a medium other than a partnership, such as a company, a trust, an agency or a joint ownership. The borderline between what can properly be described as a 'joint venture' and what should more properly be seen as no more than a simple contractual relationship may on occasion be blurred. Thus, where one party contributes only money or other property, it may sometimes be difficult to determine whether a relationship is a joint venture in which both parties are entitled to a share of profits, or a simple contract of loan or a lease under which the interest or rent payable to the party providing the money or property is determined by reference to the profits made by the other. One would need a more confined and precise notion of what constitutes a 'joint venture' than that which the term bears as a matter of ordinary language before it could be said by way of general proposition that the relationship between joint venturers is necessarily a fiduciary one: but cf. per Cardozo CJ in *Meinhard v Salmon* (1928) 164 NE545 at p 546.[62]

Commenting on this paragraph, it was said in *Schipp v Cameron, Harrison and Others*:

> The High Court [of Australia] held in *UDC v Brian* ((1985) 157 CLR 1 at 10 per Mason, Brennan and Deane JJ) that joint venturers would be subject to fiduciary obligations if their venture took the form of partnership. Joint venture agreements thus attract equitable principles attached to fiduciaries if they are analogous to a relationship which equity already recognises, namely a partnership. But it is unclear when the two relationships will be analogous. The High Court's statement in *UDC* that most joint ventures would be partnerships as a matter of ordinary language, does not finally dispose of the issue as to the circumstances in which a joint venture will bear sufficient similarity to a partnership to attract fiduciary obligations. Plainly that issue can only be decided by reference to the particular circumstances of a particular case. In order to more closely consider the issue, it is necessary to look at the characteristics of a

---

62 (1985) HCA 49; 157 CLR 1 at 10, *per* Mason, Brennan and Deane JJ; 59 ALJR 676; 60 ALR 741.

partnership relationship at law and the extent to which these characteristics are similar to, or different from, a given joint venture agreement.[63]

1.2.7 With a view of profit

The requirement of profit connotes some expectation of pecuniary gain.[64]The requirement is not that profits be actually generated but that the parties are involved in the association with a view to profit, rather than for some other dominant objective.

According to the well-known definition of Fletcher Moulton LJ in *Re the Spanish Prospecting Company Limited:*

> The word 'profits' has in my opinion a well-defined legal meaning, and this meaning coincides with the fundamental conception of profits in general parlance, although in mercantile phraseology the word may at times bear meanings indicated by the special context which deviate in some respects from this fundamental signification. 'Profits' implies a comparison between the state of a business at two specific dates usually separated by an interval of a year. The fundamental meaning is the amount of gain made by the business during the year. This can only be ascertained by a comparison of the assets of the business at the two dates.[65]

This has been criticised for its inclusion of gains in asset values as well as trading profits. Nonetheless it has been consistently adopted and applied in that sense. However, it does not encompass every advantage or benefit which the parties might derive from their association or activities undertaken pursuant to it. In *Duke Group Ltd (in liq) v Pilmer* it was said:

> [However] profit may be identified or calculated, it connotes a direct and definable pecuniary gain. It does not mean the receipt of some other type of benefit or advantage, even if some benefit ultimately leads to a pecuniary gain.[66]

Cummings v Lewis and Others[67] concerned an arrangement between a racehorse trainer and accountants promoting a scheme relating to a racehorse owing syndicate. Wilcox J, following the approach above, said:

63 [1998] NSWSC 997 at para 710.
64 *Duke Group Ltd (in liq) v Pilmer* [1999] SASC 97; 73 SASR 64.
65 [1911] 1 Ch 92 at 98.
66 [1999] SASC 97; 73 SASR 64.
67 (1991) unreported, Federal Court of Australia, 2 August, No G668/89.

It is true that, in acquiring the horses and issuing the prospectuses, both Mr Cummings and the accountants were profit-motivated. The syndicates offered the prospect for each party to increase their professional earnings. But, as is explained in *Lindley on Partnership* (15th edn) at p 12, the effect of this third element is that it 'is essential that what is to be shared is the profits of the business in the sense of the net gain resulting after payment of all outgoings'.[68]

It is clearly that case that the mere fact that the members of an association stand to derive some benefit does not mean that they are associated with a view to profit.[69] Profit implies some sense of prospective financial gain over and above expenses.

Duke Group Limited v Pilmer was a case involving a scheme of participation in Australia of several state-based partnerships in a wider national association. The South Australian Court of Appeal held that there was no carrying on of a business for a profit. The court said:

> It may not be necessary to go as far as Wilcox J went in *Cummings v Lewis and Others* (1991) to say that the sharing of profits is essential to a partnership. What is essential is that the relevant business being carried on in common must be carried on with a view of profit. We take that to mean that the would-be partners must have as an object in carrying on the relevant business the deriving of profit from the carrying on of that business.
>
> [There] was never any sense [from the formation of a national alliance] in which the profits of a particular firm were to be shared with members of another firm. There were mutual benefits to be had in the form of retention of clients, expansion of practices, ability to attract national and international work etc, but there was never any view of deriving profits from any common business ...
>
> So far as the activities of the licensors and their successors were concerned, they may have been carrying on business in common in the provision of services and benefits to particular firms. We are prepared to assume for present purposes that they were. However, that activity was never carried on with a view of profit. The terms of the deed made that quite clear, and the practice over many years confirmed it. No profits were in fact made, but small surpluses were merely carried forward to the next year and sufficient called by way of levy to make up the actual costs of providing the services. The national arrangement may perhaps better be described as an arrangement to share expenses in areas where there were obvious economies and benefits to the individual firms in doing so. The national arrangement could not be described as a relationship

---

68 Upheld on appeal. Approved in *Duke Group Ltd v Pilmer* [1999] SASC 97, *per* Wilcox J approved the definition of partnership, defined by Fletcher Moulton LJ in *Re the Spanish Prospecting Company* [1911] 1 Ch 92 at 98, in the context of circumstances in *Cummings v Lewis and Others* (1991) unreported, Federal Court of Australia, 2 August, No G668/89.
69 See *Wise v Perpetual Trustee Co Ltd* [1903] AC 139 at 149, *per* Lord Lindley.

which subsisted between persons carrying on business in common with a view of profit.[70]

1.3 Statutory rules for inferring a partnership

Whether the particular arrangement satisfies all of the conditions set out above is the overriding test. However, the Partnership Acts of the various South Pacific jurisdictions contain some guiding rules to be considered when the question of a possible partnership is laid open to decision.[71] Section 3 of the Fiji Partnership Act is typical in this regard. It provides:

3 In determining whether a partnership does or does not exist regard shall be had to the following rules –

(a) joint tenancy, tenancy in common, joint property, common property or part ownership does not of itself create a partnership as to anything so held or owned whether the tenants or owners do or do not share any profits made by the use thereof;

Sharing gross returns

(b) the sharing of gross returns does not of itself create a partnership whether the persons sharing such returns have or have not a joint or common right or interest in any property from which or from the use of which the returns are derived;

Effect of sharing profits, etc

(c) the receipt by a person of a share of the profits of a business is *prima facie* evidence that he is a partner in the business, but the receipt of such a share or of a payment contingent on or varying with the profits of a business does not of itself make him a partner in the business; and, in particular –
  (i) the receipt by a person of a debt or other liquidated amount by instalments or otherwise out of the accruing profits of a business does not of itself make him a partner in the business or liable as a partner;
  (ii) a contract for the remuneration of a servant or agent of a person engaged in a business by a share of the profits of the business does not of itself make the servant or agent a partner in the business or liable as a partner;

---

70 [1999] SASC 97 at paras 976, 977, 979.
71 Partnership Acts: s 5 (CI), (S), (Tu); s 3 (N); ss 11, 12–15 (Ni), under Partnership Law Act 2019 which repealed the Partnership Act 1908; ss 16–20 (MI) in Division II (Nature of Partnership); s 2 (V); s 2 Partnership Act 1890 (UK) (T), (SI), (K).

     (iii) a person being the widow or child of a deceased partner and receiving by way of annuity a portion of the profits made in the business in which the deceased person was a partner is not by reason only of such receipt a partner in the business or liable as a partner;

Loan at interest varying with profits

     (iv) the advance of money by way of a loan to a person engaged or about to engage in any business on a contract with that person that the lender shall receive a rate of interest varying with the profits or shall receive a share of the profits arising from carrying on the business does not of itself make the lender a partner with the person or persons carrying on the business or liable as a partner:

Provided that the contract is in writing and signed by or on behalf of all parties thereto;

     (v) a person receiving by way of annuity or otherwise a portion of the profits of a business in consideration of the sale by him of the good-will of the business is not by reason only of such receipt a partner in the business or liable as a partner.

1.3.1 Sham transactions

The advantages of adopting a partnership as the particular legal structure for a business have been discussed above. Often there is a question of the taxation benefits that can arise from a sole trader splitting his or her income with members of his or her family. By splitting income between all partners, the trader hopes to take advantage of a lower progressive tax rate that applies to lower levels of income in some countries, such as in the Fiji Islands. Forming a partnership with family members can achieve that objective. But the partnership, like any other arrangement, will only be recognised if it was intended as a genuine arrangement, as opposed to a mere pretence or sham.

In other words, a purported partnership agreement will not be given legal effect by the courts if they are satisfied that the transaction, whatever the motives, was a sham. As to what constitutes a sham transaction, Lockhart J said in *Sharrment v Official Trustee*:

> A 'sham' is for the purposes of Australian law, something that is intended to be mistaken for something else, or that is not really what it purports to be. It is a spurious imitation, a counterfeit, a disguise or a false front. It is not genuine or true, but something made in imitation of something else or made to appear to be something which it is not. It is something which is false or deceptive.[72]

---

72 [1988] FCA 266; 18 FCR 449.

In *Paintin & Nottingham Ltd v Miller, Gale & Winter*,[73] Turner J of the New Zealand High Court said:

> The word 'sham' is well on the way to becoming a legal shibboleth; on its mere utterance it seems to be expected that contracts will wither like one who encounters the gaze of a basilisk. But by a 'sham' is meant, in my opinion, no more or no less than an appearance lent by documents or other evidentiary materials, concealing the true nature of a transaction, and making it seem something other than what it really is.

1.3.2 Commencement of partnership

When does a partnership commence? In other words, when does it take effect? That is essentially a matter of determining, objectively and on the evidence, the point in time at which the arrangement as required under the legislation comes into effect. Normally, this will be the date upon which the partners actually agree to commence the carrying on of the partnership business.

However, it is possible that the partners might agree on some earlier date, and this will be given effect by the courts. Does this mean that the partners become liable to third parties (creditors) in respect of debts prior to the actual commencement date?[74] The answer to this would usually be negative. Such a conclusion is reinforced by the provisions of s 6 of the Fiji Partnership Act, quoted above. It is a case of not being able to 'alter the past in that way'.[75]

There have been doubts about the evidential value of such an agreement between the parties when a third party seeks to rely on it, because the third party was not privy to the agreement.[76] However, if the evidence is such that it goes to the establishment of the actual date of commencement of the partnership on an objective basis then it would be of value. The agreement between the parties would be evidence to be considered along with other evidence in determining the actual date when the partnership commenced.

1.4 Partnership and agency

A partnership is usually treated, as noted above, as a consensual arrangement which gives rise to relations of agency between the partners, however many there might be, and whatever the precise terms of their defined relationship under the

---

73 [1971] NZLR 164 at 175; see also *Sharrment Pty Ltd v Official Trustee in Bankruptcy* (1988) FCA 266; 18 FCR 449 at 453–54.
74 See Roderick l'Anson Banks, RC, *Lindley & Banks on Partnership*, 21st edn, 2022, London, Sweet & Maxwell, Part 3, Chapters 12–14.
75 *Waddington v O'Callaghan* (1931) 16 TC 187 at 197, *per* Rowlatt J.
76 *Lindley and Banks, op cit* fn 74.

partnership agreement. Each partner is regarded as being an agent of the others, and so the partners are thus also principals as regards each other.

However, the question of the nature of agency is itself a vexed one. Lord Pearson observed in *Garnac Grain Co Inc v HMF Faure & Fairclough Ltd* that:

> The relationship of principal and agent can only be established by the consent of the principal and the agent. They will be held to have consented if they have agreed to what amounts in law to such a relationship, even if they do not recognise it themselves and even if they have professed to disclaim it.[77]

The elements of agency in this particular context were subject to analysis in *South Sydney District Rugby League Football Club Ltd v News Ltd,*[78] where it was pointed out that it has been conventional to take the principal and agent relationship itself as a focus of agency itself.[79] This approach emphasises that the relationship 'can only be established by the consent of the principal and the agent'.[80] However, the court noted that the consents so given 'need not necessarily be to a relationship that the parties understand, or even accept, to be that of principal and agent'.[81] It is sufficient if 'they have agreed to what amounts in law to such a relationship',[82] even though they may have 'artfully disguised' by express disclaimers.[83]

The court further noted that there is no uniformly agreed definition of agency.[84] In fact, there is a certain ambivalence about it. However, two predominant definitions of agency appear in the literature: the US Restatement, Second, Agency, §1 and *Bowstead & Reynolds*[85] (the latter being based upon the Restatement provision) have become authoritative. The definition in the Restatement, as referred to in the judgment, is as follows:

> §1 Agency is the fiduciary relation which results from the manifestation of consent by one person to another that the other shall act on his behalf and subject to his control, and consent by the other so to act.

---

77 [1968] AC 1130 at 1137.

78 [2000] FCA 1541.

79 Cf. *International Harvester Co of Australia Pty Ltd v Carrigan's Hazeldene Pastoral Co* (1958) HCA 16; 100 CLR 644 at 652.

80 *Garnac Grain Co Inc v HMF Fanre & Fairclough Ltd* [1968] AC 1130 at 1137; see e.g. Peter Watts KC, F.M.B. Reynolds KC (ed), *Bowstead & Reynolds on Agency,* 23rd edn, 2023, London, Sweet & Maxwell, Chapters 2, 3, 6, 7.

81 *Branwhite v Worcester Works Finance Ltd* [1968] 3 All ER 104 at 587.

82 *Garnac Grain Co Inc v HMF Fanre & Fairclough Ltd* [1968] AC 1130 at 1137; *Nichols v Arthur Murray Inc* 56 Cal Rptr 728 (1967) at 730–31.

83 *Board of Trade v Hammond Elevator Co* 198 US 424 (1905) at 441–42.

84 *South Sydney District Rugby League Football Club Ltd v News Ltd* [2000] FCA 1541.

85 *Op cit* fn 80, Chapters 2, 3, 6, 7.

That in *Bowstead & Reynolds* is as follows:

> Agency is the fiduciary relationship which exists between two persons, one of
> whom expressly or impliedly consents that the other should act on his behalf
> so as to affect his relations with third parties, and the other of whom similarly
> consents so to act or so acts.

The court was of the view that, the necessary consents apart, the required characteristics of the agency relation could thus be put in the following way. First, it is
required that one party acts on the other's behalf. Secondly, it is required that one
party, the agent, is subject to the other's (the principal's) control or direction. There
is no logical inconsistency between the two. It is common enough that a person
who acts on behalf of another is subject to the control of that other with regard to
how his or her functions are to be performed.

However, of these two, the second, so it was said, had not figured prominently
as a decisive indicator of agency at common law save in two settings.[86] The first is
where it is contended that a company is an agent of its parent company, shareholders or of particular officers because of the control it or they exercise over the company. This seemed to follow from the separate identity principle in company law,[87]
although in that area the control characteristic had undergone much subsequent
refinement.[88] The second situation is where a party who is 'expressed to stand in
the relation of independent contractor to another is claimed as well to be the agent
of that other'. The court here indicated that:

> the two relationships are not mutually exclusive[89] – the 'acting on behalf of'
> or 'representative' characteristic must be able to be discerned in the factual
> relation of the parties – where that characteristic can properly be inferred in
> circumstances in which the alleged principal exercises, or is entitled to exer-
> cise, a significant degree of control over the contractor's performance of its
> services (and in particular over contracts entered into), the contractor is apt in
> consequence to be characterised as an agent. ... It probably is the case that the
> control exercisable by one party can in some settings itself bear on the deter-
> mination whether the other acts on its own account or on behalf of the former
> when dealing with a third party.[90]

86 *South Sydney District Rugby League Football Club Ltd v News Ltd* [2000] FCA 1541.
87 As established in *Salomon v Salomon & Co* [1897] AC 22.
88 Referring to *Gramophone and Typewriter Ltd v Stanley* [1908] 2 KB 89; *Briggs v James Hardie
    & Co Pty Ltd* (1989) 16 NSWLR 549; see also *op cit* fn 80, Chapters 2, 3, 6, 7.
89 Referring to *CFTO-TV Ltd v Mr Submarine Ltd* (1994) 108 DLR (4th) 517; affirmed (1997) 151
    DLR (4tn) 382; *Lower Hutt City v Attorney-General* [1965] 2 NZLR 65 at 71 in para 137.
90 Referring, to e.g. *CFTO-TV Ltd v Mr Submarine Ltd* (1994) 108 DLR (4th) 517; *Northern v
    McGraw-Edison Co* 542 F 2d 1336 (1976); *Condus v Howard Savings Bank* 986 F Supp 914
    (1997) in para 137.

Just how far and in what way the relationship involved in a partnership (that is, in all partnerships) evinces this element of control, which also is implicit in agency, is perhaps a matter for debate. Whilst partners act on behalf of the firm, and therefore on behalf of the other partners, it is not clear that there is, or needs to be, any real expectation or right of control by the partners over the activities of each other partner. What is common to both definitions mentioned is in fact the fiduciary obligation of agents to their principal. That obligation is imputed generally where there is an absence of control rather than the presence of it. It is more generally imputed where one party is obligated to act in the interests of or for the benefit of another.

However interesting that might be, the law clearly imposes an agency relationship on partners by statute. Sections 6–11 inclusive of the Fiji Partnership Act, like their counterparts, clearly impute an agency relationship to partners in the most direct way. Sections 6 and 7 make this clear enough:

> 6 Every partner is an agent of the firm and his other partners for the purposes of the business of the partnership; and the acts of every partner who does any act for carrying on in the usual way business of the kind carried on by the firm of which he is a member bind the firm and his partners unless the partner so acting has in fact no authority to act for the firm in the particular matter and the person with whom he is dealing either knows that he has no authority or does not know or believe him to be a partner.[91]

> 7 An act or instrument relating to the business of the firm and done or executed in the firm-name or in any other manner showing an intention to bind the firm by any person thereto authorised, whether a partner or not, is binding on the firm and all the partners:[92] Provided that this section shall not affect any general rule of law relating to the execution of deeds or negotiable instruments.

1.4.1 The description affixed by the parties

The parties might describe the arrangement they have brought into being as a partnership or as something else. However, what the parties have termed the relationship is not determinative. It is a matter for the courts to determine what the legal effect of the arrangement is in terms of the criteria laid down. They construe the intention of the parties, but this has little to do with what the parties might have called the arrangement. Something that has been called a partnership could in fact be held to be a joint venture, and vice versa. What the parties have called

---

91 Partnership Acts: s 18 (Ni); s8 (Tu), (CI); s 22 (N); s5(V); ss 51, 58 (MI); s 6 (S); s 5 Partnership Act 1890 (UK) (SI), (K), (T).
92 Partnership Acts: s 7 (S); s 20 (Ni, (Tu), (CI); s 23 (N); s6 (V); s 6 Partnership Act 1890 (UK) (SI), (K), (T).

the particular arrangement is simply one factor amongst others to be weighed up by the court.[93]

In *Duke Group Limited v Pilmer*[94] it was said:

[The court] must examine the substance of the relationship and not merely what the participants called themselves.

Indeed, in that case, the court approved the following comments in *Weiner v Harris*:

Two parties enter into a transaction and say 'It is hereby declared there is no partnership between us'. The court pays no regard to that. The court looks at the transaction and says 'Is this, in point of law, really a partnership? It is not in the least conclusive that the parties have used a term or language intended to indicate that the transaction is not that which in law it is'.[95]

Likewise, in *Commissioners of Inland Revenue v Williamson* it was said:

My Lords, you do not constitute or create or prove a partnership by saying that there is one. The only proof that a partnership exists is proof of the relations of agency and of community in losses and profits and of the sharing in one form or another of the capital of the concern; the only proof of a partnership consists in proof of these things. No doubt the proof may be supplied by what in fact the persons alleging themselves to be partners have done during the currency of the alleged partnership.[96]

In *South Sydney District Rugby League Club Ltd v News Ltd* the issue involved a deed containing a clause denying agency between the parties. In that context, the court said:

It is legitimate for parties to avoid the 'unwanted consequences' of a particular category of legal relationship by seeking to cast it in a form that takes it outside that category of relationship: *Colbron v St Bees Island Pty Ltd* (1995) 56 FCR 303 at 314. But whether or not they are successful in achieving that end does not depend simply upon whether, in an express provision of their agreement, they attribute or deny to their relationship a particular legal character – be this, for example, employer and employee: *Australian Mutual Provident*

---

93 *South Sydney District Rugby League Football Club Ltd v News Ltd* [2000] FCA 1541 at para 928.
94 [1999] SASC 97.
95 [1910] 1 KB 285 at 290 *per* Cozens-Hardy MR.
96 (1928) 14 TC 335 at 340.

Society v Chaplin (1978) 18 ALR 385; principal and principal or principal and agent: *Board of Trade v Hammond Elevator Co*, above; or partners: *Ex parte Delhasse; In re Megevand* (1878) 7 Ch D 511. The parties cannot by the mere device of labelling, no matter how genuinely intentioned, either confer a particular legal character on a relationship that it does not possess or deny it a character that it does possess: *Ex parte Delhasse*, above, at 532; see 2A Corpus Juris Secundum, 'Agency', §7; see also the observations of Lord Denning in *Massey v Crown Life Insurance Co* quoted in the *Australian Mutual Provident Society* case, above, at 389. ...

Save where an express labelling provision is shown to be a sham, the provision itself (as a manifestation of the parties' intent) must be given its proper weight in relation to the rest of their agreement and such other relevant circumstances as evidence the true character of their relationship. This may lead to its being disregarded entirely: *Ex parte Delhasse*, above, *Board of Trade v Hammond Elevator Co*, above; or to its being given full force and effect: *Australian Mutual Provident Society v Chaplin*, above. And such will depend upon whether, given the actual incidents and content of the relationship (i.e. 'the factual relation') to which the parties have consented, they have consented 'to a state of fact upon which the law imposes the consequences which result from agency': *Branwhite*'s case, above, at 587; Restatement, Second, Agency, §1 comment b.[97]

The parties might have agreed on a future date for commencement of the partnership. If, despite this, they begin to operate the partnership business together before that time, they will be held to be partners from that earlier date.[98] However, this will not be so if all that was involved were acts of a preparatory or preliminary nature undertaken by the partners prior to entering into business.[99]

It is possible that a new partnership can be deemed to come into existence on the dissolution of another partnership with a different constitution of partners. However, this gives rise to a number of juristic problems,[100] and such an inference cannot be made where it does not fit the essential commercial and financial structure on which all of the relevant parties were agreed.[101] In some cases it is possible that the agreement of the parties might have been that any preliminary agreement between them was subject to a formal partnership agreement being entered into.

---

97 [2000] FCA 1541 at paras 134.3, 134.4.
98 *Lindley and Banks, op cit* fn 80, Chapters 2, 3, 6, 7; *South Sydney District Rugby League Football Club Ltd v News Ltd* [2000] FCA 1541 at para 375.
99 *Lindley and Banks, op cit* fn 80, Chapters 2, 3, 6, 7.
100 See the discussion by Gowans J in *Banfield v Wells-Eicke* [1970] VR 481 and *Carlton Cricket & Football Social Club v Joseph* [1970] VR 487.
101 *Henderson v Amadio Pty Ltd and Others* [1995] FCA 1029; 140 ALR 391.

In other words, legal relations as partners were not to have commenced until the formal agreement was executed.

This was the view taken by Brooking J in *Toyota Motor Corp Australia Ltd v Ken Morgan Motors Pty Ltd*. Where the conclusion on the facts is that the parties did not intend that a partnership agreement would come into existence until they (or their attorney) had executed a formal document dealing with 'matters which are ordinarily agreed upon in transactions of the class in question', then there will be no partnership until that agreement is in fact executed.[102] If the parties merely executed something which was an 'informal, vague and relatively short document', on this basis it would not normally be legally binding. It is possible that in the interim, pending the execution of the partnership agreement, the rights and obligations of the group of parties as, say, investors would be adequately governed by the law relating to co-owners and guarantors. But they would not be partners.

As noted above, it is the intention of the parties, as settled by the court, that is determinative in settling whether or not a partnership exists. Interpretation of the words and conduct of the parties is the key element here rather than determining subjective states of mind. Intention, in other words, is a matter of the court attributing meaning and in light of that meaning determining whether the arrangement meets the legal criteria required of a partnership. Thus it is normally said that the existence of a partnership is determined by reference to the true contract and intention of the parties as appearing from all of the facts and circumstances relevant to the relationship of the parties.[103] The events occurring after the execution of an agreement might be relevant to this issue, to the extent that the conduct of the parties after that date might itself be relevant.[104]

It is possible that multiple partnerships can exist between the same partners. In each case, however, the relevant criteria for the existence of a partnership must be independently established. The New South Wales case of *Hitchins v Hitchins and Another*[105] is illustrative of this situation. One of the main issues in that case was whether the relationship between the parties involved was one of partnership for the purposes of the definition in s 1(1) of the Partnership Act 1890 (NSW). The definition in that section is the same as that which appears in the legislation of the South Pacific jurisdictions. The plaintiff and her two brothers entered into partnership with a number of other people in respect of the operation of a hotel. The business and the property on which it was run were owned by all the partners jointly.

---

102 [1994] 2 VR 106 at 130–34.
103 See *Cox v Hickman* (1860) 8 HLC 268; *Jolley v Federal Commissioner of Taxation* (1989) 86 ALR 297 at 306–8, *per* Burchett and Lee JJ; *Amadio Pty Ltd and Others v Henderson* [1998] FCA 823 (14 July 1998) at para 3.2 (Full Federal Court of Australia); ss 5, 6 Partnership Act 1958 (Vic).
104 See *Lindley and Banks, op cit* fn 80; *Robinson v Federal Commissioner of Taxation* (1986) 17 ATR 1068 at 1071–72.
105 (1998) 47 NSWLR 35.

The joint share of the three family members in the partnership was a minority of the total interests.

The share of the three in respect of the profit of the hotel business was paid to them jointly. A dispute arose between them concerning the disbursement and application of the share of those profits when received into their hands. The plaintiff, the sister, alleged that they should have been divided equally. The first defendant had allegedly failed to do so. The plaintiff alleged, as one of her claims, that the arrangement for the distribution of the share of profits from the hotel business constituted a separate partnership between the three siblings. The plaintiff alleged that under partnership law, as partners in this particular partnership, entitlement to the share of these profits generated by the other business was equal between them. The plaintiff also claimed entitlement to an account of the dealings of this alleged recipient partnership.

The Supreme Court considered the combined effect of ss 1 and 2 of the Partnership Act (NSW). As noted above, s 1(1) provides specifically that a partnership is 'the relation which exists between persons carrying on business in common with a view of profit'. Section 2(1) provides that co-ownership of property does not of itself create a partnership in the property so held. Section 2(2) is to the effect that the sharing of gross returns does not in itself establish the existence of a partnership, whether or not the persons have a common interest in the property from which the returns are derived.

Taking account of these three provisions together, it was held that the arrangement in this instance whereby the three siblings invested in a share in the hotel partnership and then received drawings from it, did not constitute a partnership. In particular it did not constitute the carrying on of a 'business in common'. The activity was nothing more than an investment. This was because there were no elements of undertaking trade or business. There was no flow of underlying transactions or systematic organisation of the operation that would amount to the carrying on of a business. The parties may have been partners in the hotel business, but this did not carry through to establish a separate partnership business in respect of the joint ownership of the share of profits generated from the hotel partnership. Whether there was a separate partnership had to be judged independently of the first business. The court did, however, find on other grounds that the plaintiff was entitled to an equal share of the profits received by the three siblings.

2

THE PARTNERSHIP AGREEMENT
AND PARTNERSHIP INTERESTS

2.1 Terms of the partnership

Partnerships can be created in various ways:

(a) by express agreement, either wholly in writing, wholly oral or a combination of both;
(b) by agreement implied wholly or partly from surrounding circumstances;
(c) by estoppel;
(d) by statute.

We will concentrate on the first two types. The partnership agreement is of central importance in determining the rights and obligations of partners and the general basis for the operation of the partnership. There is no legal requirement that a partnership be in writing. Many partnerships are formed wholly orally whilst others are formalised in written agreements. In some cases, a combination of writing and oral discussions might provide the basis for the content of the partnership agreement.

As partnerships are intentional creations, they are usually formulated after considerable negotiation. Most usually they will involve some formal deed or instrument under seal, or some agreement drawn by one or more legal advisers for the parties involved. In some cases, however, a partnership agreement is something which, in the absence of any express or formal agreement, the courts will infer from the circumstances. This is much like they will do in respect of any other contract.

The partnership agreement, whatever form it should take, constitutes a contract between the parties involved. Consideration is implied from the mutual promises

DOI: 10.4324/9781003428060-3

of the parties to be bound by the terms of the agreement. The commercial element is always present in view of the fact that the parties are involved in an agreement to carry on business with a view to profit. Whilst it is common to embody the partnership agreement in a deed or indenture which is executed by the parties under seal, there is strictly no need for the agreement to take this form. Whilst deeds take effect without consideration, in this case, the deed is superfluous because mutual consideration moving from both parties' promises will always be present.

A partnership can also be created by estoppel, without the need for consideration in the strict sense understood in contract law. Seeing as it is now widely accepted that equitable estoppel[1] can give rise to substantive legal rights, rather than merely defensive equity, the position is much better established than perhaps it once was. Estoppel in equity can arise where one or more parties make some statement, whether as to law or fact, or some promise, undertaking or representation with actual or imputed knowledge that it would be relied on as material by some other party. If the statement (and so on) is in fact relied on by another party to their detriment, there is an estoppel situation whereby the maker or makers of the statement is/are bound by the terms of the statement which has been made and relied on.[2] Substantive legal rights are established in this situation. Clearly enough, these substantive legal rights could involve the imputation of a partnership or partnership rights on dissolution where, for example, this has been the subject of the statement or representation in question.

It is one thing to establish an agreement. It is another to decide what the actual terms of the partnership agreement were or are. Often this is a crucial matter, for the rights and liabilities of the partners will depend very much on the actual terms of the partnership. In some cases, these terms, as we have already noted, will be implied by the Partnership Acts, but only where there is no agreement to the contrary.

In order to decide what the terms of the partnership are in a given case, regard must be given to various factors. These are:

1 See e.g. *Amalgamated Investments v Texas Commerce* [1981] 3 All ER 577 at 584–85; *Legione v Hateley* (1983) HCA 11; 152 CLR 406; *Commonwealth of Australia v Verwayen* (1990) 170 CLR 394; *Waltons Stores (Interstate) Ltd v Maher* (1988) HCA 7; 164 CLR 387. It is not entirely clear whether the development of equitable estoppel along these lines will be accepted in the South Pacific jurisdictions. See e.g. *Paul v Tuanai* [1994] WSSC 15 (6 December 1994) referred to in *Lafaele v Talipeau* [2014] WSSC 18 (15 May 2014) which dealt with a counter-claim to proprietary estoppel on the basis of *Willmott v Barber* [1880] UKLawRpCh 183; (1880) 15 Ch D 96, 106; *Patel v Patel* [1992] FJCA 22 (18 November 1992); *Jamnadas Sports Fiji Ltd v Stinson Pearce Ltd* [1994] FJCA 20. In all of these cases, there appear to be some reservation about applying estoppel based on a broad principle of unconscionability. We suggest, however, that these limitations are likely to be dispensed with in future cases, except perhaps in Tonga where s 103 Evidence Act (Cap 15) imposes some limitations on the development of the doctrine. See *Fie'eiki v 'Ilavalu* (No. 2) [1996] TOLawRp 4; [1995] Tonga LR 192 (12 April 1996).
2 See e.g. *Waltons Stores (Interstate) Ltd v Maher* (1988) 164 CLR 387; *Commonwealth of Australia v Verwayen* (1990) 170 CLR 394.

(a) the express agreement of the parties if there is one;
(b) terms implied from the factual circumstances as within the intention of the partners;
(c) terms implied by operation of law, whether on general contract principles in cases of efficacy, as a matter of construction of the agreement or by imputation in an estoppel situation;
(d) terms implied by statute, particularly the Partnership Acts,[3] and the rights and obligations implied by the general law of partnership.

Most partnerships are, as we have said, created by express agreement. Often the agreement is embodied in a deed under seal. More often the agreement is reduced to some written form without execution under seal. There is no prescribed legal form for a partnership agreement. These are traditionally perceived as private law arrangements where the parties are free to settle the terms of their own arrangement to a considerable degree.

2.1.1 The terms of the partnership

Leaving aside estoppel and statutory situations, the terms of a partnership are most commonly determined either by express or implied agreement or by the operation of law. In the former instance, partnerships are consensual arrangements between two or more individuals. Traditionally, the area of partnership law was conceived as part of private law. Thus, it was to be regarded as an arrangement that, like a contract, was understood in terms of a coming together of the parties to constitute their own arrangement, the terms of which were enforceable at law. The law simply enforced the arrangement that the parties had, by agreement or consent, brought into existence.

The primacy of the partnership agreement as a source of rights and duties of the parties is preserved by s 20 of the Partnership Act of Fiji. It reads as follows:

> 20 The mutual rights and duties of partners, whether ascertained by agreement or defined by this Act, may be varied by the consent of all the partners, and such consent may be either expressed or inferred from a course of dealing.[4]

Whilst this indicates a power of variation of existing terms by consent, it is clear that it would extend to any variation (or exclusion) of the terms implied by the statute achieved by the partnership agreement itself. Thus, the statutory terms, noted

---

3 Partnership Act (F), (V), (Ni), (Tu), (MI), (N), (CI); UK Partnership Act (K), (SI), (T).
4 Partnership Acts: s 25 (Ni), (CI), s 22 (Tu), s 36 (N), s 19 (V); s 20 (S); s 19 Partnership Act 1890 (UK) (SI), (K), (T).

below, apply only to the extent that they have not been excluded by the consent of the parties at the time of the making of the partnership or in fact afterwards.

The same applies specifically as regards the rights and duties of the partners, which are specified in s 25 of the Fiji Islands Partnership Act.[5] This section imports various provisions relating to matters such as entitlement to a share of profits, indemnity rights, shares of profits, the admission of new partners and dissolution. It is in the following terms:

25 The interest of partners in the partnership property and their rights and duties in relation to the partnership shall be determined subject to any agreement, expressed or implied, between the partners by the following rules:

(a)   all the partners are entitled to share equally in the capital and profits of the business and must contribute equally towards the losses, whether of capital or otherwise, sustained by the firm;

(b)   the firm must indemnify every partner in respect of payments made and personal liabilities incurred by him
(i)   in the ordinary and proper conduct of the business of the firm; or
(ii)   in or about anything necessarily done for the preservation of the business or property of the firm;

(c)   a partner making for the purpose of the partnership any actual payment or advance beyond the amount of capital which he has agreed to subscribe is entitled to interest at the rate of five per cent per annum from the date of the payment or advance;

(d)   a partner is not entitled before the ascertainment of profits to interest on the capital subscribed by him;

(e)   every partner may take part in the management of the partnership business;

(f)   no partner shall be entitled to remuneration for acting in the partnership business;

(g)   no person may be introduced as a partner without the consent of all existing partners;

(h)   any difference arising as to ordinary matters connected with the partnership business may be decided by a majority of the partners, but no change may be made in the nature of the partnership business without the consent of all existing partners;

(i)   the partnership books are to be kept at the place of business of the partnership (or the principal place if there is more than one) and every partner may, when he thinks fit, have access to and inspect and copy any of them.

5 Partnership Acts: s 20 (V); s 21 (S); s 23 (MI); s 36 (Ni), (CI); (Tu); s 37 (N); s 24 Partnership Act 1890 (UK) (SI), (K), (T).

A partnership need not be created expressly as a contract. However, most partnerships do in themselves constitute a contract, in that the elements of agreement and consideration, which are the fundamentals of contract, will be present in most partnerships. Consideration is constituted by the mutual promises made by the parties and by the agreement to share in the profits of the undertaking. Very often the partnership agreement is referred to as a partnership contract. Some partnership agreements are created by way of a deed or indenture between the parties, but this is not strictly necessary, given that the elements of consideration will usually be present.

There can be an enforceable contract to create a partnership at some future time.[6] Furthermore, a partnership can be created by estoppel. This has long been acknowledged in restricted cases.[7] However, the doctrine of estoppel has undergone considerable evolution in comparatively recent times and its basis has been broadened. It is no longer a merely defensive equity, but can be used effectively to create substantive legal rights. It can do so even where consideration in the sense required by contract law is absent, a development which some fear undercuts the jurisprudential basis for the law of contract.

It is normal, but not obligatory, that there be a written partnership agreement or deed embodying the main terms that the parties have agreed on. The agreement will usually cover such matters as the following, although this list is not exhaustive:

- Date of commencement of the partnership. If no date is specified, it is to be determined by evidence as a matter of fact. The partnership can commence before the actual partnership business commences to operate, but in the absence of a specified date of commencement, this would be presumed to be the date of commencement of the business.
- Duration of the partnership. A partnership might be for a fixed period of time only, or subsist only until the happening of some event or be for an indefinite period.
- Nature of the partnership business. The partnership might relate to one business undertaking or several together. It might commence with an existing business or be open to expansion into other areas of business.
- Entitlement of the partners to shares of profits and losses of the partnership. These are usually presumed to be equal unless the contrary intention is shown.
- Rights, duties and obligations of partners: including prohibitions, if any, against the partners carrying on business in competition.
- Contributions to partnership capital and how, when and by whom they are to be made. These are most often equal, but need not be so.

---

6 See *South Sydney District Rugby League Football Club Ltd v News Ltd* (No 5) [2000] FCA 877.
7 See Roderick l'Anson Banks, RC, *Lindley & Banks on Partnership*, 21st edn, 2022, London, Sweet & Maxwell, Part 3, Chapters 12–14.

- Entitlement of the partners to a share of partnership property. There is a presumption that these are equal, but this can be displaced by agreement.
- Management of the partnership business: some partners might not be expected to participate in the management or running of the business, being, in effect, 'silent partners'.
- Provisions governing retirement of existing partners and pre-emptive purchase rights of remaining partners. It is usual that in the event of the retirement of a partner, the remaining partners have the first right to purchase the interest of that partner at a price determined according to a specified formula.
- Admission of new partners.
- Assignment of interests in the partnership. It is to be noted that an assignment does not generally make the assignee a new partner with rights and duties as a partner as against the existing partners.
- Mortgages and charges against partnership interests and partnership property. Sometimes this is permitted and sometimes not.
- Circumstances under which a partnership is dissolved. The statutes make provisions as to dissolution that apply in the absence of agreement to the contrary. Some factors might give rise to an immediate dissolution of the partnership whilst others might involve an election to be made by the partners or some of them.
- Remuneration rights of partners. Some partners who participate in the running of the partnership business might be entitled to remuneration over and above their share in profits.
- Powers of a partner to obtain advances or to borrow against shares of profits.
- Termination of partnership. Usually, the partnership agreement stipulates that on the happening of certain events as regards one partner or more generally, the remaining partners have the right to terminate the partnership agreement by written notice. This might or might not lead to the dissolution of the partnership. Usually, the remaining partners will be given the right, for example, to continue the partnership and to operate its business on buying out the relevant partner.
- Circumstances under which a partner might be excluded from the partnership for some form of specified misconduct.
- The keeping and auditing of the accounts of the partnership.
- The employment of lawyers, accountants and auditors of the partnership.

There is nothing either in the Partnership Acts or elsewhere that imposes a formal requirement as to writing in the creation of a partnership. Nor are there other particular formalities required for the creation of a partnership. Being largely governed by equity in early times, the issue of whether a partnership was created was one of substance rather than one of meeting formal requirements.

Orally created partnerships are enforceable, provided, of course, that the arrangement that is constituted meets the definitional elements to make it a valid partnership under the relevant legislation. It is possible that a partnership agreement, like an ordinary contract, could be constituted by terms that are partly in writing and partly oral. This creates substantial scope for dispute between parties as to whether the writing constituted the whole of the transaction between the parties or not. Where there is some writing purporting to record the transaction, there might be some evidential presumption that this was to represent the totality of the agreement, but this can be rebutted by proof that the writing did not represent all terms that the parties agreed to.

The Partnership Acts supplement this agreement by implying some terms only if the partnership agreement does not otherwise provide. In a few cases, the Act supersedes the agreement of the parties, but this is the exception rather than the rule. A partnership can be created by a wholly oral agreement between the parties or by a combination of a written document and an oral agreement. It is a matter for the court to determine, first, that a partnership has been created by the parties in accordance with the requirements discussed elsewhere and, secondly, what the constituted terms of the partnership are in any case. Obviously, where the court is faced with a mixture of oral and written terms this will be no easy task, but it is one that the court must nevertheless perform.

Terms implied by operation of law could refer, on the one hand, to those terms which a statute implies or deems to exist in the partnership, such as those under s 25 of the Fiji Islands Partnership Act (mentioned above). On the other hand, it could refer to those terms that the courts imply themselves in order to give better effect to the intentions of the parties or to require the partners to better fulfil their obligations to one another. Those that arise by way of the construction of the partnership agreement are considered further below. Others arise not by the construction of the agreement but by the operation of law in a wider sense. One of the more important of these implied obligations is the fiduciary obligation which the partners owe to one another. This obligation will be examined further in due course.

2.1.2 Adding to the terms of the partnership

The terms of a partnership can be varied by further contract of variation between the partners. As a partnership is created by contract, any variation of it cannot usually be effective unless any agreement as to variation is supported by independent consideration.[8] As there is no legal requirement that a partnership be in writing, a written partnership agreement can be varied (or discharged) by an oral agreement.[9] The variation of the rights of the partners itself does not provide sufficient consideration.

---

8 Generally referred to as accord and satisfaction. See *Tallerman & Co Pty Ltd v Nathan's Merchandise (Victoria) Pty Ltd* (1957) HCA 10; 98 CLR 93.
9 See *Berry v Berry* [1929] 2 KB 316. This applies even where the partnership agreement was embodied in a deed.

However, the doctrine of estoppel may play a part here as well. Where one partner, by some representation, promise, undertaking or course of conduct, has encouraged another partner or the other partners to rely on an assumption to the effect that the rights of the first party under the partnership will not be enforced, and this is actually relied on by the others to their detriment, then the first party might be estopped from enforcing those rights.[10] Another situation involves estoppel by convention. In contract situations,[11] it is now clear that parties might enter into a formal contract and then proceed by virtue of certain assumptions to trade or carry out the contract according to certain assumptions (or assumed states of affairs) which do not have a clear basis in the express terms of the contract. This assumed state of affairs can give rise to what is called an estoppel by convention. According to one formulation, an estoppel by convention will arise in the following circumstances:

(i)   the parties have assumed a state of affairs whether it be factual, legal or both;
(ii) the assumed state of affairs is the basis for action or inaction in the dealings between the parties;
(iii) the departure by one party from the assumption would result in a detriment being suffered by the other party.[12]

The older cases appear to lay greater emphasis on the idea that the representation or otherwise should have caused a party to change their position. The later cases tend to speak of detriment.[13] It has been suggested that 'convention' here refers to 'mutual representations' of the parties.[14] Yet there is some doubt about whether the assumptions on which the parties proceed should have some reference to the contract, its construction or its legal effect, or in fact any reference to the pre-existing contract at all. The above analysis suggests that one perhaps looks to the effect of the assumptions on the contract rather than to assumptions deriving from the contract in some way. However, some judicial statements suggest that there should

---

10 See the cases referred to under fn 1 above.
11 Although it need not be confined to contract situations: see *Downderry Constructions Ltd v Secretary of State for Transport Local Government and the Regions and Caradon District Council* [2002] EWHC 2 (Admin); *Republic of India and Others v India Steamship Company Ltd* [1997] UKHL 40, [1997] 4 All ER 380, [1997] 3 WLR 818, the latter appearing to suggest that cases of estoppel by convention and estoppel by acquiescence are not examples of the operation of the same overarching principle.
12 *Powercor Australia Ltd v Pacific Power* [1999] VSC 110 at para 451, relying on the principles enunciated by Dixon J in *Grundt v The Great Boulder Proprietary Gold Mines Ltd* (1938) 59 CLR 641.
13 See *Commonwealth v Venoayen* (1990) HCA 39; 170 CLR 394 at 415 referred to in *Kramer v Stone* [2023] NSWCA 270 at para 181; *Waltons Stores (Interstate) Ltd v Maher* (1988) HCA 7; 164 CLR 387 at 419.
14 *Mirvac Homes Pty Ltd v Parramatta City Council* [1999] NSWLEC 239 at para 32.

be a referential nexus. In *Hamel-Smith v Pycroft & Jetsave Ltd*,[15] in a passage later endorsed by Bingham LJ in *The Vistafjord*,[16] Peter Gibson J said that the estoppel applies where:

(1) parties have established by their construction of their agreement or their apprehension of its legal effect a conventional basis;
(2) on that basis they have regulated their subsequent dealings; and
(3) it would be unjust or unconscionable if one of the parties resiled from that convention.

However it is formulated, the notion of estoppel by convention might appear at once to fall foul of the settled principle relating to the interpretation of contracts. It is well established that a court in construing a contract is not permitted to look at the subsequent conduct of the parties. For example, in *James Miller & Partners Ltd v Whitworth Street Estates (Manchester) Ltd*, Lord Reid said:

> It is not legitimate to use as an aid in the construction of the contract anything which the parties said or did after it was made. Otherwise one might have the result that a contract meant one thing the day that it was signed, but by reason of subsequent events meant something different a month or a year later.[17]

However, the courts have treated estoppel by convention cases as involving something other than construction of contract issues, notwithstanding that estoppel in this context, as in fact in most others, can be seen as an *ex post facto* variation of the settled basis of the contract. It is not really a case of adding to the contract as such. Rather it is a matter of doing justice to the state of affairs established by the parties. In *Amalgamated Investment and Property Co Ltd v Texas Commerce International Bank Ltd*, Lord Denning said:

> Although subsequent conduct cannot be used for the purpose of interpreting a contract retrospectively, yet it is often convincing evidence of a course of dealing after it. There are many cases to show that a course of dealing may give rise to legal obligations. It may be used to complete a contract which would otherwise be incomplete. It may be used so as to introduce terms and conditions into a contract which would not otherwise be there.
>
> If it can be used to introduce terms which were not already there, it must also be available to add to, or vary, terms which are there already, or to interpret them. If parties to a contract by their course of dealing put a particular

15 (1987) unreported, 5 February.
16 [1988] 2 Lloyd's Rep 343 at 351–2.
17 [1970] AC 583 at 603.

interpretation on the terms of it – on the faith of which each of them – to the knowledge of the other – acts and conducts their mutual affairs – they are bound by that interpretation just as much as if they had written it down as being a variation of the contract. There is no need to inquire whether their particular interpretation is correct or not – or whether they were mistaken or not – or whether they had in mind the original terms or not. Suffice it that they have, by their course of dealing, put their own interpretation on their contract, and cannot be allowed to go back on it.[18]

In *Republic of India and Others v India Steamship Company Ltd*, the House of Lords said:

> It is settled that an estoppel by convention may arise where parties to a transaction act on an assumed state of facts or law, the assumption being either shared by them both or made by one and acquiesced in by the other. The effect of an estoppel by convention is to preclude a party from denying the assumed facts or law if it would be unjust to allow him to go back on the assumption: *The August Leonhardt* [1985] 2 Lloyd's Rep 28; *The Vistafjord* [1988] 2 Lloyd's Rep 343; Treitel, *Law of Contracts*, 9th edn, at 112–13. It is not enough that each of the two parties acts on an assumption not communicated to the other. But it was rightly accepted by counsel for both parties that a concluded agreement is not a requirement for an estoppel by convention.[19]

2.1.3 Construction of the partnership agreement

A partnership agreement is taken to express the terms of the arrangement made between the parties. It is a matter for the court to determine what the intention of the parties might have been. Where they are written, partnership agreements vary in size and sophistication depending partly on the complexity of the arrangement and sometimes on whether the agreement has been drawn up by a lawyer or an accountant.

As noted above, partnership agreements are not required by law to be in writing. Thus, the courts, in interpreting the terms, do not adhere to the written document as much as if the document is a will or a statute, where the writing is taken as fundamental to the legal act in question. However, the most basic rule is that the words which appear in a document, or which are otherwise treated as making up the terms of the partnership, are to be given their plain and ordinary meaning. Although the task of the court is to give effect to the words used in this way, this is seen as the best way of giving effect to the intention of the parties. This intention

---

18 [1982] 1 QB 84, [1981] 3 All ER 577.
19 [1997] UKHL 40, [1997] 4 All ER 380, [1997] 3 WLR 818.

is to be determined objectively as far as possible, rather than inquiring into what the actual state of mind or intentions of the parties were at the time they made the agreement. Put another way, it is not a matter of seeing what went on at the time in the minds of the parties.[20]

Accordingly, in *Barker Gosling Group Pty Ltd v Lilley*, it was said:

> Although the task of the Court is to give effect to the plain and ordinary meaning of the words used, it does so with the object of giving effect to the intention of the parties to the contract, which is to be ascertained objectively.[21]

The terms of the partnership will usually be expressly formulated, but they can also be implied by the courts from the circumstances in which the parties found themselves or from the conduct of the parties at the time of entry into the partnership. Terms can be implied according to certain factual assumptions or as a matter of law.

In *South Sydney District Rugby League Football Club Ltd v News Ltd*,[22] it was said:

> Where a term is implied in fact rather than in law, the implication is based upon the presumed or imputed intentions of the parties. Where the contract is a formal one complete on its face, if a term is to be implied it must be reasonable and equitable; necessary to give business efficacy to the contract so that no term will be implied if the contract is effective without it; so obvious that 'it goes without saying'; capable of clear expression; and must not contradict any express term of the contract,[23] ... Where the contract is an informal one that has not been reduced to any complete written form, the test for implying a term is whether the implication of it is 'necessary for the reasonable or effective operation of the contract' in the circumstances of the case.[24] ... In such a case,

---

20 See *Codelfa Construction Pty Ltd v State Rail Authority (NSW)* [1982] HCA 24; 149 CLR 337 at 346–52, *per* Mason J. See also *Barker Gosling Group Pty Ltd v Lilley* [2000] FCA 999.

21 Para 29, referring to *Codelfa, ibid.* at 346–52, *per* Mason J.

22 Para 392.1, referring to *Byrne and Frew v Australian Airlines Ltd* (1992) 45 IR 178 at 422 *per* Hill J. An appeal was heard before the Full Court of the Federal Court by Black CI, Keely, Beaumont, Gray and Heerey JJ (1994) 52 IR 10. For commentary on the case, see Anthony Forsyth, "Contractual Incorporation of Award Terms: Byrne and Frew v Australian Airlines Ltd" (1994) 36 JIR 417. On the apparent differences between the tests for formal and informal contracts, see Tolhurst, GJ and Carter, JW, 'The new law of implied terms' (1996) 11 CLJ 76; Tolhurst, GJ and Carter, JW, 'Implied terms: refining the new law' (1997) 12 CLJ 152.

23 Referring to *BP Refinery (Westernport) Pty Ltd v Shire of Hastings* (1977) UKPCHCA 1; 180 CLR 266 at 283; *Codelfa Construction Pty Ltd v State Rail Authority (NSW)* [1982] HCA 24; 149 CLR 337; *Byrne v Australian Airlines Ltd* (1995) HCA 24; 185 CLR 410 at 441–42.

24 Referring to *Breen v Williams* (1996) HCA 57; 186 CLR 71 at 123–24.

though, it is necessary to arrive at some conclusion as to the actual intention of the parties before considering any presumed or imputed intention.

The courts can also imply a term into the partnership agreement as a matter of law, which it regards as a legal incident of a particular class of contract.[25] This is quite different from the implication of a term as a matter of fact, where it is a matter of reconstructing the intention of the parties. In such a case the implication made by the court does not depend upon the intention of the parties at all.[26] It is regarded more or less explicitly as a policy issue.[27]

2.2 Exclusion clauses

Partnership agreements, like insurance policies, are commercial documents. They should thus be given a businesslike interpretation.[28] According to *McCann v Switzerland Insurance Australia Ltd*, '[interpreting] a commercial document requires attention to the language used by the parties, the commercial circumstances which the document addresses, and the objects which it is intended to secure'.[29] In this context, exclusion clauses will be given effect as regards liability which is clearly within the ambit of the words used. That includes cases of fraud and dishonesty.[30]

So far as interpretation of these clauses is concerned, the High Court of Australia in *Darlington Futures Ltd v Delco Australia Pty Ltd* said:[31]

> the interpretation of an exclusion clause is to be determined by construing the clause according to its natural and ordinary meaning, read in the light of the contract as a whole, thereby giving due weight to the context in which the clause appears including the nature and object of the contract and, where appropriate, construing the clause *contra proferentem* in case of ambiguity.

---

25 See also *Australis Media Holdings Pty Ltd v Telstra Corp Ltd* (1998) 43 NSWLR104 at 122–23.

26 See also *Breen v Williams* (1996) HCA 57; 186 CLR 71 at 103.

27 See *South Sydney District Rugby League Football Club Ltd v News Ltd* [2000] FCA 1541; *Simonius Vischer & Cov Holt & Thompson* [1979] 2 NSWLR 322 at 348.

28 *Hydarnes Steamship Co v Indemnity Mutual Marine Assurance Co* [1895] 1 QB 500 at 504.

29 [2000] HCA 65 at 22; *Lake v Simmons* [1927] AC 487 at 509, *per* Viscount Sumner.

30 *McCann v Switzerland Insurance* [2000] HCA 65 at para 23; see also *Australian Breeders Co-Operative Society Ltd v Griffith Morgan Jones and Others* [1997] 1405 FCA; *Lynch & Co v United States Fidelity and Guarantee Co* [1971] 1 OR 28; *Crowe v Wheeler and Reynolds* [1988] 1 Qd R 40. On the dishonesty exemption clauses in insurance policies, see generally *McMillan v Joseph* (1987) 4 ANZ Insurance Cases 60–822; *Crowe v Wheeler and Reynolds* [1988] 1 Qd R 40 *East End Real Estate Pty Ltd v CE Heath Casualty & General Insurance Ltd* (1991) 7 ANZ Insurance Cases 61–151; *Chittick v Maxwell* (1993) 118 ALR 728; *HG & R Nominees Pty Ltd v Fava* [1997] 2 VR 368.

31 (1986) 161 CLR 500 at 510. See also *Underwriters at Lloyd's and Ors v Ellis* [1998] NSWCA 242, *per* Powell J.

2.2.1 Restraint of trade terms

It is not uncommon that a partnership agreement will contain a restraint of trade clause that provides, on the face of it, that a partner who leaves the partnership cannot carry on business in competition with the remaining partners for a speci-fied term and within a specified area.

Clauses of this nature have traditionally been viewed with some suspicion but can be enforceable on certain conditions. In *Amoco Australia Pty Ltd v Rocca Bros Motor Engineering Co Pty Ltd.*, it was said that 'a restraint will not be enforce-able, unless it affords no more than adequate protection to the interests of the cov-enantee [partner] in respect of which he is entitled to be protected'.[32] In *Geraghty v Minter*, Mason J said: 'Whether the restraint which is accepted is reasonable depends initially on the nature and the extent of the interest which is sought to be protected, for the restraint must not exceed that which is necessary for the legiti-mate protection of the interest'.[33]

These clauses are available for the protection of partners just as much as employers. Master and servant situations are earlier examples of the use of such clauses and there has been some confusion about whether they applied only to partnership situations in which the partner was previously an employee or not. The position now is that this is seemingly irrelevant. The High Court of Australia has held, assuming applicability,[34] that 'in no circumstances can there be any rea-son for regarding covenants made between partners more strictly than those made between employers and employees'.[35] Furthermore, as Stephen J said in *Geraghty v Minter:*

> There is nothing unreasonable about a 'unilateral' restraint clause where a new partner is admitted into an existing business venture; nor in such a case is it necessarily remarkable that the partnership should be terminable at short notice without cause. All must depend upon the particular circumstances of the parties who have chosen these terms as appropriate to govern their partnership relationship. A 'unilateral' restraint clause is not merely reasonable, it is com-mercially essential where the intention of the parties is that on a dissolution a particular partner is to retain for himself the benefit of the goodwill of the busi-ness. That intention is, of course, made manifest when such a restraint clause is coupled with an express provision entitling that partner, upon dissolution, to retain sole property in and the exclusive use of the existing partnership name.[36]

---

32 (1973) HCA 40; 133 CLR 288 at 306; and see pp 315–16.
33 (1979) HCA 42; 142 CLR 177 at para 14.
34 See *Fitch v Dewes* [1921] AC 158; *Scorer v Seymour Jones* [1966] 1 WLR 1419, [1966] 3 All ER 347.
35 *Geraghty v Minter* (1979) HCA 42; 142 CLR 177 at 185, *per* Gibbs J.
36 (1979) HCA 42; 142 CLR 177 at 190.

Where a person seeks equitable relief, such as by way of injunction, the relief is discretionary. Whoever comes to equity must do equity. Thus, it has been said that persons who seek equitable relief by injunction to enforce a covenant in restraint of trade "cannot obtain such relief unless they allege and prove that they have performed their part of the bargain hitherto and are ready and able also to perform their part in the future".[37]

Those who seek to enforce the clause have the onus of showing that the clause is in all respects reasonable as regards the restraint which it seeks to impose. A restraining clause which, having regard to all of the circumstances between the parties, is unreasonable as to either the area within which it was intended to operate or the time for which it was to endure will not be enforced. A clause will only be enforced, in other words, if it provides no more than adequate protection for the interest of the remaining partner or partners. Furthermore, it must be shown that the restraint which is actually imposed is not described in terms that are so wide as to make it unreasonable.[38] The remaining partner or partners also have to show that the interest which they are seeking to protect by way of the restrain clause is one which they are entitled to protect.[39] Where, for example, the remaining partners have the sole right to continue to use the firm name, it is clear that the restraint of trade covenant is incidental to the enforcement of that right.[40]

The validity of the restraint of trade clause is to be determined at the time the partnership agreement was made.[41] In *Shell UK Ltd v Lostock Garage Ltd*,[42] Lord Denning MR acknowledged this as the general rule. However, he suggested an exception: the court should not enforce a contract in restraint of trade if circumstances afterwards arise in which it would be unreasonable or unfair to enforce it. This was not accepted by the majority[43] and is a proposition of dubious status. The court failed to approve it in *Geraghty v Minter*. In that case, Mason J (as he then was) seems to have had some reservations about the issue being wholly considered at the date of the agreement, saying:

---

37 *Measures Brothers Ltd v Measures* [1910] 2 Ch 248 at 254; approved in *Kaufman v McGillicuddy* (1914) 19 CLR 1 at 10–11. See also *Shell UK & Co v Lostock Garage Ltd* [1976] 1 WLR 1187 at 1199, 1202, 1206; [1979] 1 All ER at 490, 492, 496; *Geraghty v Minter* (1979) HCA 42; 142 CLR 177, *per* Gibbs J.

38 *Geraghty v Minter* (1979) HCA 42; 142 CLR 177 at 186, *per* Gibbs J.

39 *Ibid.* at 187.

40 *Ibid.*

41 See *Lindner v Murdoch's Garage* (1950) 83 CLR 628 at 653; *Amoco Australia Pty Ltd v Rocca Bros Motor Engineering Co Pty Ltd* (1973) HCA 40; 133 CLR 288; 1 ALR 385.

42 [1976] 1 WLR 1187 at 1196, *per* Lord Denning MR.

43 *Ibid.* at 1201–02, 1203.

it should not apply so as to exclude from consideration a subsequent agreement by which the parties divide the ownership of that goodwill which the restraint was designed to protect.[44]

In *Souster v Draper*,[45] a partnership agreement contained a clause to the effect that each partner would 'be just and faithful to the other and shall devote that partner's best efforts and whole time and attention to the partnership business'. The partnership agreement divided entitlement to the share of profits between the two partners on a 60:40 basis. It was claimed by one partner (entitled to 40%) that the failure of the other partner to produce 60% of the income of the firm constituted a breach of this term. The High Court of New Zealand rejected this contention both as a matter of fact and in terms of the established legal nature of the relationship between partners, in the latter respect following *Gallagher v Schulz*.[46]

2.2.2 Breach of terms

The general consequences of a breach of partnership are similar to those that apply to a breach of a simple contract. However, it must be kept in mind that a partnership gives rise to fiduciary obligations on the partners, unlike simple contracts generally. A breach of a partnership agreement might lead to a right to damages or a right to terminate, or a range of other consequences. Very often the express terms of the partnership agreement will specify the consequences of particular breaches. These could include termination of the partnership or the exclusion of the partner who is guilty of a breach. In other cases, the occurrence of a particular breach might lead to the dissolution of the partnership altogether.

It is clear that, as with any contract, a partnership agreement may be breached, and such breach may involve repudiation of the partnership.[47] Defined in its narrow sense, repudiation of a contract may occur when a party manifests an inability or unwillingness to perform it or evinces an intention no longer to be bound by the partnership agreement. It would be likewise where a partner indicates an intention to fulfil the partnership obligations only in some way that is substantially inconsistent with that party's obligations. In such cases, the innocent partner is entitled either immediately to accept the repudiation and treat the partnership as at an end, or to ignore the repudiation and claim damages or other remedies for breach.

---

44 (1979) HCA 42; 142 CLR 177 at 200.
45 CA156/98, 26 April 1999 at para 7.
46 (1988) 2 NZBLC 103,196 at 103.
47 See e.g. *Hurst v Bryk* [1997] 2 All ER 283 at 289 and 303 and the cases cited there; [2000] 2 WLR 250.

2.2.3 Shares in a partnership

It is common enough to talk of a share in a partnership. But there is a need for caution in doing so. The expression 'share in a partnership' does not refer to a share like that of a member of a proprietary company, which is a legal property interest. Holding a share in a company makes a person a member of the company and gives that person a special form of property. The latter is not an interest in the property or assets owned by the company itself, even though the underlying asset value might have some impact on the value of the share. It is independent property in itself, which is owned by the shareholder.

In contemporary legal theory, a company share is a type of personal property which is in nature distinct from the property owned by the relevant company.[48] Formerly, as recently as the 18th century, a company was taken to be a trustee of its assets for the benefit of its members, which meant that remedies in equity could be available against it for a breach of trust.[49] Under some circumstances, the members of the company, as trust beneficiaries, could be regarded as owning an interest in the assets of the corporation.[50] Later, however, in the 19th century, company shares came to be treated as personal property – a move which denied the shareholder the possibility of an interest in the underlying assets of the company.[51] The property held by the shareholder was thereafter regarded as the shares themselves and not any interest in the underlying corporate assets.

A share in a partnership is something different again. This is due to a partnership being a different kind of association from a company. A partnership is generally not incorporated. The share of a partner must therefore be something more direct, in that it involves direct participation in the property of the partnership. Even so, that hardly clarifies all of the senses in which we can speak of a share in a partnership. It has been said:

> The phrase 'share in a partnership' can be used to convey a number of different meanings. It can be used to refer to the right of a partner to share in any surplus of partnership assets over partnership liabilities upon dissolution and the associated beneficial interest in the totality of partnership assets prior to dissolution (*Arbuckle v Federal Commissioner of Taxation* (1964) 13 ATD 378; *Bakewell v Deputy Federal Commissioner of Taxation (SA)* (1937) 58 CLR, p 770). It can, in some contexts, be used to refer to the 'capital' directly or indirectly contributed to the partnership and which is distinct from, and may be

---

48 See *Archibald Howie Pty Ltd v Commissioner* of *Stamp Duties (NSW)* (1948) HCA 28; 77 CLR 143 at 156–57. The same applies to shares in other corporations such as cooperatives and credit unions.

49 *Ashby v Blackwell and The Million Bank Co* (1765) Amb 503; 27 ER 326.

50 This was so as regards real estate of the corporation.

51 *Bligh v Brent* (1836) 2 Y & C Ex 268; 160 ER 397.

unrelated to, his interest in any surplus of assets on dissolution (see *Lindley on Partnerships*, 13th edn, p 347). As a matter of convenience, it can be used to refer to the total aggregation of a partner's rights under a particular partnership agreement (his part 'of the whole adventure': *Hocking v Western Australian Bank* (1909) 9 CLR, p 743). While the phrase is a useful one and is to be found in the various Partnership Acts and in judgments of the highest authority, it is important to ensure that its latent ambiguity does not conceal a need for precision and that its use does not camouflage either the true nature of the particular partnership relationship or the fact that generalisations as to the content of the rights and duties, *inter socios*, of the members of a partnership are liable to be misleading.[52]

What, then, is the nature of a share in a partnership? This issue was considered in *Everett v Federal Commissioner of Taxation*, where Bowen CJ in the Federal Court of Australia said:

[A partner has] ... a beneficial interest in the partnership assets. That interest is not to be described as a title to specific property but as a right to his proportion of the surplus after the realization of assets and the payment of debts and liabilities (*Bakewell v Deputy Federal Commissioner of Taxation* (SA) (1937) 58 CLR 743, p 770; *Canny Gabriel Castle Jackson Advertising Pty Ltd v Volume Sales (Finance) Pty Ltd* (1974) 131 CLR 321, p 327). Notwithstanding the peculiar fluctuating character of the interest of a partner, it is regarded as an interest in every asset of the partnership and is properly described as a beneficial interest (*Livingston v Commissioner for Stamp Duties* (Q) (1960) 107 CLR 411, p 453). So far as profits are concerned the partnership accounts for purposes of the agreement between partners and the income tax legislation were maintained on an accruals basis.[53]

In *Chan v Zacharia*, Dean J said:

It is now established, under the general law as reinforced by the provisions of Partnership Acts and in the absence of overriding provisions of a particular partnership agreement (see *Attorney-General v Boden* [1912] 1 KB 539), that the legal representative of a deceased partner has 'an unascertained interest in every single asset of the partnership, and it is not right to regard him as being merely entitled to a particular sum of cash ascertained from the balance sheet of the partnership as drawn up at the date of his death' (*per* Romer J, *Manley*

---

52 *Commissioner of Taxation of the Commonwealth of Australia v Everett, Peter R* [1978] FCA 89; 21 ALR 625; 38 FLR 26 at 40, *per* Deane J.
53 38 FLR 26. Upheld on appeal by the High Court: [1980] HCA 6; 143 CLR 440; 54 ALJR196.

v Sartori [1927] 1 Ch 157, pp 163–64) ... Notwithstanding the strictures of [some] authorities ... there is neither metaphor nor inaccuracy in the description, in the ordinary case, of a partner or of a surviving partner as a trustee of a particular item of partnership property which is legally vested in his name but the 'beneficial interest' in which 'belongs to the partnership'.[54]

An interest or share in a partnership is equitable property. A share in a proprietary company is legal property. Both are choses in action. A partnership share is distinct from the underlying assets of the partnership which might in some sense comprise it. Each partner thus has distinctive equitable property. Section 33 of the Partnership Act 1895 of Western Australia, for which there is no corresponding provision in the South Pacific legislation, provides that the share of a partner in the partnership property at any time is the proportion of the then existing partnership assets to which he or she would be entitled if the whole were realised and converted into money, and after all the then existing debts and liabilities of the firm had been discharged. But, as is shown by the heading of Part III of the Act, in which s 33 appears, this is one of the provisions which regulate the relations of partners to one another, and it does no more than give statutory effect to the view always maintained by the courts[55] as to the 'indefinite and fluctuating interest' of each partner vis à vis the others. In *Sharp v Union Trustee Co of Australia Ltd*, Rich J said:

> No doubt, as between himself and his partners, his interest in individual items is subject to their right to have all the assets of the partnership for the time being dealt with in accordance with the partnership agreement, but his interest in them is none the less real for that.[56]

In *Haque v Haque (No 2)*,[57] the issue was the location of the interest of the deceased in various partnerships for the purposes of succession law. This depended on how the interest of the deceased partner was to be classified. Private international law has different rules for moveable and immoveable property. The partnership owned land in Western Australia. Did this mean that the interest of the deceased in the partnership was to be regarded as an interest in immoveable property; that is, the real estate itself? If it were, then the law of Western Australia would apply, seeing as the land was located in that jurisdiction. Having found that both partnerships were solvent at the date of death and that the death of the deceased did not terminate the partnership, Kitto J held that the interest in

---

54 [1984] HCA 36; 154 CLR 178 at para 16.
55 See *Bakewell v Deputy Federal Commissioner of Taxation (SA)* [1937] HCA 11; 58 CLR 743 at 770, and the cases cited there.
56 [1944] HCA 35; 69 CLR 539 at 551.
57 [1965] HCA 38; 114 CLR 98.

the partnership, whatever underlying assets it might relate to, remained personal property:

> [In] relation to both the partnerships with which we are concerned the pre-liminary question is: what asset of the estate is it material to consider for the purpose of deciding the right of succession? The deceased in his lifetime had, in relation to each partnership, rights of two kinds. On the one hand he had rights with respect to each individual item of partnership property, constitut-ing an interest in each such item, which he was entitled to assert as against all the world. ... On the other hand he had his share in the partnership as a whole, consisting of a right as against his co-partners – and this was his whole right as against them – to have the assets realized on dissolution of the partnership, to have the proceeds applied in discharging the debts and liabilities, and to have his share of the surplus paid to him. ... When he died, his beneficial interest in the individual assets no doubt devolved upon his executor, but the executor could not realize such an interest or dispose of it as if it were by itself an asset of the estate. The asset to be administered was (in the case of A & N Haque) the share in the partnership as a whole, and (in the case of A Haque & Co) the money which the partnership agreement provided should be paid to the estate by the surviving partners in satisfaction of the share. The question of succes-sion therefore arises with respect only to the share in the partnership in the one case and the obligation of the co-partners in the other. These assets, being choses in action, are in my opinion to be classed as movables.

Thus, the partnership interest of the deceased was to be regarded as an item of moveable property. Even though it might reflect interests in underlying assets which are themselves immoveable property (real estate or interests in real estate), the interest as such is moveable. Thus, it was subject to the succession laws of the deceased's place of domicile.

2.2.4 Assignment

As we have just noted, an interest in a partnership is equitable property. It consti-tutes a form of personal property vested in the partners individually. This form of property is known as an equitable chose in action. Normally one would assume that this would mean that it is assignable only in equity rather than as a legal chose in action. The courts, however, have consistently held that equitable choses in action are within the meaning of 'legal chose in action' as this term is employed in the Property Law Act provision dealing with assignment.[58] Thus, they are assigna-

---

58 See e.g. s 113 Property Law Act Cap 130 (F) and the authorities discussed below; Property Law Act (UK) 1925 (Ni), (N), (Tu), (T), (V), (K), (CI), (MI), (S), (SI).

ble by notice under the section. This, however, is an optional or alternative method of assignment which does not preclude equitable assignment. Thus, an interest in a partnership is assignable by a legal means and an equitable means.

The Property Law Act provision follows what was first introduced as s 25(6) of the Supreme Court of Judicature Act 1873 (UK), thereafter s 136 of the Law of Property Act 1925 (UK). These provisions have been adopted in the South Pacific jurisdictions in one form or another. Section 113 of the Property Law Act Cap 130 of Fiji Islands is one relevant provision. It reads as follows:

> 113 (1) Any absolute assignment by writing under the hand of the assignor (not purporting to be by way of charge only) of any debt or other legal chose in action, of which express notice in writing has been given to the debtor, trustee, or other person from whom the assignor would have been entitled to receive or claim that debt or chose in action, is effectual in law (subject to equities having priority over the right of the assignee), to pass and transfer from the date of the notice
>
> (a)   the legal right to that debt or chose in action;
> (b)   all legal and other remedies for the debt or chose in action; and
> (c)   the power to give a good discharge for the debt or chose in action, without the concurrence of the assignor.
>
> (2) Where the debtor, trustee, or other person liable in respect of the debt or chose in action referred to in subsection (1) has notice –
>
> (a)   that the assignment so referred to is disputed by the assignor, or any person claiming under him; or
> (b)   of any other opposing or conflicting claims, to the debt or chose in action, he may, if he thinks fit, either call upon the persons making claim thereto to interplead concerning the debt or chose in action, or pay the debt or other chose in action into court, under the provisions of the Trustee Act.

It has been held in many jurisdictions that this applies in respect of partnership interests, and it would also appear to be the case in South Pacific jurisdictions. In *Federal Commissioner of Taxation v Everett,* it was said:

> the assignment does not constitute the assignee a partner or pass to him the powers of management, administration and inspection of books and accounts which repose in the assignor as a partner. What is more, legal title to the assets of the partnership continues to vest in the partners to the exclusion of the assignee and he has no access to the assets. The extent of the assignee's equitable interest is ascertainable only on dissolution. These considerations

lead us to the conclusion that the assigning partner continues to stand in the relationship of a trustee to the assignee, notwithstanding that the assignee may be entitled to receive payments from partnership profits direct from the partnership.[59]

Generally, an assignment is possible only in respect of presently existing property. A partnership interest as such is a presently existing chose in action which can thus be assigned. Sometimes, however, a partner might attempt to assign not the chose in action which he or she has but the interest in future income to be generated by the partnership and to which he or she would become entitled. This is what is termed future property, which is a mere expectancy or speculative interest and which is not regarded as immediately assignable. As a general proposition, future property is not assignable at common law,[60] but it could be assigned in equity because after-acquired or future property was assignable for value.[61] Consideration was required even where the assignment was effected by deed.[62]

Thus, Windeyer J in *Norman v Federal Commission of Taxation* said:

> But in equity a would-be present assignment of something to be acquired in the future is, when made for value, construed as an agreement to assign the thing when it is acquired. A court of equity will ensure that the would-be assignor performs this agreement, his conscience being bound by the consideration. The purported assignee thus gets an equitable interest in the property immediately the legal ownership of it is acquired by the assignor, assuming it to have been sufficiently described to be then identifiable. The prospective interest of the assignee is in the meantime protected by equity. These principles, which now govern assignments for value of property to be acquired in the future, have been developed and established by a line of well-known cases, of which *Holroyd v Marshall* (1862) 10 HLC 191 (11 ER 999); *Collyer v Isaacs* (1881) 19 Ch D 342; *Tailby v Official Receiver* (1888) 13 App Cas 523; and *In re Lind; Industrials Finance Syndicate Ltd v Lind* [1915] 2 Ch 345 are the most important.[63]

Any partner is entitled to make an equitable assignment of his or her share for value or, conceivably, by way of gift. In *United Builders Pty Ltd v Mutual Acceptance Ltd*, it was said:

---

59 [1980] HCA 6; 143 CLR 440 at 448.
60 *Lunn v Thornton* (1845) 1 CB 379; 135 ER 587.
61 See *Taitby v Official Receiver* (1888) 13 App Cas 523 *per* Lord Macnaghten.
62 *Norman v Federal Commissioner of Taxation* [1963] HCA 21; 109 CLR 9 at para 7, *per* Menzies J; referring to *In re Ellenborough* [1903] 1 Ch 697.
63 *Ibid.*, para 3. See also *Palette Shoes Pty Ltd v Krohn* (1937) HCA 37; 58 CLR 1 at 26, 27, *per* Dixon J.

It is trite law that a member of a partnership may not, without the consent of his partners, introduce a stranger into the partnership. Hence no assignment of his share in the partnership to a stranger, whether absolute or by way of security, will entitle the assignee to meddle in any way in the affairs of the partnership. This principle of partnership law now finds expression in s 31 of the Partnership Act[64] 1890 (UK) and in its counterpart, s 34 of the Partnership Act of 1891 (Q). Those sections restrict the right of such an assignee of a partnership share by denying him any right 'to interfere in the management or administration of the partnership business or affairs, or to require any accounts of the partnership transactions, or to inspect the partnership books'. So long as the partnership continues as a going concern, the assignee's only right 'as against the other partners' is to receive the assignor's share of profits; on dissolution he is entitled to the assignor's share of the partnership assets and, for the first time, to an account as from the date of dissolution.[65]

Where the assignment is for value, equity will enforce the assignment because it is for value according to the maxim 'equity regards as done that which ought to be done'. A partner may assign the partnership interest in whole or in part.[66] The assignment might be by way of deed but need not be. The assignment will not make the assignee a partner or confer on the assignee any right to interfere in the management or administration of the partnership. The assignment gives the assignee certain rights, such as the right to income, as part of the bundle of rights which are assigned. But that does not include the right to participate in or manage the partnership business nor the immediate right of access to the assets of the partnership. Without these rights being vested in the assignee, the assignee cannot be held to be a partner.[67] The assignment will be valid even where it has the consequence of avoiding the payment of income tax of a former partner by way of assigning income,[68] although it might be struck down where the transaction was a sham or constituted an evasion of taxation.[69]

The majority of the High Court in *Federal Commissioner of Taxation v Everett* pointed out that a partner has no title to any specific property owned by the

---

64 This applies for Kiribati, Solomon Islands, Tonga; and also in the Partnership Acts, s 35 (MI); s 32 (S); s 48 (N); s 31 (V); s 57 (CI), (Ni); s 34 (Tu).

65 [1980] HCA 43; 144 CLR 673 at 679.

66 See *Norman v Federal Commissioner of Taxation* [1963] HCA 21; 109 CLR 9 at 29; *Shepherd v Federal Commissioner of Taxation* (1965) 113 CLR 385 at 396; *Commissioner of Taxation of the Commonwealth of Australia v Everett, Peter R* [1978] FCA 89; 21 ALR 625; 38 FLR 26.

67 See *Commissioner of Taxation of the Commonwealth of Australia v Everett, Peter R* [1978] FCA 89; 21 ALR 625; 38 FLR 26; *Dodson v Downey* [1901] 2 Ch 620 at 622.

68 *Commissioner of Taxation of the Commonwealth of Australia v Everett, Peter R* [1978] FCA 89; 21 ALR 625; 38 FLR 26.

69 See *Arbuckle v Federal Commissioner of Taxation* (1964) 13 ATD 378.

partnership, but the partner has a beneficial interest in its assets.[70] This is an interest 'in each and every asset of the partnership as well as a right to a proportion of the surplus after the realisation of its assets and payment of debts and liabilities'.[71] For income tax purposes, in the Australian context at least, this did not deny that the amount a partner may receive from the partnership may include a share of income earned by the use of assets. Nor does the description of the interest of the partners as an equitable chose in action prevent it from being treated, again for income tax purposes, as a share of income.[72]

As regards assignments of partnership property, it is clear enough that equity will permit an assignment according to the requirements of equity, which are much less in relation to assignments than those for assignments at common law. In the latter case, strict compliance with prescribed formalities is necessary. Equity is much more relaxed regarding the method of assignment required, preferring to look to the substance rather than the form. In general, it mandates no requirement as to writing or any particular form of assignment. As a general proposition, all that is required to assign property in equity is a clear manifestation of the intention to assign the property in question.[73]

It is established that an assignee of a partnership interest is, by virtue of a valid assignment at the date of the assignment, entitled to "an unascertained interest in every single asset of the partnership, and it is not right to regard him as being merely entitled to a particular sum of cash ascertained from the balance sheet of the partnership as drawn up at the date of dissolution".[74] At the same time, the assignment of a share in a partnership cannot assign more than the partnership interest actually represents at the time of assignment.[75]

Most often a share in a partnership will consist of a right to a proportion of the surplus after the sale of the land and payment of the debts and liabilities of

---

70 [1980] HCA 6; 143 CLR 440, pp 452–55, referring to reasoning of Kitto J in *Stewart Dawson Holdings Pty Ltd v Federal Commissioner of Taxation* (1965) 39 ALJR 300 at 301.

71 *Commissioner of Taxation v Walsh, Peter Joseph* [1983] FCA 140; 48 ALR 253; 83 ATC 4415; 69 FLR 240.

72 See *Walsh, ibid., per* McGregor J, referring to *Livingston v Commissioner for Stamp Duties* (1960) 107 CLR 411, which, he said, "does not decide to the contrary, preoccupied as it was with the problem where is situate the right of a residuary legatee or next of kin to have an estate duly administered. So far as Kitto J in that case referred at p 453 to the interest of a partner, the reference was to a right to a proportion of the surplus after the realization of assets and payment of debts and liabilities of the partnership".

73 The requirements are the same as for assignments of a beneficial interest under a trust. See Chapter 3.

74 *Manley v Sartori* [1927] 1 Ch 157 at 163, 164; *In re Fuller's Contract* [1933] Ch 652 at 656; *Trustees Executors & Agency Co Ltd v Federal Commissioner of Taxation* [1944] HCA 20; 69 CLR 270 at 285.

75 See also *Maslen v Perpetual Trustees & Agency Co (WA) Ltd* [1950] HCA 55; 82 CLR 101.

the partnership.[76] As between members of a partnership, the relationship is contractual in nature, or at least primarily contractual. It is the terms of the partnership agreement (both express and implied) which set up the partnership and therefore provide the substratum on which the rights and duties of the parties are constructed. As Deane J has commented:

> Questions of illegality aside, any implication, by statute or rule of law, of provisions into the relationship between partners is ordinarily subject to any contrary intention appearing from the agreement between the partners. The rights of a member of a partnership will commonly (but not necessarily) include rights relating to any partnership assets which may exist. They will almost invariably (but, conceivably, not necessarily) include rights relating to any partnership profits which may be earned.[77]

Thus:

> In the absence of agreement to the contrary, a member of a partnership has no definite or separate share or interest in any particular partnership receipt or other item of partnership property. He has an undivided beneficial interest in the totality of partnership assets (including receipts and choses in action) and is entitled to insist that they be applied for legitimate purposes of the partnership. The precise content of that undivided beneficial interest will be affected by any separate right of the partner to share in any partnership profits or in any distribution of partnership assets in the sense that the distribution of partnership profits and assets, in accordance with the provisions of the partnership contract, is a legitimate purpose of the partnership. If the partnership agreement so provides or all the partners so agree, there is no general rule of law which prevents the partners dividing or applying partnership receipts and other assets at any time or in such manner as they see fit. In the absence of such provision or consensus, however, a partner's separate interest in relation to partnership assets is to share, either equally or in such other proportion as the partners may agree, in any surplus remaining, upon a dissolution, after the realization of the assets and payment of the debts and liabilities of the partnership. His separate entitlement in relation to any partnership profits is, in the absence of such provision or consensus, to share, either equally or in such other proportions as the partners may agree, in partnership profits if and when they are earned in

76 *Darby v Darby* (1856) 3 Drew 495 at 503–04, 61 ER 992 at 995; *Rodriguez v Speyer Bros* [1919] AC 59 at 68; *Bakewell v Deputy Federal Commissioner of Taxation (SA)* (1937) HCA 11; 58 CLR 743 at 770; *Commissioner of Taxation of the Commonwealth of Australia v Everett* (1980) HCA 6; 143 CLR 440 at 446.

77 *Commissioner of Taxation of the Commonwealth of Australia v Everett, Peter R* [1978] FCA 89; 21 ALR 625; 38 FLR 26, p 40.

respect of any accounting period which the partners accept (or, in the absence of agreement, the overall circumstances indicate) as appropriate or in respect of the whole or a particular part of a partnership venture.[78]

The question arises as to whether there be an assignment of a partnership interest in equity by way of gift which takes place without complying with the requirements of the likes of s 113 of the Property Law Act of Fiji, noted above. As indicated, the section does apply with respect to partnership interests. The problem here is rather narrower than the 'vexed' question of equitable assignments by way of gift of equitable property. As noted above, the view has been taken that the section provides only an alternative. Equitable choses in action are legally assignable by notice or by way of equitable assignment, which normally requires only a manifestation of intention rather than compliance with some formal method. In *Norman v Federal Commissioner of Taxation*, Windeyer J, after having stated that there was authority for the proposition that there could be a valid equitable assignment independent of the requirements of the statute, added:

> If an attempt is made to assign, by way of gift, a chose in action assignable under the statute, then, as I see the matter, the requirements of the statute cannot be ignored; for the general rule of equity is that an effective assignment occurs only if the donor does all that, according to the nature of the property, he must do to transfer the property to the donee. But the weight of authority is, I think, in favour of the view that in equity there is a valid gift of property transferable at law if the donor, intending to make, then and there, a complete disposition and transfer to the donee, does all that on his part is necessary to give effect to his intention and arms the donee with the means of completing the gift according to the requirements of the law: see *Brunker v Perpetual Trustee Co Ltd* (1937) 57 CLR 555, pp 600-02, *per* Dixon J; *Re Smith* (1901) 84 LT 835; *In re Rose* [1949] Ch 78; *In re Rose* [1952] 1 Ch 499. On this basis, if a man, meaning to make an immediate gift of a chose in action that is his, executes an instrument that meets the requirements of the statute and delivers it to the donee, actually or constructively, he has put it out of his power to recall his gift. It is true that until notice is given to the debtor or person against whom the chose is enforceable at law, all the requirements of the statute have not been complied with. But the notice can be given by the donee; and, if the donee has express or implied authority to give it, I think that equity would not allow the donor to deny the right of the donee to do so and so intercept his gift. I reach this conclusion with some hesitation, for it involves some departure from the majority view in *Aiming v Aiming* (1907) 4 CLR 1049.[79]

78 *Ibid.*
79 [1963] HCA 21; 109 CLR 9.

The section applies only where there is an absolute gift of the whole of the chose in action.[80] It will not apply where the transaction is one of charge or where only a part of the interest is sought to be assigned. It does not apply in respect of declarations of trust over the interest concerned. However that might be, it is a significant fact that under the section the notice can be given by either the assignee or the assignor. If the issue is one of arming the assignee or donee with power to complete the assignment, then surely the assignee would always be in a position to complete the assignment by giving the notice to the remaining partners. Even trying to rationalise the situation in terms of the rule in *Milroy v Lord*, which would be to assimilate assignments in equity of *legal* interests, the assignee would have power to complete. Hence, provided the gift is one of the whole of the partnership interest of the donor, then the donee could give the notice as a matter of principle. All other things being equal, the gift is perfectible without the intervention either of the donor or of equity.

2.2.5 Charge on partnership interest

'Charge' is a legal term which can include many different types of arrangement. It generally indicates something that is less than an assignment of property: it is, rather, a security interest in property. An assignment is the passing of ownership or title to property from one person to another. A charge, however, is in the nature of a security interest in the sense that the charge is created by the owner (as chargor) in favour of a chargee in order to secure some interest, usually a loan or a debt. Hence it is common to refer to a mortgage as a type of charge. However, at common law, a mortgage involves the transfer of title to the mortgagee (or borrower) for the duration of the mortgage subject to reconveyance, enforceable in equity, when the loan is repaid.

The term 'charge', however, most commonly refers to the creation of an interest without such a transfer. It can give the chargee rights, such as possession or sale of the property concerned, in the event of default on payment or repayment by the chargor, but it need not involve a situation where the chargee has title to or ownership of the property. Hence whilst the term might include a mortgage it also includes debentures, fixed and floating corporate charges, various liens and the like. In many respects, the types of charges that can be created over partnership interests are the same as those that can be created over the assets of a company, as discussed in Chapter 6.

In principle, a partnership interest, as a form of equitable property, can be made subject to an equitable charge. The manner of creation of such a charge is, in equity, a matter of intention rather than precise form. The creation of a charge by one partner will not affect the rights of the other partners, but at the same time, the

---

80 *Williams v Atlantic Assurance Co* (1933) 1 KB 81; *Re Steel Wing Co Ltd* (1921) 1 Ch 349.

existence of the partnership cannot unduly restrict any rights that the chargee has under the instrument creating the charge.

In *United Builders Pty Ltd v Mutual Acceptance Ltd*,[81] two companies were the only partners in an enterprise. One company executed a charge in favour of the other. The deed of charge provided that United Builders 'hereby charges all its right title and interest in the partnership … to the following intent and effect'. This was followed by a statement that this would be so notwithstanding anything to the contrary contained in the deed of partnership. Another clause provided: "(iii) Save as provided for in this deed the rights, powers, interest and entitlement of United Builders Pty Ltd as a partner under the said Deed of Partnership are not abridged or affected in any way".

On construction of the partnership deed, it was held that the rights of United Builders in the partnership were not limited to the right of a party on dissolution of partnership to a proportion of any surplus after realisation of assets and payment of debts. They included, according to the court, "the *sui generis* interest which a partner has in partnership assets, being his beneficial interest in every asset of the partnership, although not including title to any specific property of the partnership".[82] The court held that they also

> comprised various rights conferred upon each partner under the partnership agreement, such as the right to participate in the management of the partnership through appointees to its committee of management, the right to receive half yearly such net profits of the partnership as might be available for distribution and the right to determine the partnership in the events specified in the partnership deed.[83]

The respondent, Mutual Acceptance, argued that the charge created by the deed of charge was a fixed rather than a floating charge over United Builders' interest in the partnership in the narrowest sense. The court held that this was not a case of assignment or attempting to bring a partner into the partnership. It was an arrangement between two partners to alter the terms of the arrangement and significantly there were no 'other partners' or third parties whose interests might be affected by what they put in train.

The High Court took the view that as a matter of construction, this was a floating charge only. It said:

---

81 [1980] HCA 24; 144 CLR 673.
82 Referring to *Canny Gabriel Castle Jackson Advertising Pty Ltd v Volume Sales (Finance) Pty Ltd* (1974) HCA 22; 131 CLR 321 at 327–28.
83 [1980] HCA 24; 144 CLR 673 at 679.

In the absence of statutory impediment and of infringement of any principle of partnership law, the charge is free to operate according to its terms; 'the rules as to partners' can no more regulate the position than they could in *Rome v Wood*. Those rules being inapplicable, the effect of the charge extends to the whole of United Builders' rights and interest in the partnership. It is in this situation and in the light of the terms of cl 1 that it must be determined whether the charge operates as a fixed charge or as a floating charge.

Whether a charge is floating or fixed will depend upon the intention of the parties, to be gathered from the terms of the document creating the charge and from surrounding circumstances.[84] In the present case the words of charge are equivocal as to its precise nature but the surrounding circumstances, together with [the deed], sufficiently reveal an intent that the charge should be a floating, not a fixed, charge.[85]

The court was of the view that this interpretation was supported by the fact that, had the deed been intended as a fixed charge, the right of United to continue to exercise normal rights in the partnership, such as the right to participate in management and to vote, would have been negated.[86] The nature of a floating charge, however, permits the partners to carry on much as before notwithstanding the charge. Thus:

> Ordinarily, a floating charge is a charge granted over the whole of a company's undertaking or over a class of its assets, such as stock-in-trade or book debts. While the company continues to carry on business, the property so charged will necessarily be subject to change. Unless the charge is permitted to float over the changing mass of charged assets, rather than to fasten upon them once and for all when created, the company will be unable to carry on its business. It is this intention of the parties, that despite the charge, the company should still continue to carry on its business, which, once made manifest, leads to the conclusion that the charge is a floating charge: *In re Panama, New Zealand and Australian Royal Mail Co* (1870) LR 5 Ch App 318, p 322, *per* Giffard LJ; *Illingworth v Houldsworth* [1904] AC 355, p 358, *per* Lord Macnaghten; *Evans v Rival Granite Quarries Ltd* [1910] 2 KB 979, p 994, *per* Fletcher Moulton LJ. The characteristic of a floating charge, which enables it to be employed so as to give effect to such an intention of the partners, is that, although it creates an existing charge, it does not 'specifically affect any asset subject to it until it crystallises into a fixed security': *Luckins v Highway Motel (Carnarvon) Pty Ltd* (1975) 133 CLR 164, p 173, per Gibbs J, and see *Biggerstaff v Rowatt's*

---

84 See also the discussion in Chapter 6 as to floating and fixed charges provided by the companies.
85 [1980] HCA 24; 144 CLR 673 at 681.
86 *Ibid.* at 683.

Wharf Ltd [1896] 2 Ch 93, p 106; *Evans v Rival Granite Quarries Ltd* [1910] 2 KB 979.[87]

The Partnership Acts contain special provision relating to the charging of the interest of a partner. Section 24(2) and (3) of the Fiji Islands legislation is typical in that regard:

24 (2) The Supreme Court may, on application by summons of any judgment creditor of a partner, make an order charging that partner's interest in the partnership property and profits with payment of the amount of the judgment debt and interest thereon and may, by the same or a subsequent order, appoint a receiver of that partner's share of profits (whether already declared or accruing) and of any other money which may be coming to him in respect of the partnership, and direct all accounts and inquiries and give all other orders and directions which might have been directed or given if the charge had been made in favour of the judgment creditor by the partner, or which the circumstances of the case may require.

(3) The other partner or partners shall be at liberty at any time to redeem the interest charged or, in case of a sale being directed, to purchase the same.[88]

2.2.6 Capital and assets

The capital of a partnership is not the same as the assets of the partnership. These are different legal concepts. In *Reed v Young*, it was said:

The capital of a partnership is the aggregate of the contributions made by the partners, either in cash or in kind, for the purpose of commencing or carrying on the partnership business and intended to be risked by them therein. Each contribution must be of a fixed amount. If it is in cash, it speaks for itself. If it is in kind, it must be valued at a stated amount. It is important to distinguish between the capital of a partnership, a fixed sum, on the one hand and its assets, which may vary from day to day and include everything belonging to the firm having any money value, on the other (see generally *Lindley on the Law of Partnership*, 14th edn, 1979, p 442).[89]

---

87 *Ibid.* at 682; see also *Rowe v Wood* (1822) 2 Jac & W 553, 37 ER 740; *Cavander v Bultee* (1873) LR 9 Ch App 79; *Palmer v Thompson* (1879) OB & F (SC) 182.

88 Partnership Acts: s 25 (S); s 24 (V); s 38 (MI); s 44 (Ni), (CI); s 41 (N); s 27 (Tu); s 24 Partnership Act 1890 (UK) (SI), (K), (T).

89 [1984] STC 38 at 57. Seemingly approved by the House of Lords on appeal: see [1986] 1 WLR 649 at 654. See also *Popat v Shonchhatra* [1997] EWCA Civ 1966 at para 11.

In s 24(1) of the Partnership Act, the reference to capital does not include partnership property. The section, which applies subject to any express or implied agreement between the partners, reads as follows:

> 24 (1) All the partners are entitled to share equally in the capital and profits of the business, and must contribute equally towards the losses whether of capital or otherwise sustained by the firm.

In *Popat v Shonchhatra*, the following interpretation of the section was adopted:

> If it be proved that the partners contributed the capital of the partnership in unequal shares it is presumed that, in the absence of an agreement to the contrary, on a final settlement of accounts, the capital of the business remaining after the payment of outside debts and liabilities, and of what is due to each partner for advances, will, subject to all proper deductions, be divided amongst the partners in the proportions in which they contributed it and not equally.[90]

Furthermore, according to Nourse LJ in that case, there is no authority and nothing in principle to support the view that s 24(1) was only intended to apply to revenue profits up to the date of dissolution. The section is entirely general in its terms and thus applies equally both before and after dissolution.[91]

---

90 [1997] EWCA Civ 1966 at para 16.
91 *Ibid.* at para 23.

3

TRUSTS

3.1 Defining a trust

Let us attempt a basic definition of a trust.[1] As with many legal concepts, there is considerable dispute regarding the most effective definition. We can say that a trust is essentially a property-holding arrangement under which a person or persons (called 'the trustee' or 'the trustees') hold property or hold property exclusively for the benefit of another or others (called 'the beneficiary' or 'the beneficiaries') or for other legitimate purposes. The property is held by the trustee or trustees subject a special equitable obligation known as a fiduciary obligation, which is conceived of as attaching to the trust property.

These principles and doctrines continued to apply post-independence without substantive modification. The Trustee Act 1925, as amended to the relevant cut-off date, provides the model for local trustee legislation in these countries. In some countries such as Vanuatu and the Solomon Islands that legislation continues to apply. We will discuss new laws on trusts from Nauru and Samoa, and recent cases according to the classification of trusts in the South Pacific. Further to Chapter 1, we also explore some of the taxes and tax penalties associated with trusts across the South Pacific region.

A trust cannot be created without there being property which is subject to the trust. Basically, however, any legal or equitable property (meaning anything that

---

1 *The Law of Trusts Looseleaf 4th ed.* (Ford, HAJ, Lee, WA, Bryan, M, Glover J, Fullerton, I. 2019, Sydney, Thomson Reuters Australia Subscriptions) is a suitable reference for the historical development of the trust; see Holdsworth, WS, *A History of English Law*, 1972, London, Methuen, Sweet and Maxwell – it provides another useful overview of the development of the trust during that particular period of English legal history.

DOI: 10.4324/9781003428060-4

is recognised within the legal system as a whole as in the nature of property) can be the subject of a trust. There is a legal requirement of certainty of subject matter of the trust. In other words, there must be trust property which is readily identifiable as subject to the trust obligation. Although trusts are freely recognised in England and other English law-based jurisdictions, and often form the basis for a diversity of business operations and estate-planning schemes, they are not a worldwide phenomenon. That is, neither the trust institution nor the peculiar legal relations to which they give rise are recognised by all legal systems.

As we noted before, trusts are frequently used as structures for commercial enterprise. This is so even though trust law has traditionally regarded a trustee's engagement in commerce or business as being risky in nature and therefore to be discouraged. Indeed, a trustee usually requires the grant of an explicit power, whether in the trust instrument or by statute, to carry on a business on behalf of the trust. Such a power will not be inferred. Despite this somewhat limiting factor, trusts are frequently established with no other objective in mind than to carry on business.

In this chapter, we will look at some of the common understandings and challenges in establishing a trust, as well as some of its conventionally accepted legal features. We will then consider principles that purport to differentiate a trust from other types of legal arrangement, such as agency and partnership. We do not propose to recount the history of the trust in English law fully here, as it is beyond the scope of this work. This chapter will examine the basic concept of a trust as it applies in the South Pacific region. In the South Pacific jurisdictions, the law of trusts formed part of the received law of the countries when the common law and the doctrines of equity were applied during colonial times. These principles and doctrines continued to apply after independence without substantive modification. The Trustee Act 1925, as amended to the relevant cut-off date,[2] provides the model for local trustee legislation in these countries. In some countries, such as Vanuatu and the Solomon Islands, that legislation continues to apply.[3]

A trust is a very specific type of legal arrangement or institution. Some trusts are creatures of private law. They are created by consensual undertakings between particular parties or by the declaration of intention of one person. Most such trusts are created for the benefit of individuals or groups of individuals. In many cases, these beneficiaries are named specifically, whilst in other cases they are defined as members of a class of potential beneficiaries.

---

2 This refers to the date of the reception of former colonial law within the various countries; see Jennifer Corrin and Don Paterson, *Introduction to South Pacific law* (4th edition), 2017, Cambridge, Intersentia Ltd.

3 On the reception of their principles and trust law in particular, see Hughes, R.A, *Trust Law of the South Pacific*, 1999, Suava, IJALS, Chapter 2. On the reception of the doctrines of common law and equity, see Corrin Care *et al., ibid.*, pp 30–34.

Other trusts are more public in nature. Some valid trusts are created so as to benefit purposes rather than a particular individual or group of individuals. In general, the only legitimate purpose trust is a trust for charitable purposes. These are known as charitable trusts, and the law has its own rather narrow concept of what a valid charitable purpose is. Other trusts are public, in that either they are creatures of special legislation (many trusts are established by statute for public purposes) or they are established by the courts themselves.

We will encounter both types later on. An example of the first is the Vanuatu National Provident Fund, which is created under the Vanuatu National Provident Fund Act Cap 189. It exists for the purpose of receiving provident or superannuation contributions from employees in that country. Examples of the second type, which we normally call trusts created by operation of law, include constructive trusts and resulting trusts. These are most often used by the courts as a kind of remedial institution. They are imposed by equity to achieve or to do justice in particular situations, for example where there is grossly improper conduct or where, as a matter of implicit legal policy, it would be unjust to deny someone an interest in particular property.

A trust gives rise to quite distinctive legal arrangements which are to a large degree the product of the peculiar evolution of the trust in the English legal system. Other legal systems contain legal institutions that are similar in some respects to trusts. In the South Pacific region, some customary practices regarding the disposition and/or use of communal or family property approximate to trust relationships, although not exactly. Most usually, the courts have been wont to distinguish clearly between trusts and customary rights.

The trust is a product of English legal history. It is part of the introduced law of the South Pacific countries. From the purist point of view, the trust is, as Maitland described it, 'the greatest and most distinctive achievement performed by Englishmen in the field of jurisprudence'.[4] The legal relations to which it gives rise are, in that sense, often regarded as unique to common law systems.

A trust creates a division of interests in property between a trustee and the beneficiaries. However, this division of interests under a trust is a product of the unique conditions of English legal history. Historically, the English courts of common law (the King's Courts) regarded the trustee as the full legal owner of the property in question. It was only the courts of equity (or Chancery) which regarded the beneficiaries as having a rightful (or equitable or beneficial) claim to the trust property. They recognised this entitlement by imposing special obligations on the trustee to deal with the property concerned wholly for the benefit of the beneficiaries. This obligation was and is known as a fiduciary obligation, which was, again, a special development of the courts of equity.

---

4 Maitland, FW, *Selected Essays*, 1936, Cambridge, CUP, p 2.

It is this duality of the court system in English legal history that gives rise to the distinctive elements of a trust. Without the existence of courts of equity, which pretended to supplement and expand the legal principles applied by the common law courts, there may well have been nothing today that we would call a trust. Other legal systems do not have this duality. They may give recognition to obligations that we would like to call fiduciary obligations. However, this is never quite in the sense in which we now speak of the fiduciary obligation of a trustee.

3.1.1 Standard definitions of a trust

There is no comprehensive definition of a trust. There are many different types of trust arrangement which do not easily lend themselves to reduction to a simple set of principles. The evolution of the concept of a trust has been largely left to case law. A traditional definition of a trust can be found in Jacob:

> A trust is an institution developed by equity and cognisable by a court of equity. A trust is not a juristic person with a legal personality from that of the trustee and beneficiary. Nor is it merely descriptive of an equitable right or obligation … More particularly, a trust exists when the owner of a legal or equitable interest in property is bound by an obligation, recognised by and enforced in equity, to hold that interest for the benefit of others, or for some object or purpose permitted by law.[5]

According to Watson and Taylor, a trust is:

> an equitable obligation binding on one person to deal with property for the benefit of another person. Trusts are created by a trust deed. By means of a trust deed, the settlor settles assets on trustees who have legal ownership of those assets. However, the trustees hold the assets in trust for the beneficiaries who have beneficial or equitable ownership.[6]

These definitions contain a common core of reference to essential elements of the trust despite some variation in emphasis. They are legal or juristic definitions which have some primacy bearing in mind that the trust is essentially a creation of the law or, more specifically, of the equity courts. Because the courts of equity and those of common law were historically distinct from one another, at least prior to the United Kingdom Judicature Acts of 1873 and 1875, it was appropriate to

---

5 Heydon, JD and Leeming, MJ, *Jacob's Law of Trusts in Australia*, 2016, NSW, LexisNexis Butterworths, 8th edn, p 1 at [1–01].
6 Watson, S and Taylor, L. *Corporate Law in New Zealand*, 2018, Wellington Thomson Reuters New Zealand Ltd, p 41 at 2.4.4., *op cit* fn 3, p 3.

distinguish between the types of interest recognised by each. The interests of the beneficiaries under the trust were recognised only by the equity courts and were not recognised by the common law courts at all.

On this basis, one could distinguish between legal and equitable interests. This distinction is still maintained, although the jurisdictions are no longer completely separate. The distinction has never been without its theoretical difficulties, particularly if we begin to talk about two distinct 'ownerships', namely legal ownership and equitable ownership of the same property. According to Maitland, the conflict could be dissolved by accepting that what the equity courts set up in terms of a trust was not a form of ownership vested in the beneficiaries which then denied legal or common law ownership. In his view, they conceded that the trustee was the legal owner of the trust property but imposed a special form of obligation on the trustee to deal with the property exclusively for the benefit of the beneficiary, which obligation was personally enforceable against that trustee.[7] It is only in that sense that it remained appropriate to talk of equitable 'ownership' of a beneficiary under a trust. It was just a case of equity grafting special obligations which would restrain the free exercise of legal rights according to the maxim 'Equity follows the law, but not slavishly'.

Legal definitions aside, a trust does perform a number of social and economic functions. These functions are perhaps too diverse to enable them to serve as a means of understanding the proper nature of the trust. Furthermore, there seems to be no good reason why the trust should not be distinguished from other types of social institution, even though it may overlap in function with corporate or other types of association, such as a partnership. Some trusts certainly have this overlap, but others do not. A trust is a legal institution. To what extent does it bear the common understanding of the term 'trust', in other words a relationship evocative of confidence, benevolence, goodwill, faith, faithful understanding and so on? It does to some extent. This holds at least in respect of the type of legal obligation that equity courts impose upon the trustee. It is this obligation, the fiduciary obligation (fiduciary being a derivative from the Latin *fides*, for 'faith'), which determines many of the essential features of a trust, particularly as regards the trustee's duties and functions. However, being a fairly technical and sophisticated type of legal relationship, much more than this needs to be said in order to understand what is involved.

Let us look at some practical examples which illustrate how we need to distinguish between a legal trust and common understandings of trust:

- Alanieta may trust her uncle Sailasa when he says that when he dies his house property will be hers. The fact that she 'trusts' him or has confidence in him

---

7 Maitland, F, *Equity*, 1969, Cambridge, CUP, p 17.

will not alone constitute Sailasa as a trustee of the house for her, nor will it make her a beneficiary in the legal sense.

- So also, if Timaima gives her son Ioane a motor vehicle on his express promise that, on penalty of returning the vehicle to his mother, he will not exceed the speed limit, a breach of this promise by Ioane (being a breach of the trust reposed by Timaima in Ioane's promise) does not make Ioane a trustee in law of the vehicle.

- Similarly, where Eseta says to Willie, 'Come and live with me and take care of me for the rest of my life and you can trust that I will buy a house for both of us', and Willie takes up the offer, the purchase of a house by Eseta in which they both live does not alone constitute a trust. The reason here and elsewhere is that although the legal notion of a trust does involve something of the common understanding of trust, the mere existence of this common sense of trust in a given relationship is not sufficient to establish the existence of a trust at law. The legal sense and the common sense are not commensurate because the law recognises only certain types of relationships founded on trust as enforceable legal relationships.

The point is that not every occasion of trust or promise of faith constitutes an enforceable trust, just as not every agreement involves a legally binding and enforceable contract. In some legal systems this may be true where, for example, agreements are enforceable simply on the basis of the morality of keeping of promises. In English-based legal systems, however, something more is required. In respect of contracts, there must be something of value given in return for the promise (the factor of consideration). In respect of trusts, other elements must be shown to exist before an arrangement will warrant the court's protection as a trust. It is usual to reduce these to four vital elements, which we will discuss immediately below.

A final point to note is that the question of whether a trust does or does not exist is a matter for the law (and particularly that part of the law which we call equity) to determine. The courts have the final say in determining whether an arrangement satisfies the essential features of a trust. What the parties choose to call their arrangement will be largely irrelevant. They may call it a trust, but it may amount in law to a contract, a lease or, in fact, nothing at all. They may call it a licence, a contract of some kind or an option, but the court might say, in the final analysis, that they have created a trust.

3.1.2 The four elements of a trust

The four necessary elements of a trust are usually put in this way. For any trust to exist there must be:

(a) a trustee;

(b) a beneficiary or a legitimate purpose;

(c) trust property; and

(d) a trust obligation, binding on the trustee, which attaches to the trust property.

These elements must be present in all trusts of whatever type, even though some trusts, such as resulting and constructive trusts, being largely the creatures of legal policy, come into being by operation of law. Let us look at the four elements in turn.

3.1.3 The trustee

All of the above definitions purport to make it clear that the trustee's status and role are crucial elements in the trust arrangement. The trustee will be regarded by the equity courts as the outward owner of the trust property. In other words, the title to the trust property is vested in the trustee.[8] However, the trustee is forbidden from dealing with that property as if it is their own. An exception would be where the trustee is also a beneficiary under the trust, but this does not deny the general import of what has been said, nor does it deny the existence of the obligation placed on the trustee by virtue of the existence of the trust itself.

The obligation is a fiduciary obligation imposed by equity rather than by the terms of a private bargain settled between the parties. Certainly, in many cases, it will arise as a consequence of a private bargain or arrangement. But it is, strictly speaking, an obligation imposed by the law itself – a legal policy intrinsic to the recognition of the trust as a valid form of legal arrangement.

The following are significant factors in relation to the position of the trustee:

(a) the form of the trustee's ownership;

(b) the obligations of the trustee;

(c) the source of the trustee's obligations;

(d) the range of the trustee's duties.

The form of ownership

As has already been indicated, it is conventional to think of a trust as creating something like a divided form of ownership, although many have been keen to point out that this is not strictly accurate. Certainly, lawyers continue to talk in terms of the trustee having the legal estate, interest or ownership in the trust property, whereas the beneficiary or beneficiaries are said to have the equitable estate, interest or ownership. This is a convenient but misleading way of describing the

---

8 It is sometimes said that the trustee holds the legal title, but this is not strictly correct, in that a trust can be created over property interests which are equitable rather than legal.

situation. The trustee does have the outward interest in the property (which may be, strictly speaking, either legal or equitable property) and this creates the appearance to the outside world that the trustee is in fact the absolute owner. In the case of a trust over land, for instance, the trustee will appear as the registered owner on the title deeds to the property. Frequently there is no public acknowledgment that the trust exists at all – at least as far as public records go.

The obligation of the trustee

Despite the fact that the outward title is vested in the trustee, equitable doctrine holds, where is clear that a trust relationship exists in the first place, that the trustee is subject to an obligation enforceable in equity to deal with the trust property not for the trustee's own benefit but for the exclusive benefit of the beneficiaries of the trust. In this sense, the beneficiaries might be said to have something in the nature of an equitable 'ownership' of, or at least an equitable interest in, the trust property. In some cases, their claim to something like title or ownership may be more justified than in others. For example, where the beneficiaries are all over the age of 18 years, and are not subject to any legal incapacity, they may have the right to terminate the trust and require that the trust property be transferred to them. This right exists only where the trust is what is called a bare trust, the trustee having no active duties to perform. In such a case, there is no real difficulty in approximating the beneficiaries' interest to that of ownership.

In other cases, given that interests under a trust can be defined in a great variety of ways, one cannot extend this notion of ownership to the beneficiaries so easily. More strictly, and as has already been said, they have a right to have the trust administered and the obligation of the trustee enforced. In some cases, the beneficiaries might not have fully vested interests at all. Their right to receive the trust property might be postponed pending the occurrence of certain conditions or it might be subject to defeasance in the event that certain things occur. Their right to take an interest out of the trust might be subject to the trustee exercising a discretion or power to allocate such an interest to them. However, even in those cases, the beneficiaries are granted enforceable rights against the trustee as a result of the creation of the trust and the trustee's position as apparent owner is restricted in light of the obligation to observe those rights. The most basic of the obligations to which the trustee is subjected is called the fiduciary obligation.

The trustee's duties, powers, rights and liabilities

We will look closely at the duties, powers, rights and liabilities of a trustee in Chapter 9. For the moment we will note some of the more important of these by way of introduction. The primary duty of a trustee is the fiduciary duty or obligation just mentioned. Others include a duty to carry out the terms of the trust, which serves to define the scope of authority of the trustee. A trustee is under a duty to abide by the terms of the trust, having regard to both the trust instrument and any statutory powers and duties. There is an absolute duty on the trustee not to take an interest in the trust property. There is a duty on the trustee to properly account for the trust property and a duty to act without reward, unless the trust instrument provides specifically for remuneration.

A trustee also has certain powers, such as a power of sale or lease of the trust property or a power to employ agents. Trustees are also entitled to certain rights as a consequence of the office which they hold, such as the right to be indemnified out of the trust assets in relation to the claims of creditors of the trust. The trustee has a right to obtain directions from the court wherever there is a matter of possible contentiousness or doubt in relation to the administration of the trust.

Some of these obligations, duties, liabilities, powers and rights have their source in the decisions of the courts, which have elaborated the role of the trustee over time. Others are implied by the legislation, primarily in the Trustee Acts of the various jurisdictions in the South Pacific. There is sometimes, however, legislation which needs to be referred to in the case of particular trustees and particular types of trust. Corporate legislation in England, Fiji, Samoa, Vanuatu, New Zealand and Australia makes special reference with respect to the trustees of what are termed corporate unit trusts, which can include time-sharing schemes, cash management funds, real property trusts, etc. Some trusts, such as Crown land trusts, may be created by legislation and impose special duties, rights and liabilities.

A third source of these duties, rights and so on may not apply as regards all types of trust. It will apply only in the case of what are termed express trusts; that is, those trusts established by agreement between individuals, by will on the death of an individual or by the declaration of trust of one or more individuals. Here the instrument creating the trust will be an important source of rights, powers, duties and liabilities of both the trustee and the beneficiaries. As the most common form of trust is that established expressly, the law tends, as with contracts, to give some degree of priority to the express terms created by the parties themselves. In that sense trust law involves an area of private law. Thus, it will always be important to have regard to the trust instrument itself. Even in relation to statutory duties and powers, it is often the case that the trust instrument can override the provisions of the statute. In some cases, the statutory provisions are said to apply only in the absence of the provisions of the trust instrument.

Anyone of full legal capacity, whether a natural person or an artificial legal person, such as a company or other type of corporation, can be appointed as a trustee. In some countries, the trustee may be an infant, although, upon application, the court has the power to appoint another trustee until the infant becomes of age. The basic requirement, in the absence of legislation to the contrary, is that the trustee appointed be a person legally capable of holding property. It is no disqualification that the trustee has an interest in the trust property. The trustee may be the person who creates the trust in the first place. This situation will involve what is called a declaration of trust.

The court has the inherent power to remove a trustee. Alternatively, the trust instrument may provide that a trustee can be removed in certain situations such as bankruptcy, insolvency, death of the trustee, commission of a felony or loss of capacity to carry out the office of trustee. The Trustee Acts also make special provisions in relation to the removal and replacement of trustees and these provisions tend to be fairly similar throughout the jurisdictions. A detailed examination of these provisions is, however, beyond the scope of the present work.

3.1.4 The beneficiary or special purpose of the trust

It will be noted from the definitions above that they refer not only to the existence of a beneficiary (or perhaps a number or class of beneficiaries), but also to trusts that exist solely for the carrying out of some special purpose allowed by law. In this respect, the definitions encountered above sought to accommodate certain types of trust which may exist for purposes rather than for individuals. The only valid form of this is a charitable trust. The notion of special purpose trusts which are non-charitable in nature, for example a trust to benefit animals, has not received wide acknowledgment in English law. What is charitable for these purposes is a matter for legal definition rather than common understanding. This is discussed further below.

In general, and leaving aside purpose trusts, there is a requirement that the trust have an ascertainable beneficiary or class of beneficiaries. This is usually said to be the requirement that there be certainty of objects. If this requirement is not met, there will be a resulting trust in favour of the settlor (the person who created the trust).[9] The trustee cannot take the property beneficially (i.e. as his or her own) because it would be unjust to do so. It may not be the case that the class is completely ascertainable at the time the trust is established. Provided the trust also complies with certain other rules of law as to the vesting of interests, the trust will be valid so long as there is some mechanism set out in the trust instrument itself whereby the range of beneficiaries can be ascertained with reasonable certainty at some future time. Thus, a person may seek to make provision for children not yet born. A trust which provides for 'all my children' will generally be held valid even though they may not be born at the time the trust comes into effect.

The beneficiaries of a trust have certain rights which, as in the case of the trustee, may arise from the general law and practice of the equity courts in dealing with trusts, from statute or from the trust instrument. As has been suggested above, the beneficiary is commonly said to have equitable ownership of the trust property, although this is a somewhat clumsy expression. The beneficiary has, at least, a right enforceable against the trustee personally, and attaching to the trust

---

9 As will be seen later, a resulting trust is a trust which arises by operation of law, particularly where, as here, there has been a failure in the carrying into effect of a proposed legal arrangement.

property, to have the trust carried out and properly administered. If the trustee fails to carry out the trust, the beneficiary has a right to approach the court to have the estate administered by the court itself, or possibly to have the trustee removed, or to have compensation awarded. The beneficiary also has the right to follow the trust property into the hands of persons who knowingly receive it from a delinquent trustee in certain circumstances.

For some time, there has been a contentious issue as to whether the beneficiaries can ever be said to have an interest more directly in the trust assets themselves. According to the approach advocated by Maitland, the beneficiaries' interest was primarily one which consisted of a right to have the equity courts make an order against the trustee that the trust be properly administered or carried out.[10] It was a right *in personam* only.[11] If this was so, in general, the beneficiaries' interest under a trust could be described only very loosely and inaccurately as one of ownership. 'Ownership' in legal parlance usually implies some sense of dominion over property, or rights in specific property – such as in the trust assets in this case. But according to Maitland's view, the assertion of a claim to assets of the trust could only be properly made by invoking the assistance of the court in an administration suit. Maitland's view appeared to be reinforced by the decision of the House of Lords in *Lord Sudeley v Attorney General*,[12] but it is a matter of some dispute, as we will discuss later when considering the position of the beneficiary further.[13]

However, there has been frequent dispute as to the appropriateness of this view regarding all types of trust. Take the case of a trust known as a bare trust; that is, one where the trustee has no duties of management to perform but merely holds the property on behalf of the beneficiaries. Equity has usually treated these situations as though the beneficiaries were in fact the owners of the trust property. This is because the trustee is merely holding property at their direction. Another instance might be where the rule known as the rule in *Saunders v Vautier*[14] applies. This rule states, in effect, that where the beneficiaries are all of full age and legal capacity, they are able collectively to terminate the trust and call on the trustee to transfer the trust property to them, even though the trust instrument might provide for a longer continuance of the trust. In both cases, there would appear to be some merit in regarding the beneficiaries as having ownership in some sense (that is to say equitable ownership) of the trust property.[15]

However, this cannot apply in respect of all types of trust. The fact is that beneficial interests under a trust can be defined in an infinite variety of ways. This factor makes it extremely difficult to generalise, and almost impossible to say that

---

10 Maitland, *op cit* fn 7, pp 46 ff.
11 That is to say, a personal right exercisable against the trustee. It is not a right in property at all.
12 [1897] AC 11.
13 See Chapter 9.
14 (1841) 41 ER 482; 4 Beav 115.
15 See Chapter 4 for a discussion of this rule in more detail.

trust beneficiaries attain ownership interests in all cases. For example, there are types of trust known as discretionary trusts where the beneficiaries' interests are conditional on a power or discretion of the trustee to allocate interests out of the trust to them. Their interest is speculative only because it depends on the trustee making a decision in their favour at some particular time. Until that discretion is exercised in their favour, they are in reality potential beneficiaries only.

In any event, there are some trusts which are created in such a way that the beneficiaries' interests can never be taken to approximate full ownership. Much depends on how the interests of the beneficiaries are set up under the terms of the particular trust. A particular beneficiary might have been granted a life interest only, or perhaps a right for some other limited time. A beneficiary's interest can be absolute, conditional, defeasible, vested or contingent. In some cases, the beneficiaries' interests might be vested in the sense that they are clearly established by law, although they are not vested absolutely in the sense that they are free from conditions which have to be met before entitlement is established. In other words, the beneficiary may not be entitled to call for termination of the trust and the transfer of whatever entitlement they might appear eventually to be entitled to. There could be some legal impediment to the beneficiary's right to obtain the interest immediately. In this case, the beneficiary's interest is vested contingently, or subject to some condition, or otherwise incomplete in nature.

In other cases, the actual vesting of the trust interest may be postponed in such a way that there is no presently established interest of the beneficiary. The entitlement of the beneficiary may be postponed until the beneficiary is entitled to show that some condition is fulfilled. There is a difference, for instance, between a trust '*for X to be paid to him when he attains 18 years*' and one which provides '*only if X attains 18 years, then for him*'. In the latter case, the taking of the interest by the beneficiary will be conditional upon him attaining the requisite age. If he does not reach 18, his estate will not be entitled to anything out of the trust. There are also what are termed defeasible interests; that is, interests which are given but which are subject to a provision that should certain things occur or not occur then the beneficiary will lose the interest. Conceptually they would best be regarded as vested interests which are subject to a defeasance.

In all of these cases, it is a difficult matter of construction of a trust instrument and sometimes reconstruction of the circumstances surrounding the creation of the trust to ascertain just what the interest taken by the beneficiary amounts to in law. The differences between categories of interest are fine and yet they may be of considerable consequence so far as the beneficiary's entitlement is concerned. As a general proposition, it appears safe enough to say that in most cases what the beneficiary acquires under the trust is an independently constituted equitable chose in action. A chose in action is usually regarded as a form of proprietary interest at law within the general framework of what we call personal property. However, there are numerous exceptions and anomalies. It will not always be regarded as an interest which is assignable or transferable, as are most proprietary interests. It is simply not possible to say that all such interests lead inevitably to the postulation of an interest in the underlying assets of the trust. It is possible in some cases, and not in others.

3.1.5 The trust property

As already noted, one of the main features of the trust is that it is an arrangement for the holding of property. It is because of this that the duty of the trustee to preserve trust property (which we will examine later) is one of the more fundamental duties of the trustee – although the scope of this duty may be curtailed in some cases by specific powers given to the trustee in certain cases. In short, however, without property, there is no trust. This applies both at the time of creation of the trust and throughout the entire existence of the trust.

What counts as property in terms of this requirement? Property is a difficult and extensive legal concept and an examination of its full ramifications is beyond the scope of this book. So also is a discussion of the many different types of property over which a trust may reign. Unfortunately, there is no unified regime for dealing with all possible types of property. The consequence of this is that the manner in which property is to be dealt with is the subject of fragmented provisions. Some of these are a product of past commercial practices, others the subject of extensive statutory provisions. The ways in which trusts over property are created are capable of at least as many variations and permutations as the property system itself provides. In principle, however, a trust can be created over any type of lawful property, whether it be real property (land or interests in land), intellectual property, goods and chattels, negotiable instruments, debts due, contractual rights or indeed beneficial interests under other trusts.

The idea that there cannot be a trust without trust property leads directly to the rule that there must be certainty of the subject matter of a trust. 'Subject matter' in this context refers to the trust property. The rule requires that when an attempt is made to create a trust, whether by instrument or otherwise, the terms of the trust must specify with reasonable certainty what property it is that is to be subject to the trust obligation. If this obligation is not met, the putative trust will be void, which is to say, no trust will have been created. The rule is, in essence, a requirement as to the adequate identifiability of the trust property. Put another way, the terms of the proposed arrangement, whether embodied in writing or not, must provide a clear definition as to what the trust property actually is.

3.1.6 The trust obligation

The trust obligation is usually conceived of as the duty imposed on the trustee(s) to deal with the trust property not for his, her or their own benefit but exclusively for the benefit of the beneficiaries in terms of the trust. It is to be noted that the duty is both negative and positive in nature. In the negative sense, it prohibits the trustee from gaining personal advantage, directly or indirectly, out of the trust.

In a positive sense, it imposes a duty on the trustee to carry out the trust on the particular terms laid down. It is from this obligation, as has been said, that most of the basic rights, duties, privileges and obligations of the parties to a trust seem to follow, if not as a matter of logical necessity, then certainly in terms of practical consequences. Indeed, it is this obligation that defines the relationship between the parties to the trust and provides the focal point of the trust obligation. Much of trust law is concerned, in fact, with the articulation of this relationship. It is a relationship that admits considerable variation, simply because trusts themselves admit of diverse adaptations.[16]

It is often said that the trust obligation attaches to the trust property itself. This may seem an unusual proposition in itself. It is meant, however, to convey the idea that the beneficiaries' rights are not only against the trustee personally. A breach of trust committed by the trustee will result in a right to a range of possible remedies that can be sought from the courts. Some are in the nature of personal remedies against the trustee. For example, the beneficiaries might elect to claim equitable compensation from the trustee. However, some remedies are what we call proprietary remedies, in the sense that they are oriented towards the recovery of property or gains which have been misappropriated. In this case, equity usually accords rights to recover trust property which has been lost or misappropriated by a trustee in breach of trust. This might extend to recovery of property or gains flowing from it from third parties or strangers to the trust.

Usually, these remedies are alternatives; that is to say, the beneficiary must make a choice between these personal and proprietary remedies. However that might be, the beneficiary usually has rights to follow the trust property into the hands of another where the trustee has disposed of the property to a third party with that person's knowledge, actual or constructive, of the breach of trust.[17] This is one form of what is known as the equitable remedy of tracing. In these circumstances the beneficiary, through the agency of the courts, may intervene to recover the property from the third party and, as it were, restore the trust. This would usually involve the courts imposing a constructive trust[18] on the recipient to ensure the return of the beneficial interest to its rightful place.

3.2 Classification of trusts

Trusts used for commercial purposes will most usually be in the form of what we call express trusts. We will examine these in greater detail in the next chapter. One simple way of classifying trusts is by the manner of their creation. For instance, some trusts are brought into existence by express agreement by consenting parties,

---

16 See the discussion of the fiduciary obligation in Chapter 9.
17 The conditions on recovery from third parties are usually determined according to the rule known as the rule in *Barnes v Addy* (1874) LR 9 Ch App 244.
18 On which, see below.

others by legal inference from the conduct of parties and others are created by statute or imposed by the courts in order to do justice to the interests of a party. This method of classification is useful, although, on a strict analysis, it tends to break down in certain cases. The following is intended more to introduce the legal terminology regarding certain types of trust. This is by no means an exhaustive classification.

3.2.1 Express trusts

An express trust is one created by the expressed intentions of certain parties. Trusts of this type are seen as the product of actual intention or deliberate design. In other words, in order to create such a trust there must be a manifest intention by the parties to bring about a trust.

Some trusts must be created in writing to be enforceable. For instance, an express trust created by will must be in writing because the law of succession, which deals with the passing of property on death, requires that wills both be made in writing and comply with other formal requirements.[19] Similarly, a trust created over an equitable interest, such as the beneficial interest in another trust, must be usually in writing, although this depends on the substantive law of the jurisdiction in question.

An express trust may be fixed or discretionary. In the first case, the interests of the beneficiaries are settled or determined by the terms of the trust. This is not the case with discretionary trusts, as will be seen below. Express trusts may also be private, in the sense that they are for the benefit of private individuals, or public, such as a charitable trust (see below).

3.2.2 Implied trusts

The intention to create an express trust can be implied from the surrounding circumstances rather than explicitly formulated. An implied trust in this sense is strictly a matter of legal inference from the evidence available. Parties may have acted over time in a way that makes it clear that all the necessary elements of a trust were present and were assumed to apply to the property. However, sometimes trusts that arise by operation of law, independent of the intentions of the parties, are also referred to as implied trusts. We will reserve the use of the term 'implied trust' to those which are the product of intention.

19 See e.g. s 6 Wills Act Cap 59 (F), although there are limited exceptions in the case of privileged wills: see s 17, Part V of the Act.

3.2.3 Resulting trusts

A resulting trust is a trust implied by the operation of law in the absence of an express or implied intention of the parties. However, intention is relevant in so far as, in these cases, the existence of the trust is based on certain presumed, rather than actual, intentions of the parties. The law presumes an intention in certain circumstances even though there might not have been one expressly stated or capable of inference from the conduct of the parties.

This is a limited form of trust best illustrated by an example. Suppose that a person (the settlor) creates an express trust, transferring his property to the trustee upon trust for all of the settlor's children. At the time of creation of the trust, the settlor has no children, but creates the trust in the fecund expectation of fatherhood at some future time. The settlor then dies, leaving no children. Here the object of the trust has failed. There are a number of other circumstances where this situation might arise. A trust may be created for a certain purpose which is frustrated. Property may be given to another on certain conditions that are not fulfilled.

In such a case, the law does not allow the recipient of the property, whether trustee, donee or otherwise, to keep the property for themselves. Instead, the law says that there is a resulting trust arising in favour of the original settlor or donor. This effectively allows the arrangement to be reversed. The property is said to result (i.e. in the sense of revert) to the original party. In the example given, the trustee could not acquire the beneficial ownership of the property. Instead, the trustee would hold the property on a resulting trust for the original settlor or, in practical terms, for the estate of the deceased settlor. The estate of the deceased would now include the value of the property over which the trust was created. There are other circumstances where resulting trusts might arise, but a discussion of them is outside the scope of this book.

3.2.4 Constructive trusts

A constructive trust is a type of trust that arises not out of the actions, agreement or intentions of the parties but as a matter, more or less, of legal policy applied by courts of equity. They are used in many circumstances for remedial purposes where it is appropriate to recover property, for example, from a trustee or other fiduciary who has misappropriated property or made gains in breach of their obligations. However, the circumstances in which constructive trusts have been employed are somewhat wider than this. There appears not to be any overarching theory or principle which guides the courts as to the use of constructive trusts. In some jurisdictions they are thought to be based on the need to prevent unjust enrichment, whilst in others they are thought to be grounded on principles of unconscionability (or grossly unfair or unjust conduct) or perhaps enforcing reasonable expectations of parties.

3.2.5 Discretionary trusts

The nature of these trusts, which are brought into existence as express creations, was briefly mentioned above. They are in frequent use for taxation and estate-planning purposes because the existence of the discretion in the hands of the trustee usually allows the taxpayer to readjust the entitlement of the beneficiaries at the end of a given financial year. The term 'discretionary' in these contexts usually applies because the trustee has discretion as to whether or not to apply income to the beneficiaries. However, the nature of the discretionary power may be otherwise. It may apply to the shares in capital under the trust, to the sale of trust property, to carrying on a business and otherwise.

3.2.6 Bare trusts

As indicated above, these are trusts under which the trustee has no active duties to carry out, for example, the active management of the trust property. The trustee merely holds the property for the beneficiaries and nothing more. In such cases, it is of interest to note the rule in *Saunders v Vautier*,[20] which holds that where there is a bare trust and the beneficiaries are of full age and legal capacity, the beneficiaries are entitled by collective action to terminate the trust by calling on the trustee to transfer the trust property to them.

3.2.7 Unit trusts

These trusts fall into two categories, namely the public unit trust and the private unit trust. In both cases, the trust instrument provides for the creation of units to be held by beneficiaries. The number of units held by any given beneficiary determines the entitlement of the beneficiary to a share in the total trust property. The units therefore function rather like the shares in a company. The trust will be called public or private depending upon whether or not the units are made available for public subscription. If the trust is a public unit trust, there are strict investment controls to be met by the trust in some jurisdictions such as Fiji, Samoa and Vanuatu. The interests that public investors acquire are treated as more or less the same shares under a public issue.[21]

3.2.8 Statutory trusts

This category of trust includes trusts created by legislation. The legislation often makes extensive provisions as to the extent of the trustees' obligations and powers. It may provide for the precise terms of the trust to be gleaned partly from

---

20 (1841) 41 ER 482; 4 Beav 115.
21 Unit trusts are discussed further in Chapter 4. See pp 99 ff.

the legislation and partly from the terms of trust instruments settled by Crown authorities pursuant to delegated powers under the legislation. Certain Crown land trusts fall into the latter category. The beneficiaries may be the public generally or some more limited section of the public. In a strict sense, there need be no ascertainable class of beneficiaries at all. The trust may simply be established for Crown purposes or for management purposes. One important sub-class is the trust which arises on intestacy.

One example of a statutory trust is that provided for under Part XX of the Niue Act 1966 with respect to Niuean persons with a disability such as mental infirmity and who, in the opinion of the Land Court, are deemed unfit to have the management of their property. Pursuant to s 501 of the Act, the Land Court, on proof of the disability, can make a trustee order appointing persons to be trustees of the property of the person concerned.

In Fiji, the Native Lands Trust Board Act Cap 134 constitutes, by s 3, a Native Lands Trust Board as a body corporate which is the trustee of all so-called native lands in Fiji. Section 4 of the Act vests all native land in the country in the control of the Board for the benefit of the Fijian owners. By s 2, 'native land' means land which is neither Crown land nor the subject of a Crown or native grant, but includes land granted to a *mataqali* (a clan group of indigenous Fijians) under the Act. The Board has exclusive power to grant interests including leases over such land and to apply funds received for the benefit of Fijians.

Statutory trusts are also provided for under the legislation pertaining to intestate succession in many of the Pacific countries. For example, ss 44 and 45 of the Administration Act 1975 of Samoa provides that where certain persons such as brothers and sisters become entitled to the property of an intestate, it is to be held on statutory trust for them. This ensures that the property passes to them in equal shares and through them to their lineal issue according to what is known as the *per stirpes* principle of distribution.[22]

Other well-known trusts in the South Pacific region are provident funds, which are established through contributions by employers and employees to a fund which is in turn invested, in order to provide benefits for employees within a country in the event of their retirement or death. One example of this kind of trust is the entity established under the Vanuatu National Provident Fund Act Cap 189 of Vanuatu. Section 2 of that Act constitutes a body corporate known as the Vanuatu Provident Fund Board, with certain specific functions and powers to carry out the objectives of the Act. Section 14 of the Act establishes the Vanuatu National Provident Fund and s 15 provides that the Board is the trustee of the fund. The moneys in the fund must be invested by the Board according to guidelines laid down by the relevant Minister and the Central Bank of Vanuatu from time to time. By s 38 of the Act, moneys standing to the credit of a member's account may be withdrawn only on

---

22 This means according to class or group entitlements rather than on a *per capita* basis.

certain conditions, these being where the member (a) has attained 55 years of age; (b) has died; (c) has become permanently physically or mentally incapable of engaging in employment of any kind; or (d) is about to leave or has left Vanuatu with no intention of returning to it – whichever condition is first met.

3.2.9 Charitable trusts

A charitable trust is a trust for a purpose or purposes rather than for the benefit of individual beneficiaries or classes thereof. They are types of express trust. A charitable trust is the only trust for purposes allowed under English law. Such trusts must meet the legal requirement of being established for a charitable purpose, although some trusts that do not quite meet the strictness of the legal definition can be saved from invalidity in certain circumstances.

Charitable trusts are created as express trusts. What constitutes a charitable purpose is a complex issue and one of marginal relevance to us in this book. However, the most common view is that in order to be charitable, the relevant purposes must be limited to (a) the relief of poverty; (b) the advancement of education; (c) the advancement of religion; or (d) other purposes beneficial to the community not included in the foregoing.[23] In addition to being charitable in this rather narrow sense, all such trusts much exhibit an element of public benefit before they can be held valid. The exception to this is trusts for the relief of poverty, where public benefit is presumed without further proof. What constitutes public benefit varies somewhat from case to case. Where, for example, the right to receive the benefits of a particular trust purpose is limited to an extremely small and closed group of persons, the required element of public benefit will not usually be found.

3.3 Trusts and other interests

In this final section, we will discuss the differences between a trust and certain other types of legal interest. By appreciating these differences, it will be easier to understand the nature of the trust as a distinctive type of arrangement recognised and enforced within the legal system.

3.3.1 Trust and agency

A trust is similar to an agency relationship in many ways. The main point of similarity is that, like a trustee, the agent is subject to a fiduciary obligation. An agency arises wherever one party is empowered to do certain things on behalf of another – the latter being called the principal. The agent is in a position of trust taken in

---

23 See *Commissioners for Special Purposes of the Income Tax v Pemsel* [1891] AC 531 at 580; 22 QBD 290.

a very loose or common sense. The agent is bound to account to the principal for any property or money that comes into the agent's hands. The agent is bound to act in good faith in all dealings on the principal's behalf.

Whilst this similarity holds, the main point of difference is perhaps that the agency relationship is much more general than that involved in the trust. An agency may involve dealing in property of a principal, but it need not do so. There may be a valid agency involving no property at all. An agent may simply be empowered to do certain acts for a principal. In a trust, however, there must be property and, unlike an agency, that property is vested in the trustee subject to the trust obligation.

3.3.2 Trust and partnership

We noted in the Introduction and in Chapter 1 that, strictly speaking, a trust is not a legal form of association at all. Whilst a trust may involve the carrying on of a business by the trustee (and this is frequently the case), and may be formed for strictly commercial purposes, trusts are not associations. A trust is a legal institution for the holding of property. The differentiation is based on the mid-19th century decision of *Smith v Anderson*,[24] which still seems to be authority within the English legal system and former British colonies.

3.3.3 Trusts and corporate forms

In some respects, the role of the trustee is like that of a corporate director. They are under various duties, such as the duty to act in the best interests of the company and to act in good faith. Many trusts, such as public unit trusts, are similar to corporate enterprises, especially in the investment field.

The corporate form involves the corporation having an independent legal personality. It is a separate person or a separate entity at law. It is distinct from its members and the directors' duties are owed to the corporation, not to the aggregate of members. The trust, on the other hand, is not a distinct legal entity. The trust, as such, cannot sue or be sued, nor can it perform acts in its own name. Only the trustee can perform these acts and functions on behalf of the trust. In this respect, it is more like a partnership than a company. It is an aggregation of distinct interests.

3.3.4 Trust and contract

As we noted above, a contract in common law systems such as those of the South Pacific is an agreement which is legally binding. To be binding and for the

---

24 (1880) 15 Ch D 247.

obligations to be enforceable, there is a requirement of valuable consideration. This is not the case where the agreement is embodied in a deed, but that is a rather special exception. Consideration lends a commercial flavour to the agreement, such that the law is satisfied that the agreement is one which ought to be enforced. The finer points of the theory of consideration need not be entered into here, although it should be noted that the doctrine of consideration has been undermined considerably by developments in the area of equitable estoppel, which is based on notions of enforceability of obligations which are similar in many ways to those of trusts.

However, it is clear that the trust cannot be wholly assimilated with a contract or contractual obligation. The two areas of law developed separately, although the fact that equity courts developed particular remedies in relation to contract enforcement means that there was bound to be some overlap. The obligations and rights under a trust are not wholly contractual. As has been said above, often a trust may be created by a contract, although this is not universally the case. Normally a contract is enforceable only by the parties who entered into the contract. In a trust, however, beneficiaries under the trust will be entitled to enforce the trust obligation even though they were never parties to its creation. Sometimes a fiduciary obligation will be Imposed on contracting parties, but this is rather exceptional. Furthermore, the notion of fiduciary obligation applicable in respect of trustees is, of itself, not contractual in nature. For one thing, parties to a contract are usually considered to be on equal terms. In a fiduciary relationship, this is not so. A contracting party is placed under an obligation to perform the contract. But this is not a fiduciary obligation in the sense discussed before. It is an obligation created specifically by the enforceability of the contractual agreement itself. Here, perhaps, it is the public nature of the trust obligation that makes the difference.

3.3.5 Trust and debt

A debt is legally due wherever one person is entitled to recover a sum of money from another. Debt is traditionally a common law right of action. Whilst there are circumstances where beneficiaries or the settlor of a trust are entitled to recover moneys from the trustee, this is not a right of action in debt. A debt does not always involve the holding of property, although in some cases – e.g. in relation to a secured debt such as a mortgage – this might be so. Again, the debtor is not placed under a fiduciary obligation to pay the moneys due or otherwise in relation to the creditor. In this respect, the relationship involved in debt is much closer to that of contract than it is to the trust relationship.

4

EXPRESS TRUSTS

4.1 The creation of express trusts

Express trusts *inter vivos* (that is, during the lifetime of the creator of the trust) and those that are created by will (i.e. a testamentary trust) can be created by contract, either by a settlement (that is, where a person as settlor confers property on a trustee subject to the trust obligation) or by declaration of trust (that is, where a person who is the holder of the beneficial interest in property declares himself or herself to be a trustee of that property in favour of others). However, a trust needs no contract to be enforceable. The trust obligation is one which equity enforces in its own right, independently of any notion of contractual obligation. It requires no legal element of consideration in its formation, as is required of contracts. Consideration, in a sense, provides the element of commerciality in a contract and justifies its enforcement. However, a trust involves a departure from such a rationale altogether. As was said in *Jones v Lock*: 'If I say, expressly or impliedly, that I constitute myself a trustee of [property], that is a trust executed and capable of being enforced without consideration'.[1] It is enough that the trustee has assumed the trust obligation. As this is an obligation to deal with property for the benefit of others, the trustee will be compelled to abide by the terms of the trust simply because it would be wrong to allow that person to deny the interests of others thereby created.[2] However, if the

---

1 (1865) LR 1 ChApp 25 at 28, *per* Lord Cranworth, LC.
2 In that sense, equity acts on conscience. See *Commissioner of Stamp Duties (Qld) v Joliffe* (1920) 28 CLR 178, *per* Isaacs J.

DOI: 10.4324/9781003428060-5

transaction creating the trust is complete, then property is vested according to the trust without more.[3]

However created, these trusts generally have immediate effect from the time of assumption of the trust obligation.[4] This will usually be the date on which the trust instrument, if there is one, comes into effect. In the case of a will, which, as we shall see, requires that certain formal requirements be met, the position is different. A will operates from the date of death of the testator rather than the date on which it is made. Furthermore, a will may create trusts in favour of beneficiaries, but these would not generally begin to operate until the duties of administration of the deceased estate have been completed by the executors or administrators. This may be some time after the date of death. We will return to that issue later.

Equity requires no particular form to be adopted in order to create a trust. There are some exceptions to this, as noted below. Basically, however, any clear manifestation of intention to create a trust is sufficient. It is a matter for the court to determine whether what was intended was a trust or some other non-trust arrangement. Neither the use of nor the failure to use the term 'trust' when settling the trust terms is conclusive. What is described specifically as a trust may treated by the courts as an outright gift. Alternatively, a transaction may have been one involving a transfer of property to a second person with the intention that that person confer benefits on a third person. Such a transaction might appear superficially to be a trust, but on closer examination, this might not be the case at all. The transaction might have involved a conditional gift of property rather than the setting up of a trust. For example, the recipient of the property may receive it on condition that he or she makes a gift of other property to, or confers other benefits on, a third party. Or the donee may take subject to a charge on the property in favour of a third party. In neither case is there a trust.[5] In *Countess of Bective v Federal Commissioner of Taxation*, it was said that a condition imposed on a recipient of property to confer benefits on third parties might have at least four different effects. These were:

> (1) a statement of the donor's motive or of his expectation. If so the first person [the recipient] takes the gift absolutely and incurs no legal or equitable obligation to fulfil the purpose. ... (2) The purpose may be so stated as to amount to a condition upon and subject to which the first person takes beneficially. By accepting it the donee incurs an equitable duty to perform the condition which

---

3 *Collinson v Pattrick* (1838) 2 Keen 123; 48 ER 575; *Kekewich v Manning* [1851] 1 De G, M & G 176; *Commissioner of Stamp Duties (Qld) v Joliffe* (1920) 28 CLR 178.

4 It is possible that the coming into being of the trust might be postponed by the terms of the trust to some date after the date of the execution of the trust instrument.

5 *Re Hodge* [1940] Ch 260; *Countess of Bective v FCT* (1932) 47 CLR 417; *Re Lester* [1942] Ch 324; *Re Frame* [1939] Ch 700. But as the last of these cases shows, the mere use of the words 'on condition' does not necessarily make it a conditional gift rather than a trust.

is annexed to the gift. ... (3) The first person may take the gift beneficially, but the statement of the purposes, particularly if it involves the payment of money, may operate as an equitable charge thereon in favour of the other or others. Bequests and devises to parents for the maintenance and benefit of their children are from their very nature peculiarly susceptible of this interpretation. ... (4) The direction to pay the first person may be regarded as conferring no beneficial interest upon him, and, whether he receives it in the character of a trustee or in some other character such as guardian, the expression of the purpose may amount to a statement of objects to which he is bound to apply the fund.[6]

Technical language is certainly not required to create an express trust and, even when it is used, it is a matter for the court to settle the nature of the arrangement in question.[7] For example, where property is transferred to a person and the arrangement is held to be one of trust rather than assignment of the beneficial interest, then, in the event of bankruptcy of the holder, the property would not be available to creditors.[8] However, the use of merely precatory terms, such as terms of request or statements of desire, will not be enough to bring a trust into existence. In *In Re Adams and the Kensington Vestry*,[9] a testator had left his estate to his wife 'in full confidence that she will do what is right as to the disposal thereof between my children, either in her lifetime or by will after her decease'. It was held that the issue was one of giving effect to the intention of the testator as expressed in the whole document. In this case, it was held that the words were not enough to create a trust despite the use of the word 'confidence' and that what was intended was a gift to the wife absolutely. Even where precatory words are used, however, the outcome depends upon the view the court takes of the whole document and the occurrence of precatory words may not in all cases deny the existence of a trust.

In South Pacific communities, it might be difficult in many instances to determine whether a trust has been constituted according to the requirements of introduced law or whether the parties have attempted to set out some customary obligation. The Nauru Supreme Court in *In the Matter of James Ategan Bop*[10] was faced with such a situation. A number of years after the death of a Chief, it was alleged that he had expressed a wish that his heir should distribute certain land to certain named persons. The court held that this was to be taken as placing on the heir not a trust obligation but an obligation of honour, leaving him free to

---

6 (1932) 47 CLR 417 at 419–21.
7 *Richards v Delbridge* (1874) LR 18 Eq 11; *Re Armstrong* [1960] VR 202; *Re Potter* [1970] VR 352.
8 See *Toovey v Milne* (1819) 2 B & A 683, 106 ER 514; *Edwards v Glynn* (1859) 2 E & E 29, 121 ER 12; *Re Drucker (No 1)* [1902] 2 KB 237; *Barclays Bank Ltd v Quistclose Investments Ltd* [1970] AC 567.
9 (1884) 27 ChD 394.
10 Land Appeal No 29 of 1969.

determine what to allocate and to whom. This provided the disappointed 'beneficiaries' with no remedy at law or in equity.

Equity can give effect to a number of different arrangements regarding the disposition of property. Even the trust itself can be highly diverse in terms of the interests that it sets out to create.[11] Some of these may be taken to have effect only on the death of a particular person, but this does not necessarily amount to a disposition by will such as would amount to testate succession. This may be an important issue where the formal requirements for the making of a will have not been observed.[12] It may have been intended that the arrangement should operate with immediate effect rather than from the moment of death, and thus it may be considered a trust rather than a testamentary disposition.

However, what is required in respect of express trusts is a manifestation of an intention to create a trust. Issues have sometimes arisen as to the question of intention itself. In this regard, it has frequently been said that equity 'fastens on the declaration' of intention to create the trust.[13] The court searches for a clear declaration of intention and if it finds one, that is the end of the matter. It is viewed in objective terms by reference to the meaning of the words employed rather than by inquiry into the inner or subjective meaning attributable to the particular user. Psychological considerations of intention tend not to be considered except in so far as trusts must, like contracts and gifts, be voluntary creations. Where, for example, the will of the party creating the trust is overborne by duress, coercion or equitable fraud, such that the transaction cannot be considered a free and voluntary act, the courts will set it aside. In other respects, the declaration of trust (taking 'declaration' in its widest sense) will be taken as self-contained and the court will ask itself whether on the face of it there was an intention to bring a trust into being. It has been said that this is because it is the declaration itself which, like a conveyance of property, vests the property in the beneficiary of the trust.[14] Where the declaration is in writing, oral or extrinsic evidence will not be admitted to reveal an undisclosed or secret intention on the part of the author, although such evidence may be admitted to show that the settlor or declarer of the trust established the arrangement with the fraudulent intention of defeating the claims of creditors.[15]

Very often, the creation of an express trust is a matter of inference from a set of facts before the court. These are cases where there is something less than a clear expression of intention to create the trust, such as in a declaration or other instrument. These are trusts which are inferred from the conduct of the parties or from the circumstances rather than involving the direct use of express words. In other

---

11 *Russell v Scott* (1936) HCA 34; 55 CLR 440 at 454.
12 *Re Potter* [1970] VR 352.
13 See *McFadden v Jenkyns* (1842) 1 Hare 458; 41 ER 589.
14 *Commissioner of Stamp Duties (Qld) v Joliffe* [1920] HCA 45; 28 CLR 178, *per* Isaacs J.
15 *Johns v James* (1878) 8 Ch D 744.

words, the court might not be able to find any clear declaration of trust but might be prepared to imply one from the conduct undertaken. Here, it is suggested, some additional evidence of intention must be found because the court will not impose the trust obligation if none was intended at all.[16] Such an issue arose in the Fiji case of *Nagaiya v Subhaiya*.[17] This involved an allegation that land purchased in the name of the defendant but which had been used ever since by his immediate family as a place of residence was held by him as trustee for the family members and, in particular, his brothers. Not only had the brothers resided on the property for a number of years, but some of them had undertaken work on the property. There were allegations that the purchase money had been contributed by members of the family, although these were disputed by the defendant and the court seems to have found that these allegations were inconclusive. The Fiji Court of Appeal, and subsequently the Privy Council, held that there was insufficient evidence to establish the existence of a trust. Such an allegation needed to be established with a sufficient degree of certainty and here the evidence was insufficient to do that. At the appellate level, the court would not readily interfere with the finding of the court of first instance where there was a conflict of evidence between the parties and the matter involved some necessary attempt to assess the credibility of the parties. However, it appeared relevant that the allegation of the existence of a trust was not made until a number of years had elapsed since the purchase in the defendant's name.

4.1.1 Vesting property in the trustee

As indicated above, there are two methods whereby a trust *inter vivos* can be created. The first is where a person (or persons), called the settlor, transfers property to a person to hold it as trustee for others or for a legitimate purpose. The second is where a person who is the owner of property declares himself or herself to be a trustee in favour of another. Where the first of these is involved, the property must be legally vested by the settlor in the trustee. In the second case, vesting is not necessary, bearing in mind that the declarant already has title to the property and, provided that the trust is to have immediate rather than future effect, it is enforceable immediately.[18]

So far as the first situation goes, the property must be legally vested according to the legal or equitable rules relating to assignment of property. These are the same rules that apply to all assignments of property, not just in the trust situation. Legal rules for the assignment of property vary from one kind of property to another, but usually they require strict compliance with some settled form or legal

---

16 See *Vandenberg v Palmer* (1858) 4 K & J 204; *Hughes v Stubbs* (1842) 1 Hare 476; 66 ER 1119.
17 [1969] FJLawRp 38; [1969] 15 FLR 212 (7 November 1969).
18 *Ex parte Pye* (1811) 18 Ves. Jun. 140; (1814) 34 ER 271.

procedure. However, in general, property is assignable in equity simply by way of clear expression of an intention to assign. No particular form is required. The purported assignment must constitute a genuine attempt to create legal relations.[19] The court must be satisfied that a particular transaction involves an attempted assignment of property to a trustee, rather than a declaration of trust. The position relating to validity may rest crucially on how the court construes the transaction. It will not attempt to artificially reconstruct a particular transaction just to make it valid; for example, by casting it as a declaration of trust rather than an assignment.[20] Where, for example, a trust is sought to be created voluntarily, it will be important to decide whether it is an assignment or a declaration of trust. In the latter case, the transaction, even if voluntary, is complete when the declaration is made. In the former case, the rule is that equity will not perfect an imperfect gift. The first may be valid; the second may not be valid in some circumstances. Let us consider the equitable rules in relation to assignment a little further.

Equity treats assignments in a particular way which does not in all respects follow the common law approach. It is necessary to make some basic distinctions. The first is the distinction between property which is assignable at law, i.e. there exists some particular method of assignment of the property in common law, and property which is assignable in equity only. The latter will be the case with respect to what is known as equitable property, which the common law does not recognise as constituting a proprietary interest. Examples include partnership interests, equitable mortgages and the interest of a beneficiary under a trust. The second distinction is between assignments that are voluntary and those that are for value. The latter involves a contract to assign the property in question. This distinction is particularly important because equity has always treated voluntary transactions or gifts in a way which is distinct from transactions or assignments which are for value. The first of these tends to invoke the maxim that 'equity will not assist a volunteer'. In the case of assignments by contract, however, the relevant maxim is most often 'equity will regard as done that which ought to be done'. The sense of this is that equity will often treat an interest under an incomplete but enforceable contract as if the contract had been completed. We will deal here firstly with the case of voluntary assignment.

4.1.2 Voluntary assignments

Historically, equity has treated with disfavour the enforcement of gifts. Where there is consideration, equity will go to some lengths to save a transaction which

---

19 *Toara v Simbolo* [1998] VUSC 62; Civil Case 152 of 1996 (1 October 1998), referred to in *Simbolo v Government of the Republic of Vanuatu* [2018] VUSC 49; Civil Case 165 of 2017 (14 May 2018).
20 *Milroy v Lord* (1862) 4 De GF & J 264, 45 ER 1185; *Re Rose* [1952] Ch 499; *Anning v Anning* (1907) HCA 13; 4 CLR 1049.

is legally incomplete. But in respect of incomplete gifts of property, it prefers not to lend assistance. This is not without some anomalies. For example, where a trust is created there is no requirement of consideration. Yet where this was clearly intended equity will freely enforce the trust. Where there is a voluntary assignment that purports to achieve effects which are very similar in some ways to the outcome of a gift, it will not intervene. Thus, the intention of the parties in bringing about the transaction in a certain way can be crucial.

There are two operative equitable maxims in relation to assignments by way of gift or voluntary assignments. These are: (a) equity will not assist a volunteer; and (b) there is no equity to perfect an imperfect gift. If a disposition is by way of gift and, as a matter of construction of the arrangement, the transaction is completed in the required sense, then equity will fully protect the donee's interest. However, there will be problems here in determining whether the gift is complete to the required degree. Where there is a gift, and it was intended by the parties that the gift would take effect in the future, then the donee will not be regarded as having any equity which is enforceable. This will arise in situations where there was no clear intention that the gift would take effect as a present assignment or present transfer of property.

In the case of voluntary assignments proper, the distinction between legal property (property assignable at law) and equitable property (property assignable in equity only) becomes rather crucial. The mere fact that the property is assignable at law does not necessarily exclude the role of equity. This is because there will be situations where the assignment has not followed the prescribed legal form. At this stage, it should be appreciated that the common law generally requires some particular form in which property is to be assigned and this form of assignment varies from case to case. For example, real property is sometimes assignable under old or general system conveyancing, which is a distinct system from that applicable to property held under the state-guaranteed system of title in place in some jurisdictions (generally called Torrens title). In respect of the former, there is a requirement as to writing, but the latter requires a statutory form of transfer or other dealing to be registered. Entire choses in action, such as debts, are assignable under s 136(1) of the Law of Property Act 1925 (UK) and its equivalents in the Pacific countries.[21] Shares are to be assigned in accordance with requirements of the Companies Acts,[22] and so on. In some instances, there are legal methods of assignment of equitable property, e.g. trust interests. We will return to this point later on.

The question will arise as to whether equity will protect the interests of a voluntary assignee in a situation where property is assignable at law according to some specified form, but the actual form of assignment has not been complied

---

21 E.g. s 113 Property Law Act Cap 130 (F).
22 On which, see later.

with. This involves the application of the rule in *Milroy v Lord*.[23] The judgment put forward rules which are relevant to the purported assignment in equity of property which is assignable at law. The main rule is usually put in this way: "The transferor must have done everything which, according to the nature of the property in question, was necessary to be done in order to transfer the property and to render the transaction binding". This, as might be appreciated, is a somewhat loaded statement of a legal rule because of the occurrence of the words 'necessary', 'transfer' and 'render binding'. The two main issues of concern in this regard are: (1) What needs to be done in relation to the particular property? and (2) By whom must that thing be done?

Both of these questions have given rise to some dispute as to the rule's correct application. The approach put forward in the Australian High Court in *Anning v Anning*[24] by Griffiths CJ was that it was necessary from the donor's point of view to have done everything in his or her power to make the transaction binding on himself or herself. If anything remains to be done by the donor (in the absence of which the donee cannot obtain title against a third party), then the gift will be imperfect and equity will not perfect it. If the donee can do whatever is required of him or her without the assistance of the court, then the gift is complete in the required sense and the donee's title will be recognised as such in equity. Where the gift is incomplete by reason, for example, of the absence of government consent to transfer, the transaction would be revocable by the donor.[25] In the same decision, however, Isaacs J adopted a different interpretation of the *Milroy v Lord* rule. It was said by him that the donor must have perfectly effectuated the gift so far as the nature of the property admits. If the property is assignable at law (i.e. if there is some legal method of assignment), it must be assigned correctly. If the property is not assignable at law, equity requires only a clear expression of intention to assign. The real test so far as legally assignable property was concerned was, he said:

> If the legal title is assignable at law it must be so assigned or equity will not enforce the gift. If for any reason, whether want of a deed by the assignor or a specifically prescribed method of transfer, or registration or statutory notice, the transfer of legal title is incomplete. When the law permits it to be complete, equity regards the gift as still imperfect and will not enforce it. In such a case, the fact that the assignor can do all that he can be required to do is not applicable.[26]

Higgins J adopted a rather more extreme view: the donor must have done everything he or she could have done to perfect the gift, even where this covers things

---

23 (1862) 4 De GF & J 264; 45 ER 1185.
24 (1907) HCA 13; 4 CLR 1049.
25 See *Hedmon v Ika* [1980] NRSC 2; [1969–1982] NLR (B) 148 (5 November 1980).
26 (1907) HCA 13; 4 CLR 1049.

which are not in their nature obligatory. This is a very harsh interpretation of *Milroy v Lord*. It has not generally been followed, perhaps because it creates expectations which are wholly unreasonable. However, subsequent cases have not satisfactorily resolved the issue as between the interpretation of Griffiths CJ and that of Isaacs J. The former is, it is suggested, the more reasonable and should be the one applied in the South Pacific jurisdictions.

4.1.3 Assignments for valuable consideration

Where there is an assignment for valuable consideration, the position regarding the effect of the assignments is in one way a little simpler. First of all, let us assume that the transaction has been completed by the payment of the price, i.e. the transaction is legally executed. The position is then whether the property is legally or equitably assignable, i.e. whether it is regarded as complete in equity as well. This will be so, notwithstanding any non-compliance with statutory or other formal requirements. Such a position stands in direct contrast to the position regarding voluntary assignments as discussed above. Assume, however, that one has a valid contract for the assignment of property, but it is not yet completed, i.e. the contract is executory in nature. The question is then whether there is a basis for saying the assignee is, at some point prior to completion, the equitable owner or the owner as far as equity is concerned. Does completion of the assignment or the vesting of the interest sold, arise only on completion of the contract? Does the assignee acquire an equitable proprietary interest at some earlier point in time?

On this issue, the decided cases suggest that the assignee's interest is an equitable proprietary interest as and when the contract arises. This would seem to suggest that property is vested in the trustee and the trust arises when the contract to assign the property is executed. This, it is contended, is so whether the property is legal or equitable. In the decision in *Lysaght v Edwards*, Jessel MR said:

> The moment you have a valid contract for sale the vendor becomes in equity a trustee for the purchaser of the estate sold, and the beneficial ownership passes to the purchaser, the vendor having a right to the purchase money, a charge or lien on the estate for the security of the purchase money, and a right to retain possession of the estate until the purchase money is paid, in the absence of express contract as to the time of possession.[27]

The guiding principle behind this decision was that the equity regards as done that which ought to be done. As to the precise nature of the interest, it was contended that when the vendor had made out a title to convey under the contract, or where the purchaser had accepted what the vendor had got to give (i.e. if the vendor sought to

---

27 (1876) 2 Ch D 499 at 506.

convey an interest which was less than that for which he or she contracted), there was a constructive trust on the vendor in favour of the purchaser. Prior to that time, the vendor was to be regarded as a type of quasi-trustee, or what was called a trustee *sub modo*.[28] It seems undeniable in light of the established authorities that equity will regard a purchaser under an unconditional contract which is capable of being subject to an order of specific performance as having beneficial ownership as at the date of making of the contract. In *Legione v Hateley*,[29] it was held per Gibbs CJ and Murphy J of the High Court of Australia that "[there] is no doubt that when the purchasers executed the contract and paid the deposit the beneficial ownership of the land passed to them subject to the payment of the purchase price".[30]

This has usually been taken to be the case where the contract is specifically enforceable, but not otherwise. Nonetheless, there has been some academic conjecture about whether this can be taken as the exact position in all cases. There is a line of authority which suggests that the availability of specific performance is not of itself the key. The issue is whether the purchaser's interest in the subject matter of the contract is capable of protection in some other way, for example by way of injunction. This opts for a much broader approach, which follows from some of the older authorities such as *Tailby v Official Receiver*,[31] *Hoysted v Federal Commissioner of Taxation*,[32] *Redman v Permanent Trustee Co of NSW*[33] and, perhaps, *Brown v Heffer*.[34] Such a view is also consistent with the approach of Mason and Deane JJ of the High Court of Australia in *Legione v Hateley*, above. However, the predominance of current authority tends to be that the availability of specific performance is in fact central.

4.1.4 Assignments of future property

In order to make an effective assignment, there must be a proprietary interest. At law and in equity, a proprietary interest is regarded only as a presently existing interest in the rather general sense of something which is established at the present

28 See *Chang v Registrar of Titles* [1976] HCA 1; 137 CLR 177 at 184–85 *per* Mason J.
29 (1983) HCA 11; 152 CLR 406.
30 See also *KLDE Pty Ltd v Commissioner of Stamp Duties of Queensland* [1984] HCA 63; 155 CLR 288 at 295–97; *R v Broadcasting Tribunal; Ex parte Hardiman* [1980] HCA 13; 144 CLR 13 at 31. In *Haque v Hague (No 2)* [1965] HCA 38; 114 CLR 98, it was said (at 124): "the making of the contract had to an extent transferred the beneficial ownership to the purchaser. The deceased [vendor] was not a mere trustee for the purchaser, but his position was something between that of a mere trustee and a mortgagee. He could exercise for his own benefit such rights with regard to the land as were consistent with the contractual rights of the purchaser until payment of the purchase money in full and until that event he had a lien or charge for the unpaid purchase money".
31 (1888) 13 App Cas 523.
32 [1920] HCA 29; 27 CLR 400.
33 (1916) HCA 47; 22 CLR 84.
34 [1967] HCA 40; 116 CLR 344.

time and gives the required degree of dominion over an object. The term 'future property' is something of an oxymoron because there is no proprietary interest which can exist only in the future. It must be a presently existing right to be a property right. Furthermore, it must be ascertainable or identifiable as such. The right to future income by way of salary or wages is one example of property that cannot be assigned by an immediate assignment. What would happen if the person were to lose their employment? The quantum of the alleged property is indeterminate and not presently existing. Where a person falls within one of the classes of potential beneficiaries under a discretionary trust, where they take no interest until the trustee exercises the discretion in their favour, they cannot be said to have any property interest.[35] They have a mere expectancy which is not assignable. Hence no trust over such an interest can be created because it is impossible to vest it in the beneficiary.

It has been held that a residuary beneficiary under the will of a deceased person whose estate has not been administered cannot have a presently existing property interest in the assets of the trust. It has been held to be impossible to assign that interest to another or *a fortiori* to create a trust over such an interest. In *Sherani v Jagroop*,[36] a residuary beneficiary had purported to enter into a contract to lease part of the estate property in which he had a possible share as residuary beneficiary under the will of a deceased person. The Fiji Supreme Court held that this was ineffective, as the administration of the estate had not been completed. However, the decision is to be questioned on some grounds. It is correct to say that such a person cannot be said to have a property interest in the specific assets of the deceased estate. But the authorities relied on by the court merely speak of an interest in specific assets comprising the estate. The fact that administration is not completed implies that any such specific assets cannot be identified. So much follows from *Livingston's Case*,[37] which, incidentally, was not referred to by the court. However, there is good authority to the effect that the residuary legatee does have an equitable chose in action or a property interest in the entire and undivided mass of the assets. In *Comptroller of Stamps v Howard-Smith*,[38] it was held by the High Court of Australia, relying on many of the same authorities, that such an equitable chose in action was assignable by the residuary legatee. On this basis, it would appear that the decision is clearly against the weight of authority.

Furthermore, the decision appeared to miss the point regarding the assignment of expectancies or future property. A person can make a present assignment of an interest which will only come into existence as a proprietary interest in the future where the assignment is by way of contract. Provided that the contract is

---

35 See Chapter 6.
36 [1973] FJLawRp 18; [1973] 19 FLR 85 (24 October 1973). Relying on *Lord Sudeley v Attorney General* [1897] AC 11 and *Barnardos Homes v Special Income Tax Commissioners* [1921] 2 AC 1. To the same effect, see *Commissioner of Stamp Duties (Qld) v Livingston* [1965] AC 694.
37 *Commissioner of Stamp Duties (Qld) v Livingston* [1964] HCA 54; 112 CLR 12; [1965] AC 694.
38 (1936) HCA 12; 54 CLR 614.

specifically enforceable, equity will enforce the contract and regard the purchaser as having an equitable interest under a constructive trust from the vendor. What the judgment leaves unclear is whether the conclusion reached by the court was on the basis that the contract in this case was specifically unenforceable. It did conclude that there was an 'overwhelming practical problem of enforcement' but the court appears not to have related that to the issue in hand. The agreement to lease clearly constituted a contract to assign and an interest by way of lease. Hence if it were specifically enforceable, the contract would be enforced by equity as a contract to assign the interest when it had been fully ascertained.

However, future 'property' cannot be assigned by way of gift because of the operation of the maxim 'There is no equity to perfect an imperfect gift'. Where the assignment is for value, a different maxim will be applied, and that is 'Equity regards as done that which ought to be done'. The existence of consideration or value is regarded as sufficient equity to warrant enforcement of the contract, and therefore enforcement of the assignment as a contract to assign the property when it comes into being in the future. Very much will depend on the intention of the parties, or how that intention is construed by the court. It must be construed as a contract to assign the property as and when it comes into being. If the arrangement is construed as an attempt presently to assign property, which does not presently exist as such, then the assignment will fail because the property does not presently exist. One is required to distinguish between situations where there has been an attempt not to assign anything which could be called future property or future benefits, but to assign present property to which those future benefits or future rights will accrue. An example of this might be a situation where a person assigns a royalty but in reality, the right to future royalty is attached to some existing intellectual property. The copyright is assigned and the royalty rights accrue to the assignee as a consequence only of the passing of the property from which they accrue. The assignment of the intellectual property will be effective immediately. Something which appears as an attempt to assign future royalties or future income from that property might conceivably be construed as merely part and parcel of the assignment of the intellectual property itself. Clearly much will hang on the construction of the arrangement in question.[39]

4.2 Formal requirements as to creation

In the case of trusts *inter vivos* of certain interests and in relation to the assignment of interests, formal legal requirements are imposed. These apply to the creation of trusts in land. Even the assignment of interests which are equitable interests, such as beneficial interests under a trust (over which a further trust can

---

39 See generally *Norman v Federal Commissioner of Taxation* [1963] HCA 21; 109 CLR 9; *Shepherd v Federal Commissioner of Taxation* (1965) 113 CLR 385; *Taylor v Federal Commissioner of Taxation* (1969) 123 CLR 206; *Palette Shoes Pty Ltd v Krohn* [1937] HCA 37; 58 CLR 1.

be created), falls within these requirements. These are statutory provisions which are derived with some modification from the Statute of Frauds. Obviously, this is a case where a legal form of transfer is required. On the basis that equity follows the law, the existence of these formal requirements will have a direct effect on the creation of trusts by assignment. It should be pointed out that these requirements also apply in some instances to declarations of trust of interests in land as well as those created by intermediate assignment. Their operation is limited to express trusts and trust implied by conduct. They do not affect the operation of resulting or constructive trusts.

As regards trusts created by will, there are formal requirements as to the making of a will which derive from the (UK) Wills Act 1837.[40] These requirements are that the will be in writing, signed by the testator at the foot or end of it and that it be attested by at least two attesting witnesses who also subscribe their names as witnesses. A testamentary trust must meet these requirements. In some jurisdictions, the courts have power to uphold the validity of a will even though it does not meet the formal requirements.[41] Whether the creation of the trust involves a testamentary disposition requiring its embodiment in a will is to be determined largely by reference to the concept of a will itself. A secret trust, which is a form of resulting trust rather than an express trust, is allowed to obviate these requirements.

A will is a document which purports to affect the property of a person and which is to come into effect only from the moment of the death of the maker of it. If this is the manifest intention of the document, then it must be made according to the formalities specified in the Wills Acts. If it is not, the whole document will be struck down. This will include the terms of any trust intended to have been created by the putative will. As mentioned above, certain trusts might be validly created *inter vivos* but purport to create interests which take effect by reference to the death of the creator of the trust or of another person. For example, a person could establish a trust whereby he or she reserves an interest for life and, from death, for his or her children. This is not a testamentary disposition because it is intended to take effect immediately. In *Russell v Scott*, it was said:

> Succession post mortem is not the same as testamentary succession. But what can be accomplished only by will is the voluntary transmission on death of an interest which up to the moment of death belongs absolutely and indefeasibly to the deceased.[42]

---

40 The legislation of the South Pacific countries and the formalities required are discussed in Hughes, RA, *Succession Law in the South Pacific*, 1999, Suva, IJALS, Chapters 2, 3 and 4.

41 This is so in several of the Australian jurisdictions. See e.g. s 18A Wills, Probate and Administration Act 1898 (NSW) and generally Mackie, K and Burton, M, *Outline of Succession*, 2000, Sydney, Butterworths, 2nd edn, pp 65 ff.

42 (1936) HCA 34; 55 CLR 440 at 454. See also *Baird v Baird* [1990] 2 WLR 1412; *Re MacInnes* [1935] 1 DLR 401; *Williams v FCT* [1950] HCA 21; 81 CLR 359.

4.2.1 Certainty of subject matter

At all times during the continuance of the trust, there must be certainty of subject matter. As a trust is effectively an arrangement regarding the holding of property, the requirement is that it can only exist where there is separately identifiable property to which it relates. This is a condition in relation to the creation of trusts. It is also a requirement as to continuing validity. If the trust property should cease to exist, then the trust will be at an end. So far as creation goes, the trust instrument must identify the subject matter of the trust, otherwise the trust will fail for uncertainty. Nor can it exist if there is a basic uncertainty about the property over which the trust obligation is supposed to range.

There are two aspects of this requirement. The first is that a trust can only be created with respect to something which equity regards as a proprietary interest. Thus, a trust cannot be created with respect to future property or speculative or expectant interests in the sense discussed above. These interests are neither assignable nor can they be the subject matter of the trust. Secondly, there is the requirement of identifiability. A trust cannot range over property which cannot be determined. Obviously, this will be a matter requiring clear definition in the trust instrument where there is one. In other respects, this issue has to be determined at least when the trust is created but also thereafter. This does not mean to say that a trust has to be limited to specific property in a specific form only. The nature of the trust property may undergo conversion after the trust is created, for example where a trustee pursuant to a power or a trust for sale sells trust real estate and then invests the proceeds. A trust may generate further property where the trustee is empowered to acquire it. Trust investments may yield interest, or the trust property may generate other income which is accumulated. Trustees may under certain circumstances borrow money or improve trust property. Whatever the case, this after-acquired property certainly becomes part of the subject matter of the trust obligation and there is nothing in this which infringes the rule as to certainty of subject matter.

4.2.2 Certainty of objects

A trust must have certainty of objects in order to be validly created. This also is a continuing requirement. Generally, a trust requires a separation of legal and equitable interests. Where these are merged, for example where a person appears to be both the trustee and the sole beneficiary of the same property, the trust is invalid or terminates from the time when the merger occurs.[43] 'Objects' for these purposes means either the individual beneficiaries of the trust or the purposes of the trust. If the objects who are to benefit from the carrying out of the trust are not stated

---

43 See *The Law of Trusts Looseleaf 4th ed.* (Ford, HAJ, Lee, WA, Bryan, M, Glover J, Fullerton, I. 2019, Sydney, Thomson Reuters Australia Subscriptions), p 153.

with a sufficient degree of certainty, then, again, the trust will fail for uncertainty. In relation to private trusts, this is known as 'the beneficiary principle', based on the decision in *Morice v Bishop of Durham*[44] (or at least the dominant interpretation of the *ratio* in that case). According to this principle, a trust can only be valid if it is for (legal) persons or groups of persons or for some charitable purpose. Taken strictly it would mean that there can be no trust for purposes which are not charitable. Such trusts are known as trusts of imperfect obligation. There has been some inconsistency about this in England, for example, where some types of non-charitable purpose trust have been upheld.[45] In Australia, the tendency is to exclude the possibility of any such trusts being treated as valid. The reason for this prejudice against trusts of imperfect obligation is that there is no one who could enforce the obligation of the trustee in the event of maladministration. In the case of a charitable trust, the Attorney General could at least intervene and bring the matter to court. But where there is a private purpose, this is not possible, and the court cannot intervene of its own motion.

It is conventional to interpret the certainty of objects requirement with two senses. The first is that the recipients under the trust should be identifiable with certainty and, secondly, the interests that they take should be discoverable with certainty. The emphasis of the requirement will shift depending upon whether the trust is fixed or discretionary. It is not necessary that all of the persons who might benefit as beneficiaries be precisely ascertainable at the moment when the trust is created. Gifts to classes of individual beneficiaries can under certain circumstances be valid, that is, provided that the criteria for class identification dictate that it is possible to identify whether any particular individual is or is not a member of the class in question. The operation of the requirement is particularly relevant in the case of discretionary trusts where there is a range of potential objects whose interest in the trust depends upon the exercise of a discretionary power of determination by the trustee.

In relation to public purpose or charitable trusts, there are special issues which apply. In such cases, the purpose must indeed be identifiable with some measure of certainty, but furthermore, it must both be exclusively charitable[46] and evince an element of public benefit. As a general rule, these are the only types of trust where trusts which are focused on providing for the furtherance of purposes rather than for individuals or groups of individuals will be treated as valid under introduced

---

44 (1804) 9 Ves Jun 399.

45 Ford and Lee *(op cit* fn 43, p 178) indicate that the following trusts for non-charitable purposes have been upheld in England: "trusts for the maintenance of particular animals; trusts for the construction of graves and sepulchral monuments; trusts for the maintenance of graves and sepulchral monuments and trusts for the saying of masses, in jurisdictions where these are not regarded as charitable".

46 This is the general rule but there are some statutory exceptions in the case of mixed charitable and non-charitable purposes. See Ford and Lee, *op cit* fn 43, pp 883 ff.

law. It is on this basis that trusts for the benefit of collective groups or entities, such as 'that he [the trustee] would continue it [the property] in the family'[47] or 'consider the testator's relations',[48] have generally been struck down as uncertain. Similarly so with trusts for the purposes of 'This Week's Good Cause' [of the BBC],[49] trusts 'for parochial purposes',[50] for 'generally useful purposes',[51] for 'parish work' as opposed to 'the inhabitants of a parish',[52] for 'hospitable purposes',[53] 'benevolent' purposes[54] and 'philanthropic' purposes.[55] These were trusts which were held to contain no charitable purpose, even implicitly.[56] Such issues are beyond the scope of this book.

However, it should be noted that the application of this approach in the South Pacific jurisdictions is to some degree problematic. In these jurisdictions, the traditional culture veered strongly in the direction of the recognition of communal entities and communal rights rather than those which are premised on the rights of the individual. There is now a tendency in the post-colonial era to look towards other sources of law rather than introduced law and, in particular, to accept that the premises of introduced law are often inconsistent with those of traditional custom and culture. This was aptly put by the High Court of Western Samoa in *Kaliopa v Silao*:

We, western judges, schooled in the common law, valiantly attempt to support the matati system and communal land tenure and, in so doing, all too often confuse the issues by attempting to apply common law labels with which we are comfortable to factual situations which are controlled by Samoan custom and tradition. Accordingly, the average opinion sets forth a factual situation, states the controlling Samoan custom, then attempts to apply a common law principle – together with supporting citations – in an attempt to justify the decision. We should also stop trying to rationalize Samoan customs and traditions by recourse to common law principles and precedents. We should accept Samoan customs and traditions as controlling authority. These customs and traditions need no common law support. Actually common law principles which are

---

47 *Harland v Trigg* (1782) 1 Bro CC 142.
48 *Sale v Moore* (1827) 1 Sim 534; 57 ER 678.
49 *Re Wood (dec'd)* [1949] Ch 498.
50 *Farley v Westminster Bank Ltd* [1939] AC 430.
51 *Kendall v Granger* (1842) 5 Beav 300; 49 ER 593.
52 *Re Norton's Will Trusts; Lightfoot v Goldson* [1948] 2 All ER 842.
53 *Re Hewitt's Estate; Gateshead Corp v Hudspeth* (1883) 53 LJ Ch 132.
54 *Chichester Diocesan Foundation v Simpson* [1944] AC 341.
55 *Re Macduff; Macduff v Macduff* [1896] 2 Ch 451.
56 An implicit charitable purpose was held to be present, however, in a trust 'for my country England' in *Re Smith, Public Trustee v Smith* [1932] 1 Ch 153; cf *Williams' Trustees v Inland Revenue Commissioners.* [1947] AC 447.

based on private ownership of land are often the antithesis of Samoan customs and traditions which are based on communal land tenure.[57]

Furthermore, so far as the recognition of charitable purposes is concerned, it needs to be said that the concept of what is charitable, and hence a charitable object, is one which is to some extent culturally relative. Whilst this might theoretically be a question merely of adjusting the concept of a charity to local circumstances, it does raise the somewhat deeper question as to the relative importance of the objectives of charitable trust law to these countries. They are countries where the creation of charitable purpose trusts is limited. Many of them are insufficiently economically developed, in the Western sense, to encourage the creation of large charitable trusts. Such issues raise some fundamental issues which have yet to be addressed fully by the courts and by legislators. Inevitably, they might impact on the approach to basic issues such as those we have under consideration here. To date, there are no clear guidelines.

In *Volavola v Mara*,[58] the issue involved a clause in a trust deed over land at Yanuca Island in the Fiji Islands. This was not native land and was therefore outside the operation of the Fijian customary system acknowledged pursuant to the Native Lands Act Cap 133. However, the deed purported to identify the beneficiaries by listing certain living persons and "their lawful heirs and successors according to Native custom as though they constituted one Mataqali and the provisions of s 5 and s 6 of the Native Land Ordinance (Cap 109) apply to their land". It was argued that the trust should fail because this definition purported to constitute the land as native land which must then be treated to all intents and purposes as if it were *mataqali* land. Such a claim, if upheld, would have ousted the jurisdiction of the court to entertain the suit of the plaintiff alleging mismanagement by the trustee, as in *Kaliavu v Native Land Trust Board*,[59] where it had been held that the members of custom or *mataqali* land could not maintain a suit for any wrong concerning the *mataqali*. In this case, however, it was held that the description in the trust deed could not be treated as constituting a *mataqali*. This was impossible by way of a private law trust deed. Such lands were outside the scope of introduced trust law in any event. The description above was to be taken only as an attempt to describe the beneficiaries of the trust in an appropriate way. However, the description of the objects was sufficient to meet the required test of certainty and the trust was upheld.

One issue that is suggested by this ruling is whether in the South Pacific jurisdictions the certainty of objects requirement, put in terms of the beneficiary principle, is likely in the future to be interpreted more liberally than it has been in other jurisdictions. The reason for this might be that traditional South Pacific societies

---

57 [1981] ASHC 1; HC-LT NO (1 January 1981), p 2.
58 [1986] FJLawRp 2; [1986] 32 FLR 9 (16 May 1986).
59 [1956] FJLawRp 16; [1956–57] 5 FLR 17 (27 August 1956).

have always been disposed to the recognition of communal entities, which English law's individualistic bias might treat as philosophically untenable.

4.2.3 Other issues affecting validity

As we shall see later, the vesting of interests in beneficiaries of a trust must comply with certain rules relating to the remoteness of vesting or the rule relating to perpetuities. Where the trust fails to do so, it will be invalid. In the Fiji Islands, the perpetuities rule is that which has been modified by the Law of Property Act Cap 130. Section 36 of that Act refers to 'limitations' which, for these purposes, can be treated as provisions purporting to create the beneficial interests under a trust. The section provides:

> 36 In determining whether any limitation is invalid as infringing the rule of law known as the rule against perpetuities, the perpetuity period is, for the purposes of that rule, such period of years not exceeding eighty as may be specified in the instrument creating that limitation or, if no such period of years is specified in such instrument, the period that is applicable under that rule at law.

Under section 38(1), limitation is not to be declared or treated as invalid as infringing the perpetuities rule unless and until it is certain that the interest it creates cannot vest within the perpetuity period. If the limitation creates or confers a general power of appointment over or in connection with property – and that could relate to a general power of appointment contained in a trust instrument – it will not be treated as invalid unless it is clear that the power cannot become exercisable within the perpetuity period. However, if the power becomes exercisable within that period, it is valid. Section 29 permits the likes of trustees to apply to the court to obtain a declaration of validity.

It is common enough in relation to trusts to have a provision which requires, or at least permits, the trust income to be accumulated for a period. The question will be whether such accumulations of income offend the perpetuities rule. In England, special time constraints were put on the period for which income could be accumulated by the so-called Thellusson Act in 1880 which was then re-enacted by the Law of Property Act 1925 (UK), ss 164–66. These provisions were repealed in several jurisdictions in the second half of the 20th century. In the Fiji Islands, the relevant provision is now s 48(1), which assimilates the permissible accumulations period to the perpetuities period. It reads as follows:

> 48 (1) Where property is settled or disposed of in such manner that the income thereof may or shall be accumulated wholly or in part, the power or direction to accumulate that income is valid if the disposition of the accumulated income is, or may be, valid and not otherwise.

(2) Nothing in this section affects the right of any person or persons to terminate an accumulation that is for his or their benefit or any jurisdiction or power
of the court to maintain or advance out of accumulations or any powers of a
trustee under Part V of the Trustee Act.

In jurisdictions in the South Pacific where such statutory provisions do not exist,
the position is somewhat more problematic. It has not been determined whether,
in the case of Vanuatu for example, the UK perpetuities legislation to the same
effect applies by virtue of the general provisions relating to the reception of UK
statutes. It must be doubtful whether such legislation could be held applicable to
local circumstances as regards land where all land in that country is vested in
custom owners under the Constitution.

There will also be certain putative trusts which will be held void on the grounds
of illegality, public policy or otherwise. For example, trusts which are created for
the purposes of defrauding creditors have long been voidable at the instance of the
Official Receiver, Trustee or other appropriate officer in bankruptcy. In Australia,
trusts established for the purposes of evading or avoiding income taxation can
be set aside for certain purposes pursuant to general anti-avoidance provisions.[60]
This applies by legislation.[61] However, more generally, trusts created for fraudulent or wrongful purposes will be set aside in equity. Similarly so with trusts for
other illegal purposes, although much now depends on the nature of the illegality.
On the issue of whether property is recoverable, this might depend on whether the
illegal purpose has been put into effect.[62]

4.3 Interpretation of trust instruments

The question of interpretation of the terms of the instrument creating a trust, be it
a will or other instrument, is especially appropriate with regard to express trusts
rather than trusts implied by the operation of law. We will address this issue here.
Of course, care must be taken in the creation of the trust to ensure that the various
requirements as to certainty are met and that the trustee has appropriate powers. The wording used in the trust instrument assures a paramount importance
in determining the trust relationship. There are numerous examples of situations
where these two issues of interpretation and administration arise together. The
proposed acts of a trustee have to be within the terms settled by the trust. The trustee's rights may be subject to considerable variance from trust to trust. The rights
of beneficiaries or proposed beneficiaries to benefits under the trust will
often depend upon the terms of the instrument, which determine those rights.

---

60 See Part IV Income Tax Assessment Act 1936 (as amended). Similar provisions, although perhaps
not so elaborate, exist in other jurisdictions.
61 This legislation derived from the statute 13 Eliz I c 5 of 1571, which was subsequently adopted in
altered form in s 175 of the Law of Property Act 1925 (UK).
62 See *Nelson v Nelson* [1995] HCA 25; 184 CLR 538, referred to in *Li v Tao* [2023] NSWCA 310.

Thus, although certain of the duties, rights, obligations and powers of the parties to a trust are matters of legal policy (in other words, they are a consequence of the public nature of the trust institution), in most circumstances, the trust instrument plays a vital role in determining just what the parties are entitled to do or to demand. The trust instrument, in that sense, is part of the constitution of a particular trust.

Sometimes it is not possible authoritatively to resolve problems of construction and interpretation to enable a trustee or an executor to carry out the trust in confidence that its terms and effect are as they appear to them. There needs to be a variety of mechanisms put in place to protect a trustee who acts reasonably and in good faith in carrying out the trust. The trustee legislation sets out certain mechanisms which allow a court to absolve a trustee from liability that has been innocently incurred. It also provides certain procedures which can be undertaken by a trustee in order to protect themselves against unknown claimants against the trust estate. Also, a trustee who acts on advice from appropriate experts in the appropriate field will be entitled to argue that they have acted in good faith in the performance of their duty, as well as having a source of indemnity should the advice in question prove to be wrong. These issues will be discussed in Chapter 9. But, more directly in point, the trustee faced with possible ambiguities and uncertainties concerning the proper legal effect of the wording of a trust instrument or a will is always able to apply to the equity court for directions as to how they should act. The direction of the court on issues such as entitlement to trust property, the powers of the trustee, the proper carrying out of the terms of the trust and other issues of construction will finally settle the matter in the sense that the trustee can act on the court's order in full confidence that in so doing they will be absolved from liability. The circumstances in which this protection will not be afforded are limited to cases where the trustee, in seeking the court's opinion, has misled the court, or negligently or wilfully withheld relevant facts from it.

Let us look for the moment at some of the basic approaches to the interpretation of trust instruments.

4.3.1 The construction of legal arrangements generally

Legal arrangements such as trusts can be created in a number of ways. To ascertain the terms of those arrangements, it is necessary to have regard to the mode of their creation. Some arrangements (and this goes for many types of trust, express and otherwise) are brought into being by virtue of wholly oral arrangements. Others may be constituted partly by oral negotiation and partly by documents. Others again are created wholly in writing. Certain forms of trust must be in writing, leading one to conclude that, in such circumstances, the discussions of the creating parties are irrelevant. This, as will be seen, is not quite the case. A more accurate conclusion would be that the oral negotiations between the parties are devalued, a predominant position being accorded to the instrument that embodies the parties' agreement. This will be further considered below.

Another relevant point here is that, even where a trust (or contract or will) is created wholly in writing, there are varying degrees of sophistication attached to the composition of written documents. There is, for instance, a vast difference between a trust deed which has been prepared by a legal adviser after lengthy negotiation between independent parties on the one hand, and a document written out by a father whereby he purports to create a trust (or something like it) for the benefit of his children, on the other. The first document would be lengthy (and, too often, overly so) and would detail the rights and obligations of the parties with some stringency. It would employ a great deal of technical language, usually with fixed or relatively stable meanings to legal practitioners and judges. It would attempt to anticipate all the circumstances that may give rise to dispute or conflict between the parties and set out to defuse them. It would also attempt to foresee all the important circumstances in which a power of the trustee to act is required, or where it is appropriate that the trustee exercise a certain discretion, and stipulate the conditions or the circumstances in which these actions are to be taken. On the other hand, the unskilled draftsperson who makes a document creating a trust may not even have been aware that it was a trust which was being established. The language of the parties may be entirely banal, using words which have no precise legal connotations. Alternatively, the draftsperson may have attempted to employ sophisticated legal terminology with certain intentions in mind, yet have succeeded in expressing something which, to a lawyer or a judge, may appear either ridiculous or as intending something else.

Realistically, both of these positions ought to be taken into account when the construction and interpretation of a legal document is in issue. In one respect, the court is obliged to say just what it is that constitutes the terms of the trust, assuming that it is a trust.[63] There may be considerable argument about just this point. The parties may contend that certain things which were said were in the nature of negotiations only. In other words, they may not have intended that what was said should become binding on them. They were engaging in pre-agreement negotiations rather than settling the binding terms of the legal arrangement. One party may contend that the arrangement was constituted partly by oral terms, partly by written terms and, perhaps, partly by legally implied terms. The other party may assert that the arrangement was constituted solely by written terms or by written and legally implied terms. Alternatively, one party may contend that several documents together constitute the binding arrangement whilst the other may allege that only one of several possible documents constitutes it.

---

63 As mentioned above, the mere use of the word 'trust', or the failure to use it, does not determine the legal issue as to whether there was a trust – see *Harmer, R.W. v The Commissioner of Taxation* [1989] FCA 651; 91 ALR 550; *Kinloch v Secretary of State of India* (1880) 7 App Cas 619; *Deputy Federal Commissioner of Taxation v Trustees of the Wheat Pool of Western Australia* [1932] HCA 15; 48 CLR 5.

At this level, the court is considering the preliminary, but equally important, question of what it is that is to be construed or interpreted. It is not engaging in an interpretative exercise in itself. It is relevant to distinguish between the two types of enterprise involved here for the reason that the evidence which is admissible in relation to both issues may vary. As will be seen in due course, where the arrangement is constituted by writing alone (or written plus implied terms), a legal rule limits the admissibility of oral evidence that seeks to contradict or vary the clear import of the written document. This is called the parol evidence rule. However, where it is claimed that the arrangement is constituted by both oral and written evidence, then obviously evidence will be admitted to determine the oral, as well as the written, terms of the arrangement. In this respect, it may be vital to determine which issue is in question.

On the other hand, it would seem reasonable that, having established the manner of constitution of a legal arrangement, the court, in construing the terms of that arrangement, ought to pay some attention to the context and the circumstances in which it was created. Supposing that the terms of the arrangement are proved, there might yet arise a number of questions as to what they mean and, more to the point, their legal effect. Suppose that an arrangement is constituted wholly by a written document. There ought to be rules of law to determine how a court is to go about resolving any ambiguities in the document. There ought also to be rules to indicate whether and under what circumstances a court can go beyond the terms of the written document to clarify the meaning of the terminology used by the parties. In such cases, a court should be able to pay attention to the context in which the document was created, any special language used by the parties (such as language which has a special meaning to parties from a particular background) and what the parties consider to be the effect of the arrangement they have set about to create.

These issues are too broadly stated to accord with what the courts will in fact permit when proceeding to construe a written document. There are traditional limitations upon how far a court will go in permitting evidence of particular meanings and particular intentions. One of the reasons for these limiting rules would appear to be that, in construing a written document constituting a legal arrangement, the court is not merely trying to ascertain what was the meaning or effect intended by one party. As stated earlier, the concept of intention in this regard is misleading because it has a subjective sense of psychology about it. In this context, intention and meaning are used in a rather more objective sense. The reason is clear enough where an arrangement is constituted by agreement between several parties. Here the court is trying to construe not the intention or meaning intended by one party, but the objective sense of the arrangement constituted by all the parties.

However, even where an arrangement is constituted by the unilateral act of one party (for example, where a party declares themselves a trustee), the court will not proceed on the basis that evidence from that party in some way determines the meaning or legal effect of the document. The reason for this is that if a document constitutes a binding legal arrangement, it has already attained the mantle of objectivity. Once a party purports to create legal relations, they purport to affect the positions of him/herself and others within the legal system. In this sense, it is a matter for the courts rather than the creating party to determine the meaning and effect of that arrangement. Thus, in matters of construction, the court's primary concern is not with what the creator of the arrangement meant or subjectively intended. It is concerned with the objective legal effect of the arrangement which has been brought into existence. It is this objective legal effect that will finally constitute the binding and enforceable arrangement.

This approach is not difficult to justify, although, as will be seen, it has been necessary to admit certain exceptions to its stringent application. The circumstances of creation and the question of special or peculiar linguistic meanings are sometimes matters where the courts have seen fit to admit extrinsic evidence. They have done so to prevent gross injustice to the parties concerned with the outcome, perhaps; it is difficult to find a sustained and pervasive rationale behind all the exceptions. However, to reinforce the general approach, it can be said that to freely allow a party or parties to an arrangement which, at the point of actual creation, pretends some finality and binding effect, to be contradicted at the whim of a party, would have a tendency toward arbitrariness. The meanings that can be attributed to terminology, even legal terminology, admit a great degree of variation. Language can be twisted to suit particular ends and purposes. Language use, as most linguists would admit, changes in a disorderly and sometimes radical way.

To obviate this arbitrariness and to entrench some degree of consistency in the interpretation of legal arrangements, the courts have developed rules of construction which are of special application when a court is faced with the interpretation of written documents. One of these rules is the parol evidence rule.

4.3.2 The parol evidence rule

The parol evidence rule is of particular significance in considering the effect of trust instruments because it operates to exclude certain evidence from consideration. Normally in matters of the interpretation of trust instruments, the courts will interpret the intentions of the creator of the trust by giving the words in the instrument their ordinary or usual meaning. There are some exceptions to this in the case of ambiguities which appear in the words of the document and these allow the admission of evidence to clarify the meaning of the relevant words.[64] However, the parol evidence rule is applied rather more strictly in respect of documents which are legally required to be in writing or evidenced in writing.

---

64 There are numerous other technical legal rules of interpretation adopted by courts, but we have omitted discussion of them here.

Put simply, this rule states that where a legal arrangement is constituted wholly by writing, oral (or parol) evidence will not be admitted so as to add to, vary or contradict the terms of the written document. In other words, the court is concerned with the legal effect and meaning of the document as it stands. Evidence that purports to contradict the plain import of that document or those documents will be inadmissible in proceedings before the court. Of course, it must appear to the court that the document or documents in question constitute the whole of the arrangement. Otherwise, as has already been indicated, the court will be entitled to admit further evidence to show what additional terms were part of the arrangement.

4.3.3 Exceptions to the parol evidence rule

There are exceptions to this rule. The most notable of these are as follows:

(1) Evidence can be admitted to prove a custom or trade usage which does not appear on or is not stated in the document. In this way, the document can be added to effectively. It is questionable whether this is really an exception or merely a question of the constitution of the arrangement. That is, evidence is admitted to show that the arrangement is really constituted by the written document plus terms implied by custom.

(2) Evidence may be admitted to show that although the document has been brought into existence and executed by one or more parties, its operation was contingent upon certain events occurring, such as the consent of a third party or the occurrence of other events.

(3) Similarly, the above oral evidence is admissible to show that a document that has been executed was not intended to have immediate effect in constituting a legal arrangement. The document may have been executed by mistake or as a joke. Other instances have already been encountered – where, for example, a will has been executed without the requisite testamentary intention. It is doubtful whether, in a strict sense, this provides an exception to the parol evidence rule because such evidence is concerned with whether or not a particular arrangement was properly constituted rather than with questions of construction of the meaning of the document.

(4) It may be an exception to the rule where the circumstances are that one party has been deceived as to the content of the written document executed by them. Normally, the rule is that a party who executes a written document accepts the contents of the document even though they have not fully acquainted themselves with it. However, where a party's execution of a document has been produced by the fraudulent misrepresentation of another to the effect that the document does or does not contain certain terms, then it would seem reasonable that the parol evidence rule should not prevent evidence being given about the true nature of the arrangement which was intended, even

where this stands as a contradiction of the written document. What might be more unclear is the extent to which this exception applies to cases of equitable fraud rather than actual deceit. Equitable fraud involves conduct the equity courts would regard as unfair, unjust or an abuse of a superior position. There has been a tendency, evident in the field of contract law, to make increasing use of the legal notion of unconscionability to remedy situations where a party in a superior bargaining position fails to treat another fairly in entering into a transaction. For instance, a particular party may have suffered some physical or mental impairment at the time a transaction is entered into. The other party, knowing of the impairment, fails to take steps to ensure that the person is fully aware of the nature of the transaction. The usual consequence of this is that the transaction fails to be completely set aside. Oral evidence is, of course, admitted to establish the relevant facts. But it is difficult to imagine precise cases where a party would be relying on the principle as an exception to the parol evidence rule. It may be appropriate to raise the issue in a case where there has been a representation by one party (in an appropriately superior position) that a certain clause in the document has an effect which is entirely at odds with the normal legal effect of the clause in the document itself. It may also be appropriate to raise it in cases where one party suggests that although a certain clause appears in a legal document at the time of execution, it is not to be regarded as enforceable. Such an occurrence is not altogether unusual, especially in a situation where the arrangement is embodied in a standard or prepared form. One party may question the existence of a particular clause only to be told that it is merely there for appearance's sake, or that is merely legal jargon of no effect.

4.3.4 Rectification

Rectification is a remedy available in the equity courts. This may be seen as another exception to the parol evidence rule. This remedy is available where parties have reached a concluded agreement and, as the result of an error or oversight, the written document that is supposed to embody that agreement does not accurately reflect it. Thus, the court has the power to order that the written document be rectified by including what has been omitted or varying what departs from the prior agreement. It would be inappropriate to grant the remedy where the court could simply as a matter of construction remedy the situation to accord with what was actually intended. In other words, the court may be able to resolve the situation simply by interpreting the document in a way that removes the cause for concern. As with other equitable remedies, rectification is a discretionary remedy. It will not be granted if some other remedy is available. A party may lose their rights to an order through a variety of equitable remedies, such as inexplicable delay.

Rectification may be granted in a bilaterally created arrangement (such as a trust created by agreement between parties) or a unilateral arrangement (such as a declaration of trust by an individual). The requirements as to the relevant mistake will vary in both cases. Where the arrangement is unilaterally created, the mistake of the creating party will be sufficient. It does not matter that the arrangement may have been entirely voluntary, as with a settlement by way of gift. The court will nevertheless proceed with some caution in order to prevent a party from simply changing their mind at a later stage.

4.3.5 Bilateral creations

Where an arrangement has been bilaterally created, it is the rule that a mistake by one party is not enough to warrant rectification. It must generally be a mistake that affects the concluded agreement reached by both parties – i.e. the oral agreement objectively concluded. There are some exceptions to this rule, however:

(1) Unilateral mistakes will be sufficient to ground rectification in cases of fraud, actual (intentional deception) or constructive (that is, equitable fraud in the sense mentioned above).
(2) Rectification is available in cases of estoppel. This encompasses situations where one party makes a mistake and the other, knowing of the mistake, does nothing to correct it. This other party will be prevented from denying the availability of rectification.
(3) In cases of election, a unilateral mistake will suffice. This involves situations where one party knows of the mistake of the other but the situation does not quite amount to fraud. The court will put the party to their election, requiring them to either submit to rectification or have the entire arrangement rescinded by the court. This order may be appropriate in cases of unconscionability, as discussed above.

Rectification is available in a wide range of legal arrangements. However, it should be noted that rectification will not normally be granted for a will except in the case of fraud. The reason for this appears to be that the requirements in relation to the making of a will (including the requirement that it be made in writing) are strict and usually presuppose that a testator will have been careful to scrutinise what they are bringing into being. The document will have mostly been the product of careful consideration and ought to be taken as a more-or-less solemn act.

By reason of these exceptions to the parol evidence rule, it can be seen that its operation is not quite as strict as it initially appears. There will be a number of cases where the courts will permit evidence to be given of extrinsic circumstances which ultimately may have the outcome of showing that a written document does not have the effect it appears to have on the face of it.

4.4 Unit trusts

As we mentioned at the outset, unit trusts are kinds of express trusts which are most often employed for commercial purposes. Although unit trusts can be either private or public in nature, we will concentrate for the most part on the latter.[65] Public unit trusts are usually subjected to legislation which is in addition to that applying to trusts or trustees in general. We will comment generally on the nature of the schemes of regulation involved in Australia, New Zealand, Fiji and Vanuatu and attempt to draw some comparisons between the different approaches to regulation which are adopted in these jurisdictions.

The division between public and private unit trusts is generally made on the basis that public unit trusts are subject to legislation which is imposed in the interests of the protection of members of the public who invest in them. They are sometimes called corporate trusts, regulated trusts or, in the United States, mutual funds. Depending on the types of schemes that are operated, they can be known by a variety of other names, such as property trusts, cash management trusts, equity trusts and so on. Their name is usually determined by the nature of the investments in which the trusts funds are primarily invested. Private unit trusts are not so regulated. Sometimes they are used for the purposes of providing the structure for small business or for the holding of property. The fact that the beneficial interests are defined by reference to the holding of units facilitates the transfer of the beneficial interests to a third party without reconstructing the whole trust. They also facilitate the changing of the structure of interests in the trust, say by the issue of further units to raise more capital for the purposes of the trust.

Some superannuation or provident schemes are structured as unit trusts. A superannuation or provident scheme is an investment scheme which provides for a person to receive accumulated investment benefits on their retirement from work either at a specified age, or through incapacity or in the event of their death. However, most often, these schemes are independently regulated by independent legislation.[66] We will not be concerned with those schemes here.

The use of unit trusts as vehicles for investment is common throughout Australia, New Zealand, the US and Europe. This is not yet so in the South Pacific, at least as regards public unit trusts. Little is known about the extent of use of private unit trusts. The only major unit trust currently in operation at the public level in Fiji is the Unit Trust of Fiji. There is little evidence in other South Pacific jurisdictions of the promotion or growth of investment in unit trusts and it would be idle to speculate on whether this form of investment is likely to prove attractive in those regions at this time. Even so, the mechanisms are in place in some

---

65 For a more comprehensive treatment of the scheme of regulation in Australia, see Hughes, RA, *The Law of Public Unit Trusts*, 1992, Melbourne, Longman.
66 We gave examples of such legislation in Chapter 3 – see p 74.

jurisdictions for the establishment of unit trust schemes. With it, there comes the vehicle for regulation of certain types of investment, but it is doubtful whether the implications of this legislation for the promotion of schemes of investment in the South Pacific are widely known, much less complied with.

A unit trust is one type of express trust. The trust instrument provides, by appropriate wording, that the beneficial interest in the trust is divided into units. These units are then allocated to beneficiaries, who are sometimes also described as unit holders. Very often, the beneficiaries or unit holders will be investors in a particular business or scheme for which the trust provides the structure of operation. Sometimes, the unit holders might originally be allocated particular units with a reserve of unallocated units which can be allocated by the trustee or by the trust manager at a later time.

In many respects, the units thus defined in the trust take on features that are similar to shares in a company. The holding of a unit carries with it certain rights that are defined by the terms of the trust instrument. Most commonly, there is a divided structure of management of the trust between a manager and a trustee. It is a division which purports to provide for the trustee as guardian or protector of the interests of the unit holders along with a separate management company (or possibly an individual) which has responsibility for the day-to-day running of the scheme to which the trust relates. The occurrence of this division, which in some cases is imposed as a legislative requirement, has created some confusion about the proper areas of authority of each office holder.

Sometimes, these entities behave in law as if they were corporate undertakings. In many respects, their activities are regulated by specific legislation requiring a specific management structure. It has often been the case that the courts have applied the principles of corporate law, such as fraud on the minority, to public unit trusts. The legislation in question generally attempts to impose certain standards on the management of the trust and to provide safeguards to investors in units. They are public vehicles of investment and are therefore subject to investor-protection policies on the same model as corporations. Often, for example, they are subject to the provisions which require that any offering of units must be accompanied by a prospectus providing certain minimum information to investors about the nature of the scheme in which they are investing.

The older types of public unit trust were either fixed trusts or flexible trusts depending on whether or not the trust must invest in specified types of assets. Most trusts now are types of flexible trust. In recent times, there has been a tendency to classify trusts according to the types of investment in which the particular trust engages; for example, equity trusts, which invest in shares, bond trusts, cash management trusts, property trusts, time-sharing schemes and even green trusts.

Notwithstanding their similarities with corporate structures, and their adoption in Australia under the wing of corporate securities regulation, public unit trusts must still be approached as trusts.[67] This basic proposition was upheld by the High Court of Australia in *Charles v Commissioner of Taxation*, where it was said:

> A unit held under this trust deed is fundamentally different from a share in a company. A share confers upon the holder no legal or equitable interest in the assets of the company; it is a separate piece of property, and if a portion of the company's assets is distributed amongst the shareholders the question whether it comes to them as income or as capital depends upon whether the corpus of the property (their shares) remains intact despite the distribution. … But a unit under the trust deed before us confers a proprietary interest in all the property which for the time being is subject to the trust of the deed … so that the question whether moneys distributed to unit holders under the trust form part of their income or of their capital must be answered by considering the character of those moneys in the hands of the trustees before the distribution is made.[68]

Put simply, the separate entity principle of a company requires that company shares be characterised as a form of property existing independently of the property which is owned by the corporation or company itself; that is, as a separate juristic entity. Shares are property in their own right. Even if the value of the share might be determined for some accounting purposes by reference to the value of the underlying assets of the company, the shares do not indicate that the holder of the shares has any direct proprietary interest in the assets of the company. Those underlying assets are the assets of the independent entity, which is the corporation itself. The shares constitute legal choses in action belonging to the shareholders. They are bundles of rights which define the rights of participation which shareholders have in the corporation or company, the rights to receive distributions of profits from the company, the right to vote and so on.

It is true that in the case of public unit trusts, the holder of units is accorded many similar rights to those of a shareholder, such as the right to receive a

---

67 It has sometimes been suggested that the rights which exist under a unit trust are really special forms of contractual relations; e.g. as subsisting between the unit holder and the management company. Such an argument is advanced by Sin, who suggests that this has always been the nature of the relationship involved in these trusts. See Sin, KF, *The Legal Nature of the Public Unit Trusts*, 1997, Oxford, OUP. The argument has some merit, particularly in dealing with the sometimes-problematic relationship between a unit holder and the manager. Sometimes, for example, the trust deed will attempt to exclude any right of interference by either a trustee or a unit holder in the manager's conduct of the trust business. However, whilst a contract is inevitably involved in the acquisition by a unit holder of units, there are doubts about whether the contract would subsist beyond the point of creation. In other words, the difficulty is whether any contractual arrangement is affected by the equitable doctrine of merger on the creation of a trust.

68 [1954] HCA 16; 90 CLR 598.

distribution of income and the right to attend and vote at meetings. These rights are defined mostly by the trust deed, which performs a function similar to the memorandum and articles of the company. But the point of difference concerns the nature of the interest of the shareholder on the one hand, and the holder of units in the trust on the other. The trust deed defines the nature of interest which the unit holder, as a beneficiary, has in the assets of the trust. It is equity which defines the nature of that interest which is enforceable against the trustee. There has long been a dispute in equity jurisprudence as to the nature of this interest – whether it is merely a right *in personam*, or whether it involves an interest *in rem*, that is, in the assets vested in the trustee. Yet, whatever the outcome of this protracted and at times tiresome debate, the interest of the unit holder is essentially the interest of a beneficiary under a trust and not that of the owner of a separate piece of legal property, as is the case with a shareholder.

There is another significant difference between corporations and unit trusts. A corporation or company is a form of legal association. The shareholders are, as a consequence of their shareholding, participants in a common form of association. In the case of a trust, this is not so because the trust developed as a form of property-holding arrangement rather than a form of association, such as a company or a partnership. According to the mid-19th century English decision of *Smith v Anderson*,[69] a unit trust was not to be considered a form of association even though the investors in it were, to some extent, investing in a common form of enterprise or undertaking. The fact that the investors were all recipients of beneficial interests in the one trust did not make the trust an association. Hence, according to that decision, the failure to register the trust as a company under the then Companies Act 1862 did not make it an illegal form of association. The Act required, as Companies legislation still does, that any association with more than a certain minimum number of members must be registered as a company under the Act.

There has been some contentiousness about the rationale for the decision in *Smith v Anderson*,[70] but it still seems to represent good law on the stated issue. The decision requires, perhaps, that rather artificial distinctions be drawn between a trust on the one hand and various legal forms of association on the other. These distinctions are not always easy to draw, given that the position of the unit holders under a very large investment trust, on an economic realist view of the matter, is hardly distinguishable in most respects from the position of the shareholder who invests in a large corporation. But the distinction is still one which the decision requires to be drawn.

---

69 (1880) 15 Ch D 247.
70 See Hughes, *op cit* fn 65, pp 5 ff.

4.4.1 The different approaches to regulation

The basic structures of various schemes of regulation in respect of public unit trusts adopted by South Pacific jurisdictions and their near neighbours are different in many ways. The current scheme of regulation in Australia was a product of an attempt in the 1950s to bring certain joint-investment schemes within the scope of corporate regulation – particularly the prospectus requirements. Promoters of various non-corporate schemes had been able to avoid the prospectus disclosure requirements because the interests offered were not shares or other interests in a corporation. In the Australian situation, it is not in fact necessary that a prescribed investment scheme to which the legislation applies should involve the setting up of a trust. In fact, some other structure such as a friendly society or cooperative could be used. However, the unit trust format remains the classic type of regulated structure.

Effectively, what the original legislation did was to bring non-corporate investment schemes within the scope of the Companies legislation by requiring that, where interests in prescribed investment schemes were offered to the public, an approved trust had to be established with an approved trustee and a management company (being a public company). The approved deed had to contain certain covenants binding the trustee and the management company. Despite a number of subsequent refinements, the same basic structure applies under the Corporation Act 2000 at the present time, although under this legislation the divided structure of management has been with a single responsible entity for the trust. Similar considerations attended the bringing into existence of the Prevention of Fraud (Investments) legislation in the United Kingdom in the late 1930s.

In fact, it should be noted that unit trusts have had a chequered history. The need for regulation of trust investments has often been brought about by the suspect activities of promoters of investment schemes which operate on the fringes of the corporate investment market. The history of the unit trust industry has been attended by a series of notable failures of large trusts and a lack of certainty about the rights of unit holders and the relationship between the two controlling entities: the trustee and the manager. In Australia in the late 1980s, a number of property trusts failed. This prompted a review of the legislation and a tightening of the obligations placed on the managing entities. However, whilst these failures no doubt damaged investor confidence in the trust market, it seemed to revive in the 1990s. No doubt this was due in large part to the relationship between the trust industry and the superannuation industry in Australia. To date, unit trusts continue effectively in competition with the corporate securities market.

The main difficulty with the Australian scheme has been with the definition of prescribed interests to which the regulatory scheme applies.[71] The policy here has been to cast a wide net, almost so broad as to include any interest (proprietary or not) in any investment scheme or undertaking, and then to enumerate a number of exempt schemes in the primary and subordinate legislation. In addition, the central regulating body, the Australian Securities Commission (ASC), has a wide discretionary power to exempt particular schemes from the operation of the provisions. The policy is obviously designed to ensure that the regulatory scheme applies in principle to almost anything, thereby countering the ingenuity of investment promotion in developing new forms of investment to attract the interest of investors. This has often created consternation on the part of legal and other advisers, who have found it exceedingly difficult to determine whether any particular scheme is or is not a prescribed interest scheme. The definition of a prescribed interest and the ancillary concept of a participation interest provide little comfort in this regard.

In Vanuatu, the scheme of legislation relating to unit trust schemes is under the Prevention of Fraud (Investments) Act, which is adapted from former UK legislation. As will be seen in due course, the scope of the legislation is limited in that it applies only to certain types of unit trusts and not others. For example, it does not apply to real property trusts or to time-sharing schemes. There is a requirement for a deed of trust that contains certain covenants aimed at protecting the interests of investors. There is also a requirement for the licensing of persons who deal in securities, including units in a unit trust and provision for a divided structure of management along the lines mentioned above.

4.4.2 Regulation in the Fiji Islands and New Zealand

In the Fiji Islands and New Zealand, the legislative model is rather different from the approach adopted in Australia. In effect, it is somewhat narrower in scope and displays a little less of the institutionalised paranoia attending the need to regulate investment in Australia. Section 3(1) of the Unit Trusts Act of Fiji prohibits the establishment of a unit trust without the prior approval of the Minister. Section 8(1) prohibits the issuing or offering of interests in a unit trust to the public except on the basis of a prescribed form of prospectus.

---

71 On this, see Magarey, D, 'Prescribed interests' (1989) 7 *Companies and Securities Law Journal* 25. The leading authority on the approach taken by Australian Courts is *Australian Softwood Forests Pty Ltd v Attorney-General (NSW)* [1981] HCA 49; 148 CLR 121. See more recently *Madison Pacific Property Management Pty Ltd v Australian Securities and Investment Commission* [1999] FCA 62; 89 FCR 263.

The definition of 'unit trust' in s 2 of the Act assumes some importance. 'Unit trust'

> means any scheme or arrangement that is made for the purpose of or has the effect of providing facilities for the participation, as beneficiaries under a trust, of subscribers or purchasers as members of the public, in income and gains (whether in the nature of capital or income) arising from the money, investments other property that are for the time being subject to the trust.

This is followed by a number of exemptions such as debentures, credit unions, friendly societies and certain superannuation schemes for income tax purposes.

The combined effect of s 3(1) and the s 2 definition would indicate that the only interests relevant for the purposes of the Fiji scheme of regulation are proprietary interests – in fact, equitable proprietary interests of a beneficiary under a trust. We might leave aside the rather vexed question of whether all beneficial interests under a trust are proprietary or not. Suffice it to say that where they are defined by reference to units in trust property, they would be proprietary unless they were the subject of a discretionary power of the trustee – which in this context is unlikely. The definition in s 2 clearly refers to participation 'as beneficiaries under a trust' and to the derivation of benefits 'arising from the money, investments and other property ... subject to the trust'. Thus, one must conclude that the provisions apply only when the interest offered is an interest in something which is already structured *as* a unit trust. Hence, the Fiji Islands and New Zealand policy is to impose a scheme of regulation of unit trust offerings *per se*.

This is not at all the Australian approach, which attempts to regulate all prescribed interest offerings; that is to say, interests in schemes which, in their inception and initial promotion, might have had nothing to do with a trust at all. The interest might have been an interest in the gains to be made by several investors in the ownership of a racehorse, a speculative interest in the possible income of a joint venture or other enterprise or an interest under certain franchise arrangements. These interests need not be proprietary in any sense, much less an interest under a trust. In Australia, a unit trust needs to be created only in order to comply with the regulatory scheme itself. Given a prescribed interest scheme, the legislation demands that it be converted into a unit trust with a certain structure as a condition of obtaining ASC approval.

4.4.3 Public offering of securities

The Corporations Law in Australia has dispensed with the notion that what needs to be regulated is the public offering of securities which are prescribed interests. The former Companies Codes of the Australian states had stated that a prospectus needed to be provided where invitations or offers of securities were to be made to the public only. This concept was deemed to include offers to a member of the public. This requirement of a public offering, as extended, attracted some consternation on the part of the courts and criticism on the part of academic writers. It was described as a minefield. How could one determine just when an offer took on the characteristic of being made to the public? What would be an offer to a member of the public rather than to an individual in their capacity as a private (i.e. non-public) individual? Usually, it was the generality of the offer making it available to all and sundry in the community which was enunciated as the guiding principle here.[72] But that was not entirely free of difficulty when confronting offers to groups of individuals and subsections of the larger community.[73] The difficulties in providing answers to these questions prompted the drafts of the Corporations Law removing the element of public offering from the prospectus provisions altogether. Effectively, any offering of or invitation with respect to prescribed interests or other securities will attract the prospectus requirements, although again there are a number of stated exceptions to this.

Under the Fiji Unit Trusts Act, however, the requirement that the issue or offer of unit trust interests be to the public is firmly entrenched in s 8(1) in respect of prospectus requirements. Furthermore, the fact that s 4(1)(b) assigns to the management company the task of issuing or offering interests 'to the public' clearly entrenches the idea that the legislation seeks to regulate only public transactions in unit trust interests. However, in this case, there is no definition of 'public' or public offering in the legislation. There is no attempt, as with s 5(4) of the former Companies Codes in Australia, to include an offer to a member of the public within that concept.[74] Nonetheless, it does leave to case law the difficult task of determining just when an offer or invitation has the required element of publicity – a task which our past experience has proved exceedingly difficult.

4.4.4 Management structures

The management structures of unit trusts are similar in New Zealand, Fiji and Vanuatu. All require a divided structure with both a trustee and a management company to be appointed. In Australia, a single responsible entity must be approved by the ASC and this usually happens at the time when the deed of trust itself is approved. The trustee need meet no qualifications stipulated in the legislation, although the ASC has certain policy guidelines to be met. The trustee can be an individual. The Australian scheme posits no particular requirement as to approval of the management company. This is presumably because the role that it plays is largely that of a promoter of a commercial scheme. The legislation provides only that the management company must be a public company. In practice, it

72 See e.g. *Lee v Evans* (1964) 112 CLR 276 at 285, *per* Barwick CJ; *Nash v Lynde* [1929] AC 158, 169 *Ex parte Lovells*; *Re Buckley* (1938) 38 SR (NSW) 153 at 159; *In re South of England Natural Gas and Petroleum Company Ltd* [1911] 1 Ch 573.
73 See *Corporate Affairs Commission (South Australia) v Australian Central Credit Union* (1985) 59 ALJR 785 at 787–88.
74 Bankruptcy Act 1991 Companies Code, s 5(4).

will usually have been formed by and be controlled by those individuals who were the promoters of the investment scheme to which the trust relaxes.

Under the Fiji legislation, there is a mechanism for approval of trustees. First, this would be a matter to be considered by the Minister when considering approval of the trust itself under s 3(1). It is certainly a factor that the Minister might consider to be material pursuant to s 3(2) of the Act. Section 6 of the Act requires that the trustee be either a trustee corporation within the meaning of the Trustee Act (Cap 65) or a company or bank approved by the Minister either generally or in respect of a particular trust. The Minister may require the deposit of a board. In respect of the manager, s 5(1) requires that it be a company. Section 5(2) prohibits a company from acting as manager of a unit trust unless a bond is lodged by a person approved by the Minister. There is no approval of the management company as such, but the provision for payment of a bond provides at least some measure of security.

As indicated earlier, one of the areas of difficulty concerning public unit trusts is the divided structure itself. It was seen as appropriate to have the trustee established independently of the promoter of the operation. At one stage, it was proposed in Australia that the divided structure be abolished in favour of having one responsible entity for public unit trusts. This would unify the total control of the trust, and both guardianship and managerial responsibilities, in one entity. However, as things stand, the trustee is invested with the trust property and is there to represent the interests of the unit holders. The management company, however, mainly has charge of the day-to-day operation of the scheme.

The division of roles, however, has always entailed some institutional confusion. At one stage, it seems to have been thought that the trustee merely played the role of watchdog and therefore was not under a duty actively to investigate the management company's conduct of the scheme. Very often, this view was reinforced by reference to clauses in unit trust deeds which prohibited the trustee or the unit holders from interfering in the management of the scheme. However, the courts have since determined the position to be otherwise, casting on the trustee an active duty to inform itself of the management company's activities. A trustee who fails to do so could be liable at the hands of the unit holders should the scheme collapse.[75]

The other issue involved here concerns the nature of the relationship between the management company and the unit holders. The manager was viewed not as one who represented the unit holders, whether directly or through the trustee. After all, those persons involved in the management company interests most likely would have established the scheme in the first place as a commercial investment opportunity. There was debate from time to time about whether the management company was a fiduciary with a corresponding obligation imputed in equity

---

75 See Hughes, *op cit* fn 65, pp 99 ff.

in favour of the unit holders. It now seems reasonably well settled that this is so.[76] Whilst not a trustee, the position of the management company equates with that of other fiduciaries, such as company directors and promoters – both of whom are regarded as under fiduciary obligations to the entity they serve. The difficulty is to work out the precise scope of the fiduciary obligation, which must be something less than that of a trustee. But that is no doubt something which will be worked out over time by the courts.

4.4.5 The Vanuatu legislation

As noted above, the Prevention of Fraud (Investments) Act Cap 70 of Vanuatu is an adaptation of earlier UK legislation of the same name. The general import of the legislation is to impose a scheme of control on dealings in securities. It requires, for example, that dealers in securities obtain licences[77] and imposes liability on dealers in securities with respect to misleading and false statements.[78] So far as unit trusts are concerned, the approach is similar to that in Australia. The legislation sets up a mechanism for public approval of unit trust schemes. It requires that there be a trust deed which contains certain provisions aimed at investor protection and mandates a divided structure of management of the trust between a trustee and a manager. The legislation does not contain any extensive specification of the roles of the trustee and manager, notwithstanding that in other jurisdictions, the differentiation of functions has proved to be a difficult one. Much is left to the trust relationship to provide protection to investors in the schemes.

Rights or interests in a unit trust are deemed to be securities by virtue of s 1(1). However, the definition is not as broad as that in Australia. The definition refers only to rights or interests

which may be acquired under a unit trust scheme under which all property for the time being subject to any trust created in pursuance of the scheme consists of either

  (a) shares, debentures or rights or interests therein;
  (b) securities of the Government of Vanuatu or of any other country; or
  (c) rights, contingent or otherwise in respect of money lent to or deposited with any industrial and provident society or building society.

Thus, the Act relates only to certain forms of equity or bond trusts. In Australia, New Zealand or Fiji, the definition of securities would cover unit trusts established

---

76 See *Elders Trustee and Executor Co Ltd v EG Reeves Pty Ltd* (1987) 78 ALR; *Perpetual Trustees WA Ltd v Corporate West Management Ltd* [1989] WAR 117.
77 See Part II of the Act.
78 See Part III.

to operate time-sharing schemes, forestry schemes, real estate investments schemes and so on.

The definition of 'dealing in securities' is also contained in s 1(1). The definition is exhaustive. Dealing in securities means:

> doing any of the following things (whether as a principal or agent), that is to say, making or offering to make with any person, or inducing or attempting to induce any person to enter into or offer to enter into:
>
> (a) any agreement for, or with a view to acquiring, disposing of, subscribing for or underwriting securities or lending or depositing money to or with any industrial or provident society or building society; or
> (b) any agreement the purpose or pretended purpose of which is to secure a profit to any of the parties from the yield of securities or by reference to fluctuations in the value of securities.

Section 2 of the Act prohibits dealing in securities without a licence, although certain transactions such as those on an approved stock exchange (which Vanuatu does not have) are excluded by s 3. Under s 8(1), the Minister is permitted to make rules relating to the conduct of business of licensed dealers, including the manner in which dealings might take place and the forms to be used in dealing contracts. Section 11 contains a general prohibition against the making of false, deceptive or materially misleading statements in relation to the offer, subscription or acquisition or disposal of securities. Section 12 sets out provisions which are in the nature of prospectus requirements relating to the making of offers and invitations for the purchase or subscription of securities to which the Act applies.

Part IV of the Act deals with unit trust schemes. Section 13(1) empowers the Minister to declare by order that any unit trust scheme is an authorised unit trust scheme for the purposes of the Act. Certain conditions set out in the section must be fulfilled. Both the manager and the trustee of the scheme must be a corporation incorporated and have a place of business in Vanuatu. The scheme must be such that effective control over the affairs of the manager corporation is and will be exercised independently of the trustee corporation. The scheme must be such as to secure that any trust created in pursuance of the scheme is expressed in a deed providing, to the satisfaction of the Minister, for the matters set out in the Schedule to the Act. However, the Minister is provided with a general power of dispensation with these requirements in special circumstances. The trustee corporation must satisfy one of the following: (a) the corporation has an issued capital of not less than 100 million vatu, of which not less than half is paid-up capital and the assets of the corporation are sufficient to meet its liabilities; or (b) more than four-fifths of the capital of the corporation is held by another corporation which meets the requirements under (a).

The requirements under the Schedule to the Act relate to certain provisions that must be included in the trust deed relating to the scheme. There must be provision made for:

- determining the manner in which the manager's prices for units on a sale and purchase, and the yield from the units, are respectively to be calculated and for entitling the holder of any units to require the manager to purchase them at a price calculated accordingly;
- regulating the mode of execution and the issue of unit certificates and, in particular, for ensuring that no unit certificate shall be executed or issued in respect of rights or interest in any property until steps have been taken, to the satisfaction of the trustee, to secure that the property will be vested in him or her or, subject to any prescribed conditions, in a nominee for him or her approved by the Minister;
- prohibiting or restricting the issue by or on behalf of the manager of advertisements, circulars or other documents containing any statement with respect to the sale price of units, or the payments or other benefits received or likely to be received by holders of units or containing any invitation to buy units, unless the document also contains a statement of the yield from units;
- securing that any advertisement, circular or other document containing any statement with respect to the sale price of units or the yield therefrom, or containing any invitation to buy units, shall not be issued by or on behalf of the manager until the trustee has had a reasonable opportunity of considering the terms of the document, and shall not be so issued if, within a reasonable time after the document first comes under his or her consideration, he or she notifies his or her disapproval of the terms thereof in writing to the manager;
- the establishment of a fund to be applied in defraying the expenses of the administration of the trust and for regulating the application of that fund;
- the audit, and the circulation to the holders of units, of accounts relating to the trust (including the accounts of the manager in relation to the trust and statements of his or her remuneration in connection therewith);
- requiring the manager (subject to any provisions as to appeal contained in the deed) to retire from the trust if the trustee certifies that it is in the interests of the beneficiaries under the trust that he or she should do so.

The Minister is given power by s 13(2) to require the manager and the trustee, in respect of any application for approval under Part IV, to supply further information. The Minister may also revoke any approved scheme on certain grounds specified in the section. These include, for example, that the circumstances relevant to the making of an order have materially changed since it was made. The Minister also has power, by the same section, to appoint investigators to investigate and report on the administration of any unit trust scheme where it appears either that it is in the interests of the unit holder to do so or that the matter is one of public concern.

5

COMPANIES

5.1 Types of company

There are basically three types of company that can be found in any of the jurisdictions. These are companies that are limited by shares (public and private), unlimited companies and guarantee companies. We will explain the meaning of these terms in a moment. The structural distinction between the three forms of companies is based on the different attributes regarding membership, capitalisation and management. The aim of the present is simply to present the main features distinguishing these companies. It does not venture into discussing their effectiveness or otherwise as business entities in the South Pacific.

5.1.1 What is a company?

The term 'company' may mean different things to a lawyer as opposed to, say, an economist, a business person or a sociologist.[1] Economists tend to emphasise the nature of a company as a vehicle for the accumulation of capital, or as a profit-making entity. Others treat them as one form of organisation of human affairs amongst the various others.[2] To lawyers, as we noted in the Introduction, a company is a very special form of legal association which obtains special characteristics as a result of its incorporation.

---

1 See other definitions in Berns, S *et al.*, *Company Law and Governance*, 1998, Oxford, OUP, pp 4–8.
2 As will be seen later, companies have a special structure of management which is essentially hierarchical in nature.

DOI: 10.4324/9781003428060-6

Gower defined a company as 'an association of a number of people for some common object or objects'.[3] Legally, a company is a form of association, as Gower's definition suggests. Most often, but certainly not always, it is an association which carries on some form of commercial or trading activity. When we speak of companies, most people have in mind the limited liability company, which has a shareholding with individual members holding shares. It is a mechanism to attract private or public investment in the company which seeks, in turn, to use the capital contributed to engage in profit-making activities of some sort or other. Trading activity is by no means an essential aspect of a company. We will see that some types of company are used as organisational structures for non-profit-making activities such as the pursuit of sporting or social purposes. Nor do all companies have either limited liability or a shareholding structure, on which see further below.

From a legal point of view, a company is an association which is created by a special procedure laid down by statute. However, it is an association that is also conceded a juristic or legal personality. This means that in law it is treated for many purposes as if it is a person with legal rights and duties, much like a natural person. It is a distinct legal entity and not merely an aggregate of the individuals who are its members, as is the case with a partnership.[4] A company must sue and be sued in its own name where the matter concerned is properly something which 'belongs' to the company.

According to this principle – called the separate identity (or entity) principle – a company is a thing which is distinct from its members, and also from its managers, directors and employees. Creditors must bring an action against the company itself in order to recover debts which are rightly owed to them by the company. The liability of the shareholders, in the case of companies with limited liability, is limited to the amount that might be outstanding in respect of their contributions to their shareholding. The same applies with all company liabilities whether based in debt, tort, contract or otherwise. There is no immediate right of action by outsiders against the members or shareholders, the board of directors or the individual directors, managers or employees of the company.[5]

The so-called separate identity theory of companies (or corporations more widely) holds that a company has a corporate status which it achieves on registration pursuant to the relevant legislation. This act of incorporation brings about the legal creation of the company, much like the birth of a natural individual does in

---

3   See Davies, P; Worthington, S; Hare, C, *Gower: Principles of Modern Company Law 10th Edition*, 2016, London, Sweet & Maxwell, p 4, at 1-1.
4   A partnership, as we noted in Chapter 1, lacks this separate legal personality. It is merely an aggregate of the individuals who are members of the association. Likewise a trust has no separate legal status as such. We noted in Chapter 4 that the trust debts and liabilities are those of the trustee personally, with rights of indemnity out of the trust assets.
5   We will return to the question of limited liability in Chapter 6.

relation to a natural individual.[6] Once properly registered according to the procedures laid down by the legislation, a company becomes a separate entity in law as a product of a legal fiction. It has rights and duties despite the fact that it is, from a realist point of view, merely an artificially created entity. However, the law does not treat a company as if it were wholly a natural individual. There are many limits to the assimilation here. It is recognised that there are certain things that a company cannot do in law bearing in mind its status as an artificial entity.

Of particular importance in the development of the separate identity principle was the late-19th century UK decision in *Salomon v Salomon & Co Ltd*.[7] The facts, briefly, were as follows. A company had been formed by a person who maintained complete control of the company in fact both as its major shareholder and as its governing director. Even though the company was effectively a vehicle for the actions directed by this person, the court nonetheless held that it persisted, against the claims of creditors, as a separate person in law. The act of incorporation of the company pursuant to the statute required the courts to uphold this status. There has been a line of authority to the same effect. In *Lee v Lee's Air Farming Ltd*,[8] it was held that the beneficiaries of a person who was in complete control of a company of which he or she was also an employee were entitled to maintain an action against the company as a separate legal entity for the purposes of recovery of compensation under the workers' compensation legislation in respect of an accident causing the death of that person during the course of employment. The *de facto* controlling situation of the deceased did not allow the court to lift the corporate veil and hold that the deceased was, in effect, self-employed.

There are also numerous exceptions to the so-called separate identity principle. Whilst the law adheres to the separate entity principle as a kind of *sine qua non* of company law, it has often been forced to create exceptions which will allow the corporate veil to be lifted where the interests of justice demand it. Although a company must sue in its own name concerning the enforcement of rights which are technically vested in the company itself, there are instances where this aspect of the principle will not be strictly adhered to. For example, minority shareholders can be permitted by the court to commence proceedings on behalf of the company, say, in cases where the controllers of the company have used their power or advantage to commit some equitable fraud against minority interests. Likewise, directors will not always be entitled to hide behind the corporate veil in order to avoid personal liability in relation to their dealings on behalf of the company. We will look at this and other reservations and exceptions in due course.

---

6 Although there is no period of minority before full legal personality is obtained, as is the case with a natural individual.

7 [1897] AC 22.

8 [1961] AC 12; [1961] NZLR 325; [1960] 3 All ER 420; see also *Ascot Investments Pty Ltd v Harper* [1981] HCA 1; 148 CLR 337.

Whilst it often appears peculiar that the law should treat an association as if it were in fact a legal person, it is in fact not so unusual an occurrence within Western legal systems. Indeed, in common and civil law systems there are other entities which have corporate status of this type. The company is in fact a species of the legal category of corporation. More accurately, it is a sub-species of what are known as corporations aggregate. It was conventional to treat the Crown and various government offices, churches and other specially created associational forms as corporations with a distinct legal status in law. Some of these might be corporations sole, which were offices occupied by one individual. Others were associations of several individuals and hence corporations aggregate. Companies are those types of corporations aggregate which are now capable of incorporation under the Companies legislation.

Historically, corporations needed to be created by Royal Charter in England by special statute or by prescription. These mechanisms for incorporation were cumbersome. They are still in use to a limited extent.[9] There were attempts to create entities known as joint stock companies by way of a deed of settlement – also common in respect of some forms of trust – which provided that the entity was to have an indefinite and perhaps infinite existence, but in terms of their actual structure, they often appeared more like a trust than otherwise.[10] From the mid-19th century in England, it became more usual to provide for their creation under mechanisms set out in a statute. In contemporary common law legal systems, there are entities such as cooperatives, friendly societies, banks and credit unions, all of which have corporate status in much the same way but conferred by legislation specific to them. We will examine some of these other forms of corporation in Chapter 7.

In 18th and early-19th century England, the term 'company' was in fact a term of rather unclear usage. It could mean what we would now call a partnership, a joint venture,[11] a trust or, indeed, a corporate entity such as we have been describing.[12] In fact, it probably meant nothing much more than a business association or structure.[13] Often the legal regulation of the rights and duties of parties involved in these entities involved the utilisation of equitable and particularly trust law principles. The term 'company' now has a more specific usage which would

---

9 The University of the South Pacific is a corporation created by Royal Charter, for example.

10 The joint stock company contributed in significant ways to the development of some principles of modern company law. The role of the deed of settlement itself produced the basic idea of memorandum and articles of association of a company. See *Peters American Delicacy Ltd v Heath* [1939] HCA 2; 61 CLR 457 at 502. Indeed, the later development of the principle of limited liability can be traced to attempts to confer such status on joint settlement companies.

11 A joint venture is technically an arrangement where parties are joined together for some common pursuit but they do not carry on business in common as such. Hence it is not strictly a partnership.

12 Indeed, terms such as 'trust' and 'partnership' were themselves no less vague at this time. See generally *Elders Trustees and Executors Co Ltd v EG Reeves Pty Ltd* [1987] FCA 603; 78 ALR 193 at 230.

13 *Re Stanley* (1906) 1 Ch 131.

distinguish it from these other entities. This distinct usage derives directly from the Companies Act 1862 (UK), drawing on the Joint Stock Companies Act 1844 (UK) in some important respects, which provided for the registration of certain types of companies according to a public process, and as a result of which independent corporate status was conferred. The statute still provides a model for much of the Companies legislation with which we will be concerned in this book.

Indeed, the statute required that all associations having more than a prescribed minimum membership were legally required to be registered under the statute.[14] In the Introduction, we gave an example of this. Otherwise, in the absence of incorporation, they would be regarded as illegal associations and contributions made by, for example, investors, and potential shareholders would be regarded as non-recoverable. This was a strange consequence of a statute which was designed, in effect, to regulate the rather rampant and questionable activities of public investment schemes at the time. However, a version of this provision is still to be found in the South Pacific legislation dealing with companies, as we shall see in due course. Trusts are not caught by this provision primarily because a trust is not a form of association at all.[15]

5.2 Companies as statutory creations

For the purposes of the legislation, a company is an entity that is legally registered under the Companies Act of a country in the South Pacific. This emphasises that a company is a creature of statute. Strict compliance with the provisions of the relevant Companies Act is required. This is not to say that the law relating to companies is to be found wholly in the statutes governing them. Company law principles were drawn from trust law[16] and general equity and continue to be so drawn. Company directors are, for example, fiduciaries, but not in the same way as are trustees. The nature and scope of the fiduciary obligation is modified substantially, bearing in mind the structure of the modern company.

5.2.1 The company constitution: Basic principles

All types of company have a memorandum and articles of association, the initial form of which must be lodged in order to obtain registration. The memorandum and articles serve as the constitution of a company in much the same way as a trust deed does for a trust, a partnership agreement functions in relation to a partnership or, in fact, a political constitution serves for a country. As we shall see later, the memorandum and articles of association of a company are of pivotal

---

14 Section 4 Companies Act 1862 (UK).
15 See *Smith v Anderson* (1880) 15 Ch D 247.
16 On early developments in this regard, see Holdsworth, W, *A History of English Law*, Vol XIII, 1952, London, Methuen, p 366.

importance in relation to the management and operation of a company and in the determination of the legal rights and duties, not only of the members of the company, but indeed of the company itself in some respects.

5.2.2 Management of a company: Basic principles

The management of a company is vested in persons who are called directors, and these persons act collectively as a board of directors, which is the major managerial organ of the company. There might be specific types of directors charged with particular sorts of responsibilities, but usually their authority is general. There are also other officers of the company, such as the company secretary and public officers, who are charged with particular responsibilities. At law, the directors are regarded as fiduciaries. They are obliged individually and collectively as a board to act *bona fide* in the best interests of the company as a whole. They are not the agents of the shareholders. Their fiduciary duties are owed directly to the abstract legal entity, which is the company itself.

The class of directors or other designated officers does not exhaust those who might be involved from time to time in the management of the affairs of the company. Depending on the size and nature of the company enterprise, there might be a number of employees who undertake various tasks on behalf of the company. A company is an abstract entity that can only act through agents.

5.3 Types of company

The Companies legislation provides for the following basic types of company: (a) a company limited by shares; (b) a guarantee company; and (c) an unlimited company.

A company limited by shares can be further subdivided into two types: namely, a public limited company and a private limited company.[17] For example, s 4(2) of the Companies Act of Fiji provides:

Such a company may be either –

(a) a company having the liability of its members limited by the memorandum to the amount, if any, unpaid on the shares respectively held by them (in this Act termed a 'company limited by shares'); or
(b) a company having the liability of its members limited by the memorandum to the amount as the members may respectively thereby undertake to

---

17 See s 9 Companies Act 2009 (SI), repealed Companies Act Cap 175 1996; Companies Act 2021 repealed Companies Ordinance Cap 10A 1980 (Kiribati), where the distinction preserved in s 10 of the former Act is no longer apparent; Companies Act 1991 [Cap 40.08] (Tu), revised the Companies Act 1991 in 2008, see s 5 for equivalent provisions.

contribute to the assets of the company in the event of its being wound up (in this Act termed a 'company limited by guarantee'); or

(c) a company not having any limit on the liability of its members (in this Act termed an 'unlimited company').

5.4 Companies limited by shares

5.4.1 Membership

A company that is limited by shares is one in which the principal method of membership is defined by holding shares. This is one of the most popular types of company, with private companies being the more frequent of the two. The word 'limited' here means that the liability of the person who holds shares to meet the debts and liabilities of the company is legally limited to the amount, if any, that might be outstanding to the company in respect of the acquisition or holding of the shares. If there are no such moneys outstanding, the shareholder cannot be called on to contribute further. This is central to the notion of limited liability, which we referred to above.

A share[18] is legally a form of legal property (that is to say, it is treated as legal rather than equitable property).[19] The shareholder enjoys certain rights of participation in the issuing company. Shares are legal choses in action,[20] a form of intangible personal property, which can be, and usually are, thought of in terms of 'bundles of rights'.[21] The rights of the holder of this 'bundle' are primarily those rights that are specified by the articles of association of the company, although there are incidental rights which exist at common law (i.e. by virtue of evolved case law).

The person who holds shares, generally described as a shareholder, has a distinct form of property in the sense just described. Normally, property rights apply, including the right to assign or transfer the interest either during a lifetime (*inter vivos*) or on death. Trusts can be created over shares held by a person. Rights of the holder in the shares held prevail over the claims of third parties. These are normal property rights.

---

18 It is important to note that 'share' in this context is used in a special legal sense. It does not have quite the same sense in which we would speak of a 'share of a business' or a 'share of a property', although there is some overlap.

19 In very loose terms, a legal interest is an interest that would have been recognised by courts of common law. An equitable interest is one that would have been recognised by courts of equity alone. Interests in a partnership and the interest of a beneficiary under a trust are what we call equitable property interests because the equity courts alone recognised those interests. They were not recognised by common law courts.

20 See e.g. *R v Williams* [1942] AC 541.

21 See *Commissioner of Inland Revenue v Grossman* [1937] AC 26; [1936] 1 All ER 762 at 789; *Archibald Howie Pty Ltd v Commissioner of Stamp Duties (NSW)* (1948) [1948] HCA 28; 77 CLR 143 at 157.

Pursuant to the separate entity principle mentioned above, the company itself owns the company assets. The shares are not interests in the company assets themselves, although the value of the shares in the marketplace might reflect the underlying value of the company's total assets. They are interests in the totality of the company and give rights enforceable by the holder against the company, but they do not of themselves designate interests in the company property or any specific part of it. They are shares in the company but not in its assets, although in practice, it will inevitably be true that the value of the particular shares is affected by the value of the underlying assets and profit-making capacity of the company from time to time.

Whilst shares are property interests, it is clear that, at the same time, they define the nature and extent of the holder's participation or membership rights of the shareholder in the company itself. They are not only property rights; they are also participation rights. The nature of the shareholder's interest is founded on a contract represented by the articles of association and confirmed by statute.[22] Put another way, the holder of shares becomes a member of the company. In respect of a company with a shareholding structure or with share capital, this is in fact the only means whereby a person can become a member. We will look at the nature of shares and holding later in the book.

As we have already noted, this type of company may be either public or private. In the case of a public limited company, there is a minimum (but no maximum) number of members. The minimum is generally seven in the South Pacific jurisdictions, and there is no upper limit. It is a usual requirement that the word 'Limited', or an abbreviation of it such as 'Ltd', is to be affixed to the name of the company at registration. Importantly, the liability of the individual members or shareholders for the debts and liabilities of the company is legally limited to the amount of shares held by them in the company.

Where the company is a private limited company, there is a requirement for a minimum and maximum number of members. The minimum is two whilst the maximum is 50.[23] Section 4(1) of the Companies Act of Fiji provides:

> 4 (1) Any 7 or more persons, or, where the company to be formed will be a private company, any 2 or more persons, associated for any lawful purpose may, by subscribing their names to a memorandum of association and otherwise complying with the requirements of this Act in respect of registration, form an incorporated company, with or without limited liability.

---

22 See *Borland's Trustee v Steel Brothers & Co Ltd* [1901] 1 Ch 279 at 288; *Re Alex Russell (Deceased)* [1968] VR 285 at 299.

23 See s 4 Companies Act 2015 (F) repealed Companies Act Cap 247 1985; ss 8, 10 International Business Companies Act (Ni), Companies Act 2006, repealed the previous Act on 31 December 2006, preventing offshore activities and status of Niue as a "secrecy haven"; s 9 Companies Act 2012 (V), repealed Companies Act Cap 191 1988; s 9 Companies Act 2009.

In the case of Tonga, however, s 13(d) of the Companies Act provides that a public company should have a minimum of one, regardless of its type. There is no maximum in either case.[24] Furthermore, the maximum number of members for a private company in the Kiribati is 25.[25] It is therefore clear that except for Tonga and Kiribati, the ten other jurisdictions have similar requirements in terms of the number of members.

In the case of a private company, the name of the company must also have in its registered name the word 'Proprietary' or an abbreviation of it such as 'Pty'. Hence a company of this type might appear under the name 'X Pty Ltd'. The purpose of this requirement is to announce to the public that the company is a private company with limited liability.

5.4.2 Directorship

It is a general requirement in the legislation of the South Pacific jurisdictions that a private company must have a minimum of two directors. Other companies are expected to possess a minimum of three directors. In the case of Tonga, for instance, it is possible to have only one director. Persons who are to hold office as directors in a public company must initially have consented to act as such. Thus, a list of persons who have consented to act as directors must be filed with the Registrar of Companies. This is not a requirement for an unlimited company or a private company.[26]

With the exception of Vanuatu, where two or more directors of a public company are to be appointed, a separate resolution is required for each director. This can be dispensed with if a single resolution to approve two directors has first been agreed to by the meeting without any vote being given against it.[27] This is not a requirement for the appointment of directors of a private company. This provision is also absent in Vanuatu.

There is also a requirement governing the residency of directors in the case of Fiji and Vanuatu. In Tonga, ss 125–71 of the Companies Act 1995 deal with the appointment, qualification and removal of directors. Section 125 even contains a

---

24 See also Part II Companies Act 2021 (K), repealed the Companies Ordinance Cap 10A 1979; s 13(d) Companies Act No 14 of 1995 (T).
25 See s 130; for Tuvalu see s 5.
26 Formerly, s 180 Companies Act Cap 248 1985 permitted this. Under s 98 of the Companies Act 2015, this is no longer the case (F); formerly, s 189 Companies Act Cap 191 1988 has been repealed. Now, s 83(4) of the Companies Act 2012, places the onus on the Registrar of Companies, to request that directors 'produce any consent specified in subsection (3)' (V); s 117 Companies Act 1991, amended by Act 5 of 1996 which repealed subsections (2), (3) and (4); see Division 3 of the Act [Cap 40.08] (Tu).
27 Formerly, under s 185 Companies Act Cap 247 1985 (F), now repealed, see Part 10, Companies Act 2015; also repealed is cf ss 43, 44 International Business Companies Act 1994 (Ni), repealed by Companies Act 2006, which removed all offshore business activities from the Act; see also ss 170, 177 Companies Act Cap 175 1996 (SI), repealed. Now Companies Act 2009.

definition of the word 'director'. It is important to bear in mind that these requirements may be different for overseas companies, especially in view of the provisions of ss 341–52 of the Companies Act 1995. In Kiribati, s 2 provides for a list of directors to be filed. Whether it is a public or private company in Kiribati, there are to be a minimum of two directors.[28]

5.4.3 Stock exchange listing

Because a private company by law cannot invite the public to subscribe to its shares or secure loan moneys from the public by creating debentures,[29] it cannot have its shares listed on the stock exchange.[30] In other words, the shares or other stocks of a private company cannot be dealt with or traded on the stock market. A stock market is a place where shares are bought or sold. On the converse, a public company can be listed on the stock market since its shares can be publicly sold.[31] In order to obtain listing on a stock exchange, the company must also comply with certain stock market listing rules. Often, this requires amendments to be made to the articles of the company in order to comply with these listing rules.

5.4.4 Sale of shares

A public company is allowed by law to advertise its shares to the public by inviting the public to subscribe to its shares. In contrast, a private company is restricted in the ways it can raise money from the public. It is therefore prohibited from inviting the public to subscribe to any of its shares or debentures. It is also restricted in the way it transfers its shares.[32] There is no equivalent provision in respect of international companies in Niue.

5.4.5 Starting business

Where a company is public, it cannot commence business unless a trading certificate is issued to it. This does not apply to a private company.[33] It is therefore

---

28 Formerly s 91 Companies Ordinance Cap 10A 1979 (K), repealed. Now s 6 Companies Act 2021. For the position in Tuvalu, see s 117 Companies Act [Cap 40.08] 1991.

29 As we will see later on, a debenture is basically a secured loan to a company, usually secured by a debenture trust deed. Debenture financing is one form of company loan financing, as distinct from equity financing, which is provided by subscription for shares.

30 See s 195 Companies Act 2015 (F).

31 See Ahmadu, M, *The Law of Banking in Fiji*, 1998, London, Avon, p 4.

32 See s 195 Companies Act 2015 (F); s 29 Companies Act Cap 175 1996, now repealed. See Division 9, Companies Act 2009 (SI); s 38 Companies Act Cap 191, now repealed. See Division 9, Companies Act 2012 (V).

33 For other restrictions affecting a public company, see ss 126–7, Division 6 and ss 422(4), 427 in Part 4 of the Companies Act 2015 (F); see s 15(3) and Schedule 4 of the Companies Act 2009 (SI); s 78 Companies Act 2021 (K).

advantageous for small and medium-sized businesses, especially those representing family interests, to register private companies, as this affords a quick start to trading. Depending upon the prevailing local conditions, it might take a reasonable length of time for the trading certificate to be processed. This might have a down-slide effect on a public company wishing to seize an immediate business opportunity after its incorporation. This does not, however, undermine the importance of public companies as business entities.

5.4.6 Meetings and proxies

Companies are generally entitled to appoint proxies in order to represent shareholders who might be absent in the meetings. It is possible to appoint more than one proxy for a public company. However, the proxy can vote but has no right to speak at the meeting. A proxy so appointed in the case of a private company has a right to speak at the meeting.[34] In the case of Vanuatu, the law is explicit on the point that only one proxy can be appointed for a private company.[35] There is no provision for voting by proxy in Tonga, either in the substantive provisions or in the rules. In Kiribati, proxies are dealt with in s 80. There is no distinction in number of proxies, whether for public or private companies. Every proxy is entitled to vote and speak at all meetings.[36]

5.4.7 Guarantee companies

In a guarantee company, the members are bound together by an undertaking to contribute to the liability of the company pro rata to their holding or pledge in the capital of the company. Instead of achieving a limit on the liability of members in terms of shareholding contributions, as noted above, the limit on the liability of members is provided in terms of an explicit guarantee provided for in the memorandum of association.

This type is thus a company having the liability of its members limited by the memorandum to such amount as the members may respectively undertake to contribute to the assets of the company in the event of its being wound up.[37] The guarantee is usually called up if the company goes into liquidation. As guarantee

---

34 See Division 6 of the Companies Act 2015 (F); s 30 Companies Act 2012 (V).
35 Formerly s 59 International Business Companies Act 1994 (Ni), repealed by Companies Act 2006, prohibiting offshore business activity; s 30 Companies Act 2009 (SI).
36 For the position in Samoa, see s 97 International Companies Act 1988, as amended by s 55 in 1991. This concerns only companies that have been designated as international in nature.
37 Section 15 (F) of the Companies Act 2015; no 'guarantee company' listed, see s 9, Part 12, Schedule 5 of 9 (SI); no 'guarantee company' listed, see s 9, Part 12, Schedule 4 of the Companies Act (V); see no 'guarantee company' listed in the Companies Act 2021 (K), nevertheless, a guarantee company may still be incorporated, see s 6, Part 2 of the Act.

companies are not for profit making, they are suitable for non-commercial ventures such as charities, religious bodies and educational foundations.

Apart from the main division of companies into those limited by shares, unlimited or guarantee, it is possible to classify companies according to how they relate to one another. This is common practice in situations where group companies exist. For this reason, companies operating in a group fashion can be holding or subsidiary.

5.4.8 Unlimited companies

An unlimited company is one that has no limit on the liability of its members. In this instance, its memorandum contains no clause dealing with the liability of the members. The implication of having unlimited liability is that members of the company can be held liable and be required to contribute in full in order to discharge the debts and liabilities of the company in the event of its insolvency.[38]

In spite of the absence of limited liability, unlimited companies have some advantages. Generally speaking, there is no public scrutiny of its accounts and financial records. Unlike a public company, an unlimited company need not file annual accounts in the company registry. There is no restriction on an unlimited company forbidding it to purchase its own shares. This is strictly forbidden in relation to public and proprietary companies.[39]

These characteristics make unlimited companies desirable business entities for professionals who want to associate together for a common business objective but would like to assume full responsibility for their practices.

5.5 Holding and subsidiary companies

Generally speaking, a company within the South Pacific[40] is regarded as a subsidiary of a holding company if the latter exercises a substantial degree of control over the former. Sections 3 and 7 of the Companies Act of Fiji, for example, give the meaning of a holding and a subsidiary company. They provide:[41]

---

38 Section 2(6), Part 20 (F); see ss 9, 10 (SI) as there are no unlimited companies registered in SI; see ss 9, 10(V); s 6(d) (K).

39 Formerly, s 33 International Business Companies Act 1994 (Ni) authorised this, until its repeal. Now the Companies Act 2006 prohibits offshore business activity.

40 Section 736 Companies Act 1985 (UK) appears to refer to an accounting definition. Since the last edition in 2006, this has become largely relevant in the South Pacific jurisdictions. Formerly, see s 156. Now Part 32 of the Companies Act 2015 covers financial reporting requirements (F); formerly, s 26 (N), now repealed under Companies Act 2006; see Schedule 1, s 3 'Meaning of subsidiary', s 4 'Meaning of holding company' and Part 7, Division 4 (SI); see Part X under the Companies Act 2021 (K); see Part 7, Division 4 (V); see Part VI (T). The definitions in the South Pacific are all legal and not accounting definitions.

41 Also see s 6 of the Companies Act 2015 (F).

3 'Holding Company', in relation to a Company, means a Company of which the first Company is a Subsidiary 'Subsidiary' means a subsidiary as defined by section 7;

7 A Company (in this section called the 'first body') is a Subsidiary of another Company only if—

(a) the other body—
    (i) controls or is in a position to control the composition of the first body's board;
    (ii) is in a position to cast, or control the casting of, more than one-half of the maximum number of votes that might be cast at a General Meeting of the first body; or
    (iii) holds more than one-half of the issued share capital of the first body, excluding any part of that issued share capital that carries no right to participate beyond a specified amount in a distribution of either profits or capital; or
(b) the first body is a Subsidiary of a Subsidiary of the other body.

The emphasis in this definition centres on the elements of control by the holding company over the subsidiary company. Control in this instance must relate to management at the board level, voting rights on the shares or investment in the equity capital of the subsidiary company. Needless to say, these are the key factors in determining the command-and-control structure of any business entity.

5.5.1 Accounting definition[42]

An alternative to the legal definition of the parent-subsidiary relationship is the accounting definition. This does not appear in the South Pacific legislation, but we mention it as a point of contrast. The accounting definition defines a parent undertaking in the context of consolidated accounts. A parent company is also considered on the same footing as a holding company. To qualify as a parent company, it should exercise dominant influence over the subsidiary company through definite clauses in the memorandum or articles of association of the subsidiary company, or should control the subsidiary company by means of a control or management contract.[43]

The significance of the accounting definition is to enable a fair and accurate description of the true relationship to be established between the parent and subsidiary by narrowing the scope of off-balance sheet financing. For this reason, a holding company must as a requirement of statute prepare in relation to it and its

---

42 A discussion on this sub-topic appears in Roach, L, *Company Law*, 2022, London, OUP, 2nd edn, pp 561, 585–6.
43 See Roach, *ibid.*, pp 73, 104.

subsidiaries a group account reflecting the financial view of the group as a single business unit.[44] The significance of the accounting definition is to reveal the true relationship between a parent company and its subsidiaries by a statement of account that shows the nexus between all the companies forming a group.[45] Through the network of holding and subsidiary companies, business risks might be spread out, especially where the subsidiaries are located in different and convenient jurisdictions.[46]

5.5.2 Incorporation

As noted before, on incorporation, a company obtains a separate legal personality. It is the company that must be sued in respect of debts that are properly those of the company itself and not those, for example, of its shareholders, directors or office holders. Likewise, it is the company itself that must bring an action concerning matters that are rightly those belonging to the company itself.

As we have also noted, a company acquires legal personality through the process of registration.[47] In this instance, an artificial entity technically becomes a person in law. The same principle applies in respect of both domestic companies and international companies registered under special legislation of some of the South Pacific countries.[48] Those seeking the formation of a company, called promoters, have to file the incorporation documents appropriate to the particular type of company and pay the prescribed fees in order to obtain registration and hence incorporation. On completion of this process, the company comes into being with an independent legal personality. It is then capable of acting on its own. It can sue and be sued in its own name, hold property and enter into contracts and is invested with perpetual succession and possesses a common seal.[49]

Prior to incorporation, a company has no independent legal status and therefore cannot enter into legal relations with others. Those who purport to contract on behalf of a company which has not yet been incorporated incur personal liability under any contracts they might have entered into. This is so even if the contract is

---

44 Section 227 Companies Act 1989 (UK).
45 See ICSA, *op cit* fn 42, pp 73, 104.
46 See ICSA, *op cit* fn 42, p 28 and the decision in *Re Southard & Co Ltd* [1979] 1 WLR 1198, *per* Templeman LJ. See also *Adams v Cape Industries Plc* [1991] 1 All ER 929; [1990] 2 WLR 657; *DHN Food Distributors Ltd v Tower Hamlets LBC* [1976] 1 WLR 852; *Multinational Gas and Petrochemical Co v Multinational Gas and Petrochemical Services Ltd* [1983] Ch 258.
47 See *Samson Poloso v Honiara Consumer Cooperative Ltd* [1985] SPLR 321; *Funaki Ofa v Tongan Wesley Church* [1988] SPLR 48; *Heinrich v Nauru Phosphates Corp* [1987] SPLR 167.
48 On international companies, see Chapter 1.
49 See Part 6 (F); formerly, s 15 International Business Companies Act (Ni), now repealed, see Companies Act 2006; s 155(SI); see Part 11 (V); see Part XV (K); s 107 and Division 12 of the Business Corporations Act 1990 (MI). See also s 18 International Companies Act 1988, as amended by s 8 of the 1991 Act (S), ss 17, 18 (T) and s 34(3) (Tu).

for professional services related to the formation of the company itself and/or the company after incorporation gets the benefit of the services rendered.[50]

There are means whereby a promoter of a company who enters into a pre-incorporation contract on behalf of the company can escape liability. First, it is possible to exclude personal liability on the basis of clear and explicit terms in the contract itself. The second means is by way of what is called novation. It is common to insert into a contract a novation clause which provides that on incorporation of the new company, the existing contract ceases, and the rights and liabilities thereunder are created or novated in terms of a fresh contract between the company and the other party. At that point, the promoter's personal liability under the contract ceases and the company assumes liability under it. But the latter situation is open to possible abuse to some extent. For this reason, promoters are regarded as fiduciaries and are under certain obligations to the new company. We will discuss the promoter's obligations in this regard in a moment.

As already noted, this principle is a major point of differentiation between companies and other corporations on the one hand, and partnerships and trusts on the other. Separate corporate personality, which is regarded as the lynchpin of the law of companies, is dictated by the legislation itself, which endows a company on registration with perpetual succession and commands that it sue and be sued in its own name.[51] This factor determines how the relations of management and control of companies and their relations to outsiders with whom they come into contact, commercially and otherwise, are resolved.

To take one instance: the directors of a company are fiduciaries. They are required to act in the best interests of the company as a whole. Their fiduciary duties are not owed to the members or shareholders of the company but to an abstract thing which is the company itself. It is the recipient of the benefit of the obligation imposed on company directors in equity. However, this is more easily said and perhaps understood than put into practice. Company law has had to grapple with the more difficult question of how to define the best interests of the company. It has sought help in other abstractions such as the interests of all members and the interests of the hypothetical average shareholder, and seems to have come to land, for the time being, on some concept of the totality of the interests of the company as a going concern. The latter concern might include the interests not only of the members or shareholders of the company but those of company creditors as well.

---

50 See the leading authorities of *Salomon v Salomon* [1897] AC 22; *Kelner v Baxter* (1866) LR 2 CP 174; *Natal Land Co v Pauline Colliery Syndicate* [1904] AC 120; and *Goh v LCL Enterprises Ltd* [1997] SBHC 20; HC-CC 138 of 1995 (12 April 1997).

51 For a rather absurd attempt to circumvent the consequences of the doctrine, see *John Beater Enterprises Ltd v Ho* [1999] FJHC 119; Hbc0249r.99s (12 November 1999).

There are many other examples. The courts have generally been reluctant to lift the corporate veil. There are, however, some exceptions to its strict application and we outline these below.

5.5.3 Exceptions to the separate entity doctrine

(1) There is a rule known as the rule in *Foss v Harbottle*. This is sometimes known as the proper plaintiff rule. It requires that a company is the proper plaintiff in all matters concerning the company's affairs. No individual shareholder or group of shareholders is entitled to bring legal proceedings asserting the interests of the company. The company itself must do this. But there will be instances where the *de facto* control of the company is vested either in directors and/or in majority or controlling shareholders. Because they have *de facto* control of the company, they can direct actions to be taken in the company's name, including the issue of whether the company does or does not institute legal proceedings. Clearly, such a control situation might be used to permit the controlling parties to commit an (equitable) fraud against the interests of, say, minority shareholders. The law will not permit this to occur. It permits the minority shareholders to bring what is called a derivative action in the company's name in order to redress the alleged fraud.

(2) As a more general proposition, the existence of the corporate veil will not be allowed to facilitate the perpetration of a fraud. Clearly, the corporate veil is one behind which individuals might seek to 'hide'.

(3) Similarly, the separate entity of a company cannot be set up as a sham in order to permit those who stand behind it simply to avoid liability. If a corporate entity has been set up as a sham in this sense, then the court will disregard it.

(4) The separate entity doctrine applies as between holding companies and their subsidiaries. Both are separate legal entities notwithstanding the closeness of their relationship.

(5) There are some statutory exceptions provided by the legislation itself. These are situations where the Companies legislation permits the court to lift the corporate veil and to look at the reality of the situation. For example, s 73(2) of the Companies Act of Fiji provides that the members of a company are personally and severally liable for debts and liabilities incurred by a company before a company is registered. In the case of a public company, the number is seven. In the case of a private company, it is two.[52]

---

52 s 41 Companies Act 1955 (NZ) were applicable until its repeal on 30 June 1997 (S), (CI); see Part 4, s 46 (SI); See Part 4, ss 45–6 (V).

5.5.4 The consequences of incorporation

The main consequences of incorporation of a company can be summarised as follows:

(1) First, there is brought into existence a separate legal entity with its own name, as explained above. This entity has perpetual or permanent existence which continues despite the death or bankruptcy of any individual member or indeed of all such members.

(2) Incorporation, with the exceptions noted in the previous chapter, brings into play the principle of limited liability of members of the company. This principle is explained further below.

(3) The interests in the company can be transferred easily in accordance with the articles of association of the company and the relevant Companies legislation. Furthermore, the share register which a company is required to keep maintains a record of the transactions concerning company shares.

(4) The memorandum and articles of association contain a formal set of objectives and rules for the company. In the articles, for example, shareholders' rights are explicitly set out and therefore a statement of those rights is readily available. Indeed, the memorandum and articles of association, because they are registered on incorporation, form part of a public record.

(5) The company, by virtue of its formal legal status, can enter into contracts and incur debts and liabilities on its own behalf, even though it necessarily acts through agents in practice. It can sue and be sued in its own right. There are some limitations on the actions that a company can take. For example, a company cannot vote or exercise other legal rights that are essentially for exercise only by natural individuals. The law has had to make some modifications to its general principles to account for the fact that a company is an artificial legal entity. It is generally liable for crimes that it commits, but the imposition of criminal liability in terms of concepts that were formulated primarily with respect to natural individuals required adjustment. A company cannot commit certain crimes, for example, the crime of rape or murder, although it seems that it could be guilty of the crime of conspiracy to commit such offences. We will deal further with these issues later on.

5.5.5 Limited liability

This is a process by which the liability of the members of the company is limited in some way. In the case of companies with a shareholding, it is determined principally by restricting liability for contribution to the debts and liabilities of the company on the winding up of the company[53] to the amount of contributions

---

53 Winding up is the process of dissolution of the company.

unpaid by the shareholder on the shares taken up by a member. In the case of companies limited by guarantee, the limitation on liability is in terms of the amount of contribution guaranteed in the memorandum of association by the subscribers to that memorandum.

In respect of shareholding companies, the liability attaches to the shares taken up by a member or to shares which are agreed to be taken up by a member. It is immaterial that the shares are unpaid by the member. Liability on the unpaid shares can be traced to the member if the company calls up the shares or where it is in liquidation. What is significant is that a member's liability to contribute to the debts or liability of the company is limited only to the amount of shares subscribed by him or her and nothing more.

The principle of limited liability enables persons to contribute to the capital of a company by taking up shares without the risk of being called upon to contribute more than they have invested or have agreed to invest in the assets of the company. More significantly, by this principle, the liability of the company cannot affect the personal assets of its members in the event of insolvency of the company.[54]

Without a doubt, the principle provides a secure forum for investment and business that is devoid of fears relating to personal accountability for losses incurred by the company. The concept of limited liability to a much greater extent explains the success of limited liability companies in the economic activities of the South Pacific countries. It is, however, clear that unlimited companies cannot by their nature benefit from the advantages of limited liability. In fact, by their very nature they profess the opposite.

5.6 Steps in registration

In order to obtain registration and hence a company, the promoters of a company must follow a set procedure of lodgement of documents such as the memorandum and articles of association of the company, a statement of first directors and other officers, other prescribed documents and payment of a prescribed fee.[55] What is required depends to some extent on what type of company is to be formed. Everything is submitted to the Registrar of Companies before a company is incorporated.[56]

The certificate of registration when issued serves as conclusive evidence that all the requirements of the relevant Companies Act have been complied with.

---

54 See the *locus classicus* of *Salomon v Salomon* [1897] AC 22.
55 See e.g. ss 208–214, Kiribati register of the Companies Act 2021 (K); s 367 Companies Act (T).
56 See s 26 Companies Act 1985 (UK). Section 4 Companies Act 1991 No 13 (Tu) specifies a set of different documents. It should also be noted that not all countries currently require all the listed documents to be filed prior to incorporating a company. However, it is envisaged that with the current trends in reform of company laws sweeping across the region, these forms will be available in future Acts in all countries. See ss 13, 15 and 16 (T).

Secondly, it evidences the fact that the company is duly incorporated by the name in its memorandum. Irregularities in the formation or mistakes in the certificate of incorporation, even if discovered later, will not affect the validity of the certificate.[57]

5.6.1 Memorandum and articles of association

These make up the constitution of a company. The memorandum defines the relationship of the company with the outside world. It normally consists of five clauses. These include the name of the company; the registered office of the company; the objects of the company; the limited liability of members or shareholders; and the authorised capital. At the end of the memorandum is a subscription clause. This is also referred to as a 'declaration clause'. This contains the names and addresses of subscribers and the total shares (if any) they intend to take. It is dated and signed by each subscriber taking at least a share each. The signatures are then witnessed.[58]

The articles of association regulate the internal matters of the company by setting out the rules governing the conduct of affairs of the company. It usually contains information on shares, powers and responsibilities of directors, meetings and rules on membership. The memorandum and articles bind the company and its members in a contractual relationship.[59]

5.6.2 Contents of a memorandum

A company memorandum must contain certain information. The first is the name of the company. The Registrar may refuse to register a company where the name in his/her opinion is undesirable. The general principles of administrative review can apply with respect to the decision of the Registrar on the naming of a company.[60] The refusal of a particular name can give the applicant the right legally to challenge the decision of the Registrar where it offends the requirements of administrative decision making.

For limited companies, the name must end with the word 'Limited' or an abbreviation of it. A guarantee company may be exempted from this requirement. Some

---

57 Section 22 Companies Act 2015 (F); s 16 Companies Act 2006 (UK); International Business Companies Act 1994, repealed. Companies Act 2006 prohibits offshore business activity. See s 6 (Ni); s 18 Companies Act (T); s 8 Companies Act 2001 (S); s 9 and Part II (K).

58 For the statutory contents of a memorandum, see s 46 and Part 4 of the Companies Act 2015 (F); s 18; ss 5, 6 Companies Act (V); s 35 Companies Act (T); s 10 Companies Act 2001 (S); cf s 8, in Part 2, and s 18 in Part 3, Chapter 22 of the Companies Act 1985 (UK).

59 See s 35 Companies Act (T); cf ss 8, 18 Companies Act (UK).

60 See *Re Mitchell Kiel and Associates* [1998] FJHC 46; Hbj0003.1998s (8 April 1998), *per* Scott J.

names are however prohibited and cannot by law be allowed.[61] Words such as 'Royal', 'Imperial', 'Chamber of Commerce', 'Building Society' and 'Cooperative' and names similar to those of other registered companies are proscribed.[62]

The matter of naming a company can raise issues of potential liability for a passing off. Passing off is an action in tort which is aimed at the prevention of interference with a person's business. It is not based on principles of unfair competition as such. Consent is a defence to such an action.[63]

The name of a company can be changed at any time, provided the requisite procedures are complied with. This is done by means of a special resolution which is lodged with the Registrar and approved by the Registrar in writing. A special resolution requires that a special majority of three-quarters of the persons entitled to vote who are present at the meeting be obtained when the resolution is passed. This is discussed later in the book. A change in name does not affect the rights and liabilities of the company.[64]

The registered office of the company must be stated in the memorandum of association of the company at the time of incorporation. The registered office must be within the relevant jurisdiction. Notice of any subsequent change in address must be communicated to the Registrar of Companies.[65] The registered office is the public office of the company and serves as the place for the service of notices and so on. It is not necessarily the place of business of the company.

Where appropriate, the memorandum in appropriate cases must contain a clause concerning limited liability. As noted before, this clause in the memorandum prescribes the liability status of the shareholder or, in the case of a guarantee company, of the members. Sometimes the memorandum might go further to specify that the liability of the managing director, directors and managers of the company is unlimited. Where a shareholder is also a director and the company is one with limited liability, that person has a dual status. As a shareholder, liability is limited in terms of the shareholding, but when acting in the capacity of a director, liability is unlimited.[66]

In the case of a limited company with a share capital, the memorandum must specify, for purposes of registration, the amount of authorised share capital of the company and the division, where appropriate, of that capital into shares of fixed

---

61 See s 25Companies Act 2015 (F); s 10 Companies Act 2006 (Ni); s 10(2)–(3) Companies Act 2001 (S); cf Part 5 Companies Act 2006 (UK).

62 See e.g. s 27 Companies Act 2015 (F).

63 See *Ervend Warnink BV v Townend & Sons (Hull) Ltd* [1979] AC 731 at 742.

64 See s 28 Companies Act 2015 (F); s 11 Companies Act 2006 (Ni); s 20 Companies Act 1972 (N); s 11 Companies Act 2001 (S); cf ss 77–81 in Part 5, Chapter 5, Companies Act 2006 (UK).

65 Sections 132–3 Companies Act 2021 (K). Note generally that the contents of the memorandum of a company can be altered by special resolution. See s 50(2) Companies Act 2015 (F); s 18 Companies Act 2009 (SI); ss 8(b), 109(3) Companies Act (Tu); cf s 87 Companies Act 2006 (UK); s 196 (T).

66 See ss 8(d), 31 Companies Act [Cap 40.08] 2008 (Tu).

amounts, usually into shares with par value.[67] The memorandum must indicate who the first subscribers are to the memorandum. Where the company is one with a share capital, a certain number of shares will be allocated to them in the memorandum. Each subscriber must take a minimum of one share.[68] Those who subscribe to the memorandum are first directors of the company (later appointments to the board of directors may be achieved through formal appointments). They are also liable to the shares subscribed, which as a rule is to be paid in cash.[69]

5.6.3 Objects of a company and the ultra vires doctrine

One of the more important clauses in the memorandum of association of a company is the objects clause. The objects for which the company is formed must be lawful. The requirement for a statement of objects in the memorandum of association is, except in Vanuatu, explicitly imposed by the statutes as a prerequisite of registration.[70] The objects define the scope of powers of the company. In effect, the objects also limit the activities or business dealings in which the company can legitimately engage.

In other words, the stated objects set the scope of the activities that a company duly incorporated may legitimately undertake. From the point of view of investors in the company and of the public at large, the requirement for stated objects provides some sort of guideline as to the nature of the company's general undertaking. In some jurisdictions, the requirement of an objects clause has been done away with altogether. In Australia, for example, the position is that a company memorandum may state objects, but it is not necessary that it do so.[71] Also, legal reforms have been introduced which seek to ensure that the consequences of a statement of objects, in terms of what is called the *ultra vires*, are substantially dispensed with.[72] Reforms in this direction have been implemented, although perhaps not to quite the same degree, in most of the South Pacific jurisdictions.

---

67 Cf s 42(1) Companies Act 1995 (T); s 16 Companies Act 1972 (N); note that Kiribati, like the UK, has a minimum paid-up share capital: see s 21 Companies Act 2021 (K): public company $20,000; private company $500. See also s 6 Companies Act [Cap 40.08] 2008 (Tu); cf ss 545–6, Part 17, Chapter 1 of the Companies Act 2006 (UK). Note that in the United Kingdom, a company's authorised capital can also be denominated in foreign currency. But see s 42(1) (T).

68 Section 82(2) Companies Act 2015 (F); s 21 Companies Act 2009 (SI); s 543 Companies Act 1955 (NZ) (CI); s 22 Companies Act 2001 (S); s 21 Companies Act 2012 (V).

69 See s 583 in Chapter 5 of Companies Act 2006 (UK).

70 Section 46 Companies Act 2015 (F); s 8 Companies Act 2009 (SI); see Part 2, Division 1 of the Companies Act 2001 (S).

71 See s 117(2) Corporations Law 2001 (Aus).

72 See ss 160–62. The process of watering down the *ultra vires* doctrine in Australia began with the state-based Companies Acts in the early 1960s, and the erosion has continued. Now, under the Corporations Law, contravention of the objects clause can only be relied on or asserted in certain limited circumstances, for example with respect to prosecution for a criminal offence under the Corporations Law or in relation to a claim based on oppressive conduct. See ss 162(7), 230, 260 and 1324.

From a common law perspective, the objects clauses in the memorandum of association serve three primary functions. Firstly, they stipulate the extent of a company's contractual powers. Secondly, they define the legal capacity of a company. Thirdly, they provide notice to the public as to the area of legitimate activity of the company, bearing in mind that they need to be in the memorandum and registered as such. This in turn determines whether and how far the *ultra vires* (meaning literally 'beyond power') rule will apply in respect of actions of the company.[73]

5.6.4 Ultra vires

Simply put, the *ultra vires* doctrine holds, in the absence of a statutory provision to the contrary, that anything done by a company which is outside the proper scope of its stated objects is void and of no effect whatsoever.[74] This includes transactions entered into by the company with third parties. As on registration of the memorandum of association, the objects clauses become part of a public record: persons who deal with a company are fixed with constructive notice of the content of the company's stated objects. This prevents an otherwise innocent third party who deals with the company from asserting innocence of the restrictions.

The company itself is entitled to rely on the *ultra vires* doctrine. Therefore, it can assert that a transaction is void even though, clearly, the expectation as to knowledge of the scope of powers of the company would be placed most firmly on those who operate the company itself. The doctrine operates at the level of public policy, which displaces argument along these lines. Furthermore, *ultra vires* does not imply illegality. This could perhaps be relied on by a person who had received property or benefit from a company as a result of an *ultra vires* transaction as a basis for not being compelled to make restitution under the *in pari delicto* principle. Here the transaction is merely void *ab initio*. Owing to this, it can be argued that the *ultra vires* doctrine produces quite artificial and unjust consequences.

The position as regards the application of the rule to dealings by third parties with a company has produced some anomalies. Third parties could have a transaction struck down by virtue of the *ultra vires* principle. At the same time, the rule in *Royal British Bank v Turquand*[75] (the so-called 'indoor management rule') holds that third parties are not bound to inquire into the scope of powers of the directors of a company. Also, the position of members and third parties was put on a different footing. Members of the company could seek an injunction to restrain a company acting outside its powers and thus were in a better position

---

73 See s 8(3) Companies Act [Cap 40.08] 2001 (Tu). It is not necessary to state the objects, but the limitations on the powers of the company have to be stated, if any. See s 20 (T).

74 On justifications for the rule, see Hicks, A and Dignam, A, *Cases and Materials on Company Law*, 7th edn, 2001, New York, Oxford University Press, pp 165–178.

75 (1856) 6 E & B 327. See also s 45 Companies Act 2015 (F); s 18 (N). In the case of Fiji and Samoa, it seems that the incidental and ancillary objects and powers are intended to cure the defects in some aspects of the *ultra vires* doctrine.

than an innocent third party dealing with the company. Given these anomalies, it is not surprising that the *ultra vires* doctrine has been either abolished altogether or severely circumscribed in many jurisdictions.[76]

Various methods have been devised to circumvent the consequences of the company objects doctrine. As noted before, a company which seeks to enter new ground would have to go through the process of amending its memorandum if the power to undertake a particular course of action does not expressly or impliedly exist. The general practice has been to draft as widely as possible the objects clauses of a company in order to avoid the consequences of the rule, although there remain certain powers which cannot, by design of the memorandum, be attributed to a company.[77] Where very restricted clauses are drafted as objects of a company, the danger is that if the main object fails, the company may be wound upon the pretension that the substratum has failed.[78]

For example, the effects of the common law *ultra vires* doctrine have been softened in some jurisdictions. Formerly, s 45 of the Companies Act [Cap. 191] 1988 of Vanuatu provided this. This Act was later repealed. The key reforms in Vanuatu had abolished the more complex legal concept of *ultra vires* from the Companies Act 2012.

The sub-section permits a member of the debenture holder in the company to seek an injunction from the court to restrain the doing of acts by a company in excess of the objects. The court may also grant compensation under certain circumstances. The proviso to s 45(1) serves as a substantial qualification of it, particularly in relation to the rights of third parties who have dealt with the company. There is no requirement that the third party should have been free of knowledge or notice of any objects limitation in order to invoke the benefits of the proviso to sub-s (1).

There are equivalent provisions in s 10 of the Companies Act 2021 of Kiribati. In Tuvalu, s 34(1)–(3) of the Companies Act [Cap 40.08] 1991 grants an unlimited capacity to a company. This is in addition to the rights and privileges of a natural person of full age and capacity that a company possesses. It is clear that by a combined reading of ss 34 and 35, the *ultra vires* rule is not meant to operate in Tuvalu. Furthermore, s 34 of the Companies Act of Tuvalu goes on to render the powers of a company as unlimited in addition to the powers conferred on it as an incorporated person.[79]

---

76 In the United Kingdom, ss 35, 25A and 35B of the Act abolished the doctrine altogether.
77 See *Bell Houses Ltd v City Wall Properties Ltd* [1966] 2 QB 656.
78 ICSA, *op cit* fn 41, p 58; see also the so-called *Cotman v Brougham* (1918) 34 TLR 410 clause. See s 3A of the Companies Act (UK) introduced in 1989, which purported to soften the effect of the failure of objects. There is no equivalent statutory provision in any jurisdiction of the South Pacific at the present time.
79 For further powers, see s 34(1) (a) and (b) Companies Act [Cap 40.08] 2001 (Tu).

5.6.5 Alteration of objects

Alteration of company objects can only be achieved by a special resolution of the company. This, in some South Pacific jurisdictions, is possible only where certain statutory conditions are complied with as well.[80] Further still, an order of the court confirming the alteration is required in order to validate the alteration. Section 48 of the Companies Act 2015 of Fiji specifies a different requirement as follows:

> A company may, by special resolution, alter the provisions of its memorandum with respect to the objects or powers of the company:
>
> Provided that, if an application is made to the court in accordance with this section for the alteration to be cancelled, it shall not have effect, except in so far as it is confirmed by the court.

Section 187 of the same Act provides that in order to effect a cancellation of any purported alteration of the company's objects, the application must have been made by holders of not less than 10% in nominal value of the company's issued share capital or any class thereof or, if the company is not limited by shares, not less than 15% of the company's members.[81]

5.6.6 Articles of association

These are rules that regulate the internal affairs of a company. They deal with, amongst others matters touching on membership, shares, alteration of the capital of a company, procedures for calling and conducting meetings, directors and their powers and appointment and removal.[82]

In the event of a conflict between the memorandum and articles, the former prevails. In general practice, it is easier to alter the articles than the memorandum. Because of this, it may be possible to include some clauses of the articles in the memorandum in order to make it more difficult for any alterations to take place.

The schedules to the various company statutes in the region contain model articles which may be adopted by a company in lieu of formulating articles of their own.[83]

---

80 See s 16 Companies Act 2031 (K), dealing with objects and powers of the company.

81 Cf s 16(SI); s 16 (V); s 16 (Ni).

82 See ss 46–9, Division 2 of the Companies Act 2015 (F), which appears to suggest that articles might not be necessary for a company limited by shares; cf s 15, see Model rules in Schedules 2–5 applicable to the four categories of companies (SI); s 8(V); s 10 (Tu).

83 Section 728(2)(b) (F); s 10 (SI); s 9 (Tu); see ss 14(1)(b), 15 and Model rules in Schedule 2, 3 and 4 of the Act (S); s 14 and Model rules in Schedules 1–4 (V); cf ss 19–20 (UK).

5.6.7 Articles and the statute

The Companies legislation, in specific cases, often allows certain things to be done if the articles also permit it. For instance, the Companies Acts of the region normally permit a company to reduce its capital in so far as the articles permit it.

Where a particular act is prohibited by the Companies Act, it cannot be permitted under the articles. For instance, the laws of most jurisdictions prohibit the issuing of shares at a discount. Shares are only to be issued at a premium. It follows, therefore, that no articles, no matter how ingeniously drafted, can legitimise shares issued at a discount.

5.6.8 Binding effects

Together, the memorandum and articles bind the members collectively and individually and the company, and as between the members themselves.[84] As between members, the articles will only have force as regards the rights and obligations which affect members in their capacity as members only. Sections 46 and 47 of the Companies Act 2015 of Fiji is a typical provision.[85]

5.7 Procedure for altering the articles

Alteration of the articles can be achieved only by a special resolution,[86] which is lodged with the Registrar. The Registrar issues a notice in the *Gazette* to this effect.[87] Once carried by a special resolution, the alteration is effective and binding on all members of the company. A company cannot fetter its rights to alter the articles. This means, for example, that it cannot declare its articles to be unalterable. It cannot make a separate contract in order to prevent it from altering its articles. It cannot make a stipulation of more than 75% of the votes as a minimum for altering the articles.

It is, however, possible for weighted shares to be used as a means of blocking the passing of a special resolution.[88] The assent principle can also be invoked to alter the articles. This is where all members agree to the alteration but without

84 See s 6–7 (F); s 16 (S); s 16 (SI); s 35 (T); s 10 (Tu); s 16 (V).
85 Since the last edition, Kiribati now holds an equivalent provision; see s17 of the Companies Act 2021.
86 Section 46(7) Companies Act 2015 (F); cf s 21 Companies Act 2006 (UK); see also *Cane v Jones* [1980] 1 WLR 1451 on situations where a resolution might not always be necessary.
87 Section 46(7) (F); s 14(2) (S); s16(1), (2) of the Companies Act 2017 (CI); s 14(2), (3) (SI); s 14(5) (V); but see s 16 (K), which imposes further special conditions.
88 See generally ICSA, *op cit* fn 41, pp 78–80.

a meeting and without a special resolution.[89] In practice, however, certain techniques may be adopted which would have the effect of preventing alterations to some provisions of a company's memorandum or articles.[90]

5.7.1 The bona fides test

Whilst in principle a company can alter its articles, a power to do so must be exercised *bona fide* and in the interests of the company as a whole. In other words, the power is fiduciary in nature. The alteration stands even if it is against the personal rights of members. Where an alteration is not unreasonable, a court may take the view that it is in the overall interest of the company.[91]

There is no direct authority in the South Pacific, but the view of Evershed MR in *Greenhalgh v Ardene Cinemas Ltd*[92] sheds some light on the rationale underlying the *bona fides*. In *Greenhalgh's Case*, the majority shareholders altered the articles to remove the pre-emption rights governing the sale of shares to an insider first before being offered to outsiders.[93] The court held (on a challenge by Greenhalgh to the alteration of article) that the alteration did not affect the rights of minority shareholders as they were also allowed to sell their shares to outsiders if they so wished. The alteration was therefore valid in that it was not against the interest of the company as a whole.

5.7.2 Promoters

Clearly, a company cannot form itself. It requires the action of natural individuals. A promoter is a person who is essentially involved in the formation of a company

---

89 See *Cane v Jones* [1980] 1 WLR 1451.
90 See the leading English Court of Appeal case of *Bushell v Faith* [1970] AC 1099. The following may be considered: "(1) By the use of entrenched provisions. A clause can be inserted in the memorandum instead of the articles and declaring it to be unalterable. (2) Weighted shares may be used to prevent the passing of special resolution to alter the articles. (3) Adoption of an absentee article. The articles may provide that where there is a proposed alteration of an article, the quorum must include the member proposing the alteration. The member may then absent himself/herself from the meeting in order to prevent passing the resolution. (4) An application can be made to a court to cancel the alteration if a move is made to alter a clause which should have been in the articles but is put in the memorandum", ICSA, *op cit* fn 41, p 79.
91 See s 21 Companies Act 2006 (UK). For detailed alteration procedures of the articles, see s 16 Companies Act 2015 (K).
92 [1951] Ch 286; see also *Ebrahimi v Westbourne Galleries Ltd* [1973] AC 360.
93 On the effect of an alteration of articles on a contract of services with an employee or director of the company, see *Hickman v Kent or Romney Marsh Sheep-Breeders' Association* [1915] 1 Ch 881; *Eley v Positive Government Security Life Assurance Co Ltd* (1876) 1 LR Ex D 88; *Beattie v E & F Beattie Ltd* [1938] Ch 708; *Rend v Astoria Garage* [1952] Ch 637; *Nelson v James Nelson & Sons Ltd* [1914] 2 KB 770.

with reference to a given project who sets it going and who takes the necessary steps to accomplish that purpose.[94] In *Tracy v Mandalay Pty Ltd*, it was said that a promoter is a person who 'gets up the company'.[95] In *Erlanger v New Sombrero Phosphate Co*, it was said that:

> They [the promoters] have in their hands the creation and moulding of the company; they have the power of defining how, and when, and in what shape, and under what supervision, it shall start into existence and begin to act as a trading corporation.[96]

It is not necessarily the person who lodges the incorporation documents who is a promoter. A promoter could include a person who is instrumental only in bringing together the interests which are required to initiate the formation of the company business which leads to incorporation. A professional who performs services merely to bring into life a company is not considered in law as a promoter. To be a promoter, one must have a direct financial benefit or connection with the company sought to be formed.[97] First directors named in the articles or subsequent directors or other such beneficiaries such as shareholders can be regarded as promoters provided that they are instrumental in the formation of the company in the appropriate way.

The position of promoters has to be looked at in the overall context of company incorporation. They play a central role in getting the relevant administrative work done. They usually have clear goals for floating the company. Very often, they are directly responsible for securing the initial working capital through direct or indirect funding and therefore in initiating the company business. At the end of the day, they stand to reap rewards flowing from the prosperity of the company. Kiribati is the only country in the region where the duties of promoters have been laid down by statute.[98]

In view of all the relative roles of promoters and the companies that they are instrumental in bringing about, they must be subjected to rather onerous standards of accountability. In equity, promoters are treated as standing in a fiduciary relationship to the company as from the time of incorporation. Because of the fiduciary roles they occupy, they are answerable to the company for breach of any

---

94 *Tywcross v Grant* (1877) 2 CPD 469. For the duties of a promoter, see *Erlanger v New Sombrero Phosphate Co* (1878) 3 App Cas 1218; cf *Salomon v Salomon* [1897] AC 22; see s 121 Companies Act 2021 (K). For the position of pre-incorporation contracts in the United Kingdom, see s 43 Companies Act 2006 (UK). Vanuatu has a specific provision on pre-incorporation contracts, presumably developed along the English lines: see s 110 (V); ss 128–131 Companies Act 2021 (K).

95 [1953] HCA 9; 88 CLR 215.

96 (1878) 3 App Cas 1218 at 1236.

97 ICSA, *op cit* fn 41, p 32.

98 See s 121 (K).

fiduciary duty. Promoters are one type of fiduciary amongst others. Generally, a fiduciary relationship exists in equity where there is a relationship of imbalance such that one party stands in a position of privilege or power against another. As between the promoter and the company, the imbalance is clear enough. The promoter is able to commit the intended company to certain legal relationships which are negotiated in advance.

It is potentially a position which lends itself to abuse by promoters in the sense that they might derive personal benefit from their position at the expense of the putative company. For example, they might enter into contracts on behalf of the intended company in which they have some direct or indirect personal interest. As a result of this, equity treats them as fiduciaries of the company itself and imposes certain expectations on them, primarily in terms of an obligation of disclosure to an independently constituted meeting of the company. Any contract or other legal arrangement entered into by a promoter will be treated as capable of rescission by the new company unless it has been ratified by an independently constituted meeting of the company after full disclosure of material factors by the promoter.[99]

Finn comments on this duty as follows:

> A promoter does not safeguard himself by making a disclosure to confederates of his on the board. To be effective his disclosure to the company must be made to a board of directors independent of him, or to the existing and intended future members of the company as a whole, the latter disclosure usually being made in the prospectus or articles.[100]

In particular, promoters are susceptible to liability in pre-incorporation contracts and other expenses incurred in the formation of the company.[101] Some provisions now appear in the Companies Acts of the region which deal with pre-incorporation contracts.[102] The general rule is that a person who enters into a transaction on behalf of a non-existent company is personally responsible for such a contract.[103] This principle works on the assumption that a non-existent person has in law no capacity to contract. However, by relying on the principle of novation, the benefits or liability under a pre-incorporation contract could be transferred to an

---

99 *Tracy v Mandalay Pty Ltd* [1953] HCA 9; 88 CLR 215.
100 Finn, P, *Fiduciary Obligations: 40th Anniversary Republication with Additional Essays,* 2016, Sydney, Federation Press, p 227.
101 See *Phonogram Ltd v Lane* (1982) 1 QB 938; cf *Cotronic (UK) Ltd v Dezonie (t/a Wendaland Builders Ltd)* [1991] BCC 200 (25 February 1991).
102 See s 110 (V); see s 33 and Part 3 (Tu); ss 127–131 (K); see ss 73–5, Part 7 (F); s 110 (SI); see ss 114–6, Part 7, Division 1, Sub-division B (S); see ss 137–141, Part 9, Subpart 2 (CI); cf see ss 191, 194, Part X(T).
103 *Kelner v Baxter* [1866] LR 2 CP 174.

incorporated company. This provides an exception to the general rule as previously discussed.

5.7.3 Change in status of a company

It is possible to bring about a change in the status of a company already formed by transforming it into a different type of company. A conversion through the process of re-registration may involve a private company becoming public; a public company becoming private; limited becoming unlimited; and unlimited becoming limited.[104]

---

104 See s 76, Part 8 (F); see ss 245–249, Part XVIII (K); s 210, Part 14, Division 4 (SI); s 344, Part 14a (S); s 407 (CI); ss 20–23, 23(2) (Tu); s 210 (V); cf see s 353, Part XIX (T).

6

CAPITALISATION OF COMPANIES

6.1 Types of company capital

The equity capital of a company can basically be sub-classified into four types:[1] authorised, issued, called-up and reserve. The authorised (or nominal) capital (whether partly or fully paid up or whether it remains unpaid) must be stipulated at the time the company is incorporated.[2] The others might come into play depending on the nature and operations of the company. Issued share capital is capital that the company has actually put out for subscription by shareholders and taken up by them. This is sometimes called 'allotted share capital' and sometimes 'subscribed capital'. This represents the nominal value of shares allotted and issued to shareholders, although sometimes the amount contributed can in fact be more than the nominal value of the shares as determined by the memorandum and articles of the company. There are no specific requirements governing the issue of a company's authorised capital within the region, including in Kiribati where formerly under s 21(1) of the Companies Ordinance, it specified certain minimum levels of capital to be on issue at incorporation, which is not the case in the Companies Act 2021 (K).

The called-up share capital is the portion of the company's capital that shareholders have actually paid for, that is to say, in terms of partly paid shares as mentioned immediately above. Where a share is partly paid, the shareholder remains liable for the unpaid portion of the price of the share.[3] Reserve capital is the portion of the company's capital that is, in effect, set aside for use in the future. Not

---

1 This classification is not hard and fast.
2 Formerly, s 41 Companies Ordinance, now repealed. See Companies Act 2021 (K).
3 Section 547 Companies Act 2006 (UK).

DOI: 10.4324/9781003428060-7

all of the authorised capital of the company needs to be issued at any given time. For this reason, such amount is referred to as uncalled capital. Reserve capital can be brought into use by a special resolution of the company where the company goes into liquidation. At this point, it can be used to offset expenses that arise out of the liquidation.[4]

In the case of Kiribati, however, a company can only increase its share capital by means of a special resolution.[5] The difference in procedure is based on the fact that in Kiribati, the share capital of a company is specified in the Constitution. In the other jurisdictions, this is found in the memorandum of association. To alter the articles would therefore require the company to use a special resolution.

In all countries of the region, the Registrar of Companies must be notified of the increase. At the time of notification, the following documents are to be filed with the Registrar: particulars of the new shares created as a result of the increase in capital; a printed copy of the resolution authorising the increase of capital; and a printed copy of the altered memorandum reflecting the new changes in capital structure.[6]

A company can make alterations to its share capital by passing a special resolution at its general meeting. The alterations may affect the issued or unissued share capital of the company, provided that the articles of the company permit such alterations.[7] Alterations relating to the consolidation of existing shares into shares of larger denominations, division of existing shares into shares of larger nominal value and the cancellation of unissued shares are allowed.[8]

6.1.1 Reduction of authorised share capital

A company limited by shares is at liberty to reduce its share capital at any time, provided that it satisfies the conditions laid down by statute. The intention of the statutory guidelines is to ensure that the company's capital is maintained in the interest of the shareholders and is not wasted to the detriment of either the shareholders or the company. These guidelines are also aimed at ensuring that creditors are not prejudiced in their later attempts to recover funds from the company.

---

4 There are no explicit provisions for 'reserved capital'; see s 21, Part 6 of the Companies Act 2015 (F); no provision for 'reserve liability' in Companies Act (SI); no provision for 'reserve liability' in Companies Act (S and CI). In Samoa, see s 34 'Reserve liability' in International Companies Act 1988.
5 See s 63 Companies Act 2021. This provision is not as explicit as the 'Alteration of capital' in the former Act (K).
6 See ss 21–27, Companies Act (UK); s 48, 90 Companies Act (F); s 24 Companies Act (Ni); s 74 Companies Act (V); ss 312 and 313 Companies Act 2021 (S); ss 16, 55 and 82 Companies Act 2017 (CI).
7 See s 16 Companies Act 2021 (K).
8 See s 177(1)(e) Companies Act 2015 (F); see Part 3 (SI); and on conversion of shares which are fully paid into stock or stock into shares, see ss 189, 198, 199 (F); see 'arrangement' provisions as the new Act does not provide for alteration to share capital (V); see Part XIII, the new Act does not explicitly provide for alteration and reduction to share capital, in comparison to the former Act (K).

The principal, and indeed the only, method of reducing the authorised share capital is for the company to pass a special resolution. Such resolution is then subject to confirmation by the court. The articles of the company must also permit a reduction of capital, although they can of course be amended by another special resolution to achieve that effect.[9] Through this process, the company may then extinguish or reduce liability on any of its shares in respect of share capital not paid up. It may also be able to cancel any paid-up share capital which is lost or not represented by available assets with or without extinguishing; reduce liability on any of its shares; or pay off any paid-up share capital which is in excess of the wants of the company.[10]

Reduction of capital raises some problems for shareholders, creditors or the company itself. Due to this reason, it is always viewed seriously by regulators in different countries. For the shareholders, a reduction in the company's capital would likely mean a cancellation of some of the existing shares held by them. This can result in shareholders losing their holdings and thus effectively being thrown out of the company. This is the greatest danger posed by a reduction of share capital to a shareholder.

Creditors might also be uneasy about a reduction in share capital, as this would mean that some of the shares of the company have not been backed by tangible assets. Assets of the company are very often likely to be wasted in the process of reduction of capital. This might weaken the asset base of the company, thereby leaving the creditors vulnerable to loss.

In respect of the company itself, reduction of capital can constrain the company's ability to garner and utilise its capital.[11] Investors are usually dissuaded from moving into companies that have recently reduced their capital. This might also indicate a weakening of the company's financial base, although this is not

---

9 See generally ss 641–653, Chapter 10 of Part 17, Companies Act 2006 (UK); see Part 18, Division 1–4 of Companies Act 2015(F); similar to V, the new Act provides no provision for this, in comparison the former Act (ss 64–69 Companies Act) (SI); s 24 International Business Companies Act (Ni) repealed. The Companies Act 2006 (N) makes no provision for this, which is similar to the situation in V and SI; unlike the former Act (ss 75–80), the new Act provides no provision for this Companies Act (V); s 63 Companies Act (N); no express provision in N, S and CI dealing with reduction of share capital (CI); ss 6 and 8 Companies Act (T) – although there is no express provision in Tonga dealing with reduction of share capital; ss 70–73, Division 5 Companies Act [Cap 40.08] (Tu).

10 Formerly, s 75 Companies Act (V), although there is no express provision for this in the new Companies Act 2012 and the new Companies Act 2009 (SI); see Part 18, Division 1–4 of Companies Act 2015 (F), although there is no express provision in Fiji dealing with reduction of share capital. Formerly, Kiribati had a different procedure specified – see s 43 and especially s 46, although there is no express provision for this in the new Companies Act 2021; no express provision in dealing with reduction of share capital in the Companies Act (S) and (CI).

11 It is important to note the distinction between issued and unissued shares of a company when discussing reduction of share capital. A limited company is at liberty to extinguish unissued shares, which may consequently reduce the authorised or nominal capital of the company. Legally speaking, by so doing, the financial buoyancy of a company will not be affected.

always the case. For all these reasons, a company cannot reduce its capital in such a way as to hamper its effective operations. This factor informs the need for any company to effectively maintain its capital.

6.1.2 Maintenance of capital

For any business entity to survive in a potentially turbulent commercial environment, it must not only be in a position to attract capital but should also be in a position to retain and improve its financial buoyancy. This, in a simple way, explains why it is important for a company to maintain its capital. But there are other justifications for such a proposition. Traditionally it was the interests of creditors or potential creditors of the company which needed to be protected. Thus, in *Trevor and another v Whitworth and others*, it was held that the creditors of a limited company "are entitled to assume that no part of the capital which has been paid into the coffers of the company has been subsequently paid out, except in the legitimate course of business".[12] This gave rise to the doctrine of maintenance of share capital, which prohibited a company from reducing its share capital. The position has been subsequently affected by various statutory provisions which permit capital reductions, but only subject to certain conditions.

A company generates its capital from members' subscriptions, whether or not the consideration is fully paid at the time of issue. It is apparent, though, that a subscriber still remains liable on the unpaid portion of the shares subscribed. In this scenario, there may legally be nothing stopping a company that is trading at loss from losing its capital. The law purports to safeguard subscribed capital which must be kept in the hands of the company in order to help it offset its debts, except to the extent that it is lost or eroded in proper trading activities. But in effect, the capital maintenance doctrine strikes down not only direct attempts to return subscribed capital to members; it also strikes down indirect methods such as where the company purports to finance the purchase of its own shares.

The following principles are relevant aspects of the capital maintenance rule at the present time:

(1) The premium amount arising from the issue of company shares at a premium must be paid into a special account called the share premium account. The issue of shares at a premium is a way of attracting an additional contribution on the shares over and above the actual issue price. Only the difference between the nominal and the premium amount of the issue is to be deposited in the share premium account. But from a technical point of view the premium, not being part of the price of the issued share in itself might not be thought to be capital. The share premium account is different from the

---

12 [1886-90] All ER Rep 46 at 423–24.

share capital account. Whilst the latter can be used in the day-to-day running of the company, the former can only be utilised by the company in special circumstances.[13] This helps to provide some measure of financial stability to the company in the event of need. Section 3 of the Companies Act of Fiji provides:

'Share premium account' means an account containing a sum equal to the aggregate amount or value of the premiums on shares issued at a premium to their par value, whether for cash or otherwise.[14]

(2) As a general rule, the shares of a company should not be allotted at a discount. In other words, the discounting of shares is a practice which infringes the capital maintenance rule, at least as a matter of principle. The objective of issuing shares is for a company to raise capital with which it can operate its business. Where shares are issued at a discount, the company is likely to be deprived of the needed revenue it would have earned if such shares were sold at the nominal value or even at a premium. By always issuing shares at the nominal or premium rate, a company would not only be in a position to raise the needed capital but could also create a strong financial base. The Companies Acts in the region have definite provisions prohibiting a company from issuing shares at a discount except in specified circumstances.[15]

(3) Companies should not generally fund the buying of their own shares. If allowed to do so, companies would often have to pay for these shares from the capital of the company.[16] This in a technical sense would amount to a depletion of the capital base of the company. Where the capital base is depleted, the shareholders, creditors and the company would certainly be affected by a loss in the value of the assets of the company. Except for Tonga, other island jurisdictions within the region have provisions[17] prohibiting companies from funding or providing financial assistance for buying their shares or those of their subsidiaries. This should not, however, be confused with a company

---

13 See s 610, Chapter 7 Companies Act 2006 (UK); s 22 (Ni); s 65 Companies Act (Tu). The share premium account: (a) may be used to pay up shares under a bonus issue; (b) may be used for pre-incorporation expenses.

14 See ss 3, 196 of Companies Act 2015 (F); formerly, s 44 Companies Ordinance, although there is no equivalent provision for share premium in the Companies Act 2021 (K), s 65 Companies Act (Tu). There is no equivalent provision in S, V and Tonga.

15 See generally, s 64–65 Companies Act (Tu); there is no equivalent provision in CI, K, NI, S, Tonga, V; s 580, Chapter 5 Companies Act 2006 (UK); redeemable shares: cf s 33, Division 6, Part 3 of Companies Act 2009 (SI); ss 684–89, Chapter 3 (UK); s 191 Companies Act (F); ss 33–34, Division 6, Part Companies Act 2012 (V); ss 40–43 Companies Act 2021 (K). See also *Ooregun Gold Mining Co of India Ltd v Roper* [1892] AC 125.

16 Cf s 224, Division 4 of Part 18 Companies Act 2015 (F); s 55 Companies Act [Cap 40.08] (Tu).

17 See, generally, ss 232–36, Division 6, Part 18 Companies Act (F); s 54 Companies Act, Division 3, Part 4 (Tu); s 35, Division 7, Part 3 Companies Act (V); s 36, Division 7, Part 3 Companies Act (S); s 44, Subpart 8, Part 5 Companies Act (CI); s 44, Part 5 (K); s 35, Division 7, Part 3 (SI); cf ss Chapter 3, Part 18, Companies Act 2006 (UK).

accepting a gift of its shares. This in normal circumstances is a permissible practice.[18] There is no statutory backing for this procedure in the Companies Acts in the region.

(4) As a general rule, public companies are prohibited from making any allotment of shares unless shareholders have paid the minimum subscription on the shares.[19] This practice is consistent with the requirement for payment of executed consideration in ordinary sale contracts. The objective is to provide the company with some funds at allotment. The balance could be followed up later. If all allotments of shares were allowed to be taken up by shareholders without any payments, no proceeds would pour into the coffers of the company. The implications for this sort of situation are not far-fetched for any new business entity eager to generate funds in order to commence business.

(5) As a general rule again, dividends cannot be paid out of capital. In the event that dividends are to be paid out of profits,[20] the company must deduct all expenses before such payments are made to shareholders. The implication of this rule in English company practice is obvious. Once declared after any given trading year, the dividends become debt owed by the company to its shareholders. If this should be paid out of capital, there is a likelihood of depletion in the asset base of the company. Whilst shareholders would go away smiling, having been paid their dividends, the company might end up in a financial straitjacket.

Except in the case of Kiribati, Tuvalu and Niue, there is no single statutory provision on this issue in any of the other South Pacific countries. In those countries, unlike the United Kingdom, the issue has been left for the articles of association to deal with.

6.1.3 Allotment of the share capital

The share capital of a company is subscribed by shareholders through the process of allotment.[21] Allotment is the mechanism through which the shares of a company are provided to prospective shareholders at the time of issue of the shares. There are other ways in which a person can become a shareholder in a company. They can receive the shares by way of a transfer *inter vivos* from an existing shareholder as a result of a gift or a purchase. Alternatively, a person might acquire them by way of transmission after the death of an existing shareholder under the deceased

---

18 *Re Castiglione's Will Trust* [1958] Ch 232, Division 4 of Part 18 Companies Act 2015; ss 677–80, Chapter 2, Part 18 Companies Act 2006 (UK).

19 See s 49, Division 2, Part IV, Companies Act 1991 [Cap 40.08] (Tu).

20 See s 687, Chapter 3, Companies Act 2006 (UK). See also *Re Exchange Banking Co (Flitcroft's Case)* [1882] 21 Ch 519 CA; cf *House of Fraser v ACGE Investments Ltd* [1987] AC 387.

21 Except the first subscribers in the registered memorandum of the company.

shareholder's will or under the intestacy rules.[22] We will deal with these situations later. However, allotment is concerned with issue of shares by the company itself.

Allotment is regarded as a form of contract. Here the prospective shareholder makes an application to the company requesting allotment of shares. Where the company accepts this offer, the shares will be allotted by the company and the applicant thus becomes a shareholder. The power to allot shares is governed by the articles and is usually vested in the directors of the company.[23]

Allotment processes are more detailed in cases of public companies than in private companies. The reason is obvious. Public companies are by law empowered to advertise their shares to the public and as a result, have to comply with stringent conditions aimed at safeguarding the public. Most public companies might also venture to trade their shares on the stock exchange, thereby exposing themselves to further regulatory requirements governing the allotment of shares.

There are no complications with allotment of shares by private companies. For public companies which are listed on the stock exchange, two steps are normally adopted: issuance of a renounceable allotment letter; and entry of applicant name on Registrar and return of allotment.[24] The effect of an allotment is to make an applicant a member of the company.[25]

As has been said earlier on, the power to allot shares is exercisable by the board of directors of the company. In most cases, it is the board that determines the terms of the contract of allotment. The directors can only exercise this power to allot where they are so authorised by the articles of association. In the alternative, they may be authorised to allot by means of an ordinary resolution of the members in a general meeting.[26]

Because allotment of shares is a contract between the company and the allotee, it has to be supported by consideration. Consideration for shares can be in cash or in kind.[27] Payment of shares is to be at the nominal value or at a premium.[28] Where allotment of shares is to be made as bonus issue, it is regarded as payment of full

---

22 Transmission can also result from bankruptcy of the existing shareholder.
23 Because this is a matter usually dealt with in the articles, there are no statutory provisions in the South Pacific.
24 See Roach, L, *Company Law*, 2nd edn, 2022, London, BPP OUP Publishing, pp 111–12 on the UK approach.
25 See ss 549–51 Chapter 2, Part 17 of Companies Act 2006 (UK); apart from s 82 Companies Act, there is no equivalent provision on 'allotment of shares' from the former Act (F) and (V).
26 See ss 549–51 Chapter 2, Part 17 of Companies Act 2006 (UK).
27 See s 553 (UK); no equivalent provision (Ni); cf s 57 Companies Act [Cap 40.08] (Tu); s 61 Tuvalu defines payment by cash.
28 But what is significant is that in allotting shares, a company is required to obtain in money or in money's worth consideration of a value at least equal to the nominal value of the shares. This explains why shares are issued at par. This is the no-discount rule. A company shall not fix a price which is less than the nominal value of the shares. See s 552 (UK); no equivalent provision (F) allowing for the issue of shares at a discount under certain conditions. No equivalent provision (K), (Ni), (SI), (V); cf in Samoa, where it is possible if sanctioned by a court.

consideration. This is because reserve funds that are regarded as shareholders' funds can then be converted into fixed capital, which is used to pay for the bonus issue on behalf of the members.[29]

The issue of shares on a no-discount basis is generally regarded as a rule affecting public companies.[30] Private companies are free to allot shares to be paid for at a discount or by means of non-cash consideration. Payment by non-cash consideration in the case of public company shares requires independent valuation in order to ascertain the full and fair price of the non-cash consideration.

It appears that the need for a valuation of non-cash consideration is as yet not a statutory requirement in any of the South Pacific island jurisdictions, especially in payment for shares of private companies. This position replicates the general common law position in respect of private companies where a company can allot shares for inadequate consideration by accepting goods or services even where they are overvalued.[31] Whilst in general terms, courts do not always interfere with valuation of shares, auditors could be challenged if the valuation was considered unfair.[32] However, the courts have the power in appropriate cases to step in and regulate an unguarded valuation.

In respect of public companies, however, the rules for payment of shares are more rigid. No private valuation of the consideration for shares is allowed. The valuation must be carried out by a competent and independent valuer. It also appears that this is not a statutory requirement for payment of shares of public companies in the region. The nearest provision to this in the region is s 59 of the Companies Act 1991 of Tuvalu. What is clear, though, in the case of Tuvalu but missing in the other island countries is that executory consideration in the form of services to be performed cannot be accepted as consideration for shares except where the services have already been performed.[33]

Furthermore, a company must, at the time of allotment, receive at least one-quarter of the nominal value of the shares. This is applicable in jurisdictions like Kiribati and outside the region in the United Kingdom where a public company has a minimum nominal share capital.[34]

6.1.4 Return of allotment

Where a company limited by shares makes an allotment of its shares, it must within a specified period deliver to the Registrar of Companies prescribed

---

29 A bonus issue is also called a capitalisation issue or scrip issue. See Chapter 5, Part 17 (UK); no equivalent provision, Companies Act 2006 (Ni).
30 No equivalent provision for the 'issue of shares at a discount' in Companies Act 2021 (K).
31 See s 59 Companies Act [Cap 40.08] (Tu).
32 See *Dean v Price* [1953] Ch 590 at 591; [1954] Ch 409.
33 Cf s 583(2) Companies Act (UK).
34 See s 552 (UK).

information regarding the allotment of shares, including the number and classes of shares allotted, amounts paid and payable and the persons to whom they have been allotted.[35] The amount of allotted shares also determines the amount of stamp duty payable upon registration. There are criminal penalties for failure to comply with statutory provisions dealing with allotment.[36] In discussing return of allotment, and especially where a prospectus is used for public subscription of the company's shares, it is now a recognisable principle that a company can give financial assistance for the purchase of its shares where an employees' share scheme is in operation.[37]

6.1.5 Effect of irregular allotment

An irregular allotment is one that contravenes statutory requirements. An irregular allotment is voidable at the instance of the applicant. This option must be exercised within a specified period, normally within one month of holding the statutory meeting.[38]

Where a director contravenes or permits a contravention of any sections dealing with allotment, s/he shall be liable to compensate the company and the allottee respectively for any loss, damages or costs which the company or the allottee might have suffered.[39]

Other common law issues can arise in respect of an allotment. Because an allotment takes place by virtue of a contract, then clearly enough the contract might be breached, with consequential rights of action arising. Allotments can be affected by issues such as fraudulent, negligent and innocent misrepresentation, which might give rise to rights to damages and/or rescission according to general law principles.

---

35 Sees 53 [Cap 40.08] (Tu).
36 See ss 555–57, Chapter 2, Part 7 of Companies Act 2006 (UK); no equivalent provision in (F), (SI) and (V).
37 See s 1166 (UK). The scheme allows employees of a company to hold some shares in the company or other company of the same group. Spouses, widows or widowers of employees as well as their children up to 18 may be eligible. The company institutes the scheme usually by means of a trust where trustees acquire and hold shares on behalf of the beneficiaries. The trust operates by using money lent to it by the company, which repayment may be considered as allowable deduction for tax purposes. Cf s 44(K); s 36 (S) and s 44 (CI) but no equivalent provision (formerly, s 67 (NZ) in CI and S, which allows a company to issue labour shares). There is no nominal value on such shares and they do not form part of the capital of the company.
38 No equivalent provision in Companies Act 2012, although it was formerly covered under s 61 (V).
39 See formerly s 59 (NZ) (S), (CI), now no equivalent provision deals with this situation in recent Acts.

6.1.6 Prospectuses[40]

In the South Pacific jurisdictions, as elsewhere, public companies must advertise their shares to the public by means of an approved prospectus document. The document contains in effect an invitation to the public at large or to specified members of the public to subscribe to the shares of the company under certain conditions. The prospectus also covers a proposed issue of debentures by a company.[41]

It is also to be appreciated that an approved prospectus is required by law to be issued by a public company where it intends to make an offer or invitation to the public or a member of the public to subscribe for shares or indeed debentures in the company. This requirement is part of a policy of protecting potential investors in a company. Because the contents of the prospectus must contain certain prescribed information and reports, it operates as a mechanism to ensure that basic information is provided to the proposed investor such that the investor can make an informed decision about whether to invest in the company or not.

Companies are prohibited from making offers or invitations of their shares or debentures to the public or to members of the public except on the basis of an approved prospectus. Where an offer is made without a prospectus, the company is liable to criminal penalties and possibly other sanctions. It is to be noted that the prospectus is required only in respect of offers or invitations to the public or to members of the public. Hence not all offers by a company to an individual to take up shares in the company necessarily require a prospectus.

The determination of what is an offer or invitation to the public or to a member of the public has long been a vexed question. The difficulty in determining such an issue led to the abolition of this requirement in Australia with the introduction of the Corporations Law 1990. A prospectus is now required there in respect of any offering, public or not, although the concept is still retained for some other purposes. However, in the South Pacific jurisdictions, the requirement of publicity remains. This suggests that the courts are able to differentiate between offers which have some public character about them and which can be differentiated from a merely private offering or an offering to a person in a purely private capacity. The mere fact that an offer is made one-off or to an individual does not necessarily mean that it falls into the category of a private individual. The lines between the two are certainly blurred. The legislation, however, contains certain deeming provisions. Section 61 of the Companies Ordinance of Kiribati provides, for example:

---

40 See generally the following statutory provisions: ss 869–73 (UK); see s 284, Part 26 (F); no equivalent provision dealing with prospectuses (CI), (K), (S), (SI) and (V); ss 31–40, Part IV (N); s 40 deals with civil and not criminal liability.
41 See e.g. formerly s 63 (V), now no equivalent provision deals with prospectuses in Companies Act 2012.

61 (1) It shall not be lawful for a public company to allot or agree to allot any shares or debentures of the company unless the person to whom the shares or debentures are allotted has had delivered to him a copy of a prospectus which has been duly registered with the Registrar not earlier than 3 months before the date of such allotment or agreement to allot, and no form of application for shares or debentures of a public company shall be issued unless it be accompanied by a copy of a prospectus which has been so duly registered:

Provided that the provisions of this section shall not apply where the allotment or agreement to allot is not made pursuant to a public offer of shares or debentures.

(2) It shall not be lawful for any person to make a public offer of any shares or debentures without the consent of the Registrar who in granting such consent may impose such conditions or restrictions as he may think proper.

(3) For the purposes of this Ordinance a public offer shall be deemed to be made if an offer or invitation to make an offer is

(a) made, whether orally or in writing, circulated, advertised, published or disseminated by newspaper, broadcasting, cinematograph or by any other means whatsoever; and

(b) made to any 1 or more persons whether selected as members or debenture holders of the company concerned or clients, customers or creditors of the company or of the person making the offer or in any other manner:

Provided that –

(a) a public offer shall not be deemed to be made in the case of –
   (i) an offer to existing holders of shares or debentures of the same class as the shares or debentures comprised in the offer without any right of renunciation; or
   (ii) an offer without any right of renunciation to the holders of convertible debentures or debentures having subscription rights in respect of shares of the class into or in respect of which the right of conversion or subscription exists, or if the offer is certified in writing by the Registrar to be an offer which the Registrar considers as not being calculated to result, directly or indirectly in the shares or debentures becoming available to more than 20 persons or to persons other than those to whom the offer is made and which the Registrar considers as being a domestic concern of the persons making and receiving the offer; and

(b) if any such offer which under the provisions aforesaid is not a public offer is made in writing or published or disseminated by newspaper, broadcasting, or cinematograph or any other means not being an oral invitation made to any individual or group of individuals not exceeding 10 the terms of such offer may be approved by the Registrar.

(4) For the purposes of this Ordinance any public invitation to deposit money with or to lend money to any company shall be deemed for the purposes of this Ordinance to be an offer to allot debentures of the company and any such public offer to deposit money or lend money shall only be made by or on behalf of a company which the Minister by order made under this section authorises to make a public invitation in terms of this section; and Minister may in granting his authority impose such conditions and restrictions as he may consider proper and, without prejudice to the generality of the foregoing, the Minister may require that a copy of an advertisement, circular or brochure relating to such invitation shall be approved by and delivered to the Registrar for registration before it is published.

The terms of s 61(3) and the exceptions provided by s 61(4) are to be noted. Certainly, an offer to an existing individual member of the company is excluded as a non-public offering, but this would certainly not exempt an offer made to a non-member on an individual basis. It is to be noted that in some circumstances an offer which is not a public offering still cannot be made without approval by the Registrar.

There are detailed provisions in the Companies Acts of the region dealing with prospectuses. A basic overview of the relevant provisions will be provided here. The following represent a summary of the matters that need to be contained in a prospectus. By law, every prospectus issued by or on behalf of a company must be dated and specify matters in the relevant schedule to the Act.[42] It must be lodged with the relevant Companies Registry for approval and registration.

Certain matters must be included in a prospectus. This includes information relating to projects for which finance is sought by way of the share issue. Financial reports and records must be provided along with supporting statements of experts, directors and auditors. Experts' consent is always required before the issue of a prospectus containing statements of the opinion of the expert.[43] After the issue of a prospectus, a public company can only alter the contents of its memorandum subject to general meeting.[44] Civil liability may visit any statement in a prospectus issued by a company that is untrue, misleading or contains omissions.[45] The stock exchange has a role to play in determining the contents of the prospectus where the company is a public company whose shares are quoted on the stock exchange.[46]

---

42 Cf s 52 Companies Act [Cap 40.08] 1991 (Tu).
43 Formerly, s 55, now no equivalent provision deals with this, Companies Act 2012 (V).
44 Formerly, s 44, now ss 291–92 of the Companies Act 2015 although no explicitly equivalent provision (F).
45 See *Derry v Peek* (1889) 14 App Cas 337. Formerly, s 56, now no equivalent provision deals with this (V).
46 As above (V).

Criminal liability surrounding conduct relating to prospectuses has been statutorily provided for in all of the jurisdictions. The statutes prescribe varying degrees of criminal sanctions for violating the provisions governing the issuance of a prospectus. A number of people in a company might be held individually or collectively responsible for inaccuracies or false and misleading statements in a prospectus.[47]

Defences are available in any claim for compensation against a company for having issued a prospectus that failed to comply with the statutory provisions. Two likely defences can avail a defendant, provided that (a) the defendant reasonably believed that there was no misstatement or omission and had taken reasonable steps to ensure that there were not any, and if there were, they were corrected; and (b) the plaintiff acquired the securities with the knowledge of the falsity of the statement or the matter omitted.[48]

6.2 Shares[49]

6.2.1 Nature of share

A share is a class of property that is intangible. It falls within the definition of a chose in action. In monetary terms, a share represents the interest a person has in a company. It is transferable. Inherent in the nature of a share is a combination of rights and obligations. The definition of a share must therefore entail some essential characteristics: liability; ability to derive dividends; and ability to influence decisions in a company through voting.[50] The share capital of a company is usually divided into units of shares, with each possessing a specific value. This denotes the nominal value of a share represented in monetary terms.

6.2.2 Types of shares[51]

Shares are classified according to the nature of rights conceded to the holders of them. The usual concept of shares is that they are, in effect, bundles of rights. These rights determine the extent of the involvement of shareholders in the distribution

---

47 There are no equivalent provisions in the Companies Act 2012 (V). Persons responsible include the issuer, directors of the company, each person who has authorised himself or herself to be named as a director, each person who accepts liability for any parts of the prospectus and each person who has authorised the contents of the particulars.

48 Formerly, s 56(2) provided for this. The new Act does not (V).

49 See generally the following statutory provisions: ss 540–46 (UK); s 237, Part 19 (F); ss 20–24, Part 3 (Ni); ss 19–23, Part 3 (SI); ss 19–23, Division 1, Part 3 (V); ss 20–24, Division 1, Part 3 (S); ss 18–22, Subpart 1, Part 5 (CI); ss 15–21 (T); ss 80–90, Division 5, Part IV (N).

50 See s 18, Part V (K); ss 19–23, Part 3 (SI); s 62 (Tu). See the dictum of Farwell J in *Borland's Trustee v Steel Bros & Co Ltd* [1901] 1 Ch 279 for a succinct definition of a share.

51 See generally ss 21(3), 40–44, 63 and 64 (K) and ss 33–34 (SI).

of dividends out of profits of the company, the right to vote at meetings and other rights such as this.

Ordinary shares are the commonest and most widely issued shares by companies. These shares are seized of two important attributes. They can participate in the distribution of dividends in the event of profits being declared as such but attract no dividends in any given trading year where the company declares a trading loss. Ordinary shares carry voting powers and can thus influence the management of companies. Preference shares carry the right to participate in the distribution of dividends. They do not usually have voting power but in particular cases they might do. Their greatest attraction is that they can (where provided by the articles) accumulate and carry over dividends to the next trading year if the company had declared losses in the previous trading year. Preference shares can also be redeemable shares.

Founders' or deferred shares, as the name suggests, are shares created and at incorporation are allotted specifically to the founders of the company. Special rights (for instance life membership) might attach to such shares. This practice is normally prevalent only in private companies.

6.2.3 Redeemable shares

A redeemable share is one which the company can at a later date take back after compensating the shareholder.[52] If permitted by its articles, a company having a share capital can issue redeemable shares. As a general rule, a company cannot have a share capital only made up of redeemable shares. If shares are not originally issued as redeemable, they cannot later be converted to such. The company can only redeem fully paid-up shares.[53] A company has power to issue preference shares that are redeemable.[54]

6.2.4 Rights of pre-emption

Pre-emptive rights are rights accorded to the remaining company shareholders giving them the right to acquire shares which one or more of the shareholders propose to sell or dispose of. The articles of association provide for this right, which is common enough in respect of private companies. When shares of a company are to be sold by the individual shareholder, they are to be offered to existing shareholders before anyone else. In other words, the other shareholders are provided

---

52 On redeemable shares, see ss 684–89, Chapter 3, Part 18 (UK); ss 3, s 191, Division 1, Part 17 (F); ss 33–34, Division 6, Part 3 (V); s 40 (K).

53 See ss 684–89, Chapter 3, Part 18 (UK); ss 3, s 191, Division 1, Part 17 (F); s 33–34, Division 6, Part 3 (SI) and (V); ss 34–35, Division 6, Part 3 (S); s 40 Subpart 7, Part 5 (CI); s 66, Division 5, Part IV (Tu).

54 See, ss 3, s 191, Division 1, Part 17 (F); ss 33–34, Division 6, Part 3 (V); s 40 (K).

with the first option to buy and thereby with the opportunity to retain ownership of the company. If the pre-emptive offering is not accepted, the shares can then be allotted to anyone willing to pay. Countries in the region deal with pre-emption rights in the articles of association of mainly private limited companies.[55]

6.2.5 Variation of class rights[56]

The share capital of a company can be made up of different types or classes of shares. As such, the rights attached to issued shares can only be altered after due consultation with the affected shareholders. The consent should accord with the stipulation of the articles of the company. This is with a view to protecting shareholders of the class of shares that will be affected by the variation. This is no such problem with unissued shares because no shareholders have as yet taken up the shares. The right subsisting on them may be cancelled at any time.

Generally speaking, an extraordinary resolution is required to grant approval to the variation. A special resolution passed at a separate meeting of the class or by written consent is required.[57] Minority shareholders have a right of appeal to a court against the decisions of the majority.[58] They should hold a certain percentage of shares in the class in question, and should not have consented to the variation; they can apply to the court, usually within 21 days, for cancellation of such variation.[59]

6.2.6 Transfer of shares

Because shares form part of intangible property, they can be transferred from one person to another, just as in cases of other classes of property. Once a share is registered, a holder becomes the legal owner of a share. Before then, the person is an equitable owner. The articles usually give directors the power to refuse to register a transfer of shares where they deem it as not being in the interest of the company.[60] The procedures for transferring shares in both public and private companies

---

55 Cf generally, Chapter 3, Part 17 (UK).

56 See, generally, the following: Division 3, Part 16 (F); s 53, Division 2, Part 4 (SI); s 53, Division 2, Part 4 (V); s 63–66, Part VI (K); s 64 (N).

57 See ss 630–35, Chapter 9, Part 17 Companies Act 2006 (UK); Division 3, Part 16 (F); 53, Division 2, Part 4 (SI); s 53, Division 2, Part 4 (V); s 54, Division 2, Part 4 Companies Act 2001 (S); see s 63, Subpart 3, Part 6, although there is no equivalent provision (CI); see ss 63–66, Part VI Companies Act 2021, although there is no equivalent provision (K); see s 117 Companies Act, although there is no equivalent provision (T).

58 See *House of Fraser Plc v ACGE Investments* [1987] AC 387.

59 See, generally, the following: Division 3, Part 16 (F); s 53, Division 2, Part 4 (SI); s 53, Division 2, Part 4 (V); ss 63–66, Part VI (K); s 64 (N).

60 See s 245 Companies Act 2015 (F); s 90 Companies Act 1991 [Cap 40.08] (Tu).

are similar, though not identical.[61] However, the end result of a transfer of shares in both cases is to confer some form of proprietary interest on the buyer.

In respect of both private and public companies in the South Pacific, the registered holder occasions a transfer by completing the stock transfer form. This is delivered to the purchaser together with the share certificate. The buyer completes the transfer and pays stamp duty before handing it over to the company for registration.[62] For the transfer of shares to be completed, certification of the shares transferred is required. Certification therefore seals the processes of share transfer from the transferor to the transferee. The company therefore becomes bound by the outcome of the certified shares.

Section 247 of the Companies Act of Vanuatu Cap 2015 provides:

247 – (1) The certification by a Company of an instrument of transfer of Specified Securities of the Company – (a) is taken as a representation by the Company to any person acting on the faith of the certification that there have been produced to the Company such documents as on the face of them show prima facie title to the Specified Securities in the transferor named in the instrument of transfer; and (b) is not taken as a representation that the transferor has any title to the Specified Securities.

Section 247(2) further provides:

If a person acts on the faith of a false certification by a Company made negligently, the Company is under the same liability to the person as if the certification had been made fraudulently. There are equivalent provisions in all the other Island jurisdictions of the South Pacific.[63]

---

61 On the processes of certification of shares, see also ss 37–38, Division 9, Part 3 (SI), viz sometimes the whole shares may be transferred by a registered holder. In this case, the following procedures are to be followed: (i) holder sends a signed 'allotment form' with his or her share certificate to the company; (ii) the transfer is returned to the holder accepting lodgement of the certificate; (iii) the holder hands over transfer to the buyer; (iv) the buyer goes on to pay stamp duties; (v) a new certificate for the sold shares is issued to the buyer by the company. See also s 775, Chapter 1, Part 21 Companies Act 2006 (UK), s 10 (K); ss 38, 40 (S), ss 54–55 (CI).

62 Public companies in the United Kingdom transfer their shares today through an automated system. The primary mechanism for securities settlement in the United Kingdom is the Central Securities Depository (CSD) operated by Euroclear UK & Ireland. The settled trades are then transferred electronically through the CSD, which holds the securities in electronic form. In the United Kingdom, this is often facilitated by CREST (CREST Co Limited), which is the United Kingdom and Ireland's central securities depository for the electronic settlement of trades. The CREST replaced the previous electronic settlement system, TALISMAN, in late April 1997.

63 See s 775, Chapter 1, Part 21 Companies Act 2006 (UK); s 247 Companies Act (F); see Division 9–10, Part 3 Companies Act (V); cf s 775, Chapter 1, Part 21 (UK). No equivalent provision, generally see ss 47–55 Companies Act 2021 (K) and s 92 Companies Act [Cap 40.08] (Tu).

6.2.7 Certification

Sometimes, a registered holder might wish to transfer all of the shares held in the company. In this case, the following procedures are to be followed: the holder sends a signed with his or her share certificate to the company. The transfer is then returned to the holder by accepting lodgement of the certificate. The holder then hands over transfer to the buyer. The buyer goes on to pay stamp duties. Finally, a new certificate for the sold shares is issued to the buyer by the company.

Certification is a representation by the company to any person acting on the faith of the certification that documents have been produced to the company which, on the face of them, show a *prima facie* title to the shares comprised in the transfer. It is not a representation that the seller has any title to them, but it does imply that the certificate will be retained.[64]

6.3 Shareholders

The effects of the articles and the memorandum at incorporation provide the foundation for membership of a company. A shareholder can loosely be regarded as a person with financial interest in a company through investing in its shares. In this segment of the book, we have taken the word 'shareholder' to be synonymous with 'member'. A shareholder acquires property in the shares. But at the same time, the shares define the right of the shareholder to participate in the company. In other words, shares are also participatory interests. The extent of the participation is defined by reference to the articles of association of the company. As shares might be issued in different classes, the right of the holder to participate in the company can vary from one case to another.

6.3.1 Becoming a member[65]

Membership of a company can be achieved in a variety of ways. Perhaps the primary method of becoming a member of a company is by subscription to the company's memorandum of association. This is done at the time of incorporation. Other methods include allotment and acquisition of the legal title to shares by either *inter vivos* transfer from an existing shareholder or transmission on the death of an existing shareholder.

---

64 See 775, Chapter 1, Part 21 Companies Act 2006 (UK); s 247 Companies Act (F); see Division 9–10, Part 3 Companies Act (V); see s 94 Companies Act 1991 [Cap 40.08] (Tu) for detailed registration procedures.

65 See generally s 112, Chapter 1, Part 8 Companies Act (UK); ss 3, 14 Companies Act (F); no equivalent provision in Companies Act 2009 (SI) and (V) and the distinction between member and shareholder is unclear (SI); no equivalent provision in the Companies Act, and distinction between member and shareholder is also unclear (S), (CI).

As regards original subscription, s 36 of the Companies Act Cap 191 of Vanuatu states:

> The subscribers of the memorandum of a company shall be deemed to have agreed to become members of the company, and on its registration shall be entered as members in its register of members.[66]

Section 36(2) permits the acquisition of membership through other means. It provides:

> Every other person who agrees to become a member of a company, and whose name is entered in its register of members, shall be a member of the company.

Based on the strength of s 36(2), the following practices have been evolved as means by which persons become members of a company. The principle of registration is central to the idea of membership and therefore shareholding. It is registration on the company's register which provides for legal ownership, although clearly a person might have a claim to ownership in equity in respect of an unregistered interest. Furthermore, membership is defined by reference to legal ownership in this sense rather than with respect to beneficial or equitable ownership of shares.[67] The register itself serves as *prime facie* evidence of the matters contained in it.

By looking at the foregoing statutory provisions, it is possible to identify several possible ways by which a person or a group of persons can become members in a company. A person whose name is entered in the register of members is automatically considered a member.[68] A person may also agree to become a member of a company. This is possible where the person has decided to subscribe to the memorandum of the company.[69]

Furthermore, a person can also become a member by applying for shares and by the company allotting the shares, so also by submitting a share transfer form for registration by the company.[70] Today, it is also possible in the South Pacific region for a person to become a member of a company by applying as personal

---

66 See, generally ss 3, 14 Companies Act (F).
67 *Re Wala Wynaad Indian Gold Mining Co* (1882) 21 Ch D 849; *Patcorp Investments v Federal Commissioner of Taxation* (1976) 10 ALR, at pp 124–125; 6 ATR at 420; *Bond Corp Pty Ltd v White Industries* [1980] 2 NSWLR 351.
68 There is no equivalent provision in the Companies Act 2009 (SI), although it was dealt with in the former Act, s 27(1), (2); s 30(1)–(2) Companies Act (T); see also *Re Nuneaton Borough Association Football Club Limited* (1989) 5 BCC 377.
69 There is no equivalent provision in the Companies Act 2009 (SI), although it was dealt with in the former Act, s 27(1), (2); s 30(1)–(2) Companies Act (Tu).
70 See *Steinberg v Scala (Leeds) Ltd* (1923) 2 Ch 452, although dealing with an infant shareholder.

representative of a deceased member or trustee of a bankrupt member to be registered as the holder of the member's shares in the company.[71]

As noted above, it is registration of a transfer on the company register which would give a transferee legal ownership of the shares to which the transfer relates. However, there are situations where a person can claim ownership in equity of the shares before registration is achieved. This is dependent on the application of equitable rules relating to the transfer of property and creation of trusts. It is first necessary to distinguish two types of transfer: those which are for voluntary consideration and those which are not.

In respect of the former, the existence of a specifically enforceable contract with respect to the shares would entitle the transferee to ownership in equity from the time of the contract and therefore before completion and registration. This is on the basis of the application of the equitable maxim, 'equity treats as done that which ought to be done'. The second situation involves transfers by way of gift; that is, voluntary transfers. This situation is covered by the rules in *Milroy v Lord*.[72] Equity will not come to the assistance of a volunteer and will not perfect an imperfect gift. The requirement of the first rule in *Milroy v Lord* is that the transferor must have done all that s/he could to perfect the assignment before the gift will be given force in equity. This would seem to mean that where a transferor has executed a transfer of shares in proper form and delivered it with the share certificate to the transferee, then the transferee is in a position to complete the registration of the transfer without any further assistance from either the transferor or the court.[73] In such a case, the transferee has the equitable ownership of the shares before registration. But where, say, the transfer is handed over and the share certificate is retained by the transferor, the gift is imperfect. This is because the transferee is not in a position to obtain registration without assistance. Hence equity will not regard the transferee as entitled to any interest.

This applies only with respect to transactions which purport to be assignments by way of gift. Where it is apparent that what was intended was a declaration of trust rather than an immediate gift, the question will be whether the declaration of trust was brought about by a sufficiently clear manifestation of intention to create the trust. However, the second rule in *Milroy v Lord* suggests that the court will not deliberately misconstrue the obvious intentions of the parties in order to salvage the transaction. It will not, for example, construe something which was clearly intended as an assignment as a trust to save it from being struck down.

---

71 There is no equivalent provision in the Companies Act 2009 (SI), although it was dealt with in the former Act, s 27(1), (2), 28; generally, see ss 3, 14 (F); s 21(2), Division 4, Part 2 Companies Act (V); ss 8(3), 33, 43(3), 93 Companies Act (T).

72 (1862) 4 De GF & J 264.

73 This seems to be the import of the majority reasoning in *Anning v Anning* (1907) 4 CLR 1049, which seems to suggest that the transferor must have done everything that was within his or her legal power to do in order to complete the gift; cf *Re Rose* [1952] Ch 499.

6.3.2 Classes of membership

The classes of members will be dependent upon the types of shares held by the company. Each type of share is seized with distinct attributes, thereby conferring on it rights or obligations that might be different from other classes of shares.[74] Thus, differences in the classes of shares mean differences in the nature of shareholders' rights.

There are fundamental restrictions on membership in the articles of the company. This may differ from company to company as well as from jurisdiction to jurisdiction. What, however, determines these restrictions is the drafting pattern adopted in the articles.

Section 81(1) of the Companies Act Cap 191 of Vanuatu provides:

> If, in the case of a company the share capital of which is divided into different classes of shares, provision is made by the memorandum or articles for authorising the variation of the rights attached to any class of shares in the company, subject to the consent of any specified proportion of the holders of the issued shares of that class.

Variation of class rights could fundamentally affect the capital structure of a company, especially in situations where it results in a reduction of capital. The losers would certainly be the shareholders whose class of shares was cancelled.

6.3.3 Termination of membership

Membership of a company will come to an end in any of the following instances: death; bankruptcy; repudiation of shares by a minor; or where an absolute transfer of shares to another person duly takes place. It will also be brought about where a company is wound up, by forfeiture or acceptance of surrender of shares or sale in exercise of lien.[75]

6.3.4 Register of members

Companies are obliged to maintain a register of their members amongst their records. There are ample statutory provisions in the region dealing with the register of members, form and inspection of the register, location as well as rectification of errors in the register of members.[76]

---

74 Classes of shares include ordinary, preference and founders' shares.
75 See *The Law of Trusts Looseleaf 4th ed.* (Ford, HAJ, Lee, WA, Bryan, M, Glover J, Fullerton, I, 2019, Sydney, Thomson Reuters Australia Subscriptions), pp 153, 260.
76 See ss 81–90 Companies Act (F); ss 188–94 Companies Act (SI) and (V); see, generally, ss 366–76 Companies Act (T); ss 126–32 Companies Act (N).

As noted above, the register is central to the system of share ownership and therefore also membership. It also provides *prime facie* evidence of what is contained in it.

6.3.5 Nominee shareholdings

Due to the fact that a number of countries in the South Pacific region are either offshore finance centres, tax havens or both,[77] nominee shareholding, especially in trust companies, is increasingly becoming a feature of the company laws in these jurisdictions.

Nominee shareholding is a system of covering up the actual or beneficial owners of shares by an arrangement that allows the shares to be registered in the name of a nominee. A nominee may be an individual or a company. In a private company, it is easy to identify the beneficial owner, whilst it is rather difficult in public companies.

In cases of nominee shareholdings, a variety of important questions are often raised by tax regulators or other authorities because of the complexities of the arrangement and the secrecy in which they are often shrouded.

6.4 Dividends[78]

One of the major attractions of being a shareholder is benefiting from the profits made by a company in the form of dividends. This ties in squarely with the objective of investing capital and the consequent expectation of a return on the capital. Dividends provide a return on capital investment in the company, although there can also be returns in the form of capital growth when or if the shares are sold.

Dividends therefore represent the proportion of profits of a company that is to be distributed to shareholders as return on their investments. This is calculated at the end of a trading year.[79] Generally speaking, the distribution is specified in the articles of the company. As a rule, the board of directors of a company declares dividends. However, in the case of Tuvalu, a company in general meeting may declare dividends in respect of any year or period.[80]

In South Pacific jurisdictions, the question of dividends is a matter properly dealt with by the articles of the company. In most instances (the exceptions being Kiribati and to some extent Tuvalu), the Acts are silent on the issue. Where the statutes are silent, such countries could still have recourse to the common law

---

77 Cook Islands, Vanuatu and Samoa (international banking sector).
78 See s 830 Companies Act 2006 (UK); s 30 Companies Act (Ni); see also the relevant provisions in model articles in the schedule of the Companies Acts in respect of the other countries in the region.
79 See s 32 Companies Act 2021 (K).
80 See s 177 Companies Act 1991 [Cap 40.08] (Tu).

rules governing the generation and consequent distribution of dividends.[81] The following are some of the rules that are now applicable:

(1) A company may only make a distribution out of profits available for the purpose.
(2) A company's profits available for distribution are its accumulated, realised profits, so far as not previously utilised by distribution or capitalisation, less its accumulated, realised losses, so far as not previously written off in a reduction or reorganisation of capital duly made.
(3) Subsection (2) has effect subject to sections 832 [F1, 833A] and 835 (investment companies [F2 and Solvency 2 insurance companies]).[82]

Section 177 of the Companies Act [Cap 40.08] 1991 of Tuvalu and s 32 of the Companies Act of Kiribati are the only statutory provisions in the South Pacific that are in *pari materia* with those which obtain in the United Kingdom. Section 32(1)–(3) of the Companies Act 2021 of Kiribati provides:

(1) A company may pay a dividend to shareholders if–
    (a) the company complies with section 29; and
    (b) the dividend is authorised by–
        (i) all the shareholders under section 62; or
(2)   (ii) the directors, if the constitution so provides. A dividend authorised by the directors must comply with any conditions or restrictions set out in the constitution.
(3) Subject to the constitution and to the terms of issue of any share, a company must not pay a dividend–
    (a) in respect of some but not all the shares; or
    (b) that is of greater value per share in respect of some shares than of others.

The new law is silent as to whether it is now a generally recognisable principle that company directors have the power to declare both interim and final dividends.[83]

Formerly, the directors were liable where they unlawfully declared and distributed dividends. Directors who either agreed or participated in the decision

---

81 See s 32 Companies Act 2021 (K).
82 Section 830 Companies Act 2006 (UK).
83 Formerly, the idea that the directors could plough the profits back into the business of the company instead of distributing dividends was clear. They could capitalise the profits as bonus issues to existing shareholders or pay the profits into the share premium account; see s 32 Companies Act 2021 (K). The new Act is silent as to whether the statutory safeguards from the former Act (ss 66(6), (8)) are carried over. On the whole, the objective is unclear as to whether the new provision makes it easily flexible for a company paying out dividends to utilise forms of payment other than cash all the time.

of the company to unlawfully declare and distribute dividends were jointly and severally liable to make good the loss to the company.[84] There is no equivalent provision in the Companies Act of 2021 which deals with this.

Consequently, the requirements affecting the distribution of dividends in both public and private companies in Kiribati are unclear. In addition to these rules, public companies in the United Kingdom, for instance, are still subject to a further rule. By s 264 of the Companies Act (UK), a public company may not make a distribution at any time unless the amount of its net assets is not less than its called-up share capital and reserves and would not become less as a result of the distribution.[85]

6.5 Debentures[86]

For a company to effectively function in today's business world, it must be in a position to raise funds from more than one source.[87] Share capital undoubtedly provides one of the most important sources of funds to a company. However, public companies often utilise the instrumentality of debentures in order to finance their activities.

Debenture finance is also referred to as loan capital, as distinct from equity financing by way of contribution of share capital. The company borrows money from the public by issuing debentures to creditors. The liability is owed to the debenture holders or lenders as creditors. These creditors have their loan secured against the property of the company by way of either a fixed or floating charge.[88] Where debentures are offered to the public, it is anticipated that there will be

---

84 See *ibid.*, s 32.

85 Section 831 of the United Kingdom Act defines undistributable reserves as: share premium account; capital redemption reserve; any surplus of accumulated unrealised profits over accumulated unrealised losses (revaluation reserve); any reserves which statutes, memorandum or articles prevent from being distributed. Cf formerly s 66(3), now the new Act makes no provision for this; see s 32 (K).

86 See generally Part 7 Companies Act 2015 (F); formerly, ss 83–100 Companies Act, although the new Act of 2009 makes no provision for this (SI); formerly, ss 93–111 Companies Act, although the new Act of 2012 makes no provision for this (V); ss 66–79, 91–100 Companies Act (N); formerly, ss 91–101, although the new Act of 2001 makes no provision for this (S); the new Act of 2017 makes no provision for this (CI); see s 253(1) of the Companies Act 2021, which allows the continuation of ss 48–52 'despite the repeal of the Companies Ordinance' (K).

87 This now brings into focus the significance of the incidental power clause in a company's memorandum. It is pointless having a company without empowering it to borrow. Limitation as to the power is found in the articles of the company. The power is generally delegated to the board of directors. It is a general presumption of law that where there is a power to borrow, there is also a power to create charges over the assets of a company. See s 48 in Kiribati, which empowers companies to borrow money.

88 See s 49(12) in s 253(1) of the Companies Act 2021 (K).

numerous lenders who take up the debenture offer. In order, however, to obviate the necessity of having individual loan agreements with every lender to the company, there is provision for a debenture trust deed to be set up with a trustee who represents the interests of all of the lenders under the one debenture issue. A public offering of a debenture issue can only be made by a public company, which must comply with the prospectus requirements as noted above.

It is appropriate to note that the term 'debenture' has many senses. A debenture is primarily a legal document acknowledging that a company has borrowed money and providing the obligation to repay it on certain specified conditions. It is generally a written acknowledgment of a debt.[89] From another perspective, a debenture can be regarded as a charge created by deed. All debenture borrowings are secured borrowings, although the statutory definition presupposes that some debentures will not involve the giving of a charge over company property but are confined to security interests of this or other types. The debenture confers power on the debenture holder to enforce his or her security by sale or appointment of a receiver or otherwise as appropriate.[90] The primary sense of it is that of a secured borrowing by a company which is embodied in a deed. A company can make other unsecured borrowings, but these are usually distinguished as unsecured notes. A debenture borrowing is supported by a charge, which might involve the giving of a mortgage over company land or might involve security against other assets of the company including trading stock. Usually the name 'mortgage debenture' is given to those debentures which involve a mortgage over company land. But debentures are what could be called corporate security interests. On most stock exchanges where the company is listed, they can be traded just as can other security interests.

There are basically two types of debenture: single debenture and series debenture.[91] In the case of the former, a single loan transaction is recorded between the company and the creditor in the instrument. In respect of the latter, the company in favour of multitudes of creditors creates a pool of debentures. Although each loan transaction between the company and the creditor is regarded as a separate transaction, all transactions are recorded in one single document which provides also for a trustee, as noted above.[92] Except in the case of Kiribati,[93] other jurisdictions in the South Pacific do not have express statutory provisions empowering them to borrow money through debentures. The power to borrow is usually found in the company's memorandum as an 'incidental power clause'.

---

89 *Ibid.*, s 49(2).
90 See s 1 of the Vanuatu statute, which states that '"debenture" includes debenture stock, bonds and any other securities of a company whether constituting a charge on the assets of the company or not'.
91 See s 49(1) in s 253(1) of the Companies Act 2021 (K).
92 *Ibid.*, s 49(4) in s 253(1) of the Companies Act 2021.
93 *Ibid.*, s 48. This power can be limited by the articles of the company.

6.5.1 Debenture trust deed

The creation of any debenture by a company has to be formalised through a document called a debenture trust deed.[94] A debenture trust deed makes provision[95] for the appointment of a trustee for prospective debenture holders,[96] and defines the nominal amount of the debenture stock. A repayment period is specified, as well as the rate of interest yearly or half-yearly. Where it creates a charge over the assets of the company, the trustee is authorised to enforce the security in the event of any default.

It will usually provide for the appointment of a manager or receiver of the company where, for example, the company has defaulted or failed to comply with some provision of the deed. By the deed, the company is subject to various covenants other than the covenant to repay the loan and to pay interest. These other covenants include the provision of proper insurance of the property or the acceptance of an obligation to limit the total borrowings. Various other breach provisions may be included, and the deed usually specifies requirements for the keeping of a register of debenture stockholders, transfer of debenture stock, issue of certificates, conduct of meetings of holders, etc.[97]

6.5.2 Types of debentures or charges[98]

A debenture charge can be made against either fixed or floating assets of the company as security for the repayment of the loan, hence they are called fixed and floating charges. Both are treated rather differently. It is to be noted that most forms of security over company assets are known as charges, although the term is broad enough to encompass a wide range of encumbrances or security interests. It might include a mortgage over land or chattels owned by the company. Technically, this involves a transfer of the legal interest of the company in the land or chattels during the period of the mortgage subject to an equitable obligation imposed on the lender to retransfer the property once the loan is properly repaid. This equitable obligation is known as the equity of redemption. A mortgage may be legal or equitable depending on whether it is created in terms of the strict requirements of the legal system or not.

But in a stricter or narrower sense, a charge also refers to a transaction whereby the ownership of the property charged does not pass to the lender at all. It is an equitable security interest which is something less than a legal or equitable

---

94 See s 50(1) in s 253(1) of the Companies Act 2021 (K); s 78 Companies Act 1991 [Cap 40.08] (Tu).
95 See s 49(7) in s 253(1) of the Companies Act 2021 (K).
96 Formerly, s 85, although the new Act of 2009 makes no provision for this (SI).
97 See s 78(6)(a)–(n) (Tu); formerly, s 83, although the new Act of 2009 makes no provision for this (SI).
98 See s 49(13) in s 253(1) of the Companies Act 2021 (K).

mortgage. What it does is provide the lender with an interest in the assets by way of security. The person who holds the charge is entitled to be paid out of the property which is charged, for example in the event that it is sold. The person with the charge (the 'chargee') thus has an equitable interest in the property but it is not the same as ownership. Usually, it can be enforced, in the event of default, by way of a court order for sale or by the appointment of a receiver.

The floating charge is a creature of equity and is a powerful instrument of corporate financing because it allows a company to continue to trade in the likes of trading stock even though it is technically subject to a charge. Thus, the charge does not limit the power of the company to trade. However, under certain circumstances, the floating charge might crystallise into a fixed charge which will prevent the company from dealing effectively with the assets as they exist at a particular time.

6.5.3 Fixed charges

This may be a legal mortgage of any property of the company such as land or shares held in other companies; an equitable charge over property such as book debts,[99] ships, aircraft and other chattels; and an equitable or informal mortgage by means of deposit of title deeds to the property of the company.

A fundamental feature of a fixed charge is that it attaches to the actual asset as soon as it is created. It is generally the best form of debenture, at least from the lender's point of view, though not necessarily the company's.[100] Where a company sells its assets, it may either repay the loan from the proceeds of the sale or hand over the assets to the purchaser still subject to the charge. This is because the debt is secured against the assets in question.

6.5.4 Floating charges

This is a charge over the undertakings and assets of a company.[101] This affects all the moveable assets of the company, including its stock in trade. The charge at creation does not fix to any particular assets of the company until crystallisation takes place.[102] This allows the company to deal freely with the subject of the charge, for example by way of sale or by way of creating fixed charges over particular assets which would then have priority over a floating charge. A company's assets include what is known as circulating capital, which might include the likes of trading stock, book debts and other items such as machinery or furniture which

---

99 *Siebe Gorman & Co Ltd v Barclays Bank Ltd* [1979] 2 Lloyd's Rep 142.
100 The ability of a fixed charge to attach to property on creation gives it priority over a floating charge. See s 49(16) in s 253(1) of the Companies Act 2021 (K).
101 Section 49(15) in s 253(1) of the Companies Act 2021 (K) gives the definition of a floating charge.
102 See *Re Yorkshire Woolcombers Association Ltd* [1903] 2 Ch 284.

are replaced or turned over on a regular basis. A floating charge permits the charge to continue to have effect over new items which are substituted for those existing at the time the charge was taken out.

The company's freedom to continue to trade in assets subject to the charge, pay debts or create fixed charges over those assets in the ordinary course of its business is something that is normally implied in the charging instrument itself without express mention. The right of the company to pay debts would give to an unsecured creditor a right to seize goods subject to the charge in execution of a judgment. However, if the charge has crystallised into a fixed charge before execution is effected, then such a right would be lost and the creditor would take subject to the charge.[103]

It was decided in the leading case of *Holroyd v Marshall*,[104] for example, that a charge over the machinery of the company would still be valid even though the charge permitted the replacement of existing machinery with new machinery from time to time. In *Re Panama, New Zealand and Australian Royal Mail Co*,[105] it was held that a floating charge could legitimately provide the creditor with security, in effect, over all of the present and future property of the company, thus providing the holder of the charge with priority over unsecured creditors on liquidation. A fixed charge over circulating assets would not normally be acceptable as the relevant property could not be sold without the liability under the charge first being satisfied. However, a fixed charge can still in principle be given over circulating assets.

The charge instrument implies freedom to deal with the present and future assets in the ordinary course of business. An exceptional or one-off transaction can still be considered in the ordinary course of business.[106] But a transaction such as one which is made merely to aggravate or frustrate the holder of the charge would not be regarded as within the ordinary course of business.[107] In any event, the implied freedom of the company to deal with its assets in the ordinary course of business can be restricted by the terms of the instrument of charge itself in a particular case.[108]

6.5.5 Crystallisation

Crystallisation is some event which converts a floating charge into a fixed charge. It ends the freedom which a company has to trade in or roll over the assets which are subject to the charge. The following are some of the events which in law have

---

103 *Taunton v Sheriff of Warwickshire* [1895] 1 Ch 734 (CA).
104 (1862) 10 HLC 191.
105 (1870) LR 5 Ch App 318.
106 See *Reynolds Bros (Motors) Pty Ltd v Esanda Ltd* (1983) 8 ACLR 422.
107 *Hamilton v Hunter* (1982) 7 ACLR 295.
108 See *Fire Nymph Products Ltd v Heating Centre Pty Ltd* (1988) 14 NSWLR 460.

been recognised as crystallisation: liquidation of a company; cessation of business; active intervention by the charge such as appointment of a receiver over the assets of the charge, or selling the subject of the charge; where the contract of charge so provides that notice can convert the charge into a fixed charge; and crystallisation of another floating charge, if it causes a cessation of business.[109]

Crystallisation can occur with respect to events which are expressly provided for in the instrument of charge, or it can come about by implication. The former is sometimes called automatic crystallisation. The relevant events will be provided for in the charging instrument between the company and the lender. Automatic crystallisation occurs whether or not the charge is aware of the events leading to crystallisation and whether or not the charge is willing to enforce the charge because of the occurrence of the stipulated event.[110] It seems that across the region, only in Kiribati is automatic crystallisation statutorily endorsed. This is found in s 49(14), which provides to the effect that a charge securing debentures shall become enforceable on the occurrence of the events specified in the debentures or trust deed constituting the same.[111] However, it is not always desirable that crystallisation should come about automatically. It might not be in the interests of the creditor, much less the company. Thus, it is open for the deed to provide the chargee with an option as to whether to intervene or not.[112] But where the clause is unambiguous that crystallisation is automatic, then it must take effect regardless of the wishes of the parties.[113]

Crystallisation by implication is usually with respect to events which cause such a disruption to the activities of the company that it is appropriate that the company's liberty to continue to carry on business should be suspended. Events such as the appointment of a liquidator, the appointment of a receiver of the company's property or the company ceasing to carry on business fall into this category.[114]

6.6 Rules of priority

The very nature of and differences between a floating and a fixed charge means that there is considerable potential for conflict between different types of chargees as well as those who deal with property of the company which is subject to the

---

109 *Re Woodroffes (Musical Instruments) Ltd* [1986] Ch 366, 377–78.
110 In *Re Brightlife* [1987] Ch 200, the court rejected as automatic crystallisation a clause which provided that the company was to cease to deal with the charged assets only on the happening of a particular event. The point here is that an automatic crystallisation clause should expressly state that on the occurrence of an event, the floating charge is converted into a fixed charge.
111 See s 253(1) of the Companies Act 2021 (K).
112 See e.g. *Dovey Enterprises Ltd v Guardian Assurance Public Fund Ltd* [1993] 1 NZLR 540 (CA).
113 See *Permanent Houses (Holdings) Ltd, Re* (1989) 5 BCC 151.
114 On the last of these, see *Hamilton v Westpac Banking Corp* (1984) 79 FLR 330; *DCT v Lai Corp Pty Ltd* [1987] WAR 15; *Fire Nymph Products Ltd v Heating Centre Pty Ltd* (1988) 14 NSWLR 460.

charges. There might also be differences in the nature of the rights in the same type of charges either because they have been created on different dates or because of differences in the dates of registration. The priority rules are essentially rules developed to resolve conflicts between different claimants to a legal or equitable interest in property. If one part has what is in effect no property interest at all, then the priority rules do not apply at all. A merely personal interest, such as an interest under a personal licence, will always yield to a property interest.

The rules of priority were adopted in an attempt to resolve competing claims of creditors in respect of different charges created over the same property. It is thus important to bear in mind that the rules of priority in relation to company charges are determined by: (a) the nature of the charges concerned and whether they are both legal, both equitable or one legal and one equitable; (b) the date of creation of the charge; (c) whether there is a requirement for registration of the particular charge or not; and (d) the date of registration of the charge where required. It is to be borne in mind that statutory priority order of preferential payments will over-ride any other rule of priority regarding the rights of debenture holders. In this context, s 99(1) of the Companies Act of Vanuatu Cap 191 provides:

> Where either a receiver is appointed on behalf of the holders of any debentures of a company secured by a floating charge, or possession is taken by or on behalf of those debenture holders of any property comprised in or subject to the charge, then, if the company is not at the time in course of being wound up, the debts, which in every winding up are under the provisions of Part VI relating to preferential payments to be paid in priority to all other debts, shall be paid out of the assets coming to the hands of the receiver or other person taking pos-session as aforesaid in priority to any claim for principal or interest in respect of the debentures.[115]

6.6.1 Rules of priority

The rules of priority are complex. This is more so when it affects company charges. For this reason, our discussion of the effect of the rule on debentures will outline only a modest but effective navigation chart for priorities. It should be borne in mind that these are only general rules which are overridden by express statutory provisions. The following basic rules will be of some assistance in understanding the concept of priority in relation to company charges:

• Legal charges rank between themselves according to the order of their crea-tion or, where they are in essence registrable charges, in respect of their order

---

115 See also s 49(21) in s 253(1) of the Companies Act 2021 (K).

of registration (that is, irrespective of their time of creation). The requirements as to registration are set out below.

- A legal charge has priority over an equitable charge. This follows from the equitable maxim, 'where the equities are equal, the law prevails'. Provided that the taker of a subsequent legal charge takes for value, in good faith and without notice of the existence of the prior equitable charge, then the legal charge will have priority.

- Two equitable charges take priority according to the time of creation. The relevant equitable maxim here is that 'where the equities are equal, the first in time prevails'.

- Where a legal chargee has notice of the prior creation of an equitable charge or has acted otherwise than in good faith, the equitable charge takes precedence over the legal charge. This will mean that the equities are not equal as required for the purpose of the maxims noted above. In appropriate circumstances, the equity court can postpone the application of the normal priority rule where the interests of justice require it.[116]

- In cases of two registered charges, priority goes with the time of registration. But there are complications here, in that not all charges are registrable whilst in other cases, one registrable charge might be registered and another not. Suppose there are two registrable charges, neither of which is registered: the rule as between competing equitable interests would apply – that is, normally the first in time prevails. If there are two registrable charges but only the first is registered, then clearly the first prevails. If it is only the second that is registered, then it prevails by virtue of registration. If one charge is registrable and the other is not, then much depends on whether their status is legal or equitable. The first is clearly equitable but the second one might be legal or equitable. The general rules above will then sort out the relative priorities.

---

116 The position can be quite complicated in view of the fact that a particular instrument of charge might contain a clause, sometimes called a negative pledge, which purports to restrict the right of the company to create further charges. In substance, this is a contractual promise which normally binds the parties to it only. But it might still be relevant for the purposes of the allocation of priorities. The issue is in part whether the subsequent chargee had notice of the restrictive clause or not. Where the charge is registered, the legislation provides (see below) that registration does not impute knowledge of the charging instrument, but this might put the subsequent chargee on proper inquiry as to the contents of the charge. There is, however, some variation between the jurisdictions on this point. Where the register is required to contain not only basic details of the charge but a copy of the charging instrument and thus also the restriction, it could stand as constructive notice of the existence of the provision. See generally *Cox v Dublin City Distillery (No 2)* [1915] 1 IR 345; *Re Castell and Brown Ltd* [1898] 1 Ch 315; *Latec Investments Ltd v Hotel Terrigal Pty Ltd (In Liquidation)* [1965] HCA 17; 113 CLR 265 and the discussion in Ford, HAJ and Lee, WA, *Principles of the Law of Trusts in Australia*, 1990, Sydney, Law Book Co, p 791.

- If a floating charge attaches to the property at the time of crystallisation, it becomes a fixed charge. Its priority over other charges will depend upon the date of creation or registration, whichever is applicable in the circumstances.
- If a fixed charge is created to secure a debt within six months of a company becoming insolvent, it may be invalid as a preference in Tonga.[117] In the case of other countries in the region, the period is 12 months.

6.6.2 Rights of debenture holders

A creditor of the company (who is a debenture holder), in addition to enjoying all the powers of a legal mortgagee, may exercise all the rights of an unsecured creditor. This means that the debenture holder or the designated trustee can sue the company for the debt and seize the property as a judgment creditor if the debt remains unpaid after both the principal sum and the interest have become due. The debenture holder can also petition the court to compulsorily wind up the company where the company has been unable to repay the sum secured by the floating charge after a demand for the repayment of same.

In addition to these remedies, a secured debenture holder or a trustee of a debenture trust deed may enforce the security by taking possession of the asset which is subject of the security where s/he is a legal chargee or by selling off the property comprised in the debenture, or by appointing a receiver[118] or applying for a foreclosing order.

In dealing with the powers of a secured debenture holder to sell, foreclose or appoint a receiver, we should note the problems surrounding retention of title by the seller. This is governed by the Romalpa clause.[119] As a general rule, a receiver has no powers of disposal over any assets of the company which are not covered by the charge under which s/he is appointed, nor over the assets of third parties in possession of the company. Where the seller retains the title but parts with the goods, it is obvious that a receiver cannot therefore deal with the property under the circumstances. A Romalpa clause may constitute a registrable charge.

6.6.3 Registration

Any charge falling within the definition provided in the legislation and created over the assets of a company, whether fixed or floating in nature, needs to be registered. The Companies Acts in the region specifically provide for the compulsory registration of debentures created by a company but the definition extends to other types of charge as well. The Registrar of Companies is the authority empowered

---

117 See also s 239 Insolvency Act 1986 (UK).
118 See s 80 Companies Act 1991 [Cap 40.08] (Tu); s 50 in s 253(1) of the Companies Act 2021 (K). (K).
119 See *Aluminium Industrie Vaassen v Romalpa Aluminium* [1976] 1 WLR 676.

to register company charges[120] and must maintain a register with information with respect to every company. The court may order the register to be rectified from time to time as necessary and grant appropriate relief.[121] As noted above, where the charge is a registrable charge under the legislation, it obtains priority according to the date on which it was registered. The registration of a charge will impute actual notice to any person subsequently dealing with the company as to the existence of the charge but not normally as to the contents of the charging instrument.

There are no equivalent provisions to the former provisions dealing with company charges in the Vanuatu Companies Act 2012. Similarly, there are no equivalent provisions found in the Companies Act 2009 of the Solomon Islands, for the Companies Act 2021 Samoa or the Companies Act 2017 of the Cook Islands, Section 51 reflected in s 253(1) of the Companies Act 2021 of Kiribati.

The application for registration is to contain certain prescribed information. Generally, the obligation to register is placed on the company itself, although in default of the company complying with its obligation, any other person can register.

The legislation defines which charges are registrable charges. For example, in New Zealand, the Companies Act 1955 was repealed, which led to the enactment of the Companies Act 1993 and the Companies (Registration of Charges) Act 1993.

---

120 See s 51 in s 253(1) Companies Act 2021 (K); cf s 830 Companies Act 2006 (UK). In the case of other instruments, registration is to be effected under the relevant stamp duties law. See e.g. the Stamp Duties Act [Cap 68] 1988 (V); Stamp Duties Act Cap 70 1988 (T).
121 Generally, see s 178 Companies Act 2012 (V).

7

COOPERATIVES, CREDIT UNIONS AND INCORPORATED SOCIETIES

7.1 Cooperatives

Cooperatives are forms of corporation which are specially created by statute. Cooperatives have long been regarded as alternatives to companies and other corporations as vehicles for the carrying on of business ventures. Traditionally, they are to be seen as self-help organisations through which individuals in local communities could pool the products of their own labour and efforts for the good of all. The word cooperative derives from the Latin *cooptare*, which meant 'to elect' in the sense of electing a colleague just as we now speak of co-opting someone to a position. More literally, the Latin conveyed the sense of 'to work together'.

Very often, cooperatives have been organisations for the marketing and sale of agricultural products both within the community and beyond. However, they are by no means confined to agricultural pursuits. The usual model is perhaps the cooperative store. But cooperative societies have engaged in banking, financial and investment business, as with the Raefeisen Banks in Germany. They were the forerunners of the building society and credit union movements designed to provide 'self-help' credit facilities to their members.

The cooperative movement has a distinctive history as both a political and social movement. The self-help ideology which has surrounded cooperatives has meant that they have commonly been put forward as an alternative to the capitalist system of investment, particularly company investment. The cooperative movement has been a worldwide movement which grew out of Owenite[1] socialism in

---

1 Robert Owens, a social reformer and former industrialist who engaged in several experiments with alternatives to capitalist organisations in the 19th century in England.

DOI: 10.4324/9781003428060-8

England and various forms of moderate socialism on the European continent in the latter half of the 19th century.

The movement which seeks to promote the alternative benefits of cooperative organisational and economic ideals has waxed and waned. It has seen many notable failures and, perhaps, an undeservedly small number of major successes. The Mondragon experiment in the Basque region of Spain is one of the most successful of all, involving a community which itself is largely run on cooperative 'political' principles. It has been promoted in many so-called third-world countries as a means of encouraging the development of commerce on a communal basis. It has been promoted in the South Pacific in similar terms, but the successes have been less than remarkable.

The strength of cooperatives is also their downfall. Their structures claim to be democratic and based on wide-scale participation and sharing by the community. However, this structure, whilst appealing, means that they cannot compete effectively with the companies which have a hierarchical organisational structure and the consequent ability to make and enforce internal decisions rapidly. Cooperatives have been less successful in the attraction of investment, for which they were not, in principle, designed. They are not fully geared towards profit making, as are limited companies.

7.1.1 Cooperatives legislation

Cooperatives came to be regulated by statute in England at the end of the 19th century. That legislation forms the basis for the legislation of most of the South Pacific jurisdictions. The legislation in most of the former British colonies is the same in content. The following legislation is now applicable in the South Pacific region:

- Cooperative Societies Regulations 1953 as amended by the Cooperative Societies Act 1966 of Cook Islands;
- Co-operatives Act 1996 of the Fiji Islands;
- Co-operative Societies Ordinance Chapter 14 1952 of Kiribati;
- Corporations and Partnerships Title 18 Cooperative Associations Chapter 7 1993 of the Marshall Islands;
- Co-operative Societies Ordinance 1952 of Samoa;
- Co-operative Societies Act Chapter 164 1953 of the Solomon Islands;
- Co-operative Societies Act Chapter 17.02 1973 of Tonga;
- Co-operative Societies Act Chapter 40.20 1952 of Tuvalu;
- Cooperative Societies Act Chapter 152 1987 of Vanuatu.

7.1.2 Types of cooperative society

Section 4 of the Cooperatives Ordinance of Kiribati limits the types of society that can be registered as cooperative societies under the Act. It reads as follows:

Subject to the provisions hereinafter contained, a society which has as its object the promotion of the economic interests of its members in accordance with co-operative principles, or a society established with the object of facilitating the operations of such a society, may be registered under this Ordinance with or without limited liability as the Registrar may decide.[2]

In Vanuatu, s 3 provides as follows:

Subject to this Act any society for carrying on any industry, business or trade in accordance with co-operative principles may be registered under this Act.

However, in none of the legislative provisions is there a definition of what constitutes 'cooperative principles'. The meaning of this phrase is to be gleaned from general usage and from those provisions of the Act which provide to cooperative societies certain of their distinctive characteristics. These include the following:

(1) the promotion of the economic interests of the members rather than of the corporate entity itself as at least one of the objectives;
(2) one vote per member in most cases – the principle of equality or democracy;
(3) restrictions on the extent of ownership of shares;
(4) enforcement of local or regional characteristics of cooperatives;
(5) entitlement to regular dividends on shares;
(6) possible requirements under the by-laws of the society regarding the use of the society as a distribution point for produce.

In the Marshall Islands, the legislation proclaims that its purpose is:

To promote, foster and encourage the intelligent and orderly marketing of certain products through the formation of cooperative associations; to eliminate speculation and waste in the marketing of certain products; to make the distribution of cooperative products between the producer and consumer as direct as can be efficiently done; and to stabilize the marketing of cooperative products.[3]

The term 'cooperative products' is defined to include 'fishery products, agricultural products, handicrafts and indigenous products and non-indigenous products'.[4] In that country, cooperative societies are deemed to be non-profit making, in the sense that they are organised not to make a profit for themselves or their members but only for their members as producers and/or procurers of cooperative

---

2 See also s 4 Cooperative Acts (F), (S), (SI), (Tu).
3 Article 202 (MI).
4 Article 203 (MI).

products.[5] In other countries, it is left to the by-laws of the society to determine whether or not the objects of a society include profit making.[6]

Generally. The definition of the objectives of a cooperative society is a matter for the by-laws of the society. Given the nature of the cooperative society, it is bound to act within its legal objects. In the Marshall Islands, however, Article 254 defines authorised activities in the following manner:

> A cooperative association may engage in any activity in connection with the marketing, selling, preserving, harvesting, drying, processing, manufacturing, canning, packaging, grading, storing, handling, or utilization of any cooperative products produced or delivered to it by its members; or the manufacturing or marketing of the by-products thereof; or any activity in connection with the purchase, hiring, or use by its members of supplies, machinery, or equipment, or in the financing of any such activities.

7.1.3 Incorporation of cooperatives

The public management of cooperatives is vested in a Registrar of Cooperative Societies or similar named functionary who also deals with both the registration of cooperative societies and ensuring that cooperative principles are observed in particular cases.[7]

On incorporation, the cooperatives society achieves the status of an incorporated body with a separate legal identity on the same basis as for companies as discussed in Chapter 5.[8] Generally, such societies may be registered with or without limited liability of members.[9] Limited liability can be obtained only where at least one member of the society is itself a registered society.[10] The name of the society on registration must include the word 'cooperative' and in the case of societies with limited liability it must also include the word 'limited'.[11] In the Marshall Islands, there is no requirement that the name of a cooperative should contain any particular words. In Samoa, the word 'Felagolagoma'i' may be used instead of 'cooperative' and the word 'Fa'atapula'aina' instead of 'limited'.[12] There

---

5 Article 204 (MI).

6 See e.g. s 34(1) (S).

7 See e.g. s 6 (F); s 3 (K); s 3 (S); s 3 (SI); s 3 (Tu) and s 2 (V). In the Cook Islands, s 4 established a Department of Co-operation under the control of the Minister of Co-operation, and provided also for the appointment of the Registrar, under the Public Service Act 1965 (CI).

8 See e.g. s 7 (Tu), s 7 (S), (SI). In the Marshall Islands, cooperatives are formed in the manner required under the Associations Law for domestic corporations and generally assimilated with them, see s 2015.

9 See e.g. s 4 (K), (Tu), (SI).

10 *Ibid.*

11 See s 20(6)(a) and (b) (F); s 5(2) and (3) (K); s 5(2) and (3) (SI); s 5(2) and (3) (Tu); s 4(2) and (3) (V).

12 Section 5(2) and (3) (S).

is no provision with respect to limited liability in the Vanuatu legislation. Section 4(3) requires, however, that the word 'limited' be the last word in the name of any registered society, which would appear to suggest that all cooperatives in Vanuatu have limited liability. In respect of membership, s 4(1)(a) and (b) of the Vanuatu Act anticipates that a registered society might have either a minimum of seven persons as members or at least one registered society as a member. Thus, there is no necessary connection here between having a registered society as a member and the attainment of limited liability status.

An application for incorporation requires a minimum number of members, usually ten,[13] who must meet certain membership qualifications specified under the legislation. For example, in Tuvalu, the Act requires that members must have attained the age of 16 years and be resident within or in occupation of land within the society's area of operations as set out in the by-laws of the society.[14] In the Marshall Islands, five or more persons, a majority of whom are residents of the country and engaged in the production of cooperative products, may form a cooperative.[15] The minority of any member does not restrict the rights of that person to carry out any acts required or permitted under the legislation.[16] The second of the requirements just mentioned seeks to ensure that cooperatives are, in effect, local, regional or communally based entities. In the case of Vanuatu, a person must be 18 years of age to be a member.[17] In Samoa, the qualification contained in s 21 of the Act is that the person shall be 18 years old and be resident within, a *matai*[18] within or a titleholder by Samoan custom within the society's area of operations.

Generally, members cannot exercise their rights as members unless they have paid all amounts required to be paid in respect of their membership or duly acquired their interest in the society. Section 24 of the Cooperative Societies Act of Vanuatu states as follows:

No member of a registered society shall exercise the rights of a member unless or until he has made such payment to the society in respect of membership or acquired such interest in the society as may be prescribed by the rules or by-laws.[19]

The first part suggests that an initial subscription for shares is not complete until all moneys due have been paid. Presumably, the second part of this provision is designed to ensure that where a person seeks to become a member of a cooperative

---

13 See s 7(a) (F); s 5(1), (K), (S), (SI), (Tu). In Vanuatu, it is seven – s 5(2)(a)(V).
14 See s 23 (a) (K), (Tu); s 20(a) (SI); s 37(1)(a) (F).
15 See Arts 212 and 242.
16 See s 28 (K), (Tu); s 33 (F). There is no such provision in the Solomon Islands legislation.
17 Section 23 (V).
18 *Matai* is a chiefly title in Samoa.
19 See also s 24 (K), (Tu); s 21 (SI); s 22 (S); s 40 (F).

society by acquisition of the shares of another person, then the legal assignment must be duly completed before membership rights can be exercised.

In the Fiji Islands and Vanuatu, provision is made for the registration of cooperative societies as probationary societies. Section 7 of the Act in the Fiji Islands provides that where the Registrar does not see fit to register a society, he or she may, by notice in writing, defer registration subject to compliance with conditions and provisions as set out in the notice. Subject to these conditions and provisions, the notice of deferment entitles the society to operate as a registered society with probationary status. It is, despite its probationary status, deemed to have the status of a body corporate with limited liability and with otherwise full rights to hold property and engage in dealings. Section 8 provides that the Registrar, on being satisfied of compliance with the provisions of the Act by the probationary society, may afterwards register the society. In that event, the society acquires full status as a registered society.[20]

7.1.4 Membership of cooperative societies

All cooperative societies generally have a shareholding, and membership of the society is defined with reference to shareholding. In the Marshall Islands, a cooperative may be formed either with or without shares. Where there are shares, they may be issued in different classes,[21] but one class must be known as common stock and voting power may be restricted to the holders of common stock.[22] Where no shares are issued, the articles must contain provisions which determine voting power and property rights of members, and particularly whether they are equal or unequal.[23]

Membership rights are generally determined by the regulations and/or by-laws of the cooperative society. Normally, the by-laws must be filed with the Registrar on the application for incorporation. In the Marshall Islands, a code of by-laws must be filed within 30 days of incorporation of the society.[24] Subject to meeting the qualifications for membership under the Act, there are no restrictions on the transfer of shares by a member of a cooperative society to another person unless specifically provided for in the by-laws. However, in the Marshall Islands, given the prescribed membership required under the legislation, Art 720 of the legislation prohibits transfer of the common stock or membership certificates to persons not engaged in the production of products handled by the cooperative association. In that country, other qualifications for membership may be set out in the by-laws.[25]

---

20 Section 13(3); see s 6(4) and (5) (V).
21 Article 216 (MI).
22 Article 248 (MI).
23 Article 217 (MI).
24 Article 219 (MI).
25 Article 223 (MI).

The legislation is silent on the question of the legal status of the by-laws as between members or between members individually and collectively and society. As we have seen, in company law, the articles of association are treated as a contract between these respective parties. One can speculate that the same approach would be adopted with respect to cooperative societies, subject of course to the provisions of the legislation in the area of the parties' rights and privileges.

For the purposes of the legislation, a member includes both a person who originally joined in an application for registration of the society as well as a person who is admitted to membership after registration of the society in terms of the relevant by-laws of the society.[26] Membership of the society is defined by reference to shareholding, just as is the case with respect to proprietary companies. There are restrictions noted above on who can be a member of a society, and the legislation endeavours in particular to ensure that cooperative societies are regionally based in terms of membership.[27]

Members are restricted to one vote only in the conduct of the affairs of the cooperative society,[28] a provision which again seeks to ensure the application of democratic principles to cooperatives. This precludes control of the cooperative being obtained by someone who has accumulated a majority or even a large quantity of shares and thus prevents them from acquiring significant controlling voting power. One registered cooperative society may become a member of another society. Where this occurs, the voting rights may be different, and this depends on the provisions made in the regulations governing the society.[29] In general, a person may become a member of more than one cooperative society. However, in the Fiji Islands, s 41 of the Act provides that one person cannot become a member of more than one society whose primary objective is to grant loans to its members. This is commonly the case with respect to building or housing societies.

There are restrictions placed on the amount of shareholding that can be held by any individual member, other than in the case of a member that is itself a registered cooperative. In the case of the Tuvalu legislation, the restriction is as to onefifth of the total share capital, and this is common in other legislation.

In addition, there are restrictions on the extent of the liability of any past member of a cooperative society in respect of the debts of a registered society. This applies regardless of any limitations which apply by virtue of the limited liability principle where it applies. In Tuvalu, s 31(1) of the Act states that the liability of a past member for debts of the society is limited to a period of one year from the date of cessation of membership. Where a member is deceased, the limitation is for a

---

26 See s 2 (F), (K), (S), (SI), (Tu), (V).
27 In the Marshall Islands, the Associations Law 1990–91 is applied to cooperative societies to determine questions relating to powers and rights, see s 205.
28 See s 26 (K), (Tu); s 24 (S); s 22 (SI); s5 (b) (F).
29 *Ibid.*

period of one year from the date of death of the member.[30] It is to be noted that in both cases the relevant provisions refer to debts and not presumably to any other forms of liability that might arise.

The shareholding or interests of members are subject to a charge in favour of the society in respect of moneys that might be due to the society by any member. The society is entitled to a statutory right of set-off against such shares or interest in respect of any amount due.[31] Subject to this right of set-off, the share or interest of any member in the capital of the society cannot be the subject of attachment or court-authorised sale in respect of any debt or liability incurred by the member. Nor is that share or interest available to the assignee or trustee in bankruptcy in the event of the bankruptcy of the member, except where the society has been dissolved.[32]

Section 14 of the Co-operative Societies Ordinance 1952 of Samoa provides for the creation of a charge in favour of the society over the produce of the member in certain circumstances. It provides:

Subject to any prior claim of the Government of Western Samoa[33] on the property of a debtor and to the lieu or claim of a landlord in respect of rent or any money recoverable as rent and in the case of immoveable property to any prior registered charge thereon –

(a) Any debt or outstanding demand payable to a registered society by any member or past member shall be a first charge on all crops or other agricultural produce, felled timber, or other forest produce, marine produce, fish (fresh water and salt water), livestock fodder, agricultural, industrial and fishing implements, plant, machinery, boats, tackle and nets, raw materials, stock in trade, and generally all produce of labour and things used in connection with production raised, purchased or produced in whole or in part from any loan whether in money or in goods given him by the society: Provided that nothing herein contained shall affect the claim of any bona fide purchaser of transferee without notice;

(b) Any outstanding demand or dues payable to a registered housing society by any member or past member in respect of rent, shares, loans or purchase money or any other rights or amounts payable to such society shall be a first charge upon his interest in the immovable property of the society.[34]

---

30 See s 31(1) and (2) (K), (Tu); s 33 (T); s 29 (S); s 25(1) and (2) (SI); s 96 (F).
31 Section 15 (K), (S), (SI), (Tu), (V); s 16 (T); s 28 (F).
32 Sections 15 and 16 (K), (S), (SI), (Tu), (V); ss 16, 17; s 29 (F).
33 Now simply Samoa.
34 See also s 14 (K), (SI), (Tu), (V); s 15 (T); s 27 (F).

7.1.5 Financing issues

Finance provided in return for shares subscribed for by members is the main form of capital-raising activity of a cooperative. The legislation imposes restrictions on various financial dealings that can be undertaken by a cooperative society. A society can also receive deposits by way of loan funds from members of a society. The legislation limits loan funding to the society from non-members to the extent only as provided for in the regulations and by-laws of the society.[35] The same regulations and by-laws may impose restrictions on transactions of a registered society with persons who are non-members.[36]

Loans by a cooperative society can only be made to members of that society, although usually with the consent of the Registrar loans can be made to another registered society.[37] However, the legislation usually provides exceptions in the case of funds to be deposited in prescribed accounts, deposits or securities.[38]

The legislation requires that a certain proportion of funds generated by the society as profits must be transferred to reserves. For example, s 36(1) of the Tuvalu Cooperatives Societies Act requires that one-quarter of the net profits of the society be carried forward to a general reserve fund which is to be used only in accordance with the regulations or by-laws.[39] The excess above that reserve may be used in three specified ways. First, in the case of a society with limited liability only, it might be used by the society for the payment of a dividend or bonus to members of the society. If the society has unlimited liability, the amount cannot be paid out in this way without a general or special order of the Minister responsible. Secondly, it might be allocated to any fund constituted by the society in accordance with the regulations or by-laws. Thirdly, after a society has transferred to reserves as required under s 36(1), it may, with the sanction of the Registrar, pay an amount of up to 10% of remaining net profits to any charitable purpose or to a common-good fund.[40]

7.1.6 Management of cooperatives

Management of cooperatives is usually vested primarily in a board of directors. Strictly speaking, the cooperatives legislation of the region does not impose a requirement that there be a board of directors. This is, however, commonly provided for in the by-laws of the society. In the Marshall Islands, there is specific provision as to a board of not less than three directors elected by members of

---

35 Section 31 (S); s 33 (Tu), (V); s 35 (T); s 33 (K); s 27 (SI); s 97 (F).
36 Section 97 (F); s 34 (K); s 28 (SI); s 32 (S), (V).
37 Section 33 (F); s 32 (K), (T), (Tu); s 28 (SI); s 32 (S), (V); cf Art 255 (MI).
38 Section 36 (F); s 35 (K); s 29 (SI); s 35 (Tu); s 33 (S), (V); s 37 (T).
39 Section 37(1) (F); s 36(1) (K); s 34(1) (S); s 30(1) (SI); s 34(1) (V).
40 Section 100 (F); s 36(2) (K); s 34(2) (S); s 30(2) (SI); s 36(2) (Tu); s 34(4) (V).

their own number,[41] and various legislative principles governing the election of directors.[42]

The legal principles relating to management and the relationship between managers and members are generally the same as those that apply to companies. Members of boards and the board collectively are fiduciaries and are thus required to act *bona fide* in the best interests of the society. These points will be taken up in Part B. Special provisions exist with respect to the winding up of cooperatives. These will be examined in Chapter 28.

7.2 Credit unions

Some countries of the South Pacific region have legislation providing for the creation of credit unions. Section 2 of the Credit Union Act Cap 165 of the Solomon Islands defines a credit union as a cooperative, non-profit organisation registered under the Act and with certain stipulated objects.[43] Under s 15 of the Act, those objects are:

(a) to promote thrift among its members;
(b) to create a source of credit at a fair and reasonable rate of interest primarily for provident and productive purposes;
(c) to receive savings of its members either as payment, shares or deposits; and
(d) to provide an opportunity for its members to use and control their own money in order to improve their social and economic well-being.[44]

The procedure for incorporation of credit unions follows the same pattern as that for cooperatives. The other provisions relating to the qualifications of members are also similar. A credit union once registered becomes a member of a credit union league which has certain duties under the legislation, including the protection of the future growth of credit unions and the provision of leadership and guidance.[45] One credit union can be a member of another credit union. The by-laws of a credit union follow a standard code of by-laws approved by the Registrar, although each credit union has its own memorandum of association dealing, for example, with the division of share capital, the name of the credit union, the registered office and the initial subscribers.[46] The words 'Credit Union' must appear in the name.[47]

---

41 Article 233 (MI).
42 Articles 227–32 (MI).
43 Also, s 2 Credit Unions Act 1990 (K).
44 Section 28 (F); s 15 (K), (V).
45 See Part X (K); Part IX (SI); Part 10 (V). In the Fiji Islands, a federation of credit unions is provided for – Credit Unions Act 1954.
46 Section 11 (F); s 6 (K), (SI); s 7 (V).
47 Section 27 (F); s 14 (K), (SI), (V).

Members hold shares in a credit union which are assignable as for company or cooperative shares. Restrictions are placed on assignability of shares. A member may assign shares only to a person who is another member of the credit union,[48] and assignments require the approval of the board of directors.[49] In Vanuatu the, Act prohibits the transfer of a share in a credit union,[50] although in the case of the death of a member, his/her shareholding must be vested in his/her personal representative.[51] The share capital is divided into shares of a small nominal value. The principle of limited liability is applied as regards the members of a credit union.[52] Usually, members are not permitted to be members of more than one credit union at a time.[53] In Fiji, membership of a credit union is limited to groups of persons having a common bond of occupation or association or to groups of persons residing within a well-defined neighbourhood, community, rural or urban district.[54] A limitation on the liability of past members and the freedom of a member's interest from attachment similar to those of cooperative members is also established by the legislation.[55] No such provisions apply in the Fiji Islands.

The legislation adopts similar rules relating to accounts, audits, investigations, creation of reserves, meetings and management as apply with respect of companies and cooperatives.[56] Finance can be raised not only by share subscription but by borrowing or by raising funds by way of deposits. There are some restrictions on the investment powers of credit unions. Section 40 of the Credit Unions Act of the Solomon Islands provides, for example:

> For the purpose of carrying out its objects, a credit union may, subject to the provisions of this Act, invest or deposit its funds –
>
> (a) with any licensed bank in Solomon Islands;
> (b) with any other credit union; or
> (c) in any other way as approved by the Registrar.[57]

Management of credit unions is vested in a board of directors and specific officers who have particular statutory duties in addition to a range of general law duties substantially similar to those of company directors. There is also provision in the legislation and the by-laws for a credit committee and a supervisory

---

48 Section 86 (F); s 39(2) (K); s 33(2) (SI).
49 Section 86 (F); s 39(3) (K); s 33(3) (SI).
50 Section 29 (V).
51 Section 29 (V).
52 Section 11–12 (F); s 9 (K); s 7 (SI); s 7 (V).
53 Section 25 (K); see s 24, although no equivalent provision deals with this in the Act (SI); s 25 (V).
54 Section 37 (F).
55 Sections 31 (K); s 25 (SI). See ss 39, 47, although there is no equivalent provision in Vanuatu.
56 See generally Part IX (F); Parts VI–VIII (K), (SI); Part 6 (V).
57 See also ss 99 (F); ss 32, 35 (K); ss 30, 33 (V).

committee in relation to any credit union.[58] The former has the primary function of overseeing members' loans, interest rates and terms of credit. The latter regularly examines the affairs of the credit union and conducts audits.

Credit unions may be dissolved. Except in the Fiji Islands, as noted below, there is no provision in the legislation for the likes of voluntary or compulsory winding up. The Registrar, with the approval of the Minster, may cancel the registration of a credit union on certain grounds. These include:

(a) where an investigation provided for in the legislation has been held;
(b) where the number of members is less than 15;
(c) where the incorporation of the credit union was obtained by fraud or mistake; or
(d) where, after notice from the Registrar, there has been a wilful violation of any provisions of the Act, the regulations or the by-laws.[59]

Cancellation of registration may lead to the appointment of a liquidator in whom all property of the credit union is vested. This gives rise to a process of liquidation and winding up similar to that which applies with respect to companies.[60]

In the Fiji Islands, there is provision for dissolution by consent of the members. In that country, s 68 of the Act permits dissolution of a credit union by order of the court, adopting the procedure for compulsory winding up under the Companies Act. As an alternative, a credit union may be wound up by the consent of three-quarters of the members signing an instrument of dissolution.

7.3 Incorporated societies

Some countries in the South Pacific region, namely Tonga and Niue,[61] have legislation providing for the incorporation of societies or associations. The purpose of this legislation is to provide the opportunity for associations to gain the benefits of incorporation. These are generally associations or societies whose primary objectives cannot include the making of profits or pecuniary gains for their members. This precludes partnerships from incorporating under this legislation. It does not mean, however, that they cannot be engaged in commerce.

---

58 Section 99 (F); ss 32 (SI); in Vanuatu, the legislation anticipates the creation of a supervisory committee, but its precise duties are not independently specified. No provision is made for a credit committee. See s 49. Similarly, this is the case in Kiribati.
59 Sections 60, 65 (K); s 58 (S); s 60 (V).
60 On which, see Chapter 28. See also Part VII (SI); s 42, Part 7 (V).
61 In both cases, the legislation is based on the 1908 legislation of New Zealand, which was extended to Niue and adopted without much significant change in Tonga.

For example, s 4(1) of the Incorporated Societies Act 1908 of Niue provides for the incorporation of a society which consists of not less than 15 persons associated for any lawful purposes but not for pecuniary gain. In the case of Tonga, it is at least five persons.[62] Section 20 prohibits a society from doing any act which, if the doing of it were one of the objects of the society, would imply that the members were associated for pecuniary gain.[63] Criminal liabilities are imposed on the society and in certain circumstances on members for breach of the section.

Section 5 of the legislation provides that persons are not deemed to be associated for pecuniary gain merely by reason of any of the following circumstances; that is:

(a) that the society itself makes a pecuniary gain or some part thereof is divided among or received by the members or some of them;
(b) that the members of the society are entitled to divide between them the property of the society on its dissolution;
(c) that the society is established for the protection or regulation of some trade, business, industry or calling in which the members are engaged or interested, if the society itself does not engage or take part in any such trade business industry or calling or any part of branch therefore;
(d) that any member of the society derives pecuniary gain from the society by way of salary as the servant or officer of the society;
(e) that any member of the society derives from the society any pecuniary gain to which he/she would be equally entitled if he/she were not a member of the society; or
(f) that the members of the society compete with each other for trophies or prizes other than money prizes.[64]

An application for registration must be lodged with the Registrar and must be made with the consent of the majority of the members of the society. Rules of the society must be lodged.[65] The rules provide for a number of specified matters, including the inclusion of the word 'Incorporated' as the last word in the name of the society.[66] On registration, the society has the status of a body corporate with perpetual succession and a common seal.[67] The Registrar is obliged to keep a register of all incorporated societies.[68]

---

62 Section 6(1) Co-operative Societies Act [Cap 17.02] 1973 (T).
63 No equivalent provision deals with this, see s 31 (T.)
64 No equivalent provision deals with this in Tonga.
65 Section 7 (N); s 7 (T). In the Marshall Islands, the equivalent legislation is Chapter 8 of Title 18, Corporations and Partnership, dealing with non-profit corporations.
66 Section 6 (N); s 6(3)(T), the Tongan equivalent is 'cooperative' or 'fetokoni'aki' in the Act.
67 Section 10 (N); s 9 (T).
68 Section 33 (N); s 2 (T).

Once registered, a society has been incorporated and it must comply with the objects contained in its rules. The Registrar has power to give a notice prohibiting a society from carrying on any activity or proposed activity which is or might be beyond the scope of its objects.[69] An incorporated society must have a registered office.[70] It must each year lodge financial statements to the Registrar containing details of income and expenditure, assets and liabilities and mortgages, charges and other securities.[71]

Provision is made for the keeping of a public register of members.[72] A corporate body is permitted to become a member of an incorporated society unless, somewhat curiously, the purposes of the society are *ultra vires* the said corporate body.[73] Where a body corporate is a member, it is deemed to be the equivalent of three individual members.[74] It would seem clear that an incorporated society can be a member of another incorporated society on this basis. Membership of the society does not impose any liability in respect of contract, debt or other obligation made or incurred by the society.[75] Members do not have any right, title or interest, legal or equitable, in the property of the society.[76]

An incorporated society may be wound up or dissolved in three ways. First, a society may be wound up voluntarily by a resolution of the society confirmed by a resolution at a subsequent meeting at least 30 days after the first resolution.[77] Alternatively, a society may be wound up by the court on a petition from the society, a member or a creditor on certain specified grounds.[78] These include where the society has suspended its operation for a year, its members are reduced to fewer than 15, it is unable to pay its debts, it carries on any operation whereby any member of it makes a pecuniary gain or where the Supreme Court is of the opinion that it is just and equitable that it should be wound up.[79] Thirdly, the Registrar can make a declaration under seal that a society is dissolved and by publication of that declaration in the *Gazette*. This can be done where a society is no longer carrying on its operations or has been registered by reason of a mistake of law or fact.[80] On winding up or dissolution, as above, all surplus assets after the payment of debts, costs and liabilities are to be divided in accordance with the rules of the society.[81]

---

69 Section 19 (N); no equivalent provision (T).
70 Section 18 (N); generally, see s 12 although no equivalent provision (T).
71 Section 23 (N); s 53 (T).
72 Section 22 (N; s 20 (T).
73 Section 29 (N); see ss 9, 25, Part IV, although no equivalent provision (T).
74 Section 31 (N); no equivalent provision (T).
75 Section 13 (N); no equivalent provision (T).
76 Section 14 (N); no equivalent provision (T).
77 Section 24 (N); it is quite the opposite, see s 43(5) (T).
78 Sections 25, 26 (N); ss 43(5), 47 (T).
79 On the just and equitable ground for winding up, see Chapter 28 below.
80 Section 28 (N); see Part VII (T).
81 Section 27 (N); s 67, although no equivalent provision (T).

PART B
Control and management of commercial entities

Introduction

In this part of the book, we will extend our consideration of partnerships, trusts and corporations by introducing legal issues relating to the management and control of those entities.

We build on our comprehensive review of relevant case law and legislation in the South Pacific with an emphasis on partnership and the relations between partners. We will also examine the powers, fiduciary duties, rights and liabilities of trustees who are in effective control of the trust. We then turn to examine corporations and companies.

DOI: 10.4324/9781003428060-9

8

RELATIONS BETWEEN PARTNERS

8.1 Partners as agents

As noted above, each of the partners is the agent of the others and each individually has power to bind the firm, and hence all of the other partners, in dealings with third parties. Thus, as against the others, collectively and individually, each partner is in a position of advantage or power and equity seeks to ensure that this be exercised both honestly and for the purposes or objects for which the power exists; namely, for the benefit of the partnership as a whole.

The Partnership Acts themselves give vent to this notion of agency and the authority of an individual partner to bind others in the firm. Section 6 of the Partnership Act of Fiji, for example, states:

> 6 Every partner is an agent of the firm and his other partners for the purposes of the business of the partnership; and the acts of every partner who does any act for carrying on in the usual way business of the kind carried on by the firm of which he is a member bind the firm and his partners unless the partner so acting has in fact no authority to act for the firm in the particular matter and the person with whom he is dealing either knows that he has no authority or does not know or believe him to be a partner.

Sections 10, 11 and 12 of the same Act, which are discussed below, provide the basis for the liability of the other partners for the debts and for the acts and wrongdoings of an individual partner. There is some variance between the various provisions as regards shared liability in this context, but this will be dealt with independently.

DOI: 10.4324/9781003428060-10

In terms of relationships between the partnership and outsiders or third parties, the principles of agency apply. Partners are deemed to be agents of one another and hence can enter into relationships with third parties which bind all partners. Additionally, the partners represent the firm for other purposes such as the receipt of legal notices.[1] In terms of agency principles, where a partner enters into a relationship with a third party within the normal course of the usual carrying on of the partnership business, the firm and the other partners are legally bound. There are two clear exceptions to this, as provided for in s 6 above. The first is where the partner has exceeded his or her authority and the third party with whom the partner deals knows that the partner is acting in excess of his or her authority. The second is where the third party does not know or believe that the partner with whom they are dealing is in fact a partner.

The authority of a partner to bind the firm will usually be a case of actual authority. However, partners also have implied authority with respect to a range of matters even though they might not be expressly provided for in the partnership agreement. For example, a partner has implied authority to sell goods of the firm and to purchase goods on behalf of the firm if those goods are necessary for the carrying on of the partnership business or are of a kind which is usually employed in the partnership business. Similarly, partners have implied authority to receive payments of debts due to the partnership and give receipts in the discharge of those debts. Usually, a partner has implied authority to employ persons on the business of the firm. Where a partnership conducts a trading business, each partner has implied authority to engage in commercial dealings which are intrinsic to the carrying on of the business.[2] This extends to borrowing money on behalf of the firm, making pledges over partnership goods and chattels,[3] giving equitable mortgages over assets of the partnership and executing negotiable instruments and bills of exchange on behalf of the firm. However, matters such as these are often subject to express restrictions or prohibitions contained in the partnership agreement. Where this is so, the firm or the other partners will not be bound where the third party has notice of the partnership agreement.

There are also instances where a partner does not have actual or implied authority to do any particular act, as well as cases where a partner has some express or implied authority but proceeds to act outside the scope of that authority. There are circumstances where a partner can still bind the firm on the basis of what is known as ostensible authority. This arises where the partners have by some course of conduct or representation held out a particular partner to the third party, either

---

1 See *Doe D Bennett v Roe* (1849) 7 CB 127; *Canas Property Co Ltd v KL Television Services Ltd* [1970] 2 QB 433 at 799; *Singh v Wilson-Speakman* [1998] FJCA 12; Abu0040u.95s (27 February 1998).

2 See generally *Molinas v Smith* [1932] QSR 77; *Goldberg v Jenkins* (1889) 15 VLR 36.

3 Although implied authority will not extend to situations where the purpose of the pledge or other credit arrangement is not connected with the usual business of the partnership.

specifically or more generally, as having authority to bind the firm with respect to the matters in question, including a holding out to the effect that a certain person is a partner when in fact he or she is not. In such a case, the 'partner' so held out might bind the firm and the other partners to the third party, unless the third party has specific knowledge of the actual lack of authority.

Where some person, not actually a partner, has either represented him or herself to be a partner in a particular firm or has knowingly allowed him or herself to have been held out to a third party as a partner, then that person might incur liability as a partner to the third party where, for example, the third party, in reliance on the representation, has extended credit to or otherwise dealt with the firm. This is governed by the general principles of estoppel.[4]

8.1.1 The liabilities of partners

Subject to whatever is contained in the partnership agreement, the liability of partners in respect of debts and contractual obligations of the partnership is joint.[5] In respect of some claims, however, the partners are jointly and severally liable. This is discussed below. Where a partner has died, his or her estate is also severally liable, on the basis discussed below, in respect of debts and contractual obligations so far as they remain unsatisfied, subject to the payment of the deceased partner's separate debts out of his or her estate.[6]

The legislation makes specific provision with respect to situations where one partner utilised the credit of the firm for purposes which are not connected with the ordinary business of the firm. Where this occurs, the firm is not bound unless the action was specifically authorised by the other partners. Such authorisation does not affect the personal liability of the partner concerned.[7] Where there is an agreement in force which restricts the power of a partner to bind the firm, it is not bound by any act done in contravention of that agreement with respect to persons who have notice of the agreement.[8]

The incurring or obtaining of credit or the giving of indemnities by a partner could in any event constitute a serious breach of the partnership agreement, especially where it exposes the firm to substantial liability. In *Fulwell v Bragg*,[9] the partners of a firm attempted to expel the plaintiff partner from a solicitors' partnership when they learnt that he had given an indemnity of £10,000 on behalf of the firm. The indemnity was given without informing his partners, although he had made some attempt to protect the firm by obtaining counter-indemnities.

---

4 See *Lynch v Stiff* [1943] 68 CLR 428.
5 See s 10 Partnership Act (F).
6 *Ibid.*
7 *Ibid.*, s 8.
8 *Ibid.*, s 9.
9 (1983) 127 S.J. 171.

The plaintiff failed to inform his partners of a letter in which it was made clear that the firm was in serious danger of being made liable under the indemnity. The duty to disclose was taken to be high. The court held that regardless of whether the indemnity situation involved a serious breach of the partnership agreement which could have led to expulsion under the explicit terms of the agreement, the failure to disclose the context of the letter amounted to a serious breach of the partnership agreement.

Joint liability means that a creditor can bring an action against any one of the partners in the firm in respect of the whole of the debt or obligation concerned; however, the partner who is sued is entitled to a stay of the action until the other partners are joined in. There is only one action available to the creditor and if judgment is obtained against one of the partners only, no further action can be brought by the creditor against the others. The right of action is exhausted by the judgment obtained even though the partner subjected to the action and judgment might not be able to satisfy the liability.[10]

In respect of wrongful acts and omissions committed by any partner in the course of the carrying out of the partnership business or with the authority of the other partners, the partners in the firm are jointly and severally liable.[11] This means that the wronged party may sue one, some or all of the partners in respect of the claim. 'Wrongful acts and omissions' extend to claims in tort such as those grounded in negligence, assault, defamation, fraud, trespass and so on. However, it must be shown that the act in question was committed during the ordinary course of the partnership business or was authorised by the other partners.[12]

With respect of the misapplication of money or property of a third party by a partner or others such as an employee, the partnership legislation makes specific provision as to the liability of the partners. Section 12 of the Partnership Act of Fiji, for example, provides two different bases for liability which might arise here. It reads as follows:

12 Where–

(a) one partner acting within the scope of his apparent authority receives the money or property of a third person and misapplies it; and

(b) a firm in the course of its business receives money or property of a third person and the money or property so received is misapplied by one or more of the partners whilst it is in the custody of the firm, the firm is liable to make good the loss.

---

10 See *Kendall v Hamilton* (1879) 4 App Cas 504.
11 See s 11 Partnership Act (F).
12 *National Commercial Banking Corporation of Australia Ltd v Batty* (1986) 65 ALR 385.

Section 12(b) clearly extends to the acts of another person such as an employee or agent of the partnership. It is not merely confined to the acts of a partner. The innocence of the other partners is irrelevant to the question of liability in either case. It should be noted that for (a) to apply, the receipt of money or property should have been within the ordinary scope of actual or apparent authority of the firm. Apparent authority may refer to situations where there is no actual authority of the partnership but a course of dealing or a holding out of the partner concerned might produce apparent or ostensible authority to receive or deal with the property in question. In the case of (b), it is necessary that the money or property should have been received by the firm within the course of its business. In respect of claims under this section, the liability of the partners is joint and several, as for wrongful acts and omissions.[13]

An incoming partner to an existing firm is not liable for debts and liabilities of the firm which were incurred before he or she became a partner.[14] As between the existing and the new partner, the terms of a contract relating to the admission of the new partner may impose liability for pre-existing debts and obligations on the new partner. This, however, is not generally enforceable by a third party and merely operates between the partners themselves.

Where an existing partner retires from the partnership, that retiring partner remains liable for debts and liabilities which were incurred before the retirement.[15] Again, the partners and the retiring partner may have entered into an express or implied contract whereby the remaining partners absolve or indemnify the retiring partner from such liabilities. Such an agreement will only absolve the retiring partner of liability to third parties where they have actually been party to the contract in question. In relation to ongoing debts and liabilities of the partnership, after the date of retirement, the retiring partner remains liable for all such liabilities because a person who continues to deal with the firm after there has been a change in its composition is entitled to assume that the composition remains the same.[16] This assumption is not available where, for example, a creditor was aware that the retiring partner had ceased to be a partner or that the firm had been dissolved.[17] In such a situation, the retiring partner can avoid continuing liability after retirement if a specific notice is provided to those persons with whom the firm has had dealings, and who would otherwise be entitled to assume that the composition of the firm continues.[18] The legislation makes specific provision with

---

13 See s 13 Partnership Act (F).
14 *Ibid.*, s 18(1).
15 *Ibid.*, s 18(2).
16 See *Scarf v Jardine* (1882) 7 App Cas 345. In such a case, the creditor will have to elect whether to proceed against the existing partners or the partners in the old firm.
17 See *Tower Cabinet Co Ltd v Ingram* [1949] 2 KB 397.
18 The partnership legislation of the South Pacific does not contain any special provisions relating to the giving of proper notice in these circumstances.

respect to guarantees given by or to the firm. In the absence of agreement to the contrary, any change in the constitution of the firm revokes such guarantees as regards transactions taking place after the change.[19]

The partnership legislation extends liability as a partner to anyone who, even though not a partner, represents himself or herself as, or knowingly suffers himself or herself to be represented as, a partner in the firm. This extends to representations which are oral, written or constituted by conduct. Such liability extends to any person who has, on the faith of such a representation, extended credit to the firm. The liability of the firm is established whether or not the representation itself was communicated to the creditor by or with the knowledge of the apparent partner making the representation or suffering it to be made.[20]

8.1.2 The general rights and duties of partners

The rights and duties of partners as between themselves are defined either by the express or implied terms of the partnership contract, by the Partnership Act of the jurisdiction concerned or by the doctrines of common law and equity. The last of these provides a kind of background of expectations as to the roles of partners and their duties in relation to one another. So far as this is concerned, s 46 of the Partnership Act (Fiji), for example, provides for the preservation of the roles of common law and equity, in the following way:

> 46 The rules of equity and of common law applicable to partnership shall continue in force except in so far as they are inconsistent with the express provisions of this Act.

The rights and duties of the partners, whether they arise under the agreement or by statute, can be varied at any time either by consent of all the partners or by a course of dealing.[21] However, there are certain rules contained in the Partnership Acts which govern how we are to determine matters such as the partners' interests in partnership property as well as questions of rights and duties of partners as regards the partnership. Section 25 of the Partnership Act (Fiji) is typical of such a provision in the legislation of the region:

---

19 See s 19 Partnership Act (F).
20 *Ibid.*, s 15. Where a partner has died, the continuing use of the old firm name or of the deceased partner's name as part of it does not make the legal personal representatives' estate or effects liable in respect of debts contracted after the death.
21 *Ibid.*, s 20. A course of dealing might also give rise to an estoppel by convention between the partners, which can also affect their substantive rights and obligations. On the general principles here, see, for example, *Con-Stan Industries of Australia Pty Ltd v Norwich Winterthur Insurance (Aust) Ltd* (1986) 160 CLR 226.

25 The interest of partners in the partnership property and their rights and duties in relation to the partnership shall be determined, subject to any agreement expressed or implied between the partners, by the following rules:

(a) all the partners are entitled to share equally in the capital and profits of the business, and must contribute equally towards the losses, whether of capital or otherwise, sustained by the firm;

(b) the firm must indemnify every partner in respect of payments made and personal liabilities incurred by him
   (i) in the ordinary and proper conduct of the business of the firm, or
   (ii) in or about anything necessarily done for the preservation of the business or property of the firm;

(c) a partner making, for the purpose of the partnership, any actual payment or advance beyond the amount of capital which he has agreed to subscribe, is entitled to interest at the rate of six per cent per annum from the date of the payment or advance;

(d) a partner is not entitled, before the ascertainment of profits, to interest on the capital subscribed by him;

(e) every partner may take part in the management of the partnership business;

(f) no partner shall be entitled to remuneration for acting in the partnership business;

(g) no person may be introduced as a partner without the consent of all existing partners;

(h) any difference arising as to ordinary matters connected with the partnership business may be decided by a majority of the partners, but no change may be made in the nature of the partnership business without the consent of all existing partners;

(i) the partnership books are to be kept at the place of business of the partnership (or the principal place, if there is more than one), and every partner may, when he thinks fit, have access to and inspect and copy any of them.

This section, and others like it, render the rules above applicable 'subject to any agreement expressed or implied between the partners'. Thus, clearly, the partnership agreement can expressly displace or modify the operation of any particular rule stated in the section.[22] However, it also seems clear that the partnership agreement itself might not be the only source of such displacement or modification. The section refers to 'any' agreement, even an implied agreement (one implied from conduct or behaviour or informal communications of the parties, for example), and this clearly indicates something other than a formal and express partnership agreement, contract or deed.

---

22 See also the possibility of variation by consent or a course of dealing, discussed above.

8.1.3 Duty to account and to provide information

The Partnership Acts impose a requirement that partners render accounts and provide full information to each other. This is in fact part and parcel of the fiduciary duty of partners, who must be honest and faithful to one another concerning partnership business. The Acts also confirm the fiduciary principle that requires a partner to account for benefits and gains received by the partner in connection with the partnership business.

The Partnership Act (Fiji), ss 29 and 30, contain the standard provisions in this regard:

> 29 Partners are bound to render true accounts and full information of all things affecting the partnership to any partner or his legal representatives.
>
> 30 (1) Every partner must account to the firm for any benefit derived by him without the consent of the other partners from any transaction concerning the partnership, or from any use by him of the partnership property, name, or business connection.

Both sections are important acknowledgments of the fiduciary principle in a partnership context. However, they are not the sole source or expression of the fiduciary duty of a partner. Section 46, as we noted above, preserves the role of the general doctrine of equity, for example.[23] Such doctrines, which include those pertaining to fiduciary obligations, are somewhat broader in the area of fiduciary obligations than the provisions contained in the Act, and it is these that we will now turn to.

8.1.4 Fiduciary obligations of partners

A partnership usually involves a fiduciary relationship and the attendant fiduciary duties resulting from that relationship.[24] The term 'usually' is quite deliberate here. Later on, the vexed question of whether a fiduciary obligation can be excluded will be considered. There are, however, partnership relationships proper as well as many relationships which approximate to them without quite conforming to all the hallmarks of a partnership as required under the Act.

Many of the principles of fiduciary obligation find expression in the partnership legislation. For example, the Fiji Partnership Act, in ss 29, 30 and 31, provides for three specific duties which are directly fiduciary in nature. These are as follows:

---

23 The doctrines would apply independently of section.
24 See *Birtchnell v Equity Trustees, Executors and Agency Co Ltd* [1929] HCA 24 (15 October 1929); 42 CLR 384 at 407, *per* Dixon J.

29 Partners are bound to render true accounts and full information of all things affecting the partnership to any partner or his legal representatives.

30 (1) Every partner must account to the firm for any benefit derived by him without the consent of the other partners from any transaction concerning the partnership or from any use by him of the partnership property, name or business connexion.

(2) This section applies also to transactions undertaken after a partnership has been dissolved by the death of a partner and before the affairs thereof have been completely wound up either by any surviving partner or by the representatives of the deceased partner.

31 If a partner without the consent of the other partners carries on any business of the same nature as and competing with that of the firm, he must account for and pay over to the firm all profits made by him in that business.

8.1.5 Partnerships and similar relationships

The existence of a fiduciary relationship might in fact follow from the finding of a joint venture rather than a partnership proper. Relationships which approximate to, but do not have all the indicia of, a partnership proper can be fiduciary in nature. However, this is not necessarily the case. Many such non-partnership relations will not be treated as fiduciary at all; for example, contractual arrangements where it is clear that the parties are holding themselves at arm's length and without the indicia of reliance, both of which are normally characteristic of fiduciary relationships.

However, it is clear enough on the basis of current authorities that joint ventures can sometimes give rise to fiduciary obligations. That is especially so where there is some high degree of assimilation to a partnership. Yet even in cases where that assimilation does not exist could fiduciary duties be implied, although they would usually be very different in nature and scope from those which pertain to partnerships. Much will depend upon the form that the particular joint venture takes and upon the content of the parties' obligations in that relationship.[25] General fiduciary principles have to be moulded to the circumstances of particular cases.

The difference is, perhaps, that in the case of a partnership, the relationship is nearly always treated as fiduciary almost as a matter of principle. Even a relationship between merely prospective partners, or participants in a proposed partnership to carry out a single joint undertaking or endeavour, will ordinarily be fiduciary if the prospective partners have reached an informal arrangement to

---

25 See *United Dominions Corp Ltd v Brian Pty Ltd* [1985] 157 CLR 1 at 11, *per* Mason, Brennan and Deane JJ; *Foxtel Management Pty Ltd v Seven Cable Television Pty Ltd* [2000] FCA 1159 (18 August 2000), para 102.

assume such a relationship some time in the future, and have proceeded to take steps involved in its establishment or implementation.[26] In the case of a joint venture, this issue depends upon whether the courts are satisfied that the relationship was 'based upon a mutual confidence' such that the participants would 'engage in [the] particular activity ... for the joint advantage only'.[27]

8.1.6 Partnerships as fiduciary relationships

In respect of partnerships in the strict sense, the statement of Dixon J of the Australian High Court in *Birtchnell's Case* has become the classic statement in this context. In this case, the partnership carried on business as real estate agents of one of the firm's clients, who had purchased land through the partnership business. The client then sold the land again in an underhand arrangement with one of the partners, under which arrangement that partner received profits. The court held that the transaction was within the scope of the fiduciary relationship arising from the partnership business and, accordingly, an accounting for the profits to the other partners was required. In the course of the judgment, Dixon J said:

> Indeed, it has been said that a stronger case of fiduciary relationship cannot be conceived than that which exists between partners. ... The relation is based, in some degree, upon a mutual confidence that the partners will engage in some particular kind of activity or transaction for the joint advantage only. In some degree it arises from the very fact that they are associated for such a common end and are agents for one another in its accomplishment. ... The subject matter over which the fiduciary obligations extend is determined by the character of the venture or undertaking for which the partnership exists, and this is to be ascertained, not merely from the express agreement of the parties, whether embodied in written instrument or not, but also from the course of dealing actually pursued by the firm.[28]

In *Cameron v Shipp*, it was said:

> Partners owe to one another duties of the utmost good faith. This includes a duty to render true accounts and full information of all things affecting the partnership; a duty of honesty in dealings with third parties, whether or not the particular transaction is of a partnership nature; a duty to account to other partners for any benefit or gain obtained in circumstances where there was

---

26 See *United Dominions, ibid.* at 12; *Foxtel Management, ibid.*

27 *United Dominions, ibid.* at 12–13; *Hall v Hall* (1994) 5 Tas R1 at para 166.

28 *Birtchnell v Equity Trustees, Executors and Agency Co Ltd* [1929] HCA 24 (15 October 1929); 42 CLR 384 at 407–8, *per* Dixon J.

a conflict of personal interest and fiduciary duty or a significant possibility of such a conflict; and a duty to account for any benefit or gain obtained or received by reason of, or by use of, their fiduciary position or of any opportunity or knowledge resulting from it.[29]

Formulations of the fiduciary obligation and the circumstances of breach are legion. The duties of a trustee in the performance of his or her role provide the guiding model, but the duties of a trustee are much higher than in the case of other fiduciaries. A trustee must act exclusively in the interests of the beneficiaries, but in the case of other fiduciaries such as partners, it is more a matter of requiring performance substantially in the interests of the beneficiaries of the obligations. In *Hall v Hall*,[30] it was said:

A fiduciary is in breach of his duty if he derives a profit by use of his position of trust as partner. A trustee can be in breach of duty if trust assets are used as security for personal business or if partnership resources are used in such a way that a personal benefit is derived to the detriment of another partner. In such circumstances the trustee must account for the use of the trust property. This is especially so where there is a mixed fund (see *Hallett's Estate; Knatchbull v Hallett* (1880) 13 Ch D 696, *Scott v Scott* (1963) 109 CLR 649 and *Hagan v Waterhouse* (1994) 34 NSWLR 308). Breach of duty may occur in the absence of fraud, dishonesty or bad faith *(Keech v Sandford* (1726) Sel Cas 61 25 ER 223). In circumstances where the transaction amounts to a breach of duty, full disclosure must be made if the fiduciary is to avoid liability (*DPC Estates Pty Ltd v Grey and Consul Development Pty Ltd* (1974) 1 NSWLR 443).[31]

However, the strictness of this formulation is subject to some limitations. For example, it was said in *Walden Properties Ltd v Beaver Properties Pty Ltd*:

The court of equity has always been a jealous guardian of the rights of the person entitled to the benefit of the performance of fiduciary duties. However, where the fiduciary duty is to provide information, and the information can be shown by the fiduciary to be incapable of affecting the result, I consider that the beneficiary cannot take advantage of the breach of duty.[32]

In *Aberdeen Railway Co v Blaikie Brothers*, the scope of the duty was stated by Lord Cranworth in the following terms:

---

29 (1929) 42 CLR 384.
30 (1994) 5 Tas R 1 at para 187.
31 See also *New Zealand Netherlands Society 'Oranje' Inc v Kuys* [1973] 2 All ER 1222. Upheld in *Hall v Hall, ibid.* at para 174.
32 [1973] 2 NSWLR 815 at 846–47.

it is a rule of universal application that no one having such duties to discharge shall be allowed to enter into engagements in which he has or can have a personal interest conflicting or which possibly may conflict with the interests of those whom he is bound to protect. So strictly is this principle adhered to that no question is allowed to be raised as to the fairness or unfairness of a contract so entered into.[33]

Deane J (as he then was) in *Chan v Zacharia* stated as follows:

The variations between more precise formulations of the principle governing the liability to account are largely the result of the fact that what is conveniently regarded as the one 'fundamental rule' embodies two themes. The first is that which appropriates for the benefit of the person to whom the fiduciary duty is owed any benefit or gain obtained or received by the fiduciary in circumstances where there existed a conflict of personal interest and fiduciary duty or a significant possibility of such conflict: the objective is to preclude the fiduciary from being swayed by considerations of personal interest. The second is that which requires the fiduciary to account for any benefit or gain obtained or received by reason of or by use of his fiduciary position or of opportunity or knowledge resulting from it.[34]

The class of fiduciary relationships is sometimes understood in terms of accepted conventional classes of fiduciary relations, of which partnership is certainly one. The courts have treated certain relationships as falling within 'accepted' or 'ordinarily recognised' categories of fiduciary relationship.[35] As was said by Mason J (as he then was) in *Hospital Products Ltd v United States Surgical Corp and Others*:

The accepted fiduciary relationships are sometimes referred to as relationships of trust and confidence or confidential relations (cf *Phipps v Boardman* [1967] 2 AC 46, p 127), viz, trustee and beneficiary, agent and principal, solicitor and client, employee and employer, director and company, and partners, approved by Deane J in *Chan v Zacharia* at 196. See also *Birtchnell v Equity Trustees, Executors & Agency Co Ltd* (1929) HCA 24 (15 October 1929) 42 CLR 384.[36]

---

33 (1854) 2 Eq Rep 1281; [1843–60] All ER Rep 249, 252 *per* Lord Cranworth.

34 [1984] HCA 36; 154 CLR 178.

35 *Hospital Products Ltd v United States Surgical Corp* (1984) 156 CLR 41 at 68, 96, 141. See also *Ardlethan Options Ltd v Easdown* [1915] HCA 53; 20 CLR 285 at 292–93; *Para Wirra Gold and Bismuth Mining Syndicate NL v Mather* (1934) 51 CLR 582 at 591, 596; and *Tracy v Mandalay Pty Ltd* [1953] HCA 9; 88 CLR 215 at 241–42.

36 *Ibid.* at 96.

All of the above statements of principle might appear to suggest certain common features such that one might find one all-embracing principle of fiduciary obligation. If so, it has never really been found. Finn suggests that there is a cluster of legal principles which make up the notion of a fiduciary obligation, and these are invoked and given different emphasis depending on the particular circumstances.[37] Sometimes it finds expression as the duty to act honestly, the duty to act reasonably, the duty to exercise powers for proper purposes, the duty to act in the best interests of those to whom the obligation is owed or the duty to avoid conflicts of duty and personal interest.

The basic notion of a fiduciary obligation can be and has been extended, however, to other types of relationship by the process of moulding and adjustment, as noted above. Hence the class of fiduciary relationships in equity is not at all closed. The comments of Dixon J in *Birtchnell v Equity Trustees, Executors and Agency Company Ltd* might thus appear to affirm that the existence of a fiduciary relationship is essential to the existence of a partnership in the first place. In support of this, there are numerous references to partnerships as being contracts of the utmost good faith and thus, one might conclude, essentially fiduciary.[38]

The fiduciary duty of a partner extends in principle to all aspects of the partnership's affairs. It can even apply in situations where some of the partners purport to dissolve a partnership without the concurrence of one of the number. Thus, in *Hurst's Case*,[39] some of the partners set out to dissolve the partnership. They signed a dissolution agreement without the plaintiff partner's agreement. The court held that the attempted dissolution was a wrongful repudiation of the partnership agreement, even though it did not excuse the plaintiff partner from contributing to partnership liabilities.

The fiduciary obligation can extend beyond the life of the partnership in some circumstances. In *Chan v Zacharia*, there was a dissolution of a partnership between two medical practitioners. However, before the partnership had been fully wound up, the defendant partner entered into an agreement for a new lease of the premises in which the medical practice had been carried on. This was even though the original lease was still in fact the property of the partnership and on that basis was still available, in the winding up, to be used for the discharge of debts of the partnership. The court, by a majority, held that the agreement for a new lease was held by the doctor on a constructive trust for those persons who were entitled to the property of the dissolved partnership.

---

37 Finn, PD, *Fiduciary Obligations*, 1977 Sydney, Law Book Co.
38 See *United Dominions Corp Ltd v Brian Pty Ltd* [1985] 157 CLR 1 at 6: Gibbs CJ quoted with approval the reference of Lord Atkin in *Bell v Lever Bros Ltd* [1932] AC 161. See also *Chan v Zacharia* [1984] HCA 36; 154 CLR 178; *Helmore v Smith* (1886) 35 Ch D 436; and *Imperial Group Pension Trust Ltd v Imperial Tobacco Ltd* [1991] 1 WLR 589 at 597.
39 *Hurst v Bryk* 2 All ER 283; [2000] 2 WLR 740.

This case, and similar cases,[40] involves an application of the well-established principle of equity known as the rule in *Keech v Sanford*[41] in the partnership context.[42] On one view, this is a special case of the application of the fiduciary duty applying in respect of renewal of lease situations. It is quite a strict rule, where equity is more concerned with laying down standards than with consequences for particular individuals. Others see it as an application of common fiduciary principles.

The expression 'renewal' in this statement includes the grant of a new lease. It appears irrelevant whether or not there was a right of renewal of the lease originally held by the partners.[43] In *Chan v Zacharia*, the partnership had been dissolved and thus the partnership was in no position to renew the lease itself. In *Keech v Sandford* itself, the landlord had refused to grant a renewal of the lease to the trust, but the renewal in the name of the trustee was not to be permitted on that account. This is a common enough principle in the area of constructive trusts in equity where the trustee or fiduciary has sometimes been denied the ability to plead the legal or practical impossibility of action by the beneficiary as grounds for taking action on his or her own part.[44]

However, one of the ongoing issues concerning the *Keech v Sandford* principle (as a seemingly independent principle) revolves around the degree of stringency with which it applies to fiduciaries other than trustees. In the case of trustees, it applies by way of absolute prohibition. In the UK authority of *In re Biss; Biss v Biss*,[45] it seemed to have been suggested that, in the case of non-trustee fiduciaries, the principle involved only the imputation of a rebuttable presumption (i.e. one of fact) that the person concerned is incapable of retaining the benefit of the lease in question. However, it might be that this is only where the class of person involved as fiduciaries is clearly outside the established class of fiduciaries.[46] If so, then, as Gibbs J suggested in *Chan v Zacharia*,[47] it is difficult to see why partners should fall within that special exception. Nonetheless, the distinction is well established.

One of the possible reasons given here is that the fiduciary obligation of partners can seemingly be excluded by the partnership agreement in any particular case.[48] Whilst that seems odd, given that the fiduciary relationship is one means through which equity courts enforce standards of conduct on particular parties,

---

40 See e.g. *Sew Hoy v Sew Hoy* [2000] NZCA 314.
41 (1726) Sel Cas 61; 25 ER 223.
42 See also *Featherstonhaugh v Fenwick* (1810) 17 Ves 298 at 311 (34 ER 115 at 120); *Clegg v Fishwick* (1849) 1 Mac & G 294 at 298–99 (41 ER 1278 at 1280); *Clegg v Edmondson* (1857) 8 De GM & G 787 at 806–7 (44 ER 593 at 601); *In re Biss; Biss v Biss* (1903) 2 Ch 40 at 56–57, 61–62.
43 *Chan v Zacharia* [1984] HCA 36; (1984) 154 CLR 178 at para 2.
44 See *Phipps v Boardman* (1967) 2 AC 46, for example.
45 (1903) 2 Ch 40.
46 See *In re Biss; Biss v Biss* [1903] 2 Ch 40 at 61, *per* Romer LJ.
47 [1984] HCA 36 at para 2.
48 See *ibid.* at para 45, *per* Slicer J.

it is a position which seems to follow the logic relating to the free operation of exclusion clauses in comparatively recent times. The issue is subject to further discussion below. However, Gibbs J commented:[49]

> The onus that lies on a partner of rebutting the presumption is not easily discharged – see *Clegg v Edmondson*, at p 807 [at p 601 of ER] cited in *In re Biss; Biss v Biss*, at p 62.

> The presumption could not be rebutted unless the partner who had obtained the renewal could at least show that it was obtained without any breach of the obligations which were cast on him by the partnership relation.

8.1.7 Remedies for breach of fiduciary obligation

In *Hall v Hall, Jones and Loquitur Pty Ltd* on the question of remedies for breach of fiduciary duty, it was stated:

> [That a] breach of fiduciary duty can give rise to the imposition of a constructive trust is effectively an application of the principles of tracing. The remedy is to enable profits gained by a fiduciary in breach of trust to be traced into an identified property (see *Phipps v Boardman* (supra), *Regal (Hastings) Ltd v Gulliver and Others* [1967] 2 AC 134 and the Partnership Act 1891, s 26). In effect where profit can be traced into identifiable property, proprietary remedies are appropriate and many include a determination that a constructive trust exists with respect to property acquired in breach of duty (see *Lac Minerals Ltd v International Corona Resources Ltd* [1989] 2 DLR 574). The discretion is wide and a court may more readily impose a constructive trust in a case of fraud than where there is a case of honest mistake (*United States Surgical Corp v Hospital Products International Pty Ltd* [1983] 2 NSWLR 157) but it is open to a court to award compensatory damages (*Commonwealth Bank of Australia v Smith* (1991) 102 ALR 453).[50]

The remedies for breach of a fiduciary duty are personal in nature.[51] As just noted, the duty will remain on the partners even though the partnership has been dissolved. It certainly applies where the partnership is still in the process of being wound up.[52] Thus, persons who are no longer strictly partners are entitled to seek remedies for breach. However, Murphy J in *Chan v Zacharia* dissented from this

---

49 [1984] HCA 36 at para 2.
50 BC9503012 at para 168.
51 See *Consul Development Pty Ltd v DPC Estates Pty Ltd* (1975) 132 CLR 373.
52 *Chan v Zacharia* [1984] HCA 36 at para 3, *per* Gibbs CJ.

view, holding that there was no such duty after dissolution. He cited in support of this a number of US decisions such as *Bayer v Bayer*[53] and *In the Matter of Silverberg*.[54] However, applying the logic of *Keech v Sandford*, one could doubt this approach and suggest that the obligation might extend even beyond the process of dissolution itself.

Three main remedies are available as a result of a breach of fiduciary duty: (a) the making of an order for the taking of accounts between the partners; (b) the restoration of property to the partners through the use of a constructive trust or tracing order if necessary; and/or (c) the making of an order for equitable compensation against the delinquent partner.[55] The approach of the equity courts is generally flexible in respect of the remedies which are appropriate. Those remedies are of course discretionary.

There are two possible approaches to determining the actual liability of a fiduciary in consequence of a breach. In *Hospital Products Ltd v United States Surgical Corp*,[56] Mason J (as he then was) said:

One approach, more favourable to the fiduciary is that he should be held liable to account as constructive trustee not of the entire business but of the particular benefits which flowed to him in breach of his duty. Another approach, less favourable to the fiduciary, is that he should be held accountable for the entire business and its profits, due allowance being made for the time, energy, skill and financial contribution that he has expended or made. ... In each case the form of inquiry to be directed is that which will reflect as accurately as possible the true measure of the profit or benefit obtained by the fiduciary in breach of his duty.

The general liability of a fiduciary, such as a partner, to account for profits was discussed in *Warman International Ltd and Another v Dwyer*,[57] where it was said:

In the case of a business it may well be inappropriate and inequitable to compel the errant fiduciary to account for the whole of the profit of his conduct of the business or his exploitation of the principal's goodwill over an indefinite period of time. In such a case, it may be appropriate to allow the fiduciary a proportion of the profits, depending upon the particular circumstances. That may well be the case when it appears that a significant proportion of an increase in profits has been generated by the skill, efforts, property and resources of the fiduciary, the capital which he has introduced and the risks he has taken, so long as they

---

53 215 App. Div. 454, 214, N.Y. Supp, 322 (1st Dep't 1926).
54 App. Div., 438 N.Y.S. 2d 143.
55 See *Nocton v Lord Ashburton* [1914] AC 932 at 956–57.
56 Referring to the statement of Upjohn J in *Re Jarvis (Deceased)* [1958] 1 WLR 815 at 820.
57 [1995] HCA 18; 182 CLR 544; 69 ALJR 362; 128 ALR 201; 46 IR 250, p 31.

are not risks to which the principal's property has been exposed. Then it may be said that the relevant proportion of the increased profits is not the product or consequence of the plaintiff's property but the product of the fiduciary's skill, efforts, property and resources. This is not to say that the liability of a fiduciary to account should be governed by the doctrine of unjust enrichment, though that doctrine may well have a useful part to play; it is simply to say that the stringent rule requiring a fiduciary to account for profits can be carried to extremes and that in cases outside the realm of specific assets, the liability of the fiduciary should not be transformed into a vehicle for the unjust enrichment of the plaintiff.[58]

8.1.8 Exclusion of the fiduciary obligation

In the discussion above, we raised the question of possible exclusion of the fiduciary obligation in the case of a particular partnership. The normal expectation would be that this would be excluded, if indeed it can be excluded, by a clause (an exclusion clause) in the partnership agreement. However, as will be seen, some of the statements of principle may be wide enough to countenance exclusion by reference to circumstances surrounding the creation of the partnership without any explicit clause.

Partnership is at the centre of a dispute as to the nature of the relationship and whether there are aspects of the relationship which are fundamental or not. Different views on this have characterised the United States as against other common law countries. Although there is no clear authority on this issue, it is most likely that the South Pacific jurisdictions would follow Australia and New Zealand, although the Marshall Islands would likely follow the US position. This is so given the background and/or training of many of their superior court and appellate judges.

On the one hand, there are those who assert that a partnership is essentially one of mutual confidence between the partners themselves. This is essential, they say, for persons to carry on business in common as the statutory definition of a partnership requires. On this basis, a partnership is to be understood as a particular legal institution, which means that there are aspects of it implied by law in every partnership regardless of the terms negotiated between the partners at the time of formation. In view of the mutual confidence required of the partners, the law imputes a fiduciary relationship to them in favour of each other partner and, therefore, this is something that cannot be excluded by the terms of the agreement between the partners.

On the other hand, there are those who claim that a partnership, if it has any fundamental features at all, is something that arises by contract between the parties. It

---

58 *Per* Mason CJ, Brennan, Deane, Dawson and Gaudron JJ.

is an intentional arrangement under which primacy is accorded to the arrangement and the terms of that arrangement are determined by the parties themselves. This is the contractarian view which is fed to some considerable degree by thinking in the area of Law and Economics. On such a view, fiduciary obligations are not essential to a partnership at all because a partnership is a contract and a commercial arrangement between arm's-length parties. These obligations can be excluded by a clearly worded clause in the partnership agreement. Perhaps, on the same logic, they could be excluded by the implied terms of the partnership agreement or contract or by the conduct of the parties, so far as this is appropriate to ascertaining questions of intention.

Such an approach might derive some support from the comments of Viscount Haldane in *Nocton v Lord Ashburton*; where he commented on the relationship between implied contract and fiduciary obligation, he suggested that a particular obligation over and above that of honesty could be raised by the circumstances and by the relationship of the parties. In this vein, he said:

> Such a special duty may arise from the circumstances and relations of the parties. These may give rise to an implied contract at law or to a fiduciary obligation in equity. ... I have only to add that the special relationship must, whenever it is alleged, be clearly shewn to exist.[59]

However, drawing comparisons with contractual doctrine is not quite the point. The issue is perhaps whether the commercial nature of the relationship ought to be emphasised, or whether some other aspect of it should be the focus. In many American jurisdictions, the courts often impose fiduciary duties directly on shareholders, directors and officers of corporate general partners. Thus, as one writer has put it:

> As a result, individuals in these positions should not rely on the argument that the corporate form of the general partner shields them from personal liability to limited partners, at least when they act opportunistically or in their own interest (or in the selfish interest of the corporate general partner) rather than in the interest of the partnership.[60]

The contractarian view is supported by some judicial authority in Australia and New Zealand. In *Hospital Products Ltd v United States Surgical Instruments*, Mason CJ held that a fiduciary obligation would, in any case, need to be moulded to fit the terms of a particular contract entered into by the parties. Presumably,

---

59 [1914] AC 932 (HL) at 955–56.
60 Hamilton, RW, 'Corporate general partners of limited partnership' (1997) 1 *J Small & Emerging Bus Law* 73, p 74.

moulding here might include exclusion altogether. This, however, was not a partnership case. In *Chan v Zacharia*, Deane J suggested that it was at least conceivable that a partnership agreement might exclude the fiduciary obligation otherwise owed by partners. These comments, like those of Mason CJ, were *obiter dicta*. The position is also supported by developments in contract law which have done away with the concept of fundamental obligations. Likewise in trust law, clauses which purport to exclude the right of indemnity of a trustee against the trust assets, or the confinement of rights of recourse to a particular fund of assets, have been held to be valid. *McLean v Burns Philp Trustee Co Ltd Pty*[61] is just one example of this line of development.

It has also been suggested that vulnerability is often lacking in commercial settings. Thus, the fiduciary concept is invoked sparingly, the courts opting instead to uphold the inviolability of business enterprise.[62] This is a variation of the standard line of argument which appeared in the 19th century against the intervention of equitable doctrine in commerce, thereby upsetting its proclaimed need for development against a background of certainty. At best, this is pure myth. Commerce requires no certainty at all. In fact, it thrives on lack of certainty and has always done so. In any event, nothing prevented the intervention of equity into commercial areas such as controlling the actions of company directors and partners. Equity always had a role to play here and did so, to a certain extent, by deploying the fiduciary principle. However, we should also note that vulnerability is merely one possible rationale for the imposition of a fiduciary relationship. The imposition of standards of conduct is an independent one.

The judiciary in Australia and New Zealand, for example, unlike the United States, have not yet made any commitment to the notion that every contract imposes on each party a duty of good faith and fair dealing in contract performance and enforcement.[63] Such a duty has been accepted as an implied legal incident of particular classes of contract,[64] especially where the contract involved is of a commercial character.[65] There is a certain degree of conceptual uncertainty involved in notions such as 'good faith' and 'fair dealing',[66] although such wording

61 (1985) 2 NSWLR 623.

62 *Ironside et al. v Smith* (1998) 223 AR 379 (CA).

63 *South Sydney District Rugby League Football Club Ltd v News Ltd* [2001] FCA 862 at para 393; cf Restatement, Second, Contracts, § 205; and see generally the discussion in *Renard Constructions (ME) Pty Ltd v Minister for Public Works* (1992) 26 NSWLR 234 at 263 ff; *Service Station Association Ltd v Berg Bennett & Associates Pty Ltd* (1993) 45 FCR 84 at 95–97; *Hughes Aircraft Systems International v Airservices Australia* (1997) FCA 558; 76 FCR 151 at 191 ff.

64 *Alcatel Australia Ltd v Scarcella* (1998) 44 NSWLR 349; *Hughes Aircraft Systems International v Airservices Australia* (1997) FCA 558; 76 FCR 151.

65 *Garry Rogers Motors (Aust) Pty Ltd v Subaru (Aust) Pty Ltd* [1999] ATPR § 41–703 at 43,014.

66 *Aiton Australia Pty Ltd v Transfield Pty Ltd* (1999) 153 FLR 236 at 255ff.

and other vague equitable concepts are now commonly imported into legislation.[67] But the concept has been accepted nonetheless. Even so, there are limitations on the free application of this principle in the absence of statute. In *South Sydney District Rugby League Football Club Ltd v News Ltd*, it was said:

> recent decisions suggest that the implied duty of good faith and fair dealing ordinarily would not operate so as to restrict decisions and actions, reasonably taken, which are designed to promote the legitimate interests of a party and which are not otherwise in breach of an express contractual term.[68]

In the Canadian case of *Litwin Construction (1973) Ltd v Pan*, which was again not concerned with a partnership at all, a developer/promoter failed to comply with a number of legislative requirements at the provincial level. In the first instance, it was held that the defaulting buyers could not rely on the non-compliance of the developer with the requirements just mentioned because the purchasers, after becoming aware of non-compliance, had affirmed the contract. It was argued that there was still a fiduciary obligation on the vendor. As to the role of the fiduciary concept in the commercial setting, the court said:

> In a commercial relationship, where the parties have different interests which they both seek to carry forward by entering into a contract or contracts with each other, it would be a most exceptional case where the law would impose a fiduciary obligation which the parties themselves did not make a term of their contracts, either expressly, or by implication through the officious bystander or business efficacy rules.[69]

This was followed in another Canadian case: *Huber Holdings Ltd v. Davidge*. There, it was held that an accounting firm which was also the sole owner of the general partner did not owe a fiduciary duty to the individual limited partner plaintiff. It was said:

---

67 In *South Sydney District Rugby League Club Ltd v News Ltd* [2000] FCA 1541, it was observed at para 393.3: "I would note in passing that the supposed uncertainty with 'good faith' terminology has not deterred every State and Territory legislature in this country from enacting into domestic law the provisions of Article 7(1) or the United Nations Convention on Contracts for the International Sale of Goods: e.g. Sale of Goods (Vienna Convention) Act 1986 (NSW)."

68 *South Sydney District Rugby League Club Ltd v News Ltd* [2000] FCA 1541 at 394.4. See *Alcatel Australia Ltd v Scarcella* (1998) 44 NSWLR 349 at 369–70; *Garry Rogers Motors (Aust) Pty Ltd v Subaru (Aust) Pty Ltd* (1999) ATPR § 41–703; see also *Asia Television Ltd v Tau's Entertainment Pty Ltd* [2000] FCA 254 at para 77; *Advance Fitness Corp Pty Ltd v Bondi Diggers Memorial & Sporting Club Ltd* [1999] NSWSC 264 at para 122; *Far Horizons Pty Ltd v McDonald's Australia Ltd* [2000] VSC 310.

69 *Revell v Litwin Construction* (1973) Ltd (1991) 86 DLR (4th) 169 at 104–5 *per* curiam judgment cited in *Shea v Manitoba Public Insurance Corporation*, [1991] ILR para 1–2721, [1991] BCJ No 711, [1991] ILR para 1–2721 *per* Finch J.

I find that the plaintiff has not established that the defendant breached any duty to the plaintiff in connection with the original investment of the funds. There is no ground for any complaint of any undue influence, or of any failure to disclose the terms of the proposal or the involvement of Johnson and the other partners of Davidge and Company in this project. The proposal and the partnership agreement set out their involvement as developers, as investors, and as shareholders in the general partner, 266548 Alberta Limited. Johnson testified that limited partners were advised that Davidge and Company would be paid a fee for putting together the project and for their services as accountants ... Further, the plaintiff has not established that the plaintiff was vulnerable to or at the mercy of Davidge and Company. The plaintiff acted in the purchase of the units as a prudent businessman, inspecting the property, studying agreements and consulting his own solicitor. Huber had prior experience in speculative land investments. In light of these facts, it is difficult to allege and establish any peculiar vulnerability.[70]

In another Canadian case, *Hodgkinson v Simms*, it was said, although by the minority of the Supreme Court of Canada:

Each relationship must be examined on its own facts. A relationship where one party unreflectively and automatically accepts the advice of the other might raise different considerations. The critical question ... is whether there is a total assumption of power by the fiduciary, coupled with total reliance by the beneficiary. In short, that the beneficiary was vulnerable in the sense of being at the mercy of the fiduciary's discretion.[71]

The majority, however, took a wider approach to the application of fiduciary concepts in commercial situations. They held that the existence of a contract does not in itself preclude the implying of fiduciary obligations. Despite the contractual basis of the relationship, 'the facts surrounding the relationship will give rise to a fiduciary inference where the legal incidents surrounding the relationship might not lead to such a conclusion'.[72]

It was suggested that some caution is required in applying fiduciary concepts in a context such as this:

---

70 (1992) 128 A.R. 268 (QB) at 274–75.
71 *Hodgkinson v Simms*, [1994] 3 SCR 377, [1994] 3 RCS 377, [1994] SCJ no 84, [1994] ACS no 84, 1994 Carswell BC 438, [1994] 3 SCR 377 at para 142.
72 *Ibid.* at para 28; see *Standard Investments Ltd v Canadian Imperial Bank of Commerce* (1985), 52 O.R. (2d) 473 (Ont., CA), leave to appeal refused, [1986] 1 S.C.R. vi. In *155569 Canada Limited v 248524 Alberta Ltd* [2000] AJ No 101, 2000 ABCA 41, 77 Alta LR (3d) 231, 255 AR 1, 30 RPR (3d) 185, 94 ACWS (3d) 776, [2000] AJ No 101, the partners were held not to be fiduciaries, but the court indicated that a general partner (company) in a limited partnership situation like unit trust could, under certain circumstances, be in a fiduciary relationship.

> Commercial interactions between parties at arm's length normally derive their social utility from the pursuit of self-interest, and the courts are rightly circumspect when asked to enforce a duty (i.e. the fiduciary duty) that vindicates the very antithesis of self-interest.[73]

In the end, it was suggested that the court, in assessing the existence of fiduciary obligations, should take a contextual approach and inquire whether, 'given all the surrounding circumstances, one party could reasonably have expected that the other party would act in the former's best interests with respect to the subject matter at issue'.[74] And, is there evidence of a mutual understanding that one party has relinquished its own self-interest and agreed to act solely on behalf of the other party? Presumably, the existence of a contract and its terms are factors to consider in assessing the nature of the relationship between the parties, and whether there is a reasonable expectation that one would act in the best interests of the other.

The contractarian position is regrettable and seems to be based on freedom of contract and arm's-length bargaining principles which are no longer tenable. The fiduciary relationship is so integral to the notion of a partnership relationship that to permit its exclusion by the partnership appears fundamentally wrong. No one would seriously suggest that a fiduciary relationship could be excluded from a trust proper because it is so integral to the idea of a trust in the first place. It is not a question of determining whether a simple contract relationship ought to be treated as fiduciary in some respect or other. The question is whether a partnership could exist in any reasonable sense if the partners are treated as non-fiduciaries. That is difficult to imagine. In fact, the effective exclusion of the obligation would perhaps better be treated as a denial of the existence of a partnership at all.

Apart from this, there is the fact that the partnership legislation seems to suggest that the relationship be treated as fiduciary in some ways, although it is not exactly forthright in saying so. It is true that sections such as s 20 of the Partnership Act of Fiji, noted above, clearly appear to suggest that any aspect of the relationship can be varied by mutual consent. It is to be noted that provisions such as this refer only to mutual rights and duties ascertained by agreement or defined by the Act. The fiduciary obligation is imposed by the doctrines of equity and does not fit neatly within either of these categories. One would hope that the South Pacific jurisdictions would go their own way on this issue.

8.2 Criminal liability

There are many circumstances under which partners can be exposed to criminal liability. It is beyond the scope of this work to discuss in detail the great variety of

---

73 *Ibid.* at 414.
74 *Ibid.* at 409.

criminal offences in which partners might become involved. There are, however, some specific offences under the Criminal Codes of the South Pacific region which deal specifically with partnership situations. It will suffice that we note these.

The Penal Code (Tuvalu), Chapter 10.20: stealing of partnership property by a partner is a separate offence:

252 If any person, who is a member of any co-partnership or is one of 2 or more beneficial owners of any property, steals or embezzles any such property of or belonging to such co-partnership or to such beneficial owners, he is liable to be dealt with, tried and punished as if he had not been or was not a member of such co-partnership or one of such beneficial owners.[75]

The Penal Code of Fiji provides for another offence in these terms:

287 (2) Any person who with intent to defraud or injure any other person–

(a) by any unlawful violence to or restraint of the person of another; or
(b) by accusing or threatening to accuse any person (whether living or dead) of any such crime or of any felony, compels or induces any person to execute, make, accept, endorse, alter, or destroy the whole or any part of any valuable security, or to write, impress, or affix the name of any person, company, firm or co-partnership, or the seal of any body corporate, company or society upon or to any paper or parchment in order that it may be afterwards made or converted into or used or dealt with as a valuable security, is guilty of a felony, and is liable to imprisonment for life.

8.2.1 Partnership property

It is a requirement that the property of the partnership should be used exclusively for the purposes of the partnership. There are several different categories of partnership property. Partnership property can consist of property which is originally brought to the partnership at the time it is created, as well as property acquired afterwards on behalf of the firm. It can also include further property contributed to the firm by the partners, property which has been acquired with the firm's money and the goodwill of the partnership which builds up over time through the conduct of the firm's business.[76] It is assumed, unless the contrary intention appears, that property purchased with the firm's money is deemed to have been bought on account of the firm.[77]

---

75 Cf s Crimes Act 2009 (F).
76 See ss 21(1) and 22 Partnership Act (F).
77 Section 22 (F).

Where land is part of the partnership property, the Act requires that it be treated as personal or moveable estate rather than real estate as between the partners.[78] If property is deemed to be partnership property, then it is available to be brought to account on dissolution of the partnership. Whether an item of property is partnership property depends on the general proposition as to whether that item ' gave rise to valuable rights which were capable of being held for the partnership in such a way as to constitute partnership property'.[79] However, it is quite clear that not all the property of each partner used for the purposes of the partnership business must necessarily be regarded as having been brought into the partnership. In some circumstances, it might persist as the separate property of one partner.[80]

Any partner has authority to sell partnership property. Where the partnership agreement places a prohibition on the sale of property by any partner, a sale would constitute a breach of the partnership terms. However, the partner could commit the firm to a binding contract with a third party to sell property, unless that third party has notice of the restriction.[81]

Issues will often arise as to whether property which is in fact owned by one of the partners has become property of the partnership as a whole. Where some item of property is contributed by one partner as partnership property, it will normally be credited in the capital account of the partnership as part of that person's contribution to the partnership. If such property were then improved, so that upon the dissolution of the partnership the sale price exceeds the value fixed at the time when the property became a partnership asset (i.e. at the time of contribution), the excess amount yielded is divisible as profits of the partnership business.[82] Often, however, the contribution of a partner is less than explicit and the issue might be whether the circumstances justify the property being treated as partnership property in the absence of express agreement on that issue. Generally, this is determined according to equitable principles, particularly that of estoppel.

Again, it will often be difficult to distinguish between cases where property is to be treated as partnership property and those where the circumstances merely give rise to some licence to use the property for the purposes of the partnership. Needless to say, in the latter case, the property is not partnership property. In the Fiji case of *Waterhouse v Grant*,[83] Byrne J held that a betting and totalisator licence and the business name under which a betting business was conducted were owned by the partnership as a whole and could not be considered the property of

---

78 See s 23(F).
79 *Kelly v Kelly* (1990) 92 ALR 74 at 78, *per* Mason CJ, Deane, Dawson, Toohey and Gaudron JJ, citing *Ambler v Bolton* (1872) LR 14 Eq 427; *O'Brien v Komesaroff* (1981) 150 CLR 310; (1981) 41 ALR 255.
80 O'Brien v Komesaroff, *ibid.*
81 See *Kelly v Kelly* (1990) 92 ALR 74.
82 *Robinson v Ashton* (1875) LR 20 Eq 25.
83 [1999] FJHC 85; Hbc0148j.98s (13 August 1999).

just one of the partners, notwithstanding that it might have been so registered. Whether or not it was a partnership asset was a matter to be determined on the evidence.

The property of a partner might be used for the conduct of the business of the partnership. However, that does not necessarily mean that it has lost its status as the property of an individual person who happens, coincidentally, to be a partner. It is certainly true that not every item of property used by a partnership is to be treated as partnership property.[84] Where the partnership, in the course of using the property, makes improvements on the property, however, or otherwise deals with it in a manner inconsistent with the retention of individual ownership, the position might be different.

This issue was taken up in *Burdon v Barkus*. The facts there were that a partnership was created in order to work a coal seam. The seam was located on land owned by one partner. When this seam was finished, the managing partner proceeded to dig another pit to get access to another seam of coal on this same piece of land. The partnership borrowed money on its own account. These loan funds, together with partnership profits, were outlaid on the project. The owner of the land was aware of the activity. No objection was made to it. Indeed, the owner might have benefited from it in the form of a share of extra partnership profits. However, in the view of the court, the circumstances were not such that the partnership had acquired any interest in the land. Despite this, the court went on hold that, on dissolution of the partnership, the non-owning partner should not be deprived of the share of the profit of the partnership which had been expended in the work of constructing the pit.

Turner LJ said:

[This] ... is a case of a partnership for working a mine, in which case, if the partnership is to continue at all, the expenditure is necessary and not voluntary, and it can hardly be that where money is necessarily expended for the benefit of a partnership, the partner expending it is not entitled to be repaid out of the partnership assets. It is true that, expenditure being out of the partnership profits, it falls upon the plaintiff no less than upon the defendant, and if, therefore, no profit can result to the defendant it may not be just that he should be charged with it; but the inquiry leaves this question open.[85]

This decision was approved by Barwick CJ of the High Court of Australia in *Harvey v Harvey* on similar facts. Here the court said:

---

84 See *O'Brien v Komesaroff* (1981) 150 CLR 310; (1981) 41 ALR 255 at 322, *per* Mason J, with whose judgment Murphy, Aickin, Wilson and Brennan JJ agreed. See also *Gian Singh & Co v Nahar* [1965] 1 All ER 768; *Harvey v Harvey* (1970) 120 CLR 529.

85 (1862) 4 De GF & J 42 at para 51; (1862) 45 ER 1098 at 1102, *per* Turner LJ.

His Lordship seemed to place the equity to such an inquiry generally upon the need to prevent an injustice as between the partners but particularly on 'the general doctrine of this Court' (i.e. the Court of Equity) 'with reference to parties standing by and encouraging expenditure'. If I may say so, I would myself prefer to express the particular ground upon which an inquiry of the kind in question should be justified by saying that the construction of the pit had become part of the partnership business, so that expenditure upon it was a partnership expense. But however that may be, the purpose of equity to prevent injustice remains as an overriding consideration in the taking of the partnership accounts.

... As in this case the improvement of the property was part of the partnership business, the making of the improvements was 'necessary' to carry on that business and not 'voluntary' in the sense of those words in the quotation I have just made. Consequently, the cost of effecting the improvements which qualified as being done in the course of the partnership business and for its purposes must be met by the partnership. If one of the partners has so far borne that expense, the other must reimburse him his share of that expenditure.[86]

On this view, there must be something more than the fact that the partnership business is conducted on property owned by one of the partners. The owner-partner must have done something which amounts in effect to an estoppel. Later, Barwick CJ added:

Of course, it is true enough that one partner may allow the partnership business to be carried on on a property or on premises which are and are to remain exclusively his: and the property will not merely by that circumstance become a partnership asset. If in the course of carrying on the partnership business, which does not include the betterment of that property itself as a purpose of the partnership, the partner's property is improved, the partnership will have no claim upon him either in respect of the expense of making the improvement or in the added value which the improvement has brought to the property. But what if the improvement of that property is a purpose of the partnership business? Undoubtedly the cost of the work which effects the improvement is then an expense of the partnership to be borne by the partners in their partnership proportions like any other expense of carrying on the partnership business. As to that, I can feel no doubt.[87]

It was not important here that there was no express agreement to pass some equitable proprietary interest to the other partner. The conduct of the parties was

---

86 (1970) 120 CLR 529 at 547.
87 *Ibid.* at para 24.

sufficient to infer an implied intention that as a result of work and improvements effected, the property was to be regarded henceforth as partnership property.[88]

However, this view was rejected by the majority of the court, who held that in the absence of something to show clearly that the parties intended that the asset be a partnership asset, it need not be treated as such. The rights of parties can still be adjusted on dissolution. Walsh J (with whom Menzies J agreed) said:

> It is true, of course, that just as money may be brought into the partnership assets by way of a contribution by one partner to the capital of the partnership, so also land may be brought in as a contribution to capital. But in any particular case in which there is no formal agreement putting the matter beyond doubt, it must be decided upon a consideration of the circumstances whether it should be concluded that this has been done or whether the partnership has acquired no more than a right to the use of the land. In the present case it may be that the fact that it was contemplated that the land would be improved and that its improvement was one of the purposes of the partnership, could be regarded, if there were no other circumstances relevant to the question, as justifying the conclusion that the land itself was brought in as an asset of the partnership. But in my opinion the other circumstances of the case require the conclusion that it was not.[89]

The making of repairs would not justify any inference that a property is partnership property because that is consistent with the right of use. The making of improvements might give rise to a stronger presumption, although it would seem from the majority view in *Harvey v Harvey* that this would not be enough in itself. There will be difficult situations where improvements are effected to property with the knowledge and consent of the owner. Improvements constitute additions to the property. They cannot be separated from the property nor set aside from it and distinctly owned. Nor can they be sold separately from the property. They are non-divisible. Hence:

> while their cost can be ascertained and their effect upon the value of the property estimated, it is only upon realization of the property that anything which could possibly be regarded as a profit could arise, i.e. the profit – the extent to which the sale price of the property is higher than it would otherwise have been simply because of the improvements effected by the partnership – would be ascertained for the first time.[90]

---

88 *Ibid.* at 550. See also *Kenny's Patent Button-Holeing Co Ltd v Somervell and Lutwyche* (1878) 38 LT (NS) 878; *Waterer v Waterer* (1873) LR15 Eq 402 at 406.

89 *Ibid.* at 563.

90 See *per* Menzies J in *Harvey v Harvey* (1970) 120 CLR 529 at 556. See also *Pettit v Pettit* [1970] AC 777.

However, more would need to be shown than that a partnership made improvements to the property concerned. Indeed, it would also appear that it would not be enough to show that the asset in question was that which produced, directly or otherwise, the partnership income or a part of it.

The real difference between Barwick CJ (and also the court below) and the majority in *Harvey v Harvey* seemed to be on the question of whether the property of one partner could or could not become partnership property on general equitable principles, including particularly estoppel. But, whilst Walsh J pointed out that none of the authorities[91] had actually upheld a case on this ground, there appeared no reason why it could not be. The majority simply seemed to say that they were not satisfied that, given the circumstances before them, there was no basis for inferring that the asset be regarded as partnership property. This does not of itself exclude the application of equitable principles. As Walsh J put it:

> It is common for agreements to be made, particularly amongst members of a family, for the use by a partnership of land which belongs to one of the partners. By such an agreement, unless a different intention is expressed or is to be inferred from the circumstances, the partnership acquires a right to have the use of the land so long as the partnership continues but no greater right or interest in it either at law or in equity than a right to use the land, a right which may be regarded as arising either from a tenancy or from a licence. Subject to that right the ownership of the property remains with its former owner. This type of arrangement is illustrated by the case of *Munro v Commissioner of Stamp Duties* [1934] AC 61 at p 67, in which transfers by way of gift by the owner of the land, upon which under an earlier verbal agreement the business of graziers had been carried on by the owner and his children in partnership, were considered to be gifts of 'the property shorn of the right which belonged to the partnership'.[92]

Walsh J went on to reject the notion that the partnership would be entitled to claim a share in the enhanced value of the owning partner's property. In the context of the above, however, he referred to cases where the asset might actually be contributed, as is common with money, as an actual contribution by a person to the partnership capital or property. His comments appear to refer to exceptions only in the case of the express or implied intentions of the parties. But it would seem that one must still be able to argue that there could be cases where a party stands by and encourages another to undertake work on the strength of an assumption

---

91 He relied on such cases as *Burdon v Barkus* (1862) 4 De GF & J 42, (1862) 45 ER 1098; *Pawsey v Armstrong* (1881) 18 Ch D 698; *Miles v Clarke* [1953] 1 WLR 537.
92 *Harvey v Harvey* (1970) 120 CLR 529 at 562, *per* Walsh J.

that a certain state of affairs would be brought about. It seems clear that this is the direction which the principles of estoppel have taken since this decision.

Accordingly, in *Hall v Hall, Jones and Loquitur Pty Ltd*, Slicer J said:

> Given the developments which have occurred in equitable principles since 1968 (e.g. *Hewett v Court* (1983) 149 CLR 639, *Legione and Another v Hateley* (1983) 152 CLR 406, *The Commercial Bank of Australia Ltd v Amadio* (1983) 151 CLR 447, *Tableland Peanuts Pty Ltd v Peanut Marketing Board* (1984) 57 ALJR 283, *Chan v Zacharia* (1984) 154 CLR 178, *Hospital Products Ltd v United States Surgical Corp and Others* (1984) 156 CLR 41 and others), it is likely that the case would be decided differently today. But one of the approaches taken by the court affords the form of remedy given to the plaintiff. The remedy is available even if the critique referred to as the 'fusion' fallacy applies (see *Daily v Sydney Stock Exchange Ltd* [1981] 2 NSWLR 179, *Cases and Materials on Equity and Trusts*, Meagher, Gummow and Lehane, 2nd ed at 221, and Malcolm, 'The penetration of equitable principles into modern commercial law, part I' (1987) Australian Bar Review Vol 3 No 3). In *Harvey* the court was dealing with a claim for equitable relief made on the basis that the contribution of labour and skill of the partnership considerably improved the property. Menzies and Walsh JJ (Barwick CJ dissenting) held that the land in question did not become an asset of the partnership nor could the additional value attributable to the improvements be taken into account. However, all three justices agreed that the final accounts of the partnership should be varied to the extent that the owner of the land had not been charged with the cost of the making of improvements and that his account should be debited with one half of the expenses. On that approach the plaintiff in these proceedings would be entitled to remedy.[93]

In the case of *Don King Productions v Warren*,[94] the issue was whether the benefit of choses in action which were not legally assignable could be transferred to a partnership and thereby become partnership property. The partnership was one involving the promotion of boxing in Europe. The partnership was dissolved after a dispute. The partnership agreement provided for assignment by each of the partners to the partnership of promotional contracts which they had entered into separately. Because these were exclusive contracts for personal services containing prohibitions against assignment, they could not be legally assigned. The High Court held in the first instance that although the contracts were not assignable, the agreement to assign could be considered in equity as a declaration of trust for the benefit of the partnership. Treated accordingly, they were partnership property

---

93 BC9503012 at 37.
94 [1999] 2 All ER 218.

and given effect as such under the relevant Partnership Act. On appeal, the Court of Appeal affirmed the decision.

In *Lukin v Lovrinov*,[95] one of the issues for determination was whether a fishing quota held by one of the partners became an asset of the partnership. The plaintiff and the defendants had entered into partnership in 1977 to operate a boat in the business of fishing for tuna out of Port Lincoln. One of the defendants was granted a federal government quota in 1984. The quota in effect limited the catch. Those quotas were transferable. After he obtained the quota in question, the defendant leased it out. The proceeds of the leasing were, however, brought into account within the partnership. The defendant afterwards sold off the quota to his son. It was claimed by the plaintiff that the sale price ought to be brought to account in the partnership because the quota had at some stage become partnership property. Perry J held that in all the circumstances, at the time of its acquisition, the quota was not an asset of the partnership.[96] He said:

> The answer is that there is no evidence of anything said or done as between the partners at any stage over the long history of the matter which could support the conclusion that the plaintiff on the one hand and the defendants on the other ever reached an agreement that the quota was to be treated as an asset of the partnership. Furthermore, I do not think that the defendants distinguished between utilisation of the quota to support fishing activities by the partnership using Torpedo as a fishing boat and utilisation of the licence as a means of generating income by leasing out the quota attaching to it.

It was significant that the partners had conducted their affairs in an informal way and had not bothered to distinguish between their personal and their partnership income. This explained the fact that the relevant income was accounted for in the partnership. There was no express or implied agreement at any time that the assets would be treated as partnership assets. Similarly, in *Kelly v Kelly*,[97] the High Court of Australia held that, despite the fact that the annual licence fees were paid by the partnership, an abalone authority attached to the licence, the proceeds of which were paid into the partnership, was not an asset of the partnership. As regards joint bank accounts to which contributions in irregular amounts are made from time to time by the partnership, the normal assumption is that it is partnership property. The onus lies with any person asserting that specific moneys found in the account

---

95 [1998] SASC 6614.
96 See also *Kelly v Kelly* (1990) 92 ALR 74; cf *Matariki Ltd v Deadman & Anor* CA 15–99, 2 September 1999 (which was argued on grounds of unconscionability and estoppel).
97 *Kelly v Kelly* (1990) 92 ALR 74.

did not belong to the partnership.[98] Where the account is held in the name of some partners only, it might be inferred that it is held on trust for all partners.[99]

The legislation contains a specific provision dealing with situations where individuals are the co-owners of land and are also partners. Where profits are generated from the land and these profits are applied in the purchase of further land, it is to be assumed, in the absence of agreement to the contrary, that the land so purchased is not to be regarded as partnership property.[100]

Contributions and entitlements to partnership capital are not the same thing as rights to partnership property. Partnership property means the items of property or the assets which are owned by the partnership as a whole. Capital is owned individually and, although it is available for use by the partners, it does not become something in which the remaining partners acquire an interest. The individual is entitled to a return of capital on dissolution. Partnership property would normally be something which is sold in the event of dissolution prior to being divided.[101] As Lord Andrews CJ said in *McClelland v Hyde*,[102] 'the capital of a partnership is something different from its property or its assets'. Capital may be introduced by a partner, which is a benefit to the partnership. But such introduction of capital does not, without more, mean that another partner becomes entitled to claim a share of that capital.[103]

The entitlement to a return to the partners of their contributed capital will normally have some priority in the event of a dissolution, subject only to the claims of external creditors. In *Binney v Mutrie*, it was said:

> Their Lordships understand that all claims of persons external to the partnership have been satisfied. That being so, it is clear that the surplus assets should be first applied in paying to each partner his claims in respect of capital. The residue will be profits, and will be divisible as such.[104]

The same approach was adopted by the High Court of Australia in *Rowella Proprietary Ltd v Abfam Nominees Proprietary Ltd*, where it was stated:

> Out of the assets of the firm, the partners are entitled to a return of the capital contributed in priority to any share in the 'ultimate residue' ... The ultimate residue ... is the surplus remaining after external creditors have been paid ...

---

98 See *Brady v Stapleton* (1952) 88 CLR 322.

99 See *Hume v Lopes* [1892] AC 112,115; *Hall v Hall, Jones and Loquitur Pty Ltd* BC9503012.

100 Section 21(1) (F) Partnership Act.

101 See further below.

102 [1942] NI 1, 7.

103 *Hall v Hall, Jones and Loquitur Pty Ltd* BC9503012.

104 (1886) 12 App Cas 160 at 165, *per* Lord Hobhouse.

and the partners have received out of the assets of the partnership a return of the advances they have made and of the capital they contributed.[105]

The existence of a partnership asset would seem to suggest a requirement as to the existence of the partnership or at least the duties of partners *inter se*. In respect of a dissolution of partnership, the obligations of the partners are continued for the purposes of winding up the affairs of the partnership after the dissolution.

In *Sew Hoy v Sew Hoy*,[106] the Court of Appeal of New Zealand had to consider a situation where a partnership which had been dissolved subsequently became entitled to property pursuant to a right which was not known to exist at the time of dissolution. A parcel of land was acquired by three brothers and their wives in 1973 as tenants in common. The land became the sole partnership asset. Three years later, the Crown compulsorily acquired the land for public works and title passed to it in 1976. One of the partners died in 1977, an event which dissolved the partnership in accordance with s 36 of the Partnership Act 1908 (NZ). The final compensation payment in respect of the land acquisition was not made by the Crown to the former owners until 1982. By then the Public Works Act 1981 had come into force and the former owners, including the estate of the deceased partner, all became entitled to the benefit of the statutory offer-back rights conferred by s 40 of that Act. Such rights did not exist under the previous legislation, the Public Works Act 1928, which vested the land in the Crown entirely free of all former claims and interests. In 1992, the Crown determined that a part of the land taken in 1976 was surplus to its requirements and proceeded to make an offer in accordance with s 40 of the Public Works Act. One former partner proceeded to take advantage of the offer to the exclusion of the others. The issue was whether this constituted a breach of duty such that the transaction could be set aside by the remaining former partners.

At first instance, it was held that the acquisition of land by the Crown was incomplete at the time of the partnership dissolution because compensation payments were not completed by the Crown until 1982. Therefore, under the general law and the Partnership Act, the obligations of the partners continued so far as was necessary to complete the transaction. However, Chisolm J considered that the offer by the Crown pursuant to s 40 of the Public Works Act was a new transaction. Thus, he found that the right to have the land offered back was not itself a partnership asset: it was not certain that the land would ever be offered back. Any other interpretation would give rise to the 'extraordinary situation' that partnerships whose land had been taken under the Public Works Act would effectively linger indefinitely. Chisolm J also found that, in the absence of continuing duties of partnership, the other partners' claim that the respondents owed them a fiduciary

---

105 (1989) 168 CLR 301 at 305, 306.
106 [2000] NZCA 314.

duty to disclose all relevant information relating to the land could not be sustained. There was nothing fiduciary in the relationship of co-owners as such. Whilst there had been a history of cooperation and a degree of mutual reliance between the various family groups represented in the partnership, this did not continue at the time the Crown made its offer under s 40 of the Public Works Act.

On appeal, the court rejected the arguments of the appellants claiming that the asset was in the nature of a substantive present property right in the nature of a pre-emption or option. It was nothing more than 'an expectation or hope (*spes*)' that might be realised at an indefinite future time.[107] Being an 'inchoate right' it was not something which was anticipated by s 41 of the Partnership Act, which deems the relationship between partners to continue after dissolution for the purposes of winding up affairs of the partnership and to complete transactions begun but unfinished at the time of the dissolution.[108]

8.2.2 Presumption of equal entitlement

In the absence of anything to the contrary in the partnership agreement, it will be assumed that the entitlement of partners to both property and profits of the partnership are equal. Section 25(a) of the Partnership Act of Fiji confirms this as follows:

> 25(a) all the partners are entitled to share equally in the capital and profits of the business and must contribute equally towards the losses, whether of capital or otherwise, sustained by the firm.

In *Joyce v Morrissey*,[109] the English Court of Appeal was faced with a dispute as to entitlement to profits. The partners were members of a rock band. In the first instance, it had been held that one of the band members was entitled to a quarter share of the profits. This relied on s 24 of the Partnership Act 1890 (UK), under which partners are entitled to an equal share of the profits of the partnership, in the absence of any contrary agreement. That provision is to the same effect as s 25(a) of the Fiji Act.

Two of the other band members appealed, claiming that they were the main instigators of the band. They relied on the existence of an understanding that they would be entitled to 40% of the profits each, 10% each going to the remaining two. This claim appeared to be supported by information contained in some of the accounts prepared by the group's accountants and provided to the plaintiff but not the subject of comment from him. The Court of Appeal upheld the High Court's

---

107 See also *Attorney General v Horton* [1999] 2 NZLR 257 at 261.
108 [2000] NZCA 314 at para 14, 28, 30.
109 [1998] TLR 707.

decision that the four band members were entitled to an equal share of the profits. It held that s 24(1) of the Act applied. The entitlement to profits was not affected by the consent of the partnership accounts sent out. Nor could it be assumed from the silence of the plaintiff (i.e. the lack of response) that there was acceptance of the revised terms. The fact that the plaintiff might not have been able to understand the accounts without advice was relevant.

8.2.3 Profits of a partnership

The profits of a partnership business belong to the partners. It is assumed, by virtue of the statutory provision just mentioned, that the partners are entitled equally to profits, but this assumption might be overridden by the terms of the partnership agreement which might allocate entitlement to profits differentially as between the partners. The partnership agreement will also usually settle when the partners are entitled to make drawings on profits from time to time. Some partners under the partnership agreement might be allocated a right to a salary over and above profits, for example in respect of the performance of a management role in the partnership.

A partner is not usually entitled to require a distribution of profits or net income until accounts have been prepared. Nonetheless, the partner still has a particular interest in the net income of the partnership. This is so even though the precise amount of this interest may not be capable of determination until the accounts are prepared for the relevant period.[110]

8.2.4 Goodwill

Goodwill of the partnership business is partnership property and must be dealt with accordingly. Goodwill has been defined as 'the benefit and advantage of the good name, reputation and connection of a business'.[111] In *Box v Federal Commissioner of Taxation*, Fullagar and Kitto JJ of the High Court of Australia said:

> Goodwill includes whatever adds value to a business, and different businesses derive their value from different considerations. The goodwill of some businesses is derived almost entirely from the place where they are carried on, some goodwills are purely personal, and some goodwills derive their value partly from the locality where the business is carried on and partly from the

---

110 See *Rowe, B. v The Commissioner of Taxation* [1982] FCA 107; (1982) 82 ATC 4243 at 4244; (1982) 60 FLR 475 at 476; *Rose v Federal Commissioner of Taxation* [1951] HCA 68; (1951) 84 CLR 118 at 124; *FCT v Galland* (1986) 162 CLR 408 at para 8.
111 *Inland Revenue Commissioners v Muller & Co's Margarine Ltd* [1905] HCA 57; 3 CLR 393; [1901] AC 217 at 223.

reputation built up around the name of the individual or firm or company under which it has previously been carried on.[112]

In *Geraghty v Minter*, Stephen J said:

Goodwill of a partnership business is an inseverable whole unless, of course, it consists in fact of a series of separate goodwills, each applicable to distinct areas in which the one business operates or to distinct business activities which the one business entity carries on. When sold, proceeds of goodwill may be divided up readily enough, but … it is inherently inseverable from the business to which it relates. It may cease to exist or may be purloined by one who falsely represents his own business as the original business, but it cannot be disposed of separately from the business which created it nor can it survive the cessation of that business. The reason is simple: since it reflects and is dependent upon the reputation of that business, to sever it from the business destroys it.[113]

It is usual practice to insert a restraint of trade clause in a partnership agreement in order to protect the goodwill of a continuing partnership against competition by outgoing partners. In *Geraghty v Minter*, it was said:

Thus where, after dissolution, the business previously conducted by a partnership continues to be carried on under the same name by one of the former parties or by a purchaser, the old goodwill will tend, at least initially, to adhere to that business. As time passes the business, under its new management, will acquire for itself its own distinctive goodwill which will gradually take the place of the old goodwill. The function of restraint clauses is the better to ensure that this initial adherence of goodwill is not interfered with by the activities of the former owners of the business.[114]

112 *Ibid.* at 397.
113 (1979) HCA 42; 142 CLR 177 at 193.
114 *Ibid.*

9

THE TRUSTEE

9.1 The trustee's duties

Let us look first at the duties of trustees. A set of given duties of any one individual gives rise to a set of corresponding rights in others. In this case, those others are the beneficiaries under the trust. The role of the trustee is pivotal in the management of affairs of the trust. We note in earlier chapters that a trustee provides the classical model of a fiduciary, in the sense that the position of a trustee under a trust is a kind of exemplar for all other types of fiduciary relationship. The trustee's fiduciary duty is more onerous than for other categories of fiduciary.

The primary duty of a trustee is as a fiduciary, requiring that the trustee act exclusively in the interests of the beneficiaries. In negative terms, the trustee, like other fiduciaries, must avoid conflicts of duty and interest. The trustee's duties are generally restrictive in nature, to such an extent that some authors have raised the question as to whether they are duties or disabilities.[1] In the commercial context, there is the added factor that the restrictive nature of the duties can make the role unsuitable to commercial decision making and activity generally. This element, coupled with the fact that the courts take a rather restrictive view of the trustee's powers and the legitimate purposes to which the trust property may be applied, suggests that there are some dangers inherent in the use of trusts for commercial purposes. It also suggests that when commercial trusts are created, considerable attention needs to be given to the definition of the trustee's powers and functions so as to make the trust more suitable to commercial activity.

---

1 Heydon, John D and Leeming, Mark J, *Jacob's Law of Trusts in Australia*, 2016, NSW, LexisNexis Butterworths, 8th edn; Watson, S and Taylor, L, *Corporate Law in New Zealand,* 2018, Wellington Thomson Reuters New Zealand Ltd.

DOI: 10.4324/9781003428060-11

Many of the trustee's duties considered below are aspects or incidents of the general fiduciary obligations of trustees.[2] Trustees, in the performance of their office, are under a duty to take care pursuant to the law of negligence, but this too is sometimes treated in trust law as one situation which might constitute a breach of trust. The office of a trustee is an onerous one. The acceptance of the office of trustee has been described as 'an act of great kindness', at least by those who are not statutory trustee companies.[3] Furthermore a trustee must, with some exceptions, act gratuitously in the performance of his or her office.[4] It has been suggested that:

In exercising his discretions a trustee must act honestly and must use as much diligence as a prudent man of business would exercise in dealing with his own private affairs; in selecting an investment he must take as much care as a prudent man would take in making an investment for the benefit of persons for whom he felt morally bound to provide. … If he takes the same care of the trust property as a man of ordinary prudence would take of his own, he will not be liable for accidental loss, such as a theft of the property while in his possession or in the possession of others to whom it has been entrusted in the ordinary course of business, or a depreciation in the value of the securities upon which the trust funds have been rightfully invested.[5]

---

2 Finn, PD, *Fiduciary Obligations*, 1977, Sydney, Law Book Co, p 15.

3 See *Knight v Earl of Plymouth* (1747) Dick 120 at 126. Statutory trustee companies are those created under specific legislation and may charge fees for their services. Their duties are, however, no less onerous in other respects.

4 Meagher, R and Gummow, W (eds), *Jacobs' Law of Trusts in Australia*, 1997, Sydney, Butterworths, p 416: "In accordance with the rule of equity that trustees must not profit by their trust, trustees are not, as a general rule, entitled to remuneration for their labours in the trust; they are entitled to no compensation either for their personal trouble or for loss of time. Equity looks upon trusts as honorary and a burden upon the honour and conscience of the trustee"; trusts are not considered to be undertaken for mercenary reasons. The reason underlying the rule is that the interest and duty of the trustee must not be brought into conflict. The rule is really an illustration of the more general principle that no one who has a fiduciary duty to perform shall place himself in such a position that his interest will, or even may, conflict with that duty, and that if interest and duty do conflict, interest must give way. See also *Robinson v Pett* (1734) 3 P Wms 249, 24 ER 1049; *Barrett v Hartley* (1866) LR 2 Eq 789; *Ayliffe v Murray* (1740) 2 Atk 58, 26 ER 433; *Bray v Ford* [1896] AC 44 at 51, (1895–99) All ER Rep 1009; *Re Corsellis, Lawton v Elwes* (1887) 34 Ch D 675 at 681; *New v Jones* (1833) 1 Mac & G 668, n, 41 ER 1429.

5 Baker, PV and Langan, K, *Snell's Principles of Equity*, 1982, London, Sweet & Maxwell, p 221, referring variously to *Re Smith, Smith v Thompson* [1896] 1 Ch 71; *Learoyd v Whitely* (1887) 12 App Cas 727; *In Re Luckings Will Trust* [1968] 1 WLR 866 at 874; *Morley v Morley* (1678) 2 Ch Cas 2; *Speight v Gaunt* (1883) 9 App Cas 1; *In re Chapman, Cocks v Chapman* [1896] 2 Ch 763.

9.1.1 *The duty to be familiar with the terms of the trust*

A trustee may assume office either at the moment of creation of the trust or at some time afterwards. In the first case, the trustee is an original trustee. A trustee may also be appointed as an additional or a replacement trustee to a trust that is already in existence.[6] The duty to be familiar with the terms of the trust will apply in either case. A trustee must know the nature and extent of the trust property under the trustee's charge and the general terms of the trust that is to be administered or managed.[7] The duty requires more than a mere reading of the trust instrument. It requires an appreciation of the meaning of its contents.[8]

9.1.2 *The duty to adhere to the terms of the trust*

A trustee must, as a general rule, adhere to the terms of the trust and act within the scope of authority conferred. Trustees who depart from the terms of the trust, even where it appears justifiable, might be held liable for a breach of trust.[9] However, a trustee need not carry out or abide by terms of the trust that are impossible to carry out or are illegal.[10] The principle is not dissimilar to that which applies to agents and partners. A trustee is personally liable for any loss which is occasioned by acting outside the scope of authority.[11] Under limited circumstances the court has power to vary the terms of the trust. Sometimes, of course, a trustee may experience difficulties in adhering strictly to the terms of the trust. The express terms may lack clarity, or it may have become impossible to carry them out. In such a case, there are two courses of action open to the trustee. First, the trustee has the right to approach the court for directions and should do so where there is any doubt about matters of interpretation of the terms of the trust. Secondly, in some cases, the trustee may depart from the terms of the trust where the beneficiaries, all of whom are *sui juris* and absolutely entitled to their respective interests, unanimously direct the trustees to do so. This is based on the principle that beneficiaries who fall into this category can, pursuant to the rule in *Saunders v Vautier*,[12] put an end to the trust.[13]

---

6 Meagher and Gummow, *op cit* fn 5, p 334.
7 See *Hallows v Lloyd* (1888) 39 Ch D 686 at 692.
8 See *Turner v Turner* [1983] 2 All ER 745.
9 *Fry v Fry* (1859) 27 Beav 144; 54 ER 56.
10 *Re Beard; Beard v Hall* [1908] 1 Ch 383.
11 Meagher and Gummow, *op cit* fn 5, p 381.
12 (1841) 41 ER 482; 4 Beav 115.
13 *Wharton v. Masterman* [1895] AC 186 at 198, *per* Lord Davey, cited in *Berwick v. Canada Trust Co*, [1948] S.C.R. 151 at p 156: "[The] principle of *Saunders v Vautier* ... would at once be applicable if this were the case of a gift to an individual. That principle is this: that where there is an absolute vested gift made payable at a future event, with direction to accumulate the income in the meantime, and pay it with the principal, the court will not enforce the trust for accumulation in which no person has any interest but the legatee, or [in other words] the court holds that a legatee may put an end to an accumulation which is exclusively for his benefit".

Generally, however, trustees are not bound to follow the directions of beneficiaries unless they are, in effect, agents of the beneficiaries.[14] The trustee is in control of the trust, not the beneficiaries, and thus independence of decision-making action is required.[15] The beneficiaries in *Saunders v Vautier* situations can, if they want, terminate the trust but cannot interfere otherwise with the independence of the trustee.

If a trustee seeks directions from the court, then the following of those directions will provide the trustee with immunity.[16] The courts have two types of jurisdiction to grant directions: inherent and statutory. The inherent jurisdiction derives from the court's supervisory function with respect to the administration of trusts in general. This power, however, is limited, in that the court will not permit dispositions of the trust property which were not originally established by the testator or settlor. In *Fitzpatrick v Waring*, it was said:

> The Court, in such a case, whether it assumes the place of the trustee, or guides him in the discharge of his duties, is still confined within the limits of the trust as constituted by its author, and has no authority to go beyond those limits. Its business is to execute the trusts, not to alter them.[17]

The right of a trustee to apply for directions is contained in the trustee legislation.[18] There are statutory powers given to the courts to authorise a departure from the express terms of a trust instrument and to vary the terms of the trust. These are further considered in Chapter 27.[19]

9.1.3 The duty to get in the trust property

The trustee has an additional duty to get in the trust property so as to administer it according to the terms of the trust. Obviously, under the terms of creation of the trust, the trust property has to be legally vested in the name of the trustee. However, 'getting in' here means exercising actual control with respect to that property. It would be a breach of this duty if the trustee allowed the property to

---

14 *Re Brockbank* [1948] Ch 206.
15 *Turner v Turner* [1983] 2 All ER 745.
16 *Re New* [1901] 2 Ch 534.
17 (1882) 11 LR Ir 35 at 44, *per* Lord Chancellor in. *Re Hazeldine's Trusts* [1908] 1 Ch 34 at 40–41, *per* Farwell LJ, as originally cited in the Court of Appeal, in *Gonzales v Claridades* (2003) 58 NSWLR 211 at 218, in para 33, as cited in *Westfield Queensland No 1 Pty Ltd v Lend Lease Real Estate Investments Ltd* [2008] NSWSC 516; BC200803975 at para 40.
18 Section 88 Trustee Act (F); s 25(4)(c) Trusts Act 2014, although no equivalent provision (S); s 66 Trustee Act 1956 (NZ), (CI); also see s 639(1) Cook Islands Act 1915; repealed in Niue, see s 703 Niue Act 1966 (Ni).
19 Section 89 Trustee Act (F); s 10(6), although no equivalent provision (S); s 57 Trustee Act (UK) (K), (SI), (V).

remain under the control of a third party and thereby inhibited his or her own power to administer. It matters little whether the trustee is an original trustee appointed at the time the trust came into existence, or a substitute or additional trustee appointed by the court.[20] The general requirement is that the trustees must have the property under their own control. Debts owed to the trust must be collected and the money brought under the control of trustees.[21]

9.1.4 The duty to preserve trust property

The duty of the trustee to preserve trust property is one of the trustee's central duties. As we have noted before, much of the conservatism displayed by the courts with respect to questions of trustee investment and trust businesses is a result of the central importance assigned to this duty. The preservation of the trust property is accorded a higher priority than the generation of trust profits by business activity. In *Speight v Gaunt*,[22] it was found that the trustee, on acquiring the trust property, is under a duty in respect of its management and administration to take all those precautions which an ordinary prudent person would take in managing similar affairs of their own. In this regard, Ford and Lee suggest:

> The way in which the trustee will perform his duty of care will depend upon the terms of the trust, the nature of the property settled upon trust and the powers conferred upon him by the trust instrument and by the law. For instance, in the case of a strict trust for successive beneficiaries it will be the duty of the trustee to maintain an even hand between the beneficiaries entitled to the capital and those entitled to the income. This duty will oblige him to invest the trust fund in securities which will preserve its capital value for the benefit of the capital beneficiaries and produce income for the income beneficiaries. On the other hand if the trustee is not required to maintain separate capital and income accounts, for instance, if the trust is a discretionary trust as to both income and capital, it may well be proper for the trustee to pursue capital appreciation rather than income production or vice versa. If the trust fund is small in size the trustee may well be within the duty of care imposed upon him in investing within the range of trustee securities permitted by statute, ... although that range may be narrow and not necessarily investment wise. This is because the high cost of seeking the permission of the court to enlarge his investment powers, followed by the relatively high administrative costs of forming and maintaining a sophisticated investment portfolio, might well outweigh the small loss

---

20 *Hallows v Lloyd* (1888) 39 Ch D 686.
21 See *Field v Field* (1894) 1 Ch 425; *Partridge v Equity Trustee Executors and Agency Co Ltd* [1947] HCA 42; 75 CLR 149.
22 (1883) 9 App Cas 1.

which a virtually cost-free investment in the financially unattractive but statutorily authorised portfolio in which case the costs of obtaining the consent of the court to an enlargement of the investment powers in order to do so would be justified.[23]

Clearly enough, the expectations will vary from one trust to another. Where the trustee is a professional trustee, the duty is no higher than for an ordinary person.

9.1.5 The duty to invest trust funds

A trustee is obliged to ensure that the funds of the trust fund are properly invested. Investment has, however, a restricted meaning in trust law. It cannot include those 'investments' which are speculative in nature. Nor does it include those, the prime purpose of which is the generation of profit alone. In this regard, the trustee's duty to preserve trust property, above, is highly influential. We will examine the issue of investment of trust funds further below.

9.1.6 The duty to keep and render accounts

A trustee must keep proper and complete records of his or her administration of the trust. Normally a trustee is obliged to make those records and accounts accessible to the trust beneficiaries, except in cases where confidentiality can justifiably be claimed. Even the potential object under a discretionary trust has a right to inspect the trustee's records.[24] A trustee is not entitled to destroy records at the termination of the trust.[25]

9.1.7 The duty to be loyal

Loyalty is one specific aspect of the trustee's fiduciary obligation mentioned above and in Chapter 3. Loyalty implies an aspect of other trustee duties such as acting exclusively for the beneficiaries, not making a profit out of the trust, not being able to purchase trust property,[26] acting impartially as between the beneficiaries, not fettering the exercise of powers or discretions in any way and setting up rights of

---

23 Heydon and Leeming, and Watson and Taylor, *op cit* fn 2.
24 See on the duty generally *Burrows v Walls* (1855) 5 De GM & G 233; 3 ER 859.
25 *Payne v Evens* (1874) LR 18 Eq 356.
26 The purchase rule, which applies to other fiduciaries as well, states that a trustee is completely incapacitated from purchasing the trust property unless the instrument or the court clearly authorises it. A second aspect of the rule is that the trustee may purchase at a fair price with the informed consent of all of the beneficiaries. See *De Bussche v Alt* (1878) 8 Ch D 286; *Nugent v Nugent* [1908] 1 Ch 546; *Queensland Mines Ltd v Hudson* (1978) 52 ALJR 399. See Heydon and Leeming, and Watson and Taylor, *op cit* fn 2.

third parties against those of the beneficiaries.[27] It is also an aspect of the duty to observe and abide by the terms of the trust.

9.1.8 The duty not to delegate

A trustee is forbidden from delegating his or her powers to another person. On acceptance of office, he or she accepts the duty to act personally in carrying out the trust. Some delegation may be permitted by the trust instrument or in cases of necessity, for example, the employment of agents and professionals. The trustee legislation also permits the employment of agents, solicitors and professionals by providing a trustee with limited powers to do so. Where the trustee has legitimately appointed an agent there is no clear indication in equity as to the degree of control that should be exercised with respect to the agent. The expected degree of control must admit variation from case to case. The trustee cannot be permitted to undertake a merely passive role at all times. Under certain circumstances, the trustee must be put on notice and there will be factors that will require the trustee to be more cautious than usual. The trustee retains the ultimate control and personal liability for the administration of the trust and therefore needs to maintain some degree of vigilance over the activity or non-activity of an agent.

The rule against delegation will prevent a trustee from giving up the primary obligations that he or she has with respect to the administration of the trust. There will be a breach of this rule where the trustee has elected to sit back and let others, beneficiaries or otherwise, undertake the primary duties of administration of the trust.

9.1.9 The duty to distribute

A trustee is under a duty to distribute the trust property to the beneficiaries entitled to it when they are all of full age and capacity and when their interests are appropriately vested and they call for the termination of the trust. The same applies when the terms of the trust itself call for distribution. Certain immunities attach to a trustee who distributes after a notice of intended distribution is given. The duty to distribute and the right of immunity are discussed further below.

9.2 The trustee's rights

We turn now to the question of the rights of the trustee. Again, some of these rights are established by the traditional role of the equity courts in the articulation of the functions of the trustee. In other cases, they have been extended in some

---

27 *Newsome v Flowers* (1861) 30 Beav 461, 470; 54 ER 968, 972, *per* Sir Romilly MR; *McGregor v McGregor* (1899) 7 NZLR 538.

respects by the trustee legislation. Whilst the trustee's duties are onerous there are certain special rights which alleviate this burden to some extent. Equity has not merely left the trustee 'out on a limb', so to speak. It would be incorrect to regard the trustee's position as one consisting merely of duties alone. For example, trustees are always reminded of their duty in equity to act gratuitously, although in law trustees may under certain circumstances have rights to receive remuneration by way of commission. We will set out some of the main rights of a trustee below.

9.2.1 The right to commission

In equity a trustee is generally expected to act gratuitously. There are, however, some well-established exceptions. A trustee can take a commission where:

(1) remuneration is provided for expressly or impliedly in the trust instrument;[28]
(2) the court expressly allows it as part of its inherent jurisdiction.[29] According to the decision in *Duke of Norfolk's Settlement Trust*,[30] jurisdiction of the court in this regard is an exceptional one to be exercised sparingly. The singular ground for allowance of commission is the necessity of obtaining the services of either some particular individual trustee, whose services were of special value to the trust, or some particular kind of trustee, such as a trust corporation;
(3) the trust property is situated abroad in a country where remuneration is permitted;[31]
(4) there is an agreement between the trustee and the beneficiaries, all of whom are *sui juris*.[32] The courts will closely scrutinise the agreement;
(5) statute so provides. Under certain circumstances, commission can be allowed to the legal personal representatives of a deceased estate under probate legislation of various jurisdictions in the South Pacific. In other cases, the trustee legislation provides for an award of remuneration to trustees by the courts;[33]
(6) the trustee is solicitor-trustee under the rule in *Cradock v Piper*.[34] The rule allows a solicitor-trustee to recover his or her profit costs as a solicitor when

---

28 *Re Pooley* (1888) 40 Ch D 1.
29 *Re Freeman's Settlement Trusts* (1887) 37 Ch D 148, 152.
30 [1979] Ch 37 at 58.
31 *Northcote v Northcote* [1949] 1 All ER 442; Bishop, W and Prentice, D, 'Some legal and economic aspects of fiduciary remuneration' (1983) 46 MLR 289 at 306.
32 *Re Will of Moore* (1896) 17 LR (NSW) B 78; *Bray v Ford* [1896] AC 44; (1895–99) All ER Rep 1009; *Robinson v Pett* (1734) 3 P Wms 249, 24 ER 1049; *Re Will of J Lockett* (1920) SR (NSW) 213; (1920) 37 WN (NSW); *Northcote v Northcote* [1949] 1 All ER 442; *Re Gee; Wood v Staples* [1948] 1 All ER 498; *Peach v Jagger* (1910) NZLR 423, Heydon and Leeming, and Watson and Taylor, *op cit* fn 2.
33 See e.g. s 94 Trustee Act (F).
34 (1850) 1 Mac & G 664; 41 ER 1422.

he or she acts in legal proceedings on behalf of himself and his co-trustee jointly, provided his or her so acting did not increase the trust expenses;[35]

(7) the trustee is a statutory trustee company which is permitted under relevant legislation, such as the Trustee Corporations Act Cap 66 of Fiji, to charge commission for its services.

The amount of commission payable in a given case to a trustee will depend on the extent of the work to be undertaken on behalf of the estate, the degree of responsibility exercised and the level of skill and specialised knowledge required.[36]

9.2.2 The right of reimbursement for expenses and liabilities

A trustee is entitled to indemnity with respect to liabilities and indemnities incurred on behalf of the trust and within the scope of his or her authority. As noted above, the debts or liabilities of a trust are really those of the trustee. A trustee may, however, avoid personal liability if they enter into, say, a contract on behalf of the trust and expressly exclude personal liability and indicate to the other party that all liabilities will be met out of a particular fund of the trust assets.[37] To do so requires a clause which is quite clear in its confinement of the creditor's rights to a particular fund and the exclusion of personal liability of the trustee. Merely including the trustee as a contractor in the capacity of trustee will not be enough. In any of these situations, the trustee may claim indemnity or recoupment out of the trust assets, or out of the assets of the beneficiaries. A trustee may also claim indemnity against a co-trustee where action has been taken against him or her on an individual basis.

There are two basic kinds of trustee indemnity. The main one is a right of indemnity out of the trust assets. The second, more restricted kind, is that against the beneficiaries personally. In general, the trustee's right extends to a recovery of any expenses or liabilities, including for example tortious liabilities,[38] debts, contract liabilities and other expenses of proper administration of the trust. The last of these might include, for example, litigation costs where they are sued by the ben-

---

35 See Bishop and Prentice, *op cit* fn 32, p 306; Martin, JE, *Hanbury and Maudsley's Modern Equity*, 1985, London, Stevens, pp 570–71.

36 *Roman Catholic Trusts Corporation for the Diocese of Melbourne v National Trustees, Executors and Agency Co of Australasia Ltd* (Kaye J, Supreme Court of Victoria, 26 June 1981, unreported) cited and approved in *Allen v Union Fidelity Co of Australia* (1986) 6 NSWLR 341.

37 *Re Anderson; Ex parte Alexander* (1927) SR (NSW) 296 and generally Heydon and Leeming, and Watson and Taylor, *op cit* fn 2.

38 Thus, in *Bennet v Wyndham* (1862) 4 De GF & J 259; 45 ER 1183, whilst woodcutters employed by the trustee carried on their work, they felled a tree and a bough injured a passer-by. The trustee was found personally liable to pay damages to the injured man. It was held further that the trustee, having acted with due diligence and employed a proper agent within the scope of his duty, was entitled to indemnity out of the trust estate.

eficiaries complaining against their administration of the trusts.[39] Where a trustee is not authorised to carry on the business, they are entitled only to expenses they incur for the purpose of realisation of that business enterprise. Where they have authority to carry on the business, they are entitled to be indemnified in priority to the rights of the beneficiaries and trade creditors of the business.[40] But if they have no authority to carry on the business beyond the period required for realisation, they have no right to indemnity in priority to the creditors unless the creditors actively and positively assented to the carrying on of the business. We will consider the rights of indemnity further below.

9.2.3 The right of contribution from co-trustees

The liability of co-trustees to creditors and other third parties is joint and several. Where one of two or more trustees personally meets any legitimate expenses relating to the trust, they are entitled to a contribution from the co-trustees for their share of the expenses incurred.[41] There are times, however, when a trustee in this position may call upon the co-trustee to meet the whole expense and not only contribute a part of it. In this case, the trustee will seek indemnity from the co-trustee. In *Bahin v Hughes*,[42] one of two trustees of a fund innocently but wrongfully invested the fund in a mortgage with insufficient security. The trustees were found to be jointly and severally liable. The trustee who had left the whole transaction in the hands of the first trustee claimed indemnity from the latter. The claim was rejected, the court saying:

> Miss Hughes was the active trustee and Mr Edwards did nothing, and in my opinion it would be laying down a wrong rule to hold that where one trustee acts honestly, though erroneously, the other trustee is to be held entitled to indemnity who by doing nothing neglects his duty more than the acting trustee. That Miss Hughes made an improper investment is true, but she acted honestly, and intended to do the best she could and believed that the property was sufficient security for the money although she made no inquiries about their being leasehold houses. In my opinion the money was lost as much by the default of Mr Edwards as by the innocent though erroneous action of his co-trustee, Miss Hughes. All the trustees were in the wrong, and everyone is equally liable to indemnify the beneficiaries.

---

39 *National Trustees Executors and Agency Company of Australasia Ltd v Barnes* (1941) 64 CLR 268.
40 *Vacuum Oil Company Pty Ltd v Wiltshire* (1945) 72 CLR 319 at 324–25; see also *Strickland v Symons* (1884) 26 Ch D 245.
41 *Chillingworth v Chambers* [1896] 1 Ch 685.
42 (1886) 31 Ch D 390.

However, it was suggested that where one of the trustees is a solicitor-trustee or similarly has a professional expertise and capacity leaving the administration to that person may be justified.[43] The maxim that 'equity is equality' applies to the working out of liabilities between trustees. The courts and beneficiaries are not concerned with the relative degree of culpability of individual trustees when a breach of trust has occurred. Trustees will be held severally and jointly liable to put right the breach. Consequently, any debt owed by the trustees can be discharged by any one trustee from their personal resources, but a contribution may thereafter be sought from the co-trustees. However, where a co-trustee is also a beneficiary under the trust, he or she is not entitled to claim a contribution or indemnity from the other trustee. In *Chillingworth v Chambers*,[44] the plaintiff and defendant, the trustees of a will, invested funds of the trust in authorised securities. The plaintiff also became entitled as a beneficiary to a share of the trust estate. The investments, some of which were made before and others after the plaintiff became a beneficiary, turned out to be insufficient. The plaintiff and defendant were declared jointly and severally liable to make good the loss to the estate. The loss was made satisfied out of the plaintiff's share of the trust estate which was in excess of the loss. The plaintiff sought a contribution from the defendant. It was held that the right of contribution for loss arising from a breach of trust for which both are culpable does not apply where one of the trustees is also a beneficiary and has received an exclusive benefit as a result of the breach of trust. It would appear that the share or interest of a beneficiary who has profited by a breach of trust must bear the whole loss. The trustee who is a beneficiary must therefore indemnify the co-trustee to the extent of his or her share or interest in the trust estate, and not merely to the extent of the benefit he or she has received.

9.2.4 The right to impound a beneficiary's interest

Both the general law and the relevant trustee legislation provide for the trustee's right of impounding of a beneficiary's interest where the beneficiary has instigated a breach of trust by a trustee. The relevant statutory provisions take the following form, following s 72 of the Fiji Trustee Act:

> 72 (1) Where a trustee commits a breach of trust at the instigation or request or with the written consent of the beneficiary, the Court may, if it thinks fit, make such order as to the Court seems just for impounding all or any part of the

---

43 *Ibid.* See also *Lockhart v Reilly* (1856) 25 LJ (Ch) 697; *Thompson v Finch* (1856) 22 Beav 316, 52 ER 1130 & 8 De GM & G 560, 44 ER 506 (CA); *Blyth v Fladgate* [1891] 1 Ch 337 at 365; cf *Head v Gould* (1898) 2 Ch 250.

44 [1896] 1 Ch 685.

interest of the beneficiary in the trust estate by way of indemnity to the trustee or person claiming through him.

(2) The provisions of subsection (1) shall be deemed to empower the Court to impound all or any part of the interest of any beneficiary who receives any pecuniary benefit from the breach of the trust.

(3) This section applies not withstanding that the beneficiary may be a married woman entitled for her separate use and restrained from anticipation.

9.2.5 The right to approach the court

A trustee might often be placed in a position of uncertainty in relation to how the trust is to be administered or whether he or she has particular powers to perform certain acts. In such a situation, it is best for the trustee to avoid risks. One primary aspect of the court's jurisdiction with respect to trusts is that of supervision and the ability to provide directions to the trustee on a range of matters. It will not direct that a discretion be exercised in a particular way, because this is a matter for the trustee's own judgment. However, it will settle such matters as interpretation of the trust instrument, the existence or non-existence of a particular power, the entitlement of putative beneficiaries and so on.[45]

9.2.6 The right to a discharge

On completion of administration and the proper vesting of the beneficial interests absolutely, the trustee is entitled to be discharged from the office of trustee. The beneficiaries, if they are all *sui juris*, must examine and settle accounts before final discharge. The court may do so in other cases.[46] Trustees have the right to pay money into court, for example where a beneficiary cannot be located for the purposes of distribution. This is now provided for in the trustee legislation.[47]

9.3 Liabilities of trustees

We turn now to the question of the liabilities of a trustee. There are two aspects to this. First, there is the question of liabilities for breach of trust and failure to perform duties. Secondly, there is the question of a trustee being liable to third parties in respect of debts and other claims in carrying out the trust. In respect of the latter, it has been noted that a trust is a distinct type of legal arrangement. A trustee is invested with authority to do certain acts on behalf of the trust. However, a trust does not exist as a juristic person like a corporation, hence the trust as such does

45 See generally Meagher and Gummow, *op cit* fn 5, pp 606–09.
46 *Chadwick v Heatley* (1845) 2 Coll 137; 63 ER 671.
47 Section 95 Trustee Act (F).

not bear liabilities to third parties. Trust law requires, therefore, that the question of trustee liabilities in respect of external debts and liabilities be understood in a special way. In basic terms, the trustee is personally liable but there are rights to indemnity which enable the trustee to seek satisfaction out of the trust assets and, in limited cases, from the beneficiaries personally. Sometimes the creditors of the trustee may avail themselves of these rights where the trustee fails to make good the liability, and this is known as the right of subrogation.

9.3.1 Personal liability of the trustee in respect of breaches of trust

Trustees can commit a breach of trust in a number of ways. The remedies which are available depend to some considerable extent on the nature of the breach. It has been indicated already that the beneficiaries of a trust have a right of action *in personam* against the trustee for any loss that flows from a breach of trust. This right of action persists despite the existence of any right of action *in rem*, to recover trust property and benefits, from either the trustee or third parties to the trust where it has been conveyed to them in breach of trust. The beneficiary remains entitled to pursue their remedies against the trustee, for equitable compensation, even where there may be no remedy to recover the property from strangers by way of remedy of tracing. Proprietary remedies include the imposition of a constructive trust. Equitable remedies are normally discretionary. However, matters pertaining to breach of trust are those which traditionally fell within the exclusive jurisdiction of the equity courts and thus the remedies in this context are not discretionary.

The meaning of the term 'breach of trust' is rather vague, although used with great frequency. In one general sense, it means any breach by a trustee of a legal obligation imposed on him or her regardless of the source of that obligation. This includes obligations arising under general equity or by statute or by the trust deed. Trustees may be liable for torts such as negligence where they have failed to act prudently in the performance of their office. They can be liable for breach of the express or implied provisions of the trust instrument itself, or for acting in excess of the authority which it confers on them. A breach of trust can be constituted by a failure by a trustee to exercise a power which is given by the trust instrument or by law – for example, a power of sale or a power to invest – in circumstances where it was highly appropriate that the power be exercised. So far as their powers are concerned, trustees are subject to the fraud on the power doctrine, which forbids them from exercising powers for an improper or alien purpose. They are also, as part of general equity, subject to a pervasive and rather strict fiduciary obligation.

So far as the scope of authority is concerned, the trust instrument will be of considerable importance. The intention of the creator of the trust, once ascertained, will be given primacy in determining what a trustee is authorised to do, or forbidden from doing. There are some obligations and duties that cannot be excluded because they are so basic to the office of a trustee as equity conceives it that to permit their exclusion would be a denial of the status of trustee itself. Into this category would fall the fiduciary obligations of the trustee and the obligation to deal with the trust property for the benefit of the beneficiaries. Furthermore, it would be contrary to the policy of the law that a trustee should be relieved of liability for acts of fraud (except by order of the court itself, as will be discussed later) and perhaps for other instances of civil liability which arise from the commission of acts of a quasi-criminal character.

A trustee must comply with the provisions of the express or implied terms of the trust. Equity expects that trustees will exercise due skill and care in the performance of their duties and in attending to the affairs of the trust. Failure on either account will amount to a breach of trust. As indicated earlier, the nature and extent of the trustee's obligations and duties will vary from case to case. The terms of one trust may impose considerably more onerous duties on a trustee than otherwise. An investment trust, one would expect, would create a set of trustee obligations that are considerably more extensive than those for a bare property-holding trust. Correspondingly, the expectations of the degree of care and skill vary considerably from one trust to another. Much will depend upon the particular nature of the trust property, the special purpose for which the trust was created and whether the trustee was appointed as a professional trustee or otherwise with the expectation that the trustee possessed a particular capacity or expertise.

So far as the duty of care and skill is concerned, there is considerable overlap with the law of negligence. This is discussed separately below. One frequently litigated question concerns the liability of any of the trustees in their exercise of, or failure to exercise, a power of sale. Trustees who have this power are under a duty to exercise it to obtain the best possible price in the circumstances. Usually, a sale by auction will be treated as a measure of guarantee that the trustees have exercised their power properly. The auction stands as a determinant of the best price available for the property at the time. Even so, a trustee should not allow the property to be disposed of at a ridiculously low price, for example as a result of either no reserve price being set, or if the reserve is set well below what could reasonably be expected. Even so, there may be circumstances justifying disposal at a price substantially less than value. The possibility of obtaining a better price after some period of delay may be outweighed by factors of urgency or necessity justifying immediate disposal. The question reduces to whether the trustee, in the exercise of his or her power, has acted prudently and reasonably in the circumstances, bearing in mind that they are dealing not with their own property but with the property of others.

Where a breach of trust has been committed, the trustee is personally liable to make good the loss suffered by the beneficiaries. Remedies in trust law, here and more generally, tend to be restitutionary, in the sense that they are primarily concerned with bringing back to the trust any property gains or profits which rightly belong to the trust. The trustee is obliged to compensate the trust to an extent that will restore the trust to its position had the breach of trust not occurred. In addition to liability for the actual loss occurring from a breach of trust, the trustee may be ordered to pay interest on the lost amount. The amount of such interest is a matter for the court and may vary between jurisdictions. In cases involving some of the more culpable instances of wrongdoing such as gross negligence, deliberate retention of trust funds or misappropriation, the courts will award a higher rate of interest.

If a trustee is successfully sued for breach of trust, then the costs of the action will usually be ordered against the trustee. The awarding of costs is a matter that lies in the court's discretion. That is to say, the court's order for the costs of proceedings is a matter for the court's discretion. There might be cases where the trustee can invoke the court's discretion in their favour, but this will generally not be the case. Liability of a trustee who has committed a breach of trust is not vitiated by the death, bankruptcy or retirement of the trustee. In death and bankruptcy, the claim will persist against the personal representatives (or the trustee in bankruptcy) of the estate of the trustee. Where the trustee has merely retired, the trustee remains personally liable.

As the question is one of personal liability, the limitation period for the bringing of any action to recover loss will generally be the same as for any other right of action such as the recovery of any personal liabilities. Under the relevant statute of limitations provisions, generally a period of six years will apply. The relevant date is the date upon which the breach of trust occurs. In cases of fraud, the period is 12 years. It is also a period of 12 years where the liability involves what is called a specialty debt, which is to say, a case where the liability arises under an instrument under seal or a deed. In some circumstances, the courts have power to extend the periods mentioned on the application of the injured party. However, it should be noted that the equity courts will not permit the statute of limitations to be used as a vehicle for fraud itself and the trustee could be estopped from relying on it.[48]

There are some circumstances where a beneficiary may be barred from bringing an action even within the limitation period mentioned above. The beneficiary may have done some action, with full knowledge of the breach, which amounts, in effect, to a release of the trustee from liability. Alternatively, the beneficiary, again with full knowledge of the breach, may have acquiesced in or consented to the breach by the trustee. The beneficiary must not have been induced by the trustee to give such consent or to concur in the breach. The knowledge required includes the beneficiary's awareness of the legal consequences of the trustee's action. The trustee has the burden of proof in this regard. Furthermore, this defence will be available only against a beneficiary who at the relevant time was of full legal capacity, i.e. was not a minor or subject to any legal disability such as mental incapacity.

---

48 *Commonwealth of Australia v Verwayen* (1990) 170 CLR 394.

9.3.2 The trustee's liability in tort

A trustee is a legal actor and therefore is as capable as any other legal actor of performing actions that give rise to liability in tort. A trustee, therefore, whether strictly within the scope of authority conferred upon them by the terms of the trust, or indeed acting wholly outside that scope of authority, may act in such a way as to become liable in a suit for damages based in tort. This refers to liability to third parties, that is, to persons who are not beneficiaries of the trust. In such cases, the trustee's liability will generally be personal, in the sense that the trustee will not be entitled to indemnity out of the trust fund in the damages payable to third parties. The operative assumption here is that the trustee is entitled to indemnification only in the performance of those acts that the trust authorised and which he or she carried out directly in the exercise of that authority.

There would be few trusts indeed which would authorise, explicitly, the performance of unlawful acts by a trustee (whether they be criminally or civilly unlawful) in such circumstances as to entitle the trustee to indemnity in the commission of a tort. Were that the case they would be void for illegality or contrary to public policy. It is possible, however, that such a situation could arise or that the trustee performs an act and performs in a manner directed by the beneficiaries of the trust. Assuming that they are all of full capacity, and that the trustee has merely acted as their agent in performing the act, the trustee would be entitled to indemnity from the trust in the act performed. The conformity with the directions of the beneficiaries as to the manner of performance may be of vital importance here. If the trustee is authorised to do something and then proceeds, on their own account, to perform it negligently or otherwise unlawfully, the right to indemnity might be lost.

The trustee who performs an unlawful act is exposed thereby to immediate liability at the hands of the third party affected. However, if the circumstances are such that the trustee is merely no more than the agent of the beneficiaries in doing the act, then the beneficiaries would themselves be liable to the third parties as authorising principals. If proceedings were commenced against the trustee alone, then they would be entitled to join the beneficiaries as parties to the action, claiming that the act was, in reality, substantially the act of the beneficiaries themselves, being performed pursuant to their express authority and direction. In some situations, indeed, the parties, trustee as well as beneficiaries, may each be liable to contribute to any damages awarded, that is, where each party is to be attributed fault of some degree. The tort of conspiracy may cover some of the ground here because the wrong is constituted by the agreement to do an unlawful act. An agreement that the trustee commit a certain act fraudulently, or, in fact, negligently may be sufficient to establish the tort of conspiracy.

However, a trustee who performs an unlawful act may expose him or herself to tortious liability not only to third parties but to the beneficiaries of the trust. Thus, liability in tort may be a cause of action that accrues to the beneficiaries in addition to any action based on breach of trust. The terms of the trust instrument may authorise the investment of funds by the trustee, or, as is commonly the case, it may authorise the trustee to carry on a certain business. Failure to exercise these powers pursuant to a reasonably expected standard of care may give rise, in the event of an occurrence of loss, to an action against the trustee based in negligence. It is appropriate, given the fact that negligence is the most commonly litigated area of tort, and one which is an omnipresent threat in the conduct of commercial affairs, that it be examined in somewhat more detail than the other torts mentioned.

Negligence formed the basis for the expansion of the area of tortious liability in commercial and social practice throughout the 20th century. One need merely mention motor vehicle personal injury claims, the vast majority based in negligence, to substantiate this claim. Additional areas, commonly acknowledged, are those involving the giving of professional advice, consumer services of various kinds and advice relating to industrial accidents and various aspects of product liability. In many such cases, it would be true to say that the common law action for negligence has been displaced, to some extent, by specific statutory provisions imposing liability. The action for negligence, however, always lingers in the background as a possible stop-gap measure in a number of areas where legislation has not caught up with commercial and social reality. Some would suggest, and it is likely true, that, bearing in mind its application to increasingly novel situations, the basis of the action in negligence has considerably changed throughout the course of this century. Indeed, it has also been claimed, contrary to the traditionalist view of English law courts, that actions for negligence have formed the arena for considerable social policy-making activities on the part of the courts themselves. These factors impose some degree of difficulty upon those who would like to find some simple basis for the application of the principles of negligence in such a way as to suitably cover all of those situations in which it either has been or will be applied. We do not propose to provide a general exegesis of the basis for liability in negligence. Rather, we will discuss the particular case of some importance in relation to a trustee's potential liability with respect to matters of investment. This is illustrative of the application of these principles.

The case of trustees who are subject to an obligation to invest trust funds deserves some special comment. There is some conjecture about the precise way in which liability, particularly in negligence, is to be determined in such cases. Some would argue that the traditional approach of the courts on questions of negligence is in need of change or reconsideration in these contexts. The suggestion here is usually that the standard of the reasonably prudent person is a not altogether appropriate criterion for measuring the adequacy of the trustee's activity or inactivity in these contexts. This standard has its origins in late 19th-century case law on negligence, and many writers claim that it is out of step with modern-day commercial and social reality.

An investment trustee for the present purposes will be considered as one who has a power to invest trust funds. This power will be derived either from the trust instrument, from the trustee legislation, possibly from special Acts of Parliament that may confer such a power on special classes of trustee or from the order of the court. Irrespective of the precise source of the power, the legal formula applied by the courts to assess the trustee's activity in this context has been that of reasonable prudence. This has not been done to discount the particular situation of the trustee. Nevertheless, the appropriate duty of care expected of a trustee has been conceived and put forward in terms of the criterion of reasonable prudence or the prudent person test. For instance, in *Re Whiteley; Whiteley v Learoyd*, it was said:

> The duty of the trustee is not to take such care only as a prudent man would take if he had only himself to consider; the duty is rather to take such care as an ordinary man would take if he were minded to make an investment for the benefit of other people for whom he felt morally bound to provide.[49]

The objection to this line of reasoning as it is applied to trustees is briefly that the focus on the standard of the reasonably prudent trustee tends to place too much emphasis upon particular transactions, or, in other words, particular types of investment. Finn and Ziegler suggest, for instance, that such a standard impels the courts to pass judgment on the activity of a trustee in relation to specific investments undertaken, whilst at the same time ignoring the total context of the trustee's investment portfolio. Specific transactions can be assessed in terms of the test just mentioned but it is peculiarly adapted to judging the activities of an individual trustee in relation to a specific transaction.[50] This case-by-case approach adopted by the courts tends to judge individual transactions in isolation, ignoring other investments made by the trustee pursuant to their investment power.[51]

The investment trustee is compelled to have an eye on both the need for capital maintenance and the level of investment return. In some cases, this will reflect the divergent interests of beneficiaries under the trust, e.g. of remainder beneficiaries who are entitled to the trust estate subject to a life interest, and of the life tenant who is entitled only to income from investment of the funds throughout their life. However, apart from the interests of beneficiaries, the trustee may find that the duty to preserve trust property will be rather precariously balanced against the duty to obtain reasonable returns on investments. Obviously, investment that is speculative and therefore likely to induce or possibly geared to inducing an increased level of return will be struck down in circumstances where it shows a failure to observe the duty to protect trust property.

---

49 (1886) 33 Ch D 347 at 355, *per* Cotton LJ.
50 Finn, FJ and Ziegler, PA, 'Prudence and fiduciary obligations in the investment of trust funds' (1987) 61 ALJ 329, particularly 333.
51 *Ibid.*

In most cases, it would seem that the courts have tended to favour the emphasis on the duty to preserve capital investment. The reasons for this are historical. Trust law has always tended to perpetrate a distinction between trust property or capital on the one hand, and trust income on the other. It is a distinction that has had an enormous influence on other areas of law, such as income taxation, where it has provided the theoretical basis for distinguishing between what is taxable (as income) and what is not (as capital). Presumably, because trusts were traditionally concerned pre-eminently with property interests, the trustee's duties were seen fundamentally as protective of those interests. In a variety of senses, English law has acted upon the presupposition of 'no property, no trust'. As has been indicated elsewhere, property is an essential element of the trust and the trustee's obligation to the beneficiaries is regarded as being annexed to it. Little wonder, then, that a particular investment that places the property of the trust at risk will be impugned by the courts, on the ground that it tends to undermine the very basis for the existence of the trust.

There are, however, a number of grounds whereby the basis for proceeding in this fashion might be questioned, at least so far as it provides a theoretical background against which to consider a trustee's performance of the duties of investment under a trust. For instance, does it take account of the appropriate environment in which a modern investment trustee is compelled to operate? Does it over-emphasise the notion of capital in some rather static or fixed sense? Does it unduly discount the sense in which investments ought to be spread in a modern market environment? Why penalise a trustee who elects to diversify trust investments as far as possible, that is, by viewing each transaction in isolation from all others? Can the trustee's action be fairly assessed without regarding the totality of their investment activity?

Whilst there is no doubt about the capital-versus-income dichotomy as intrinsic to the historical development of the trust itself along with the historical articulation of the trustee's obligations, the question is whether it serves any useful purpose in the present commercial and economic climate. The courts have recognised on certain occasions that in appropriate contexts the trustee ought to diversify the trust investments as far as possible in order to both maximise returns *and* reduce the risk of capital loss. This objective of diversification is one means whereby the trustee might achieve some balance between capital and income-related interest. But the question still remains as to whether a trustee will stand to be considered imprudent where one relatively higher risk investment fails, even where the risk is to some extent offset by other strategies in an investment portfolio. Can the trustee argue, for instance, that the whole of a particular investment strategy is the relevant context for the determination of the prudence/imprudence of their actions? Must the transaction producing an investment loss be treated as an isolated occurrence divorced from other diverse aspects of the total trust investment plan?

Finn and Ziegler argue that an affirmative answer to both of these questions is out of touch with the contemporary reality of investment strategy. They argue for a reassessment of the traditional criterion of the prudent person in terms of what they call the modern portfolio approach. Such an approach would assess the trustee's action as part of, or within the context of, a larger package. It is one that emphasises the trustee's action as part of the total portfolio strategy, the aim of which is efficiency in the sense of yielding 'the highest level of portfolio return per unit of total portfolio risk or, conversely, [achieving] for a given level of portfolio return the smallest level of total portfolio risk'.[52] These authors cite a number of justifications for their position. A good deal of academic argument stands in support of the appropriateness of such an approach. It incorporates, one might say, part of the contemporary scenarios of investment and management accounting theories. Unfortunately perhaps, it does not have any great deal of support from the courts, despite occasional suggestions as to the appropriateness of diversification. What takes place in the realm of accounting theory or commercial practice does not always find its way into legal principle, although, in the field of commercial and mercantile law, the courts have always been prepared to pay some attention to the conventions of practice. Where legal recognition of the changing realities of practice is accorded it usually takes place well after the event.

Despite the appeal of changing strategies for investment in fields such as superannuation fund investments, it is likely that the prudent person test will still be applied by the courts for some time, even if it is applied in some modified form. Whilst it might be argued that its 'running mate', the traditional emphasis on the capital risk factor, ought to be defused or relaxed in favour of an emphasis on the general fiduciary obligation of the trustee, such a change would seem to require a reworking of the very notion of the trust itself; that is, as a distinct form of property interest. To do this would require the articulation of some modified conception of the trust itself, or at least some rather novel notion of trust property.

Proponents of revision seem to be suggesting that what is of prime importance is that the trustee act for the benefit of the beneficiary. This they see as the main factor that ought to determine the propriety of trust investment action. This, rather than the attempt to counterbalance capital risk and income return (with emphasis on the former), is more appropriate to the activity of an investment trustee in a contemporary environment. An argument for revision, however, ought not to be confused with what the courts regard as authoritative legal principles at any given time.

9.3.3 Relief of a trustee from liability

The relevant trustee legislation makes provision for the relief of trustees from various forms of liability not available to the ordinary person. First, however, it might be said that, apart from the legislation, trustees are always able to approach the

52 *Ibid.*

equity courts for directions as to the course of conduct they should pursue. This is treated as part of the rights attaching to the trustee's office considered elsewhere in this chapter, and need not be pursued further at this point.

Section 71 of the Trustee Act of Fiji reads as follows:

> If it appears to the Court that a trustee, whether appointed by the Court or otherwise, is or may be personally liable for any breach of trust, whether the transaction alleged to be a breach of trust occurred before or after the commencement of this Act, but has acted honestly and reasonably, and ought fairly to be excused for the breach of trust and for omitting to obtain the directions of the Court in the matter in which he committed the breach, then the Court may relieve him either wholly or partly from personal liability for that breach.[53]

It is to be noted that relief may only be granted under the section if the trustee can show that they have acted both honestly and reasonably. These two terms are not coextensive. For example, a given act may be done honestly but with an entire lack of prudence. A person who acted on the advice of a professional adviser has been precluded from relief under the section. They may have acted honestly in relying on the advice tendered – the advice being given in a particular form to allow the adviser to misappropriate trust funds. However, the trustee might be shown to have had grounds for suspicion that the activity in question was risky. In such a case, although the trustee's action was honest, the suspicion of risk would deem it to be unreasonable.

Additionally, the courts entertain certain reservations as to the granting of relief under the section. They are mindful of the need to grant relief to trustees who have exposed themselves to liability for seemingly innocent breaches of trust. However, this has to be weighed against the interests of the beneficiaries. The granting of relief may well place the beneficiaries' interests at a considerable disadvantage, especially where they have no other remedy than a right of personal action for recovery against the trustee. This would be the case, for instance, where the beneficiaries are unable to recover the property itself by virtue of an action *in rem* such as tracing or seeking the imposition of a constructive trust in the circumstances mentioned above.

An additional requirement for the granting of relief is that the circumstances must be such that the trustee ought fairly to be excused. General formulations such as this are difficult to reduce to authoritative criteria. In fact, it seems to allow the court considerable discretion in the granting or refusal of relief. The general opinion seems to have been, nevertheless, that the words do impose an additional requirement for the granting of relief, even though many of the cited examples

---

53 Section 68(3) Trusts Act 2014, although no equivalent provision exists (S); s 61 Trustee Act (UK) (K), (T), (Tu), (SI); s 73 Trustee Act (NZ), (CI), (Ni).

overlap considerably with ordinary senses of what is reasonable. Any number of factors may arise in this regard. Have the trustees made proper attempts to recover the loss? Are there other avenues that they might have pursued or might yet pursue in relation to such recovery? Did they attempt to obtain proper advice? Was the loss the consequence of a mistake and, if so, could such a mistake have been discoverable, say, on the obtaining of proper advice? Were the trustees responsible in some other way for the loss – for example, if the trustee is a professional adviser, was the mistake contributed to by employees' supervision? Certainly, it would appear to be the case that professional trustees and trustees who are entitled to be remunerated for their services as such are generally conceived to be under a more onerous obligation in relation to their performance of trusteeship duties. So also, it might be more difficult for them to obtain relief under the section.

The section appears wide enough to cover situations where no liability has yet been established in a breach. The court's power to grant relief can be exercised provided that it is of the opinion that such liability for breach of trust might arise in the future. It should also be noted that the trustee is the one who carries the burden of establishing the matters required to the satisfaction of the court. The trustee, in other words, must make out a case that satisfies the requirements of the section. The trustee need not commence independent proceedings for such relief. It is possible for the trustee to seek such relief in proceedings commenced by the beneficiary by way of recovery for breach of trust.

9.3.4 The trustee's external liabilities

Liability of a trustee to beneficiaries is one thing; liability to creditors and third parties is another. As the trust gives rise to no independent legal personality as with a corporation, it is the trustee who will be regarded as personally liable to creditors and third parties. Where there is more than one trustee, they will be regarded as jointly and severally liable. This means that any one of the joint trustees will be liable to meet the whole of the debt or liability subject to a right of reimbursement from the other trustees for their share.

The personal liability of the trustee(s) justifies a right of indemnity given to the trustee(s) for reimbursement out of the trust property and, in some circumstances, from the beneficiaries personally. In addition, the trustee may limit personal liability in the particular dealing giving rise to a debt or a liability. The creditor may agree that recourse for payment is to be made to a particular fund, such as the assets of the trusts, rather than to the trustee personally.

Suppose a trustee is authorised by the terms of the trust instrument to carry on a business and to deploy some of the trust property for that purpose. The trustee in this situation may be either carrying on a business which was formerly conducted by the creator of the trust, or alternatively, authorised to establish a wholly novel enterprise. The question to be considered here is whether the trustee incurs any liability when, in this situation, and perhaps other analogous situations, they are merely carrying out the terms of the trust. The matters considered above are not wholly relevant because it is assumed here that the trustee has committed no breach of trust and committed no tort. Obviously, these issues may arise in this situation, but for the sake of the ensuing discussion it will be assumed that this is not so.

Obviously, the trustee, as the outward representative of a trust business, will incur liability. This will arise as an inevitable consequence of business activities. Contracts for the supply and/or purchase of goods and services as well as normal maintenance items will be entered into by the trustee on behalf of the trust. The trustee will undertake obligations in favour of third parties, and in certain circumstances it may be that, owing to no fault on the part of the trustee, the contract cannot be carried out on the trustee's part. It is a risk of carrying on any business that economic circumstances, as much as mismanagement or inefficient business planning, may lead to a lack of liquidity, insolvency and so on. What happens, then, if the trustee is unable to give due performance of a contractual obligation so incurred? The other party may claim damages for breach, or may seek some other direct remedy for breach against the trustee.

The position of the trustee in this situation is, in some respects, analogous to that of an agent. The trustee is personally liable to third parties with whom they deal in carrying on the trust business. That personal liability extends to all outgoings, liabilities, expenses and losses incurred or arising in these circumstances. The rationale for this is that the third party has dealt with the trustee personally and the trustee as such is the outward legal representative of the beneficial interests under the trust. However, this principle largely causes the analogy with agency to fall down. The acts of an agent may bind a principal to a contract with third parties, provided that the acts of the agent are within the scope of the agent's authority. This applies to contracts as much as to other acts. But the trustee's position is different. The trustee who contracts on behalf of the trust enters into a contract in their capacity as legal holder of the trust property. Thus, the trustee does not bring the beneficiaries into any contractual relationship with the third party. The beneficiaries remain outside the scope of the contract. By virtue of the doctrine of privity of contract, neither can the beneficiaries enforce the contract against the third party, nor can the third party enforce it against them.[54] This is true even though the contract may directly affect their rights or be to their general benefit or detriment. The beneficiary can only enforce the trust through the trustee. Similarly, the fact that a party to a contract enters into that contract explicitly as trustee for nominated beneficiaries does not have the immediate effect of bestowing benefits or imposing obligations on the beneficiaries so named. The trustee remains the party who is liable on, and entitled to enforce, the contract.

---

54 See *Construction Engineering (Aust) Pty Ltd v Hexyl Pty Ltd* [1985] HCA 13 (12 March 1985).

This is not to say, however, that the rights of the parties to the contract, i.e. trustee and third party, cannot be construed in such a way as to take account of the trust. The parties may specifically contract on the basis that the trustee shall have no personal liability in the contract. The parties may agree that the party other than the trustee shall have recourse only against the trust property. Bearing in mind what was said at the outset of this topic, that the trust is not a legal entity as such, this may seem to lead to absurd conclusions.

Neither the trustee, nor the trust, nor the beneficiaries (by virtue of the privity of contract doctrine) would seem to have incurred any liability under the contract. However, cases such as this have been taken to amount to a promise by the trustee to exercise their powers over the trust in order to obtain payment of the debt or to meet the liability.[55] The contract does not elevate the other party to the position of a secured creditor. Nor could such a situation be effective and totally exclude the personal liability of the trustee on the contract. It is, after all, the trustee who enters into the contract and makes a promise to the other party. Either there is a contract between the parties or there is not. If the contract purports to exclude the personal liability of the trustee to such an extent that includes basic liability under the contract, then a court may be compelled to say that either there is no contract at all or, following the approach in *West v Sydney City Council*, that the exclusion clause is inoperative to all forms of liability. (The contract may seek to limit the extent of the trustee's liability to that which could be borne by the trust property. A mere contractual reference to one of the parties contracting *as* trustee would not be sufficient to imply the limitation. The particular type of limitation needs to be clearly stated.)

9.3.5 Indemnity of trustee

The position here in relation to personal liability would be unduly onerous if it left the trustee without some means of recourse. Of course, it may be onerous in any event where, for practical reasons, such as depletion or exhaustion of trust resources through circumstances beyond the trustee's control, the rights mentioned in the following cannot yield relief. The law has long recognised that in return for the duties and responsibilities of carrying out the trust, the trustee should have a right of indemnity against the trust property for losses, outgoings and liabilities incurred in the performance of those duties. In some, perhaps limited, circumstances discussed below, this right of indemnity can be extended to include a right against the beneficiaries themselves. The right of indemnity at general law is supplemented in a limited way by the trustee legislation, which provides that a trustee may obtain reimbursement, or may pay or discharge out of the trust property, all expenses incurred in or about the execution of their trusts or powers.

---

55 *Parsons v Spooner* (1846) 5 Hare 102; *Muir v City of Glasgow Bank* (1879) 4 App Cas 337.

The trustee's general right of indemnity against the trust property is wider, however, than the legislative provision on 'expenses' would suggest. The general right of indemnity in relation to expenses has been justified on the basis that it is the price paid by the beneficiary for the (usually) gratuitous services of the trustee.[56] The existence of relatively common provisions in trust instruments entitling trustees to remuneration for services makes this justification seemingly limited. Nevertheless, the general right persists and extends to all liabilities, losses, outgoings and expenses incurred in carrying out the trust. Perhaps, if it is to be justified, the right of indemnity to a trustee is the price of the present and future benefits that the beneficiary obtains or is likely to obtain under the trust.

The right of indemnity gives rise to a first equitable charge or lien against the trust property. A lien normally implies a right of mere retention or possession pending satisfaction. In this case, if the indemnity amount is not satisfied within a reasonable time the trustee has a right of sale of the trust property.[57] There is some doubt about this where the exercise of this power would completely destroy the trust. The right of indemnity extends to both liabilities presently incurred as well as those likely to arise in the future. In the latter case, the trustee is entitled to retain from any proposed distribution of trust property an amount sufficient to meet future or contingent liabilities. Indeed, the trustee would be unwise not to do so. Unless the case is one where the right of indemnity extends to recoverability against the beneficiaries personally, the trustee may lose their indemnity by distributing the trust property. There are, of course, avenues whereby the trustee can protect themselves against future liabilities, for example by giving notice of intended distribution.

It is not necessary that the trustee should have actually paid the amount for which indemnity is sought. Liability refers to liabilities or obligations to pay which have been incurred. Presumably, the term refers also to any sense of liability which involves an obligation on the trustee to make payment to another. Thus, the right of indemnity has been held to include moneys payable under an award of damages to a worker employed by the trustee for injuries incurred in the course of employment.[58] It has also been extended to cover damages for nuisance to adjoining land arising from the use of premises in which the trustee was carrying on business.[59] In addition, it includes the costs of defending an action brought against the trustee relating sufficiently to the trust, entitlement under the trust or the carrying out of the purposes of the trust.[60] The proviso is that the trustee should not have been at fault in relation to the proceedings; for example, the proceedings might have been administration proceedings concerning the trustee's own malad-

---

56 *Re Beddoe; Downes v Cottam* [1893] 1 Ch 547 at 558.
57 See *Trautwein v Richardson* [1946] Argus LR 129.
58 *Bennet v Wyndham* (1862) 4 De GF & J 259.
59 *Re Raybould; Raybould v Turner* [1900] 1 Ch 199.
60 *Re Holden, Ex parte Official Receiver* (1887) 20 QBD 43.

ministration.[61] It also covers expenses that are reasonably and honestly incurred by the trustee in the improvement, as well as maintenance, of the trust property. The indemnity is available provided the trustee has acted in good faith. It applies even in the absence of authority derived from the trust instrument.[62]

The trustee would be entitled to a reimbursement for rates, land tax and other outgoings in respect of land held subject to the trust. In general, if a trustee advances their own money to the trust, say to pay a debt, there will be no entitlement to interest. The reason is that a trustee cannot make a profit from the carrying out of the trusteeship.[63] The exception to this is where the trust instrument provides otherwise. Also, the decision in *Re Beulah Park Estate, Sargood's Claim*[64] suggests that where the debt discharged itself carries interest, the trustee is entitled to interest on the amount so paid. The trustee is subrogated to the right of the creditor to obtain interest. The doctrine of subrogation allows a party who has discharged or satisfied a liability of another in certain circumstances to take up the rights of that other against third parties. A common example is the right of an insurer who meets the claim of an insured. By subrogation, the insurer takes over the rights of the insured to recover against third parties. The doctrine is relevant in another context below.

A trustee will potentially lose their right of indemnity in two cases: namely default by the trustee and the possibility of exclusions by the trust instrument. As to the first of these, a trustee who has committed a breach of trust will not be entitled to indemnity, at least where the breach introduces a liability on the trustee to compensate the trust. There appears to be no general disqualification arising from the commission of the breach itself, i.e. where no loss to the trust is involved.[65] A similar disqualification would obtain where the trustee is indebted to the trust. The general principle is that the trustee must make good the default or the indebtedness before the right of indemnity can be exercised.

Secondly, the right of a trustee to indemnity is a general legal right and could in some respects be thought to attach to the trustee's office. Unfortunately, the law is not at all clear on whether rights of indemnity can be excluded by the trust instrument. The issue directly affects the ability of creditors to recover by subrogation where the trustee has failed to meet the liability. The trustee's right of indemnity against beneficiaries can be excluded because it seems to be in the nature of a personal right only.[66] However, with respect to the right of indemnity against the trust assets, the right is arguably more fundamental to the trustee's office. There

---

61 *National Trustees Executors & Agency Co of Australasia v Barnes* (1941) 64 CLR 268.
62 See *Daly v Union Trustee Co. of Australia Ltd* (1898) 24 VLR 460.
63 *Re Jones* [1917] QSR 74; *Sichel v O'Shanassy* (1877) 3 VLR (E) 208.
64 (1872) LR 15 Eq 43.
65 *Staff Benefits Pty Ltd and the Companies Act, Re* [1979] NSWLR 207.
66 *Re German Mining Co; ex parte Chippendale* (1853) 4 De GM & G 19.

are authorities which suggest that it may be excluded[67] and some which suggest that it may not be.[68] If the right were conceived as part of the way in which equity requires the proper administration of the trust, then that would be a factor against exclusion. Such an argument would be based on the notion that the allocation of rights of indemnity is simply a means whereby the courts of equity brought to account the proper debts and liabilities of a trust.[69] The consideration is not merely with exclusion or non-exclusion of the private rights of a trustee. If due weight were given, perhaps on policy grounds, to the rights of creditors to recoup where the trustee has failed, that also would support non-exclusion. The position is more complicated by the fact that a right of indemnity out of assets also exists in the legislation. In some cases, it appears capable of exclusion, in other cases not. The issue in the former case is whether the legislative right absorbs the general equitable right. Perhaps it does not, bearing in mind that the original trustee legislation in England was intended to be codificatory only.[70] Unfortunately, the issue awaits authoritative determination.

The trustee's primary right of indemnity is against the trust property. If the property of the trust is inadequate to meet the extent of the liability in question, then the onus falls on the trustee. It has been acknowledged, however, that in some cases the trustee may have a right of recovery against the beneficiaries.[71] The circumstances where this may arise are perhaps not as clearly stated in the cases as they ought to be. The principle authority is the case of *Hardoon v Belilios*.[72] In this case, the Privy Council held that where the single beneficiary was of full age and absolutely entitled, the trustee has always had a right of indemnity against the beneficiary personally as well as the right against the trust property. It was not a precondition to the exercise of this right that the beneficiary should have requested the trustee either to take on the trust, to incur the liability for which the indemnity is sought or, alternatively, to have carried on the activity that gives rise to such a liability. The rationale seemed to be that the beneficiary of such a trust, in effect, owns the trust and has the trustee at their direction, certainly as to the ultimate termination of the trust. This would imply that the beneficiary implicitly indemnifies the trustee against the consequences of performance carrying out the trust. In this particular respect, if not more generally, the trustee may be likened to an agent who acts in accordance with his or her principal's delegated authority (in the

---

67 *RWG Management Ltd v Commissioner for Corporate Affairs* (1985) VR 385; *McLean v Burns Philp Trustee Co Pty Ltd* (1985) 2 NSWLR 623.

68 *Kemtron Industries Pty Ltd v Commissioner for Stamp Duties (Queensland)* [1984] 1 Qld R 576 at 585.

69 Such an approach might be supported from the reasoning in *Octavo Investments Pty Ltd v Knight* (1979) 54 ALJR 87 and the older authority of *Rowley v Ginnever* (1897) 2 Ch 503.

70 In which case it might not exclude the general equitable position that existed beforehand.

71 Hughes, RA, 'The trustee's right to a personal indemnity from beneficiaries' (1990) 64 ALJ pp 567–79.

72 *Hardoon v Belilios* [1901] AC 118.

absence of an explicit direction to do particular acts – the question always being whether the agent's acts were within the scope of the original delegation of power; if so, the principal may be bound even though the agent performs some act that he was never explicitly directed or requested to undertake).

However that might be, there is a curious anomaly so far as other decided cases go. It was once thought that *Hardoon's Case* suggested that there was a difference as regards trusts with multiple beneficiaries, but this is now baseless. This is in fact the position taken by the Victorian Supreme Court in *JW Broomhead (Victoria) Pty Ltd (in liq) v JW Broomhead Pty Ltd*,[73] which is the correct position on any reasonable reading of *Hardoon's Case*.

9.3.6 *The right of indemnity as against the trust property*

Whatever the case, the trustee's rights against the beneficiary cannot be exercised without first exhausting the right of indemnity as against the trust property. In *Wise v Perpetual Trustee Co Ltd*,[74] it was held that the members of a non-profit unincorporated association are not personally liable to indemnify the trustee. The peculiar nature of such associations, not being associations for profit or gain, excluded any question of such an indemnity. The trust was confined to a right of indemnity against the property of the club. As with the property indemnity, the trustee may pursue this right against the beneficiary without first making actual payment for the liability. The amounts to be paid by the beneficiaries will be determined by their proportionate shares in the beneficial interests under the trust. In the event that one of the beneficiaries has become bankrupt or insolvent, the remaining beneficiaries would be liable to account rateably for it. Where a beneficiary has assigned their interest under the trust, then, in the absence of a specific release by the trustee, that beneficiary remains liable to indemnify. This is the case even with liabilities that have arisen after the date of the assignment. However, unless otherwise provided in the instrument of assignment, there would be an implied term in the assignment that the assignee is liable to indemnify the assignor against such liability. The trustee in such a situation is presented with an option to seek indemnity against either assignor or assignee. This right does not apply to a trustee in bankruptcy of a bankrupt beneficiary's estate, even though such a person takes the interest of the beneficiary.

The situation where the trustee carries on a business requires special mention. Apart from the fact that cases where beneficiaries have been held personally liable to indemnify the trustee have been predominantly concerned with these circumstances, certain other issues arise. First, they illustrate certain problems about the extent of the trust property that might be available to satisfy the trustee's right of

73 [1985] VR 891.
74 [1903] AC 139.

indemnity. Secondly, they illustrate the position of creditors against the trust. As will be seen, the two issues can be interrelated in a variety of factual situations. The trustee's right of indemnity for expenses, outgoings and losses incurred in the course of carrying on the business follows from the general principles discussed above. This will apply where the trust instrument authorises the trustee to carry on a business or, alternatively, where it is authorised by an order of the court or by all the beneficiaries being of full capacity. Where there is no such authority, the trustee, on the face of it, has no right of indemnity. The authority thus derived carries with it the mandate to incur liabilities on behalf of the trust. In this situation, there is implicit recognition of the trustee's entitlement to indemnity for liabilities incurred in carrying out the trust. (Although the authority of the creator of the trust or of the court is not a matter that alone gives rise to a right of indemnity against the beneficiaries personally. The indemnity applies at least to trust property.)

Most commonly, however, the creator of the trust will not commit the whole of the trust property to the carrying on of the business. Does the trustee's right of indemnity extend to the whole of the property of the trust or only to that committed to the carrying on of the business? Is there a difference between property that is made available to the trustee though not actually committed in the conduct of the business, and property actually used in the conduct of it? On the first of these questions, *Ex parte Garland*[75] stands as authority for the proposition that the right of indemnity extends only to the property that the creator of the trust authorised to be used for the purposes of carrying on the business and any assets acquired in the course of carrying on the business. The answer to the second question seems to follow as a matter of course. It makes little difference that the trustee has not employed all the property he or she was entitled to have employed in the carrying on of the business. As long as the property is available for such employment under the direction of the creator of the trust (perhaps also under an order of the court or at the direction of the beneficiaries), then the indemnity will apply to that property, utilised or not. Nevertheless, the trustee's right of indemnity will be limited to the property so authorised. The justification for this limitation seems to have been the supposedly inherent risks involved in the conduct of a business, as contrasted with the assumed stability afforded by mere investment. The limitation was seen in effect as a type of limited liability to protect the balance of trust property from liabilities accrued in the conduct of the business. If the business failed, the trust might still continue. This position seems wholly irrelevant in a modern context and has been properly criticised as such. Nevertheless, the principle in *Ex parte Garland* has been applied in so many other cases that it seems still to authoritatively determine the issue. The trustee's right of indemnity for trading liabilities against the property of the trust will, in this case, be exhausted when that part of

---

75 (1803) 10 Ves 110; 32 ER 786.

the property authorised for business purposes and any after-acquired assets have been fully depleted. Similarly, if those business assets have been gradually eroded through trading activity, the trustee may have no recourse in liabilities or losses accrued, except where there exists a right of indemnity against the beneficiary personally.

Ought there to be a specific appropriation of assets by the creator of the trust before the trustee has a right of indemnity? *Strickland v Symons*[76] suggests that this is so. The case placed reliance upon a particular interpretation of *Garland's Case* to arrive at the conclusion that the trustee's indemnity was not available at all where there was no specific appropriation of assets for business purposes in the instrument creating the trust. The case did not concern direct enforcement of the indemnity by the trustee. The issue was whether a creditor of the business could enforce the trustee's right in such a case. This is discussed below. However, *Garland's Case* does not warrant this interpretation on its own terms. There seems to be no particular reason why either a trustee's right of indemnity or the creditor's access to it should be limited in the way that *Strickland's Case* suggests. In the absence of a specific appropriation, and bearing in mind the need for limitation of the scope of indemnity, there is no reason why reference could not be to the property actually applied in the course of business pursuant to the power given. This would act as a sufficient delineation of the property subject to the indemnity.

9.3.7 The doctrine of subrogation

Creditors of the trustee are entitled to the benefit of the trustee's right of indemnity by virtue of the doctrine of subrogation. This does not mean that the creditors have a right to proceed directly against the trust property. Subrogation will operate only where their rights against the trustee have been exhausted, without full satisfaction, or where their rights against the trustee cannot be enforced because the trustee has absconded or where the trustee is insolvent or bankrupt. The trustee must have been authorised in carrying on the business, in the manner suggested above.[77] In *Re Johnson*,[78] the justification for conceding this right to the creditor was said to be that it would be unjust to allow a beneficiary the benefit of profiting from trading activities as a result of the creditor's concession of credit, without bearing some of the burden in the event that the trustee is unable to meet the liability. However, the creditor's right to pursue this line will be restricted. Subrogation yields no greater rights for the creditor against the other party than the trustee had. If there is some essential limitation on the scope of the trustee's right of indemnity, then the creditor's right of recourse will be similarly limited. In some cases, the

---

76 (1884) 26 Ch D 245.
77 *Re Blundell* (1888) 40 Ch D 370; *Vacuum Oil Co Pty Ltd v Wiltshire* (1945) 72 CLR 319.
78 (1880) 15 Ch D 548.

trust instrument may impose such limitations on the trustee's rights. Such a situation, coupled with the existence of a trustee that is a limited liability company with no substantial assets, may leave a creditor in an unenviable position.

There are other limitations. If the trustee has committed other trust funds without authority, i.e. in breach of trust, or has borrowed from the trust, the right of set-off to which such instances give rise against the trustee would have to be satisfied in priority to the creditor's claims. In many cases, this may block the creditor's effective subrogation of the trustee's right of indemnity altogether. As was said in *Ex parte Edmonds*,[79] the creditor merely stands in the shoes of the trustee and has no higher right than the trustee's right to indemnity. Creditors do not have a proprietary interest in the funds of the trust, even though the trustee has been held to have such an interest in these circumstances.[80] There are also obvious procedural problems in admitting that a creditor has any direct access to the trust funds. The right of action exists through the trustee against the fund alone and relates only to those liabilities that can be admitted as within the scope of the authority created by the trust instrument.

Special problems exist in relation to trusts created by will. Where the will authorises the trustee to carry on a business, then no immediate problems exist. The issues are determined according to the general principles above. But where there is no such authority (apart from statute) and the trustee carries on business nonetheless, problems might arise in relation to the determination of the priorities of two classes of creditors, i.e. those who were creditors at the date of death and those who are creditors of the business carried on. The testator is generally not entitled to defeat the claims of their creditors by the provisions of their will. A provision in a will that authorises a business to be carried on could not have the effect of defeating or postponing the claims of such creditors.[81] Such a provision could, however, affect the rights of the beneficiaries; i.e. by virtue of the trustee's right of indemnity.[82]

Where the executor/trustee carries on business without authority or other than for the purpose of realisation, they do so at their own risk. The liabilities incurred in so doing are the trustee's personal liabilities and there is no right of recourse against the estate, the beneficiaries or the estate creditors. However, if a beneficiary authorises the trustee to carry on business, then the trustee, as against that beneficiary, has a right of indemnity out of the estate. Also, if an estate creditor (i.e. a creditor of the testator) actually authorises the testator to carry on the business, the trustee is entitled to a similar indemnity out of the estate, as against the claims of that creditor.[83] Any new creditors of the trustee will be entitled to the

79 (1862) 4 De G F & J 488; 45 ER 1273 at 1277.
80 *Octavo Investments Pty Ltd v Knight* (1979) 54 ALJR 87 at 90.
81 *Vacuum Oil Co Pty Ltd v Wiltshire* (1945) 72 CLR 319.
82 *In Re Oxley* [1914] 1 Ch 604 at 613.
83 *Dowse v Gorton* [1891] AC 190.

benefit of that right of indemnity in the event that they cannot obtain satisfaction from the trustee personally. Thus, the relative priorities of estate and business creditors might be reversed.

The cases suggest that this position may obtain not only where an estate creditor actually authorises the trustee to carry on business. Where the creditor 'actively and positively assents' to the trustee carrying on business, the position may be the same.[84] Knowledge of the fact that the business is being carried on without authority is not enough and nor is mere passive acquiescence.[85] The conduct must be sufficiently positive to amount to an authorisation of the trustee's activity and an acceptance of the consequent right of indemnity. Because the creditor is, in effect, giving up their right of priority, the requirement will not be lightly met. Whether the position is one of actual authority or active and positive assent, the justification for the readjustment of the priorities is that a party cannot both approbate (i.e. by authorising or consenting to the continuance of the trustee's activity) and reprobate (by denying the trustee's consequent right of indemnity and the derivative rights of the new creditors).

9.4 The powers of the trustee

The powers of the trustee set the scope of authority of the trustee in relation to the trust. Some powers are expressly or impliedly contained in the trust instrument; others are a consequence of the general functions of the trustee according to equity. Others still are conferred by the trustee and possibly other legislation. Some might arise after they are conferred by the court by way of variation of the trust deed. Here we will discuss only some of the main powers of a trustee.

As the trust instrument will play an important role in the definition of powers, there will be considerable variation from case to case as regards the particular powers. As a general proposition, in the case of commercial trusts, it is highly appropriate that the trust instrument should deal comprehensively with the powers of the trustee for the carrying on of the business concern and conferring a full range of managerial powers. One particular reason for this is that the statutory powers, such as they are, are largely inadequate for commercial trustees.

9.4.1 Power to carry on a business

The carrying on of a business by a trustee has traditionally been viewed by the courts as in the nature of a risk venture. It comes into conflict with the principle that a trustee is under a duty to preserve trust assets. The contemporary relevance of this approach is highly debatable, but it indicates the conservatism of the

---

84 *Ibid.*
85 *Vacuum Oil Co Pty Ltd v Wiltshire* (1945) 72 CLR 319.

traditional approach to the management of trusts. It will be a breach of trust where the trustee without power engages in a business venture on behalf of the trust.

A power exists only where it is conferred by the trust instrument, by legislation or by the court. Normally, caution should be taken to include such a power in the trust instrument. So far as the trust instrument is concerned there will be circumstances whereby a power might be implied from the existence of other powers. An instance of this would be where the trust property comprises in part a business carried on by the settlor with a power to sell that business as a going concern. If the business is to be sold as a going concern, this would imply a power of the trustees to carry on business pending sale but no longer than is necessary to achieve the sale. In any event, the power will be construed strictly by the courts.[86] In New Zealand, and hence in the Cook Islands and Niue, there is a statutory power to carry on a business.[87] As mentioned above, where a trustee carries on a business and incurs trade debts, it is only the assets of the trust business that are available to satisfy the trustee's indemnity against trust property. The same limitation applies to the rights of subrogation of the trade creditors as they acquire no higher rights than the trustee has. The general assets of the trust are not available in either case.

9.4.2 Power to repair and insure trust property

Trustees at general law have the power to repair the trust property. Indeed, they have a duty to do so in terms of their duty to preserve it. There is not, however, either a power or a duty to improve the property. The division between a repair and an improvement is perhaps a fine one. Repair indicates the maintenance of something in an existing condition. Improvement implies a substantive change in the condition of the property in the direction of betterment.[88] Statute provides a limited power of improvement under certain conditions.

There is no duty on a trustee to insure trust property, but he or she may do so if it is desired.[89] There is also a statutory power to insure.[90]

9.4.3 Power to lease trust property

A lease of the trust property could in certain circumstances prejudice the interests of the beneficiaries. It would also produce benefits to a life tenant who is entitled to the income from the trust property during the life tenancy. Hence it is an issue

---

86 *Re Francis* [1948] S.A.S.R. 287.
87 Section 32 Trustee Act 1956; see also s 51 Trustee Act (F); no equivalent provision in Trusts Act 2014 (S).
88 See *O'Neill v Coffill* (1920) 20 S.R. (NSW) 264.
89 *Re McEacharn* (1911) 103 LT 900.
90 Section 42 Trustee Act (F); s 42 Trusts Act 2014 (S); s 24 Trustee Act (NZ), (CI), (Ni); s 19 Trustee Act (UK) (K), (T), (Tu) (SI), (V).

which bears on striking a balance between the interests of a life tenant and those of the remaindermen under a trust. On that basis, the power to lease has been viewed with some circumspection by the courts. It has been said that the trustee may have a power to lease at general law but on the proviso that it can be shown that it was both reasonable and done in the fair management of the trust estate.[91] There are, however, statutory powers of leasing for a limited term under the trustee legislation provided to trustees with a power of sale and to those with a power to manage.[92]

9.4.4 Power of sale

Some trusts are created for no other purpose than the effecting of a sale of trust property. These are known as trusts for sale and the power to sell will necessarily be explicit in them. A power of sale exists where the trustee has a discretionary power to sell. However, in certain cases, the power is one which, on the terms of the trust instrument, must be exercised. Powers can be expressed to be exercisable at the direction of a third party. Whether the power of the third party to direct in this regard is fiduciary in nature is a matter for determination on general fiduciary principles.

There is an implied duty on the trustee to sell according to the rule in *Howe v Lord Dartmouth*.[93] This duty is implied by law rather than on construction of the trust instrument. This rule applies where there is a residuary personal estate which is left on trust for successive beneficiaries and the assets concerned are of a wasting, reversionary or hazardous nature. In such a case, it would be the duty of the trustee to sell as soon as a fair price is obtained. The trustee cannot be expected to sell whenever a sale at any price can be obtained. The rule might be displaced where there is a contrary intention expressed in the trust instrument.

Apart from statute[94] and conferral by the court, there is no general power of sale unless the trust instrument confers such a power, either expressly or impliedly. Circumstances where such a power will be implied include cases where there has been a charge imposed on realty to pay debts,[95] the existence of a direction to distribute the trust estate,[96] a power to wind up the trust[97] or a direction to divide the property between beneficiaries.[98]

---

91 *A-G v Owen* (1805) 10 Ves 555; 32 ER 960. See Heydon and Leeming, and Watson and Taylor, *op cit* fn 2.
92 Section 23 Trustee Act (F); generally, see s 56 Trusts Act 2014 (S); s 14 Trustee Act (NZ), (CI), (Ni); s 12 Trustee Act (UK) (K), (T), (Tu), (SI), (V).
93 (1802) 7 Ves 137; 32 ER 56.
94 See the provisions referred to in note 92.
95 *Seelander v Rechner* (1884) 18 SALR 82.
96 *Alston v Equity Trustees, Executors and Agency Co Limited* (1912) 14 CLR 341.
97 *Re Wheaton* [1937] SASR 19.
98 *Pagels v MacDonald* [1936] HCA 15 (29 April 1936); 54 CLR 519.

The beneficiaries, if of full age and capacity, can also authorise a sale of the trust property.[99] A power of sale is frequently accompanied by a power to post-pone sale. Such a power of postponement is also conferred by statute in certain circumstances. There are statutory powers to sell contained in the trustee legisla-tion. These are premised on the existence of a power to pay or apply capital mon-eys for any purpose. The same requirement exists in relation to the borrowing of moneys, as discussed below.

The trustee's duty with respect to sale is normally put as a duty to sell as soon as a fair price can be obtained. It depends on the construction of the instrument. Sometimes it would be better to put it as a duty to obtain a fair price within a rea-sonable time. Much depends upon whether the obligation to sell is accompanied by a power to postpone the sale either for a particular time or for a reasonable period. Where there is a power to postpone the sale, the trustee is under a duty to obtain a fair price within a reasonable time.[100] The duty will not normally be regarded as a duty to sell on any terms whatsoever, as this may sacrifice the interests of the ben-eficiaries. The general test will be whether the trustee acted prudently. There will not necessarily be a breach of trust if a delay in the exercise of the power resulted in a lower price than that which might have been obtained if the sale had taken place earlier.[101] A power as opposed to a duty to sell may be wholly discretionary in the sense that all that the trustee is obliged to do is consider whether to exercise the power or not on a regular basis. The courts will be loath to interfere with the trustee's decision to exercise or not to exercise the power.

9.4.5 The power to invest

As with powers to carry on a business, the power to invest has long been regarded with considerable circumspection by the courts. The concept of investment has a highly restrictive meaning and certainly does not accord with the meaning of the term in general usage. It has been held not to include investment in property required for the purpose of use or enjoyment.[102] Its meaning in trust law has been taken very conservatively, and has had to be seen as determined largely by the ubiquitous duty to preserve trust property. In this regard, the strong early ten-dency, deriving from the prevalence in the 19th century of trusts for successive interests, was to favour the interests of remainder beneficiaries in the capital of the trust property rather than the interests of life tenants in the production of income. Furthermore, the early tendency was to encourage investment in land rather than other forms of investments, and this was determined by reference to legal lists

---

99 Heydon and Leeming, and Watson and Taylor, *op cit* fn 2.
100 *Cox v Archer* (1964) 110 CLR 1.
101 *Marsden v Kent* (1877) 5 Ch D 598.
102 *Re Power* [1947] Ch 572; *In the Will of Sherriff* [1971] 2 NSWLR 438; *Re Peczenik's Settlement Trusts* (1964) 1 WLR 720 Ch D.

of authorised investments which were drawn up by the judiciary or embodied in legislation. These lists still exist in the legislation and remain influential in the interpretation of what is authorised. Even trust instruments which gave a general power to invest or to invest in securities were sometimes interpreted in terms of the list requirements.[103]

Another factor which tended to restrict the range of investment possibilities undertaken by trustees was the practical concerns about questions of liability with respect to failed investments. The approach of the courts was to view each investment by a trustee on an isolated basis and to determine whether that transaction, in the event of loss, could be judged prudent or not. This position is at odds with the modern so-called portfolio theory of investment management, which favours the spread of risk across a portfolio of investments and judges the prudence of the investment strategy with respect to the performance of the whole portfolio.[104]

The more modern approach to questions of investment tends to be in terms of the so-called prudent investor approach rather than the legal list approach, although the continued existence of the statutory investment lists remains a restrictive factor. This has derived much force from the US decision in *Harvard College v Amory*,[105] where it was said:

> All that can be required of a trustee is that he shall conduct himself faithfully and exercise a sound discretion. He is to observe how men of prudence, discretion and intelligence manage their own affairs, not in regard to speculation but in regard to the permanent disposition of their funds, considering the probable income, as well as the probable safety of capital to be invested.

In part the adoption of this approach, which was subsequently limited in a number of ways, was driven by the need to recognise the existence of new forms of investment. In New Zealand, the Trustee Amendment Act 1988 introduced changes to the Trustee Act 1956, which accommodated this new approach to some degree. Sections 13A, 13B and 13C of the Act now provide:

> 13A (1) A trustee may invest any trust funds, whether at the time in a state of investment or not, in any property.
>
> (2) Any such investment may be varied from time to time.
>
> 13B … a trustee exercising any power of investment shall exercise the care, diligence and skill that a prudent person of business would exercise in managing the affairs of others.

---

103 See e.g. *Bridges v Shepherd* (1921) 21 SR (NSW) 220.
104 Heydon and Leeming, and Watson and Taylor, *op cit* fn 2.
105 26 Mass (9 Pick) 446 (1830).

13C ... where a trustee's profession, employment or business is or includes acting as a trustee, or investing money on behalf of others, the trustee in exercising any power of investment, shall exercise the care, diligence and skill that a prudent person engaged in that profession, employment or business would exercise in managing the affairs of others.

The standard imposed by section 13C is a little different from that in the *Harvard* case, primarily because of the reference to 'managing the affairs of others'. This seems to require that the trustee act as a fiduciary rather than as a prudent business person. Section 13E goes on to list a number of factors that should be taken into account. Some of these include the desirability of diversifying investments, the nature of existing trust investments, the need to maintain the real value of capital or income of the trust, the risk of loss or depreciation, the potential for capital appreciation, the term of the investment and the likelihood of inflation affecting the investment. The emphasis on diversification of investment adopts the portfolio approach to investment mentioned earlier.[106]

Other jurisdictions adopt the list approach more directly by the publication of approved lists of investments in the trustee legislation. Attempts have been made to update the lists to provide for some of the newer forms of investment.[107] The lists provide for investment to be made in the likes of government stocks and securities, state-guaranteed debts, municipal bonds, mortgages of real estate, certain bank deposits and public utilities.[108]

9.4.6 The power to borrow moneys

The power to borrow moneys is slightly anomalous in some ways. An unauthorised borrowing may be made pursuant to the general power of a trustee to incur debts and liabilities on behalf of the trust; that is, provided it is within the scope of the authority of the trust. No explicit power is needed. A trustee who borrows excessively and thereby endangers the trust assets may have committed a breach of trust. But there is no requirement that there be an express or implied power to make an unsecured borrowing.[109] The trustee can then simply claim indemnity or recourse pursuant to the general right of indemnity. That in itself seems enough to justify the borrowing. In respect of secured borrowing, however, there

---

106 On these provisions see Davis, RL, *A Guide to Trustee Investments under the Prudent Person Approach*, 1990, Wellington, Butterworths.

107 As happened in Australia in the late 1980s. See Heydon and Leeming, and Watson and Taylor, *op cit* fn 2.

108 See, as an example of this approach, ss 12–22 Trustee Act (F); see, generally s 31 Trusts Act 2014 (S).

109 *Re German Mining Co; ex parte Chippendale* (1853) 4 De GM & G 19 would support such a proposition.

is no general right to borrow without an express power. This is treated, therefore, as something of an entirely different category. The English legislation, however, imported a secured power to borrow where the trustee had power to pay or apply capital moneys for any purpose. *Re Suenson-Taylor's Settlement*[110] held that such a provision did not authorise borrowing for negative gearing purposes against the trust assets, for example where the trust assets were to be used to acquire additional assets. This is so regardless of whether it might yield gains to the trust as a whole. It was regarded as essentially speculative in nature.[111]

9.4.7 Miscellaneous other powers

The trustee legislation confers on trustees a range of other powers for minor purposes. These include the power to compromise claims, to pay statute-barred debts, to employ agents, to lend trust moneys, to give receipts, to compromise claims against the estate and to convert any trust business into a company. The trustee is also given a statutory power to make payments out of income or capital for the maintenance and advancement of the lives of beneficiaries. The power to make payments to maintain an infant beneficiary exists independently of the statutory power.[112] The power to advance, which also exists at general law, is a power for the trustee to make provision out of capital moneys of the trust either to an infant or to contingent or remainder beneficiaries for their advancement in life, their education and maintenance of benefit. The power has always been widely construed by the courts. The statutory power has been interpreted in a similar light.[113] Certain qualifications are imposed in the legislation on the beneficiaries who might receive. Advancements might include payment of the debts of a beneficiary where this is necessary to avoid bankruptcy, provisions for recuperation of the beneficiary, after heavy study, the purchase of a house, provision for taxation and certain payments meeting the moral obligations of the beneficiary.[114]

---

110 [1974] WLR 1280.
111 See Hughes, RA, 'A Trustee's borrowing powers' (1998) 2(1) JSPL.
112 See *Chapman v Chapman* [1954] AC 429.
113 *Pilkington v Inland Revenue Commissioners* [1964] AC 612.
114 See Heydon and Leeming, and Watson and Taylor, *op cit* fn 2.

10

MANAGEMENT OF COMPANIES

10.1 Types of meeting

The role of these individuals and organs in the management of the company as well as the legal basis for the division of functions between them is an important one. An equally important and not unrelated issue is that of the incurring of liabilities of the company. In respect of individuals within the company, we need to understand the roles and functions of the likes of individual directors, the managing director, the company secretary and a range of other employees of a given company.

As companies necessarily act through human agents, one often needs to be able to determine whether a particular person has the required authority to bind the company legally to third parties. Likewise, there may be questions about whether or not a company has incurred criminal liability in a given case. The normal criteria for determination of criminal guilt or liability are very much premised on the assumption that it is an individual person who is the potentially guilty party. But more and more frequently during the course of the last century, companies made themselves targets for criminal liability. But seeing that a company itself cannot have a guilty mind, we need to consider the basis upon which a company can be held liable for a criminal offence. This we will do in due course. In the meantime we will concern ourselves with the internal structure of management of a company.

The primary organs for the management of a company are, most usually, the general meeting of members or shareholders, the board of directors and winding up meetings. The first two are relevant to a company still in business, whilst the third is concerned with the cessation of business of the company. This chapter will deal only with the first two. So far as this reflects a relationship between

DOI: 10.4324/9781003428060-12

directors and shareholders, it should be noted that the relationship is not based in contract. Whilst the constitution of a company constitutes a contract between the shareholders themselves and between the shareholders and the company,[1] there is no contractual relationship, collectively or individually, between the shareholders and the directors.[2] Certainly, there is no contract of agency between the shareholders and the directors. There might be a contract between individual directors and the company relating to the terms of service of the director, although sometimes there is not.

Since meetings of the relevant organs are pivotal to the management of a company, it is important to understand why it is generally necessary to hold meetings. Amongst other reasons, the calling or holding of a meeting is to communicate to or listen to other persons present. It can also be a forum through which a common or collective decision regarding company policy is arrived at. A meeting might also serve as a platform for expressing opinions or making known the views of shareholders or other participants. Sometimes, meetings can serve as a means of obstructing a decision or policy of a company. But generally, the importance of them is that of collective decision making.

It is usual that the articles of association provide that all matters pertaining to the day-to-day control of the company are vested in the board of directors collectively. The board is in other words the primary instrument of management. The articles will also make other provisions regarding the number of members of the board and their general composition, the holding of meetings, the transaction of business at board meetings, the required quorum and other relevant matters. It is normal that the board of directors serves as an independent managing organ of the company. It does not normally derive its managerial authority by way of delegation from the annual general meeting, although there have been some instances where this is so.[3] Accordingly, in the general run of cases, the board of directors is not subservient to the annual general meeting and is not obliged to follow its directions. But is the reverse the case? In other words, is the board of directors superior to the annual general meeting? This was once thought to be the case, but such a view no longer has support. The current view seems to be the organic view: namely, that the board of directors and the general meeting are independent and coordinate bodies with independent spheres of authority.[4]

As a general proposition, a registered company can hold meetings as and when it desires so long as this is in conformity with the provisions of its statute or its constitution. Depending upon the circumstances, a company may hold a general

---

1 *Hickman v Kent or Romney Marsh Sheep-Breeders' Association* [1915] 1 Ch 881. This originally implied status is now confirmed by the relevant statutes.
2 In some jurisdictions the legislation provides that the constitution also creates a contract between the company itself and both directors and other corporate officers.
3 This was in fact the early view of the relationship established in the 19th century.
4 See *John Shaw and Sons (Salford) Ltd v Shaw* [1935] 2 KB 113.

meeting,[5] a board of directors' meeting or a meeting relating to the company's dissolution. Each of these meetings has a specific objective to achieve. The size and nature of operations of each company would determine the frequency of holding the first two types of meeting. Meetings by registered companies may therefore take any of the three following forms.[6]

A company is invested with the power to control its own meetings. However, today it is also established that meetings should not only be in accord with existing laws but must equally be conducted according to certain procedural requirements. This is to ensure that the rights of the participants, as well as those of the general public, are safeguarded as far as possible. A meeting cannot be employed as an avenue for the violation of public or private rights.

To this end, a company is at liberty to hold meetings in public or in private but must take heed of public order laws. Security agencies may intervene in any company meeting where there is an imminent threat to life or property.[7] The civil law of defamation, assault or battery can in appropriate cases also sanction the organisers of the meeting, including the company. The press can also be excluded from company meetings where matters to be discussed border on confidentiality.[8]

Every company meeting must have a chairperson[9] and a secretary.[10] The meeting must also have a quorum.[11] Voting by proxy[12] might be allowed, depending upon whether it is a public or private company. There has to be an agenda and issues must be raised through motions and decisions carried through resolutions.[13] There also has to be a regulated order of debate and the chairperson must attend to

---

5 A general meeting; this is also categorised into annual general meetings (AGMs); extraordinary general meetings, class meetings and statutory meetings. See s 33, although no equivalent provision for a 'general meeting' (SI).

6 It is also possible for a company to hold class meetings where it has more than one class of shares. Class meetings are usually held with the object of varying class rights. The rights of a class are normally stated in the articles. Whenever a class variation is to be effected, the rights of the holders must be protected. In other words, their consent must be sought and obtained. The usual pattern of such a meeting is as follows: (a) a preliminary class meeting is held to agree to the variation, followed by (b) a full general meeting of the company in order to effect the variation. For a standard procedure on variation of class rights, see s 630 Companies Act 2006 (UK).

7 See s 2 Defamation Act Cap 33 (T); Public Order (Preservation) Act Cap 7.09 (T), Part III. The following offences may attract criminal penalties if committed in the course of a meeting: riot; violent disorder; affray; causing fear or provoking violence; harassment.

8 ISCA, *Meetings*, 1993, London, BPP Publishing, p 17.

9 Section 5 Companies Act 2021 (K).

10 No equivalent provision in Companies Act 2021 (K).

11 See s 28 Companies Act 2021 (K); s 160 Companies Act [Cap 40.08] 1991 (Tu).

12 Voting may be by show of hands or poll in companies. Other methods include ballot, division, voice vote and acclamation. See further s 37 Companies Act 2021 (K); s 150 [Cap 40.08] 1991 (Tu).

13 On resolutions, for instance, generally see ss 9, 14, 47, 49, although no equivalent provision in Companies Act 2009 (SI) cf formerly, s 135 Companies Ordinance [Cap 175] 1961 (SI). The types of resolutions are (a) ordinary, (b) special and (c) extraordinary. Cf ss 120–21 Companies Act (T).

interjections or points of order. The proceedings of the meetings must be recorded in the minutes.[14]

10.1.1 Annual general meeting

This is generally considered one of the most important meetings of a company. It is held once every year.[15] This meeting provides a forum where routine and topical issues affecting the company are addressed. The minimum notice period must be complied with before a valid meeting is called.[16] Proxies can attend and vote at the meeting.[17] Minutes of the meeting are to be kept. The articles may determine other matters relating to the calling and conduct of the meeting.

The meeting is to be held at any time within 18 months of incorporation. This might not be in the calendar year of incorporation or even in the following year. There may be an interval of 15 months between one annual general meeting (AGM) and the next.[18] The essence of an AGM is to allow members to question the progress of the company, direct questions to the directors or exert some form of pressure on the directors where performance is unsatisfactory.[19]

10.1.2 Extraordinary general meeting

This is any meeting called by the company or members other than the AGM. This can be summoned at any time. It is for the purpose of discussing unusual matters affecting the company or some sudden issues that require the immediate attention of the company. Discretion is vested in the directors to call an extraordinary general meeting (EGM) when they consider such as being necessary.

Members with at least a certain specified percentage of shareholding may also summon an EGM. The requisition must indicate the object of the meeting.[20] An auditor may also requisition an EGM, although this is not the case in all jurisdictions.[21] An EGM may also be called by order of the company.[22] The directors are by law mandated to summon an EGM in any or all of the following events:

---

14 See Meetings of shareholders, Part VI, although no equivalent provision in Companies Act 2021 (K); generally, see s 113, Division 2, although no equivalent provision in Companies Act 2009 (SI).

15 Compare with statutory meetings: no equivalent provision in Companies Act 2009 (SI); s 141 Companies Act [Cap 40.08] 1991 (Tu).

16 See s 145 Companies Act [Cap 40.08] 1991 (Tu); cf ss 34, 35, 37, although no equivalent provision in Companies Act 2012 (cf formerly ss 132, 134 Companies Act [cap 191] 1988) (V).

17 See s 150 Companies Act [Cap 40.08] 1991 (Tu); s 30 Companies Act (V).

18 Section 141 Companies Act (Tu).

19 Section 120 Companies Act (T).

20 Cf *ibid.*, ss 120, 121.

21 Sections 516–18 Companies Act 2006 (UK).

22 Section 34, Division 6 Companies Act 2009, although no equivalent provision cf Companies Act [Cap 175] 1961 (SI); s 143 Companies Act (Tu).

(a) on the request of members who hold a certain specified percentage of share-holding in the company;
(b) on the request of an auditor who resigns in certain circumstances;
(c) in the case of a public company where within 28 days the directors are aware that the assets of the company have fallen below half of its called-up capital; and
(d) where the court compels the holding of an EGM.

10.2 Board meetings

As noted above, the board of directors is the primary policy-making organ of the company. It also has general overview of the activities of the various committees under its direct control.[23] The frequency of a company's board meeting is generally determined by its articles. However, the chairperson of the board, the company or interested shareholders may also requisition a meeting in appropriate cases. The relevant executive officers and other staff members of the company in turn implement the decisions reached by the board of directors. Matters that cannot be executed without the concurrence of the shareholders have to be submitted to the general meeting for approval.

10.2.1 The powers of management: Division of powers

The constitution of a company sets out the way in which power is shared between the various organs in a company. There are two main organs of a company: the board of directors and the members or shareholders in a general meeting. The powers of the two are in effect balanced and limited in various ways. As we noted above, the arrangement between the two is not hierarchical. It is organic, in the sense that the two organs have separate and independent powers and functions. In Tonga, however, sections 127–29 of the Companies Act cover other important matters relating to the management of companies, such as the carrying out of major transactions and delegation of powers. These have not been left to the articles, as is the case with the other jurisdictions.

The board of directors and the general meeting are categorically different in some ways. First of all, directors are subject to fiduciary duties, which means that they are obliged to act individually and collectively in the best interests of the company. This notion is examined further below. But the members of the company are not fiduciaries and do not have to exercise their own powers as fiduciaries. Directors can be removed by the general meeting under certain circumstances, but the reverse is never the case.

23 This includes meeting by committees of the board. A board's committees may be set up to deal with appointments, welfare, finance, industrial relations, etc. For the meaning of 'board' see s 126 Companies Act (T).

The division of power is clearly outlined in the Companies Acts, as well as (usually) in the articles of the company. The members in general meeting exercise certain powers exclusive to them such as alteration of objects or capital or alteration of the articles.[24] The board exercises powers delegated to it by the company. Most important of these is the power to borrow.[25] Other delegated powers may be validated by reference to the general meeting. Delegated powers of directors generally cover matters on management and business of the company. The powers of directors are usually subject to the Companies Act, the memorandum and articles as well as any instructions contained in special resolutions.

It is important to bear in mind that the memorandum, articles and instructions by special resolutions do not have retrospective effect to invalidate a decision already taken by the directors. They can, however, impose or set new measures aimed at curtailing the powers of the directors. It is also to be noted that so long as the actions of the directors are *intra vires*, they are not subject to control or direction by the members. Furthermore, shareholders cannot direct or instruct directors individually or collectively as their agents. If anything, directors can be considered as agents only to the company and not to the body of shareholders. However, it is established practice for directors to be controlled by the shareholders by altering the articles or by passing a specific special resolution thereby imposing limits on the directors' powers.[26]

The immediate power of management is vested in the board. Generally, the annual meeting cannot interfere with the functions or actions of the board.[27] Where a particular matter is vested exclusively in the control of the board, the members of the company cannot use the power to requisition meetings and demand that the matter be put to a vote of the general meeting.[28] In fact, where the general meeting attempts to do so, the decision is nugatory.[29]

There are, however, some exceptions to this. For example, the board might, for reasons which are exceptional, be unable to act. The board might be deadlocked on a particular issue with no way of effectively resolving it. In such a case the general meeting of members has the power to assume authority to decide the matter.[30] Another instance is where the board is unable to meet owing to the continued absence of a quorum for board meetings. There might be cases where directors have resigned or died and this is the cause of the depletion in numbers. The

---

24 See ss 11, 70 Companies Act [Cap 40.08] 1991 (Tu); ss 104–09 Companies Act (T).

25 Articles often impose limitation on powers of directors. See e.g. Art 79 in Table A, Third Schedule of Companies Act 1955 (NZ) – no equivalent provision in Companies Act 1993 (NZ).

26 See s 144 Companies Act (Tu).

27 The two leading authorities on this are *Automatic Self-Cleansing Filter Syndicate Co Ltd v Cuninghame* [1906] 2 Ch 34 and *Quin & Axtens Ltd v Salmon* [1909] AC 442.

28 *NRMA Ltd v Parker* (1986) 6 NSWLR 517.

29 See *Imperial Hydropathic Hotel Co. Blackpool v Hampton* (1882) 23 Ch D 1; *Gramophone and Typewriter Ltd v Stanley* [1908] 2 KB 89.

30 See *Barron v Potter* [1914] 1 Ch 895, but cf *Berlei Hestia (NZ) Ltd v Fernyhough* [1980] NZLR 150.

situation cannot be resolved owing to the fact that it is the board of directors that is assigned the power of appointing new directors.[31] However, if the power of appointing new directors is vested in the general meeting, then the general meeting must attempt to resolve the situation by appointing new directors rather than by usurping the power of the board to make a decision.

The power of initiating and prosecuting litigation is vested in the board of directors with respect to any matter which falls within the scope of their authority under the articles. However, the general meeting might have a reserve of power with respect to litigation in some circumstances. Where the board has initiated litigation against a third party in the name of the company, then, as a general proposition, the general meeting cannot intervene and seek to stop the proceedings.[32] The rule known as the rule in *Foss v Harbottle*[33] asserts that the proper plaintiff in any proceedings to be brought concerning the company's interest is the company itself. If in fact the decision to take those proceedings is vested with the board of directors, then they are fully entitled to assert the company's name. Put another way, the corporate interest cannot be asserted by a member or by a collectivity thereof. The board normally controls the company. If, however, this control is abused, such as in a case where it is exercised for purposes which are fraudulent or oppressive, then members can bring what is called a derivative action to assert the company interest. The derivative action thus provides an exception to the proper plaintiff rule in *Foss v Harbottle*.

In *Edwards v Halliwell* [1950] 2 All ER 1064 four types of situation were suggested as justifying a derivative action. The first is where someone in control of the company has caused the company to undertake or to be about to undertake an action which is or would be *ultra vires*. The second is where the action on the part of the controller involves action which goes beyond the constitution and this requires authorisation by way of a special resolution of the general meeting but the authorisation, however, has not been obtained. The third situation involves cases where the action involves some infringement of the personal right of a member and this infringement is not one which could be remedied or legitimated by a resolution of the general meeting. The fourth involves situations where the action is something which could be condoned by the general meeting of the company, but the act of condoning it would itself amount to a fraud on the company, that is, because those who perpetrated the wrongdoing are in control of the company.

There is a possible fifth exception. Put loosely, this arises in situations where the interests of justice require that a minority shareholder be permitted to bring an action in the name of the company to address the wrongdoing. There has been some debate as to whether such an exception ought to be recognised, although there is some apparent support for it.

---

31 *Isle of Wight Railway Co v Tahourdin* (1883) 25 Ch D 320; *Foster v Foster* [1916] 1 Ch 532.
32 *John Shaw and Sons (Salford) Ltd v Shaw* [1935] 2 KB 113.
33 (1843) 2 Hare 461.

In respect of the powers of shareholders, a majority decision binds the minority of the company albeit with proper safeguards to the rights of the minority. The following are some of the safeguards to protecting minority interests in a company:

(a) An *ultra vires* action of a company cannot be sanctioned by a majority of the members. This is because the action is void as a matter of law. Illegal acts of the company are treated in the same way.
(b) Where the articles of the company specify a special procedure, the majority cannot override it except where the articles are duly amended by special resolution of the general meeting.
(c) A decision of the majority cannot stand if it is fraudulent where, for example, control by the majority is to defraud the company – the minority may bring an action against the fraudulent majority.
(d) The best way to safeguard minority interests is through an articulate drafting of the articles at the outset.

10.2.2 Directors

We have already considered the position of shareholders.[34] It is now appropriate to examine the role of directors, who play a much more direct role in the management of companies. Directors are not the only officers of a company nor the only ones who, as individuals, participate directly as agents of the company. There will be other officers of a company such as the company secretary and a public officer who have particular administrative functions. A company will usually have a managing director, who is certainly a director but who also has greater powers than other directors in relation to the day-to-day management and control of the company. The managing director's position is usually a remunerated position and most often there is a contract of service between that person and the company.

Because directors sit at the apex of a company's decision-making structure, they occupy an important position in the affairs of the company. Whilst they must meet some legal qualifications regarding their appointment and the continuing holding of office, there is no guarantee of particular experience sufficient to engage in management. Even though companies can often benefit from the experience and sound business advice given to them by the appropriately qualified directors, the directors can in some cases actually hinder the progress of the company. In any case, directors, were they freely permitted to indulge their personal interests, could deleteriously affect the interests of the company. In view of the latter risk, there are some particular duties imposed by company law, or more particularly equity, on company directors as well as on other senior executive staff of a company. These are called fiduciary duties and will be examined further below.

---

34 Refer to Chapter 6.

10.2.3 Who is a director?

A director is any eligible natural person[35] who has been appointed by a company to hold office as a director on its board of directors. This is admittedly a rather functional definition. Such a person could hold office by virtue of an appointment under the articles of the company or through an appointment by means of an ordinary resolution in a general meeting of the company. So far as legal definitions of the office go, s 73 of the Companies Act of Kiribati defines a director to mean a person, by whatever name called, who is appointed to direct and administer the business of the company.[36] In fact, directors are those whose duties extend more to management than administration because their role in relation to the making of corporate policy is a key one. Company employees normally carry out the policy decisions made by the directors. Some directors might also be employees of the company and therefore have an executive or administrative function as well.

Usually, directors are engaged in collective decision making; that is to say, as members of a collective body known as the board of directors. However, there might be particular directors, such as the managing director or a governing director, who have special powers and are able to bind the company to particular legal arrangements. The articles of the company will play a special role in defining the powers of these special classes of directors, although often there are traditional aspects of these offices which serve to define the authority of each.

The company can appoint a person to occupy the position of an ordinary (non-executive), executive, alternate or shadow director.[37] In the South Pacific countries, it is only the Companies Act of Kiribati that has a statutory provision on executive directors.[38] There is also a provision on managing directors[39] and no specific provision for alternate directors.[40] In the case of all others, the provisions for appointment of different types of directors and their specific functions and powers are found in the articles of the company.

Kiribati has now joined other South Pacific jurisdictions, making no provision for the appointment of representative directors (formerly, section 110(1) Kiribati Ordinance, repealed in 2021).

---

35 See s 122 Companies Act [Cap 40.08] 1991 (Tu); generally, see ss 74, 77 Companies Act 2021 (K); s 125 Companies Act (T). Cf *Pekipaki v O.K Toutai Co. Ltd* [1994] TOLawRp 9; [1994] Tonga LR 40 (15 April 1994).

36 Section 73 Companies Act 2021 (K).

37 See s 125 Companies Act (T); generally, see Part VII, Section 73 Companies Act 2021 (K).

38 Generally, see Part VII, Section 73 Companies Act 2021 (K).

39 *Ibid.*, ss 86-96.

40 *Ibid.*, formerly s 109(1) under repealed Companies Ordinance 1998 (K), which provides: "Unless prohibited by the Articles of the company a director may, in respect of any period not exceeding 6 months in which he is unable for any reason to act as director, appoint another director or any other person approved by a resolution of the board of directors, as an alternate director. Such an appointment shall be in writing signed by the appointor and appointee and lodged with the company and shall take effect on lodgement with the company".

However, a representative directors section has far-reaching implications, in that it has the potential to create an atmosphere of industrial harmony between employers and employees. The aim of the section is to allow workers' representatives to be appointed as directors of companies. Thus, the rift between management and labour which often threatens industrial peace will be narrowed in the interests of all concerned. This in industrial law language is referred to as the principal of codetermination.

In Fiji there must be at least three directors for a public company and two for a private company.[41] In the case of Tuvalu, the position is slightly different. Every company requires a minimum of two directors and, where a company has an even number of directors, not less than half in number or, where the number is odd, a majority of the directors must be nationals of Tuvalu.[42] Every company in Samoa and Kiribati must also have a minimum of two directors.[43] Whilst in Fiji, Kiribati and Tuvalu, companies registered under their Acts provide for resident directors, it does not seem to be the case in Samoa. On the conversion of a company in Tuvalu, the directors in the defunct companies are deemed to be the first directors of the new company. But this is only applicable when a company converts from public to private.[44] Except in the case of a public company, a motion for the appointment of two or more persons as directors of a company must be floated by separate resolutions in respect of each person put forward.[45]

Every director appointed must have his/her name entered into the register kept for that purpose.[46] Directors do not necessarily have to be shareholders, but where the articles provide for the payment of qualification shares, directors can only assume office if the qualification shares are paid.[47] Directors are disqualified from holding office where they have been found guilty in connection with misconduct relating to financial matters or administration of companies.[48]

Directors can be removed by the shareholders in a general meeting by passing a special resolution. But special notice of the resolution must be given to the director to enable him/her to show cause at the general meeting as to why he/she should not be removed. This accords with the principle of fair hearing.[49] However,

---

41 Generally, see Part 10 Companies Act 2015 (F).
42 Section 117 Companies Act [Cap 40.08] 1991 (Tu).
43 Section 49(1) Companies Act 2001 (S); ss 74, 77 Companies Act 2021 (K).
44 Section 121 Companies Act [Cap 40.08] 1991 (Tu).
45 Sections 94, 95 Companies Act 2015 (F); ss 74, 77 Companies Act 2021 (K); s 117 (Tu); s 86 Companies Act 2001 (S).
46 Generally, see Part VII Companies Act 2021 (K).
47 *Ibid.*; generally, see s 82 Companies Act 2009, although no equivalent provision (SI); s 123 Companies Act (Tu).
48 Generally, see ss 105–9 Companies Act 2021 (K). Other instances include the following: 'A director may be disqualified by an Act or rule of law (if qualification shares are lost for instance); bankruptcy; insanity; resignation; absence from meetings for six consecutive times'. See also generally, ss 97, 99 Companies Act 2021 (SI).
49 See generally s 114 Companies Act 2021, although no equivalent provision cf s 93 under former Act (K); s 43 Companies Act 2009 (SI).

the position might be affected where directors are also appointed under a service agreement with the company. Termination of a director's position unilaterally by the company might give the director rights to sue the company pursuant to the contract where the termination amounts to a breach of contract. It does not matter that the company's power of termination might appear to be absolute under the articles of association. It must still be considered whether there was an appropriate right of termination pursuant to the contract of service, otherwise the company could be liable for breach of that contract.

10.2.4 Duties of directors

It is now appropriate that we look at the duties and liabilities of directors. Directors are subject to a range of different duties, some of which have been evolved by decisions of the courts whilst others have been created by statute. In some instances, the duties embedded in the company statutes are simply limited statements of the duties found at common law or in equity. The statutory statement of the duty often does not exclude the common law or equitable duty. For example, the basic directors' duties of prudence and probity have been enacted as part of the statutory duties of directors in Kiribati.[50]

Directors are also in a special position vis-à-vis the company. They represent the company, which is merely a juristic entity. Thus, in equity they are treated as fiduciaries who are generally obliged to act *bona fide* in the best interests of the company. The equitable obligation here requires, for example, that they no make personal profit or gain at the expense of the company or misappropriate company property, nor should they conduct themselves in such a way as to create a conflict of interest between their interests and those of the company.[51] Should they be in breach of their fiduciary duties, equity can treat them as constructive trustees of profits and gains which they might have made or appropriated, or indeed impose a range of other equitable remedies.[52] There are a number of other aspects of the fiduciary position and we will look further at these below.

The liability of directors in respect of breach of their duties can be civil or criminal. Usually, the latter is imposed by the statutes concerned. The same act can give rise to both civil and criminal liability, but each is determined according to different standards of proof. In none of the South Pacific countries is there a regime of civil penalties attaching to the conduct of directors. In Australia, for example, it has been taken that the imposition of criminal liability on company directors does little to either prevent the occurrence of white-collar crime by directors or serve the interests of the company or the public interest, for example, in the recouping of losses or in the prevention of future delinquent conduct. But

---

50 See s 87 Companies Act 2021 (K); cf s 130 Companies Act (T).
51 See s 91 Companies Act 2021 (K).
52 See generally, s 95 Companies Act 2021 (K); s 136 Companies Act [Cap 40.08] 1991 (Tu).

this trend is unlikely to be adopted in the South Pacific countries for some time. Concerns about corruption in these jurisdictions have to date been focused on the activities of public officials in the traditional sense.

Directors are subject to liabilities which arise both at common law and in equity. The remedies are different in each case. However, as with criminal liability, the same act might give rise to consequences at common law as well as in equity. So far as equity is concerned, the position of company directors involves the extension of analogies between trustees and directors. As we shall see, however, the extent of the obligations imposed on the two as fiduciaries is different, although the same remedies might be available. Directors are treated less strictly than trustees. But directors are liable at common law for negligence or fraud. We have seen examples of this in respect of the prospectus provisions and share allotment situations where directors can be held liable for the likes of negligent or fraudulent misrepresentation.

Directors can also be held liable in contract where for example they have committed a breach of their contract of service. But as regards duties owed to the company rather than third parties, the same act can give rise to a breach of the equitable obligation as a fiduciary. For example, a director might be held liable for something in the nature of a breach of trust because he or she has acted without due care to the position of the company, thus giving rise to equitable remedies for the company as well as a right of action for damages at common law. The difference is that an action for breach of fiduciary duty is available even without proof of loss on the part of the company. In this area, equity is usually primarily concerned with the imposition of standards of conduct on directors.

10.2.5 Directors as fiduciaries

We have noted above that directors are fiduciaries in relation to the company. So too are trustees and partners, and we have examined the broad principles applicable to them in earlier chapters. Commercial actors such as company directors are often subject to fiduciary obligations, although the nature and scope of the duty have to be tailored to meet the particular circumstances in which the parties find themselves.

Historically, the fiduciary duty imposed on company directors was by way of extension of the duty imposed on trustees, although there was a need to modify its strictness somewhat. Trustees are expected to act exclusively in the interests of the beneficiaries or objects of the trust. Directors are different from trustees. The latter are primarily expected to preserve the property and assets of the trust. They are not expected to put it at risk. Even engaging in a business venture is traditionally regarded in trust law as putting the assets at risk, although this can be undertaken if the trust instrument permits it. In respect of company directors, however, their function is quite distinct from that of trustees. Risk taking is integral to the activity of most company directors. Most companies have historically engaged in business, although this is not necessarily the case, and those who manage them as commercial undertakings are thus required to take risks on behalf of their share-holders. Thus, the need for modification of the strict duty of a fiduciary applicable to a trustee. Company directors were and are expected only to act substantially in the best interests of the company rather than exclusively in the interests of the company.

The most general formulation of the duties of a company director is that the director must act *bona fide* in the best interests of the company. Sometimes this has been employed as if it were an additional ground of liability of a fiduciary and sometimes as if it were a guiding principle. However, this statement of the duty serves to highlight two points. First, the formulation suggests that the duty is subjective only. In other words, it suggests that as long as the director has some genuine belief that what he or she is doing is in the best interests of the company then all will be well. However, the courts have gone to some pains to suggest that this is not entirely so. Determining what is in the best interests of the company requires that objective issues be taken into account. In other words, the director's view of what is in the best interests of the company must be a reasonable one.

The second point to be considered in this formulation is the question of what is meant by 'the best interests of the company'. This issue has occasioned some difficulties, with the courts swinging from one abstraction to another. One could leap to the conclusion that the company's interests are really just the interests of the shareholders or a particular, perhaps controlling or majority, section of them. Thus, there have been attempts to take the best interests of the company as the interests of the shareholders as a whole or as the interests of the hypothetical shareholder. Both of these are generalisations that might be dangerous, in that they obscure the interests of particular classes of shareholders or minorities. But there are many other interests which the company entity might represent as well; hence this approach has been subjected to some criticism.

There are many aspects of the fiduciary duty that, it should be noted, apply to other company officers besides directors. The company secretary and the company auditor, for example, are also treated as fiduciaries. The fiduciary is, some would say, a many-headed monster. Some particular dimensions of the duty are as follows. These are often formulated as if they were separate heads of duty. However, they are not to be considered as if they were entirely separate. There is, in fact, considerable overlap between them. Sometimes the courts will proceed according to one particular head, treating others as relevant to it. They are as follows:

- The duty to act honestly. This is a subjective aspect of the duty. It is also restated in the legislation. In the case of Tonga, for instance, ss 130, 132 and 135 of the Companies Act 1995 restate this duty in statutory form.
- The duty to acquaint themselves with their power functions and powers. Directors, like other fiduciaries, are obliged to inform themselves as to the nature of the role which they undertake and its limitations. If the actions of

the directors were an attempt to exceed their own powers under the articles of the company, this could involve a breach of fiduciary duty.

- The duty to act in accordance with the constitution of the company. This is similar to the duty of a trustee to comply with the terms of the trust instrument. In the South Pacific this duty remains of a particular moment. Unlike the position in Australia, it is still possible in the South Pacific jurisdictions for the acts of a company to be judged *ultra vires* and therefore void. This would mean that on considering the issue of breach of fiduciary duty by directors, it will be a relevant consideration whether the directors' actions involved putting the company beyond its own powers.

- The duty to exercise powers for a proper purpose. This requirement was developed by the equity courts with respect to trustees. The rule in the *Duke of Portland v Topham*[53] requires that a trustee act with an entire and singular view of the objects of the trust.[54] But the strictness of the duty has been modified in respect of company directors, as noted above. This rule will bring to account directors who exercise their powers in order to confer benefits on either themselves or on third parties or to benefit foreign or alien objectives. This might include a situation where a director exercises a power to confer benefits on a third party. Where directors at the behest of majority shareholders agree not to exercise their powers, or to exercise them in a particular way, then the question of improper purpose comes into play.

One of the problem areas here is that the courts have to determine what the proper purpose of any given power is. In some cases, this might be obvious enough, although in others it will not be so easy.[55] Clearly enough, the exercise of the powers by the directors of companies can be employed in such a way as to upset the internal balance of power within a company, such as between different classes of shareholders or between majority and minority shareholders. The issue of new shares or of bonus shares provides classical examples of potential areas of conflict which touch on the propriety of the exercise of powers by directors.[56] So do situations where the exercise of directors' powers confers some additional or incidental

---

53 (1864) 11 ER 1242.

54 On the rule as it applies to trustees, see Hughes, R, *Trust Law in the South Pacific*, 2000, Suva: IJALS, p 115.

55 Cf *Howard Smith Ltd v Ampol Petroleum Ltd* [1974] AC 821; *Australian Metropolitan Life Assurance Co Ltd v Ure* (1923) 33 CLR 199. Thus, the court is left with a very wide discretion, but perhaps this is unavoidable if there is no clear statement as to the purpose for which a power is given. The same difficulty seems to arise in all areas of the application of the fiduciary duty in the corporate context given that the obligation is owed to an abstract entity, the nature and interests of which are rather amorphous.

56 Thus, the numerous decisions in this area: see e.g. *Ngurli Ltd v McCann* (1953) 90 CLR 425; *Howard Smith Ltd v Ampol Petroleum Ltd* [1974] AC 821; *Harlowe's Nominees Pty Ltd v Woodside (Lakes Entrance) Oil Co NL* (1968) 121 CLR 483; *Ashburton Oil NL v Alpha Minerals NL* (1971) 123 CLR 614, amongst others.

degree of control on the directors themselves or their associates.[57] The memorandum or articles of association might, in some cases, define or give clear directions as to what the proper purposes of a power might be. But in other cases, it will be left to the court to draw inferences and make assumptions from whatever source they can. In some cases, the memorandum or articles might even clearly authorise the use of a power for purposes which, viewed independently, might be regarded as totally foreign to the company's objectives.[58]

Aside from characterising the purpose for which the power was given, the courts must also characterise the purpose for which the power was in fact exercised by the directors. This is a factual question which is perhaps no less difficult that the determination of the proper purpose of the power itself. A given power might be exercised for numerous different reasons or purposes. It is a factual issue, but it cannot be determined simply by reference to the subjective motivations or considerations of the individual directors. Whilst the *bona fide* intentions of the individual directors are necessarily a factor, the court is concerned really with the purposes of the board as a whole; that is to say, as a collective entity. Obviously, there might be substantial differences between individual members of the board as to why a particular power is or was exercised. Some might not have had in mind any particular purpose at all when the power was exercised. However, the court has to arrive at some conclusion as to a substantial purpose behind the exercise of the power at the collective level. This will be attributed to the whole board even though some individual directors might have clearly had other purposes in mind.[59]

Much will depend on whether the dominant purpose of the directors was to exercise the power for an improper purpose such as the perpetuation of their own control of the company or the alteration of the balance of power in their own favour. The fact that the directors entertained some honest or sincere belief that they were doing the right thing or that they acted with integrity will not excuse

---

57 See e.g. *Advances Bank of Australia Ltd v FAI Insurances Ltd* (1987) 9 NSWLR 464; *Darvall v North Sydney Brick and Tile Co Ltd* (1989) 16 NSWLR 260. This would include an attempt by directors to perpetuate their own control of the company. See *Ngurli Ltd v McCann* (1953) 90 CLR 425; *Howard Smith Ltd v Ampol Petroleum Ltd* [1974] AC 821.

58 See *Whitehouse v Carlton Hotel Pty Ltd* (1987) 162 CLR 285.

59 See *Howard Smith Ltd v Ampol Ltd* [1974] AC 821; *Harlowe's Nominees Pty Ltd v Woodside (Lakes Entrance) Oil Co NL* (1968) 121 CLR 483; *Darvall v North Sydney Brick & Tile Co Ltd* (1989) 16 NSWLR 260; *Winthrop Investments Ltd v Winns Ltd* (1979) 4 ACLR 1. Clearly, the characterisation of a purpose even as dominant or singular and substantive might be problematic in particular cases. There might clearly be cases where a mixture of equivalent purposes attends the exercise of a particular power such that the attempt to attribute just one dominant purpose is not only difficult but also misleading. Thus, in *Mills v Mills* (1938) 60 CLR 150, it was suggested that it would be enough if an impermissible purpose attending the exercise of the power were causative, in the sense that without it the power would not be exercised. See *per* Dixon J at 186, approved in *Whitehouse v Carlton Hotel Pty Ltd* (1987) 162 CLR 285 at 294. On this, see further Watson, S and Taylor, L, *Corporate Law in New Zealand,* 2018, Wellington Thomson Reuters New Zealand Ltd, pp 521–24, at 18.3.2.

them. However, they might be excused where they can show that their dominant purpose in exercising the power was some commercial objective even though some incidental consequence of the exercise of the power might have been an improper one.[60]

• The duty not to fetter discretions (i.e. powers). The powers given to directors are in the nature of mere or discretionary powers, in the sense that the directors are not usually obliged to exercise them. There are some things which they are obliged to do or to do at particular times; for example, to comply with the requirements of legislation. As a general proposition, directors must exercise their own independent judgment in relation to the powers vested in them, but they must also exercise it on behalf of the company. They cannot create situations where restraints are imposed either on their independence in this regard or on the interests which might be served by the exercise of the power.[61] They cannot, for instance, leave it to others to determine how and when their power might be exercised. If, for example, an agreement were entered into with a third party which purported to deny to the company a power which it genuinely has and which is exercisable through the action of the directors, then this would be an invalid fetter.[62]

Two specific aspects of this principle are worthy of comment. The first is that company directors are not permitted to delegate their powers to others. They must exercise their powers and functions themselves. To leave it to others to make their decisions for them, whether by some formal delegation of powers or by simply waiting for others to make their decisions for them, would involve a surrender of the independence required of them. However, often the articles of the company will specifically authorise committees or some particular officer of the company such as the managing director to exercise delegated powers from the board with respect to specific matters. Clearly this is in order as it is formally authorised even where the authority of the board of directors and that of the committee or officer

---

60 This was the approach taken by the Privy Council in *Howard Smith* [1974] AC 821. See also *Piercy v Mills & Co Ltd* [1920] 1 CH 77; *Teck Corporation Ltd v Millar* (1973) 33 DLR (3d) 288.
61 Even where this is done on behalf of the majority of the shareholders. This would be just as much a compromise of their independence of judgment. See *Automatic Self-Cleansing Filter Syndicate Co Ltd v Cunninghame* [1906] 2 Ch 34; *Howard Smith Ltd v Ampol Ltd* [1974] AC 821.
62 *Russell v Northern Bank Development Corp* [1992] BCLC 431 (CA (NI)); [1992] BCLC 1016. But this does not mean that the directors of a company cannot enter into a contract, a term of which is that they will give approval to a certain course of action on the part of the company in future, e.g. that the company will approve a transfer of shares in favour of a particular person. This is the case, provided that the directors were acting in good faith in the interests of the company at the time of negotiation of the contract. See *Thorby v Goldberg* [1964] HCA 41; 112 CLR 597 and *ANZ Executors and Trustee Co Ltd v Qintex Australia Ltd (Receivers and Managers Appointed)* (1991) 2 Qd R 360.

is concurrent. Whether the board can continue to exercise those powers and so override the resolutions of the committee or officer is a matter for the construction of the articles in question.[63]

Secondly, even though the powers of directors might be discretionary in the sense described above, they cannot ignore the issue of whether to exercise them or not. There might not be any legal obligation on them to exercise particular powers, but they are still obliged as fiduciaries to give due consideration to whether or not the power should be exercised. This duty is of particular significance to trustees of discretionary trusts. Even though potential objects of a discretionary power might not have any established interest as beneficiaries, they are still entitled to have the trustee consider whether to exercise the discretion to confer benefits on them. Directors' powers are provided for the benefit of the company in terms of its overall management. They are not given to be completely ignored by the directors.

• Finally, there is a cluster of particular duties which overlap to some considerable extent. Whether there are three rules or whether they are just different contexts of application of the one rule requiring loyalty on the part of fiduciaries is a somewhat moot point. However, all of these are situations where the law is concerned with imposing standards of conduct on directors in relation to their management of the company. The first one is the duty to avoid conflicts of duty and personal interest. As we have explained above, directors are under an obligation to act substantially in the best interests of the company that they control. Their duty to the company is to be given precedence by them over their personal interest. There have been various formulations of this particular duty with varying degrees of strictness. One view is that the duty requires absolute loyalty by the directors to the company, in the sense that all potential conflict situations must be avoided.[64] There is no doubt that the duty is imposed with some strictness, as in this area equity has been more concerned with the imposition of objective standards of conduct on directors than with requiring honesty or subjective probity. It is clear that the directors can be held in breach of the duty even though there is no real possibility that the company was denied any opportunity for action on its own part.[65] But more usually the duty is taken as less than absolute or total, and this is con-

---

63 See, generally, *Totterdell v Fareham Blue Brick and Tile Co. Ltd* (1866) LR 1 CP 674; *Huth v Clarke* (1890) 25 QBD 391.

64 For various formulations of this duty, see e.g. *Phipps v Boardman* [1967] 2 AC 46. If taken as a duty of absolute loyalty to the company, then directors would be in breach of the duty if, for example, they held shares in the company or if they held directorships in other companies. As we have explained, some directors hold representative positions such that they are in effect nominees of other interests. This would also involve a situation of potential conflict if the duty were interpreted strictly. But equity has never required that a director's position be treated as though it were a 24-hour-a-day position. Normal commercial considerations require modification of the duty.

65 See *Regal (Hastings) Ltd v Gulliver* [1942] 1 All ER 378; *Phipps v Boardman* [1967] 2 AC 46.

sistent with the general approach to treating company directors as less than trustees.

Hence the more usual formulation of the principle is in terms of a requirement that the director avoid 'any real sensible possibility of conflict'.[66] This formulation is rather elastic but claims to be involved in practical considerations. There is thus considerable scope for variation from case to case. It requires consideration of a wide range of circumstances, including the nature of the company concerned and the extent of the personal interest involved. Certainly, it can encompass situations where the director's interest is indirect rather than direct. Most commonly it will be applied with respect to pecuniary interests, although there is no reason in principle why it should be restricted to these interests alone.

It should be noted that the rule applies with respect to conflicts which are both actual and potential. But, in the latter respect, the courts have experienced problems in narrowing down just what is a potential conflict. It could be either everything or nothing. Where a director is also a director of another company, there is some remote potential for conflict. But the courts have never wanted to hold that merely holding another position such as this would involve a breach of the rule. Much would depend on the relative situation of the two companies and whether, for example, they were in a situation of real or tangible competition.

The real issue seems to be whether the director has placed him/herself in a situation where s/he has effectively compromised the independence of judgment that is expected of him/her in relation to the (first) company.[67] But the conflict need not arise only with respect to external appointments or interests. Indeed, the more usual type of case is where the director is engaged in some form of dealing or transaction with the company itself.[68] Other classic situations are those where the director is presented with some opportunity which comes to him or her by virtue of his or her position as director of the company. In such situations, the opportunity is in reality that of the company itself and the director is obliged not to take up the opportunity without first presenting it to the company.[69]

---

66 *Phipps v Boardman* [1967] 2 AC 46 at 124; cf *Aberdeen Railway Co v Blaikie Bros* (1854) 1 Macq 461; *Chan v Zacharia* (1984) 154 CLR 178 at 199; *Hospital Products Ltd v United States Surgical Corp* (1984) 156 CLR 41 at 103.

67 See *Transvaal Lands Co v New Belgium (Transvaal) Land and Development Co* [1914] 2 Ch 488; *R v Byrnes* (1995) 130 ALR 529.

68 Ford suggests as follows: "The conflict rule has its most obvious application in cases where a director enters into a transaction, directly or indirectly, to which the company is a party. The clearest case of the director having a disabling conflict is when a director enters into a transaction with the company, whether by way of contract, trust or other transaction, under which the director stands to make a direct personal gain. Another category is where directors employ themselves to work for reward for the company". Ford, H, *Principles of Corporations Law*, 1990, Sydney, Butterworths, p 356.

69 There is considerable overlap in opportunity type cases with the profit-making rule. See below.

Directors in a situation of actual or potential conflict are obliged to disclose the situation to an independently constituted organ of the company. The company organ can approve or ratify any proposed action on the part of the director which would otherwise involve a breach of this duty. The disclosure must be of all material facts relevant to the situation of conflict. Anything less will be ineffective and will taint any consent that might be given on behalf of the company. Any consent must, in other words, be an informed one. Disclosure to an independent organ of the company would involve a general meeting of the company and one which is free of the control or influence of the director concerned. In the case of an individual director, disclosure to a board of directors which is independent of the control or influence of the director concerned might also be sufficient.

Secondly, directors are obliged not to make a profit or advantage for themselves as a result of their position within the company. This rule overlaps to some extent with the first rule. One area where this traditionally occurs is in the so-called opportunity cases: that is, where the director is presented with some opportunity which is claimed to have belonged to the company. Some proceed with these cases on the basis of the conflict rule, whilst others have dealt with them as cases of profit taking or, in fact, misappropriation, which is the third rule in this cluster – see below. This is perhaps because all three are expressions of the basic notion that a fiduciary has a duty of loyalty to the company, which is sometimes put in terms of the obligation to act *bona fide* in the best interests of the company. The rule here is not concerned with unfair or unreasonable transactions undertaken by a fiduciary. Showing that the transaction was fair or reasonable or indeed beneficial to the company will not excuse the director.[70] However, in bringing the director to account, the courts might make some allowance to the director for benefits to the company which his or her efforts have produced.[71]

The special difficulties that attend the operation of this rule relate to the determination of the scope of the obligation of the company director. The decisions frequently talk in terms of the prevention of gains or taking of profits which flow to a director as 'a result of' or 'in connection with' or 'as a consequence of' his or her office. In other words, the rule is concerned with preventing the taking of gains or advantages by a fiduciary in connection with or as a result of their office.[72]

---

70 See *Furs Ltd v Tomkies* (1936) 54 CLR 583; *Regal (Hastings) Ltd v Gulliver* [1942] 1 All ER 378; *Phipps v Boardman* [1967] 2 AC 46; *Parker v McKenna* (1874) LR 10 Ch App 96. But again, there have been concerns where this involves too strict an application of the equitable rules relating to trustees who are denied any possible benefit from their position. Arguably, practical considerations might justify some modification of the rule, but this has not occurred to date.

71 As occurred in *Phipps v Boardman* [1967] 2 AC 46. The court can impose a constructive trust on the director in order to recover the relevant gains but then make some allowance by way of remuneration to the director in respect of his or her efforts.

72 *Regal (Hastings) Ltd v Gulliver & Ors* [1967] 2 AC 134; it should be noted that even on the classical view of corporate opportunities, a director would not be permitted to resign his or her directorship in order to take advantage of the opportunity. The obligation arises once the opportunity

This is language which postulates a causal type of relationship. Such language appears clearly to suggest that it is possible to delineate the scope of the fiduciary obligation of the director. Were that possible, then one would assume that there are situations where opportunities might flow to a director which are not opportunities of the company but received in a private capacity.[73] If the director exploits advantages of the latter type, then, on this line of authority, there is no breach of the rule. In other words, directors are permitted a certain degree of freedom of action. There are opportunities that might be presented to them for which they are not accountable.

However, the delineation of the scope of the fiduciary relationship is one of the most problematic areas, not only in relation to company directors but also in respect of all fiduciaries. Furthermore, it must be noted that despite paying some lip service to the area of private action of directors, the courts have nonetheless taken a fairly strict view in practice of the fiduciary obligation. This is evident in some of the classic cases such as *Regal (Hastings) Ltd v Gulliver & Ors* and *Phipps v Boardman*,[74] where the directors were subjected to a constructive trust even though there was no way in practice that the company could itself take advantage of the opportunity concerned. The former case proceeded on the basis that the courts here were involved in the application of a policy which was intended to impose strict standards on fiduciaries. Thus, it was treated as an extension of the seemingly harsh rule of *Keech v Sandford*[75] applicable to trustees. Indeed, there are some more recent authorities which suggest that in talking of company opportunities it is not necessary to postulate any strict relationship between the opportunity and the director's connection with the company at all.[76] The real question is becoming a vaguer one, viz whether the appropriation of the opportunity was or would have been unconscionable or inequitable. This seems to reduce the consideration to whether the particular opportunity in question is one which ought in all the circumstances to have been presented to the company rather than retained by

---

becomes available to the director. See *Canadian Aero Services v O'Malley* (1973) 40 DLR (3d) 371. But the position could be different if the director's position were terminated by the company. See *Plateau Equipment Ltd v Marsden* (1991) 5 NZCLC 67,096, 67,101.

73 See *Regal (Hastings) Ltd v Gulliver & Ors* [1967] 2 AC 134; *Phipps v Boardman* [1967] 2 AC 46; *Peso Silver Mines Ltd v Cropper* (1966) 58 DLR 2d 1.

74 [1967] 2 AC 134; [1967] 2 AC 46.

75 (1726) Sel Cas T King 61. The application of such a principle renders rather questionable the stated moderation of trustee principles in their application to company directors, thus the impression that the talk of causally conceived limitations on the scope of the director's obligation is merely high-blown rhetoric. It is a curious twist that the breadth of commercial opportunities of a company should now be used to limit the scope of private activity of a company director, given that commerciality of the enterprise was originally one of the justifications for moderating the strictness of trustee principles in the corporate context.

76 See *Industrial Development Consultants Ltd v Cooley* [1972] 2 All ER 162; *Canadian Aero Services Ltd v O'Malley* (1973) 40 DLR (3d) 371; *Chan v Zacharia* (1984) 154 CLR 178 at 204.

the director. But whilst that formulation might, on one view, have the advantage of flexibility, it provides little practical guidance to those who are directors.

As with the first (and indeed the third) rule, the director can only avoid a breach of this rule by full disclosure of all material facts relating to the opportunity to an independent organ of the company and seeking its express or implied consent. As noted above, the director cannot seek to excuse him/herself by attempting to show that the company cannot itself take advantage of the opportunity in question. However, it appears to be suggested that the opportunity must be one in which the company has some present interest or in which it could reasonably be expected to be interested in the future. If the only impediment to the company's ability to take up the opportunity could be removed by action on the part of the director, then clearly the director cannot use this as a ground to excuse his or her taking up the opportunity. But there still appears to be a lack of clarity about the issue. One line of argument is that it is not purely an issue about whether or not the company could or could not, under its constitution, legally undertake the opportunity in question. In other words, the issue has to be seen in terms of practical considerations. But these are more highly indeterminate. Thus, for instance, s 139 of the Companies Act of Tonga 1995 requires such disclosure to be made by the affected director.

Nor is the director excused by showing that the appropriation of the opportunity was entirely fair to the company or reasonable in the circumstances. Furthermore, the director will not be excused by showing that the exploitation of the opportunity in question involved the use of some special skill or talent which that particular director had, although this might justify the court making some special allowance to the director when recouping the gains. It is concerned with preventing the taking of gains or advantages by a fiduciary in connection with or as a result of their office.[77] Often the courts here are more concerned with imposing strict standards of conduct on directors than with issues of fairness or reasonableness.

Thirdly, they are not permitted to misappropriate property or advantages of the company to their own benefit or for other persons associated with them. Again, there is considerable overlap here with the other two rules above. Indeed, it is conjectural as to whether the creation of a separate rule here is required at all.[78] The concern behind this particular rule is with misappropriation of something which can be regarded in law or in equity as the property of the company. It is not so much concerned with advantages or opportunities of the company which cannot be regarded as property. This has provoked some debate about whether information of the company is to be regarded as property or not.[79] As a general proposition

---

77 *Natural Extracts Pty Ltd v Stotter* (1997) 24 ACSR 110.
78 *Cook v Deeks* [1916] 1 AC 554 appears to support the existence of a separate rule relating to misappropriation of equitable property. But it is arguable that this situation could be brought just as easily under the second rule as appropriation of a particular sort of advantage.
79 Breach of the fiduciary rule is not the same thing as the principle involved in cases concerning the abuse of confidence by the misuse of confidential information. The latter can be established

it is not, but there are cases which appear to suggest that for these purposes it is to be so regarded.[80]

Management of companies presents significant problems to shareholders. As a matter of course, shareholders always expect diligent and efficient administration of their funds by the directors. Whilst it is true that the companies legislation in the region has outlined in clear terms the respective powers of the general meeting and the board of directors, in practice this demarcation is not always watertight. This is for the simple reason that directors, though not subject to the control of the shareholders, can nevertheless effectively be removed by the requisite resolution at a general meeting of the shareholders.

Directors are also invested with fiduciary roles in the management of companies. To this end, they are not only expected by all and sundry to perform their duties with skill and care, but are equally expected to deliver healthy financial returns to the coffers of the company through good management practice and accountability. This duality of expectations places the directors in a dilemma.

This difficulty is further compounded by the fact that the two main organs within a company – the shareholders in general meeting and the board of directors – are each seized with different powers to exercise in the discharge of their respect functions. These powers are spelt out in the Companies Acts as well as in the respective articles of association.

Lastly, the management of a company is no doubt a herculean task, especially when one takes into account that a company is an artificial legal structure that is comprised of human and material resources. For any company to operate effectively, the productivity of these two factors must be harmonised in such a way as to achieve an optimum level of performance.

---

even in cases where the person concerned is not a fiduciary at all. But it is conceivable that the actions of a director might involve both a breach of fiduciary status and a misuse of confidential information.

80 See e.g. *Phipps v Boardman* [1967] 2 AC 46.

PART C
Commercial transactions

Introduction

In this Part, we examine some of the types of transaction that are relatively basic to commerce in the region, whether it is engaged in by individual sole traders, communities or by commercial entities such as those we have examined in earlier chapters. All of these areas involve aspects or particular applications of the law of contract. We will explain some of the basic features of a contract as we proceed. There are special features attaching to each of them, largely as a result of commercial practice which developed in relation to these transactions and which, in many cases, was then incorporated in legislation. Some of the principles we have discussed in earlier chapters, such as that relating to the assignment of property and fiduciaries, will again be relevant in parts of the following discussion.

We will deal with transactions relating to the sale and purchase of goods and chattels, which are forms of personal property. We will not examine dealings with land or interests in land, although these can be involved in commercial dealing. The reason for this is that land involves special principles of property law and this would best be left to works which specialise in that subject matter.

We will also examine financing transactions such as financial leasing and hire purchase agreements. These involve means by which money is raised for any of a variety of purposes, some of which might be commercial whilst others are private or domestic in nature. The transactions themselves are, however, an integral part of commercial activity in the South Pacific region. Finally, we will look at the nature of insurance contracts and the legal provisions that apply to them.

DOI: 10.4324/9781003428060-13

In all of these areas, the law in operation in the South Pacific region is introduced law rather than contextualised to reflect the local and customary realities of region. However, we identify and draw out key aspects of the law of the region, which is different from that in other common law countries.

11

SALE OF GOODS

11.1 Concepts in sale of goods transactions[1]

Let us look first of all at some of the basic legal concepts underlying the formation of a valid sale of goods agreement in the region. We shall therefore in this context be examining concepts that are commonly and routinely encountered in any sale of goods transaction.

We shall in this section also be revisiting some of the concepts in Sale of Goods Acts in the region by trying to offer working definitions of what these concepts imply. The concepts include the following: goods; future and existing goods; property in the goods; specific goods; and ascertained and unascertained goods. Other phrases we shall be looking at are the components of a sale agreement – price, parties and the distinction between a sale and an agreement to sell.

Sale of goods transactions are the most basic form of commercial transaction. They involve the buying and selling of physical goods and the delivery or transfer of the ownership of the goods from sellers to buyers. They encompass a wide variety of transactions, from simple over-the-counter purchases in shops to more complex international dealings of significant value. In legal terms, a sale of goods transaction involves a special application of the principles of contract law, although the contract and the course of the dealing are regulated extensively by legislation known as the Sale of Goods Acts.

---

1 See generally ss 1–11 Sale of Goods Act [Cap 230] 1979 (F); ss 1–10 Sale of Goods Act 1975 (S); ss 1–6 Sale of Goods Act 1979 (UK).

DOI: 10.4324/9781003428060-14

In this chapter, we shall be discussing the topic by looking at a range of areas that are connected with any valid and enforceable sale of goods in countries of the region. Of particular significance to us are the following areas:

- concepts in sale transactions;
- transfer of property in the goods;
- transfer of title from a non-owner to a buyer;
- statutorily implied terms;
- performance of the contract;
- applicable remedies in the event of default by either party.

There are local Sale of Goods Acts for Samoa, the Cook Islands and Fiji. The laws of the other countries in the University of the South Pacific (USP) region derived their origin from the UK Sale of Goods Act 1893. A number of these countries also rely on adopted or extended versions of the relevant English Sale of Goods Acts.

11.1.1 Definition of goods

Goods are tangible or moveable property which can be physically transferred by delivery from one person to another. Intangible or incorporeal property such as choses in action are not goods.

By way of example, we shall make reference to the definition of 'goods' offered by statute. Section 2(1) of the Sale of Goods Act (Fiji) defines 'goods' along the following lines:

> 'Goods' includes all chattels personal, which are the subjects of trade or commerce and component parts of any such chattels. The term includes emblements, industrial growing crops and things attached to or forming part of the land which are agreed to be severed before sale or under the land which are agreed to be severed before sale or under the contract of sale or things annexed to the land which in contemplation of law do not become part of the land.[2]

As we can see from this definition, goods must have some trade or commercial application, in that they must be capable of being sold. Even if such goods were fixed to the land, they may be defined as goods and for purposes of sale, so long as they are to be detached or can actually be detached from the land. An item or object that cannot physically be detached or disentangled from land is not capable of being sold under the Sale of Goods Act. This definition therefore excludes fixed and landed structures like homes or other properties that are immobile. It also excludes the transfer and assignment of forms of intangible rights such as patents,

---

2 The Sale of Goods Act 1975 (S) has an almost equivalent provision.

trade marks, copyright, rights issues in shares, etc. These categories of rights are dealt with by other relevant laws.

11.1.2 Specific goods

Specific goods are goods that are agreed upon and identified at the time of sale by the parties. In this instance, both the buyer and seller are aware of what exactly constitutes the subject matter of their transaction. The goods may have been specified with reference to their characteristics or location or transformed into this state by means of appropriation. We shall be dwelling more on the processes of appropriation when we discuss transfer of property.

11.1.3 Future goods

These are goods whose existence has not (as yet) been established at the time of sale. They are contemplated to come into being at a future time. As the type of goods implies, both the buyer and seller are aware that such goods were not in existence at the time of their agreement. Future goods are therefore a type of goods that will come about at a later date, either by manufacture or purchase or through other appropriate processes.

11.1.4 Unascertained goods

These are goods that have not been appropriated to the contract. Technically speaking, they are the opposite of specific goods. It is possible that unascertained goods are in existence. It may even be known to the parties, but cannot actually be defined as the subject matter of the agreement until some steps have been taken by either the buyer or the seller to make it so. Appropriation converts unascertained to ascertained goods.[3] In reality, there is little difference between specific and ascertained goods.

11.2 Property in goods

Goods are a type of personal property which is sometimes referred to as moveable property. When we refer to property in the goods we are referring to legal interests in that property, in other words, to the bundle of legal rights which a person may exercise over the relevant goods, whatever they are. In a given case these might be interests of ownership or lesser interests such as a leasehold or a security interest. A person can also acquire possessory rights with respect to goods. Ownership and

---

3 See *Morgan v Russell and Sons* [1909] 1 KB 357; *Saunders (Inspector of Taxes) v Pilcher* [1949] 2 All ER 1097.

possession are two different things and one may pass from the seller to the buyer without the other accompanying it.

Ownership implies complete control or dominion over all aggregated rights in the goods or in fact any other type of property such as real estate, or intangible property such as company shares, partnership interests and trust interests, as we examined earlier. Ownership is the highest type of interest in property that a person might have. The most immediate consequences of ownership are: (1) that the owner's interest can be transferred to or alienated from another person, for example by sale or gift; (2) that lesser interests such as a lease, mortgage or other security interest can be created out of them by the owner merely by virtue of the fact that he or she is an owner; and (3) that the rights of an owner endure, in principle at least, against any other claimant to the property; in other words, the rights of an owner are in principle exclusive of the interests of all third parties.[4] Ownership carries with it the right to possession of the property as this is one aspect of dominion or control, although the right of the owner to possession might be postponed where, for example, the owner has given legal rights to possession to another person, as in the case where the owner has given or is subject to a valid lease of the property in favour of another.

Possession is conceived as a lesser right with respect to property which does not carry with it the emblement of legal or equitable title. The possessor has a right to use the item of property concerned. Possession denotes the ability to exercise immediate physical control over the goods or to possess them, but normally possessory rights do not extend beyond that. Possessory rights can go beyond a mere immediate or temporary right to have possession of the property in question. They can be created by contract, for example, where a person has tenancy rights for a period of years or where there is a right of bailment for a period of years under a contract.[5] They can be set up against the owner's rights to possession, for example, where the owner's right to possession is excluded by the terms of a contract. Possessory rights can sometimes be passed from one person to another and in some situations, the long possession of property can give rise to better rights to possession than the owner in fact has, for example, where the legal right of action for recovery of possession by the true owner of the property has expired due to the lapse of the Statute of Limitations recovery period.

However, only an owner can be said to have complete or absolute rights in property in the form of legal title. In a given situation, an owner may well also have physical possession of goods. However, it is clear that in certain situations a non-owner may also exercise possessory rights over the goods even whilst legal ownership or title is vested elsewhere. In the present context it is important to

---

4 There are many exceptions and qualifications to these principles, in particular ownership situations.
5 Bailment interests vary considerably, however. Some can be wholly gratuitous rights of possession whilst others are contractual.

recognise that a sale of goods refers to a situation where an owner transfers, by way of sale and hence by contract purports to transfer, the legal title or ownership in goods from himself or herself to another person. Under most circumstances, it would be understood that the transfer of title by way of sale also includes the transfer of possession at some point. However, the transfer of possession might take place at the point of completion of the contract (when the price is paid) or at the time the contract is entered into, or in fact at some other time in the interim.

11.3 Formation of sale of goods contract

The normal rules of contract formation apply in respect of sale of goods transactions. Contracts are legally enforceable agreements.[6] They are consensual arrangements between two or more parties in the sense that they involve the exchange of mutual promises. It is not the case that any promise by one person to another is enforceable at law. Nor does the making of a promise by one party to another constitute a contract. As it is conventionally conceived, to constitute a contract, there must be established the elements of offer, acceptance, consideration and intention to create legal relations. Offer here indicates some form of proposal on specified or specifiable terms made to another person or persons to enter into a contract. It is made by the offeror, who may be the buyer or seller. Acceptance is a process of responding to the offer by agreeing to it on its own terms. The offeree communicates acceptance to the offeror.

Consideration, at least in the present context, can be taken as the price to be paid under the terms of the contract by the buyer to the seller. Consideration must be provided by or move from both parties to the contract. On his or her part, the buyer provides consideration by way of payment of the agreed price. On the seller's part, he or she agrees to transfer the legal title to the goods to the buyer. In other contexts, the rules relating to consideration can be much more complicated. As a general rule, the consideration for a contract must be sufficient, in the sense that it must be intended as genuine, although there is no requirement that it be adequate. For example, the consideration does not have to represent the payment of a fair price or market value for the goods on the part of the buyer in a sale of goods transaction.[7]

---

6 See generally *Ululoloa Dairy Co Ltd v Minister of Health* [1961] SamoaLawRp 1; [1960–69] WSLR 45 (16 November 1961); *Storage & Export Trading Co Ltd v Tu'ipulotu* [1990] TongaLawRp 6; [1990] Tonga LR 174 (5 October 1990); *Re Polly Peck International Plc (In Administration) (No 4)* [1996] 2 All ER 433.

7 There can be situations, however, where the inadequacy of the price provides evidence of an unconscionable transaction involving radical inequality of bargaining power which is exploited by one party to a transaction. This can give rise to a contract being set aside in equity at the instance of the other party.

The fourth element, namely intention to create legal relations, is in effect a requirement that the transaction in question can be reasonably construed, by the courts if the need arises, as one which the parties intended as an enforceable legal arrangement between them. If it is clear that one or both parties had no intention to be bound by the transaction concerned, then it does not amount to a contract. If it was a mere sham, or intended as a joke, or if it lacked the features of a genuine consensual arrangement, then this element is missing. Similarly, there are situations where the parties might appear to have achieved genuine consent but through fundamental mistake or misconception as to the nature of the transaction they are undertaking, there is a complete failure of consent.

The terms of any contract, that is to say, the mutual promises which the parties are bound to carry out, and which are legally enforceable by the parties against one another, will be determined by the course of bargaining – the process of offer and acceptance – undertaken by the parties. Many of these terms will be matters on which there has been explicit negotiation. The terms will be more or less clearly stated, either in writing or orally. These are the express terms of the contract. However, much is often left unsaid or assumed in the course of negotiations. Often the terms of a contract will be left as matters to be inferred from what has been said or from the course of conduct or dealing between the parties. Others will be a matter for legal inference by the courts in order to give proper effect to the contract. These are known as implied terms. Sometimes these implied terms relate to matters which are assumed from commercial practice or usage which provides the context or background against which the parties proceeded to contract. Sometimes again, as a matter of legal policy, a statute which applies to a particular transaction will provide that, under certain conditions, terms are deemed to be implied in a particular contract. The latter is the case, as we will see, with respect to contracts for the sale of goods pursuant to the Sale of Goods Act.

11.3.1 Sale and agreement to sell

The distinction between a sale and an agreement to sell has to be made. The former is an executed transaction whilst the latter is executory in nature. In a sale, all formalities relating to the agreement have been agreed upon even if not fully completed. The parties are clearly aware of the expectations of the agreement and the level of their obligations. Where it is an agreement to sell, the terms and conditions of the agreement are to be performed not instantly but at a future time. The non-occurrence of any of the future conditions may even lead to the ultimate collapse of the agreement.

An agreement to sell goods is normally employed in situations where a number of steps have to be taken to put the goods into a deliverable state, or where the performance is dependent upon the processing of permits or other requirements, without which the agreement cannot be legally executed.

11.3.2 Price

In a sale of goods, the price is the consideration on the buyer's part that supports an agreement. This must be sufficient as to be able to render the transaction enforceable but need not be adequate or fully paid at the time of the contract.[8] In a typical sale of goods transaction, it is not even necessary to specify the price at the time of the contract, so long as it is within the contemplation of the parties that it exists. The price may also be fixed by a third party acting on behalf of the buyer and seller. The third party fixes an independent price.

11.3.3 Parties

The parties to a contract for the sale of goods are the buyer and the seller. Depending on the circumstances, one might be both the offeror and offeree at various points during the course of negotiations leading to the contract. This, however, is of little consequence once the contract has been formed. Third persons appointed by the terms of the contract to negotiate or fix prices or arbitrate in some other way are not considered parties to the contract. The position might be different where they are acting under the express or ostensible authority of either the buyer or seller. In this case, the situation is to be effectively dealt with by the law of agency, which is outside the scope of this chapter.

11.3.4 Distinction between contract for services, skill, labour and materials and sale of goods

In real life, it is not all that simple to distinguish a normal sale of goods transaction from one in which skill, labour or services are provided resulting in the supply of an accompanying object. This is why for our purposes we shall attempt to differentiate the two.

A contract of sale occurs when goods are sold by the seller to a buyer. The goods we are referring to here have already been discussed. They are physical objects capable of delivery. If such goods were to be delivered to the buyer, the buyer would have both the possession and ownership of the goods.

Akin to this may be a transaction that looks like a sale of goods but is not. In this instance, whilst goods may be delivered by the seller to the buyer, the most important aspect of the transaction is the utilisation of the skill, labour or services of the supplier in producing or making the goods.[9] Thus, where skill, labour or service plays an important role in the selling of the goods, such a transaction is to

---

8 See *Roscorla v Thomas* (1842) 3 QB 234.

9 See *Lee v Griffin* (1861) 1 B & S 272; *Robinson v Graves* [1935] 1 KB 579; *Hyundai Heavy Industries Co Ltd v Papadopoulos* [1980] 2 All ER 29; *Cammell Laird Ltd v Manganese Bronze & Brass Co Ltd* [1934] AC 402.

be regarded as a contract for services, skill, labour and materials and not one for the sale of goods.

This development is now further complicated by the introduction into commerce of computer programmes or software, which may consist of both the utilisation of skill and a physical product in the form of a diskette or CD-ROM. Much depends on how the contract is characterised in the particular case.

11.4 Transfer of property[10]

A contract for the sale of goods anticipates a transfer of property at some time from the seller, as the anticipated owner of the goods in question, to the buyer as the transferee of the legal title to those goods. Depending on the terms of the contract, possession will also pass to the buyer, most usually as a consequence of the transfer of title. However, as we have indicated, the passing of title or ownership and the passing of possession might take place at different times. It is also possible that under the terms of the contract, possession might be intended to pass not to the buyer but to some third party, for example, to an agent of the buyer. The terms of actual delivery of possession of the goods will in any case be determined by the terms of the contract that the parties have entered into.

11.4.1 Mechanisms for transfer of property

The processes by which property in goods pass on from buyer to seller must be looked at in the context of the nature of the goods. In the case of specific and ascertained goods, the rule is fairly straightforward. Property in the goods passes at the time of the sale.

In unascertained goods, no property in the goods passes on to the buyer until they are ascertained either through appropriation or by other means of ascertainment such as delivery or assent.[11]

11.4.2 Property transfer rules

There are generally five rules applicable in respect of different types of goods and in different situations to transfer property in the goods from the seller to the buyer. However, this is subject to any contrary expression of intention by the parties to the sale of goods transaction. We shall now examine each of these five rules.

---

10 See ss 17–19 Sale of Goods Act (UK); ss 18–27 Sale of Goods Act (F); ss 17–26 Sale of Goods Act (S); *Varley v Whipp* [1900] 1 QB 513; *Kursell v Timber Operators & Contractors Ltd* [1927] 1 KB 298; *Healey v Howlett* [1917] 1 KB 337; *Kirkham v Attenborough* [1897] 1 QB 201.

11 Note that the rule is stated negatively. The Act has not defined unascertained goods. Note also that the intention of the parties is made a condition of transferability of property.

(1) Specific goods in a deliverable state

Under this rule, property in the goods passes from the seller to the buyer where the contract for sale is unconditional. This is very much applicable to executed contracts where the terms have been agreed upon by the parties at the outset.[12]

(2) Specific goods to be in a deliverable state

Where the goods are specific, but certain steps have to be taken to put the goods into a deliverable state, unless such steps are undertaken no property will pass.[13] Before property in goods under this rule passes, it is expected that the buyer or seller may have to take additional steps to render the goods deliverable.

(3) Specific goods to be weighed

Where the goods are specific and in a deliverable state, but the price is to be determined as a condition of the sale, unless that is done no property in the goods passes to the buyer.[14] This rule would require the doing of extra acts, but only by the seller in order to make the goods ready for delivery. The rule is ideally situated to deal with goods that can only be sold with reference to weight and measurements or where special scientific or chemical analysis is required to put the goods in a deliverable state.

(4) Sale-or-return basis

There are instances when a buyer may be sent unsolicited goods by the seller or when a buyer requests goods for inspection before deciding whether or not to buy them. Where such goods are despatched by the seller to the buyer in any of these circumstances, unless a buyer indicates approval of the goods and especially when on a sale-or-return basis, no property in the goods is transferred to the seller.[15]

(5) Unascertained or future goods

In any agreement to sell unascertained future goods, unless the goods have been ascertained, no property in the goods passes from the seller to the buyer. Appropriation is the legal mechanism for converting unascertained into ascertained goods. We shall pay some attention to a more detailed meaning of appropriation below.

---

12 See *Tarling v Baxter* (1827) 6 B & C 360.
13 See *Underwood Ltd v Burgh Castle Brick and Cement Syndicate* [1922] 1 KB 343.
14 See *Nanka-Bruce v Commonwealth* [1926] AC 77.
15 See *Kirkham v Attenborough* [1897] 1 QB 201.

11.4.3 What is appropriation?[16]

Appropriation as a legal process has the effect of converting unascertained goods to ascertained goods. This is effective in any of the following ways: delivery of the goods by the seller to the buyer; manufacturing of the goods; assent by the buyer to purchase the goods; and where a seller exercises the disposal right in respect of the goods.

11.4.4 Romalpa clause and transfer of property

In dealing with any of the five rules for transfer of property, careful attention should be paid to the retention of title by the seller. Once goods are sold and delivered to the buyer, the seller has lost any ability to exercise control over the goods. It may arise in practice that the buyer has not yet completely paid for the goods. A common and effective way of preserving the rights of the seller is to include a Romalpa clause in the terms of sale.

The following are some implications of a Romalpa clause:

• Ownership of goods manufactured and supplied rests with seller.
• The buyer is to act as a constructive trustee by holding the proceeds of sale on behalf of the seller.

The retention of title clause is not featured in any of the Sale of Goods Acts in the region, but is generally applicable as a common law rule.[17] The underlying consideration of the clause is to protect the security interest of the seller until such a time as the buyer fully discharges the price.[18] It is also a flexible device, in that the buyer will be at liberty to have possession of the goods even though the full payment has not been tendered.

Where goods are subject to a Romalpa clause, any subsequent disposal of the goods to a third party by the buyer is subject to the subsisting rights of the seller. The seller's equity over the goods has priority over that of any third party who acquires the goods with notice.

---

16 See ss 2–105(4) of the Uniform Commercial Code, which allows for property to pass in unsegregated goods. This is now introduced in the UK 1979 Act by virtue of s 20A and 20B of the Sale of Goods (Amendment) Act 1995.
17 See *Aluminium Industrie Vaassen BV v Romalpa Aluminium Ltd* [1976] 2 All ER 552.
18 See generally Ahrnadu, ML, 'The Romalpa clause: commercial and legal implications' [1995] FLT 9.

11.4.5 Passing of risk[19]

Closely tied to the issue of property is that of risk. Risk has been defined to mean 'a multitude of mishaps, from slight damage to theft or total destruction'.[20] Risk cannot stand on its own without attaching to property in the goods. Depending upon the situation, risk may reside with ownership or possession or with both. The time of passing of property in the goods is therefore crucial to determining whether risk has also passed with the property in the goods.

As a general rule, unless a contrary intention is indicated, risk resides with the seller. But where property in the goods is transferred to the buyer, the goods are at the buyer's risk, whether or not delivery is effected.[21] This assertion makes it possible for the risk to be separated from the property by an agreement.

There are a number of exceptions to the rule on the passing of risk. Risk in the goods will not pass together with the property to the buyer if there is delay in delivering the goods. Whoever delays (whether the buyer or the seller) takes responsibility for the delay and the attendant risk.

11.5 Transfer of title[22]

This section of the chapter examines how title in goods is transferred from the seller to the buyer. Title represents the interest embodied in goods. In general, title is also a means by which ownership in goods may be ascertained. There are different processes by which title in goods is transferred from the seller to the buyer.

11.5.1 General rule for transfer of title

A person who is a non-owner of goods cannot confer a valid title on a supposed buyer of the goods. This is stated in the Latin maxim as: *Nemo dat quod non habet.* It means 'one cannot give what one does not have'. To this general rule are a number of exceptions which we shall consider below.

11.5.2 Exceptions

We shall be looking at some exceptions regarding transfer of title. In any of these exceptions, it is possible for a non-owner of goods to confer through sale or other methods of disposition a valid title to a buyer. The six exceptions are estoppel; sale

---

19 See *Stern v Vickers Ltd* [1923] 1 KB 78.
20 Marsh, SB *et al., Business Law*, 1992, Maidenhead, England, McGraw Hill, p 200. Two decades later, this principle still stands today.
21 See *Stern v Vickers Ltd* [1923] 1 KB 78.
22 See generally ss 23–27 Sale of Goods Act (F); ss 22–26 Sale of Goods Act (S); *Johnson v Credit Lyonnais Co* (1877) 3 CPD 32; *Worcester Works Finance Ltd v Cooden Engineering Ltd* [1972]1 QB 210.

in a market overt; sale under a voidable title; sale under the Factors Act; sale under special powers; and sale by seller or buyer in possession.

- **Estoppel.** As a general rule, where a representation is made to a buyer by the seller that the latter had a right to dispose of the goods, the seller will be precluded from denying the existence of such authority at the conclusion of the sale.
- **Sale in a market overt.** A market overt is defined as a legally constituted place of sale opened between the hours of sunrise and sunset.[23] The market must maintain an overt posture in order to allow free entry and exit by members of the public. Sale of goods by a non-owner in a market overt has the effect of transferring a valid title to the buyer. This exception to transfer of title is still an applicable common law principle in the 12 jurisdictions making up the USP region, although it has now been abolished in the United Kingdom.[24]
- **Sale under a voidable title.** Where a seller disposes of goods with a voidable title, but the title had not been avoided before the sale, the law confers a valid title in the goods to the buyer.[25] In this instance, nothing will impeach the title of the buyer provided there was no illegality or fraud surrounding the sale.
- **Sale under the Factors Act.** A factor is an agent who has custody of the goods before sale. Where a factor sells goods, a valid title is transferred to the buyer.[26] An important characteristic of a factor as an agent is that the factor has physical control over the goods before sale.
- **Sale under special powers.** Where sale is conducted through the instrumentality of a court order, statute or common law, the seller confers a valid title on the buyer.[27] A court of competent jurisdiction may in appropriate cases order that particular goods belonging to a judgment debtor be sold in order to pay a judgment creditor. Here it is not the owner who is selling the goods but a court.
- **Sale by a seller or buyer in possession.** A sale of goods to a third party by a seller who retains possession of the goods can confer a good title on that third party as against the buyer. Similarly so as regards a sale by a buyer in possession prior to formal transfer of title. In either case, the third party must receive the goods in good faith and without notice of the other claimant's (buyer or seller respectively) interest.[28]

---

23 See the *Case of Market-Overt* (1596) 5 Co Rep 83 b.
24 See s 1 Sale of Goods (Amendment) Act 1995 (UK).
25 See ss 23, 24 Sale of Goods Acts (S) and ss 24, 25 Sale of Goods Act (F), respectively.
26 See *Weiner v Harris* [1910] 1 KB 285.
27 See *Larner v Fawcett* [1950] 2 All ER 727 (CA).
28 See *Forsythe International (UK) Ltd v Silver Shipping Co Ltd* [1994] 1 WLR 1334; 1 All ER 851, and s 26(1)(2) (F); s 25 (S).

11.6 Implied terms[29]

In this part of the chapter, we shall examine what implied terms are and their effect on the validity of a sale of goods contract. Implied terms are terms which are statutorily incorporated into any sale of goods transaction, regardless of what the parties have initially agreed to.

An agreement for sale or a contract of sale is an expression of the intentions of the buyer and the seller. The intentions are usually represented orally, in writing or by conduct. Implied terms, however, are statutory or common law stipulations that are automatically imported into any contract made between the buyer and the seller. We shall therefore look at the nature of these terms and how they affect the position of the seller or the buyer.

11.6.1 Nature of terms[30]

Implied terms are terms that are normally implied in favour of the buyer. The implication of these terms is also in line with the concept of *caveat emptor*. Implied terms are classified for the purposes of the Sale of Goods Acts into conditions and warranties. They form part of a contract for the sale of goods.

Generally speaking, a condition is a stipulation in a contract, breach of which will enable either the buyer or seller to repudiate the contract. The consequence is of major importance to the validity of the contract. A warranty is a term of a contract, breach of which will not enable the buyer or seller to repudiate the contract but only to sue for damages. General contract law provides a third possibility: that of an intermediate term which lies somewhere between these two extremes. A serious breach of an intermediate term might give a right to terminate the contract.[31] However, we will confine ourselves to implied conditions and warranties under the Sale of Goods Acts.

As a general rule, sale of goods statutes have imposed certain terms in favour of the buyer. These include the following:

- *Correspondence with description.*[32] As a requirement of law, goods sold must correspond with the description where the sale is by description. Description is the process by which goods may be identified in an intelligible and functional way.

---

29 See generally *Rowland v Divall* [1923] 2 KB 500; *Grant v Australian Knitting Mills Ltd* [1936] AC 85; *Mason v Burningham* [1949] 2 KB 545; *Aswan Engineering Co v Lupdine* [1987] 1 ALL ER 1; *Lambert v Lewis* [1981] 1 All ER 1185.
30 See generally ss 12–15 Sale of Goods Act (UK); ss 12–16 Sale of Goods Act (F); ss 11–15 Sale of Goods Act (S).
31 See *Hong Kong Fir Shipping Co Ltd v Kawasaki Kisen Kaisha Ltd* [1962] 2 QB 26 at p 65; *Cehave NV v Bremer Handelsgesellschaft mbH (The Hansa Nord)* [1976] QB 44.
32 See *Grant v Australian Knitting Mills Ltd* [1936] AC 85; *Harlingdon & Leinster Enterprises Ltd v Christopher Hull Fine Art* [1990] 3 WLR 13.

- *Merchantable quality.*[33] It is a requirement of law that any goods sold must be of merchantable quality. This simply means that without any improvements to the goods, they should be in a state that can easily be re-sold. There would be no meaningful commerce if this important feature was lost.

- *Fitness for purpose.*[34] It is also a cardinal requirement of the law that goods sold must demonstrate a capacity to be utilised for the purpose for which they were bought. In short, goods are expected to perform as they should and be in such condition as to fulfil their purpose. Goods described as 'brand new' are expected to perform at higher standards when compared to those described as 'second hand'.[35]

- *Correspondence with sample.*[36] It is a necessary requirement that where sale is by sample, goods sold must correspond with the sample. This means that the bulk, when examined, must match the sample displayed by the seller. The buyer must have had an opportunity of comparing the sample with the sale before the contract.

- *Freedom from encumbrances.*[37] Encumbrance means a charge on the goods. It is a restriction on a person's final right of disposal. The law implies in a contract for sale that a buyer should, on purchasing goods from the seller; take them free from any encumbrances. The seller should therefore before the sale have a complete and unfettered right to dispose of the goods.

- *Enjoyment of quiet possession.*[38] The buyer must at law be capable of freely enjoying the unhindered possession and use of the goods after sale. This warranty will be breached if a third party interferes with the buyer's enjoyment of quiet possession over the goods.

11.7 Performance of contract[39]

Here, we shall be covering the obligations that are to be performed by the buyer and seller under a contract of sale. Performance may loosely be equated to matters

---

33 See *Niblett Ltd. v Confectioners' Materials Co. Ltd.* [1921] 3 KB 387; *Aswan Engineering Co v Lupdine* [1987] 1 ALL ER 1.
34 See *Business Application Ltd v Nationwide Credit Ltd* [1988] RTR 332; *Lambert v Lewis* [1981] 1 All ER 1185; *Ashington Piggeries Ltd v Christopher Hill Ltd* [1972] AC 441.
35 See *Rogers v Parish (Scarborough) Ltd* [1987] QB 933.
36 See *FE Hookway & Co Ltd v Alfred Isaacs & Sons* [1954] 1 Lloyd's Rep 491.
37 See *Rowland v Divall* [1923] 2 KB 500.
38 See *Mason v Burningham* [1949] 2 KB 545; *Rubicon Computer Systems Ltd v United Paints Ltd* (2000) 2 TCLR 453.
39 See generally *Bowes v Shand* (1877) 2 App Cas 455; *Miliangos v George Frank (Textiles) Ltd* [1976] AC 443; *Reuter, Hufeland & Co v Sala & Co* (1879) 4 CPD 239; *Warinco v Samor SPA* [1979] 1 Lloyd's Rep 450; *Robert A Munro & Co Ltd v Meyer* [1930] 2 KB 312; *Hartley v Hymans* [1920] 3 KB 475; *Bunge Corporation v Tradax SA* (1981) 2 All ER 513; *Commerciale Sucres et Denrees v Czarnilow (The Naxos)* [1990] 1 WLR 1337; *Phibro Energy AG v Nissho Iwai Corporation (Honam Jade)* [1991] 1 Lloyd's Rep 38; *Rosenthal & Sons Ltd v Esmail* [1965] 1 WLR 1117; *Arcos Ltd v EA Ronaasen & Son* [1933] AC 470; *Shipton Anderson & Co v Wheil Bros & Co* [1912] 1 KB 574; *Gabriel, Wade & English Ltd v Arcos Ltd* (1929) 34 Ll L Rep 306.

relating to the delivery of goods by the seller and the acceptance or rejection of the goods by the buyer. For performance to be complete, there are some conditions to be fulfilled before delivery of goods is considered valid under statute.

11.7.1 Delivery of goods[40]

This area basically covers issues that touch on the delivery of goods from the seller to the buyer. Some important points that should be borne in mind include the following: What is it to be delivered by the seller to the buyer? When must delivery be made and how is delivery made? Sale of goods statutes in the region have outlined in detail how these questions are to be resolved.

In dealing with delivery as a cardinal aspect of performance of the contract by the seller, it is important to closely examine three elements. These are:

- **Delivery of wrong quantity or description (rejection and its consequences).** This brings into focus the *de minimis* rule.[41] Delivery of the wrong quantity of goods by the seller to the buyer amounts to a breach of the sale contract. In this situation, the buyer is entitled to reject the goods so supplied. What is to be noted, though, is the fact that this right is fettered by the application of the microscopic deviation rule. This rule states that where the wrong quantity of goods so delivered is of negligible proportion when compared to the total quantity, the buyer cannot reject the consignment but can only sue for damages.
- **Delivery to carrier as buyer's agent.**[42] In this instance, delivery is deemed to have been effected to the buyer. This means that the risk also goes with the goods. Delivery of the goods to a common carrier or to the seller's agent is not covered by this rule.
- **Instalment deliveries.**[43] This is the process of breaking down the quantity into portions and delivering in pieces. In the sale of goods, it is permissible to conclude deliveries in instalments where this has been agreed by the parties at the outset of the contract. The following questions need to be asked: Would a breach in the delivery of one instalment amount to a breach of the whole

---

40 See ss 27–33 Sale of Goods Act (UK); ss 28–38 Sale of Goods Act (F); ss 27–37 Sale of Goods Act (S); *Hartley v Hymans* [1920] 3 KB 475; *Bunge Corp New York v Tradax Export SA Panama* [1981] 1 WLR 711 at 718; 2 All ER 513; *The Naxos* [1990] 1 WLR 1337; *The Honam Jade* [1991] 1 Lloyd's Rep 38.

41 See *Arcos Ltd v EA Ronaasen & Sons* [1933] AC 470; *Shipton Anderson & Co v Wheil Bros & Co* [1912] 1 KB 574; *Gabriel, Wade & English Ltd v Arcos Ltd* (1929) 34 Ll L Rep 306.

42 See s 33 Sale of Goods Act (F). Generally, see s 32 Sale of Goods Act (S), although there seems to be no equivalent provision. See also *Galbraith & Grant Ltd v Block* [1922] 2 KB 155.

43 See *Reuter, Hufeland & Co v Sala & Co* (1879) 4 CPD 239; *Warinco v Samor SPA* [1979] 1 Lloyd's Rep 450; *Robert A Munro & Co Ltd v Meyer* [1930] 2 KB 312.

contract? Can the principle of divisibility of contract be applied to cure the breach of the delivery of one instalment?

11.8 Remedies[44]

We conclude our discussion of sale of goods by looking at remedies. A buyer or seller may claim for breach of contract by relying on any or some of these remedies. Courts grant remedies to aggrieved parties for a variety of reasons. This usually occurs where there has been a breach of the terms of the contract by either party. Remedy is therefore a compensatory relief issued in favour of an affected party against the actions of a defaulting party to a contract of sale.

11.8.1 Seller's remedies[45]

In determining whether a seller is entitled to make claims against a defaulting buyer, the seller must satisfy the statutory requirements of being an 'unpaid seller'.[46] The following are some of the seller's rights or remedies.

- **Lien.**[47] A seller has a right of lien over the goods sold pending completion of the contract. A lien is a right of possession of the goods which holds even though title might have passed to the buyer in law or equity. The intention is to compel the buyer to tender the price to the seller or take some steps towards facilitating payments. The right of a seller to exercise a lien over the goods are subject to some qualifications.
- **Stoppage in transit.**[48] This right can be exercised by a seller to stop goods that are in transit and on their way to the buyer. The right is usually exercisable where the buyer has not paid the price and the goods have been despatched by the seller but have not yet reached the buyer. By utilising this remedy, the seller will be in a position to resume possession of the goods until the price is

---

44 See generally ss 39–54 Sale of Goods Act (F); ss 38–19 Sale of Goods Act (S); *Esteve Trading Corporation v Agropec International (The 'Golden Rio')* [1990] 2 Lloyd's Rep 273; *Lazenby Garages Ltd v Wright* [1976] 1 WLR 459; *Charrington & Co Ltd v Wooder* [1914] AC 71; *Jones v Just* (1868) LR 3 QB 197; *H. Parsons (Livestock) Ltd v Uttley Ingham & Co Ltd* [1978] QB 791; *Hadley v Baxendale* (1854) 9 Exch 341; *Braithwaite v Foreign Hardwood Co* [1905] 2 KB 543; *Colley v Overseas Exporters* [1921] 3 KB 302; *Stein Forbes & Co v County Tailoring Co* (1916) 86 LJKB 448; *The Tigress* (1863) 32 LJPM & A 97; *The Constantia* (1807) 6 Rob. Adm. R. 321; *Ex parte Chalmers Re Edwards* (1873) 8 Ch App 289; *Ward Ltd v Bignall* [1967] 1 QB 534.

45 See ss 39,40 Sale of Goods Act (F); ss 38, 39 Sale of Goods Act (S).

46 See *Ward Ltd v Bignall* [1967] 1 QB 534 at 550, especially the *dictum* of Lord Justice Diplock.

47 See ss 41–43 Sale of Goods Act (F); ss 40–42 Sale of Goods Act (S); see also *Ex parte Chalmers Re Edwards* (1873) 8 Ch App 289; *Jeffcott v Andrew Motors Ltd* [1960] NZLR 721.

48 See ss 44–46 Sale of Goods Act (F); ss 43–45 Sale of Goods Act (S); *The Tigress* (1863) 32 LJPM & A 97; *The Constantia* (1807) 6 Rob. Adm. R. 321; *Johann Plischke & Sohne v Allison Bros Ltd* [1936] 2 All ER 1009.

paid by the buyer. The right of stoppage in transit cannot be exercised by the seller if the goods have reached the buyer.

- **Action for price**. The ultimate reason for selling goods is for a seller to be paid. Where the buyer fails to pay the price for the goods so delivered, the seller is entitled to maintain an action in court for the price.[49] Recovery of the price by the seller is crucial to a seller's business and its ability to maintain a steady cash flow.
- **Action for non-acceptance**. The seller can institute an action for damages against a buyer who refuses to accept goods ordered by him/her.[50] This remedy can be enforced against a buyer provided that the seller has also fulfilled its part of the sale agreement.

11.8.2 Buyer's remedies

The buyer is at liberty to rely upon any of these remedies to redress any breach of the sale contract by the seller. These remedies include:

- **Specific performance**. This is an order of court that compels the seller to carry out the terms of the agreement, in short, to deliver the goods to the buyer. Specific performance is applicable only in instances where the sale was for specific or ascertained goods.[51] The remedy cannot be granted to compel the performance of a personal service by the defendant.
- **Action for non-delivery**.[52] A buyer can claim damages for the price of the goods against a seller who has refused to deliver goods already paid for by the buyer. The quantum of damages claimable by the buyer is dependent on the circumstances of the case.
- **Action for breach of warranty**.[53] In this instance, the buyer's right to damages is restricted to a claim for a breach of a warranty by the seller. It does not extend to a complete repudiation of the contract by the buyer on account of breach of warranty by the seller.

---

49 See *Stein Forbes & Co v County Tailoring Co* (1916) 86 LJKB 448; s 49 Sale of Goods Act (F); s 48 Sale of Goods Act (S).

50 See *Colley v Overseas Exporters* [1921] 3 KB 302. On a different point, would you consider the doctrine of equitable right of tracing as an appropriate remedy for an unpaid seller to exercise? This remedy has not been provided for by statute. Can an unpaid seller apply for the remedy of rescission? If so, what conditions are to be satisfied before rescission could be relied upon by a seller? See *Braithwaithe v Foreign Hardwood Co Ltd* [1905] 2 KB 543; s 50 Sale of Goods Act (F); s 49 Sale of Goods Act (S).

51 See generally *Sky Petroleum Ltd v VIP Petroleum Ltd* [1974] 1 WLR 576; *Re Wait* [1927] 1 Ch 606; *Phillips v Lamdin* [1949] 2 KB 33; s 52 Sale of Goods Act (F); s 51 Sale of Goods Act (S).

52 See *Hadley v Baxendale* (1854) 9 Exch 341; s 51 Sale of Goods Act (F); s 50 Sale of Goods Act (S).

53 See *Colley v Overseas Exporters* [1921] 3 KB 302; *Jones v Just* (1868) LR 3 QB 197; *Parsons (Livestock) Ltd v Uttley Ingham & Co Ltd* [1978] QB 791.

12

BILLS OF SALE, FINANCE LEASES AND HIRE PURCHASE

12.1 Bills of sale

A bill of sale is one of the most common forms of security arrangements in use in the South Pacific at the present time. It is a relatively simple way of obtaining loan funds secured over goods or chattels.[1] In this chapter, we will look at the legal incidents governing the issuing and validity of bills of sale primarily in Fiji, Kiribati, Solomon, Samoa and Vanuatu.

12.1.1 Definition

A bill of sale is a means of raising money by way of loan. It is a form of chattel mortgage. It is formally defined in the legislation as follows:

> 'Bills of sale' includes bills of sale, assignments, transfers, declarations of trust without transfer, inventories of goods with receipt thereto attached, or receipts for purchase moneys of goods, and other assurances of personal chattels, and also powers of attorney, authorities, or licences to take possession of personal chattels as security for any debt, and also any agreement, whether intended or not to be followed by the execution of any other instrument, by which a right

---

1 See generally *Nausori Daily Transport Ltd v Shiu Narayan* [1981] FJLawRp 9; [1981] 27 FLR 131 (27 May 1981); *BNZ v Ripikoi* [1992] FJLawRp 21; [1992] 38 FLR 1 (22 January 1992); *Niranjans Autoport Ltd v Narayan* [1992] FJLawRp 7; [1992] 38 FLR 12 (31 January 1992); *ANZ Banking Group Ltd v Merchant Bank of Fiji* [1994] FJLawRp 23; [1994] 40 FLR 266 (24 November 1994). See also the Bills of Sale Act Cap 225 (F); Bills of Sale Act Cap 174 (SI); Stamp Duties Act Cap 68 (V) (especially ss 1, 6, 16 and 17) which affect bills of sale.

DOI: 10.4324/9781003428060-15

in equity to any personal chattels, or to any charge or security thereon, is conferred, but does not include the following documents–

(a) assignments for the benefit of the creditors of the person making or giving the same;
(b) marriage settlements;
(c) transfers or assignments of any ship or vessel or any share thereof;
(d) transfers of goods in the ordinary course of business of any trade or calling;
(e) bills of sale of goods in foreign parts or at sea;
(f) bills of lading;
(g) warehouse-keepers' certificates;
(h) warrants or orders for the delivery of goods; or
(i) any other documents used in the ordinary course of business as proof of the possession or control of goods, or authorising or purporting to authorise, either by endorsement or by delivery, the possessor of such document to transfer or receive goods thereby represented.[2]

In essence, the borrower who owns chattels[3] obtains an advance by way of a loan of money from the lender in return for providing a security in the form of a mortgage over goods or chattels. The terms of the mortgage constitute a contract for the loan between the parties, the terms of which are binding and enforceable as contractual terms. The legislation, however, imposes certain formal legal requirements. In terms of the policy behind the current Fiji legislation, Adams JA in *Faiz Sherani v Latchman and Others*[4] said:

There is no doubt that the Fiji Ordinance is founded on [the Bills of Sale Act 1878 (UK)] and like it and its predecessor, was directed against frauds on creditors by means of secret bills of sale … In England the Act of 1878 is supplemented by the amending Act of 1882 and except for two later amending Acts irrelevant for present purposes, the English law is still to be found in the Acts of 1878 and 1882. No provisions derived from the latter have been adopted in Fiji. … The Act of 1882 applied only to bills of sale given as security for the payment of money. There is no such distinction in Fiji, and the proper construction

---

2 See s 3 Bills of Sale Act Cap 225 (F).
3 On the question of proof of ownership, see *Nand v Indra* [1993] FJCA 41; Abu0035j.91s (26 November 1993) and *Buli v National MBF Finance (Fiji) Ltd* [1998] FJHC 90; Hbc0489j.97s (3 July 1998).
4 [1968] FJLawRp 35; [1968] 14 FLR 31 (5 April 1968) at 42; see also *The Manchester, Sheffield, and Lincolnshire Railway Co v The North Central Wagon Co* (1888) 13 App Cas 554 at 561; *D Chand Bothers Ltd v BPT (South Sea) Company Ltd* [1998] FJHC 32; Hbc0088r.98s (16 March 1998).

of the Ordinance must be one that will apply to all sorts of bills of sale, whether securities for money or 'absolute' bills of sale.

Every bill of sale must have a schedule attached to it detailing an inventory of the goods subject to the charge.[5] Every bill shall be executed by and attested to by at least one witness and shall be registered with the relevant stamp duties office.[6] The lender takes a charge on the subject property as the security until the borrower repays the loan and all interest and charges provided for in it. Where the borrower fails to repay the loan or to pay as otherwise required, the lender can take possession of the chattel or sell it in order to recover the money.[7] In this context, s 2 provides:

> This Act shall apply to every bill of sale whereby the holder or grantee has power, either with or without notice, at any time to seize or take possession of any personal chattels comprised in or made subject to such bill of sale.[8]

However, in equity, a borrower under a bill of sale has a right to redeem the bill by full payment at any time before the property is forfeited or sold in consequence of default.[9] Provided that transaction is an arm's-length transaction involving no element of unconscionability or equitable fraud, the courts will enforce the terms of the contract as between the parties, including the rights of the lender on default by the borrower in meeting the express terms of the contract of loan.[10]

Under the legislation, personal chattels include goods, furniture or other articles which can be transferred by delivery. The term also extends to fixtures, stocks and growing crops. Chattels exclude interest in real property and thus the legislation has no application to finance obtained by way of mortgage or charge over land. The bills of sale provisions do not apply either with respect to debentures or charges given by companies, which must apply with the companies legislation.[11] In *Nausori Daily Transport Ltd v Skiu Narayan,*[12] in holding that a bill of sale granted by an incorporated company over its property is not a bill of sale to which the provisions of the Bills of Sale Act apply, the court said:

---

5 See s 4 Bills of Sale Act Cap 174 (SI).
6 See *ibid.*, s 6.
7 See *ibid.*, s 7.
8 Sees 2 Bills of Sale Act Cap 225 (F).
9 See *Stanley v Wilde* [1899] 2 Ch D 474; *Parkin v Thorold* (1852) 16 Beav 59; *Ex parte Ellis* [1898] 2 QBD 79, applied in *Niranjans Autoport Ltd v Narayan* [1992] FJHC 10; Hba0013j.91s (31 January 1992).
10 See *Mussen v Van Diemen's Land Co.* (1938) Ch D 253; *Knightsbridge Estates Trust Ltd v Byrne* [1940] AC 613.
11 See *In re Standard Manufacturing Company* (1891) 1 Ch 627 at 648.
12 *Nausori Daily Transport Ltd v Shiu Narayan* [1981] FJLawRp 9; [1981] 27 FLR 131 (27 May 1981) at 135.

The legislature has expressly excluded a Bill of Sale over chattels owned by an incorporated company from the operation of the Act by the definition of 'personal chattels'. While the plaintiff's Bill of Sale does confer power on the defendant to seize or take possession of the plaintiff's personal chattels referred to in the Bill of Sale, they are not 'personal chattels' as defined by the Act.

All bills of sale must be registered. This is a process for both authenticating bills of sale and providing public notice of the existence of the charge over the property concerned. Bills of sale must be duly executed and attested and then registered within a reasonable period of creation, usually within one month of the creation date. Longer periods are allowed for bills made outside metropolitan and city areas.[13]

By way of example, s 7 of the Bills of Sale Act of Fiji provides:

Every bill of sale to which this Act applies shall be duly attested, and shall be registered, within seven days after the making or giving thereof if made or given in Suva, or within twenty-one days if made or given elsewhere than the city of Suva, and shall set forth the consideration for which such bill of sale was given; otherwise such bill of sale shall be deemed fraudulent and void:

Provided that the provisions of this section shall be deemed to have been complied with in respect of any bill of sale made or given in Rotuma if within seven days after the making or giving thereof such bill of sale is lodged with the District Officer, Rotuma, for transmission to the Registrar and the date of such lodgement shall be deemed to be the date of registration of such bill of sale for the purposes of this Act.[14]

Bills of sale may be attested before an officer of the court such as the registrar, deputy registrar, commissioner for oaths, notary public or a justice of the peace.

The following are some practical points governing the operation of bills of sale:

• *Once registered, a bill of sale confers priority on the holder of the document at the point of registration.* The interest of the holder (lender) becomes paramount over all other subsequent interests acquired in the subject property.[15] The holder of a registered bill of sale is thus protected against further dealings by the owner/borrower with the subject property. The issue is more complex than that because there are circumstances under which a registered legal holder can have his or her priority postponed in favour of persons who

13 See generally s 13 Bills of Sale Act Cap 174 (SI); s 7 Bills of Sale Act Cap 225 (F); s 6 Stamp Duties Act Cap 68, Laws of Vanuatu 1988.
14 See s 7 Bills of Sale Act (F).
15 See s 12, which provides: 'In case two or more bills of sale are given comprising in whole or in part the same chattels, they shall have priority in the order of their registration'.

subsequently acquire legal or equitable interests in the subject property, for example, where the registered holder has encouraged another to acquire an interest in the belief that his or her priority will not be enforced.[16] The general principles of equitable estoppel may apply to upset the priority situation.[17] This is determined by legal and equitable priorities rules, which are beyond the scope of this book. Non-registration will render a bill of sale inadmissible in evidence or in any civil proceedings. This means that the lender cannot rely on an unregistered bill of sale to prove the loan or advance made to the borrower as a secured creditor, but may do so as an unsecured creditor.

• *The registration of bills of sale must be renewed every five years.*[18] Registration, as noted, is a requirement as to the validity of a bill of sale. It is certainly also an important element in determining the priority of a bill of sale. However, failure to register a bill of sale may not be completely fatal. A bill of sale constitutes a contract to give a mortgage or charge over the chattel concerned. Notwithstanding the requirements of the legislation, a bill of sale may still be enforceable by courts of equity as a contract to grant an interest in property rather than as a legal interest *per se*. The contract as such gives enforceable rights in equity to the parties involved and thus the parties can be compelled as between themselves to carry out their contract. An equity court would, if necessary, compel the parties to give effect to their contract by completing the registration of the bill. Furthermore, as equity regards as done that which ought to be done, the contractual obligation would be treated as giving rise to an equitable security interest in the property at least as between the parties to the contract. In some circumstances, this equitable interest may have priority over subsequent equitable interests.[19]

The main objective of having a bill of sale is to allow the borrower to obtain some loan finance from the lender. The lender may not want to advance the money without holding onto some form of security over a chattel. The security can be over a chattel which is already owned by the borrower, or it could be over assets that the borrower is intending to acquire. In the latter respect, the purpose of the bill of sale is to fund the acquisition of the chattel itself.

---

16 On questions of priority between holders of registered bills of sale over the same property, see *National Bank of Fiji v Batiratu* [1994] FJHC 14; Hba0009j.93s (28 January 1994).

17 *Fiji Development Bank v Lutunatabua* [1993] FJHC 95; Hbc0014j.93s (18 October 1993).

18 See s 17 Bills of Sale Act Cap 174 (SI); s 14 Bills of Sale Act Cap 225 (F).

19 Or indeed other legal interests where there is reason in equity to postpone the priority of the holder of a particular legal interest.

12.2 Financial leasing

Generally speaking, a leasing agreement is both a security transaction and an important method of financing transactions, for example, in international trade. This security- and trade-financing mechanism works on the basis that equipment or goods can be bought or sold through a leasing agreement between the purchaser, seller and financier.

As we have noted elsewhere, a lease is essentially an agreement which provides the lessee or tenant with a right to exclusive possession of the property concerned in return for the payment of rental; that is to say, the lease grants the tenant a right for some period of time to use and enjoy the property to the exclusion of all others, including the landlord or lessor. Leases are common enough with respect to residential housing arrangements or otherwise with respect to real estate. However, any property which is capable of possession or enjoyment can be the subject of a lease agreement. The lease provides the tenant or lessee with an interest in the property concerned and that interest can, subject to any prohibition by the terms of the lease, be assigned or sub-let to another. In standard leases, this requires the consent of the lessor.

The international legal instrument regulating leasing agreements is the International Convention on Leasing 1988 formulated in Ottawa, Canada. It falls under the auspices of the International Centre for the Unification of Private International Law (UNIDROIT). In this chapter, we will only be looking at the commercial legal aspects of a finance leasing agreement.

12.2.1 Operation of a lease

For the provisions of the Convention to apply to a financial leasing agreement, the lessee must have entered into an agreement with a third party whereby the lessor acquires the plant, capital, goods or equipment on conditions that are acceptable to the lessee. The lessee should also have entered into an agreement with the lessor permitting the former to use the equipment in return for payments of rentals.[20] The Convention also governs an operating as well as a financial lease proper.[21]

It is the lessee's responsibility to ensure that the equipment under hire is maintained in good condition and should be returned in that condition if at the end of the lease, the lessee exercises the option not to purchase the equipment.[22] Except with the consent of the lessor, a lessee cannot unilaterally terminate the leasing agreement.[23] Whilst a lessor has a general right to deal with the equipment including a transfer (subject to the lessee's interest), a lessee cannot transfer the

---

20 See Art l(a)(b) UNIDROIT Convention 1988.
21 See *ibid.*, Art 1 (4).
22 See *ibid.*, Art 9(1)(2).
23 See *ibid.*, Art 10(2).

interest in the equipment without having first sought and obtained the consent of the lessor.[24]

Going by Arts 9, 10 and 14 of the Convention, it is possible to assert that these provisions of the Convention are titled in favour of the lessor. If the imbalance is not redressed, lessees might always have to argue in favour of the exclusion of the provisions of the Convention when they contract with the lessor. This is likely to endanger the acceptability of the Convention as an international method of harmonising financial leasing agreements around the world.

The Convention outlines the basic constituents of leasing agreements. The lease must be couched in a form of agreement in order to bind the parties to it. The subject matter of the lease must be identified. The terms and conditions governing the transfer, hire or rental of the equipment must be outlined and agreed upon. The lessee is saddled with the responsibility of choosing the equipment/goods that would form the subject of the lease.[25]

After choosing the equipment/goods, the lessor then acquires the equipment/goods. A designated amount of rental is to be paid by the lessee to the lessor. The rental sum must be structured in such a way as to amortise both the principal sum as well as the interest. The parties to a leasing arrangement can by Art 5 exclude the application of the Convention from their agreement.[26]

The lessor and lessee are bound by the terms of the lease agreement. In the event of any breach, the aggrieved party is legally entitled to enforce the terms of the agreement.[27] In this context, Art 12(1) of the Convention provides:

(a) the lessee has the right as against the lessor to reject the equipment or to terminate the leasing agreement; and
(b) the lessor is entitled to remedy the failure by tendering equipment in conformity with the supply contract;
(c) the lessee may withhold payment of the rental until the lessor has made a remedial tender of the equipment.

Article 13 stipulates the applicable remedies. These include damages and other remedies, but punitive damages are categorically excluded.

12.2.2 Types of lease

Two basic types of leasing agreement are employed in this context: operating and financial leases. An operating lease has been defined by Art 2 as "one under which

---

24 See *ibid.*, Art 14(1)(2).
25 See *ibid.*, Art 1(2).
26 See *ibid.*, Art 1(2).
27 See *Lombard North Central plc v Butterworth* [1987] QB 527; *Jobson v Johnson* [1989] 1 All ER 621.

equipment is let out on lease to a series of different lessees in sequence each taking the equipment for the period for which he needs it and paying a rent reflecting its use-value". A financial lease has also been defined as 'a financial tool, in which the lessor's retention of ownership is little more than nominal'.[28] Furthermore, a finance lease has been defined as:

> A lease that transfers substantially all the risks and rewards of ownership of an asset to a lessee. It is to be presumed that such a transfer of risks and rewards occurs if at the inception of a lease the present value of the minimum payments, including an initial payment, amounts to substantially all (normally 90 per cent or more) of the fair value of the leased asset. The present value should be calculated by using the interest rate implicit in the lease.[29]

An important distinction between a finance lease and an operating lease is that in the latter case, the hirer takes the goods for a determinate period of hire, whilst in the former, ownership and property in the goods are transferred to the hirer at the end of the lease agreement. Apart from this main distinction, both leases could be premised on similar conditions regarding rental payments, calculation of interest and depreciation rates.

In an operating lease, the lessor has retained title in the goods but parts with the possession so long as rental payments are kept up to date by the lessee. In a finance lease, the rental payments by the lessee go towards the final payment of the total cost of the goods under hire. This becomes a sale at the expiry of the lease agreement.

12.2.3 Amortisation plan

The objective of a leasing agreement is to allow the lessee to have a fair and reasonable use of the goods whilst at the same time paying back to the lessor a commensurate amount as rent for the use of the goods within the agreed period. In this regard, the lessee is expected to pay back at the rental rate part of the capital cost and the accrued interest. The payment is graduated to accommodate the fair use value of the goods. To amortise the loan means to repay the capital cost of the goods.

---

28 See Miller, L and Barber, M. *Understanding Commercial Law*, 2019, Wellington, LexisNexis, 9th edn.
29 Practice note, *A guide to Practical Law's UK corporate governance materials* (2024), Practical Law Corporate, Thomson Reuters, UK.

12.2.4 Uses of leases

One of the major advantages of using a leasing agreement as a security arrangement and as a means of financing trade is that the buyer may want to purchase the goods, but may usually be prevented from doing so because of the prohibitive cost of the goods. By resorting to a leasing agreement, this obstacle can be overcome. A leasing agreement is therefore a good means of financing the purchase of durable and large capital goods or equipment by using the goods as effective security for repayment.

A leasing agreement provides a good security arrangement for the payment of the price. In this way, a lessor is able to retain title in the goods until the lessee makes the final payment. This is a good security measure to safeguard the interest of the lessor against unauthorised disposal of the goods by the lessee. The need to restrict unauthorised disposal of the goods is especially important where the lessor and the lessee are resident in different countries.[30]

The cost of rental or amortisation in a leasing agreement is regarded as an allowable deduction for income tax purposes. This means that the lessee is entitled to deduct all expenses made on the purchase or rental of the goods before their tax is assessed. This provides some financial relief to the lessee.[31]

12.2.5 Registration

An international leasing agreement creates a security interest, in that the goods are charged as security for the rental payments. The lessor is also entitled to repossess the goods where the lessee has defaulted in rental payment. Because of the existence of a charged interest on the subject matter of the lease, its enforceability would depend on registration. The leasing agreement is also subject to the appropriate stamp duty payment. Except as specifically provided, the leasing agreement is subject to the registration and stamp duty laws of the country of execution. Article 3(1) of the Convention provides:

> If the lessor and the lessee have their places of business in different States and: (a) these States and the States in which the supplier has its place of business are Contracting States; or (b) both the supply agreement and the leasing agreement are governed by the law of a Contracting State.

The act of registering the leasing agreement perfects it as a dependable and enforceable security in favour of a lessor. Non-registration would render the

---

30 For a general discussion on the retention of title clause, see Ahmadu, M, 'The Romalpa clause: commercial and legal implications' [1995] FLT, January, p 9; Everett, D, 'Romalpa clause: the fundamental flaw' (1994) 68(4) ALJ 404.
31 See Miller and Barber, *op cit* fn 28, pp 383–84, at Chapter 9.

leasing agreement unenforceable in law. By this, it also loses priority as against a subsequent sub-lessee. Importantly, where the leasing agreement has not been registered, it cannot be relied upon as evidence in court.[32] This makes it admissible in evidence where the lessor sought to rely on it to recover any outstanding sum. The lease agreement is therefore void, but money secured by it becomes payable as in a claim for ordinary debt.

By its very nature, a leasing agreement is fraught with difficulties usually arising from conflicts of law. This is more so where the lessee had disposed of the property to a third party in a third country. If the third country is not a signatory to the Convention, this creates an insurmountable recovery problem both for the sum secured and for the equipment itself. The Convention needs, therefore, to improve its conflict of law provisions. The current provisions cannot adequately cover this situation.

Furthermore, since the subject matter of the Convention is capital goods or equipment or other forms of durable goods, problems could arise where the equipment becomes fixed to land. This is more so in countries where customary ownership of land prohibits any form of alienation or sale of land to or by non-customary owners. This problem is more conceivable in the context of the South Pacific, where customary land ownership is the norm. Parties dealing with equipment or other leased goods that are fixed to such customary lands are to take heed of conceptual difficulties relating to the seizure or disposal of such equipment. Maybe a new principle of law should emerge in future amendments to the Convention to consider issues surrounding restricted disposal rights in customary ownership.

The degree of restriction placed on the alienability of customary land varies from country to country. However, the general intent of the laws in all cases is similar, namely, to prevent non-custom owners from having absolute ownership of land. All that is available is a lease for a term of years.[33] Since large portions of lands in all South Pacific island states are designated as customary in tenure, it is obvious that these laws would pose serious challenges to the validity of international leasing agreements where they attempt to tamper with the rights of custom landowners.

12.3 Hire purchase

Hire purchase agreements are in wide use as a means of financing the acquisition of goods and chattels. They have been enforced by common law courts since at

---

32 See s 9 Stamp Duties Act Cap 126 (SI); formerly, s 100 Stamp Duties Act Cap 205 1920 repealed in 2020 (F); ss 36, 37 Stamp Duties Act 1971–72 (CI); Stamp Duties Act Cap 70 (T); ss 2, 6 Stamp Duties Act Cap 68 (V).

33 See generally the Non-Native Land Restriction of Alienation Ordinance Cap 63 (K); Land Act Cap 46.02 (T); Property Law Act 1952 (CI); Constitution of the Republic of Vanuatu 1980.

least the 1873 decision in *Helby v Matthews*.[34] In that case, the plaintiff agreed to hire a piano to a third party, who in turn pledged the piano with the defendant for some money. The court held that because the agreement between the plaintiff and the third party was a hire purchase, the plaintiff was entitled to retrieve the piano from the defendant. The seller was entitled to repossess or seize the goods in the event of any default by the hirer. Since that time, the use of hire purchase agreements has expanded considerably. They are no longer confined to use with respect to personal chattels of this nature.

A hire purchase agreement is essentially an agreement whereby a lender or financier acquires goods or chattels from a seller or dealer and then proceeds to hire them out to the buyer for a fixed term. As between the financier and the hirer, there is a contract of bailment, a bailment being a right of possession regarding goods or chattels. Subject to the rental and other charges, including interest being paid to the lender, the hirer/buyer is given an option to purchase the goods at a stipulated residual amount. A hire purchase agreement is not a mortgage as between the lender and the hirer/buyer. Thus, the Bills of Sale Acts do not apply to it so far as it is concerned with sale of goods. In *McEntire v Crossley Brothers Ltd*,[35] it was said:

> it seems to me impossible to bring the case within the Bills of Sale Act because the transaction may bear a resemblance to a transaction which would be within it on the ground that it is within the mischief, when the initial step to bringing the Bills of Sale Act into operation at all fails, namely, that there should have been an assurance, or an assignment or a licence to seize ... given [by the owner] to some other person.

A hire purchase agreement, although it does provide for finance, does not constitute a mortgage or charge over the asset in question. In *Australia and New Zealand Banking Group Ltd v Merchant Bank of Fiji*,[36] the Court of Appeal of Fiji held that (a) a hire purchase agreement of the kind found in the present case is neither a bill of sale nor any other kind of charge which requires registration; (b) it is neither a loan upon security nor a conditional sale agreement; and (c) there was no statutory provision in Fiji for the registration of hire purchase agreements such as the agreement – there called an 'asset purchase agreement' – was. A hire purchase agreement is not the same as a financial lease agreement owing to the purchase option. The difference can be crucial in some jurisdictions when considering the various remedies under existing hire purchase legislation. However, common law

---

34 [1895] AC 471.
35 [1895] AC 457 at 466.
36 [1995] FJSC 10; CBV0001.1995 (21 November 1995); see also *Credit Corp (Fiji) Ltd v Kennedy Hotel Ltd* [1999] FJCA 14; Abu0009u.97s (12 February 1999).

remedies for fraud or other forms of misrepresentation involved in either kind of dealing are the same.[37]

As between the hirer/buyer and the seller, the Sale of Goods Acts do not generally apply because the sale takes place between the seller and the lender, the latter being the initial buyer.[38] As between the hirer and the lender, the hire purchase agreement is not a sale agreement because it merely gives the hirer an option to purchase the property under certain conditions.[39] Furthermore, the legislation might apply in cases where the lender is also the seller. However, that legislation does deem the supply of goods to include supply pursuant to a hire purchase agreement,[40] and thus the conditions as to quality or fitness and the like apply.[41]

In jurisdictions such as Australia and New Zealand, there are separate legislative regimes dealing with hire purchase agreements partly because the use of such agreements is frequently subject to abuse of consumer rights which are not adequately dealt with by the sale of goods legislation. In the South Pacific, the Cook Islands alone have their own hire purchase legislation at the present time. Section 2 of the Consumer Credit Act 1999[42] of that country provides as follows:

'Hire purchase agreement' includes a letting of goods with an option to purchase and an agreement for the purchase of goods by instalments (whether the agreement describes the instalments as rent or hire or otherwise), but does not include any agreement–

(a) whereby the property in the goods comprised therein passes at the time of the agreement or at any time before delivery of the goods; or

(b) under which the person by whom the goods are being hired or purchased is a person who is engaged in the trade or business of selling goods of the same nature or description as the goods comprised in the agreement.

---

37 See *Woodleigh Nominees Pty Ltd v CBFC Leasing Pty Ltd* [1999] NTSC 74.

38 *Australia and New Zealand Banking Group Ltd v Koi* [1994] FJHC 7; Hbc0231j.92s (10 January 1994).

39 On whether a hirer could be considered a 'mercantile agent' for the purposes of s 26(3) Sale of Goods Act [Cap 230] 1980, see *ibid.*, and *Staffs Motor Guarantee Ltd v British Wagon Co* [1934] 2 KB 305 at 313.

40 See s 2 Sale of Goods Act (F).

41 See s 16(1) (F) for example.

42 There are other locally enacted Hire Purchase Acts in the region: Hire-purchase Act [Cap 252] 1966 (PNG); Hire Purchase Act 1986 (Cook Islands). English Hire Purchase Acts are used as statutes of general application in most cases. For this reason, we focus only on the Cook Islands law because of its identical nature with the other English statutes. A 1998 report of the Fiji Law Reform Commission recommended the introduction of such legislation. A bill was introduced into parliament in 1999 which led to the enactment of the Consumer Credit Act 1999, which provides for the regulation of consumer credit agreements, consumer leases as well as hire purchase agreements.

In the case of that legislation, extensive provision is made with respect to implied terms and conditions in the agreement, many of which mirror those applicable in sale of goods transactions.[43] It also provides the purchaser with a number of statutory rights such as the right to receive a copy of the agreement, the right to discharge the agreement by full payment at any time, the right to a statutory rebate of interest and charges on the hiring and the right voluntarily to return the goods.[44] The power of the financier in respect of repossession of the goods is curtailed, requiring a notice of default prior to the exercise of those powers and imposing other duties to protect the interest of the purchaser in the goods.[45] Section 5 requires that a hire purchase agreement must be in writing. If this is not complied with, the agreement is not enforceable by the vendor.[46] The agreement must contain certain basic terms.[47] If it does not, then the purchaser is not liable to pay the costs of credit, such as interest, and any such costs already paid have to be refunded,[48] although this might not be the case where it can be shown that non-compliance was not of such a nature as to mislead or deceive the purchaser to his/her prejudice.[49] Similarly so, where the vendor has promptly remedied the non-compliance on its being discovered or brought to its notice and has, where appropriate, compensated or offered to compensate the purchaser for the prejudice caused to him/her.[50]

12.3.1 Basic features

There are usually three parties to a hire purchase arrangement. These are the hirer, the seller (sometimes called the 'dealer') and the financier. In another variant of hire purchase, the seller may be the financier. The seller or the dealer will be regarded as the agent of the lender for certain purposes. In *Financings Ltd v Stimson*,[51] it was held that the dealer should, amongst other things, be regarded as the agent of the finance company to receive, and accept, a notice by the hirer of revocation of his offer to buy. In *Branwhite v Worcester Works Finance*,[52] it was said:

> The matters included within the [agency relationship] should be the fixing and receipt of the deposit, representations as to the goods, probably, … delivery

---

43 See ss 11–17 Hire Purchase Act 1986 (CI).
44 See *ibid.*, ss 19–24.
45 See *ibid.*, ss 26–35.
46 *Ibid.*, s 4(1).
47 *Ibid.*, s 6.
48 *Ibid.*, s 4(2).
49 *Ibid.*, s 4(3)(a).
50 *Ibid.*, s 4(3)(b).
51 [1962] 3 All ER 386.
52 [1968] 3 All ER 104 at 122.

of the goods to the hirer. As to all these matters, the dealer should be treated as the finance company's agent and the finance company accordingly bound, irrespective of whether or not an effective hire-purchase transaction comes into existence.

It has been held that in considering the question of obligations of the finance company under the Sale of Goods Act, regard may be had to the negotiations that took place between the hirer and the dealer and in particular to representations which the dealer might have made regarding the quality of the goods and other matters. In *National MBf Finance (Fiji) Ltd v Lee*,[53] it was said:

> Furthermore the term '*antecedent negotiations*' although undefined in the Sale of Goods Act would, in my considered opinion, include any negotiations conducted or arrangements made between the oven supplier and the first defendant whereby the latter was induced to enter into the Hire Purchase Agreement with the plaintiff company or which otherwise promoted the transaction to which the Hire Purchase Agreement relates.

The basic features of hire purchase transactions may be summarised as follows:

- The hirer has an option to purchase the goods. This also means that the hirer is not duty-bound to eventually buy the goods and may opt out of the transaction at any given time.
- The hirer pays the price by means of instalments. This enables the hirer to take immediate possession of the goods but to make periodic payments as agreed until the full purchase price is discharged.
- The seller can exercise the power to repossess the goods or chattel if there has been a default by the hirer. This, though, is not an automatic power. It exists by virtue of rights under the contract. Where it is exercised, the hirer who then sells the goods is obliged to act in good faith and must not wilfully or recklessly sacrifice the interest of the hirer on any sale.[54] It is an extension of the duty which applies to any mortgagee who exercises a power of sale on default under the mortgage.
- The seller must notify the hirer before the power to repossess is exercised. This gives the hirer an opportunity to rectify the default and resume payment. It is also consistent with the right to a fair hearing.

The terms of a hire purchase agreement are contractual terms. In interpreting them the courts have often taken a sceptical view of them and adopted, in the interests of consumer protection, an approach to interpretation against the finance

---

53 [1997] FJHC 96; Hbc0052j.96s (29 July 1997).
54 *CBFC v Austin* [1999] NSWSC 1025 (13 October 1999).

company.[55] In *Slater v Finning Ltd*,[56] it was said in referring to the seller's obligations under s 14(3) of the Sale of Goods Act 1979 (UK):[57]

> the old rule of caveat emptor has become the rule of *caveat venditor* in order to meet the requirements of modern commerce and trade … While the implied condition that the goods are reasonably fit is inherently a relative concept, it is well established that the liability under Section 14(3) is strict in the sense that the seller's liability does not depend on whether he exercised reasonable care.

In *Lowe v Lombank Ltd*, it was said:

> under modern conditions many transactions, particularly of hire purchase, are entered into by ignorant persons whose only choice is either not to enter into the transaction at all or to enter into it on the terms of a standard agreement, drafted by the hire purchase company, and containing numerous clauses printed in miniscule characters which the hirers do not in fact read and, if they did, would be incapable of understanding.[58]

A noticeable feature of hire purchase is the option given to the hirer to elect whether to complete the full purchase price and thereby become the outright owner of the goods. It is an option which generally takes the form of an open offer to purchase at a specified price. Depending on the terms of the particular agreement, there may be a right in the hirer to terminate the agreement by paying out an agreed amount of interest and to exercise the option to purchase at an earlier date.

12.4 Credit sales (formerly, conditional sales)

A credit sale is an agreement for sale under which the title remains in the seller until the purchase price has been paid in full or the buyer has complied with any other conditions prescribed by the agreement for the transfer of title to him or her.[59]

A credit sale is a type of a credit sale which has the following features:

- There is a commitment by the buyer to pay the full price of the goods at the time of the agreement, even though property in the goods is retained by the seller.

---

55 *Lowe v Lombank* [1960] 1 All ER 611; *Financings Ltd v Stimson* [1962] 3 All ER 386 at 388.
56 [1997] AC 473 at 200.
57 Which is identical to s 16(3) (F).
58 *Lowe v Lombank* above, at p 614. See also *Olds Discount Co Ltd v John Playfair Ltd* [1938] 3 All ER 275.
59 See Miller and Barber, *op cit* fn 28, p 401, at Chapter 9; *Forthright Finance Ltd v Ingate (Carlyle Finance Ltd, third party)* [1997] 4 All ER 90.

- The buyer assumes possession of the goods and is at liberty to use them, but not in a manner inconsistent with the rights of ownership.
- Payment of the price is by instalment, which can be spread over a period of time or as agreed by the parties.

In *Lee v Butler*,[60] L entered into an agreement to hire some pieces of furniture from H. The repayment period was three years. The furniture was to be owned by L after payment of the price. The court held that this was a conditional sale. The court further held that it did not matter that the word 'hire' was used, as the circumstances showed that the hirer was bound to make full payments towards the purchase price.

12.4.1 Distinction between hire purchase and conditional sale

The hirer under a hire purchase agreement has the option to terminate the agreement at any time by giving notice in writing to the owner. Furthermore, it is essentially an agreement for hiring of the goods but subject to an option to purchase. In a conditional sale, the hirer is under no obligation to complete the purchase price. However, in a conditional sale, the buyer is committed to paying the full price for the goods from the commencement of the transaction. The goods are purchased at the time of the sale, although the actual transfer might be postponed. However, it would appear that conditional sales fall within the definition of a hire purchase agreement under the Hire Purchase Act of the Cook Islands, in that it includes:

> an agreement whereby goods are let or hired with an option to purchase and an agreement for the purchase of goods by instalment payments (whether the agreement describes the payment as rent or hire or otherwise) under which the person who agrees to purchase the goods is given possession of them before the total amount payable has been paid.[61]

Thus, a conditional sale agreement could need to comply with the formal provisions of that Act as to enforceability and otherwise.

There are two final points of difference worth mentioning. In some jurisdictions, a conditional sale is within the ambit of consumer credit legislation, at least where such legislation exists, whilst a hire purchase agreement is not. Furthermore, a purchaser by way of conditional sale is able to sell the goods during the currency of the agreement. The purchaser can transmit good title as a buyer in possession pursuant to the Sale of Goods Acts. Under a hire purchase agreement, the hirer is not able to do that.

---

60 [1893] 2 QB 318; *Branwhite v Worcester Works Finance Ltd* [1969] 3 All ER 104; *Andrews v Hopkins* [1957] 1 QB 229.
61 Section 2(1) Hire Purchase Act 1986 (CI).

13

INSURANCE CONTRACTS

13.1 Definition of an insurance contract

The law relating to insurance is to a considerable extent an application of the law of contract. A policy of insurance is in effect a contract between the insurer and the insured to protect or indemnify the insured against those particular risks of damage or loss that are identified in the policy document. Special principles have developed in the area of insurance law, partly as a result of mercantile practice bearing in mind the peculiar features of insurance business, and the courts have been instrumental in the incorporation of such practice into the law in this area.[1] It has been said:

> Insurance is a contract between the insurer and the insured. The primary obligation of the insurer is to provide the insured with some benefit, usually by way of replacement of property or the payment of money, on the happening of a specified uncertain event. The insured's primary obligation is to pay the premium.[2]

---

1 See generally *Lord Napier and Ettrick v. Hunter* [1993] 2 WLR 42; *Munro Brice & Co. v War Risks Association Ltd* [1918] 2 KB 78; *Pan Atlantic Insurance Co Ltd v Pine Top Insurance Co Ltd* [1995] 1 AC 501; [1994] 3 All ER 581; *North & South Trust v Berkeley* [1971] 1 WLR 470; *Falcon Investments Corporation (NZ) v State Insurance General Manager* [1975] 1 NZLR 520; *Leyland Shipping Co Ltd v Norwich Union Fire Insurance Society Ltd* [1918] AC 350; *Esso Petroleum Co Ltd v Hall Russell Ltd & Co Ltd* (1988) 2 WLR 730; *Department of Trade and Industry v Christopher Motorists' Association Ltd* [1974] 1 WLR 99; *Medical Defence Union Ltd v Department of Trade* [1979] 2 WLR 686.
2 See Borrowdale, A, *Butterworths Commercial Law in New Zealand,* 1996, Wellington, NZ, Butterworths, p 445; see Miller, L and Barber, M. *Understanding Commercial Law,* 2019,

Effectively, an insurance contract or policy transfers the risk concerned from the insured personally to the insurer. Thus, it provides the insured with protection against loss or damage occurring in a particular way or through a particular cause and this is loss or damage that would normally be serious from the point of view of the insured. Marine insurance providing protection against loss of goods in transport by sea was one of the earliest forms of insurance. Later on, other forms of insurance developed. Broadly speaking, the types of insurance now available include marine, accident, life and fire insurance, although there are many other types.

Insurers sell a variety of insurance policies to meet the demands of the public. Different policies are geared towards covering specific losses, whether against property or human life or injury. Other contracts are geared specifically towards the financial products market, for example, in providing insurance against movements in international monetary exchange rates. A quick overview of the types of policies now available indicates: *fire* – this takes care of all contingencies of destruction or loss caused by fire to property of the insured; *vehicle insurance* – which may be third party[3] or comprehensive, covering road-related accidents or other mishaps; *life* – whereby a person or his or her family members can insure against the death of that person; *professional indemnity* – which basically protects a practitioner from liability in relation to dealings with, advice to or treatment of clients or patients as the case may be; *public or occupiers' liability* – wide-scale coverage of profound losses likely to inflict damage to human life or perhaps to the environment; *motor vehicle insurance* – as indicated above; *theft* – indemnity against loss through misappropriation by another; *property damage;*[4] *mortgage insurance*; and *loss of rental insurance*. Others include: *personal accident* – which covers work-related occupational hazards; *medical, sickness or health* – covering one-off or ongoing medical care for the insured; *life* – which assures payment to the next of kin at the death of the assured; *marine* – covering shipping and all marine-related risks; *aviation* – which covers air safety and transportation of both goods and passengers; *endowment* and *retirement* – assure an annuity or lump-sum payment over a period or at a specific time. The categories mentioned here

---

Wellington, LexisNexis, 9th edn; *Department of Trade and Industry v Christopher Motorists' Association Ltd* [1974] 1 WLR 99; *Medical Defence Union Ltd v Department of Trade* [1979] 2 WLR 686.; *South Pacific Manufacturing Co Ltd v New Zealand Security Consultants and Investigations Ltd; Mortensen v Laing* [1992] 2 NZLR 282 (CA).

3 See *Bans v Jan's Rental Cars (Fiji)* Ltd [1992] FJLawRp 20; [1992 38 FLR 158 (7 August 1992). A substantial aspect of insurance business now is third-party personal injuries insurance with respect to injuries sustained in motor vehicle accidents, insurance for which is compulsory under the likes of the Motor Vehicles (Third Party Insurance) Act Cap 177 1954 of Fiji. However, third party here refers to protection only against damage caused by the insured to others; in other policies, this might provide coverage with respect to either personal injuries or property damage.

4 See *Stinson Pearce Ltd v Queensland Insurance (Fiji) Ltd* [1993] FJLawRp 2; [1993] 39 FLR 282 (15 October 1993) on whether forceful entry into premises amounted to riot and fell within the policy.

are certainly not exhaustive. Many modern policies now also provide comprehensive coverage against a collection of different risks, as in, for example, the case of travel or householder's insurance.

There are some important points regarding the nature of insurance, as follows:

(a) An insurance contract is fundamentally a contract. This means that all rules of contract such as offer, acceptance, consideration and intention to create legal relations apply.[5] An insurance contract is also referred to as a policy. The contract is a special one. As with hire purchase contracts, the interpretation of insurance contracts and attendant documentation has usually acknowledged that the insurer has a predominance of bargaining power as against this insured. Hence the courts invoke what is called the *contra proferentem* rule. This requires the court to adopt a construction favourable to the insured and against the insurer who issued the documents.[6] In other respects, the words in a contract of insurance are to be given their ordinary and natural meaning.[7] However, as stated by the Court of Appeal of Vanuatu in *In re The Estate of Francesco Picchi*:[8]

The wording of the policy will usually make the situation plain, but sometimes, as in this case, the policy wording is not clear whether separate rights and interests are insured for the benefit of each interest holder individually. Where the policy is not clear, it is permissible to look not only at the policy but to the background facts which provide the context in which the insurance was effected: *Halsbury's Laws of England*, 4 Ed, vol 25, para 416.

The normal course of formation of an insurance policy is that a proposal form is completed by the intended insured. This is an offer by the person to the company. On the basis of that proposal, the insured issues a policy which is usually in terms of the policy treated as the fundamental basis of the contract. In some cases, a person can obtain a cover note as a preliminary to obtaining full insurance. A cover note provides insurance cover on standard terms and conditions for a limited period of time, say one month, pending the full contract of insurance being issued. It is an interim insurance contract pending completion and acceptance of the proposal and the issue of

---

5 *Wight v National Pacific Insurance* [2001] TOSC 38; C 1101 2000 (11 October 2001).

6 *Fowkes v Manchester and London Assurance and London Association* (1863) 3 B. & S.917; 122 ER 343. See also *Dominion Insurance Ltd v Westpac Banking Corp* [1998] FJCA 48; Abu0005u.97s (27 November 1998).

7 See *London and Lancashire Fire Insurance Co v Bolands Ltd* [1924] AC 836; *Singh v Sun Insurance Co Ltd* [2001] FJLawRp 55; [2001] 1 FLR 231 (24 July 2001); *Charter Reinsurance Co Ltd v Fagan* [1997] AC 313 at 387–88; *Investors Compensation Scheme Ltd v West Bromwich Building Society* [1998] 1 WLR 896.

8 [1997] VUCA 8; Civil Appeal Case 01 of 1995 (21 October 1997).

the policy. The obligation of the insured to make disclosure, discussed below, applies also to cover notes.

The insured will be required to pay a premium before the policy comes into effect and usually before issue. However, as was said in *Dominion Insurance Ltd v Sea Island Paper & Stationery Ltd*:[9]

> In an insurance policy the insurer may require that payment of premium for which it undertakes to indemnify the insured must be paid before liability arises. ... However, the law is clear that notwithstanding such a requirement the insurer may extend time for payment of the premium and the validity of the insurance policy is not affected by the non-payment at the time of the risk.

(b) It is peremptory in nature. This arrangement is not based on any set of defined or certain happenings. Parties cannot insure an event which they are certain will take place at a definite time; such as the rising of the sun tomorrow morning. There must be a genuine element of risk. The loss must be unforeseen by the parties such as arising from accidents, emergencies or contingencies.

(c) Most contracts of insurance are in the form of an indemnity against specified types of loss or damage sustained by the insured. Precise obligations to indemnify will be subject to variation from case to case, depending on the terms and conditions of the policy.

(d) Given that an insurance policy is a contract, there is the requirement of consideration to make that contract valid and enforceable at law. On the insured's side, this takes the form of a premium which is payable by the insured to the insurer on such terms as are agreed.[10] On the insurer's side, the provision of the legal obligation to provide indemnity or otherwise meet the consequences of the risk should it materialise is an adequate consideration moving from it.

13.1.1 Who can be an insurer?

Legislation in the region imposes requirements on persons or entities which can issue contracts of insurance. For example, the Insurance Act Cap 82[11] requires that no insurance business must be carried on in or from within the country except by a registered insurer or by a member of an association of registered underwriters. Section 4 of the Act imposes certain requirements in relation to the registration of a company as an insurer. There are certain financial and asset holding requirements. Where the company is carrying on life assurance business, it must have a specified paid-up share capital. Other companies are required to have a certain value of assets. By s 2, 'insurance business' means the soliciting, effecting or carrying out

---

9 [1998] FJCA 17; Abu0008u.97s (15 May 1998); see also *Wooding v Monmouthshire and South Wales Mutual Indemnity Society* [1939] 4 All ER 570 at 581.

10 See *Capital Plumbing Service Pty Ltd v FML Assurance Ltd* (1986) 4 ANZ Ins Cas 60–734.

11 See also Insurance Act 2007 (S).

of contracts of insurance as an insurer and includes re-insurance business. By the same section, 'insurer' is defined as a person effecting and carrying on insurance business. This includes each member of an association of underwriters.

The legislation contains numerous other provisions in relation to the refusal and cancellation of registration, the manner in which insurance business is to be carried on and the conduct of insurance business by the likes of insurance brokers and agents.[12] There are other provisions dealing with compliance requirements for insurers.[13] There are provisions dealing, for example, with the written form in which policies are to be issued and imposing liabilities for false and misleading representations made by insurers and their agents.[14]

There are several important principles affecting insurance contracts. These are indemnity, insurable interest, utmost good faith and subrogation.[15] We will now comment on each of these in turn.

13.1.2 Indemnity

Most insurance contracts other than life and accident policies are contracts of indemnity. There is a well-established rule to the effect that contracts of insurance which provide cover for loss or damage are to be construed by the courts so as to extend only to loss of or damage to the subject matter of the insurance itself, unless the contrary is clearly stipulated.[16] In other words, the indemnity principle requires, unless it is displaced or modified by the actual terms of the policy, that the obligation of the insurer is only to pay out the actual loss or damage suffered by the insured as a result of the occurrence of the risk. The insured cannot by insuring for an excess over the real value of property, for example, make a profit out of the policy. Replacement value policies where the insurer agrees to pay the replacement value of the goods are a slight variation on this principle. Normally the extent of actual loss has to be assessed by a loss assessor and agreed by the insured. In the absence of any agreement, the insurer has to litigate the claim under the policy.

Sometimes, in a case where an indemnity policy is involved, an insured might have taken out policies with more than one insurance company. This is known as double insurance. Clearly, the indemnity principle would prevent an insured from benefiting twice to the same degree out of the respective policies. That would be to allow the insured to make a profit out of the insurance policies. The insured must elect which of the two or several policies he or she is to make a claim against. In

---

12 See Parts II, III and IV. See also Insurance Act [Cap 217] 1998 (F).

13 See ss 55(2), Part V.

14 See s 128.

15 On the operation of these principles, see generally *WR Carpenter (South Pacific) Ltd v Jewett Cameron (South Pacific) Ltd* [1994] TOLawRp 3; [1994] Tonga LR 5 (10 January 1994).

16 See *Mitsui v Mumford* [1915] 2 KB 27; *Campbell & Phillips Ld v Denman* (1915) 21 Com Cas 357; *Moore v Evans* [1918] AC 185; *Queensland Insurance (Fiji) Ltd v Aziz* [1998] FJHC 27; Hba0015j.97b (4 March 1998).

such a situation, the insurer who satisfied the claim is entitled, by way of the equitable principle of subrogation discussed below, to seek appropriate contribution from the other insurer or insurers. Contribution can only be called for from those other insurers who are liable in whole or in part to indemnify the insurer in respect of the particular risk which gives rise to the claim for indemnity.[17]

13.1.3 An insurable interest

It is a requirement that the insured must exhibit some degree of insurable interest in the subject matter of the insurance.[18] Whilst this is a requirement in all types of insurance policy in South Pacific island countries, the requirement has now been abolished in the case of life assurance in some jurisdictions. For example, in the case of New Zealand, s 6 of the Insurance Law Reform Act 1985 excludes insurable interest as a requirement in life assurance policies. The interest must exist at the time of the contract and at the time of the loss in the case of policies of general insurance. In respect of life policies, at common law, the interest must exist at the time of the making of the insurance contract only.

Historically, the existence of an insurable interest is that which differentiates a contract from insurance from a contract of betting or wager.[19] The latter are illegal and unenforceable. In the case of an insurance contract, the insurer is undertaking the risk of indemnification or coverage of loss or damage in the event that a certain risk materialises which causes that loss or damage. Where the policy provides for coverage of loss in the value of property owned by the insured occasioned by the likes of fire or theft, then clearly the policy will be in order. The insured owns the property and has an insurable interest in the sense that he or she can legitimately protect him or herself against the loss or damage to the property.

A mortgagee or a lessee of property has an insurable interest in property subject to the lease or mortgage. In the case of a mortgagee, it was said in *Royal Insurance Co Ltd v Mylius*[20] that when mortgagees insure tangible securities against the risk of fire, they insure not their debt but their security and not as mere creditors but as holders of the security. However, an unsecured creditor has no insurable interest in the property of his or her debtor.[21] A shareholder has no insurable interest in the assets of the company given that the holding of shares does not give the holder a direct interest in the assets of the company.[22] A buyer of a property who has not

---

17 *Albion Insurance Co Ltd v Government Insurance Office (NSW)* (1969) 121 CLR 342.

18 See *Macaura v Northern Assurances Co* [1925] AC 619; *Nandan v Queensland Insurance Co. Ltd* [1992] FJLawRp 27; [1992] 38 FLR 220 (27 November 1992).

19 Also, it allegedly discourages the insured from deliberately seeking to set up a claim under the policy by, for example, deliberately destroying the subject matter of the policy.

20 [1926] HCA 49; 38 CLR 477 at 489; see also *Westpac Banking Corp v Fiji Forest Sawmilling Ltd* [1998] FJCA 37; Abu0045u.96s (23 September 1998).

21 *K & F Nurse Pty Ltd and Speedway Caterers Pty Ltd v AFG Insurances* (1974) 4 ACTR 25.

22 *Macaura v Northern Assurances Co* [1925] AC 619.

yet entered into an enforceable contract for purchase does not have an insurable interest in the property which he or she is proposing to acquire. However, after the contract is properly executed, such an interest arises.[23] Indeed, where the contract is one that is specifically enforceable, the property is at the risk of the buyer as from the date of execution of the contract.[24]

13.1.4 Utmost good faith

The principle of utmost good faith applies to insurance contracts. It requires disclosure by the insured and by the insurer to each other of material facts affecting the actual or proposed insurance contract.[25] The duty applies to both parties, but it mostly affects the interest of the insured. It also extends to misstatements made in the course of filling out the insurance proposal form. It is a requirement of law that both the insured and the insurer must make adequate and truthful disclosure of matters regarding the insurance, and failure to do so may render the insurance policy unenforceable. Where the insured has failed to disclose a material fact in the proposal document or in other negotiations leading to the issuing of the policy, the insurer has the right to avoid the policy. 'Material' has been taken as follows:

> A fact is material if it would have reasonably affected the mind of a prudent insurer in determining whether he will accept the insurance, and if so, at what premium and on what conditions.[26]

The insured is under an obligation to complete the proposal form accurately. But that is only one aspect of the disclosure obligation on the insured.[27] Often the proposal form is made out to be the basis of the contract between the parties and there is a clause in it which makes the accuracy of the details provided and the truth of the answers a condition to the validity of the policy which is issued. The insured cannot contend that an insurance agent was the agent of the insured where he or she completed the policy proposal on behalf of the insured. Nor can it be claimed that the agent necessarily had authority to receive money from the insured on behalf of the insurer.[28]

---

23 *Turan Earthmovers Pty Ltd v Norwich Union Fire Insurance Society Ltd* [1976] 17 SASR 1.
24 *Ziel Nominees Pty Ltd v VACC Insurance Co Ltd* (1975) 7 ALR 667.
25 See *Banque Keyser Ullmann SA v Skandia (UK) Insurance Co Ltd* [1987] 2 WLR 1300; *Banque Financiere de la Cite SA v Westgate Insurance Co Ltd* [1990] 2 All ER 947; *Joel v Law Union & Crown Insurance Co* [1908] 2 KB 863.
26 *Mayne Nickless Ltd v Pegler* [1974] 1 NSWLR 228.
27 See generally *Khoury v GIO (NSW)* (1984) 54 ALR 639. The insured's duty also applies in respect of the issue by the insurer or its agents of cover notes.
28 See *Norwich Winterthur (Australia) Limited v Con-Stan Industries of Australia Pty Ltd* [1983] 1 NSWLR 461; *North & South Trust Co v Berkeley* [1971] 1 WLR 470; *Falcon Investments Corporation (NZ) v State Insurance General Manager* [1975] 1 NZLR 520.

Given the nature of the insurance transaction and the fact that the insurer needs to make a full assessment of the nature of the risk against which it is providing insurance, a principle evolved that an insurance contract was a contract *uberrimae fidei*, or a contract requiring the utmost good faith on the part of the insurer. According to this principle, the insured is required in the completion of the proposal form to make a full and complete disclosure of all material facts, being facts which would affect the ability of the insurer to determine the full nature of the risk against which it is providing indemnity. The duty is not merely a duty not to make misrepresentations. That of itself might ground an action for cancellation of the contract on general contract law principles even where the misrepresentations are innocent. The discourse duty arises independently of the Insurance Acts of other legislations dealing with insurance contracts.[29] It also arises independently of any express or implied terms or conditions in the policy document.[30] The position with respect to disclosure is something more because it is a positive duty. It was summarised by the Court of Appeal of Fiji in *Blueshield (Pacific) Insurance Ltd v Wati*[31] as follows:

> The duty of disclosure is distinct from the requirement not to misrepresent facts. It arises out of the fact that a contract of insurance is a contract *uberrimae fidei*. A person seeking to be insured must disclose to the intended insurer any facts within his or her knowledge that are material, that is to say which would affect the mind of a prudent insurer in deciding whether or not to provide cover (*Mayne Nickless Ltd v Pegler* [1974] 1 NSWLR 228). Facts are material if the person seeking the insurance knows that the intended insurer regards them as so, even though he or she might otherwise not regard them as material (*Glicksman v Lancashire and General Insurance Co Ltd* [1925] 2 KB 593). The manner in which a person seeking insurance generally finds out what the intended insurer regards as material is by reference to the questions that the intended insurer requires him to answer. Of course, some persons may have such knowledge by reason of their having worked in or in connection with the insurance industry.

The same principle extends to answers to questions put to an insured by an insurer at the time when a claim is made under the policy.[32] However, an insurer cannot

---

29 *March Cabaret Club & Casino Ltd v London Assurance* [1975] 1 Lloyd's Rep 169; *Dinh v Commercial Union Assurance Company of Australia* [1998] VUSC 35; Civil Case 032 of 1997 (10 August 1998).

30 *Dinh, ibid.*; although the Vanuatu Supreme Court in that case placed some reliance on the incorporation by reference in the policy in that case to some of the provisions of the Insurance Contracts Act 1974 (Cth) of Australia.

31 [1997] FJCA 25; Abu0048u.95s (14 August 1997).

32 *Mereki v Kiribati Insurance Corp* [1997] KICA 17; Civil Appeal 03 of 1996 (25 March 1997).

expect more than is reasonable. It is entitled to put questions to the proposer and to gain reasonable answers to those questions. If upon the fair construction of a question which an insurer requires to be answered the person seeking to be insured gives a truthful answer, the insurer cannot later contend that it wanted more information.[33]

13.1.5 Subrogation

The principle of subrogation is a right of recourse that exists in equity. It permits a person who has claims against one party to assume the rights of legal recourse which that party has against third parties or against property. A creditor of a trustee, for example, has rights of subrogation such that he or she can take over the rights of the trustee to claim an indemnity out of the trust assets or against the beneficiaries personally.

In the insurance context, this principle entitles the insurer who has met a claim under a policy to step into the shoes of the insured to take action in the name of the insured against third parties from whom the insured might have rights of indemnity. It also entitles an insurer who has paid out a property damage claim to assume ownership of what remains of the subject under insurance when the insured has been compensated for the loss.[34] This is sometimes called a salvage right. Where the insured has been indemnified for the loss, any salvaged items belong to the insurer, who is entitled to enter into possession and ownership or to dispose of the items as it deems fit in the circumstances.

In the Samoan case of *National Pacific Insurance Ltd v Taofinuu*,[35] the subrogation doctrine was explained as follows:

> Under the doctrine of subrogation, once the insurer has admitted its liability under the insurance policy and has paid the amount of the loss payable under the insurance policy to the assured, the insurer is placed in the position of the assured against third parties in respect of the subject matter of the insurance policy. In other words, the insurer is subrogated to the rights and remedies of the assured in respect of the subject matter of the insurance policy.

The principle is central to insurance business. As noted above, the principle also applies in double insurance situations where there is more than one indemnity insurer. Let us illustrate the application of the principle in a common enough situation of motor vehicle property damage insurance. Assume that an insured has

---

33 See *Condogianis v Guardian Assurance Company Limited* [1921] UKPCHCA 1; 29 CLR 341; [1921] 2 AC 125; 27 ALR 238; 25 Beav 444; [1875] 44 LJ Ch 683.
34 See *Lord Napier and Ettrick v. Hunter* [1993] 2 WLR 42; *Esso Petroleum Co Ltd v Hall Russell & Co Ltd* [1988] 2 WLR 730.
35 [1994] WSSC 13 (5 September 1994).

made a claim on a policy with his or her insurance company in respect of damage to the insured's vehicle in a road accident in which the insured's car was struck by another vehicle. Assume that the accident occurred because of the negligence of the other driver. In such a case, the insured can do one of two things. He or she can sue the driver or owner of the other vehicle for the recovery of the loss and damage which he or she has suffered as a result of the accident. Alternatively, he or she can claim on the insurance policy and obtain payment from the insurer, assuming the claim is within the terms of the policy. If the insured takes that course of action, the insurer claims subrogation to the legal rights of the insured against the other driver or owner to recover the amount it has paid out under the policy. The insurer can use the name of the insured in initiating legal proceedings.

13.2 Claims

As a general rule, an insured has to be compensated for the loss being claimed.[36] Much depends on the nature of the policy as to how the amount to which the insured is entitled is calculated. Some policies provide for reimbursement of actual loss, whilst in others the loss might be set at a predetermined value. It is the responsibility of the claimant to prove his or her case for entitlement to indemnity under the policy. The policy itself usually outlines the steps that have to be taken by the insured before any compensation is to be paid out by the insurer.[37]

In the event of accidents or where injury or death takes place, or where crime is suspected, the police have to be notified and a police report submitted to the insurer. Where it is alleged that a claim is fraudulent, the insurer has the onus of proving that fact. In *Jin Ying Company Ltd v Progressive Insurance Co Ltd*:[38]

> where a defendant, as insurer, alleges that a claim or part of a claim for stock by a plaintiff, as insurer, under an insurance policy is fraudulent, the onus is on the defendant who makes the allegation to prove fraud on a very high balance of probabilities. The plaintiff will not be permitted at common law to recover anything at all if his claim is proved to be fraudulent.[39]

Where the insurer alleges that it is entitled to deny liability under the policy, by reason, for example, of fraud on the part of the insured or because the loss

---

36 See *Queensland Insurance (Fiji) Ltd v Wong's Shipping Ltd* [1985] FJLawRp 20; [1985] 31 FLR 124 (8 November 1985).

37 See generally *Leyland Shipping Co. Ltd. v Norwich Union Fire Insurance Society Ltd* [1918] AC 350; *Munro, Brice & Co v War Risks Association Ltd* [1918] 2 KB 78.

38 [2002] WSSC 6 (22 March 2002).

39 Referring to *Britton v Royal Insurance Co* (1866) 4 F & F 905; 176 ER 843; *Orakpo v Barclays Insurance Services* [1995] LRLR 443; *Nsubuga v Commercial Union Assurance Co plc* [1998] 2 Lloyd's Rep 682; *Galloway v Guardian Royal Exchange (UK) Ltd* [1999] 4 Lloyd's Rep IR 209; see also *Sampson v Gold Star Insurance Co Ltd* [1980] 2 NZLR 742 (SC).

occurred as a result of the insured's deliberate act, the burden of proof likewise rests with the insurer as to those matters.

13.2.1 Assignment

An insurance policy can be assigned by an insured to another party. Usually, where there is relevant legislation, this requires that a note of assignment be endorsed on the policy document and the consent of the insurer. However, in the absence of legislation, the assignment is governed by the principles of common law and equity.

In respect of marine insurance policies, United Kingdom legislation applies as received law in the South Pacific countries. This is the Marine Insurance Act 1906. Section 50 of that Act provides:

(1) A marine insurance policy is assignable, unless it contains terms expressly prohibiting assignment. It may be assigned either before or after loss.
(2) Where a marine policy has been assigned so as to pass the beneficial interest in such policy, the assignee of the policy is entitled to sue thereon in his own name; and the defendant is entitled make any defence arising out of the contract which he would have been entitled to make if the action had been brought in the name of the person by or on behalf of whom the policy was effected.
(3) A marine policy may be assigned by indorsement thereon or in other customary manner.

In other cases, the policy may be assigned as a chose in action pursuant to provisions such as s 136 of the Property Law Act 1925 (UK), which has been re-enacted in some Pacific jurisdictions but would apply as received law in others.[40] This enables assignment of the whole of the policy. The section reads as follows:

(1) Any absolute assignment by writing under the hand of the assignor (not purporting to be by way of charge only) of any debt or other legal thing in action, of which express notice in writing has been given to the debtor, trustee or other person from whom the assignor would have been entitled to claim such debt or thing in action, is effectual in law (subject to equities having priority over the right of the assignee) to pass and transfer from the date of such notice: (a) the legal right to such debt or thing in action; (b) all legal and other remedies for the same; and (c) the power to give a good discharge for the same without the concurrence of the assignor.

---

40 See s 113 Property Law Act [Cap 130] 1978.

Finally, the policy could be assigned in equity by equitable rules relating to the assignment or property discussed in Chapter 2. A chose in action such as an interest under a policy is assignable if supported in equity where it is supported by consideration, even though it might amount to a future interest or an expectancy. Equity regards a clear manifestation of intention to assign only without requiring any particular form. The assignment is an alternative to assignment under s 136 of the Property Law Act (above). In *Raiffeisen Zentralbank Österreich AG v Five Star General Trading LLC*,[41] it was said:

> there may be an equitable assignment, which, once notified to the debtor, will have the effects of obliging the debtor to pay the assignee, of preventing further equities attaching to the debt and of protecting the assignee against subsequently notified assignments. An equitable assignment may relate either to the whole interest in a thing in action or to a partial interest: see *Chitty on Contracts* (28th edn) Vol 1, paras 20–037 to 20–040. *The Evelpidis Era* (cited below) is an example of the latter. There is a rule of practice that the assignor should be joined, but that rule will not be insisted upon where there is no need, in particular if there is no risk of a separate claim by the assignor: *Central Insurance Co Ltd v Seacalf Shipping Corp (The Aiolos)* [1983] 2 Lloyd's Rep 25, 33–34; *Weddell v JA Pearce & Major* [1988] Ch 26, 40–41; and a decision of my own in *Sim Swee Joo Shipping Sdn Bhd v Shirlstar Container Transport Ltd* (Com Ct, 17 February 1994).

In relation to life insurance policies, a special mechanism of assignment of the proceeds of the policy in the event of the death of the life insured is provided for by legislation. For example, s 83 of the Insurance Act Cap 217 of Fiji provides:

(1) The holder of a policy of ordinary life insurance may, when effecting the policy or at any time before the money secured thereby becomes payable, nominate a person or persons to whom it shall be paid in the event of his death: Provided that, where any nominee is a minor, it shall be lawful for the policy holder to appoint in the prescribed manner any person to receive the money in the event of his death during the minority of the nominee.

(2) A nomination under subsection (1) shall be incorporated into the text of the policy; or

(b) be made by an endorsement on the policy; in which case written notice thereof shall be communicated to the insurer who shall record it in the register maintained under section 49(1)(a).[42]

---

41 [2001] EWCA Civ 68; QB 825.

42 On the effect of such a provision, see *Colonial Mutual Life Assurance Society Ltd v Shandil* [1997] FJLawRp 32; [1997] 43 FLR 209 (27 August 1997).

PART D
Banking

Introduction

In this part, we will examine the legal principles and regulatory framework of banking in the South Pacific region. As a central feature in modern commerce and the economy, banks are commercial and financial institutions which, at one level, have characteristics common to other such institutions. We explore the nature of banks, the basis for their operation and provide a more comprehensive and focused discussion on the specific types of transactions, such as those relating to bills of exchange, cheques and other forms of documentary credit, which form a constituent part of modern banking transactions in the region.

DOI: 10.4324/9781003428060-17

14
BASIC PRINCIPLES OF BANKING

14.1 Definition of 'bank' and 'banking business'

The interpretation section of the Financial Institutions Act is also referred to as the definition section of the Act. It explains the meaning of the words and phrases used in the context of the statute. In the case of the Financial Institutions Act [Cap 254] 1999 of Vanuatu, the interpretation section is contained in s 2. According to that section, the term 'bank' means 'a financial institution whose banking business includes the acceptance of deposits of money that are withdrawable or transferable by cheque'. This is similar to the definitions found in s 2 of the Banking Act 1995, Fiji and Financial Institutions Act 1998, Solomon Islands.[1]

The definition section also provides the meaning of the phrase 'banking business'. According to the interpretation section of the Financial Institutions Act 1998 of the Solomon Islands, for instance, banking business means:

(a) the business of accepting deposits of money from the public or members thereof, withdrawable or payable upon demand or after a fixed period or after notice, or any similar operation through the frequent sales or placement of bonds, certificates, notes or other securities, and the use of such funds, either in whole or in part, for loans or investments for the account and at the risk of the person doing such business; and

---

1 Cf s 2 Financial Institutions Act 1996 (S), which provides: '"bank" bears the meaning given to it by the Central Bank of Samoa Act 1984'. See also s 2(1) Banking Act 1975 (N) which provides: '"bank" means a commercial and trading bank or a savings bank'. See also Title 17 Banks and Financial Institutions Act 1987 (MI).

DOI: 10.4324/9781003428060-18

(b) any other activity recognised by the Central Bank as customary banking practice which a licensed financial institution engaging in the activities described
   in paragraph (a), may additionally be authorised to do so by the Central Bank
   or any related activity which the Central Bank may consider appropriate

This definition is slightly different from that which is found in the interpretation section of the Banking Act 1975, Nauru.[2] These definitions are important
to the extent that they are likely to aid the courts in clearly ascertaining the relevant meanings of the words and phrases used in the statutes. In Vanuatu, Fiji,
the Solomon Islands and Samoa, the words 'bank' or 'banking business' are to be
construed with reference and limitations to the legislation. This has the advantage
of achieving uniformity in judicial interpretation, but it may have the converse
effect of restricting the interpretation of the phrases, especially if the courts are
not judicially proactive.[3]

As we have seen in all these definitions, a bank is defined as either a financial
institution or a company. Before commencing banking business, a bank needs to
be incorporated as a company. In this regard, it should therefore comply with the
provisions of the appropriate companies law in that country.[4] Only after being
incorporated as a company will it be granted a banking licence by the reserve or
central bank, as the case may be.

14.2 Banking limitations

All the relevant banking legislation imposes some form of limitation on the types
of institution that can carry on banking business. There are specific provisions in
the laws prohibiting banks from engaging in activities that fall outside their mandate.[5] Banking legislation across the South Pacific region has specific provisions
restricting banks from engaging in certain activities. The essence of these restrictive provisions is to ensure that only licensed financial institutions are allowed to
operate as banks. In this respect, the law appears mindful of the need to protect
depositors as well as to ensure that there is proper regulation of any company
willing to undertake a risky investment such as banking business. The legislation generally prohibits a company from carrying on banking business unless it

---

2 See s 2: "'banking business' means the business of accepting deposits of money withdrawable or
   repayable on demand or after a fixed period or after notice and the employment of those deposits in
   whole or in part by lending or any other means for the account and at the risk of the person accepting such deposits".
3 In contrast, the Banking Act 1975 (N) in s 2 contains elaborate definitions not only of a 'bank' or
   'banking business' but goes further to define the terms 'commercial and trading bank', 'financial
   institution' and 'savings bank'.
4 See ss 20–22 Companies Act 2015 (F).
5 See s 6 Financial Institutions Act [cap 254] 1999 (V); s 3 Financial Institutions Act 1998 of (SI); s
   4 Banking Act 1975 (N); s 4 Financial Institutions Act 1996 (S).

is a licensed financial institution and no person other than a bank can use the title 'bank'.[6]

The focus of these restrictions centres on the fact that no banking business shall be executed except through the instrumentality of a company which is in turn a licensed financial institution. A financial institution is generally defined to mean a company authorised by law to conduct banking business.[7] This restriction is aimed at excluding all other classes of companies from engaging in banking business, except those which possess the requisite banking licence.

It is a contravention of the relevant legislation for any person to engage in banking business without being in possession of a valid banking licence. There are both criminal and civil sanctions for violating the Act.[8] Except with the permission of the Minister responsible for finance, no person other than a licensed bank is entitled to use the designation bank or any derivatives associated with the generic word 'bank'.[9] However, there are exceptions allowed in this instance. The exemptions include an association of banks or their employees, formed for the protection of their industrial or trade union interests; a body formed outside Fiji which has added to its name the word 'bank'; and any subsidiary of a licensed financial institution that is authorised by the reserve bank to use the title 'bank' or any of its derivatives.[10] Any violations may lead to criminal penalties and sanctions.[11]

14.3 Capital requirements

Every bank which is to operate as a financial institution has a duty, just as with other companies, to establish a minimum amount of capitalisation before it can

---

6 Cf ss 4, 9 Banking Act (N); s 103 Banking Act (MI); s 4 Banking Act 2011 (CI); s 3 Financial Institutions Act 1998 (SI); s 18 Financial Institutions Act 1996 (S); s 6 Financial Institutions Act [Cap 254] 1999 (V).

7 Cf ss 2(1), 4 Niue Bank Act 1994; the position in Nauru requires further examination. This is because s 4 Banking Act (N) permits the establishment of entities other than companies to engage in banking business. The significance of this is that it empowers the relevant government department to engage in banking activities, if and only if a licence is obtained on that department's behalf by the Minister.

8 Other restrictions are found in ss 4, 5 Banking Act 1995 (F); generally, see ss 4, 50, 54, although no equivalent provision deals with this in the Banking Act 2011 (CI); generally, see ss 116, 117 Banking Act 1987 (MI).

9 See ss 6, 7 Financial Institutions Act [Cap 254] 1999 (V); s 24 Financial Institutions Act 1998 (SI); s 9(1)(a) Banking Act 1975 (N); s 19 Financial Institutions Act 1996 (S).

10 See ss 12, 30, although no equivalent provision in the Banking Act 1995 (F). Cf s 9 Banking Act 1975 (N), which stretches the definition of the term 'bank' under the Nauru Banking Act to include a 'savings bank'. It is therefore only logical to restrict the use of the term except in instances authorised by law. Cf ss 103, 107 Banking Act 1987 (FSM); ss 35, 60 Banking Act 2011 (CI).

11 Cf Niue Banking Act 1994 (Ni), which is silent on the applicable penalties where s 3 Act is contravened.

carry on banking business.[12] The solvency or financial buoyancy of a banking institution is crucial to instil public confidence in the capacity of a bank to meet its short- and long-term financial commitments. This is important not only in relation to its routine transactions but also in relation to its future expansion. The requirement of law that a bank has to first be incorporated as a company before it can venture into banking business is an attempt to ensure that strict monetary controls are maintained in relation to banking investments. A company can easily be supervised by the companies registry through the vetting of its annual returns. This information is available and may be accessed by the reserve or central bank because annual returns filed by public companies are documents whose contents are in the public domain.

The various banking laws of the region do not define the term 'capital' in this context. For our purposes, it may be defined as: 'the funds a company has for use in the business, representing its assets'. A company is seized of different types of capital which may be classified as the following: 'authorised'; 'issued'; 'called up'; and 'reserved' capital.[13]

Closely related to the issue of capitalisation is the requirement for the maintenance of minimum capital for a bank. By way of example, s 6(1) of the Banking Act 1995 of Fiji provides:

> Every financial institution licensed under this Act shall maintain–
>> if incorporated in Fiji, paid up capital and unimpaired reserves; and
>> if incorporated outside Fiji, assigned capital and unimpaired reserves in Fiji;

in such minimum proportion in relation to its assets, liabilities or risk exposures as the Reserve Bank may specify from time to time.

There are equivalent provisions in s 8 of the Financial Institutions Act 1996 of Samoa; s 7 of the Financial Institutions Act 1998 of the Solomon Islands; s 31 of the Financial Institutions Act 1999 of Vanuatu; and s 120 of the Banking Act 1987 of the Marshall Islands. The Banking Act 1975 of Nauru is silent on this issue.

It is apparent from the wording of s 6 in Fiji and similar provisions in Samoa, the Solomon Islands and Vanuatu that these sections attempt to distinguish between the minimum capitalisation requirements for a bank incorporated locally and that incorporated overseas. The provisions of the law are, however, not clear on whether 'assigned capital' is different from 'paid-up capital'. The question is: should the assigned capital of a bank incorporated overseas be considered as 'paid up' for the purpose of the laws in the countries?

---

12 See s 6 Banking Act 1995 (F); s 31 Financial Institutions Act [cap 254] 1999 (V); s 8 Financial Institutions Act 1996 (S).
13 See ICSA, *Company Law, 1993*, London, BPP Publishing, p 109.

In relation to all the provisions in the different countries dealing with this issue, the reserve or central bank is empowered to determine the minimum amount of paid-up capital or assigned capital and unimpaired reserves which are to be maintained by a licensed financial institution locally. In any case, the minimum amount of paid-up capital allowed for a licensed bank is $2 million in Fiji; 'not less than' $2 million in Samoa; and 200 million vatu in Vanuatu.

By stipulating a minimum cut-off point for capitalisation, two objectives are likely to be met. First, no company will contemplate venturing into banking business unless it is prepared to commit, in terms of resources, a minimum of the specified amount. It means that only well-intentioned business concerns may consider engaging in banking business. Secondly, the capitalisation level may be increased to match the level of inflation without the need for the reserve or central bank to seek any legislative amendment to the provision. This is because no upper limit of capitalisation is stipulated by the Act.

14.4 Issuance of banking licence

Any entity wishing to carry on banking business must first be an incorporated company. Once incorporated, it must also apply for and be granted a banking licence by the reserve or central bank before it can carry on banking business.[14] In making the application for the licence, the proposed bank must first of all satisfy the conditions attached to the grant of the licence.[15] These procedural requirements enable the reserve or central bank to determine the suitability or otherwise of the applicant company to carry on banking business.

For instance, in the case of Fiji, an application for a banking licence is made to the reserve bank. As a rule, an application is only made by a company which is duly incorporated in Fiji. By s 8(1) of the Act, no body other than a registered company is entitled to apply for a banking licence.[16] By s 8(2) of the Banking Act 1995 of the Fiji Islands, an application for a banking licence is made in writing by a company and addressed to the reserve bank. The reserve bank is empowered to determine where it deems necessary the format of the application.[17] The

---

14 See s 7(1)–(3) Financial Institutions Act [Cap 254] 1999 (V); s 3(1)–(7) Financial Institutions Act 1998 (SI).

15 See s 11 Financial Institutions Act 1999 (V); s 5 Financial Institutions Act 1998(SI); s 5 Banking Act 1995 (N); s 6 Financial Institutions Act 1996 (S); s 108 Banking Act (FSM).

16 Section 2 Banking Act 1995 (F) defines a company to mean (a) a body corporate established under any written law relating to the formation and registration of companies; (b) a statutory corporation; or (c) a body corporate which is established whether under a law relating to the formation and registration of companies or by any other method of incorporation outside Fiji. See also s 2 'corporation' in Banking Act 1987 (MI); s 2 Banking Act 2011 (CI).

17 Cf Niue, where the application is made to Cabinet; see s generally, ss 6, 17 Banking Act 1994 (Ni); s 5 Financial Institutions Act 1998 (SI); ss 10–16 Financial Institutions Act [Cap 254] 1999 (V); s 6 Banking Act 1975 (N); s 6 Financial Institutions Act 1996 (S).

requirements for the application of a banking licence by a locally registered company are different from those to be satisfied by a foreign incorporated company.[18] This is also the case in Vanuatu,[19] but there are no equivalent provisions on this point in Nauru, Samoa or the Solomon Islands.

The law permits the reserve or central bank, as the case may be, to investigate an applicant company before the licence is approved.[20] The reserve or central bank may only approve a banking licence where it is satisfied that it is in the public interest to do so. The reserve or central bank is equally empowered to monitor compliance with existing laws and regulations; certify that the applicant company possesses the minimum capitalisation required under the law; and be satisfied of the competence and integrity of the promoters or shareholders of the applicant company to be able to effectively administer a bank. This degree of regulatory control is necessary to ensure that a lesser number of banks are put in financial distress or receivership after having been issued with banking licences. This also incorporates minimum guidelines of the right to a fair hearing in favour of applicant banks, in the event that an application for a banking licence is rejected.[21]

A valid banking licence granted by the reserve bank is to be set out in writing. Conditions for issue may also be spelt out in the licence.[22] Where a financial institution incorporated overseas wishes to do business locally, an additional condition may be stated requiring that, before the commencement of business, the institution files a written nomination of a local agent for the service of notices.[23]

The banking laws of the different countries in the region set out a number of conditions for granting banking licences to potential applicant companies. The reserve or central bank may by notification in writing directed to a licensed financial institution impose new or additional conditions relating to a licence already granted. The reserve or central bank also has the power to remove or vary conditions already imposed on a licensee.[24] This power is necessary in view of the dynamic nature of the banking industry.

The banking system operates within the larger sector of the economic system. Economic upturns or downturns may have fundamental effects on the financial

---

18 For a company incorporated outside Fiji, ten documents are to be submitted. For a company incorporated in Fiji, eight documents are required to be filed by the reserve bank; see ss 8(2), 20, 24 Banking Act 1995 (F); ss 13, 14 Financial Institutions Act [cap 254] 1999 (V); s 5 Financial Institutions Act 1998 (SI); s 6 Financial Institutions Act 1996 (S); ss 5, 12 Banking Act 1975 (N).

19 See ss 13,14 Financial Institutions Act [Cap 254] 1999 (V).

20 See s 9 Banking Act 1995 (F); cf s 12 Banking Act 1975 (N); ss 11(4), 15 Financial Institutions Act [Cap 254] 1999 (V).

21 See s 9(2), (3), (4) Banking Act 1995 (F); s 6 Financial Institutions Act 1998 (SI); ss 10–16 Financial Institutions Act [Cap 254] 1999 (V); s 7 Financial Institutions Act 1996 (S).

22 See s 10(1) Banking Act 1995 (F); s 107 Banking Act 1987 (MI); s 7 Banking Act 2011 (CI).

23 See s 10(2) Banking Act 1995 (F).

24 Section 11 Banking Act 1995 (F); ss 13, 14, 15(3) Financial Institutions Act [cap 254] 1999 (V); s 12 Banking Act 1975 (N); cf s 12 Banking Act 2011 (CI).

and banking sector. Sometimes this may require some changes in banking policies. In the event that this change is to be reflected in the conditions of the banking licence, the reserve bank can easily do so by relying on these powers. There will be no need for any tedious process of legislative amendment where the minimum paid-up capital is to be raised by the reserve bank.

The laws implore all banking institutions holding valid banking licences to conspicuously display them in public areas of all places of their business. Criminal sanctions may be enforced against every director or manager of a licensed financial institution for not displaying the licence. A fine is normally imposed on a violator by the reserve bank.[25]

After the grant of a banking licence, the reserve bank is invested with the power to suspend or revoke the licence so granted. In most of the countries in the region, the grounds for suspension or revocation are normally spelt out in the empowering provision.[26] Apart from instances where evidence of the financial and managerial failure of a bank is required in order to justify suspension or revocation of licence, discretion is generally conferred on the reserve or central bank to determine when to suspend or revoke a banking licence, provided the normal procedural safeguards of hearing fairing are observed. Note, however, that except in the case of Fiji, where suspension as distinct from revocation of the licence is possible, in the cases of the Solomon Islands, Samoa and Nauru no such power to suspend the licence exists. The only power granted to the reserve or central bank is to revoke the licence.

In either case, the effect of a suspension or revocation of a banking licence is to effectively prevent a licensed financial institution from carrying on any banking business by itself or through intermediaries until the suspension or revocation is rescinded. This is very clearly stated in the case of Vanuatu. By way of example, s 18 of the Financial Institutions Act [Cap 254] 1999 provides: 'A financial institution whose licence is revoked under s 17 or 46 must cease to carry on all banking business on and from the date on which the revocation takes effect'.

The immediate effect of either a suspension or revocation is the same, namely, to stop the financial institution from operating as a bank. In the case of Fiji, it is still not clear whether under the Banking Act the suspension of a banking licence can be converted into revocation or vice versa. This question is necessary when we look at s 21(2) of the Banking Act of Fiji. Here, the law contemplates equating the consequences of revocation with those of a suspension. In legal terms, the effect of a suspension is different from that of a revocation.

25 Section 13 (F) – not exceeding $1,000; and s 17 Banking Act 1987 (MI).
26 See s 21 Banking Act 1995 (F); s 6 Financial Institutions Act 1998 (SI); s 21 Banking Act 1975 (N); s 7 Financial Institutions Act 1996 (S); s 113 Banking Act 1987 (MI); s 14 Banking Act 2011 (CI).

The power to rescind a suspension or revocation is vested in the High or Supreme Court as the case may be. Where an application for review or rescission is made to the court, the reserve or central bank is entitled to be heard.[27] The effect of rescinding a suspension or revocation is to restore the licensed financial institution to its *status quo ante*. And without the need for any further formalities, it can recommence banking business. The reserve or central bank is, however, at liberty to impose further conditions as it deems fit before the bank may recommence business.[28]

The various banking laws in the region do enshrine the right to a fair hearing in the process of suspension or revocation of a banking licence. In these countries, the power of the central or reserve bank to suspend or revoke banking licences is reviewable by the court, except in the case of Samoa and the Solomon Islands, where the laws are silent. The final authority to confirm the suspension or revocation of a licence therefore rests with the court and not the reserve or central bank of the country.[29]

14.5 Maximum shareholding or equity ownership

There are provisions in the Banking Act 1995 of Fiji, the Financial Institutions Act 1996 of Samoa, s 621 of the Banking Code 1982 of the Federated States of Micronesia, s 44 of the Banks and Financial Institutions Act 1987 of the Marshall Islands and the Financial Institutions Act 1998 of the Solomon Islands dealing with equity shareholding and ownership of shares in banks. No such provisions are found in the Banking Act 1975 of Nauru. By way of example, in the case of Fiji, equity ownership is covered in s 7. It states:

(1) An individual together with his relatives within the second degree of consanguinity or affinity shall be allowed to own or control the exercise of up to 15% of the voting shares of licensed financial institution:
Provided that–
   (i) if. the ownership is through a company, the company may own or control the exercise of up to 30% of the voting shares of the licensed financial institution; and
   (ii) that the individual together with his relatives within the said degree and one or more companies which he or his relatives within the same degree

---

27 See s 21(4) Banking Act 1995 (F).
28 *Ibid.*, s 21(5).
29 Similar provisions are found in s 21 Banking Act 1975 (N). A significant feature of the position in Nauru is that under sub-s (3) of the same section, a bank is entitled to continue operations for three months after the revocation of its banking licence. See s 21(6) and (7) Banking Act 1995 (F); s 20 Financial Institutions Act [Cap 254] 1999 (V); s 21(3) Banking Act 1975 (N); cf s 7 Financial Institutions Act 1996 (S); s 6 Financial Institutions Act 1998 (SI).

control, shall not in the aggregate own or control the exercise of more than 30% of the voting shares of a licensed financial institution incorporated in Fiji which may be increased to 50% subject to the approval of the Minister.

(2) Subsection (1) of this section shall not preclude the establishment in Fiji of branches or subsidiaries incorporated in Fiji of 100% non-resident controlled financial institutions.

There are two primary reasons why it is necessary to put a cap on the distribution pattern of equity holding in banks. By specifying the maximum equity holding individuals are permitted to hold in banks, a potential investor will be able to determine where the locus of control in the bank lies, should he or she wish to invest in the shares or stocks of the bank. This may affect any investment decision. Secondly, as domestic banks are becoming more and more integrated into the global financial system, the reserve or central Bank may want to be in a position to accurately ascertain the scheme or distribution of the share ownership in a bank. This will give it an accurate projection of the foreign currency status of the nation, especially in relation to the inflow or outflow of investments conducted through the bank.

By way of comparison, s 35 of the Financial Institutions Act [Cap 254] 1999 of Vanuatu is similar to s 7 of the Banking Act 1995 of Fiji and s 144 of the Banks and Financial Institutions Act 1987 of the Marshall Islands. However, sub-s 35 (1) conveys a different structural meaning when compared to sub-s (1) of Fiji. For clarity, it is reproduced here:

A licensee must not for its own account acquire or hold share capital in a financial, commercial, agricultural, industrial or other undertaking if to do so would result in the combined value of that share capital exceeding 25 percent, or such higher percentage as the Reserve Bank approves in writing, of the value of the licensee's eligible capital.

We shall return to the implications of differences soon. Section 18 of the Financial Institutions Act 1996 of Samoa and s 23 of the Financial Institutions Act 1998 of the Solomon Islands deal with the issue but also in a slightly different way. However, the overall import is akin to what obtains in s 7 of Fiji. Sub-section (3) of s 18 in Samoa which is *in pari materia* to that of the Solomon Islands provides:

For the purpose of this Section, 'transfer of control' refers to any event specified in Subsection (2) that results in a person acquiring ownership or exercising power over twenty percent (20%) or more of the voting stock of a licensed financial institution.

In examining s 35(1) of the Financial Institutions Act [Cap 254] 1999 of Vanuatu, it is clear that the word 'licensee' used in the section should have read 'individual' or 'person'. The import of the section, as is the case with s 7(1) of Fiji, is to prevent individuals or family members from holding more than the percentage of shareholding allowed by the law. A licensee in this case means the bank because only a registered corporate entity like a company is entitled to a banking licence. If the intention is to prevent only companies who are holders of banking licences from holding more than the desired number of shares in banks, then the provision is meaningless because it can be circumvented by individuals and their family members. The better formulation is what s 7(1) of the Banking Act 1995 of Fiji says. The effectiveness of the position in s 35(1) of the Financial Institutions Act 1996 of Samoa is open to question. It only applies in cases of transfer of ownership of shares and does not deal with first-time shareholders.

Generally speaking, the effect of the provision even in the case of Fiji is to merely prohibit individuals from acquiring a certain percentage of voting shares in a bank. Thus, the section has not taken into account the problems of interlocking ownership control of businesses which can be used as a means of circumventing the above provision. Section 7 of the Banking Act of Fiji, s 18 of the Financial Institutions Act of Samoa and s 34 of the Financial Institutions Act of Vanuatu do not appear to anticipate the possibility of acquiring equity ownership and control of a bank by means of investing through affiliated or group companies. This device is equally capable of negating the restriction imposed by sections.

In view of this, it is necessary to suggest that amendments to the laws should be considered, especially when dealing with the control of equity ownership through the use of affiliates and interlocking shareholding. Though in the case of Fiji, s 7(2) of the Banking Act prevents the establishment of 100% 'non-resident controlled financial institutions', including foreign-controlled banks, this is far from being satisfactory. The relationship between equity and control of investment is not usually measured in percentages. Through the use of weighted shares, even minority shareholders can control the affairs of a company.[30] This may amount to a circumvention of the restriction on equity ownership imposed by the laws in the different countries.

14.6 Payment of dividends

Before we examine the requirements regulating the payment of dividends, we shall begin by looking at what dividends mean. None of the banking laws in the region has defined the term 'dividends'. What the laws have done is to provide ways by which dividends are distributed to shareholders of the bank.

30 See the views of Biersteker, TJ, 'Transnational corporations and the neutralisation of legislation', in Ghai, Y *et al.* (eds), *The Political Economy of Law*, 1987, Delhi, OUP, pp 465–73.

What, therefore, is dividend? A working definition may refer to dividend as the portion of the profits generated by a company and distributed to shareholders at the end of a trading period. Dividend given to shareholders is the return on their investing in the shares of the company. The procedure for the distribution of dividends is contained in the articles of the company. As a general rule, it is the responsibility of the bank's board of directors to declare either interim or final dividends before eventual distribution to the bank's shareholders.

In respect of all the laws, licensed financial institutions are prohibited from declaring or paying any dividend or making any transfers or remittances from their gross profits which will adversely affect the bank's paid-up capital. This is to protect the paid-up capital of the bank. The provisions also prohibit licensed financial institutions that are incorporated overseas from paying dividends on their shares and from remitting funds overseas until all capitalised and other expenses have been deducted from the gross profits. The restrictions are directed at ensuring that no bogus dividends are declared without first having deducted expenses reasonably incurred by the company. This also helps to ensure a true and fair assessment of a bank's profitability during the last trading year.

Dividends are only to be declared when all capitalised expenditures have been deducted from the gross profits generated in the last financial year. This includes preliminary expenses, organisation expenses, share selling commission, brokerage and amount of losses incurred (not represented by tangible assets) that have been completely written off.[31]

More importantly, it is to be observed that certain phrases used in connection with the payment of dividends have not been defined by the Acts of either Fiji or Vanuatu. This means that phrases such as 'preliminary expenses' and 'organisation expenses' may likely be subject to conflicting interpretations by the courts. They might, for example, imply the use of accounting techniques. This difficulty would be obviated if the interpretation section defined the word 'dividend'.

Section 23 of the Banking Act 1995 of Fiji; s 32 of the Financial Institutions Act [Cap 254] 1999 of Vanuatu; s 620 of the Federated States of Micronesia Bank Act of 1980; and s 147 of the Banking Act 1987 of the Marshall Islands are aimed at controlling the quality of dividends declared out of the profits of a bank. This reduces the risks of falsifying expenditure in the bank's balance sheet as a way of misleading either the shareholders or the public. There seem to be no direct equivalent provisions in the Financial Institutions Act 1996 of Samoa or the Banking Act 1975 of Nauru.

---

31 See s 23 Banking Act 1995 (F); s 32 Financial Institutions Act [Cap 254] 1999 (V).

14.6.1 Reorganisation

By 'reorganisation' we mean restructuring the corporate foundation of a company, in this case a bank. Reorganisation of banks or companies is generally achieved by amalgamation, merger or reconstruction. This is a process whereby different companies are integrated or constituted into a new entity. It may assume a vertical or horizontal dimension. Horizontal reorganisation involves companies in the same line of products or services, whilst vertical reorganisation is between companies in different lines of products or services.

A number of factors are responsible for the reorganisation of businesses. Notable amongst these are the following: declining profitability; inefficiency and the avoidance of waste; the need for corporate expansion into new lines of product or for controlling and utilising existing marketing; and the creation of retailing outlets of established products. The basic objective of corporate reorganisation is to achieve economies of scale.

Corporate reorganisation is a basic feature of company law.[32] This is, however, integrated into the Banking Acts of some jurisdictions in the South Pacific region.[33] By way of example, in Fiji, it is found in s 22 of the Banking Act. In any corporate reorganisation process, the approval of the reserve bank must be sought and obtained. This approval validates any scheme of arrangement or corporate reorganisation in which a bank may wish to engage. There are important procedural requirements to be complied with before any corporate reorganisation process is validated. These include the provision of full particulars of any alterations made to the memorandum or articles of association of a licensed financial institution, which should then be forwarded to the reserve bank, followed by verification of these alterations by a statutory declaration made by a director of the licensed financial institution.[34] The notification of alteration is necessary because it is possible for the corporate structure of a company to be altered only by means of an amendment to some provisions of the articles of association.

Generally speaking, licensed financial institutions and their subsidiaries, whether incorporated locally or overseas, are prevented from making arrangements or entering into agreements to sell or dispose of their business by amalgamation or otherwise reconstruct their capital or make any arrangement or enter into an agreement for the purchase or acquisition of the business of any financial institution.[35]

---

32 See ss 437–40 Companies Act 2015 (F); see also Davies, P; Worthington, S; Hare, C, *Gower: Principles of Modern Company Law 10th Edition*, 2016, London, Sweet & Maxwell, Chapter 29.

33 See s 22 Banking Act 1995 (F); s 149 Banking Act 1987 (MI); s 17 Financial Institutions Act 1996 (S).

34 See s 17 Financial Institutions Act 1996 (S); cf s 19 Banking Act 1987 (MI).

35 See s 22(1), (2) Banking Act 1995 (F).

These restrictions are aimed at safeguarding the financial and other assets of the bank. They are likely to protect investors or depositors who may be adversely affected by the reorganisation. This is because reorganisation is a process which usually alters the legal rights of shareholders or other creditors of the company. The process may result in either a diminution or increment in the asset holding of the company or the proportion of investors' equity or other participation in the company.

To enhance its control over corporate reorganisation processes affecting banks, the reserve or central bank has the power to intervene if it appears to it that a particular process of reorganisation is detrimental to depositors.[36] The reserve or central bank is also empowered to take appropriate steps to minimise the effects of the corporate transformation process on the depositors or creditors of a licensed financial institution so as to assist in improving the viability of the nation's financial system.

Where corporate reorganisation of banking enterprises is not properly monitored by the reserve or central bank, it is possible that the country's economy will be affected. For any business, the continuous preservation of its corporate and financial identity is a vital element in its success. If this is changed without proper notice, the confidence of the investing public may be shattered and sometimes beyond redemption. This uncertainty therefore justifies the need for specific provisions on corporate reorganisation in the various banking laws in the region.

The banking laws across the region also obligate transnational enterprises to inform the Reserve or Central Bank regarding matters affecting their corporate reorganisation. This is aimed at preventing their parent companies from changing their corporate structures through the use of their subsidiaries located overseas. Should this happen, the reserve or central bank would find it difficult to determine the true corporate structure of the affiliated company domiciled locally. This is more of a concern in countries like Samoa, Vanuatu, the Cook Islands and to some extent Nauru because of their offshore finance status.

14.7 Relaxation of banking rules

In spite of the rigidity of the various banking laws in the region, as we have already noted, some have still made provisions allowing for the relaxation of the rules in their practical application to different circumstances. By way of example, s 79 of the Banking Act 1995 of Fiji empowers the Minister of Finance, acting on the recommendation of the reserve bank, to relax the operation of the Act in respect of any financial institution where in doing so the object of the Act will be attained. For the relaxation to be effective, it must be published in the *Gazette*. The order must specify the extent and duration of the relaxation and any of its

---

36 See *ibid.*, s 22(3).

conditions. There are no equivalent provisions found in the Banking Act 1975 of Nauru, Financial Institutions Act 1996 of Samoa, Financial Institutions Act [Cap 254] 1999 of Vanuatu or Financial Institutions Act 1998 of the Solomon Islands.

In the case of Fiji, therefore, we may note the following points. The discretion to order relaxation is only vested in the Minister, who in turn cannot exercise this discretion without the recommendation of the reserve bank. Where there is no recommendation, the Minister cannot invoke the provision of s 79 of the Act. This means that the Minister's discretion is not absolute. Furthermore, the provision permits the Reserve Bank of Fiji to adapt its operations to the exigencies of the prevailing economic situation in the country. The financial and banking environment is dynamic and sometimes fluid in nature. The banking laws should be flexible enough to accommodate changing circumstances in order to foster economic growth and prosperity. This seems to be a discernable objective of s 79. But this flexibility should not be achieved at the expense of prudential supervisory standards of the banking institution.

14.7.1 The legal relationship between a customer and banker[37]

In order to understand the scope of the relationship between a client and a bank, it is imperative first to examine the legal attributes of who is a 'customer' as well as who is a 'banker'. As a matter of general legal practice, a natural or artificial being (who is a legal person in law) can be a customer to a bank. An artificial person is usually a body corporate recognised as such through legal fiction. This includes incorporated bodies such as companies and other legally registered entities such as partnerships and cooperatives.

14.7.2 Who is a customer?

There is as yet no statutory definition of the term 'customer' in the banking laws of the region.[38] In this respect, we can therefore have recourse to the traditional legal definition offered in other jurisdictions. Through judicial pronouncement, a customer is generally defined as 'a person who has some sort of account either current or deposit with a bank'.[39]

Therefore, to be legally considered a customer to a bank, a person must exhibit some recognisable course of dealing in the nature of banking business with the bank. This assertion is broad to encompass a person conducting a temporary

---

37 This segment is based on a revised chapter in Mohammed L. Ahmadu *The Law of Banking in Fiji* (1998) Avon Books, London.
38 See s 75 Bills of Exchange Act [cap 227] 1978 (F).
39 See the definition by Lord Dave in the old English case of *Great Western Railway v London and County Banking Co Ltd* [1901] AC 414; see also *United Dominions Trust Ltd v Kirkwood* [1966] 2 QB 431; *Wong Kam Chung v Republic* [2001] KICA 17; Criminal Appeal 01 of 2001 (5 April 2001).

transaction with a bank. But what cannot readily be established is whether this is also flexible enough to accommodate off-the-record and over-the-counter spot transactions such as foreign currency exchange.

14.7.3 Who is a banker?

There are statutory definitions of the word 'bank'. It should be noted that the words 'bank' and 'banker', for the purpose of discussion under this heading, are used interchangeably. A definition of one would suffice for the other. The Banking Act defines the word 'bank' as 'any financial institution whose operations include the acceptance of deposits of money withdrawable or transferable by cheque or other means of payment transfer'.[40] The Bills of Exchange Act,[41] in s 2, defines the word 'banker' as encompassing 'a body of persons whether incorporated or not, who carry on the business of banking'. In view of the supremacy of the provisions of the Banking Act over the Bills of Exchange Act, it is doubtful whether this definition will now stand, especially in view of the fact that all banking institutions are required to be incorporated companies.[42]

14.7.4 Operating accounts

The intention here is not to accord any detailed treatment to accounts,[43] but rather to discuss the possible means by which accounts could be operated. Thus, in discussing the relationship between a customer and a banker, it is equally important to state, even if briefly, that it is possible for a person to open and operate a deposit (savings) or current (cheque) account. The account can be denominated in either local or foreign currency. Alongside the introduction of electronic banking, we have seen an increase in the number of services now marketed by banks through these accounts. By operating a current account, a customer may now be entitled to use a variety of credit cards for transactions through the bank.

Though not generally part of the banking laws in the South Pacific region, it is still possible to operate bank accounts through the instrumentality of intermediaries or authorised agents. The two most common means of operating accounts by intermediaries are delegated authority and power of attorney.

---

40 See s 2(1) Banking Act 1995 (F).
41 Contained in the Laws of Fiji 1978.
42 See the definition of 'financial institution' under s 2(1) Banking Act 1995 (F).
43 For a detailed treatment of the area, refer to Chapters 12, 15, 16 and 17 of Penn, GA *et al.*, *The Law Relating to Domestic Banking*, 2000, 2nd edn, London, Sweet & Maxwell.

14.7.5 Delegated authority

The practice of using delegated authority to operate an account by one on behalf of another has no statutory backing in the countries of the region. As a general common law practice, it can however not be discounted because of the pervasive application of English in all the countries in the region. As this practice becomes widely used in the near future, it is expected that future enactments may also come up with limitations to the exercise of the authority. This is simply to protect customers of the bank.

Delegation as a legal principle implies that powers are committed to a person or body which as a rule is always subject to resumption by the delegating authority.[44] The process of delegation therefore allows a person (transferor) to transfer an authority to another person (transferee) in order to enable the transferee to function in place of the transferor. This transfer of power can be used as a means of operating a bank account. But before there is considered in law to be a proper exercise of delegated authority, the delegation has to be evidenced in writing. It is also important that a bank should obtain the precise details of the delegated power from the customer before acting on a delegated mandate. This is necessary in minimising future controversies as to whether or not the delegate acted without or in excess of authority.

14.7.6 Power of attorney

A power of attorney is by law a written authority. It is made out in the form of a deed which is signed, sealed and delivered by the parties to it. The purpose of the document is to empower a donee to act on behalf of a donor of the authority. A power of attorney as a matter of practice can be impregnated with as many powers as the donor desires. It is common practice to first spell out specific powers. These are then followed by an omnibus clause containing incidental or general powers which may also be exercised by a donee in furtherance of the specific powers. The authority to operate or service a bank account can also be stipulated as one of the powers to be exercised by a donee. The power of attorney is generally considered to be a contractual document.

It is a cardinal requirement of law that where a transaction is constituted by deed, a person appointed to execute the terms of the deed must also be appointed by deed. In this case, where a donee executes instructions relating to land matters, it is imperative that for the actions to be validated, the donee must also be appointed by deed. This generally underscores the importance of power of attorney. Closely related to the foregoing is the rule that a person who has the capacity to contract can therefore engage in transactions by means of an attorney.[45]

---

44 *Bamgboye v University of Ilorin* (1991) 8 NWLR 1 (Part 207) 1.
45 See *Bamgbose v Jiaza* (1991) 3 NWLR (Part 177) 64.

What is significant about the power is that for it to be legally enforceable, the various registration laws in the region require that the instrument be registered by either the Titles or the Lands Registry.[46] After it is issued, a delegated authority and a power of attorney may legally be countermanded by the issuing authority. Whilst the former may be annulled by a simple written instruction of a customer directed to the bank, a power of attorney can only be terminated by means of a deed revoking it. To obviate this rather complex process, it is possible for termination or breach provisions to be inserted into the instrument at the time of its construction. This will enable either or both parties to the deed to determine it in accordance with the breach provisions contained therein. This, it is suggested, is a more practical and efficient way of dissolving a deed. It avoids the dual costs of preparing and registering the instrument.

Generally speaking, the constitution, operation or dissolution of a power of attorney is not covered by the banking laws of the countries in the region. It is an area of property law which over a period of time has found its way into the arena of banking law.

14.7.7 Nomination of accounts

The Banking Act 1995 of Fiji contains a provision dealing with nomination of accounts. There are no equivalent provisions in Samoa, Kiribati, Tonga, Tuvalu, Samoa, Niue, the Cook Islands, the Federated States of Micronesia or the Marshall Islands. This should not in any case be confused with a power of attorney. For this reason, it is considered necessary to briefly examine this novelty in the Fiji position. Sections 63–66 of the Fiji legislation allow for nomination of accounts. It is very prudent that a definition of what constitutes nomination is found in the Act. For clarity, s 63 provides:

> In this Part of this Act, unless the context otherwise requires, the term 'nomination' means the nomination by any person (in this part referred to as the nominator), pursuant to any enactment, of any person (in this Act referred to as the nominee or nominees) to whom any amount standing to the credit of the nominator in any account at the time of his death is to be paid on his death.

The significance of this provision can be summarised as follows: (a) The purpose of a nomination under the section is to allow someone to benefit from the account of the nominator. (b) The nomination only becomes operative at the death of the nominator. (c) The beneficiary can only benefit if the account is in credit. (d) Since it is a gift, it can be revoked by the nominator.

---

46 See e.g. ss 19, 20 Land Transfer Act [Cap 131] 1971 (F); cf s 2 Property Law Act [Cap 130] 1978, although no equivalent provision (F).

These essential features of a nominated account clearly distinguish it from a power of attorney. Whilst in the former a person is to benefit from the account of the nominator through the instruction of the nominator, in the latter a person is simply directed by an instrument to execute the instructions of the donor of the power. Further, whilst a donee in the case of a power of attorney is an agent, a nominee is not. As can be deduced now, nomination of account and power of attorney are therefore governed by different legal principles and the two should not be confused.

14.7.8 Nature of the relationship between a customer and banker

The relationship between a client and a bank is basically governed by the general principles of the law of contract. Apart from the general contractual principles, it is possible for the principles of other specialised contracts to apply. These include banking and agency laws. In appropriate cases, the relationship between a customer and a bank may also be termed as that of a bailor and bailee. The complexity of applicable rules in this area of the law quite often generates profound legal confusion in trying to determine the precise nature of the relationship between a client and a bank. There is no statutory provision in the various banking laws in the region outlining the legal nature of the relationship between a customer and a banker. This is a matter entirely left to the principles of common law position as they apply in contract.

Because a person is generally required to show proof of some ascertainable course of dealing between them and a bank before there can be a banker and customer relationship, the most obvious means of establishing this relationship is by opening and operating an account. The client in procuring the operation of an account with a bank invokes the application of the principles of contract.[47]

Ordinarily, the relationship between a client and banker is regarded as one between a debtor and creditor.[48] The client is a creditor where there is sufficient credit balance in the client's account. The bank in this case becomes a debtor to the customer since it has to pay the client on demand. It is, however, possible for these roles to be swapped. Where the client is indebted to a bank, the client is a debtor whilst the bank becomes the creditor.

It is also possible for a bank to act as an agent of its customer. There may be instances where the client specifically instructs the bank to act as such, or such a situation may arise in the course of banking transactions where in discounting bills of exchange a bank is generally regarded as an agent of the customer in whom the bill is endorsed.

---

47 The basic principles of contract are offer, acceptance, consideration and intention to create legal relations.
48 See the case of *Midland Bank Ltd v Conway Corp* [1965] 2 All ER 972.

A bailor-bailee relationship arises where articles or valuables are deposited by a customer for safekeeping in a bank. Here possession of the deposited items rests with the bank whilst ownership of the items is still retained by the customer. The bank normally charges a fee for the safekeeping of customers' valuables or for the rental of its safe deposit boxes.

The dimension of the relationship between the customer and a bank is fundamentally expanded by the intrusion of the elements of tortious liability.[49] A bank may be liable in tort for negligence where it provides a statement of the financial standing of its customer which turns out to cause damage to a third party who may have relied on it. It is also possible for the customer to proceed against the bank where the information is untrue so as to cause some damage to that person.[50] The effect of negligent misstatement as a foundation for tortious liability is now firmly entrenched in the law of banking, especially in the sphere of the customer and banker relationship.

14.7.9 Rules of banking confidentiality

The relationship between a customer and a banker is confidential, albeit subject to some exceptions. The requirement for confidentiality is deeply rooted in the fiduciary nature of banking transactions. This involves the reposing of some degree of trust and confidence by the customer on a banker. To be able to fully appreciate the nature of this concept in the conventional law of banking, an historical discussion may certainly be appropriate as a prelude to analysing the concept of confidentiality.

The evolution of banking secrecy as a cornerstone of the banking industry can historically be traced back to developments in Ancient Greece. At the time of early Greek civilisation, banking secrecy was equated to some aspects of political freedom and the right to privacy. The modern foundation of banking secrecy was however laid down by Frederick the Great in the 1765 banking statute.[51]

With the foundation of banking secrecy firmly laid in 1765, other countries improved upon it by taking further legislative measures. In 1939, Switzerland promulgated a federal legislation to protect confidentiality in banking transactions.[52] In the case of France, clause 378 of the Penal Code entrenches a definition

---

49 For a more detailed discussion, see Perm *et al.*, *op cit* fn 43, p 33.
50 See the case of *Hedley Byrne & Co Ltd v Heller & Partners Ltd* [1964] AC 465. Interestingly, this case redefined classifications of the traditional principles of tortious liability by introducing the concept of 'negligent misstatement'.
51 Naher, J, 'Why secrecy is crumbling', *International Herald Tribune*, 13 July 1987.
52 Article 47 guarantees a privileged relationship between a customer and a banker whilst Art 274 provides a penalty for any breach of this confidentiality.

of banking secrecy. This is meant to satisfy the banking secrecy requirements under clause 16 of the French Banking Law of 1981.[53]

Whilst the above countries have passed specific legislation dealing with banking secrecy, the vast majority of countries, including Fiji, still rely on the orthodox common law position as enunciated in *Tournier v National Provincial Bank and Union Bank of England*.[54] Banking secrecy rules operate on the assumption that for public confidence in the banking industry to be maintained and for the integrity of the banking institution to be protected, the relationship between a customer and a banker should be considered as privileged. *Tournier's Case*, whilst laying down this general principle, was also quick to point out some exceptions to the rule. It therefore means that the confidentiality rule can be waived where disclosure is required by law,[55] or where it is necessary in the public interest[56] or in furtherance of the legitimate interests of the bank, or where the client consents to waiver of the secrecy.[57]

The extent to which these exceptions are to be applied has not been the subject of any major judicial decision in the region as yet. This is in contrast to the position in some jurisdictions[58] where the courts have held that disclosure in the public interest is a potent exception which may be used in a variety of cases to circumvent the common law requirement of secrecy. It remains to be seen to what extent this judicial line of reasoning will be accepted or rejected in the region.[59]

The basic regime of banking business in the region is aimed at imposing restrictions on the conduct of banks and their relationship with customers with a view to securing the maximum degree of protection for depositors or creditors. In a general sense, the basic principles are directed at creating a conducive atmosphere for banking activities as a means of enhancing economic growth. In the case of Fiji, for instance, the relaxation provisions are meant to assist the economic deregulation drive. However, whether this is entirely successful or not is another matter.

---

53 Achleiter, P, *Secret Money*, 1989, London, Unwin, p 32.
54 [1924] 1 KB 46.
55 See s 6 Banker's Book Evidence Act [Cap 45] 1932 (F); Banker's Book Evidence Act 1879 (UK) (V), (SI), (N), (T), (Tu). See also *Robertson v Canadian Imperial Bank of Commerce* [1994] 1 WLR 1493.
56 See *Weld-Blundell v Stephens* [1920] AC 956.
57 The nature of the consent will depend upon the circumstances of each and every situation. Whilst in glaring instances express consent may be required, in some other less demanding cases it is possible to recognise implied consent of the customer.
58 This is especially so in instances where criminal offences are perpetrated through the banks.
59 Perhaps the 1995 National Bank of Fiji saga will provide the litmus test for a critical appraisal of the common law principle in Fiji.

15

BANKING REGULATION AND PRUDENTIAL SUPERVISION

15.1 Audit and direct control of banks

In the region, there are specific provisions dealing with this area of law. For instance, s 21 of the Financial Institutions Act [Cap 254] 1999 of Vanuatu; s 8 of the Financial Institutions Act 1998 of the Solomon Islands; ss 142–43 of the Banking Act 1987 of the Marshall Islands; and s 601 of the Federated States of Micronesia Bank Act of 1980 are illustrative examples in this regard. Prudential supervision is effected, in the case of Fiji, through a range of provisions but there is nothing in the Banking Act 1975 of Nauru on the issue. By way of example, s 21 of the Financial Institutions Act 1999 of Vanuatu provides:

(1) The functions of the reserve bank include:
   (a) to collect and analyse information in respect of prudential matters relating to licensees; and
   (b) to encourage and promote licensees to carry out sound practices in relation to prudential matters; and
   (c) to evaluate the effectiveness and carrying out of those practices.
(2) In carrying out its functions under this section in relation to a licensee, the reserve bank must have regard to the following:
   (a) the capital adequacy of the licensee in relation to the size and nature of its banking business;
   (b) the asset concentration and risk exposure of the licensee;
   (c) the separation of the banking business of the licensee from the financial interests of any person owning or controlling the licensee;
   (d) the adequacy of the liquidity of the licensee in relation to its liabilities;
   (e) the asset quality and adequacy of provisions for losses of the licensee;

DOI: 10.4324/9781003428060-19

      (f) the internal control, risk management and accounting systems of the licensee;

      (g) such other matters as the reserve bank considers relevant.

(2A) The Reserve Bank may formulate in writing guidelines and issue directives in relation to prudential matters to be complied with by:

      (a) all licensees; or

      (b) a specified class of licensees; or

      (c) one or more specified licensees.

(2B) The directives issued by the Reserve Bank must be published in the Gazette.

(2C) The Reserve Bank may vary or revoke a directive or guideline.

(3)   This section does not limit any provision of the Reserve Bank Act [Cap 125].

The reserve or central bank exercises direct control over activities of commercial, merchant and to some extent even development banks operating in the country. The overall objective of these powers is to ensure prudential supervision and effective banking regulation. Prudential supervision is central to fiscal stability in the region.

Generally speaking, the reserve or central bank is empowered by law to determine and protect the priority of claims by local creditors and depositors over all other liabilities. This is in the event of liquidation, bankruptcy or dissolution of a licensed financial institution operating locally, but incorporated overseas.[1] This ensures the protection of local creditors of a bank by compensating them for losses which they might otherwise have suffered without the protection offered by this section of the Act. In order to safeguard the interests of local depositors or creditors of foreign incorporated licensed financial institutions, banks are generally required (except with the permission of the reserve or central bank) to hold assets in the country of not less in value than the total amount of their deposit liabilities.[2]

By way of example, the regulatory powers of the reserve or central bank are found in s 30 of the Banking Act of Fiji 1995 and by contrast in s 9 of the Financial Institutions Act 1996 of Samoa. No equivalent provisions are found in the Financial Institutions Act 1998 of the Solomon Islands and the Banking Act 1975 of Nauru. We shall refer in detail to the position in Fiji as an illustration of the point. It provides:

Where–

(a) a licensed financial institution informs the reserve bank–

      (i) that it considers that it is likely to become unable to meet its obligations; or

---

1 See generally, s 40 Reserve Bank Act 1983 (F).

2 See *ibid.*, s 40(3); cf s 44 Financial Institutions Act [Cap 254] 1999 (V); cf s 122 Banking Act 1987 (MI); ss 609–11 FSM Bank Act of 1980 (FSM).

(ii) that it is insolvent or about to suspend payment

(b) a licensed financial institution becomes unable to meet its obligations or suspends payment;

(c) the reserve bank is of the opinion that a licensed financial institution–

   (i) is carrying on its business in a manner detrimental to the interests of its depositors or of its creditors; or

   (ii) is insolvent or is likely to become unable to meet its obligations or is about to suspend payments; or

   (iii) has contravened or failed to comply with any provisions of the Act; or

   (iv) has contravened or failed to comply with any condition attached to its licence;

(d) the reserve bank has reasonable grounds to believe that any associated person of a licensed financial institution is–

   (i) likely to become unable to meet its obligations; or

   (ii) insolvent or about to suspend payment; or

   (iii) subject to conditions described in paragraphs (a), (b) or (c) of this subsection;

(e) The reserve bank considers it necessary in the interest of the soundness of the financial system or to minimise detriment to the interest of depositors or creditors of the licensed financial institution to do so, the reserve bank may exercise such one or more of the powers specified in subsection (2) of this section as may, from time to time, appear to it to be necessary.

There are three points worth noting about the foregoing section. First, it places a duty on an ailing bank to inform the reserve bank of its condition.[3] However, the section is silent on the consequences of an ailing bank deliberately concealing its condition until discovery is made by the reserve or central bank. The same argument may be canvassed for sub-s (b) of the same section.

Secondly, discretion is conferred on the reserve or central bank to take appropriate measures against a bank where it decides to exercise its discretion in this regard.[4] The inclusion of the word 'opinion' grants wide discretionary powers to a reserve bank to take action. What the same section has not answered is the question of how wide this discretion might be. Where the reserve or central bank decides to intervene, the bank's 'opinion' may be subject to administrative review according to so-called the *Wednesbury* principles.[5]

---

3 See s 30(1)(a)(i), (ii) Banking Act 1995 (F).

4 See s 30(1)(c) Banking Act 1995 (F). Cf s 142 Banking Act 1987 (MI); s 602 FSM Bank Act of 1980 (FSM).

5 See Chapter 13 High Court Rules 1988 (F); *Council of Civil Service Unions v Minister for Civil Service* (1984) 3 WLR 1174; *Ridge v Baldwin* [1964] AC 40. It is now an established principle that

Thirdly, we are of the view that s 30(d) contains more refined powers than those obtained in the preceding sub-s (c). Here, there must be reasonable grounds for the exercise of such powers. This in essence makes the exercise of power by the reserve or central bank subject to the *Wednesbury* principles. Thus, aggrieved parties affected by the actions of the reserve or central bank are likely to be accorded some measure of legal protection.

The ultimate consequences for an ailing bank are for the reserve or central bank to take the following actions: (a) issue corrective directives to the bank; (b) appoint a person to either advise the licensed financial institution or conduct its business; (c) assume control of the ailing bank where consent is given by the Minister of Finance; (d) have the bank wound up by the High Court; or (e) revoke or suspend the licence of the bank.[6] In order to perfect any or all of these powers, notification of assumption of control is required to be published in the *Gazette*.[7]

Apart from instances where the controller is empowered to appoint auditors for the purpose of executing a controllership in respect of a licensed financial institution (which we shall be referring to later), it is also a requirement of law in the region that every licensed financial institution (not subject to controllership) shall maintain the services of an auditor.[8]

By way of example, the role of auditors in Fiji may be gleaned from s 58 of the Banking Act 1995. In this section, every licensed financial institution is to appoint an auditor annually. The auditor/s so appointed is/are expected by law to hold a current certificate of public practice issued by the Fiji Institute of Accountants. The duties of such auditors include preparing reports based upon information on the annual balance sheet and profit and loss account of the bank and its subsidiaries, if any.[9]

For a bank domiciled in a country in the region, the auditor's report will be tabled together with the report of the directors of the bank at the annual general meeting of the shareholders. Copies of these reports are also to be sent to the reserve or central bank.[10] The aim is to provide the shareholders of the bank with reasonable information relating to the affairs of the bank operating in the country.

---

an administrative action can be challenged by an applicant in court on the ground of being unreasonable. This is what in a general sense the *Wednesbury* principle is all about.

6 For a detailed consideration of these powers, refer to sub-ss 30(2)(a)–(e) Banking Act 1995 (F).

7 See s 30(4) Banking Act 1995 (F). Cf ss 47–49 Financial Institutions Act [Cap 254] 1999 (V); s 18 Financial Institutions Act 1998 (SI); s 15 Financial Institutions Act 1996 (S).

8 See s 58 of Banking Act 1995 (F); s 22 Financial Institutions Act [Cap 254] 1999 (V); s 9 Financial Institutions Act 1998 (SI); s 10 Financial Institutions Act 1996 (S); cf s 15(1) Banking Act 1975 (N), where a six-month time limit is stated within which the accounts of the bank must be audited.

9 See s 58 (3) Banking Act 1995 (F); s 134 Banking Act 1987 (MI); s 47 Banking Act 2011 (CI); s 22 Financial Institutions Act [Cap 254] 1999 (V); s 15 Banking Act 1975 (N); s 10 Financial Institutions Act 1996 (S).

10 See s 58(4) Banking Act 1995 (F). Non-compliance with the provision of sub-s (4) constitutes an offence punishable under sub-s (5).

By furnishing a copy to the reserve or central bank, the latter is also kept informed on the state of affairs of the bank.

A depositor, director, employee or agent of a licensed financial institution is disqualified from being appointed as an auditor.[11] In any or all of these instances, it will be extremely difficult for such an appointed person to exhibit a transparent degree of fairness and impartiality in the conduct of their audit. Auditors who are interested in the financial or other affairs of the bank definitely stand to gain or lose from the results of an audit.

The reserve or central bank has a statutory right to request that any information, data and returns of a licensed financial institution be audited by an approved auditor, on such conditions as may be specified by it.[12] This is an important and useful regulatory power that can be used by the reserve or central bank where it suspects that the affairs of a bank are not being properly conducted or that the bank is showing signs of imminent financial collapse. This section provides a rapid intervention tool which will certainly assist the reserve bank in effectively discharging its regulatory functions, especially those listed in Part V of the Banking Act of Fiji 1995.

It is important for auditors to be independent and fearless in the discharge of their responsibilities if they are to be protected from liabilities that may arise in the conduct of their duties. Ordinarily, auditors are bound by the rules of confidentiality[13] in the performance of their responsibilities. However, s 61 of the Act provides a statutory exception to the rule of confidentiality. The section provides:

> Every person who holds or at any time has held, office as required by any enactment, as an auditor of a licensed financial institution, shall disclose to the reserve bank information relating to the affairs of the financial institution obtained in the course of holding that office, if in the opinion of that person–
>
> (a) the licensed financial institution is insolvent or likely to become unable to meet its obligations or is about to suspend payment; or
>
> (b) the licensed financial institution is carrying on its business in a manner detrimental to the interests of its depositors or of its creditors; and
>
> (c) the disclosure of that information is likely to assist, or be relevant to, the exercise by the reserve bank of its powers under this Act.

Before there can be any disclosure of information affecting it, a bank is entitled to reasonably be informed in advance of the intention of the auditor to disclose such

11 See *ibid.*, s 58(7).

12 See *ibid.*, s 59(1); s 58 Financial Institutions Act [Cap 254] 1999 (V).

13 See *Galoo Ltd v Bright Grahame Murray* [1994] 1 WLR 1360. Cf s 154 Banking Act 1987 (MI).

information.[14] Further, an auditor is screened from any civil or criminal proceedings emanating from the disclosure of information to the reserve or central bank, provided that it is done in good faith.[15]

It is important to note that s 61 of the Banking Act 1995 of Fiji raises some interesting points for consideration. First, an auditor's right to disclose information pertaining to an audit is restricted to matters specified in s 61(1)(a), (b) and (c). If an auditor ventures out of these defined parameters, he/she loses the protection afforded by s 61(3) of the Act. Secondly, disclosure of such information can only be made to the reserve bank and the affected bank. The question is, would authorised agents of the reserve bank and the affected licensed financial institution be entitled to receive the audit report or information from it? There is no express statutory provision on this.[16]

15.1.1 Investigation of banks

This is an indirect means of control which may be used by the reserve or central bank to regulate the activities of licensed financial institutions. The reserve or central bank, when it deems fit (from time to time), can investigate the books, accounts and transactions of an affected bank with or without prior notice to it. These powers are to be exercised without prejudice to other provisions of the legislation.[17] There are procedural requirements to be complied with before an investigation into the affairs of a bank is commenced. Shareholders holding an aggregate of not less than one-third of the total issued shares of the bank shall request the investigation. If they are depositors, then the request should be by those holding not less than one-half of the gross amount of total deposit liabilities.[18]

Shareholders or depositors who apply to the reserve or central bank to conduct an investigation are expected to pay security for costs to cover the investigation.[19]

---

14 See s 61(2) Banking Act 1995 (F); cf s 6 Banking Act 1975 (N); s 11 Financial Institutions Act 1998 (SI).

15 See *ibid.*, s 61(3). As additional protection, sub-s (4) protects such an auditor from any proceedings against his professional conduct; sub-s (5) renders inadmissible against the auditor, in any proceedings, any information so disclosed to the reserve bank by the said auditor.

16 In this case, reliance may be placed on the provisions of s 41 Interpretation Act [Cap 7] 1967 (F). By virtue of this section, it may be argued that the reserve bank can receive contents of an audit report on its behalf. It may also be a matter for the judiciary in Fiji to decide should an opportunity come up. See also the Interpretation and General Clauses Ordinance [Cap 46] 1968 (K); Interpretation and General Provisions Act [Cap 85] 1978 (SI); Acts Interpretation Act 1924 (NZ) (CI); Acts Interpretation Act 1924 (NZ) (Tokelau); Interpretation Ordinance 1956 (N); Acts Interpretation Act 1924 (NZ) (Ni). Cf s 138 Banking Act 1987 (MI); Arts 406, 609 FSM Bank Act of 1980 (FSM); cf s 10 (2) Financial Institutions Act 1996 (S).

17 See s 11 Financial Institutions Act 1998 (SI).

18 See s 31 Banking Act 1995 (F).

19 The provision of security for cost is a normal legal procedure. For lodgement and prosecution of appeals in the High Court, Court of Appeal and Supreme Court, appellants in Fiji are to provide payments as security for costs to support their applications.

This may be necessary in order to prevent frivolous applications for investigation from unscrupulous shareholders or depositors on the slightest pretext of not being satisfied with the way the affairs of the bank are being conducted.

In the case of both the Solomon Islands and Samoa, on-site inspection by the central bank may be initiated against the activities of banks. By way of example, s 11 of the Financial Institutions Act 1996 of Samoa provides:

(1) The central bank may, under conditions of confidentiality, initiate on-site examinations of the accounts and affairs of any licensed financial institution and any of its branches, agencies or offices by central bank officers or by other persons designated as examiners by the central bank.

(2) A licensed financial institution under examination shall make available for the inspection of examiners designated by the central bank all cash and securities of the institution and all accounts, books, vouchers, minutes and any document or record that are relevant to its business and shall supply all information concerning that business as may be required, within the time specified by the examiners.

(3) The central bank officers or designated examiners may make copies of and take away for further scrutiny, any papers or electronically stored data they require.

(4) An on-site examination may extend to any of the subsidiaries and affiliates of a licensed financial institution. Accordingly, the provisions of Subsections (2) and (3) shall apply in the conduct of any examination of that institution's subsidiary or affiliate.

There are equivalent provisions in s 16 of the Banking Act 1975 of Nauru and s 11 of the Financial Institutions Act 1998 of the Solomon Islands.

15.1.2 *Effect of assumption of control*

The assumption of control of affairs of a licensed financial institution means that the reserve or central bank or any person appointed by it may carry on all or part of the business hitherto undertaken by that licensed financial institution. It may therefore be vested with all such powers or authority as may conveniently enable it to discharge that responsibility.[20] Except with the consent of the reserve or central bank, the board of directors, directors, officers or other agents of a licensed bank are disqualified from managing or conducting the affairs of the bank in any

---

20 See s 32(1)(3) but importantly (4) of the Banking Act 1995 (F).

way. Any such management of the affairs of the bank subject to the control of the reserve bank is unlawful.[21]

In the event that an associated person of a licensed financial institution is subject to controllership, any reference made in Part V of the Act to a licensed financial institution is also to be construed as a reference to that associated person.[22] The implication of this reference is to enable the controller to effectively apply the resources of the licensed financial institution to discharge the debts and obligations of the said associated person.[23]

This provision will go a long way in forestalling the manipulation and even concealment of debts or other obligations, by an overseas-based parent or holding bank in favour of its subsidiary or branch office located in the country. It is to be observed that there may be practical difficulties in trying to implement this provision of the Act. This is basically because of the absence of an 'arm's length' or 'open market price' for services such as management fees, directors' fees, expenses on research and development, etc., charged by a parent company against its subsidiary.[24]

All costs, charges and expenses incurred by the controller in the discharge of his/her obligations are to be deducted from the property of a licensed financial institution subject to controllership.[25] The controller is also expected to disclose such expenses to creditors of the licensed financial institution.[26] It is the duty of holders of the bank's books and property to deliver such to the controller. It is therefore an offence to refuse delivery of such documents or information when demanded by the controller. It is equally an offence to destroy, alter or conceal any records of a bank under controllership. Should this happen, the reserve bank is mandated to impose a fine for any violations of the section.[27] Parliament, by prescription of law, can impose liabilities on persons or bodies.[28] What is debatable, however, is whether the reserve bank (as a statutory body) is capable of performing a purely judicial function in relation to the imposition of a fine. The section is silent on whether there first has to be a demand for the documentation before

---

21 See s 32(5) Banking Act 1995 (F); cf s 18 Financial Institutions Act 1998 (SI); ss 43–44 Financial Institutions Act [Cap 254] 1999 (V); ss 3, 15 Financial Institutions Act 1996 (S).

22 See s 32(6) Banking Act 1995 (F).

23 See also *ibid.*, s 32(7).

24 An arm's length price is a price fixed for commodities which are traded between a parent company and its subsidiaries. See Murray, R (ed), *Multinational Beyond the Market: Intra Firm Trade and Control of Transfer Pricing*, 1981, Brighton, Harvester, p 5, for a detailed discussion on transfer pricing between parent companies and their subsidiaries. For the specific effects of transfer pricing on developing countries, refer to Ahmadu, ML *et al.*, 'Transnational companies and transfer pricing: legal and corporate problems' (1993) 1 *Company Law Journal*, India, 7.

25 See s 33(1) Banking Act 1995 (F).

26 See *ibid.*, s 33(3).

27 See *ibid.*, ss 35, 36.

28 See *ibid.*, s 35(2).

a penalty can be imposed by the reserve bank for violating this provision. It is submitted that in view of the constitutional principle of separation of powers, it is not conclusive that the reserve bank can implement the provisions of s 35(2) of the Banking Act 1995 of Fiji without the potential of the action being challenged in court.

The positive aspect of the section is that the quantum of fine is likely to serve as a deterrent to a breach of the provision. More of a deterrent is the upper-limit $30,000 fine in s 36 of the Banking Act 1995 of Fiji. Interestingly, sub-s (2) of the same section reverses the traditional burden of proof in criminal law by placing it on the accused where such matters are within the peculiar knowledge of the accused.[29]

15.2 Termination of controllership

Controllership over the affairs of a bank can be terminated by the Minister of Finance on the advice of the reserve bank.[30] This is distinct from terminating the appointment of a controller, which may simply be executed by the reserve bank but with the consent of the Minister of Finance.[31] There are various grounds[32] upon which the appointment of a controller could be determined. It is also possible for a controller on its own accord to resign the appointment.

15.2.1 Moratorium[33]

This is to be discussed basically in the context of Nauru and Fiji. Moratorium freezes all actions against a licensed financial institution that is subject to controllership. It is important to bear in mind that even though all proceedings or actions against a licensed financial institution are frozen when a bank is under controllership, it is still possible to commence proceedings in court if the remedy being sought is merely declaratory. The reasoning here is that whilst legislation can put a stop to certain activities including a limit on the functions or powers of a court, it is also a recognisable principle of law that there can never be an absolute ouster clause to the inherent powers of the court. This leads us to focus on the ability of

---

29 In some instances, this is likely to conflict with the right of an accused to protect him/herself from self-incrimination.

30 See s 37(1) Banking Act 1995 (F).

31 See s 38(1) Banking Act 1995 (F). Cf generally, s 15(5) Financial Institutions Act 1996 (S), although no equivalent provision.

32 These include disability, bankruptcy and neglect of duty or misconduct proved to the satisfaction of the reserve bank.

33 The list of actions falling within the heading is found in s 43 Banking Act 1995 (F); cf s 17 Banking Act 1975 (N) where moratorium can only be brought into effect on an *ex parte* application by the Secretary of Justice.

aggrieved citizens to seek redress in court by means of a declaratory judgment. In this respect, s 43(2) of the Banking Act 1995 of Fiji provides:

> Notwithstanding subsection (1) of this section, an action or proceeding may be commenced or continued against a licensed financial institution for the purpose of determining whether any right or liability exists, if the leave of the controller or the High Court is first obtained.

In contrast to what obtains in Nauru, s 17 of the Banking Act 1975 provides:

(1) The Supreme Court, on application made *ex parte* by the Secretary for Justice, may, if it considers it to be in the interests of the depositors of a bank licensed under section 5 of this Act to do so, make an order:
   (a) prohibiting that bank from carrying on any banking business in Nauru, if it is a corporation incorporated in Nauru, in Nauru and elsewhere; and
   (b) staying the commencement or continuance of all suits against that bank in regard to any banking business in Nauru, for a specified period of time from the date of such order on such terms and conditions as to the Court seem reasonable, and may from time to time extend the period, so, however, that the total period of such a moratorium shall not exceed six months.
(2) So long as an order under the preceding subsection remains in force the licence granted to the bank under section 5 of this Act shall be suspended.

For practical purposes, it is better to seek leave from the High or Supreme Court. If this is declined, then an applicant can proceed on appeal to the Court of Appeal. An applicant can only approach the court where leave is declined by a controller. This is why an application for leave should start from the High or Supreme Court.

There are no equivalent provisions on moratorium in the Financial Institutions Acts 1996 and 1998 of Samoa and the Solomon Islands, although generally covered in ss 15 and 18, respectively.

15.2.2 Limitations of the controller to deal with native lands

The controller is limited in its ability to exercise control over native lands. This is a peculiar feature of the Banking Act 1995 of Fiji only. No equivalent provisions are found in Nauru, Samoa or the Solomon Islands.

By s 50 of the Banking Act of Fiji 1995, the provisions of any enactment or agreement requiring any consent, licence, permission, clearance or other authority do not apply to any sale or other disposition of property of a licensed financial institution[34] which is being undertaken by a controller. The aim is to facilitate a

---

34 See s 49 Banking Act 1995 (F).

rapid and efficient operation of a controllership instituted by the Reserve Bank of Fiji. This also helps to prevent the wasting of assets which might otherwise be profitably disposed of.

The issue for our consideration is the proviso to s 50 of the Act, which states that the section is not to apply to any consent, permission, clearance or other authority required under the provisions of the Native Land Trust Act. The implication here is that where a disposition of property under s 49 of the Banking Act 1995 of Fiji touches on the provisions of the Native Land Trust Act, such disposition can only be validated where the necessary consent, permission, clearance or other authority is obtained. The crucial question is, should this really be so in view of the fact that both laws are in the form of legislation?[35]

15.2.3 The difference between audit and controllership

Controllership is the process of taking over the entire administration of the business and other activities of a licensed financial institution. Just as in the conduct of normal activities of a bank, the role of internal and external auditors cannot be overemphasised. Auditors have a significant role to play in ensuring that accounts are properly scrutinised, thereby presenting a true and fair assessment of the financial position of a company.

Generally speaking, companies are by law compelled to appoint auditors.[36] An auditor is regarded as a 'watchdog' in respect of the financial affairs of a company. In recent times, however, the role of auditors has come under severe criticism for not really doing enough to assist regulatory agencies in monitoring the activities of banking institutions.[37] The laxity in attitude is more pronounced where auditors are retained at very fat fees by their client banks. It is now clear that courts are increasingly prepared to hold auditors liable where negligence is established in the discharge of their responsibilities.[38] Today, auditors, like any other professionals, are expected to discharge their duties with the requisite standard of skill and care expected of their profession.

Under the Banking Act, s 53 deals with the appointment of auditors by a controller, albeit subject to the blessing of the reserve bank. The term of appointment does not exceed a period of two years, but an auditor is eligible for reappointment. For an auditor so appointed to be able to fully assist the controller, such an auditor by s 53(3) is entitled to have the right of access to all books and papers of the

---

35 The answer is found in s 100 Constitution of Fiji (defunct), which elevates the provisions of the Native Land Trust Act to the position of a constitutional provision. Because the Constitution is supreme law in Fiji, it takes precedence over an Act of Parliament.
36 See s Part 34 Companies Act 2015 (F), allowing for the appointment and remuneration of auditors. Cf s 134 Banking Act 1987 (MI); s 47 Banking Act 2011(CI).
37 Truell, P *et al.*, *BCCI*, 1992, London, Bloomsbury, pp 288–89.
38 For the statutory position, see generally s 101 Companies Act 2015 (F); for a detailed exposé on negligence and auditors' responsibilities, see *Caparo Industries Plc v Dickman* [1990] 2 AC 605.

bank and is also competent to request information and explanation from officers and employees of the bank. Whilst this may be considered as a potent power given to an auditor to enable it to perform its duties diligently, a noticeable defect of the provision is that there is no liability imposed by law on any officer or employee of the bank who refuses to accede to the request of the auditor. Furthermore, whilst the power to appoint an auditor under s 53 of the Act is vested in the controller, the removal of the auditor from office can only be effected by the reserve bank with the concurrence of the Minister of Finance, and even then, only under some specified grounds.[39]

15.3 The reserve or central bank[40]

In this part of the discussion, we shall examine the position in Fiji, Vanuatu, Samoa, the Solomon Islands and Tonga. A reserve bank or central bank, as it is referred to in other jurisdictions, is usually established by the central government of a country, which in most cases is the main shareholder of the bank. A reserve bank is normally set up by an Act of Parliament.[41] A reserve bank exercises supervisory control over commercial banks and its main functions range from administrative to commercial tasks. They may also extend to quasi-legal functions.

The powers of the bank are generally spelt out in detail in the Act establishing the bank. As was observed earlier, this is usually an Act of Parliament. In some jurisdictions, however, it is possible to find some powers of the bank in the Banking Act.[42] Generally speaking, these are powers that are exercised by a reserve bank to control the activities of commercial and other banks, including credit and financial institutions subject to its jurisdiction. This chapter, however, addresses the powers and functions of a reserve bank as are usually spelt out in the Act of Parliament establishing it.

The complexity of banking activities and the enormous volume of financial transactions processed through banking institutions require that for financial probity to prevail in the banking industry, supervisory authorities must be placed in a strong position to effectively police the affairs of licensed financial institutions.

The large-scale failures of banks[43] and related institutions in recent times prompted central banks across the globe to initiate and implement iron-clad super-

---

39 See s 53(4) Banking Act 1995 (F).
40 This section is based on a revised chapter from Ahmadu, ML, *The Law of Banking in Fiji*, 1998, London, Avon Books.
41 In the case of Fiji, see the Reserve Bank of Fiji Act [Cap 210] (F) 1983; Central Bank Act 2015 (S); Reserve Bank Act [Cap 125] 1980 (V); Central Bank Act [Cap 49] 1976 (SI); National Reserve Bank of Tonga Act [Cap 38.20] 1989.
42 See Part V Banking Act 1995 (F); Chapter 6 FSM Bank Act of 1980 (FSM).
43 See Truell *et al.*, *op cit* fn 37, pp 1 ff detailing the collapse of Bank for Credit and Commerce International in 1991. See also Ahmadu, ML *et al.*, 'Dissolution of Bank for Credit and Commerce International: the search for legal basis' (1991) XLVIII *Punjab University Law Journal* 1.

visory and control regimes for financial institutions operating within their juris-dictions. The most noticeable in this regard is the use of legislation to strengthen the regulatory powers of the reserve or central bank.[44] The current spate of bank-ing failures has also engendered a debate on the scope of auditors' responsibilities and their role in aiding the proper supervision of the banking industry.

It is not so far clear how effective these powers are for reserve or central banks in the region. Nevertheless, it is important that the relevant provisions dealing with such powers are analysed with a view to seeing how practical their imple-mentation may be.

15.3.1 Establishment

The reserve or central bank is established by an Act of Parliament.[45] By this, the bank becomes a body corporate with perpetual succession and a common seal. It also has the power to enter into contracts and sue or be sued in its own name subject to the provisions of the Act. It equally possesses the power to hold and dis-pose of real or personal property.[46] The bank shall be headquartered in the capital city or at such place as may be determined by the Minister of Finance. It can also establish branches in the country, as well as appoint agents and correspondents locally and overseas.[47] As a general principle, a board of directors is constituted to oversee the smooth running of the bank.

15.3.2 Responsibility

The primary objectives of the bank are spelt out in the Act.[48] These include regulat-ing the issuance of currency and the supply, availability and international exchange of money; promoting monetary stability; promoting a sound financial structure in

---

44 See generally Part V Banking Act 1995 (F); the 1995 collapse of Barings Bank is another pointer in the same direction. Closer to home, the liquidity problems of the National Bank of Fiji in 1995 illustrate other dimensions of the situation. For the position in the European Union, see the First Banking Co-ordination Directive (77/17/80 EEC) and the Second Banking Co-ordination Directive (92/30/EEC) relating to the need for member states to promulgate statutes to regulate banks; cited in Swan, EJ, *The Development of the Law of Financial Services*, 1993, London, Cavendish Publishing, pp 95–96.

45 See s 3(1) Reserve Bank of Fiji Act [Cap 210] (F) 1983; cf s 4 Niue Bank Act 1994 (Ni); s 2 Reserve Bank Act [Cap 125] 1980 (V); s 3 Central Bank Act 2015 (S); s 3 Central Bank Act [Cap 49] 1976 (SI); s 3 National Reserve Bank of Tonga Act [Cap 38.20] 1989 (T).

46 See s 3(2) Reserve Bank of Fiji Act [Cap 210] 1983 (F).

47 See *ibid.*, s 5; s 4 Reserve Bank Act [Cap 125] 1980 (V); s 5 Central Bank Act 2015 (S); s 6 Central Bank Act [Cap 49] 1976 (SI); s 5 National Reserve Bank of Tonga Act [Cap 38.20] 1989 (T).

48 See s 4 Reserve Bank of Fiji Act [Cap 210] 1983 (F); s 4 Central Bank Act 2015 (S); s 4 Central Bank Act [Cap 49] 1976 (SI); s 4 National Reserve Bank of Tonga Act [Cap 38.20] 1989 (T).

the country; and fostering credit and exchange conditions in an attempt to achieve orderly and balanced national economic development.[49]

To be able to achieve the objectives as outlined in the Act, the bank is also expected to perform a variety of functions. It has the sole prerogative of issuing legal tender currency;[50] it is also empowered by the Act to determine the features of banknotes and coins for use as legal tender. The bank has the additional obligation of arranging for the printing of the notes and minting of the coins.[51] The features of the currency are also to be gazetted to ensure effective public notice.[52] The reserve or central bank is also invested with the power to recall from circulation currency already issued by it.[53] The power to recall currency is complemented by the power to reissue currency for circulation in the country.[54]

The reserve or central bank, in order to achieve its objectives as enshrined in the Act, is also empowered to assist in the implementation of any law affecting the counterfeiting of currency in the country.[55] In this regard, it is expected to cooperate with other agencies of government, especially those in the area of law enforcement. In furtherance of its objectives, the bank is also allowed to deal in gold or silver coins or gold bullion or other metals. It can also deal in foreign exchange, treasury bills or other securities, open and maintain accounts with central banks or other banks, borrow foreign exchange and establish foreign credits.[56]

49 See *Reddy's Enterprises Ltd v Governor of the Reserve Bank of Fiji* [1991] FJCA 4; Abu0067d.90s (9 August 1991), which deals with a request for permission to invest offshore funds overseas. This was refused by the reserve bank. A point for consideration of the court was whether ss 4, 7, 8, 9 and 26 were intended to deal with payments in Fiji.

50 See s 22(1) Reserve Bank of Fiji Act [Cap 210] 1983 (F). By s 22(2), a contraction of sub-s (1) attracts conviction for an offence, with an imprisonment term not exceeding 14 years.

51 See s 25(1). It is important to note that by sub-s (2), the reserve bank, with the approval of the Minister, shall determine the denomination, composition, form, design, content and material of its currency. See also s 17 Reserve Bank Act [Cap 125] 1980 (V); s 24 Central Bank Act [Cap 49] 1976 (SI); s 18 Central Bank Act 2015 (S); s 22 National Reserve Bank of Tonga Act [Cap 38.20] 1989 (T).

52 See s 25(4) National Reserve Bank of Tonga Act [Cap 38.20] 1989 (T).

53 See s 26 National Reserve Bank of Tonga Act [Cap 38.20] 1989 (T); the only qualification to the section is that the holders of the currency so withdrawn shall be entitled at any time to demand payment from the reserve bank to the equivalent of the amount withdrawn.

54 See s 27 of the Act (F); cf s 26 National Reserve Bank of Tonga Act [Cap 38.20] 1989 (T).

55 See s 29; the same section considers certification by a duly authorised officer of the reserve bank that an item in question is or is not genuine to be *prima facie* evidence of the fact in any legal proceedings in Fiji. See also s 24 Central Bank Act 2015 (S); s 29 National Reserve Bank of Tonga Act [Cap 38.20] 1989.

56 See s 32(a), (b), (c), (d), (e), (f) and (g) Banking Act (F). For other related functions, see ss 38 and 39. By s 42 of the Act, the bank may determine (a) the maximum amount of the working balances that the financial institutions may hold in foreign currencies generally or in any specified currency; and (b) the maximum amount of indebtedness in foreign currencies generally or in any specific currency which financial institutions may incur. Cf s 24 Reserve Bank Act [Cap 125] 1980 (V); ss 29, 20 Central Bank Act 2015 (S); s 35 Central Bank Act [Cap 49] 1976 (SI); s 32 National Reserve Bank of Tonga Act [Cap 38.20] 1989 (T).

The bank also determines the exchange rate of the national currency vis-à-vis other currencies.[57] In addition, the reserve or central bank regulates the minimum and maximum rate of interest and the aggregate ceilings on advances to be made by banks.[58]

The bank determines the minimum holdings of unimpaired liquid assets by banks operating in the country.[59] In addition to the foregoing functions, the reserve bank acts as a banker to the government. It is also charged with the duty of maintaining and managing the country's foreign reserves.[60] The bank is generally regarded as a lender of last resort to commercial banks. In exercising this function, it comes to the rescue of financial institutions facing short-, medium- or long-term liquidity problems by providing the necessary funds at a determined rate of interest.

Apart from the foregoing specific powers, the bank is also charged with the general responsibility of promoting the country's economic and monetary stability by ensuring that commercial and other banks including financial and credit institutions are properly regulated and administered.[61] This in a broad sense is geared towards instilling public confidence in the operations of the country's financial and banking institutions. This may in turn attract direct and indirect foreign investment into the country.

15.3.3 Administrative and commercial roles

There is as yet no judicial authority in Fiji, or indeed anywhere in the region, outlining the legal status of the reserve bank. However, by way of example, Part IX of the Act deals with the relationship between the reserve bank and the government of Fiji. It is apparent from the provisions of s 47(1)(a), (b), (2) and (3) of the Act that the bank is to be regarded as a banker, fiscal agent and depository to the government. Sub-section (1) of the section provides:

---

57 See s 35. For other related functions, see ss 38 and 39 Banking Act 1995 (F).

58 See ss 40, 41, 42 Reserve Bank of Fiji Act [Cap 210] 1983 (F); s 34 Reserve Bank Act [Cap 125] 1980 (V); s 33 Central Bank Act 2015 (S); s 34 Central Bank Act [Cap 49] 1976 (SI); s 40 National Reserve Bank of Tonga Act [Cap 38.20] 1989 (T).

59 See s 43 Reserve Bank of Fiji Act [Cap 210] 1983 (F); s 33 Reserve Bank Act [Cap 125] 1980 (V); s 34 Central Bank Act 2015 (S); s 33 Central Bank Act [Cap 49] 1976 (SI); s 39 National Reserve Bank of Tonga Act [Cap 38.20] 1989 (T).

60 See s 30 Reserve Bank of Fiji Act [Cap 210] 1985; cf ss 10,11,15 Niue Bank Act 1994.

61 See ss 40, 43 Reserve Bank of Fiji Act [Cap 210] 1985 (F); cf ss 6, 96–100 Niue Bank Act 1994, where the Niue Bank is invested with a dual role. It acts as a central bank to Niue and also as Niue's International Commercial Bank. The reasons for this are not far-fetched. The increasing moves by the government to institutionalise Niue as an offshore financial centre is the prime motive for investing the bank with this dual role. Cf ss 22, 23 Reserve Bank Act [Cap 125] 1980 (V); ss 25, 36 Central Bank Act 2015 (S); ss 31, 35, 37 Central Bank Act [Cap 49] 1976 (SI); ss 30, 31, 41 National Reserve Bank of Tonga Act [Cap 38.20] 1989 (T).

The reserve bank shall be the banker and fiscal agent of the Government and shall be the depository of Government funds:

Provided that–

(a) the reserve bank may also act in such capacities to any ministry or department of Government or any statutory corporation; and

(b) the Government may maintain balances with and generally use the services of financial institutions on such terms and conditions as may be agreed between the reserve bank, the Minister and the parties concerned.

The reserve or central bank is an agent for the government in relation to matters affecting the country's exchange control and regulation of financial institutions, and as may be delegated to it by the Minister of Finance.[62]

The often-raised question in this regard is whether the reserve bank, in the exercise of its legislative functions, is to be considered an administrative outfit (which is an extension of the department of government). In the alternative, should it be considered as acting in the nature of a commercial enterprise?[63] The answers to these posers are not all that straightforward or easy.

This is because for an answer to be put forward, especially in the case of Fiji, s 3(2) of the Act has to be read in line with s 48 of the Reserve Bank Act of Fiji. There may be no apparent conflict between the two sections, but when read together they provide some difficulties in delimiting the true status of the reserve bank.[64]

It may nevertheless be stated that a reserve or central bank performing purely governmental functions on behalf of the government is to be considered as performing purely administrative functions. At this juncture it can be regarded as an extension of the department of government. But in performing commercial roles on behalf of either the government or commercial institutions, it cannot be regarded as a department of government.[65]

---

62 See s 48 Reserve Bank of Fiji Act [Cap 210] 1985 (F).

63 Section 52 empowers the Minister of Finance, after consultation with the board, to issue written directions of a general nature to the reserve bank as may seem necessary to give effect to economic policies of the government. See the English Court of Appeal decision of *Trendtex Trading Corporation v Central Bank of Nigeria* [1976] 3 All ER 437; and *Empressa Exportadora de Azucar v Industria Azucarera Nacional SA*, The Playa Larga [1983] 2 Lloyd's Rep 171.

64 Penn GA *et al.*, *The Law and Practice of International Banking*, 2005, 2nd edn, London, Sweet & Maxwell, p 67; generally, see Chapter 3, where they argue that: 'Not all state owned or controlled entities can be treated as part of the state. Many are separate entities'. This assertion may also be true of the reserve bank of Fiji having regard to s 3(2) of the Act.

65 Cf the views of Penn GA *et al.*, *ibid.*, p 67, who assert that: "The central Bank's property is not to be regarded as being for commercial purposes. The result is that the bank is liable only if it consents to enforcement. However, if the property is not that of the Bank, but that of the state (if perhaps, it is held in a separate account) then it may available if for commercial purposes".

The necessity for this split in the analysis of the functions of the reserve bank is simply to prevent the government from shielding itself from contractual liabilities in commercial transactions with other parties by relying on the doctrine of state immunity. If it is at a material time regarded as performing an administrative function on behalf of the government, it is then protected by the doctrine of state immunity. The implications of invoking the doctrine of state immunity by the reserve bank are potentially damaging for a commercial enterprise having legitimate claims against the reserve bank, which by virtue of this doctrine cannot be enforced against the bank.

In determining the legal status of the reserve or central bank, it is important that we do not confuse the corporate personality of the bank with its role as an agent of the government. There is no doubt that the Acts confer a distinct and separate legal personality on the bank, thereby making it a distinct entity from the government.[66] This, however, does not prevent the bank from still being an agent of the government.[67] Thus, to truly determine whether the bank is a department of government or not, the logical thing to do is simply examine the nature of the function being performed by the bank at the material time in question.

15.3.4 Administrative responsibilities

The statutory functions of the reserve or central bank are generally meant to be accomplished over a given period of time. This is normal where a country has a fixed-term development plan.[68] In contrast, there are short-term objectives of the bank that cannot be readily achieved via medium- or long-term statutory directives. In this case, the bank may devise and implement annual administrative directives.[69] These directives are couched in the form of monetary circulars or policies. In order to achieve the government's fiscal policy objectives, central banks in some jurisdictions issue annual credit guidelines to supplement the long-term statutory objectives of the bank. These circulars are normally released to augment annual budgetary pronouncements of the central government.[70]

---

66 See s 3(2) Reserve Bank of Fiji Act [Cap 210] 1985 (F); s 3 Reserve Bank Act [Cap 125] 1980 (V); s 3 Central Bank Act 2015 (S); s 3 Central Bank Act [Cap 49] 1976 (SI); s 3 National Reserve Bank of Tonga Act [Cap 38.20] 1989 (T).

67 See s 48 Reserve Bank of Fiji Act [Cap 210] 1983 (F); s 41 Central Bank Act 2015 (S); s 35 Reserve Bank Act [Cap 125] 1980 (V); s 46 National Reserve Bank of Tonga Act [Cap 38.20] 1989 (T).

68 Fiji has a five-year development plan. See s 44 Reserve Bank Act [Cap 125] 1980 (V).

69 See s 52 Reserve Bank of Fiji Act [Cap 210] 1983 (F); s 42 Central Bank Act 2015 (S); s 50 National Reserve Bank of Tonga Act [Cap 38.20] 1989 (T).

70 For instance, the Annual Monetary Policy of the Central Bank of Nigeria stipulates some forms of administrative controls which are exercised by the central bank over the activities of commercial banks. These are: stipulation of annual interest rates; determination of the level of localised lending; ceiling on aggregate advances; and specification of what percentage of lending should go to particular sectors of the economy. This is referred to as sectoral distribution lending. Cf s 50 National Reserve Bank of Tonga Act [Cap 38.20] 1989 (T); s 42 Central Bank Act 2015 (S).

15.3.5 Equity ownership

In the case of Fiji, for instance, the reserve bank has an authorised capital of $5 million. This may be increased from time to time by any amount proposed by the board of directors of the reserve bank, and after having been approved by the Minister of Finance.[71] However, it is not clear from the Act whether the authorised capital of the bank is equivalent to its paid-up capital.[72] There is also no provision in the Act empowering the bank to raise capital by means of public subscription to their shares or by funding the purchase of their shares through private treaties.[73] The government is the only subscriber to the authorised capital of the bank.

On a more general note, it is suggested that there is a need to publicly capitalise the reserve or central bank, especially with the current economic clamour for privatisation of public enterprises. As far as s 6 of the Banking Act 1995 of Fiji is concerned, there is no provision for reduction of the authorised capital.[74] Furthermore, if the reserve bank is to function as a truly commercial entity that is devoid of bureaucratic red-tapism, then it has to be publicly capitalised as a way of fully integrating it into the private domestic economy.

15.3.6 Management

The reserve or central bank is usually managed by a board of directors.[75] The board is charged with the responsibility of formulating the broad policies of the bank as well as ensuring that the activities of the bank are implemented in accordance with the objectives of the law. Apart from these general powers, the Act establishing the bank also spells out the duties of the board.[76] The composition of

---

71 See s 6(1) Reserve Bank of Fiji Act [Cap 210] 1985 (F); s 5 Reserve Bank Act [Cap 125] 1980 (V); s 18 Central Bank Act [Cap 49] 1976 (SI); s 6 National Reserve Bank of Tonga Act [Cap 38.20] 1989 (T).

72 For a detailed discussion of the types of company capital, see Davies, P; Worthington, S; Hare, C, *Gower: Principles of Modern Company Law 10th Edition*, 2016, London, Sweet & Maxwell, Chapter 11. See also s 6(1) Reserve Bank of Fiji Act [Cap 210] 1983 (F).

73 The absence of capitalisation for a central bank is surprising even for a country like Niue, where the bank performs the dual role of central bank to Niue as well as acting as an international commercial bank. Capitalisation is one of the important attributes of a commercial bank. See s 99(2) (a), (b), (c) and (3) Niue Bank Act 1994.

74 Cf see Division 2, Part 18 of the Companies Act (F) 2015.

75 See s 9 Reserve Bank of Fiji Act [Cap 210] 1983 (F).

76 See s 9(2) Reserve Bank of Fiji Act [Cap 210] 1983, which empowers the board to: (a) make by-laws with the approval of the Minister of Finance for the conduct of the business of the reserve Bank; (b) make regulations with the approval of the Minister generally for giving effect to the purposes of the Act; (c) issue directives for the purpose of giving effect to the provisions of the Act. Cf s 22 Niue Bank Act 1994.

the board's membership is equally defined by the Act. The membership includes the governor plus other members as may be specified by the Act.[77]

By way of example, in the case of Fiji, the governor is appointed by the Minister of Finance for a period not less than three years and not more than five years in the first instance, but may be eligible for reappointment. As a statutory requirement for appointment, the person to be appointed must have considerable experience in financial matters.[78] The Act has not laid down any guidelines for interpreting the phrase 'recognised experience in financial matters'. This is a discretion vested in the Minister of Finance to exercise. It is important to point out that the Act is also not clear on the extent to which this discretion can be challenged by means of a judicial review application in the High Court.

A significant defect of the various provisions of the Acts in the region dealing with the appointment of the board of directors is the absence of the non-executive directors in the membership of the board of the reserve or central bank.[79] This should seriously be considered in any future amendments to the Act. The role of non-executive directors cannot be overemphasised in today's boardroom settings. The appointment of non-executive directors to a board ensures to some extent that the board is constituted in such a way as to guarantee some degree of impartiality in the deliberations, by the members. This is because non-executive directors are to be appointed from outside the bank's corporate structure. They are therefore outsiders who contribute in an impersonate way to the decision-making processes of the bank.

15.3.7 Conflict of interest and secrecy

The directors are expected to avoid any sort of conflict of interest in the discharge of their statutory duties.[80] Where members have any vested interests, they are to be fully disclosed to the board. Such tainted members are also barred from voting on matters where their interests are manifest.[81] What is not clear, however,

---

77 See s 10 Reserve Bank of Fiji Act [Cap 210] 1983 (F). The directors are the governor, the permanent secretary for finance and five other members. See also s 10 National Reserve Bank of Tonga Act [Cap 38.20] 1989 (T).

78 See s 11; see also s 12 for the qualifications of other directors. Other directors must be persons of recognised standing in agricultural, commercial, financial, industrial or professional matters.

79 The position of non-executive directors in the management of public companies is attracting increasing attention since the publication of the *Cadbury Report* (UK); cf generally, Part VII of the Companies Act 2021(K), which specifically allows for the appointment of non-executive directors on the boards of companies.

80 See s 18(1) Reserve Bank of Fiji Act [Cap 210] 1983 (F): "No director shall act as a delegate of any commercial, financial, agricultural, industrial, or other interest, or receive or accept directions therefrom in respect of duties to be performed under this Act". See also sub-s (3). See s 18 National Reserve Bank of Tonga Act [Cap 38.20] 1989 (T).

81 Section 18(2) Reserve Bank of Fiji Act [Cap 210] 1983 (F).

is whether disclosure of interest to the board means disclosure to the full board. In other words, would disclosure to a duly appointed standing committee of the board dealing with such matters suffice, or would such disclosure have to be made to the full board at any of its regular sittings? It is apparent that the provisions of the Act are silent on this. What is clear is that a member with some vested interest which is already disclosed to the board will not be excluded from the formation of a quorum of the board.[82]

Except where disclosure of information is required by a written law or as required by the nature of the director's or officer's responsibilities, activities relating to the affairs of the bank are not to be divulged to any person. Using Fiji as an example, s 19 of the Act qualifies the nature of the information sought to be protected by using the word 'material'. The simple conclusion that can be drawn from this is that employees of the bank, including directors, are at liberty to disclose information concerning the operations of the bank to persons outside the bank so long as the information so disclosed is not 'material'. The question is, who determines whether the information is material or not? Is it the employee acting in a reasonable belief, or is it the bank? Another related question is, would the provisions of the Official Secrecy Act also apply to employees and directors of the reserve or central bank in the region?

In addition to the foregoing, the Act confers immunity on directors, officers or other employees of the reserve bank in respect of actions or defaults done or omitted to be done in good faith and without negligence in the course of the operations of the bank.[83] The criteria for immunity are 'good faith' and 'without negligence'. Perhaps a better proposition is to substitute 'good faith' with the word 'lawful'. The reasoning is that a person may act in good faith whilst at the same time be acting illegally. Here, the determination of one's degree of culpability in respect of a delict is 'intention' and not 'action'. This, we submit, is not a satisfactory position. There are no equivalent provisions in Vanuatu, Samoa or the Solomon Islands.

The primary responsibility of the reserve or central bank is to regulate commercial banking in the country. The powers are derived from the relevant law. Increasing pressure is now on reserve or central banks to take leading roles in effective monetary and fiscal policies of their countries by addressing both micro- and macro-economic issues and their relationship to development. This is a task that would set the agenda of national development policies in years to come in the region.

---

82 See the proviso to s 18(2) Reserve Bank of Fiji Act [Cap 210] 1983 (F).
83 See s 20 Reserve Bank Act (F); s 20 National Reserve Bank of Tonga Act [Cap 38.20] 1989 (T).

16

BILLS OF EXCHANGE, CHEQUES AND PROMISSORY NOTES

16.1 The operative laws

In simple terms, a bill of exchange is a document which takes the form of an unconditional order drawn by one person ('the drawer') to another (called 'the drawee') to pay a specified amount of money either to the drawer of the instrument or to a third party who is called 'the payee'. The drawee on the bill may or may not accept the order contained in the bill. Where he or she does so in writing, there is what is called an acceptance of the bill which amounts to an agreement to pay the amount specified on the bill at the time indicated or on demand and otherwise as directed. On acceptance, the drawee becomes known as the 'acceptor' of the bill. The drawer of the bill can then transfer the bill to the payee, who, by virtue of the acceptance and the transfer, is entitled to demand payment under the bill. The payee is then entitled to transfer or negotiate the bill to some other person, and this would most usually be a person to whom the payee is indebted. There might be many subsequent transfers or negotiations of the bill to and as between other persons who become entitled to the benefit of the order. When the bill matures, that is, when the time comes for the amount to be paid, the holder of the bill at the time is entitled to present the bill to the acceptor for payment.

The advantages attaching to negotiable instruments are to some extent obvious. They permit the transfer of money by way of credit and hence do away with the need for immediate payment of cash. The bill itself provides clear documentary evidence of the debt in question and if it is dishonoured at the due time, the holder of the bill can sue the acceptor on the bill itself.

Bills of exchange can also be made payable to third parties. Let's consider an example. Suppose Salote is indebted to Sailasa for the sum of FJ$1,000. At the same time, Sailasa owes FJ$1,000 to Jone. It does not really matter how the debt in

DOI: 10.4324/9781003428060-20

each case arose. Sailasa can draw against the credit he has with Salote by drawing a bill on Salote for FJ$1,000, which is made payable either on demand or at some specified time in favour of Jone. Supposing the bill has been accepted by Salote, she is bound to honour the bill on the terms stated and pay Jone when called on to do so. But Jone is also entitled to transfer his interest under the bill to another party; say, Seini, one of his creditors. Thus, Jone can use his interest under the bill to satisfy the debt he owes to Seini by, in effect, transferring or negotiating the bill to her. Negotiation with other holders can proceed by whoever owns or is the holder of the bill at any particular time. At any point in this sequence of transactions the holder of the bill can, if need be, sell the bill at a discount to a bank (discounting). In this way, the holder can in effect cash in the bill, leaving it to the bank to collect at the appropriate time.

The above example assumes that the original bill of exchange was created in order to draw against an existing debt owed by the drawee to the drawer, and sometimes these are known as 'commercial bills'. This need not always be the case. There are some types of bills, called 'accommodation bills', which are used directly as instruments to obtain finance by way of loan. A party who is providing loan finance in respect of a bill can do so in a number of ways. The lender or accommodating party might be the drawee of the bill in some cases. However, in other cases it might be the original drawer of the bill or an endorser of the bill. Much depends on the circumstances of the particular case. An accommodating party who has signed the bill will be liable on the bill to any holder for value (as discussed below), whether or not the holder for value knew that the person signing the bills was in fact an accommodating party. Yet there is an implied understanding that should the accommodating party have been forced to pay on the bill, there will be right of recovery from any other parties who bear primary liability on the bill.

There are laws in the region regulating the issuance and utilisation of bills of exchange. These are as follows: the Bills of Exchange Act Cap 227 of Fiji; the Bills of Exchange Act 1976 of Samoa; the Bills of Exchange Act Cap 108 of Tonga; the Bills of Exchange Act 1908 (NZ) applicable in the Cook Islands, Tokelau and Niue; and the Bills of Exchange Act 1879 applicable in Vanuatu and the Solomon Islands. Except where indicated, the discussions below refer to the same sections in all these laws.

16.1.1 Concept of negotiability

Negotiability refers to the element of transferability or legal assignment of the bill, along with certain other special features. This element emerged from customary mercantile practices and dealings many centuries ago in Europe. Negotiability enhances the proprietary value of documents which are used in financing trade and commerce.

The methods of negotiation of a bill are set out in the Act. Section 31 provides:

(1) A bill is negotiated when it is transferred from one person to another in such a manner as to constitute the transferee the holder of the bill.

(2) A bill payable to bearer is negotiated by delivery.

(3) A bill payable to order is negotiated by the endorsement of the holder completed by delivery.

(4) Where the holder of a bill payable to his order transfers it for value without endorsing it, the transfer gives the transferee such title as the transferor had in the bill, the transferee in addition acquires the right to have the endorsement of the transferor.

(5) Where any person is under obligation to endorse a bill in a representative capacity, he may endorse the bill in such terms as to negative personal liability.

There are three basic characteristics of negotiable instruments. First, a negotiable instrument is transferable free of equities. This means that it is capable of being transferred even if there exists on it a lien or equitable charge against it. The holder of it can acquire a title to the bill which is in fact better than the title of the person who transferred it to him or her. Secondly, it can be transferred for value. In this regard it is treated legally as a form of property in its own right and capable of transfer. Whoever acquires a bill for consideration and without notice of any defects which might exist on the bill by way of charges or otherwise becomes a holder in due course and acquires a good title clear of any such defects. Thirdly, it can be transferred from one person to another without the requirement that the previous holder be notified of the transfer.

In the case of a bill of exchange payable to bearer, the bill is negotiable by actual delivery of possession of the document from the holder or bearer to another person. In other cases, the bill is negotiable only by transfer plus endorsement on the bill in favour of another person or to bearer followed by delivery of possession of the bill.

16.1.2 Definition of a bill of exchange

Section 3(1) defines a bill of exchange as an unconditional order in writing, addressed by one person to another, signed by the person giving it, requiring the person to whom it is addressed to pay on demand or at a fixed or determinable future time a fixed sum of money to a specified person or according to his order, or to the bearer of the bill.

Before discussing the conditions governing the validity of a bill of exchange in Fiji, it is important to mention that an instrument which fails to comply with any of the conditions outlined in s 3(1) of the Act is not a bill of exchange.[1] Consequently,

---

1 Section 3(2).

a bill is not invalid only by reason that it is not dated, does not specify the value given or does not indicate the place of drawing or payment.[2]

16.1.3 Requirements for validity of a bill of exchange

The legal criteria for the constitution of a bill of exchange are laid out in the legislative definitions. These are as follows:

(a) It must be an order. The order is to originate from one person and is to be directed to another. The terms in which the bill is expressed must be imperative rather than in terms of request, hope, promise, wish, authorising or otherwise precatory in nature.[3] There should be no conditions attached to the order.[4] Furthermore, the order must be in writing.

(b) It must be addressed by one person to another. Parties who are subjects under the bill must also be specified with reasonable certainty.

(c) The bill is to be signed by the person giving it. Signature can legally cover a range of different modes of execution of a document. The reference to a signing indicates that it requires that a person use their own handwriting on the instrument.[5] Whatever mode is used, and this might include a mark, the signature must be effective as an adoption or authorisation of the relevant document as a whole. Indeed, it must be intended as such. If the signature is forged or appended by a person who has no authority to do so, then this is of no effect. Bills can be executed in a representative capacity, however. In addition, it appears that the authorities are confused on the question of whether an agent can actually write the name of one of the parties on a bill of exchange and thus constitute a signature. English authorities seem to suggest that they cannot.[6] Australian authorities tend to go both ways but the weight of authority seems to suggest that this can be done, making no distinction between execution explicitly in a representative capacity, or by signing the name of another.[7] There is no clear authority either way in the South Pacific countries, but it is suggested that the more liberal Australian view might well prevail in this instance. In situations where a signature on a bill of exchange or a cheque has been forged, the position is that the instrument is a nullity. The signature

---

2 Section 3(4).

3 *Little v Slackford* (1828) 173 ER 1120; *Hamilton v Spottiswood* (1849) 154 ER 1182.

4 Section 3(3) (F) and see *Bavins Jr and Sims v London and South Western Bank* [1900] 1 QB 270.

5 See *Goodman v J Eban Ltd* [1954] 1 QB 550, in which Denning LJ, at 561–62, said that, when a document is required to be 'signed by' someone, what is meant is that 'he must write his signature with his own hand'. See also *London County Council v Agricultural Food Products* [1955] 2 QB 218 and, more recently, *Firstpost Homes Ltd v Johnson* [1995] 1 WLR 1567.

6 *Ibid.*

7 See *McRae v Coulton* (1986) 7 NSWLR 644; *Muirhead v Commonwealth Bank of Australia* [1996] QCA 241.

is of no effect at all. However, there are some exceptions. There may be situations where a person allegedly drawing the bill is estopped from denying as against some other party relying on the bill from the genuineness of the signature; for example, where there has been some representation to the effect that the party signing had authority to do so.[8] Another situation is where, after the forgery occurs, the drawer ratifies the signature.

(d) It must be to pay on demand or at a fixed or determinable future time. The legislation provides that a bill is payable on demand if it is expressed to be so payable or is payable at sight or on presentation, or if no time for payment is expressed. It is payable at a determinable future time if it is expressed to be payable either (i) at a fixed period after date or sight; (ii) on or at a fixed period of time after the occurrence of a specified event which is certain to happen, though the time of happening may be uncertain.[9]

(e) It must relate to a sum certain in money. The order must be drawn for a certain sum for which payment is to be effected by legal tender or as indicated. Payment of the stated sum may be made by instalments. It may also be made according to some indicated rate of exchange. Payment of interest may also be included in the sum payable.[10]

(f) It must be payable to the order of a specified person or to bearer. This is important to determine the manner in which the bill is negotiable, whether by endorsement plus delivery or, in the latter case, by delivery only. A bill can be drawn in favour of a number of persons. Where the bill is drawn in favour of a fictitious or a non-existent person, the bill may be treated as a bearer bill.[11]

16.1.4 Parties to a bill of exchange

As indicated above, there are usually three original parties to a bill of exchange. There may be two only where the drawer of the bill is also the payee of it. Once drawn and accepted in this form, the bill can be negotiated by the drawer/payee to other parties. Some parties, as we noted above, might be accommodating parties as well. Bills of exchange can be transferred or assigned to other parties once they are created. Hence rights and liabilities with respect to the bill as originally drawn may change over time.

---

8 See *Tina Motors v Australia and New Zealand Banking Group Ltd* [1977] VR 205. The customer who becomes aware of a possible forgery on a cheque is under a duty to notify the bank as to the existence of the possible forgery.

9 Sections 15, 16 Bills of Exchange Act (F).

10 *Ibid.*, s 9(1).

11 This would seem to include a case where the drawee of the bill is a person who actually exists, but the bill was never intended to have been drawn in favour of such person. See *Bank of England v Vagliano Bros* [1891] AC 107.

These original parties are commonly referred to as the drawer, drawee and payee. The drawer of a bill is the one who authorises a payment to be made by drawing up the bill. The drawee is the person to whom the order is addressed. In other words, it is the person on whom the bill is drawn. Once that person accepts the bill by endorsing the acceptance on it, that person becomes known as the acceptor of the bill. The drawee only becomes liable on the bill if it has in fact been accepted. The payee is the person who is to obtain the payment under the bill. He or she is technically the beneficiary under the bill.

Some bills are made payable to the bearer of them for the time being. In such cases, the bill is called a bearer bill. The holder of it is called a bearer. These bills are negotiable from one holder or bearer of them to another person by delivery possession of the bill alone to that other. Other bills are payable to the order of a specified person or persons only. These are called order bills. These bills are negotiable only by written endorsement on the bill plus delivery of possession of the document. The holder of an order bill who transfers it to another is called an endorser. The person to whom it is transferred is called an endorsee.

In the case of a drawee, it is a requirement of law that he or she must be named or otherwise indicated in a bill with reasonable certainty.[12] This is aimed at dispelling any problems of mistaken identity as to who the drawee actually is. A bill may be addressed to two or more drawees, whether or not they are partners. But where the order is addressed to two drawees in the alternative or two or more drawees in succession, such an order cannot be regarded as a bill of exchange.[13] A drawee is under no liability to accept a bill. The contract constituted by the bill arises as regards this party by the act of acceptance only. However, where the drawee refuses to accept a bill drawn against him or her, that bill is said to have been dishonoured by non-acceptance. Under these circumstances, the holder of the bill (see below) will have rights of recourse against the drawer of the bill and any prior endorsers of the bill, where there are any.

In the case of a payee, he or she must be named or sufficiently identified in the bill of exchange. It is also possible for a bill to be payable to two or more persons either jointly or in the alternative.[14] Where a payee is a fictitious or non-existent person, the bill may be treated as payable to the bearer. A bill of exchange can be drawn in favour of the drawer. In such a case, where it has been drawn in favour of a bank, the bank as drawee is, it has been held, entitled either to debit the drawer's account or to negotiate the bill.[15]

There are commonly other parties to a bill which arise from subsequent negotiation of the bill. A person who holds a bill of exchange to order may negotiate

---

12 Section 6(1).
13 Section 6(2).
14 Section 7(1).
15 See *Rigg v Commonwealth Bank* (1989) 97 FLR 261 at 266.

the bill by written endorsement of transfer on the bill in favour of another person. When that person endorses the bill, he or she is known as an endorser. The person to whom it is endorsed is known as an endorsee. The endorsee becomes a holder of the bill, as explained below. The endorsee under one particular endorsement may in turn negotiate the bill further by further endorsement, and so on. In fact, in any case, an endorsement can be either to bearer or to order of a subsequent endorsee. In the first case as regards subsequent dealings with the bill, it is now regarded as a bearer bill which can be transferred by delivery unless it is again closed by a subsequent endorsement by the then holder or bearer.

The Act makes specific provision with respect to endorsement. Section 32 states as follows:

An endorsement in order to operate as a negotiation must comply with the following conditions, namely:

(a) it must be written on the bill itself and be signed by the endorser. The simple signature of the endorser on the bill, without additional words, is sufficient. An endorsement written on an allonge, or on a 'copy' of a bill issued or negotiated in a country where 'copies' are recognised, is deemed to be written on the bill itself;

(b) it must be an endorsement of the entire bill. A partial endorsement, that is to say, an endorsement which purports to transfer to the endorsee a part only of the amount payable, or which purports to transfer the bill to two or more endorsees severally, does not operate as a negotiation of the bill;

(c) where a bill is payable to the order of two or more payees or endorsees who are not partners all must endorse, unless the one endorsing has authority to endorse for the others;

(d) where, in a bill payable to order, the payee or endorsee is wrongly designated, or his or her name is mis-spelt, he or she may endorse the bill as therein described, adding, if he or she thinks fit, his proper signature;

(e) where there are two or more endorsements on a bill, each endorsement is deemed to have been made in the order in which it appears on the bill, until the contrary is proved;

(f) an endorsement may be made in. blank or special. It may also contain terms making it restrictive.

A person may also add credit to a bill by endorsing the bill as what is called a 'backer', or 'quasi-endorser' or 'stranger' to the bill. A backer is a person who endorses the bill otherwise than as an ordinary drawer, acceptor or endorser of a bill. Such a person, possibly a bank, might endorse the bill not as a transferee of the bill but as a provider of credit or collateral security to one of the parties to the bill. It might be by way of providing some form of guarantee by the backer to one of the parties (say, a seller) as regards the underlying transaction in respect of which the bill arose. However, a backer who endorses a bill becomes liable on the bill as an ordinary endorser to any person who is a holder in due course of the bill. This does not include the drawer or the payee of the bill.

The Act also refers to a holder of a bill of exchange. Basically, a holder of a bill is the person who has the primary right to enforce the bill of exchange. However, there are different categories of holder: an ordinary holder, a holder for value and a holder in due course. These notions will be examined further below. In basic terms, anyone who is a holder has rights against the drawer, the acceptor and any prior endorsers of the bill. There is no such right against the drawee under a bill which has not been formally accepted. The holder has the right to present a bill to the acceptor for payment. Assuming the time for payment has arrived, the failure of the acceptor to pay the holder according to the tenor of the bill means that the bill is dishonoured by non-payment. In such a case the holder then has a right of recourse against the drawer and any prior endorses of the bill for payment.

16.2 Capacity of parties to a bill of exchange

The capacity of a party to incur liability under a bill is the same as with the legal capacity to contract. In the case of minors, however, it has been held that a bill cannot be enforced against a minor who is a party to it even where the underlying transaction relates to the provision of necessities to that minor.[16] One partner in a trading partnership has implied authority to execute a bill of exchange on behalf of the firm as a whole. This does not apply in respect of non-trading partnerships, but there might be cases where the other partners are estopped from denying the authority of a partner to bind the firm by reason of an established course of conduct or a holding out of a partner to others as if he or she had such authority.[17] Any corporation which is competent under the law to enter into a contract can be made liable as a drawer, acceptor or endorser of a bill.[18] This argument becomes even more important in Fiji and other Pacific jurisdictions where companies are still bound by the doctrine of *ultra vires*.

A lack of capacity of one party might not be completely fatal as regards recovery under a bill. Where a bill is drawn by a person lacking legal capacity, such as an infant, a minor or a corporation, it is nevertheless possible for a holder of the bill to receive payment of the bill where it is made and to enforce it against any other party to the bill who is not incapacitated.

A bill can be executed by an agent of a party in a representative capacity. Usually, the execution of a bill in this way will make the person executing it personally liable unless it is clearly stated on the face of the bill that the bill is

16 See *Re Soltykoff ex p Margrett* [1891] 1 QB 413. Thus, this is at odds with the normal position in contract law where minors' contracts relating to necessities can be enforced on certain conditions.
17 See *London Chartered Bank of Australia v Kerr* (1878) 4 VLR 330.
18 Section 22.

executed on behalf of another, in such a way as to exclude personal liability. The courts are bound to give such an interpretation to the execution as would favour the validity of the bill.[19]

16.2.1 Types of bills of exchange

Section 4 of the Act in Fiji, as elsewhere, recognises two types of bills: foreign and inland bills. An inland bill is one which is or on the face of it purports to be (a) both drawn and payable in Fiji or within the Commonwealth of Australia, New Zealand or Papua New Guinea; or (b) drawn within Fiji or within the Commonwealth of Australia, New Zealand or Papua New Guinea upon some person resident therein. A bill other than the foregoing is a foreign bill. It appears from the wordings of s 4 that bills emanating from New Zealand, Australia and Papua New Guinea, which are foreign jurisdictions, can nevertheless be construed as inland bills for the purpose of the Act.

16.2.2 Liability of parties to a bill of exchange

Liability of an acceptor of a bill is dealt with in s 54 of the Act. By accepting a bill, an acceptor undertakes liability to pay the sum specified in the bill according to the terms of acceptance. The acceptor is estopped from denying to a holder in due course, the existence of the drawer, the genuineness of his or her signature and his or her capacity and authority to draw the bill; in the case of a bill payable to drawer's order, the capacity of the drawer to endorse, but not the genuineness of the endorsement; in the case of a bill payable to the order of a third person, the existence of a payee and his or her then capacity to endorse, but not the genuineness or validity of the endorsement.

Section 55 deals with the liability of the drawer or endorser. The implication here is that the drawer, by drawing a bill, guarantees that at the time of being presented, it will be honoured and paid according to its terms. Where it is dishonoured, the drawer will compensate the holder or endorser who is compelled to pay it, provided that the requisite proceedings on dishonour be duly taken. The drawer is also estopped from denying to a holder in due course the existence of the payee and his or her then capacity to endorse.[20] It is important to note that where a person signs a bill otherwise than as a drawer or acceptor, s/he incurs the liabilities of the endorser to a holder in due course.[21]

---

19 On the question of personal liability, see generally *English, Scottish and Australian Chartered Bank v Gunn* (1871) 10 SCR (NSW) 244 and *Elliot v Bax-Ironside* [1925] 2 KB 301.
20 Additional conditions are found in s 2(a), (b) and (c) of the Act.
21 Section 56.

16.2.3 Holders

The legislation refers to three different types of holder. These are: (a) a 'holder' in the sense of a mere or ordinary holder; (b) a 'holder for value' who is in effect a holder who has given value or consideration for the bill; and (c) a 'holder in due course'. Each of these has different rights and entitlements as regards the bill, so the determination of status is important.

A holder is defined to mean the payee or endorsee of a bill or note or the bearer thereof. A bearer is a person who is in possession of a bill or note which is payable to bearer.[22] A mere holder cannot enforce a bill, although in actions concerning the bill he or she is entitled to sue in his or her own name.[23] In order to enforce the bill, the holder must be a holder for value. The legislation provides that where an accommodation party has executed a bill, that party is liable to an action on the bill by a holder for value irrespective of whether, at the time the holder for value took the bill, he or she was aware that the party was an accommodation party.[24]

The concept of a holder for value assumes that someone who is first of all a holder, as above, has provided valuable consideration to acquire his or her interest under the bill. There is a statutory presumption as to a holder for value under s 30(1). It provides that every party whose signature appears on a bill is *prima facie* deemed to have become a party thereto for value. Otherwise, the normal contract rules relating to the provision of consideration which moves from the holder apply in this context, with two exceptions.[25] The first is that, by virtue of the legislation, the consideration may be past consideration, such as an antecedent debt or liability which would not be good consideration at general law.[26] The second is that a holder for value can enforce a bill where he or she has provided consideration for it at any time.[27] That is to say, the bill will be enforceable by a holder for value against another party who stands in an indirect relationship to the holder, even though the consideration provided by the holder did not move directly from the holder to that party. This is the case with respect to either an acceptor of the bill or any party who became a party to the bill prior to the holder for value.[28] Thus, consideration provided by a holder at any stage in the life of the bill, whether at issue, acceptance or further negotiation, would enable the holder for value to enforce the bill against all such other parties to the bill, whether their relationship to the holder is direct or indirect. Where the holder of a bill has a lien on it, whether that lien arises from

---

22 Section 2.
23 See *Stock Motor Ploughs Ltd v Forsyth* (1932) SR (NSW) 259.
24 Section 28(2).
25 See *Bonior v A Siery Ltd* [1968] NZLR 254.
26 See s 27(1)(b) Bills of Exchange Act.
27 See *Diamond v Graham* [1968] 2 All ER 909.
28 Section 27(2) Bills of Exchange Act.

contract or by legal implication, he or she is deemed to be a holder for value to the extent of the sum for which he or she has a lien.[29]

A holder in due course is one who has taken a bill, complete and regular on the face of it provided that: (1) he or she became the holder of the bill before it became overdue, and (2) without any notice of its being dishonoured if it was; (3) he or she took the bill in good faith and for value; and (4) at the time the bill was negotiated to him or her, he or she had no notice of any defect in the title of the person who negotiated it.[30]

The legislation requires the making of a presumption as to the status of a holder in due course. Section 30(2) provides that every holder of a bill is *prima facie* deemed to be a holder in due course. However, if in any action on a bill it is admitted or proved that the acceptance, issue or subsequent negotiation of the bill was affected by matters which would render the bill defective, the burden of proof is shifted. The holder will not be a holder in due course unless and until that holder proves that, subsequent to the occurrence defective matter, the bill was taken in good faith and for value. Relevant matters that would render the bill defective are fraud, duress, force and fear or illegality.[31]

A holder, whether for value or not, so long as s/he derives title to a bill through a holder in due course and is not a party to any fraud or illegality affecting the bill, is regarded in law as having all the rights of a holder in due course as regards the acceptor and all parties to the bill prior to the acceptor.[32] Being a holder of a bill confers with it other duties which have to be satisfied under that Act. These include the rights of the holder, as discussed below.[33]

The holder in due course is entitled to payment on the bill at the due date by virtue of the bill itself and independent of considerations that might arise with respect to underlying transactions. Defences based on underlying transactions cannot usually be set up in order to defer liability to meet the bill. In *Cebora SNC v SIP (Industrial Products) Ltd*,[34] it was said:

Any erosion of the application by our courts of the law merchant relating to bills of exchange is likely to work to the detriment of this country, which depends on international trade to a degree that needs no emphasis. For some generations one of those certainties has been that the bona fide holder for value of a bill of

---

29 *Ibid.*, s 27(3).
30 *Ibid.*, s 29(1). See generally *Durack v West Australian Trustee Executor and Agency Co Ltd* (1944) 72 CLR 189 and *Lombard Banking Ltd v Central Garage and Engineering Co Ltd* [1963] 1 QB 220.
31 See also s 29(2) Bills of Exchange Act.
32 *Ibid.*, s 29(3).
33 The general duties are found in ss 39–52, whilst the rights are set out in s 38 of the Act.
34 [1976] 1 Lloyd's Rep 271 at 278, Approved by the Fiji High Court in *In re Ramans Emporium Ltd* [1997] FJHC 6; see also *Deoji and Sons Ltd v Sagar Trading Co* [1995] FJCA 21.

exchange is entitled, save in truly exceptional circumstances, on its maturity to have it treated as cash, so that in an action upon it the court will refuse to regard either as a defence or as grounds for a stay of execution, any set-off, legal or equitable, or any counter-claim, whether arising on the particular transaction upon which the bill of exchange came into existence, or a fortiori, arising in any other way. This rule of practice is thus, in effect, pay on the bill of exchange first and pursue claims later.

16.2.4 Rights of the holder of a bill of exchange

The rights of a holder in due course are set out in s 38 of the Fiji legislation. This section provides:

The rights and powers of the holder of a bill are as follows–

(a) he may sue on the bill in his own name;

(b) where he is a holder in due course, he holds the bill free from any defect of title of prior parties, as well as from mere personal defences available to prior parties among themselves, and may enforce payment against all parties liable on the bill;

(c) where his title is defective–

(i) if he negotiates the bill to a holder in due course and that holder obtains a good and complete title to the bill; and

(ii) if he obtains payment of the bill the person who pays him in due course gets a valid discharge for the bill.

16.2.5 Where presentment of a bill of exchange is necessary

Where a bill is payable at sight, presentment for acceptance is necessary in order to fix the maturity of the instrument. Where a bill expressly stipulates that it is to be presented for acceptance, or where a bill is drawn and payable elsewhere than at the residence or place of business of the drawee, it must be presented for acceptance before it can be presented for payment. In no other case is presentment for acceptance necessary in order to render liable any party to the bill. Where the holder of a bill which has been drawn payable otherwise than at the place of business or residence of the drawee presents the bill for acceptance before presenting it for payment on the day that it falls due, the delay caused by presenting it for payment on the day it falls due is excused, and does not discharge the drawer and endorsers. This is on the proviso that it is presented by the holder with due diligence.

16.2.6 Rules as to presentment for acceptance of bills of exchange

Section 40 of the Bills of Exchange Act of Fiji outlines the rules to be complied with at the presentment of a bill for acceptance. There are identical provisions in the legislation of the other countries of the region.[35] The section states:

(1)
  (a) the presentment must be made by or on behalf of the holder to the drawee or to some person authorised to accept or refuse acceptance on his behalf at a reasonable hour on a business day and before the bill is overdue;
  (b) where the bill is addressed to two or more drawees, who are not partners, presentment must be made to them all then presentment may be made to his personal representative;
  (c) where the drawee is dead, presentment may be made to his personal representative;
  (d) where the drawee is bankrupt, presentment may be made to him or to his trustee;
  (e) where authorised by agreement or usage, a presentment through the post office is sufficient.
(2) Presentment in accordance with these rules is excused, and a bill may be treated as dishonoured by non-acceptance
  (a) where the drawee is dead or bankrupt, or is a fictitious person or a person not having capacity to contract by bill;
  (b) where, after the exercise of reasonable diligence, such presentment cannot be effected;
  (c) where, although the presentment has been irregular, acceptance has been refused on some other ground.
(3) The fact that the holder has reason to believe that the bill, on presentment, will be dishonoured does not excuse presentment.

16.2.7 Dishonour through non-acceptance

By s 43(1), a bill is dishonoured by non-acceptance:

(a) when it is presented for acceptance, and such an acceptance as is prescribed by this Act is refused or cannot be obtained;
(b) when presentment for acceptance is excused and the bill is not accepted.

---

35 See s 38 Bills of Exchange Act (S); s 45 Bills of Exchange Act (CI), (T), (Ni); s 41 Bills of Exchange Act (Tu).

By s 43(2), when a bill is dishonoured by non-acceptance, an immediate right of recourse against the drawer and endorsers accrues to the holder of the bill, and no presentment for payment is necessary.

16.3 Duties as to qualified acceptances

By s 44 of the Act, the holder of a bill may refuse to take qualified acceptance and, if he or she does not obtain an unqualified acceptance, may treat the bill as dishonoured by non-acceptance. Where a qualified acceptance is taken and the drawer or an endorser has not expressly or impliedly authorised the holder to take qualified acceptance or does not subsequently assent thereto, such drawer or endorser is discharged from his liability on the bill. The proviso to this sub-section does not apply to a partial acceptance, whereof due notice has been given. Where a foreign bill has been accepted as to part, it must be protested as to the balance. When the drawer or endorser of a bill receives notice of a qualified acceptance and does not within a reasonable time express his dissent to the holder, he or she shall be deemed to have assented thereto.

16.3.1 Presentment for payment

By s 45 of the Act, a bill must be duly presented for payment. Where it is not so presented, the drawer and endorsers are considered discharged from any liabilities under the bill. To be able to satisfy the requirement of the Act regarding presentment for payment, certain rules are outlined by s 45 as to when it is to be considered that there is due presentment of a bill. A bill is duly presented for payment where the bill is not payable on demand but presentment is made on the day it falls due. Where the bill is payable on demand, presentment must be made within a reasonable time after its issue in order to render the drawer liable, and within a reasonable time in order to render the endorser liable. In determining what is a reasonable time, regard must be had to the nature of the bill, the usage of trade with regard to similar bills and the facts of the particular case.

It is also a requirement that presentment must be made by the holder, or by some person authorised to receive payment on his or her behalf at a reasonable hour on a business day, at the proper place therein defined. It must be presented either to the person designated by the bill as payer, or to some person authorised to pay or refuse payment on his or her behalf, if with the exercise of reasonable diligence such person can there be found.

16.3.2 Excuses for delay or non-presentment for payment

By s 46, a delay in presentment for payment is excused when the delay is caused by circumstances beyond the control of the holder, and not imputable to his or her default, misconduct or negligence. Such circumstances may include an Act of God, belligerence between nations, floods, earthquakes and other natural disasters. When the cause of delay ceases to operate, presentment must be made with reasonable diligence.

16.3.3 Dishonour by non-payment

This is covered by s 47 of the Act. A bill is dishonoured by non-payment where it is duly presented for payment and is refused or cannot be obtained. It is also considered as dishonoured when the presentment is excused and the bill is overdue and unpaid. It is also important to point out that when a bill is dishonoured by non-payment, an immediate right of recourse against the drawer and endorsers accrues to the holder.

16.3.4 Notice of dishonour

By s 48, where a bill is dishonoured due to non-acceptance or as a result of non-payment, notice of the dishonour must be given to the drawer and endorser, and to any drawer or endorser to whom such notice is not given.[36] Certain rules are set out in s 49 of the legislation which must be followed on dishonour. In *Bank of Tonga v Shell Company (Pacific Islands) Ltd*,[37] it was stated that the procedures for dishonour are independent of the liability which may arise under the common law relating to the liabilities of a bank to its customers in respect of the collection of cheques.

16.4 Measure of damages

According to s 57 of the Act, where a bill is dishonoured, the measure of damages, which shall be deemed to be liquidated damages, are to be assessed as follows:

(a) The holder may recover from any party liable on the bill, and the drawer who has been compelled to pay the bill may recover from the acceptor, and an endorser who has been compelled to pay the bill may recover from the acceptor or from the drawer, or from a prior endorser–
   (i) amount of the bill;
   (ii) the interest thereon from the time of presentment for payment if the bill is payable on demand, and from the maturity of the bill in any other case;

---

36 This is subject to the proviso in the same section.
37 [2000] TOSC 53.

      (iii) the expenses of noting, or, when protest is necessary, and the protest has been extended, the expenses of the protest.

(b) In the case of a bill which has been dishonoured abroad, in lieu of the above damages, the holder may recover from the drawer or an endorser, and the drawer or an endorser who has been compelled to pay the bill may recover from any party liable to him, the amount of the re-exchange with interest thereon until the time of payment.

(c) Where interest may be recovered as damages, such interest may, if justice require it, be withheld wholly or in part, and where a bill is expressed to be payable with interest at a given rate, interest as damages may or may not be given at the same rate as interest proper.

16.4.1 Extinction or discharge of bills

A bill becomes extinguished where the terms or conditions of the bill are performed. In this case, the bill is considered discharged. Extinction of a bill can arise in any of the following ways.

(a) **By payment.** According to s 59, a bill is discharged by payment in due course by or on behalf of the drawee or acceptor. Payment in due course means payment made at or after the maturity of the bill to the holder thereof in good faith and without notice that his or her title to the bill is defective.

(b) **Bank paying where endorsement is forged.** By s 66, when a bill payable to order on demand is drawn on a bank, and the bank on whom it is drawn pays the bill in good faith and in the ordinary course of business, it is not incumbent upon the bank to show that the endorsement of the payee or any subsequent endorsement was made by or under the authority of the person whose endorsement it purports to be, and the bank is deemed to have paid the bill in due course, although such endorsement has been forged or made without authority.

(c) **Acceptor as holder at maturity.** According to s 61, when the acceptor of a bill is or becomes the holder of it at or after its maturity, in his own right, the bill is discharged.

(d) **Express waiver.** According to s 62, when a holder of a bill at or after its maturity absolutely and unconditionally renounces his or her rights against the acceptor, the bill is discharged. The renunciation must be in writing, unless the bill is delivered up to the acceptor. The liabilities of any party to a bill may in like manner be renounced by the holder before, at or after its maturity, but nothing in this section shall affect the rights of a holder in due course without notice of the renunciation.

(e) **Cancellation.** By s 63, where a bill is intentionally cancelled by the holder or his or her agent, and the cancellation is apparent thereon, the bill is discharged. In like manner, any party liable on a bill may be discharged by the intentional cancellation of his or her signature by the holder or his or her agent. In such a case, any endorser who would have had a right of recourse against the party whose signature is cancelled is also discharged. A cancellation made unintentionally, under a mistake or without the authority of the holder is inoperative, but where a bill or any signature thereon appears to have been cancelled, the burden of proof lies on the party who alleges that the cancellation was made unintentionally, under a mistake or without authority. However, in the case of Tonga, cancellation is covered in s 62 of the Bills of Exchange Act.

(f) **Alteration of bill**. According to s 64, where a bill or acceptance is materially altered without the assent of all parties liable on the bill, the bill is voided except as against a party who has made him or herself, authorised, or assented to the alteration, and subsequent endorsers. However, in the case of Tonga, the alteration of bill is covered by s 63 of the Bill of Exchange Act Cap 108.

16.5 Cheques

A cheque is defined in the legislation as a bill of exchange drawn on a bank payable on demand.[38] Thus, a cheque must meet all of the legal criteria set down for a bill of exchange, except that the drawee on the cheque is always a bank. Furthermore, it is in the nature of cheques that they are always payable on demand rather than at some future specified time or on the occurrence of some event. As with bills of exchange, cheques can be payable to bearer or they may be to the order of a specified person.

Cheques take a specific legal form. The duties of a bank, for example, as well as the rights of the holder to receive payment, only arise where the instrument in question complies specifically with the legal requirements for a cheque. When a cheque account is opened at a bank, the bank and the customer enter into a contract relating to the use and application of the funds deposited by the customer in the account from time to time. The customer has the right to draw on those funds and direct that they be paid by the bank in a certain way and subject to certain conditions. The contract might or might not expressly state what form the customer's directions or demands are to take, but it will be legally implied in any event that the customer's direction is to take the form of a cheque complying with the legal criteria. For one thing, this creates a situation in which the bank is capable of clearly understanding what is expected of it in relation to the use and application of the funds in the customer's account from time to time.

---

38 Section 73 of the legislation of all countries except Tonga, for which see s 72 Bills of Exchange Act Cap 108 (T).

The primary relationship is between the bank and the customer as regards the use of the funds in the cheque account. This is a contractual relationship.[39] Hence the main duty of the bank in relation to cheques drawn against the account is to the customer rather than to the third party in favour of whom the cheque is drawn or any subsequent holder of it. The holder of a cheque does not have rights against the bank. The holder's rights may be against the customer who draws the cheque or some other party such as an endorser.

In addition, as a result of mercantile practice, there has developed the practice of marking cheques in certain ways by crossing them. There are various types of crossings of legal significance, and we will examine these in a moment. The crossings serve basically to provide certain instructions to the bank against whom the cheque is drawn as to the conditions under which payment of the cheque is to be made.

The nature of the relationship between a bank and its customer is a fiduciary one,[40] but it is not one of trustee and beneficiary. It is not a relationship in which undue influence might be presumed in equity.[41] The relationship is determined essentially by the contract between them but subject to statutory rights and duties of each and to implied rights and duties arising by commercial practice.[42] The moneys to the credit of the customer in the account are in effect bank borrowings from the customer, the bank being subject to an obligation to repay or to pay them on demand by the customer, at the branch of the bank where the account is kept during ordinary banking hours.[43] The bank is obliged to give reasonable notice before refusing to do business on behalf of the customer.[44]

16.5.1 Banks' duties as to payment of cheques

At common law, the relationship between a bank and its customer as regards funds held in a current or cheque account is that of debtor (the bank) and creditor (the customer). The bank holds the funds in the account and must pay the amount

---

39 On the question as to whether a bank can by way of an exclusion clause contract out of or limit its common law liability to the customer, see Edwards, R, 'The rights of banks to contract out of common law liabilities arising in the banker/customer relationship' (1989) 63 ALJ 237.

40 On various aspects of the relationship, see Weaver, GA and Craigie, CR, *Bank and Customer in Australia*, 1975, Sydney, Law Book Co, p 2514; *Foley v Hill* (1848) 9 ER 1002; *R v Davenport* [1954] 1 WLR 569; *Currabubula Holdings & Paola Holdings v State Bank of NSW* [1999] NSWSC 276.

41 *National Westminster Bank v Morgan* [1985] 1 AC 686 at 707; *Fonua v MBf Bank Ltd* [1999] TOSC.

42 *Commercial Bank of Australia Ltd v Hulls* (1884) 10 VLR (L) 110.

43 Weaver and Craigie, *op cit* fn 40; *Joachimson v Swiss Bank Corp* [1921] 3 KB 110; *Parker v Gordon* (1806) 7 East 385, (1806) 103 ER 149; *Arab Bank Ltd v Barclays Bank (Dominion Colonial and Overseas)* [1954] AC 495.

44 *Prosperity Ltd v Lloyds Bank Ltd* (1923) 39 TLR 372.

held in it at the direction of the customer. The cheque is in effect a direction or demand to the bank to pay certain of the moneys held in the account in a certain way, whether to the order of a third party or to bearer or otherwise. The bank is obliged to comply with the customer's mandate as regards accounts which it holds on behalf of the customer. As regards a cheque account, that mandate is exercised by the drawing of a cheque in proper form.[45] It has been said:

A bank is under a contractual obligation to honour its customer's cheques [on presentment for payment by the holder], provided that:

(a) each cheque is an effective instrument in proper form;
(b) there are sufficient funds to meet it; and
(c) there is no legal impediment (such as a garnishee order, injunction, exchange control requirement etc) to the bank's honouring the cheque.[46]

The bank is entitled to expect that the terms of the cheque will be free of ambiguity. Otherwise, it will not be under an obligation to pay on the cheque. If the cheque is ambiguous, the bank is entitled to act on a reasonable interpretation of the customer's demand. If no such interpretation is possible, the bank is entitled to refuse to take action on the cheque.

The bank is under an obligation to pay if there are sufficient funds in the account at the time of presentment. If there are insufficient funds to meet the whole amount of the cheque, the bank is not liable to pay at all. It is under no obligation to make a pro rata payment of the cheque. The cheque cannot be treated as an assignment to the holder of so much of the amount as stands in the customer's account at the time payment on the cheque is called for. Cheques, like other negotiable instruments, are types of property. Thus, there are obligations at common law, as well as by statute, which apply concerning the manner in which a bank must deal with such cheques on behalf of the customer. In *Marfani and Co Ltd v Midland Bank Ltd*,[47] it was said:

At common law, one's duty to one's neighbour who is the owner, or entitled to possession, of any goods is to refrain from doing any voluntary act in relation to his goods which is a usurpation of his proprietary or possessory rights in them. Subject to some exceptions which are irrelevant for the purposes of the present case, it matters not that the doer of the act of usurpation did not know,

---

45 See e.g. *Foley v Hill* (1848) 9 ER 1002; *Joachimson v Swiss Bank Corp* [1921] 3 KB 110. It is sometimes debated whether a bank is obliged to comply with an oral order from a customer to the bank to pay moneys in an account to a third party. Given the requirement that cheques be in writing, it would seem that the bank is not obliged to comply with an oral order to pay in this way.
46 Weaver and Craigie, *op cit* fn 40, p 344.
47 [1968] 1 WLR 956 at 970–71.

and could by the exercise of any reasonable care have known, of his neighbour's interest in the goods. The duty is absolute; he acts at his peril.

In *Papandony and Another v Citibank*,[48] commenting on the above paragraph, it was said:

> A bank's business, of its very nature, exposes him daily to this peril. His contract with his customer requires him to accept possession of cheques delivered to him by his customer, to present them for payment to the banks upon which the cheques are drawn, to receive payment of them, and to credit the amount thereof to his own customer's account, either upon receipt of the cheques themselves from the customer or upon receipt of actual payment of the cheques from the banks upon which they are drawn. If the customer is not entitled to the cheque which he delivers to his bank for collection, the bank, however innocent and careful he might have been, would at common law be liable to the true owner of the cheque for the amount of which he receives payment, either as damages for conversion or under the cognate cause of action, based historically upon assumpsit, for money had and received.

Where a bank makes payment of a cheque on which the signature of the customer has been forged, the bank will be liable to the customer. In view of the forgery, there is no proper mandate or direction given by the customer to make drawings on the customer's account. However, the same statutory exceptions that apply with respect to forged signatures on bills of exchange, as discussed above, apply with respect to cheques.

16.5.2 Presentment for payment

According to s 74 of the Act, where a cheque is not presented for payment within a reasonable time of its issue, and the drawer or the person on whose account it is drawn has the right, at the time of such presentment, as between him or her and the bank to have the cheque paid and suffers actual damage through the delay, he or she is discharged to the extent of such damage. In other words, the discharge is to the extent to which the drawer or person is a creditor of the bank to a larger amount than he or she would have been had the cheque been paid.[49]

In determining what is a reasonable time, regard is to be had to the nature of the instrument, the usage of trade and of banks and the facts of the particular case.[50]

---

48 [2002] NSWSC 388.
49 Section 73 Bills of Exchange Act Cap 108 (T).
50 It is to be noted that what is a reasonable time is not stated by the Act. It is customary banking practice to regard six months as a reasonable time.

The holder of the cheque as to which the drawer or person is discharged shall be a creditor, in lieu of the drawer or person, of the bank to the extent of such discharge and entitled to recover the amount from him or her.

According to s 75,[51] the duty and authority of a bank to pay a cheque drawn on it by its customer are determined by countermand of payment and notice of the customer's death.[52]

16.5.3 Types of crossing

It is conventional that cheques contain crossings. It is not required that they do so. Cheques without crossings are called 'open cheques'. These take the form of shorthand instructions to banks in relation to the payment of cheques and are designed to provide extra protection to the drawer of the cheque in case the cheque should fall into the hands of persons who are not entitled to it. The law here, as elsewhere, has absorbed commercial practice. The existence of crossings will be relevant to situations in which a bank makes payment of cheques; this is discussed further below.

There are basically two types of crossing: general crossing and special crossing. In all the countries in the region except in Tonga,[53] this is covered by s 76. Section 76 states that where a cheque bears across its face an addition of:

(a)   the words 'and Company' or any abbreviation thereof between two parallel lines, either with or without the words 'not negotiable'; or

(b)   two parallel lines simply, either with or without the words 'not negotiable', that addition constitutes a crossing, and the cheque is crossed generally;
      (2) where the cheque bears across its face an addition of the name of a bank either with or without the words 'not negotiable', that addition constitutes a crossing and the cheque is crossed specially and to that bank.

These are in effect the only types of crossings recognised as valid crossings. The mere writing

of the words 'not negotiable' on a cheque has no effect as a crossing unless it appears in the manner indicated above. Negotiability is one of the fundamental aspects of a cheque, as with other bills of exchange. A non-negotiable crossing removes this element of negotiability in important ways. It does not prevent the instrument from being transferred from one party to another. But that is only one aspect of negotiability. What it does is remove the possibility of a transferee of such a cheque obtaining a title free of equities, or, in other words, obtaining a

---

51 See s 74 Bills of Exchange Act Cap 108 (T).
52 Bills of Exchange Act Cap 108 (T).
53 Section 75 Bills of Exchange Act Cap 108 (T).

better title to the cheque than the previous holder or holders might have had. The transferee takes subject to whatever defects of title might have existed at the time he or she acquired the cheque.[54]

16.5.4 Banks' duties in relation to the collection of cheques

A bank is under a duty to collect cheques deposited to the account of a customer. Failure to do so may result in liability in damages for negligence or conversion. In *Bank of Tonga v Shell Company (Pacific Islands) Ltd*,[55] it was said:

> A bank's duties to its customer in regard to the collection of cheques are well established at common law. As its customer's agent in this regard, a bank is bound to use reasonable care and diligence in presenting and securing payment of such cheques; accordingly, a bank must always choose the speediest section of the clearing house system when presenting a customer's cheques for payment ... As a corollary of this general principle ... a collecting bank must always give prompt notice to its customer upon dishonour. But this general law duty should be viewed as something which is quite independent of the operation of ss 48 and 49 [of the Bills of Exchange Act] for other purposes.

On the question of the measure of damages which might be awarded, the court added:

> Whilst the existence of the bank's common law duty to inform its customer promptly of dishonour is plain, the measure of damages to be awarded for breach of such a duty is another question. This will depend upon the particular circumstances, but generally speaking damages will be awarded to compensate for any losses flowing directly and naturally from the breach. Ordinarily, in a case such as the present, that is, the alleged failure to warn of an adverse event, the measure of damages will comprehend expenditure thrown away by the customer as a consequence of the bank's failure to warn the customer of the dishonour of the drawer's cheque. This could pick up any unrecovered cost of goods supplied by the customer on credit to the drawer, where that supply occurs in the customer's ignorance of the dishonour of the cheque as a consequence of the bank's failure to act promptly.

Conversion is an action based on dealing with property wholly inconsistent with the immediate right of possession of another person who has property or special

---

54 See *Commissioners of State Savings Bank of Victoria v Permewan Wright & Co Ltd* (1914) 19 CLR 457.
55 [2000] TOSC 53.

property in it. The action is available with respect to negotiable instruments.[56] The true owner of the cheque can sue a bank in conversion where a collecting bank has dealt with the cheque inconsistent with the owner's right to immediate possession. As a general proposition, where a cheque has been drawn or obtained through fraud of another party, the cheque remains the property of the drawer.[57] However, much appears to depend on whether or not the cheque was given in performance of some underlying contract. Where there is a completed contract to which the cheque was given in payment, it would seem that the transaction is at best void-able on the part of the drawer. However, property in it passes to the drawee and may be passed to others. In such a case, the right of avoidance may be lost and the drawer may no longer have the right to sue in conversion. However, where there is no contract involved, the fraud will render the transaction completely void such that no property in the cheque passes, and the drawer will remain the true owner of it. In such a case, an action in conversion can be maintained by the original drawer of the cheque.[58]

16.5.5 Duties of a bank where cheques are crossed

Section 79 of the Act lays down certain duties of a bank in situations where cheques have been crossed.[59] Where a cheque is crossed specially to more than one bank, except when crossed to an agent for collection being a bank, the bank on whom it is drawn must refuse payment thereof. Where the bank on whom a cheque is drawn which is so crossed nevertheless proceeds to pay the cheque, it is liable to the true owner of the cheque for any loss he or she may sustain owing to the cheque having been so paid.[60] The same applies where the bank pays a cheque crossed generally, or otherwise than to a bank. Likewise, it applies if the cheque is crossed specially and the paying bank pays otherwise than to a bank to whom it is crossed, or its agent for collection, being a bank.

---

56 *Lloyds Bank Ltd v Chartered Bank of India, Australia and China* [1929] 1 KB 40.
57 *Midland Bank Ltd v Reckitt* [1933] AC 1; *Great Western Railway Co v London and County Banking Co Ltd* [1901] AC 414; *Morison v London County and Westminster Bank Ltd* [1914] 3 KB 356; *Lloyds Bank Ltd v Chartered Bank of India, Australia and China* [1929] 1 KB 40.
58 See *Great Western Railway v London and County Banking Co* [1901] AC 414; *Australian Guarantee Corp Ltd v State Bank of Victoria* [1989] VR 617; *Harrisons Group Holdings Ltd v Westpac Banking Corp* (1989) 51 SASR 36; *Hunter BNZ Finance v ANZ Banking Group* [1990] VR 41; *Papandony and Another v Citibank* [2002] NSWSC 388.
59 See s 78 Bills of Exchange Act Cap 108 (T).
60 See the proviso to the section.

16.5.6 Protection to bank and drawer where a cheque is crossed[61]

Section 80 of the Act provides certain protections to banks in respect of crossed cheques. These apply to a bank on whom a crossed cheque is drawn where the bank pays the cheque in good faith without negligence. It applies in the case of a cheque crossed generally where the payment is made to another bank. If it is specially crossed, it applies where the payment is made either to the bank to whom it is crossed or to its agent for collection also being a bank. The section provides that the bank paying the cheque, and the drawer also, if the cheque has come into the hands of the payee, shall respectively be entitled to the same rights and be placed in the same position as if the payment of the cheque had been made to the true owner thereof. The protection is particularly relevant to protect the bank against liability in conversion, as discussed above.

16.5.7 Effect of crossing on holder

According to s 81 of the Act, where a person takes a crossed cheque which bears on it the words 'not negotiable', he or she does not have, and is not capable of giving, a better title to the cheque than that of the person from whom it was taken.

16.5.8 Protection of banks collecting payment of cheques

The Act provides certain protections to a bank in dealing with cheques. Section 86 of the Act[62] provides one of the main protections, as follows:

> Where a banker in good faith and without negligence:
> (a) receives payment for a customer of an instrument to which this section applies; or
> (b) having credited a customer's account with the amount of any such instrument,[63] receives payment thereof for himself, and the customer has no title or a defective title to, the instrument the banker shall not incur any liability to the true owner of the instrument by reason only of having received payment thereof. ...
> (3) A banker shall not be treated for the purposes of this section as having been negligent by reason only of his failure to concern himself with the absence of, or irregularity in, endorsement of an instrument.

---

61 On liability on post-dated cheques, see generally Hamilton, JW, 'The Canadian law on postdated cheques: indeterminate rules, unpredictable results' 35(2) *Canadian Business Law Journal* 280. See also s 2 Cheques Act No 17 of 1960 (CI).

62 See s 84 Bills of Exchange Act Cap 108 (T). Cf s 3 Cheques Act No 19 of 1960 (CI).

63 On the issue of dishonoured cheques, see generally Bradley Crawford, B, 'Return of dishonoured cheque' 36(1) *Canadian Business Law Journal* 1.

Sub-section (2) deems a cheque to be an instrument. The phrase 'without negligence' has received considerable interpretation by the courts. In *Commissioners of Taxation v English Scottish and Australian Bank Ltd*,[64] it was said:

> The test of negligence is whether the paying in of any given cheque, coupled with the circumstances antecedent and present, was so out of the ordinary course that it ought to have aroused doubt in the banker's mind and caused the banker to make inquiries.[65]

16.6 Promissory notes

16.6.1 Definition

Promissory notes are another type of negotiable instrument. Unlike cheques, they are not bills of exchange, although they are provided for under the same legislation.[66] Compared to cheques, promissory notes are not of very significant use in commerce in the region. Their usage is limited to small-scale business transactions, usually between traders who are well known to each other. Section 88 of the Act defines a promissory note as an unconditional promise in writing made by one person to another signed by the maker, engaging to pay, on demand or at a determinable future time, a sum certain in money to, or to the order of, a specified person or to bearer.

An instrument in the form of a note payable to maker's order is a promissory note unless it is endorsed by the maker.[67] A note is not invalid by reason only that it also contains a pledge of the collateral security with authority to sell or dispose thereof.[68] A note which is, or on the face of it purports to be, both made and payable in Fiji or within the Commonwealth of Australia, New Zealand or Papua New Guinea is an inland note. Any other note is a foreign note.

16.6.2 Presentment of note for payment

By s 92 of the Act, where a promissory note is made payable at a particular place, it must be presented for payment at that place in order to render the maker liable.[69]

---

64 [1920] AC 683 at 688.
65 See also *Commissioners of State Savings Bank of Victoria v Permewan Wright & Co Ltd* (1914) 19 CLR 457; *Marfani & Co v Midland Bank Ltd* [1968] 1 WLR 956.
66 There are other types of negotiable instrument, such as bills of lading.
67 It appears that a promissory note may also serve as a memorandum in writing for the purposes of the Moneylenders Act Cap 234 (F). See *Singh v Sarup* [1962] FijiLawRp 39; [1962] 8 FLR 107 (4 May 1962). A document which fails to stand up as a promissory note for the purposes of s 88 can satisfy the requirement in respect of a money-lending transaction. See *Ram Autar and Another v Penaia Rokovuni* 11 FLR 226; *Singh v Wati* [1997] FJHC 160; Hba0009j.97b (24 October 1997); *Singh v Wati* [1997] FJHC 160.
68 See s 86 Bills of Exchange Act (T); s 84 Bills of Exchange Act (NZ) (CI), (T), (Ni).
69 See s 90 Bills of Exchange Act (T); s 88 Bills of Exchange Act (NZ).

In any other case, presentment for payment is not necessary in order to render the maker liable. Presentment for payment is necessary in order to render the endorser liable. Where a note is made payable at a particular place, presentment at that place is necessary in order to render an endorser liable, but when a place of payment is indicated by way of a memorandum only, presentment at that place is sufficient to render the endorser liable, but a presentment to the maker elsewhere, if sufficient in other respects, shall also suffice.

16.6.3 Liability of the maker

According to s 93 of the Act,[70] the maker of a promissory note, by making it:

(a) engages that he will pay it according to its tenor;
(b) is precluded from denying to a holder in due course the existence of the payee and his then capacity to endorse.

16.6.4 Delivery

By s 89 of the Act, a promissory note is inchoate and incomplete until delivery thereof to the payee or bearer.[71] By s 90 of the Act, a promissory note may be made by two or more makers, and they may be liable thereon jointly, or jointly and severally according to its tenor. Where a note runs 'I promise to pay' and is signed by two or more persons, it is deemed to be their joint and several note.[72]

16.6.5 Note payable on demand

According to s 91 of the Act,[73] where a note payable on demand has been endorsed, it must be presented for payment within a reasonable time of the endorsement. If it is not so presented, the endorser is discharged. In determining what is a reasonable time, regard shall be had to the nature of the instrument, the usage of trade and the facts of the particular case. Where a note payable on demand is negotiated, it is not deemed to be overdue for the purpose of affecting the holder with defects of title of which he or she had no notice, by reason that it appears that a reasonable time for presenting it for payment has lapsed since its issue.

---

70 Section 91 Bills of Exchange Act (T); s 89 Bills of Exchange Act (NZ).
71 Section 87 Bills of Exchange Act (T).
72 *Ibid.*, s 88.
73 *Ibid.*, s 89; s 87 Bills of Exchange Act (NZ).

17

DOCUMENTARY OR COMMERCIAL CREDIT

17.1 Definition

A banker's commercial (documentary) credit is defined as:

> an undertaking by a bank to pay a sum of money to whom the credit is addressed, or to accept or purchase a bill of exchange drawn or held by that person and this is either absolute or more usually is given on condition that the person fulfils the requirements set out in the credit.[1]

17.1.1 Operation of the credit

The discussion now turns attention to documentary credit. This type of transaction is known by a variety of names, including letters of credit, banker's commercial credit and simply credit. It is one of the commonest methods of financing international trade. It involves another kind of negotiable instrument. Documentary or commercial credit is another method of financing trade, usually between domestic and foreign traders. In normal circumstances, the seller, who may be based overseas, is not aware of the financial standing of the buyer. Likewise, the buyer may not be in a position to readily ascertain the propriety of the seller to supply the goods. To obviate this handicap to commerce, the use of a commercial credit may be called into play.

Because of the general hazards of moving physical cash across international frontiers, commercial and merchant usage saw the introduction of credit to

---

1 See Pennington, RR *et al.*, *Commercial Banking Law*, 1978, London, Macdonald and Evans, p 1.

DOI: 10.4324/9781003428060-21

commerce as a necessary innovation. The aim of a credit is to provide a guaranteed means of payment for transactions between a buyer and seller. As a result of this development, certainty in discounting and payment of a credit is assured because of the use of and the involvement of banks. Very often banks act as agents to the buyer/importer or seller/exporter.[2]

The law regulating banker's credit at the international level is the Uniform Customs and Practice for Commercial Documentary Credit.[3] This was developed by the International Chamber of Commerce and was later endorsed by the United Nations Centre for Trade Law (UNCITRAL).

The basic foundation of the credit is anchored on the premise that the buyer should at the end of the transaction obtain the goods ordered. The seller must also receive payment for the goods. In fact, this is the underlying consideration in any sale of goods transaction. The intention to show good faith in a sale is meaningless unless it is backed up by the execution of agreed contractual responsibilities – the buyer receiving the goods and the seller receiving the payment.

There are normally four parties to a letter of credit. Loosely speaking, these are the buyer/importer, the issuing bank, the confirming bank, and the seller/exporter. A credit therefore contemplates the use of intermediaries in the form of either the issuing or the correspondent bank.

The buyer initiates the process of opening a credit by completing all the necessary banking formalities. If the issuing bank accepts the credit application, a contractual relation is created between the banker and the buyer. The limit and purpose of the credit is then specified. The importer then asks its bank to open a credit in favour of the exporter through a correspondent bank in the exporter's country.[4] The importer then has to produce a notarised sale contract between it and the exporter to his bank. The importer/buyer's bank is normally referred to as an issuing bank.[5] The bank in the seller's country then informs the seller of the credit. On the strength of this arrangement, the seller then dispatches the goods to the buyer. The seller/exporter will be paid when the contract and shipping documents are produced. The buyer is able to take possession of the goods on the presentation of the relevant contract documents.[6]

---

2 See *Guarantee Trust Co of NY v Hannay* [1918] 2 KB 623 at 625, where Scrutton LJ upheld the position of a bank as a financial intermediary with respect to the issuing of a banker's commercial credit. For a discussion of the duties of local banks regarding the issuing of commercial credits, see the Nigerian Court of Appeal's decision in *African Continental Bank Ltd v Obmiami Brick and Stone* [1990] 5 NWLR 230.

3 ICC Publication No 500 (1993). For matters dealing with collection of credits, see ICC Publication No 522 (Uniform Rules for Collections 1995).

4 Schmitthoff, C, *Export Trade*, 1999, London, Stevens & Sons, p 403; see also *Trans Trust SPRL v Danubian Trading Co Ltd* [1952] 1 All ER 970.

5 Article 10B.

6 See generally Goode, R, *Commercial Law*, 2nd edn, 1995, Harmondsworth, Penguin Books, pp 966–70.

The relationship between the buyer/importer and the issuing bank is contractual.[7] So also is the relationship between the correspondent bank and the seller/importer. There is, however, no privity of contract between the buyer/importer and the corresponding bank or between the seller/exporter and the issuing bank. The general remedies in contracts govern consequences arising from a breach of the terms of a credit. The measure of damages is also governed by the existing contractual principles. In other words, where the buyer breaches the terms of the credit, the seller (creditor) is entitled to claim damages just as in an ordinary contract. The creditor may also treat the contract as repudiated.

It is important to bear in mind that by Art 3 of the Uniform Customs and Practice for Documentary Credits (UCP) (500), a letter of credit is by its nature independent of the sale contract executed between the importer/buyer and the exporter/seller.[8] This prevents the parties from tying the performance of the credit to their respective obligations under the contract of sale. Even in the event that a performance becomes impossible, this should not be taken as having any effect on the validity of the credit.

A standard form credit usually contains a banker's exemption clause.[9] For a letter of credit to be legally enforceable, it must contain in its terms an expiry date. This will determine the legal limits of its operations.[10]

17.1.2 Types of credit[11]

There are two basic types of credit: revocable and irrevocable credits. These are outlined in Art 6.

17.1.3 Revocable credit

Article 8 provides for the issuance of a revocable credit. This can be cancelled by the buyer/importer at any time without recourse or notice to the seller/exporter. This makes it inadvisable for the exporter/seller to rely upon it. The seller stands to lose in the event of any cancellation of the credit by the buyer/importer.[12]

---

7 See *Jaks (UK) Ltd v CERA Investment Bank SA* [1998] 1 Lloyd's Rep 89.
8 See *Power Cuber International Ltd v National Bank of Kuwait* [1981] 1 WLR 1233.
9 Articles 15 and 16 state that a banker assumes no liability for the genuineness or accuracy of the documentary credit.
10 Article 44 UCP 500; see also *Offshore International SA v Banco SA* [1976] 2 Lloyd's Rep 402.
11 Credits can also be classified as 'confirmed' or 'unconfirmed'.
12 See *WJ Alan & Co Ltd v El Nasr Export and Import Co* [1972] 2 QB 189.

17.1.4 Irrevocable credit

Article 9 provides for the issuance of a revocable credit. Once confirmed, this credit cannot be cancelled. It is therefore a secured means of payment.[13] Credits must indicate whether they are revocable or not. If not, the law regards them as revocable.

An irrevocable documentary credit is more generally in use because it is free from all the defects of a revocable credit. The importance of irrevocable credit in *Akinsanya v United Bank for Africa*[14] led the Supreme Court in Nigeria to assert:

> The whole commercial purpose for which the system of confirmed irrevocable documentary credits has been developed in international trade is to give the seller an assured right to be paid before he parts with the control of the goods that does not permit of any dispute as to the performance of the contract of sale being used as a ground for non payment or reduction or deferment in payment.

17.1.5 Transferability and negotiability of credit

Article 48 allows for the divisibility of credits in order to finance the different aspects of the sale agreement that have been performed by the seller/exporter. In this case, a beneficiary other than the seller/exporter might be able to receive payment where the credit has been assigned to it. It is possible to assign or transfer the benefits embodied in a letter of credit because it is a chose in action.[15] A better understanding of how a credit is transferred can be gleaned from the provisions of Article 48 of the UCP (500). It provides:

(a) A transferable Credit is Credit under which the Beneficiary (First Beneficiary) has the right to request the bank called upon the bank to effect payment or acceptance or any bank entitled to effect negotiation to make the credit available in whole or in part to one or more other parties.

(b) A Credit can be transferred only if it is expressly designated as 'transferable' by the Issuing Bank...

(c) The Transferring Bank shall be under no obligation to effect such transfer except to the extent and in the manner expressly consented to by such bank.

(d) The bank requested to effect the transfer (transferring bank), whether it has confirmed the credit or not, shall be under no obligation to effect such transfer except to the extent and in the manner expressly consented to by such bank.

(e) Transferring Bank charges in respect of transfers including commissions, fees costs or expenses are payable by the First Beneficiary unless otherwise

13 Article 7.
14 [1986] 4 NWLR 273.
15 Schmitthoff, *op cit* fn 4, p 433.

agreed. If the Transferring Bank agrees to transfer the Credit it shall be under no obligation to effect the transfer until such charges are paid.

(f) Unless otherwise stipulated in the Credit, a transferable Credit can be transferred only once. Consequently, the Credit cannot be transferred at the request of the Second Beneficiary to any subsequent Third Beneficiary. For the purpose of this Article, a retransfer to the First Beneficiary does not constitute a prohibited transfer.

In analysing the transferability of credits in Article 48 of the UCP (500), we should note the following points:

* The benefits in a credit can be transferred from one beneficiary to another. In this case, the instrument can technically be regarded as a negotiable instrument or at the very least be an instrument whose benefits can be negotiated in favour of a third party.
* A credit embodies intangible rights, which give rise to propriety interests. These rights are enforceable both at law and in equity.
* The interests created by a credit have limited rights of transfer, in that only one transfer is permitted, namely a transfer from the first beneficiary to the first and only assignee. This phenomenon prevents the multiple endorsements of a credit.
* Assignment relates only to the proceeds, whilst transfer relates to the obligation to be performed under the credit. The two, though interrelated, are treated separately by the law. This is dealt with by Article 49 of the UCP (500). It provides:

> The fact that a Credit is not stated to be transferable shall not affect the Beneficiary's right to assign any proceeds to which he may be, or may become, entitled under such Credit, in accordance with the provisions of the applicable law. The article relates only to the assignment of proceeds and not to the assignment of the right to perform under the Credit itself.

17.1.6 Liability of issuing or correspondent bank

The liability of the issuing or corresponding bank will very much depend on the nature of the breach. This is also dependent upon the performance of obligations and on the content of instructions of the buyer/importer and seller/exporter to their respective banks. The extent of a banker's obligations is governed by some procedural rules in the UCP (500).

17.2 What is the nature of a bank's undertaking under a credit?

Credit is available by acceptance if the issuing bank undertakes to accept a draft drawn on it.[16] The bank in honouring the terms of the credit will not examine documents that have not been stated in the credit.[17] A bank has a reasonable time of seven banking days following the day of receipt of such documents to reject them.[18] A banker has the right to examine the documents presented to it. If there are any problems with the documents, the banker is expected to notify the buyer by the most expeditious means.[19]

17.3 Documents in support of credit

Generally speaking, a credit opened by the buyer/importer in favour of a seller/ exporter is discounted or paid against the presentation of the contract documents. Depending upon the terms of the contract of sale, an exporter/seller is expected to present the following documents in support of the credit:[20]

(1) **Bill of lading**. This refers to the shipping documents supporting the sale of goods. A bill of lading is indicative of the fact that the goods have been sent by sea freight.
(2) **Insurance policy**. This is a cover for the risks associated with transporting the goods from the seller/exporter to the buyer/importer. The type of policy is usually defined in the contract of sale between the parties.
(3) **Invoice**. This is also a necessary document that should accompany a commercial credit. An invoice details the cost price and other attendant charges on the goods. The invoice also states the quantity, quality and the type of goods.

The correspondent bank can only effect payment to the seller/exporter where the complete and correct documents are presented in support of the payment. The documents should be free of any intentional error or defect.

Hence, a credit can only be paid on the basis of authentic, complete and correct documents. This is referred to as the principle of strict performance of a credit.[21]

---

16 Article 9(a).
17 Article 13(a).
18 Article 13(b).
19 See *Seaconsar Far East Ltd v Bank Markazi Jomhouri Islami Iran* [1991] 1 Lloyd's Rep 36; see also Article 13(b) of the UCP 500.
20 Articles 20–23 UCP (500).
21 See Day, DM, *The Law of International Trade*, 1993, London, Butterworths, p 164 for other reasons on why there should be strict performance of credits.

17.3.1 *Practical issues regarding documentary credits*

- Whether a credit is revocable or not, it must stipulate the expiry date of the presentation of the documents for purposes of effecting payment. It is not sufficient to only provide for the latest date of shipment as the date on which the bill is to be paid. This is an unsatisfactory arrangement as it creates a lot of uncertainty about the actual date the bill is due.
- The effect of price fluctuation must be noted in the terms of the credit. This is especially so where the currency in which the credit is denominated is subject to the vagaries of international commerce. The international trading system cannot be divorced from other sectors of the global economy. Changes in oil, share and stock prices affect international price levels. Very often these distortions are not reflected in prices embodied in credits. At the moment, laws relating to credits offer no solution to the problem. We should therefore be looking to international commerce practice to provide a solution.

The use of documentary or commercial credits facilitates the payment procedures for imports and exports. A confirmed credit is a convenient method of paying for goods purchased from overseas. The greatest advantage is that the issuing and correspondent banks act as agents to the buyer and seller, thus minimising the chances of misunderstanding between parties.

From the point of view of the buyer/importer, there is a degree of certainty that payment would only be made when the goods have been dispatched or received. This is the condition under which a buyer/importer would part with its money. On the part of the seller, there is the assurance of being paid through the correspondent bank for the goods sold. The added advantage for the seller/importer is that it will receive payment in the country of residence without having to pay heavily for external bank charges. The intermediary role of the issuing and correspondent banks is therefore indispensable to any successful negotiation and utilisation of a credit.

18

DIGITAL CURRENCY

18.1 South Pacific context

For the deployment of digital currency in the form of cryptocurrency to be successful, the conventional use of currency as legal tender in the South Pacific has to be re-examined. The scope of legal tender has to be recalibrated to encompass aspects of transactions that can be paid for and settled through cryptocurrency. The South Pacific needs to take advantage of its size and economy, vis-à-vis its standing in the global financial system, within the greater Pacific Rim to optimise the use of digital currency such as cryptocurrency.

Countries of the South Pacific are beginning to look into the direction of utilising digital currency as a payment system to support commercial transactions in goods and services. By way of example, Palau has begun the trial for a new digital coin. This coin is supported by the US dollar and will be launched on the XRP Ledger, a technology provided by Ripple. This new coin, called Palau Stablecoins (PSCs) or Kluk, will first be given to government workers. The Kluk is the newest coin to be launched on Ripple's Central Bank Digital Currency (CBDC) platform, a system for creating digital coins that was released in May 2018. In the same vein, a number of other South Pacific nations are also eying the use of digital currencies and their supporting range of technologies. It is of note also that the Marshall Islands has begun developing its own digital coin. Similarly, Tonga wanted to make Bitcoin a legal form of money. Importantly, Vanuatu is home to Satoshi, a tech-savvy group of cryptocurrency experts.[1] By way of contrast and

---

1 See https://coinpaprika.com/news/a-group-of-islands-in-the-pacific-ocean-launch-their-digital-c urrency/#:~:text=Many%20other%20Pacific%20island%20nations,a%20community%20for%20c ryptocurrency%20enthusiasts, visited on 28 January 2024.

DOI: 10.4324/9781003428060-22

as examples, the Bahamas, Jamaica and Nigeria have already introduced CBDCs into their economies. A large number of countries are working very hard through their central banks to introduce digital currencies. A few such examples include the European Union, China, India, the United Kingdom, Brazil and many others.[2]

18.2 Definition[3]

As a digital currency, cryptocurrency[4] is simply a digital payment that rides on the back of computer networks working in coordination and using cryptography to authenticate or validate the transaction. It is simply a virtual payment initiated and concluded electronically with algorithms sanctioning, tracking and authorising it. This provides the validation process. Bitcoin (BCH)[5] is a cryptocurrency.[6] There are other important types of cryptocurrencies in vogue today. These include Ethereum (ETH), Litecoin (LTC), Cardano (ADA), Polkadot (DOT), Dogecoin (DOGE), etc.[7]

In a legal sense, cryptography[8] is the process of using algorithmic processes to confirm a transaction. An algorithm is a set of instructions for accomplishing a task or solving a problem.[9] It is a critical process for the generation of cryptocurrency.

18.3 Crypto-tech infrastructure[10]

The development and adoption of digital currency in the South Pacific may face challenges related to the existing technological infrastructure. Robust crypto-tech

---

2 *Ibid.*
3 Fanny Grace, S and John F, 'Types, Uses and Regulations of Cryptocurrency' (2018) *IJRAR-International Journal of Research and Analytical Reviews*, ijrar.org; and Bolotaeva, OS, Stepanova, AA and Alekseeva, SS, 'The Legal Nature of Cryptocurrency', (2019) *IOP Conf. Series: Earth and Environmental Science* 272, iopscience.iop.org.
4 Juels, A and Rahman, F, 'Systems and methods for securing cryptocurrency purchases', US Patent App. 15/337,481, 2017, Google Patents, Research Gate, visited on 21 December 2021.
5 Invented by Satoshi (Dorian) Nakamoto, it is by far the industry standard. The current price is $47,710 with a market capitalisation of over one trillion USD. The transaction ledger started on 3 January 2009 (visited on 21 December 2021).
6 Zavorin, I *et al.*, 'Cryptocurrency' (2017) *Widening Our Horizons: The 12th International Forum for Students and Young Researchers*, 20–21 April 2017, ir.nmu.org.ua; and Prayogo, G, 'Bitcoin, regulation and the importance of national legal reform' (2018) 1 *Asian Journal of Law and Jurisprudence* 1, 1–9.
7 See https://www.investopedia.com, visited on 29 December 2021.
8 See generally, 'Legal Tender', https://blog.sagipl.com/legality-of-cryptocurrency-by-country/#Cryptocurrency_is_legal_in_the_following_countries; European Central Bank, *Virtual Currency Schemes* (October 2012), European Central Bank, (PDF). Frankfurt am Main, Germany.
9 See https://www.investopedia.com, visited on 29 December 2021.
10 Lingappa, PR, 'Cryptocurrency infrastructure system', US Patent App. 14/749,573, 2015, Google Patents [PDF] businessperspectives.org; and Hays, D, 'Legal Aspects and Regulatory Issues of Cryptocurrencies – EU Perspective' (2018) Cryptoresearch.report, visited on 30 December 2021.

infrastructure, including secure networks and platforms, is crucial for the successful implementation of digital currencies. Cryptocurrency works on the information technology (IT) platform. It uses extensive computing power to complete a set of tasks. This is possible because algorithms can most effectively be processed with quantum processing capabilities.[11] Cyber-security and privacy considerations also have to be factored in when deploying a cryptocurrency system. High-end computing facilities and software development capabilities are also needed to smoothen the functioning of a viable cryptocurrency system.

Developing countries in the South Pacific are to therefore consider the introduction of a legal regime for cryptocurrency as a deliberate policy to be anchored by the government. However, the cryptocurrency system has to be market-driven by the private IT and financial sectors of the economy. In this regard, the South Pacific[12] may also learn from countries that have already taken the lead in introducing cryptocurrency.

18.4 Legal issues[13]

In discussing digital cash in the form of cryptocurrency in the South Pacific, there are a number of legal issues worth considering. Legal frameworks for digital currency need to be established. Clarity on issues such as the legal status of digital currencies, consumer protection and regulatory compliance is essential for fostering a secure and transparent environment. These include the principles regulating money and commodity systems; the nature of centralised banking regulation; the highly speculative and risky nature of cryptocurrency ventures; the occurrence of potentially fraudulent transactions; the spatial legal vacuum; emerging tax matters; and the comparative economic profiling power of cryptocurrencies. Each will be considered seriatim – beginning with money and commodity systems.

18.4.1 Money and commodity systems

The introduction of digital currencies may impact traditional money and commodity systems. Governments and financial institutions need to assess how digital currencies fit into existing economic structures and regulatory frameworks. Digital currency, especially in the form of cryptocurrency raises a number of

---

11 Segura, J, 'A look into the global drive-by cryptocurrency mining phenomenon' (2017) Malwarebytes Technical Report, go.malwarebytes.com [PDF] cryptoresearch.report (visited on 30 December 2021).

12 El Salvador is one such example. Hughes, SD, 'Cryptocurrency Regulations and Enforcement in the U.S.' (2017) 45 W. St. L. Rev. 1, HeinOnline, visited on 23 December 2021.

13 Bolotaeva, OS, Stepanova, AA and Alekseeva, SS, 'The Legal Nature of Cryptocurrency' (2019) *IOP Conf. Series: Earth and Environmental Science* 272, iopscience.iop.org; and Vandezande, N, *Virtual Currencies: A Legal Framework*, 2018, Intersentia.

novel but surmountable challenges, in that its profile stretches the conventional limits of legal principles defining the scope of money or commodity.[14] Money in the traditional legal sense falls within the definition of currency, which is legal tender. This sharply contrasts with the recognition granted a chattel, which is a commodity. In between is the grey area where cryptocurrency is situated.

A cautious approach to this legal position is provided by the European Central Bank, which classified Bitcoin as 'convertible decentralised virtual currency'.[15] This gives cryptocurrency a tinge of currency and commodity attributes, but without expressly recognising it as legal tender *per se*. The proactive side of this development is that Bitcoins can be used to settle virtual payments undertaken by parties to a transaction.

18.4.2 Centralised banking regulation[16]

This is one of the most important legal drawbacks to the recognition of cryptocurrency as a legal tender in most countries. Cryptocurrency works through a decentralised chain of command and often bypasses conventional banking regulatory processes for payments and settlements of accounts. In fact, it can operate as a parallel financial payment system. The role of central banks in regulating and overseeing digital currencies needs to be defined. Centralised banking regulations will influence how digital currencies operate within the broader financial ecosystem. Central and reserve banks of many countries, whilst acknowledging the potential financial benefits of cryptocurrency, are nonetheless apprehensive of its disruptive fiscal power to the financial system.

Central currency boards like the central or reserve banks take the primary responsibility for issuing and regulating legal tender currency in their countries. Foreign exchange regulations are also being superintended by these statutory agencies of government. Cryptocurrency is a disruptive deviation from these well-established fiscal regulatory mechanisms. This partly explains the reluctance of

---

14 Hale, V, *Launch an ICO & Token Crowdsale: The Complete Guide to Prepare your Startup for Launching Successful Initial Coin Offering, raising Venture & Cryptocurrency Capital*, 2018, dl .acm.org.

15 See generally, 'Legal Tender', https://blog.sagipl.com/legality-of-cryptocurrency-by-country/#Cryptocurrency_is_legal_in_the_following_countries; European Central Bank, *Virtual Currency Schemes* (October 2012), European Central Bank, Frankfurt am Main, Germany.

16 Nabilou, H, 'How to regulate bitcoin? Decentralized regulation for a decentralized cryptocurrency' (2019) *International Journal of Law and Information Technology* 27:3, 266–91, DOI: 10.1093/ijlit/eaz008; and Jaroslav, D and Jiří, S, 'Monetary Aspects of Cryptocurrency Behavior' in Ministr, J and Tvrdíková, M (eds), IT for Practice 2018, *21st International Conference on Information Technology for Practice*, Ostrava, Czach Republic, 17–18 2018; Bala, S, Kopyściański, T and Srokosz, W, 'Cryptocurrencies as electronic means of payment without the issuer. Computer science, economic, and legal aspects' (2016) Wrocław; and Fomina, O *et al.*, 'Current aspects of the cryptocurrency recognition in Ukraine' (2019) 14 *Banks and Bank Systems* 2, 203–13, DOI: 10.21511/bbs.14(2).2019.18.

many countries, both developed and developing, to fully embrace cryptocurrency as legal tender currency, at least for now.

18.4.3 Highly speculative and risky venture[17]

On the one hand, dealing in cryptocurrency involves taking an uncalculated and potentially extensive business risk. Digital currencies, especially cryptocurrencies, are often characterised by price volatility and speculation. Investors and regulatory bodies need to be aware of the risks associated with these ventures and implement measures to protect stakeholders. This is because of cryptocurrency's speculative and volatile trading nature. The actors are invisible and the economic or financial dynamics supporting its fluctuation are not transparent and cannot be easily calculated. This type of financial transaction is a departure from the already established scope of financial or business risk in law.

On the other hand, and by way of comparison, speculative trading in foreign exchange, commodities, stock, shares and other derivatives is regulated by established centralised boards. These transactions are subject to clear legal rules and violations can be detected and sanctioned. As it stands, there is as yet no definitive legal basis for holding cryptocurrency to the same operating or trading standards as regulated commodities or securities.

18.4.4 Potentially fraudulent transaction[18]

Risk of fraud in itself is not always the main concern for law. Due to the pseudonymous nature of many cryptocurrencies, there is a risk of potentially fraudulent transactions. Regulatory frameworks should include mechanisms for preventing and addressing fraudulent activities in the digital currency space. This is because the law has laid down numerous ways of addressing fraudulent transactions in a variety of scenarios. However, what is disruptively different is that cryptocurrency is underlined by the utilisation of algorithms based on exponential computing power. As it is now, the ability to manipulate and distort cryptocurrency is real, never mind its 'tamper-proof' configuration.

In addition, cyber-security is still in its infancy and has no definitive safeguards that are easily publicly available. In this respect, the law would expect the technology not only to be able to self-regulate the cryptocurrency process but also to provide transparent detection and validation mechanisms for establishing and eliminating fraudulent cryptography.

17 Drozd, O, Basai, O and Churpita, H, 'The Specificities of Using Cryptocurrency in Purchase and Sale Contracts' (2018) 4 *Baltic Journal of Economic Studies* 2, 274–81, DOI: 10.30525/2256-0742/2018-4-2-274-281.
18 Zaytoun, HS, 'Cyber Pickpockets: Blockchain, Cryptocurrency, and the Law of Theft' (2019) 97 NCL Rev. 395.

The other dimension to the argument of fraud is in relation to civil liability,[19] especially in breach of contract. Since essentially cryptocurrency transaction is peer-to-peer (P2P), the possibility of one of the parties breaching any terms of the contract cannot be entirely ruled out. The conventional contractual rules may effectively apply where the transaction is *inter partes*. However, it is conceptually difficult to establish liability in cross-border virtual breaches relating to cryptocurrency transactions.

18.4.5 Spatial legal vacuum

Digital currency, especially in the form of cryptocurrency, has emerged as a technology-driven process by introducing new legal principles that, at the moment, do not have clear jurisprudence in support.[20] Currency is legal tender, whilst a chose in action like Bitcoin is generally within the purview of intangible property. There are clear and enforceable rules relating to property rights. Currency is also centrally regulated. The cross-border nature of digital currencies may create legal challenges and regulatory gaps. International cooperation and agreements are needed to address issues that may arise in a spatial legal vacuum.

However, because Bitcoin can be used to effect digital payment for goods and services, it can transfer value and can as well settle payments just like conventional currency. This digital duality creates a new legal vacuum to be addressed. This legal gap is further compounded by the fact that only private players are involved in the generation of the value intrinsic in Bitcoin – to the exclusion of central monetary authorities. The question of state sovereignty[21] is pivotal when granting recognition to any payment process that is virtually settled by independent and private actors.

18.4.6 Emerging tax matters[22]

Virtual transactions have created an extended dilemma for tax regulation in most jurisdictions. This is especially so for countries that did not anticipate the

---

19 See Drozd, O, Lazur, Y and Serbin, R, 'Theoretical and Legal Perspective on Certain Types of Legal Liability in Cryptocurrency Relations' (2017) 3 *Baltic Journal of Economic Studies* 5, 221–28, DOI: 10.30525/2256-0742/2017-3-5-221-228.

20 See Jafari, S *et al.*, 'Cryptocurrency: A Challenge to Legal System' (2018) available at SSRN: ssrn .com/abstract=3172489, visited on 20 December 2021.

21 See, Abramowicz, M, 'Cryptocurrency-Based Law' (2016) 58 Ariz. L. Rev. 549.

22 Emelianova, NN and Dementyev, AA, 'Cryptocurrency, Taxation and International Law: Contemporary Aspects', in Popkova, EG and Sergi, BS (eds), *Artificial Intelligence: Anthropogenic Nature vs. Social Origin*, Cham, Springer International Publishing, 2020, pp 725–31; and Chohan, UW, 'Assessing the Differences in Bitcoin & Other Cryptocurrency Legality Across National Jurisdictions' (20 September 2017), available at SSRN: ssrn.com/abstract=3042248, visited on 20 December 2021.

sudden and extensive impact of online transactions, digital payment and settlement processes. In the physical environment, tax is levied based on the concept of permanent establishment. Where transnational trading groups or companies are involved, tax is levied on the basis of the global appointment principle. In the case of virtual transactions, a new concept has to be developed and invoked – the 'virtual' profit allocation principle. Taxation policies for transactions involving digital currencies need to be established. Governments must adapt their tax regulations to account for the unique characteristics of digital currencies. South Pacific countries have not yet satisfactorily repositioned themselves in this regard in order to effectively tax the magnitude of virtual transactions conducted in the Pacific's electronic space today.

18.4.7 Comparative economic profiling power[23]

A basic challenge for the law to contend with is how to precisely measure the parity of the intrinsic value of the different cryptocurrencies used across divergent financial sectors and even across various national jurisdictions. Adopting a universal legal yardstick may prove challenging, especially in the absence of either a national regulatory or an agreed global regulatory framework for determining the parity of cryptocurrencies. The adoption of digital currencies can influence economic profiling and financial inclusion. Governments and financial institutions should consider the potential impact on economic structures and demographics.

Different cryptocurrencies can be affected by different computing algorithms, economic power, investment in research and development and the sheer popularity or personality of the innovator/inventor or even investors. The solution is the adoption of a universally agreed electronic parity regulator for cryptocurrencies. There can be a global model which can then be cascaded to regional and subregional frameworks.

18.5 Paradigm shift

Cryptocurrency as a virtual payment system for goods and services is here to stay. The opportunities and threats presented by it are real, but the prospects are equally genuinely enticing. The South Pacific needs to therefore strike a balance by leaning more towards the advantages, whilst at the same time putting in place

---

23 Chohan, UW, 'Assessing the Differences in Bitcoin & Other Cryptocurrency Legality Across National Jurisdictions' (20 September 2017), available at SSRN: ssrn.com/abstract=3042248, visited on 20 December 2021; and Khulup, D, 'Legal status of cryptocurrency as a new phenomenon of digital economy' *ECON – 2018: world economy and international business: abstracts of the 5th interuniversity research student conference*, Minsk, Belarus, 13 April 2018, pp 123–25, available at: edoc.bseu.by:8080/handle/edoc/75380, visited on 20 December 2021.

safeguards to minimise the adverse effects of the virtual payment technology. It is against this background that this paradigm shift is analysed.

18.5.1 Legal enablers[24]

The passage of the Electronic Transactions Bill into an Act of Parliament in South Pacific jurisdictions is now apt. Attendant to this is the need to also have in place a digital data protection law and an electronic evidence law. Importantly, more attention should also be paid to the enforcement mechanisms in the various laws. If enacted, these laws will provide a solid legal framework along which the progressive regulation of cryptocurrency can smoothly proceed. This can be preceded by the current central or reserve bank approach in trying to establish the initial parameters for the introduction of cryptocurrency in the different countries in the South Pacific.

18.5.2 Reappraising equity and debt financing portfolios[25]

The introduction of digital currencies may impact traditional equity and debt financing models. Financial institutions and investors may need to reassess their portfolios and strategies in response to the changing financial landscape. Goods and services are usually paid for, and payments settled using conventional currency whose value is denominated by the central or reserve bank as the case may be in the South Pacific. This underpins the use of currency as legal tender to finance and pay for these transactions. The usual way of raising money in a conventional economy is through equity or debt financing. These methods are intractably tied to the use of currency as legal tender.

Online transactions have now provided for the use of virtual payments to settle digitally based transactions. Here, equity and debt financing have no direct bearing on attributing values to these online transactions. South Pacific countries have to take advantage of both processes as ways of stimulating their economies. They also have to make themselves fully compliant with the emerging virtual payment solutions in the information superhighway. South Pacific countries cannot ignore the benefits of participating in the evolving cryptocurrency economy.

---

24 Schaffner, D, 'Policy-Based Control and Augmentation of Cryptocurrencies and Cryptocurrency', US Patent App. 14/691,463, 2015, Google Patents, [PDF] acc.com, visited on 20 December 2021.

25 Drozd, O, Basai, O and Churpita, H, 'The Specificities of Using Cryptocurrency in Purchase and Sale Contracts' (2018) 4 *Baltic Journal of Economic Studies* 2, 274–81, DOI: 10.30525/2256-0742/2018-4-2-274-281; and Srokosz, W and Kopyściański, T, 'Legal and Economic Analysis of the Cryptocurrencies Impact on the Financial System' (2015) 4 *Journal of Teaching and Education* 2, 619–27.

18.5.3 Digital certification authority[26]

Establishing a reliable digital certification authority is crucial for ensuring the security and authenticity of digital transactions. This includes measures to prevent fraud and unauthorised access. A digital certificate authority (DCA) is a trusted entity that manages and issues security certificates and public keys that are used for secure communication in a public commercial network. In cryptography, a certificate authority or certification authority (CA) is an entity that issues digital certificates.[27]

A digital certificate certifies the ownership of a public key by the named subject of the certificate. This allows others (relying parties) to rely upon signatures or on assertions made about the private key that corresponds to the certified public key. A DCA acts as a trusted third party – trusted both by the subject (owner) of the certificate and by the party relying upon the certificate. The format of these certificates is specified by the X.509 standard. A DCA signs certificates used in HTTPS, the secure browsing protocol for the world wide web. It is also used in issuing identity cards by national governments for use in electronically signing documents[28] and sealing documents for e-banking transactions.

Due to the fact that cryptocurrency employs the use of public and private keys for cryptography, the central or reserve banks in the South Pacific can and indeed have the legal mandate to regulate the establishment of a CA for cryptocurrency. The aim is for the authority to process digital signatures to validate automated cryptocurrency transactions. There are financial and technical issues associated with the validation and storage of digital signatures and the protection of such databases from viral and other attacks. For a CA to be a reliable manager of digital signatures, it must eliminate the major risks of using digital signatures between the sender and recipient of cryptocurrency. The central or reserve banks in the South Pacific are well-suited to provide this value-added service of cyber-security to the region.

Finally, in this regard, the role of the central or reserve banks in the South Pacific is to be seen more as complementing the activities of private actors in the cryptocurrency space rather than as a statutory regulator impeding the process. The independence of cryptocurrency as a virtual payment system can still be maintained, whilst some degree of oversight is exercised by the bank to regulate fraud, terrorism financing and money laundering. These illicit activities are

---

26 See generally, Ahmadu, ML, 'Background Study on Cyber-Legislation in the South Pacific', International Telecommunication Union, Geneva (United Nations), Doc. No. ITU.RWG.ASP, *APT/ITU/PITA Workshop on Principles of Cyber legislation for the Pacific Island countries*, New Zealand, March 2007; and Ahmadu, ML, *Cybercrimes in Nigeria*, 2020, University Press Limited, p 1 et seq.
27 See www.bing.com (visited on 30 December 23).
28 See www.bing.com (visited on 30 December 23).

inimical to the maintenance of a sound financial system and a viable cryptocurrency system in the South Pacific. The successful integration of digital currency in the South Pacific requires addressing technological, legal, regulatory and economic aspects. Clear frameworks, collaboration among stakeholders and careful consideration of risks are essential for a sustainable and secure digital currency ecosystem in the region.

PART E

Termination and winding up

Introduction

In this part of the book, we will be examining legal principles underpinning the process of winding up or termination of business of business entities. Global trends have indicated the need for caution in the way businesses are to be halted, closed down or liquidated. Some recent developments in the global commercial arena leading to mass business failures in some of the most developed economies provide some justification for a detailed analysis of this aspect of the law in the South Pacific context.

We have chosen a few of the many types of registered entities which could undergo winding up or be subject to the legal processes of termination. In general, bankruptcy proceedings are directed at natural persons whilst partnerships, trusts and other corporate entities could be wound up or dissolved as artificial entities as required by law.

The chapters in this Part attempt to shed some light on these legal principles, as well as the procedures governing the termination or dissolution of commercial activities and/or structures of these entities.

DOI: 10.4324/9781003428060-23

19

BANKRUPTCY

19.1 Definition of a bankrupt

The most common understanding of a bankrupt is perhaps a person who is unable to pay his or her debts to creditors when they become due. This more accurately describes insolvency. In fact, what is required is the commission of an act of bankruptcy which is defined in the relevant legislation and is not coextensive with the notion of insolvency.

The legislation provides that a person may be declared a bankrupt when he or she commits an act of bankruptcy. By way of example, s 3 of the Bankruptcy Act of Fiji provides:[1]

A debtor commits an act of bankruptcy in each of the following cases:

(a) if in Fiji or elsewhere he makes a conveyance or assignment[2] of his property to a trustee for the benefit of his creditors generally;
(b) if in Fiji or elsewhere he makes a fraudulent conveyance, gift, delivery or transfer of property, or of any part thereof;
(c) if in Fiji or elsewhere he makes any conveyance or transfer of his property, or any part thereof, or creates any charge thereon, which would under this Act or any other Act be void as a fraudulent preference if he were adjudged bankrupt;

---

1 See s 3 Bankruptcy Act Cap 3 (SI).
2 See *Re Hughes* [1893] 1 QB 595.

DOI: 10.4324/9781003428060-24

(d) if with intent to defeat or delay his creditors he does any of the following things, namely, departs out of Fiji, or being out of Fiji remains out of Fiji, or departs from his dwelling-house, or otherwise absents himself, or begins to keep house, or removes his property or any part thereof beyond the jurisdiction of the court;[3]

(e) if execution against him has been levied by seizure of his goods in any civil proceedings in any court and the goods have been sold or held by the sheriff for twenty-one days;

(f) if he files in the court a declaration of his inability to pay his debts or presents a bankruptcy petition against himself;

(g) if a creditor has obtained a final judgment or final order[4] against him for any amount, and, execution thereon not having been stayed, has served on him in Fiji, or, by leave of court, elsewhere, a bankruptcy notice under this Act...;

(h) if the debtor gives notice to any of his creditors that he has suspended, or that he is about to suspend, payment of his debts.

To initiate any bankruptcy proceeding, a notice in the prescribed form must be issued against a debtor requiring him or her to pay the creditor the stated amount in satisfaction of either a judgment debt or sum ordered.[5] If it is established to the satisfaction of the court that the debtor has committed an act of bankruptcy, a receiving order will then be made by the court. In this case, either the debtor or creditor will be able to present a bankruptcy petition, subject however to a number of conditions. For instance, s 6(1) of the Bankruptcy Act of Fiji states:[6]

A creditor shall not be entitled to present a bankruptcy petition against a debtor unless–

(a) the debt owing by the debtor to the petitioning creditor, or, if two or more creditors joint in the petition, an aggregate amounts of debts owing to the several petitioning creditors, amounts to one hundred dollars; and

(b) the debt is a liquidated sum payable either immediately or at some certain future time; and

(c) the act of bankruptcy on which the petition is grounded has occurred within three months before the presentation of the petition; and

(d) the debtor is domiciled in Fiji, or within a year before the date of the presentation of the petition has ordinarily resided, or had a dwelling-house

---

3 See s 26 Bankruptcy Act (1908) (NZ) (S); s 3 Bankruptcy Act Cap 3 (SI); and *Barton v DCT* (Cth) (1974) 131 CLR 299 for the interpretation of s 40(c) Bankruptcy Act 1966 (Aus).

4 See *Licul v Coorney* (1976) 50 ALJR 439.

5 See s 4 Bankruptcy Act (F).

6 See s 27 (NZ) (S); s 6 (SI).

or place of business, or has carried on business, in Fiji, personally or by means of an agent or manager, or is within the said period has been a member of a firm or partnership or persons which has carried on business in Fiji by means of a partner or partners, or an agent or manager.

It is a general requirement that a petition for bankruptcy must be supported by an affidavit of the creditor or any person who is conversant with the facts leading to the petition.[7] If it is a debtor's petition, it should clearly state that the debtor is unable to pay the debts. Once filed, a debtor's petition can only be withdrawn with the leave of court.[8]

People engage in commercial transactions on the quite reasonable assumption that all underlying obligations will be fulfilled by both sides. In the ensuing transactions, those who owe money are expected and legally obliged under most circumstances to make payment to those to whom the money is owed. Basic commercial transactions most often give rise to a debtor-creditor relationship in respect of the amount or debt that is expected to have been paid. Many other forms of liability might arise from commercial dealings which are not strictly accounted for as debts or demands for the payment of liquidated amounts.[9] The bankruptcy legislation normally limits the types of claims that can be proven in bankruptcy proceedings.[10] In most cases, there is no problem with the payment of sums of money due. However, every now and then, instances arise where individual debtors are either unwilling or unable to pay their creditors when called upon to do so. It is in this context that bankruptcy proceedings assume relevance.

Bankruptcy is a legal situation where the rights and liabilities on either side of the relationship are in effect suspended. The primary objective of bankruptcy is to ensure that an equitable distribution of the proceeds available from assets of the debtor is made to creditors, whilst at the same time providing safeguards ensuring the humane treatment of the debtor through established legal processes. Because of this consideration, it is now possible for formerly adjudged bankrupts to be discharged at a later time to enable them to re-organise their lives again.[11]

Bankruptcy proceeds on the assumption that the debtor's property or assets, whether tangible or intangible, are taken over by persons appointed by the court in an official capacity. This official proceeds to administer the estate of the bankrupt person in order that some reasonable settlement of the debts is achieved, so

---

7 See s 6(2) (F).

8 See s 8 (F); s 30 (S); cf *Hood ex p ES & A Bank* [1970] Tas SR (NC) 2.

9 See generally, Keay, AR, 'The fundamentals of presenting a creditor's petition under the Bankruptcy Act (1991)' 21 QLSJ 137.

10 See e.g. s 32 Bankruptcy Act Cap 48 (F), which provides that claims for unliquidated damages which arise otherwise than from a contract, promise or breach of trust cannot be proven in bankruptcy proceedings.

11 See Goode, R, *Commercial Law*, 2nd edn, 1995, Harmondsworth, Penguin, p 848.

far as possible, in favour of all of the creditors. The legal right of all creditors to recover their debts and liabilities is legally suspended by the making of a bankruptcy order. Instead, they have a right to prove their claims in the bankruptcy. Creditors rank in order of priority when it comes to the settlement of their claims against the bankrupt. This order of priority is laid down by the relevant legislation. The bankrupt person is prohibited from dealing with his or her assets for the most part. Ultimately once the administration of the estate has been completed so far as possible and after a certain time has elapsed, the bankrupt is discharged from all debts and liabilities as existed at the time of the bankruptcy.

There are two main classes of creditor: secured and unsecured. The former holds security for the debt which is owed to them such as by way of mortgage or charge over the debtor's property. They are entitled to enforce the security interest they have against the property concerned and, if that should prove insufficient to satisfy the total debt, they can claim along with other creditors against the other assets of the bankrupt. Unsecured creditors hold no security for the moneys due to them. They will only recover to the extent that the realisation of the assets of the bankrupt can provide. Rarely will this be the full amount of their debt. Most often they will receive only a proportion of it by way of dividend out of the bankrupt's estate.

19.1.1 *Effect of a receiving order*[12]

A receiving order is aimed at collecting all assets or property of the debtor into a centrally administered pool and thence to be available for distribution to creditors. The effect of a receiving order made by the court is to constitute the official receiver as the legal holder and controller of the property of the debtor for the purposes of administration of the bankruptcy.[13] The law vests the power to realise the debtor's property or assets in the hands of this official receiver. The official receiver is an officer of the state,[14] but may in certain cases appoint trustees to administer the property on behalf of creditors.

19.1.2 *Public examination of the debtor*[15]

A public examination of the debtor is to be conducted by the court in order to clearly establish the claims presented by creditors as well as to give the debtor an opportunity to affirm or disprove the claims.[16] The sitting is open to the public and

---

12 See s 12 Bankruptcy Act (SI); *Ram Dutt Prasad v ANZ Ltd* 45 FLR 101; *Chand v Velson Service Station* [1986] FJLawRp 19; [1986] 32 FLR 150 (4 July 1986).

13 See s 9 Bankruptcy Act (F).

14 See ss 71–73 of the Fiji Act for duties and responsibilities of the official receiver.

15 See s 19 Bankruptcy Act (SI); *Official Receiver v Goverdhanbhai & Co* 12 FLR 70.

16 See *Re Ratu Osea Gavidi* 30 FLR 166.

may be attended by the debtor and creditor and their representatives if necessary. The debtor will be on oath and must be prepared to answer all questions put to him/her by the court.[17] The purpose is to examine the debtor in relation to his/her conduct, dealings and the property under the receiving order.[18]

19.1.3 Arrangement to pay creditors

There is nothing legally preventing a debtor from proposing to the official receiver any suitable methods of paying the debts.[19] This has to be done before the conclusion of the public examination of the debtor. A copy of the proposed arrangement, composition or scheme to settle the debt is to be given to all creditors before the meeting to consider the proposal.[20] If the debtor's proposal is accepted by the creditors, the official receiver will then seek a court order to confirm the scheme of arrangement to pay the debts. Once confirmed by the court, the scheme of arrangement will be binding on all creditors.

However, by s 19(19) of, for example, the Fiji legislation, the scheme of arrangement may not in certain cases be binding on the creditor/s. It provides:

Notwithstanding the acceptance and approval of a composition or scheme, the composition or scheme shall not be binding on any creditor so far as regards a debt or liability from which, under the provisions of this Act, the debtor would not be released by an order of discharge in bankruptcy, unless the creditor assents to the composition or scheme.

19.1.4 Priority of payment of creditors

We noted the position of secured creditors above. Their rights to enforce their claims against the property over which they have security are preserved. They can, if they wish, elect to surrender their security for the benefit of all creditors. If they retain their security but the proceeds of realisation of the property secured do not realise sufficient funds to satisfy their debt or liability, they can prove for the balance on the same basis as other unsecured creditors of the bankrupt.

In the event that a receiving order results in the eventual distribution of the assets or property of the debtor, the creditors will be ranked for payment in a certain order of priority. However, all state taxes and local rates paid; state rents; salaries or wages of ex-employees of the bankrupt; labourer's wages not exceeding, in the case of Fiji, $50; and workmen's compensation are to rank equally. If the proceeds are insufficient to satisfy the claims collectively, then the claims

---

17 See s 17 Bankruptcy Act (F).
18 See s 35 Bankruptcy Act (SI).
19 See s 118 (NZ) (S); s 21 (SI).
20 See *Field v CBC (Sydney) Ltd* (1978) 22 ALR 403.

abate in equal proportions between the creditors.[21] In most cases, the creditors' claims will not be satisfied in full.

19.1.5 Discovery of debtor's property

An adjudged bankrupt has a duty to ensure that he or she provides such information and renders sufficient assistance to enable the official receiver to obtain control of, and to realise where necessary, all the assets or property for effective distribution among creditors.[22] In this regard, s 24(2) of the Fiji legislation, for example, states:

He shall give such inventory of his property, such list of creditors and debtors, and of the debts due to and from them respectively, submit to each examination and in respect of his property or his creditors, attend such other meeting of his creditors, wait at such times on the official receiver, special manager, or trustee, execute such power of attorney, conveyances, deeds, and instruments and generally do all acts and things in relation to his property and the distribution of the proceeds amongst his creditors, as may be reasonably required by the official receiver, special manager or trustee, or may be prescribed by the general rules, or be directed by the court by any special order or orders made in reference to any particular case, or made on the occasion of any special application by the official receiver, special manager, trustee or any creditor or person interested.

Failure to comply with the above provision amounts to contempt of court. This will lead to committal proceedings issued against the debtor.[23] It is also possible in certain instances to order the arrest of the debtor and for the police to be authorised to seize any books, papers, money and goods in the possession of the debtor.[24]

19.1.6 Discharge of bankrupt

After being adjudged bankrupt, a person may apply to the court to be discharged from bankruptcy on a day to be appointed by the court.[25] The application for an order of discharge will only be entertained by the court after a public examination of the debtor is done. The court in considering the application will take into

---

21 See ss 35, 52 (F); s 38 (SI); and the FSM case of *Re Mid Pacific Construction Co Inc* [1988] SPLR 70; cf the FSM case of *Re Island Hardware* [1988] SPLR 101.
22 See *Re Bhagtu (A Bankrupt)* 13 FLR 57.
23 See s 24(4) (F); s 88 (NZ) (S).
24 See ss 25, 51 (F). See also s 137 (F) dealing with failure to keep proper books of accounts; s 89 (NZ) (S).
25 Cf *Re Arons ex p The Bankrupt* (1978) 19 ALR 633; *Pegler v Dale* [1975] 1 NSWLR 265.

account the report by the official receiver and may thereafter determine whether or not to order a discharge, suspension or variation of the bankruptcy order. The report of the official receiver shall be taken by the court as *prima facie* evidence of the statements therein contained.

The order of discharge is to operate subject to the requirements of s 30(1) of, for instance, the Fiji legislation. This section provides:

An order of discharge shall not release the bankrupt

(a) from any debt on a recognizance nor from any debt with which the bankrupt may be chargeable at the suit of the Crown or of any person for any offence against any law relating to any breach of the general revenue of Fiji, or at the suit of the sheriff or other public officer on a bail bond entered into for the appearance of any person prosecuted for any offence; and he shall not be discharged from such excepted debts unless the Chief accountant shall verify in writing his consent to the bankrupt being discharged therefrom; or

(b) from any debt or liability incurred by means of any fraud or fraudulent breach of trust to which he was a party, nor from any debt or liability whereof he has obtained forbearance by any fraud to which he was a party; or

(c) from any liability under a judgment against him in an action for seduction, or under an affiliation order, or under a judgement against him as co-respondent in a matrimonial cause, except to such an extent and under such conditions as the court expressly orders in respect of such liability.

19.1.7 *Release from burdensome obligations*

Trustees[26] appointed to manage the estate of the bankrupt are able to avoid onerous property or transactions connected with such property, if it would amount to unnecessary difficulty administering or managing such property. This may be any time within the first 12 months of the appointment of the trustee. By way of example, s 55(1) of the Fiji legislation provides:

Where any part of the property of the bankrupt consists of land of any tenure burdened with onerous covenants, of shares or stock of companies, of unprofitable contracts, or of any other property that is unsaleable, or not readily saleable, by reason of its binding the possessor thereof to the performance of any onerous act, or to the payment of any sum of money, the trustee, notwithstanding that he has endeavoured to sell or has taken possession of property, or

---

26 See *Re Alafaci; Registrar in Bankruptcy v Hardwick* (1976) 9 ALR 262.

exercised any act of ownership in relation thereto, but subject to the provisions of this section, may, by writing signed by him, at any time within twelve months after the first appointment of a trustee or such extended period as may be allowed by the court, disclaim the property:

Provided that, where any such property has not come to the knowledge of the trustee within one month of such appointment, he may disclaim such property at any time within twelve months after he has become aware thereof or such extended period as may be allowed by the court.[27]

The bankruptcy procedures dealt with here are relevant only to natural persons or individuals. Partnerships, companies and other incorporated associations are dealt with under other different schemes, although these are similar in some respects to the procedures relating to bankruptcy.

The modern procedures dealing with bankruptcies of individuals were born out of the realisation that the old practice of immediate arrest and detention in prison of debtors serves only to worsen the financial plight of creditors instead of ameliorating it. Furthermore, it served little purpose in achieving satisfaction of the claims of creditors. By sequestrating[28] and applying the proceeds from the debtor's property to satisfy the claims, creditors themselves tend to be in a far better position to at least minimise their losses.

The various bankruptcy provisions as are found today in countries of the region are aimed at facilitating procedural regularity in handling the property of persons adjudged bankrupt by courts. This gives both the creditor and the bankrupt an opportunity of a fair hearing and the possibility of legal discharge from bankruptcy, after, of course, having met some conditions. Where no specific legislation has been mentioned as in Nauru, Tonga,[29] Tuvalu, Kiribati and Vanuatu,[30] the equivalent English Act applies as a statute of general application before the relevant cut-off date for reception of the law of the former imperial country. In the case of the Cook Islands, Niue and Tokelau, the New Zealand statute applies.

---

27 See s 84 (NZ) (S); s 59 (SI).

28 *Practice Direction No 4 of 1992* on bankruptcy proceedings in Tonga. Part IX of the English Insolvency Act 1986 and the Insolvency Rules 1986, when read together with the Tongan Civil Law Act (Cap 25), apply to bankruptcy proceedings brought in the Supreme Court of Tonga.

29 The English Bankruptcy Act 1914 is applicable as a statute of general application in Vanuatu. See also *Geoffrey Bruce Clements and Anne Patricia Clements v Hong Kong and Shanghai Banking Corp* (1980–88) 1 VLR 416.

30 See s 672 Niue Act 1966.

20

PARTNERSHIP DISSOLUTION AND EXPULSION

20.1 Dissolution of partnership

Section 39 of the Partnership Act of Fiji[1] provides in fact for the continuation of the partners' authority as follows:

> After the dissolution of a partnership the authority of each partner to bind the firm and the other rights and obligations of the partners continue notwithstanding the dissolution so far as may be necessary to wind up the affairs of the partnership and to complete transactions begun but not finished at the time of the dissolution but not otherwise:
>
> Provided that the firm is in no case bound by the acts of a partner who has become bankrupt, but this proviso does not affect the liability of any person who has, after the bankruptcy, represented himself or knowingly suffered himself to be represented as a partner of the bankrupt.

Both the substantive rights, duties and liabilities of the partners also continue. In *Chan v Zacharia*,[2] the court held, for example, that the fiduciary duties of partners in a partnership which had been put into dissolution were still current notwithstanding the dissolution.

As to the effect of dissolution and the various provisions under the Act, it has been said that:

---

1 Section 41 Partnership Act (CI), (Ni) also see Partnership Application Act 1994, (Tu); s 160 Partnership Act (MI); s 38 Partnership Act (N), (V).
2 Supra.

DOI: 10.4324/9781003428060-25

Dissolution of partnership, and the consequences of dissolution, are provided for in ss 32 to 44 of the [Partnership Act 1890 (UK)] ... These provisions are important in characterising dissolution as envisaged in the Act. ... On dissolution the individual partner's authority to bind the firm changes. It subsists thereafter 'so far as necessary to wind up the affairs of the partnership' and to complete unfinished business, but not otherwise: s 38. Subject to that limited exception, the mutual agency of the partners defined in s 5 is at an end. Apart from contrary provision in the partnership agreement, there are prescribed rules for the application of partnership property and the distribution of surpluses and incidence of deficiencies. But the almost infinite flexibility of partnership is also reflected. In ss 42 and 43, for example, it is clearly envisaged that, despite dissolution, the business may continue, and that there may be a relationship among some former partners that makes it sensible to provide that the sum brought out on an accounting with an outgoing partner or that person's representatives is a debt. The creditor is identified, but the debtors can only be those who have in some way which is not defined continued to have possession of the former firm's assets. ... Dissolution refers to an event on which the relationship of partnership ceases as among the partners of the dissolved firm. That firm terminates as part of the dissolution. ... But these are relatively limited in scope.[3]

The Act does not in general prescribe for the wider consequences of dissolution in an unqualified way. Dissolution involves procedures beyond termination of the partnership. These procedures are those that will bring about "crystalisation of the interests of the partners both *inter se* and in questions with third parties ... The partnership continues, and the rights and duties of the partners remain as they were 'so far as is consistent with the incidents of a partnership'".[4] In *Inland Revenue v Graham's Trustees*, it was said that the purpose of a provision such as s 39 above was to deal with 'unfinished operations necessary to fulfil contracts of the firm which were still in force when the firm was dissolved'.[5] In *Sew Hoy v Sew Hoy*, the section was taken to enable the winding up of the dissolved partnership but to provide that the rights and obligations of former partners continue 'so far as may be necessary to wind up the affairs of the partnership' and 'to complete transactions begun but unfinished'.[6] The rights and obligations of former partners do not continue for other purposes, however. The surviving partners do not have

---

3 *Maillie v Swanney* [2000] SLT 464.
4 *Ibid.*
5 1971 SIT 46 at 48.
6 [2000] NZCA 314 at para 32; see also *Chan v Zacharia* supra, above; *Don King Productions Ltd v Warren*; *Perpetual Executors and Trustees Association of Australia Ltd v FCT* (1948) 77 CLR 1; *Re McDonald (Deceased)* [1972] NZLR 845; cf *Thompson's Trustee in Bankruptcy v Heaton* [1974] 1 All ER 1239.

any right to bind the assets of the firm by making new bargains or entering into new transactions. Pursuant to the section, the partnership is deemed to continue as to the fiduciary relationships between the partners.[7]

The Partnership Acts make provision for the division of property and profits of the partnership after dissolution. The legislation also sets out certain rules according to which the distribution of assets is to proceed on settlement of the final accounts of the partnership.[8] Section 40 of the Fiji Act[9] provides:

> On the dissolution of a partnership every partner is entitled as against the other partners in the firm and all persons claiming through them in respect of their interests as partners to have the property of the partnership applied in payment of the debts and liabilities of the firm and to have the surplus assets after such payment applied in payment of what may be due to the partners respectively after deducting what may be due from them as partners of the firm and for that purpose any partner or his representatives may, on the termination of the partnership, apply to the court to wind up the business and affairs of the firm.

Where the partnership was dissolved on grounds of fraud or misrepresentation of one of the parties thereto, the party entitled to rescind is, without prejudice to any other right, entitled to certain rights of lien on the surplus of the partnership assets, to rights of subrogation to any claims of creditors against the firm which that partner might have met and to certain other indemnity rights.[10] Where any member of a firm has died or otherwise ceased to be a partner and the remaining partners continue to carry on the business of the firm with its capital or assets without any final settlement of accounts, the outgoing partner or his or her estate is entitled to a share of the profits made since the dissolution. The court can determine the share of the partnership assets, or the outgoing partner can elect a statutory amount of interest.[11] This applies only where there is no contrary agreement. The partnership agreement sometimes provides an option for the surviving or continuing partners to purchase the interest of the outgoing partner. If this is the case, and the option is exercised, the outgoing partner or his or her estate, as the case may be, is not normally entitled to any further or other share of profits from the partnership.[12]

---

7 *Ibid.*

8 See s 45 Partnership Act (F); s 47 Partnership Act (CI), (Tu); s 44 Partnership Act (N), (V).

9 Section 42 Partnership Act (CI), (Ni) also see Partnership Application Act 1994, (Tu); s 39 Partnership Act (N), (V).

10 Section 42 Partnership Act (F); s 44 Partnership Act (CI), (Ni) also see Partnership Application Act 1994, (Tu); s 41 Partnership Act (N), (V).

11 Section 43 Partnership Act (F); s 45 Partnership Act (CI), (Ni) also see Partnership Application Act 1994, (Tu); s 42 Partnership Act (N), (V).

12 *Ibid.*

20.1.1 Grounds for dissolution

Dissolution can arise broadly in three ways: (a) by virtue of some provision of the partnership agreement, (b) by an order of the court or (c) by operation of law or of legal policy. The Partnership Acts provide several methods by which a partnership can be put into dissolution. These are as follows:

By effluxion of time for a fixed term partnership in accordance with the partnership instrument.[13]

Where the partnership was entered into for some single adventure or undertaking, then by the termination of that adventure or undertaking.[14]

Where the partnership was entered into for an undefined time, then by any partner giving notice to the other partners of his intention to dissolve the partnership.[15]

By the death or bankruptcy of any partner.[16]

Where one partner causes partnership property to be subjected to his or her own separate debts.[17]

By the happening of some event which makes it unlawful for the business of the firm to be carried on or for the members of the firm to carry it on in partnership.[18]

When one partner becomes of permanently unsound mind.[19]

When one partner becomes in any way permanently incapable of performing his or her part of the partnership agreement.[20]

When a partner other than the partner suing has wilfully been guilty of certain conduct.[21]

When a partner wilfully or persistently commits a breach of the partnership agreement which breach is calculated prejudicially to affect the carrying on of the business.[22]

When a partner wilfully or persistently conducts himself or herself in relation to the partnership business that it is not reasonably practicable for the others to carry on the partnership business.[23]

---

13 Section 33(1)(a) (F); s 35(1)(a) (CI), (Ni), (Tu); s 161(1)(a) (MI); s 32(a) (N), (V).
14 Section 33(1)(b) (F); s 35(1)(b) (CI), (Ni), (Tu); s 32(b) (N), (V).
15 Section 33(1)(c) (F); s 35(1)(c) (CI), (Ni), (Tu); s 161(1)(c) (MI); s 32(c) (N), (V).
16 Section 34(1) (F); s 36(1) (CI), (Ni), (Tu); s 31(3) (N), (V).
17 Section 34(2) (F); s 36(2) (CI), (Ni), (Tu); s 162(1)(c) (MI); s 33(2) (N), (V).
18 Section 35 (F); s 37 (CI), (Ni), (Tu); s 162(4), (5) (MI); s 34 (N), (V).
19 Section 36(1)(a) (F); s 38(a) (CI), (Ni), (Tu); s 163 (MI); s 35(a) (N), (V).
20 Section 36(1)(b) (F); s 38(b) (CI), (Ni), (Tu); s 163(1)(b) (MI); s 35(b) (N), (V).
21 Section 36(1)(c) Partnership Act (F); s 38(c) Partnership Act (CI), (Ni) also see Partnership Application Act 1994, (Tu); s 163(1)(c) Partnership Act (MI); s 35(c) Partnership Act (N), (V).
22 Section 36(1)(d) (F); s 38(d) (CI), (Ni) also see Partnership Application Act 1994, (Tu); s 163(1)(d) (MI); s 35(d) (N), (V).
23 Section 36(1)(d) (F); s 38(d) (CI), (Ni) also see Partnership Application Act 1994, (Tu); s 163(1)(d) (MI); s 35(d) (N), (V).

When the business of the partnership can only be carried on at a loss.[24]

By other circumstances which in the opinion of the court render it just and equitable that the partnership be dissolved.[25]

By unanimous agreement between the partners.

By other circumstances provided for in the partnership agreement.

Those grounds referred to in 1–4 inclusive are expressly made subject, by the legislation, to the provisions contained in the partnership agreement. However, the ground of unlawfulness of the partnership business cannot be excluded or overridden by the agreement. That ground, referred to in 5 above, is available to the other partners as an option.

The grounds provided for in 7–13 inclusive are substantive grounds whereby the court can order the dissolution of partnership. On an application for dissolution, all of the partners should be joined in the proceedings, although there may be cases where proceedings with respect to partnership affairs might be brought against some partners only. These will be cases where there is no general dissolution, account or other matters touching on the partners' interests as a whole.[26] The occurrence of the grounds specified do not of themselves determine the partnership but require that the court satisfy itself first that the grounds are made out on the balance of probabilities. In this vein, it was said in the Scottish case of *Maillie v Swanney and Others*:

> [The relevant section] provides for dissolution by the court on a discretionary basis where a ground of dissolution is made out. There is no common characteristic among the prescribed grounds other than that they are examples of relatively extreme situations in which it may be appropriate for the court to intervene in business affairs and order dissolution. But together they are incompatible with any notion that an individual partner has a general right of some kind to bring about dissolution at his own hand.[27]

Dissolution of the partnership can clearly be occasioned by one partner committing an anticipatory or repudiatory breach of the partnership agreement. The general principles of contract law apply in this context. These are as stated in *McDonald v Dennys Lascelles Ltd*:

> When a party to a simple contract, upon a breach by the other contracting party of a condition of the contract, elects to treat the contract as no longer binding upon him, the contract is not rescinded as from the beginning. Both parties

---

24 Section 36(1)(e) (F); s 38(e) (CI), (Ni) also see Partnership Application Act 1994, (Tu); s 163(1)(c) (MI); s 35(e) (N), (V).

25 Section 36(1)(f) (F); s 38(f) (CI), (Ni), (Tu); s 163(1)(c) (MI); s 35(f) (N), (V).

26 *Patel v Patel* [1992] FJCA 22; *Hills v Nash* (1844) 1 Phillips 594 at 598.

27 [2000] SLT 464.

are discharged from the further performance of the contract, but rights are not divested or discharged which have already been unconditionally acquired. Rights and obligations which arise from the partial execution of the contract and causes of action which have accrued from its breach alike continue unaffected.[28]

However, it has been suggested that repudiation cannot be automatic. Partnership arrangements may be multilateral instead of bilateral. Some partners might accept a repudiation and others might not. The position thus has to be viewed in terms of the totality of the partnership arrangement. In *Hurst v Bryk*, the House of Lords said:

> The doctrine of accepted repudiation is of general application in the law of contract, and there is no reason why it should not apply to an agreement to enter into partnership or to the contractual obligations which the partners mutually undertake to observe after the partnership has come to an end. But I have considerable doubt that it can be employed to bring about the automatic dissolution of the partnership itself.[29]

The broadest of the enumerated grounds which can be invoked before the court is that provided for under 13, the so-called 'just and equitable' ground which provides the court with considerable breadth of discretion in relation to the ordering of a dissolution. A similar ground is provided for under companies legislation.

That mentioned in 14 arises by virtue of the general law rather than the partnership agreement, although the partnership agreement might make some provision to that effect. Given that a partnership arises by agreement, it can also be terminated by the agreement of all partners. This is on the proviso that the requirements of independent consideration for the dissolution agreement exist as required by contract law. We will now look at some of the above grounds in a little more detail.

20.1.2 Termination by notice

Subject to the partnership agreement, a partnership at will or for an unfixed term can be terminated by notice given by one or more of the partners. The partnership is dissolved as from the date mentioned in the notice as the date of dissolution. If no date is mentioned in the notice, the dissolution will be as from the date of the communication of the notice.[30]

---

28 (1933) 48 CLR 457 at 476–77, approved by the House of Lords in *Johnson v Agnew* [1980] AC 367 and in *Bank of Boston Connecticut v European Grain and Shipping Ltd* [1989] AC 1056.
29 2 All ER 283; [2000] 2 WLR 740 *per* Lord Millett; distinguishing *Hitchman v Crouch Butler Savage Associates* (1982) 80 LS Gaz 550.
30 Section 33(2) (F); s 35 (CI), (Ni), (Tu); s 32 (N), (V).

The situation here is not quite the same thing as the service of a notice of dissolution in the event of, say, a breach of a partnership term by one of the partners. It is common enough to serve a notice in these cases, but this is not the act which itself achieves the dissolution. The notice in such cases is merely for the purposes of advice to the other partners. It is not a legal act of itself.

The notice must constitute notice of intention of the partner giving it to dissolve the partnership in question. It cannot be in the form of a request, nor can it be ambiguous or hesitant on the question of intention to dissolve. A notice that is precatory or by way of request or pleading will not constitute notice.

As a general proposition, the place for service of the notice will be determined by the partnership agreement if it makes a stipulation as to the address for service of notices. Otherwise, it is a question of service at the usual place of residence or place of business of the other partners. However, legislation applies here, for example s 74(2) of the Interpretation Act Cap 1A of Tuvalu, which provides:

A document or notice required or permitted to be served on, or given, delivered and notices or sent to, a person under or for the purposes of a written law, may, unless the contrary intention appears, be served, given, delivered or sent–

(c) in the case of a partnership–

(i) by serving it personally on a partner or the person having the control or management of the partnership or by sending it by pre-paid post to him at his usual or last known place of abode; or

(ii) by leaving it at or sending it by pre-paid post to the principal office of the partnership.

No particular mode of giving the notice is required or stipulated. The real question seems to be whether the notice was most likely to be brought to the attention of the other partner or partners. Service by post or personally is possible and in fact usual, but evidence must be provided in any case that the notice was in fact properly served. In such a case, registered or certified mail is commonly used, a receipt is required or the use of a process server or an independent witness as to service is provided.

20.1.3 Unsoundness of mind

In respect of this ground, it must be shown to the satisfaction of the court that it is a case of permanently unsound mind, rather than a mere temporary or transient condition. An application can be made to the court on this ground by one or more of the other partners or the committee or next friend of the affected partner, or by any other person having title to intervene.

20.1.4 Incapacity

The incapacity must be shown to be, again, something that is a relatively permanent rather than temporary condition. The incapacity is not a matter of any general incapacity, whatever that might be. It requires proof of some condition of the partner which renders him or her incapable of performing his or her part of the partnership agreement.

20.1.5 Bankruptcy, death and charge

Dissolution occurs automatically in the event of the bankruptcy or death of a partner. So also where a partner charges partnership property with his or her own separate debts. This is provided for under s 34 of the Partnership Act of Fiji and similar provisions in other jurisdictions.[31] No notice is required, as the occurrence of the event itself achieves the dissolution.

Bankruptcy does not include an order for the administration of affairs. Nor does it apply in cases where a person merely becomes insolvent or unable to pay his or her debts as they become due. Bankruptcy is a formal legal state brought about by a formal order of a court. It means, in other words, a final order suspending a person's ability to deal with their own affairs and property and vesting official control of them in an official called the official receiver or similar title. This is provided for under the independent bankruptcy legislation of the various jurisdictions.

It is to be noted that under the statutory provision here, the death or bankruptcy of one partner dissolves the partnership as against all partners. In other words, the partnership is completely dissolved. It is quite usual that this provision be overridden by the partnership agreement by a term which provides, in effect, that the death or bankruptcy of one partner does not effectuate a dissolution. To the contrary, the partnership is to continue as between the remaining or surviving partners. Provision is then made for the share of the bankrupt or deceased partner to be purchased by the other partners according to some agreed mechanism.

For example, the partnership agreement might provide that the interest of the deceased or bankrupt partner is to be valued by an independent valuer and the net value properly determined after allowance is made for a proper share of debts and liabilities. The remaining partners are then conceded the right to purchase the interest of their former partner at a price equal to the net value. It is also possible to provide that the outgoing partner's share can be purchased by an incoming partner approved by the partners at a price determined according to a standard formula. There are other ways of proceeding, but these need not concern us here.

---

31 Section 36 Partnership Act (CI), (Ni) also see Partnership Application Act 1994, (Tu); s 33 Partnership Act (N), (V).

20.1.6 Illegality

There are two types of illegality or unlawfulness which are anticipated by s 35. These are: (a) where it is or becomes unlawful for the business of the firm to be carried on *per se*; and (b) where it is or becomes unlawful for the members of the firm to carry it on in partnership. The legislation is dealing here with situations where a partnership has at one time come into existence but some event happens which produces the condition of unlawfulness on either of these two bases.

Both of these cases are slightly different from situations where the partnership was never properly brought into existence because it was tainted with some illegality right from the start, i.e. a situation where the partnership is void for illegality *ab initio*. In such a case, the partnership never existed at all on grounds of public policy. In such a case, the terminology of dissolution is inappropriate.

20.1.7 Misconduct

Section 36(c) and (d) of the Partnership Act of Fiji[32] provide two grounds for dissolution by the court based on misconduct. These are as follows:

(c)   when a partner other than the partner suing has wilfully been guilty of such conduct as in the opinion of the court, regard being had to the nature of the business, is calculated prejudicially to affect the carrying on of the business; or

(d)   when a partner other than the partner suing wilfully or persistently commits a breach of the partnership agreement or otherwise so conducts himself in matters relating to the partnership business that it is not reasonably practicable for the other partner or partners to carry on the business in partnership with him.

It is to be noted that the conduct in question must have been wilful rather than negligent, although unlike the provisions of employment legislation of the region, there is no requirement that the conduct in question should constitute gross or serious misconduct.[33] Furthermore, it is a specific type of conduct rather than some misconduct in a general sense. That is, it must be shown to have been calculated to prejudicially affect the carrying on of the partnership business.[34]

---

32 Section 38(c), (d) (CI), (Ni), (Tu); s 163(c), (d) (MI); s 35(c), (d) (N), (V).
33 See e.g. *Ferrieux v Banque Indosuez Vanuatu Ltd* [1990] VUSC 1; *National Bank of Vanuatu v Cullwick* [2002] VUCA 39.
34 See *Waterhouse v Grant* Civil Action No HBCO 148 of 1998.

20.1.8 The just and equitable ground

The court may dissolve a partnership where the circumstances are such as to render it just and equitable that the partnership be dissolved. It covers the classic situations where for example management of the partnership or its business has become deadlocked, or where a partner or partners have been excluded from participation in the decision-making process.

However, the phrase 'just and equitable' is used in many contexts and provides the court with a wide discretion as to the circumstances in which an order might be made.[35] It is also a ground for the winding up of companies.

20.2 Dissolution by agreement

A partnership is created by agreement. Thus, as we noted above, as a matter of principle it can also be dissolved by agreement, provided the dissolution agreement itself is embodied in a deed or has separate consideration. Where this occurs, the deed or agreement for dissolution can be affected by a number of factors that might lead to its being set aside. For example, in the Fiji case of *Ranchod v Lallu*,[36] the Court of Appeal of Fiji set aside a deed dissolving a partnership on the ground of equitable fraud or undue influence, although on the facts it would seem that a more appropriate ground in equity might have been unconscionability. The fact that the controlling partners had not disclosed to the plaintiff the true picture with regard to partnership profits and matters of this nature and had also failed in honouring the fiduciary duty they owed to the plaintiff provided clear grounds to set aside the dissolution.

A deed whereby one partner releases other partners from claims in respect of the partnership after dissolution is open to be set aside on various grounds. These might include misrepresentation or undue influence. As we noted earlier, the partners stand in a fiduciary relationship to each other even though there has been a dissolution.[37] A misrepresentation could be constituted by, for example, the nondisclosure of crucial information in respect of partnership profits or property. Similarly, it could be in relation to the trading activities of the partnership, or the hiding of assets bought by one partner with partnership funds. These could provide a basis for the setting aside of the deed of dissolution.[38] Undue influence or unconscionability might give rise to rights of termination where one partner or

---

35 See, in the matrimonial context, *Devi v Singh* [1985] FJCA 2; *Shakuntala v Karan* 24 FLR 87; *Lata v Ram* [2001] FJHC 117; and, in the corporate context, *In re Anshal Transport Services Ltd* [1997] FJHC 138.

36 *Ranchod v Lallu* [1993] FJHC 56; Hbc0488j.91s (29 June 1993).

37 See *Chan v Zacharia*, supra, *Geraghty v Miller*, supra and *Sew Hoy v Sew Hoy*, supra.

38 See *Dimmock v Hallett* (1806) LR 2 Ch App 21.

partners is or are in a position of control or dominion over the other and there is a situation of inequality of bargaining power which affects the dissolution.[39]

In *Patel v Patel*, the Fiji Court of Appeal held that a clause in a dissolution deed could be subject to waiver or estoppel preventing its enforcement by one or more of the partners, for example, in a situation where a party has clearly abandoned reliance on it.[40] The defendants had asserted that the right of the plaintiff to sue under a particular clause of the partnership agreement had been waived by the plaintiff's participation in an agreement by all partners not to enforce claims under the clause or, alternatively, lost through delay. The waiver argument appears to have been accepted by the trial judge as an additional basis for dismissing the plaintiff's action. The Court of Appeal held that the ground of waiver could perhaps be considered in the nature of a claim of promissory estoppel, the two terms being sometimes synonymous, or perhaps an abandonment. If it were an estoppel, it was not necessary to prove consideration for such a promise, but other factors would need to be approved. Whatever the case, the Court of Appeal, faced with an apparent inability to distinguish conceptually between cases of waiver, acquiescence, promissory estoppel and laches, held that on the facts there were sufficient grounds to deny equitable relief to the plaintiff in respect of the action under the clause.[41]

20.3 Dissolution without express agreement

The partners might, by their conduct, bring into effect a *de facto* termination of the partnership without any express agreement to that effect. For example, it was said in *GH and UP Spencer v Wenlock*:

> Out of the monies which were received, the outstanding liabilities of the partnership were discharged and the balance was applied in reducing the overdraft on the partnership account at the bank and the payment of a small dividend. That I think amounted to a dissolution of partnership, and after that date it seems to me that the former partners were not carrying on any business.[42]

In the New Zealand case of *Smith v Baker*, it was commented that:

> I think it was in fact a partnership at will, determinable by either partner giving notice to the other of his intention to dissolve. There was no evidence of any such notice having been given. The business of the partnership ended with

---

39 *Sundarlal Lallu v Parvati Manilal*, unreported, Fiji Court of Appeal, Action No CAN ABU0053 of 1995S. See Corrin Care, J, Case Note (1998) 2(2) JSPL.
40 [1992] FJCA 22.
41 *Ibid.*
42 (1922) WAR 114 at 117.

the sale of the motel by the defendant and he in his pleading denied the very existence of the partnership. In those circumstances I think I can infer that the partnership was dissolved.[43]

A partner can abandon his or her interest in a partnership and thus bring the partnership to an end. In *Palmer v Moore*,[44] the Privy Council held that a document signed by a partner addressed to his co-partners explaining that he was unable to make any further contribution to the partnership and telling them to do whatever they wished with the partnership property constituted an abandonment of his interest in the partnership. In *Jorgensen v Boyce*,[45] it was held, in the case of a working partnership, that it might be terminated by one of the partners ceasing to work.

The situation in *Lukin v Lovrinov*[46] was as follows: in 1993, one of three partners in a fishing business which had been established for several years told the other partners that he was no longer interested in the partnership. He informed them that he only wanted his share of a fishing quota attached to the licence of one of the other partners, which had been leased out for the benefit of the partnership. This brought to a head the fact that the partner had for some time refused to make any real contribution to the operation of the partnership. Perry J of the South Australian Supreme Court held that notwithstanding provisions in the partnership deed providing for written notice of termination, the statement and conduct of the partner constituted an abandonment by him of his interest in the partnership and operated to determine the partnership.

In *Jorgensen v Boyce*,[47] it was held that, in the case of a working partnership, the partnership might be terminated by abandonment through one of the partners ceasing to work. Where the partners have settled accounts between themselves with some finality, then it is open for the court to infer that the partnership was dissolved even in the absence of express agreement. In *Vidotto v Kovacevic*, it was said in this regard:

> The question whether the dealings between the parties were such that the partnership was dissolved on the basis of settled accounts between the parties is one in respect of which the onus lies on the party alleging that the accounts were settled, that is in the present case the defendants ... I think that it must follow from the nature of partnership and dissolution that until there is a taking of accounts and realisation of the assets and payments of debts and discharge of liabilities of the partnership from partnership property, the quantification of

43 (1977) 1 NZLR 511 at 513.
44 [1900] AC 293.
45 (1896) 22 VLR 408.
46 [1998] SASC 6614.
47 (1896) 22 VLR 408.

the right of any one partner to a share in the surplus (if there is one) of assets over liabilities, is at large: see *Livingston v Commissioner for Stamp Duties (Q)* (1960) 107 CLR 411 at 453. Hence if one party asserts that the partners have at dissolution quantified their respective interests so as to avoid a realisation of assets and payments of debts from partnership property an issue is raised on which the party making the assertion bears the onus.[48]

20.3.1 Consequences of dissolution

Where a partnership is dissolved, then normally the assets of the partnership business must be sold.[49] The partnership instrument might in a given case prescribe some particular method that the parties must adopt in respect of the winding up of the partnership property after legal dissolution. The intentions of the parties as expressed in the deed will normally be followed. If, however, no method of winding up is set out in the instrument, then unless the partners can come to some agreement as to what is to be done, usually all the partnership property must be converted into cash. The situation will be the same where there is a method prescribed by the partnership instrument but this method cannot be carried out by the partners. Furthermore, this presupposes that the partners cannot themselves come to some other agreement on the method of winding up. This fund of cash, after the payment of the partnership debts, is to be divided amongst the partners according to their proper entitlements to it.[50]

Any partner has the right to force such a sale whether or not such a sale of assets is necessary for the payment of debts.[51] The method of sale which each partner is entitled to insist upon will usually be by way of public auction: that is, a sale to the highest bidder. A partner has no vested right of purchase, nor can a partner compel his or her partners to purchase at valuation or on other terms unless there is some specific agreement to that effect.[52] If there is no express agreement otherwise, the surviving partners cannot assume any right to take the share of the deceased partner at a valuation or otherwise. Such rights arise usually only as a product of agreement, express or implied, between the parties themselves. Conversion into cash is the most reasonable and efficacious method of settling the accounts of the partners between themselves once and for all. Whilst other methods might appear

---

48 [1994] ACTSC 105 at para 55.

49 *Waterhouse v Grant* above.

50 See Scammell, EM and l'Anson Banks, RC, *Lindley on Partnership*, 15th edn, London, Sweet & Maxwell p 199. Also see generally Higgins, PFP, *The Law of Partnership in Australia and New Zealand*, 2nd edn, Pyrmont, NSW, LBC Information Services, pp 185, 203 and 206, adopted in *Waterhouse v Grant* above.

51 Lindley, *ibid.*, p 598.

52 *Ibid.*, p 601.

to have their advantages, conversion is far more capable of settling the accounts on equitable terms and with a minimum of dispute.[53]

20.3.2 Entitlement to account on dissolution

On dissolution of the partnership or on retirement, the partners or outgoing partner might be entitled to an account against the other partners on general equitable principles. Account is an equitable remedy which requires an inquiry and determination of an amount which is owing in a particular case, including profits and gains where appropriate. It is sometimes used in conjunction with the imposition of a constructive trust or an order for equitable compensation.

Being an action in equity, the normal range of equitable defences such as delay, waiver and acquiescence will usually be available. As noted above, normally this will be an action to which all of the other partners should be joined. In *Hills v Nash*, the court said:

> It is a general rule that an action for an account of the partnership transactions by one of the partners against some of the others, all the rest should be joined as parties to the suit.[54]

As to the general entitlement to an account, in *Chetty v Vijayaraghavachariar*,[55] the Privy Council said:

> At any rate, in all cases where for any reason it did occur that after the dissolution and complete winding up of a partnership an asset which had not been taken into account fell in, it ought to be divided between the ex-partners or their representatives according to their shares in the former partnership.
>
> If on the other hand no accounts have been taken and there is no constat that the partners have squared up, then the proper remedy when such an item falls in is to have the accounts of the partnership taken; and if it is too late to have recourse to that remedy, then it is also too late to claim a share in an item as part of the partnership assets, and the plaintiff does not prove, and cannot prove that upon the due taking of the accounts he would be entitled to that share.[56]

In *Marshall v Bullock*,[57] Gibson LJ was confronted with a situation where a partnership between two partners had been dissolved. At the time of dissolution there were partnership liabilities and possibly assets of the partnership. One of the

---

53 *Ibid.*, p 657.
54 (1844) 1 Phillips 594 at 598.
55 [1922] 1 AC 488.
56 *Ibid.*, p 496.
57 [1998] EWCA Civ J0327–15.

partners appropriated the assets and discharged the relevant liabilities. Some six years after the dissolution, but within six years of the discharge of the liabilities, the same partner brought proceedings to recover from the other partner his share of the discharged liabilities. The first partner had at no stage accounted for any of the partnership assets appropriated by him on dissolution, nor had any account been taken of partnership assets. The time for bringing an action for an account had expired long ago. The first partner asserted that there was a right of contribution from the second partner.

The court denied that there was a right to proceed for contribution as this was an action in the nature of an account. The same would apply if this were cast as an action for recovery of a share in a partnership. Both contribution and recovery of a share of the partnership are elements in an action for account. It was said:

> There are good policy reasons why this should be so. When a partnership comes to an end, there is an obligation on the partners to agree, or to have determined by the court, their respective liabilities and their respective entitlements. Once partners have dissolved the partnership, each should after six years be free of the risk of any claims being made by another partner. ... It would be unfortunate if the court were to encourage partners who have failed to obtain an account or who have allowed the time for an action for an account to be brought to expire, to rely years later on an individual item which would and should have featured in that account to make it the subject of a separate action for recovery. As I have already said, that is simply not fair, because, in ascertaining what is due from one partner to another, one has to look at both sides of the balance sheet, both sides of the account.[58]

However, the court appeared to acknowledge three exceptions to any general rule, as follows:

> One is where accounts have been finally settled. In such a case it will be known what the respective entitlements are as between the partners, and who is liable for what. In such a case it would not be necessary to seek from the court an order for an account. The second possible exception is where an asset is unexpectedly recorded (or, by like reasoning, a liability to contribution unexpectedly arises) after a final settlement of accounts and the recovery of the asset (or the discharge of the liability) is made more than six years after the dissolution of the partnership.[59] ... It may be arguable that in such a case a separate action

---

58 *Ibid.*, paras 30, 31.
59 See *Knox v Gye* (1872) LR 5 HL 656 at 678; see also *Meyer & Co v Faber (No 2)* [1923] 2 Ch 421.

will lie. The third exception is where an account would serve no useful purpose. Equity will not act in vain.[60]

Normally a former partner is not entitled to pick and choose which of several partners should be subjected to an account.[61] Yet the action must involve something which is genuinely in the nature of an action for dissolution or taking of accounts rather than, say, an action for debt against the other partners. This was applied in the Fiji case of *Patel v Patel* where, after citing *Hills v Nash*, above, it was held:

> Firstly the action brought by the plaintiff was not for an account of any sort; it was for a debt alleged to be owing by the defendants to him. The case referred to by the learned Judge was a suit for winding up; it is clear law that in an action for dissolution or the taking of accounts, all partners within the jurisdiction should ordinarily be joined; there are some exceptions, but basically this is mandatory. The same rule applies in cases of partnership disputes which 'involve the taking of some account in which all the partners are interested or the granting of an injunction or the appointment of a receiver' (*Lindley on Partnership*, 14th edn, p 522). But none of those things applied here. There was no challenge to the accounts, there was no claim to surcharge or falsify, or otherwise to re-open them in any way. There is no reason to suppose that if the plaintiff was entitled to interest on undrawn profits a calculation could not be made that would show the proportion payable by the defendants out of their share of the proceeds on dissolution. The particulars which the statement of claim alleges had been supplied to the defendants might have shown just such a calculation, and resulted in the defendants not challenging the amount nor raising any defence other than the two that we have mentioned earlier, and which had nothing to do with the accounts. If such a calculation could be and was made, then it did not involve the other partners at all.[62]

The court held that the action was not one that was in the nature of a partnership action. But if there were any necessity to join the other partners, it was a procedural failure which should not have been used by the trial judge as a basis for dismissal of the action by the plaintiff given that the rules of court contained a mechanism for remedying such defects.[63]

The Act makes some provision as to the right of partners in respect of profits derived where the business has been carried on after dissolution. Section 42 of the (Fiji) Act reads as follows:

---

60 At para 27.
61 *Ibid.*
62 [1992] FJCA 22.
63 The court referred to Ord 15 r 6 of the High Court Rules.

42 (1) Where any member of a firm has died or otherwise ceased to be a partner, and the surviving or continuing partners carry on the business of the firm with its capital or assets without any final settlement of accounts as between the firm and the outgoing partner or his estate, then, in the absence of any agreement to the contrary, the outgoing partner or his estate is entitled at the option of himself or his representatives to such share of the profits made since the dissolution as the Court may find to be attributable to the use of his share of the partnership assets, or to interest at the rate of five per cent per annum on the amount of his share of the partnership assets.

(2) Provided that where by the partnership contract an option is given to surviving or continuing partners to purchase the interest of a deceased or outgoing partner, and that option is duly exercised, the estate of the deceased partner, or the outgoing partner or his estate, as the case may be, is not entitled to any further or other share of profits; but if any partner assuming to act in exercise of the option does not in all material respects comply with the terms thereof, he is liable to account under the foregoing provisions of this section.

It was held in *Barclays Bank Trust Co Ltd v Bluff*[64] that s 42(1) did not apply to capital profits made during the period subsequent to dissolution. This view was approved by the Privy Council in *Chandroutie v Gajadhar*.[65] It is to be noted that the section provides for an exception to the general provision made by s 24(1) (above) only in the 'certain cases' (see the marginal note) in which its requirements are satisfied.[66]

Where a partner has retired and an amount is found due to him or her, the amount is due by way of a simple contract debt. Any amount found to be owing to a retired partner is to be treated as a simple contract debt.[67] As such, an action to recover it would be subject to the usual limitation period of six years under the relevant Limitations Acts.[68] This includes a situation where the retired partner commences proceedings seeking an account in equity rather than directly claiming a debt. Where law and equity give concurrent remedies of the same kind, for example, where the plaintiff seeks an account, equity will apply the Limitations Act by analogy.[69]

---

64 [1982] Ch 172.

65 [1987] AC 147 at 154.

66 See *Popat v Shonchhatra* [1997] EWCA 2327 at para 23.

67 See Higgins and Fletcher, KL, *The Law of Partnership in Australia and New Zealand*, 7th edn, 1996, Pyrmont, NSW, LBC Information Services, p 248; and see *Knox v Gye* (1872) 42 LJ Ch 234 at 237–38.

68 See *Phillips-Higgins v Harper* [1954] 1 QB 411 at 418–19.

69 *Levi v Stirling Brass Founders Pty Ltd* (1997) 36 ATR 290 at 296–97; *Knox v Gye* (1872) 42 LJ Ch 234 at 238–39 and 242–43.

However, there are circumstances where proceedings for an account might be ordered notwithstanding expiry of the limitation period. Aside from estoppel situations, this would appear to be the case in respect of error or fraud in the partnership accounts where the action can still be taken outside the limitation period. In *Williamson v Barbour*, Jessel MR said:[70]

> I have one other observation to make, which is that, where you shew a single fraudulent entry in the case of persons occupying the position of principal and agent, or trustee and *cestui que trust*, the court has actually opened an account extending over a greater number of years and closed for a much longer period than the account I have before me; I mean in the case of *Allfrey v Allfrey*, before Lord Cottenham (1 Mac & G 87). We therefore have this sort of guide without laying down any general rule, because every case must depend on its own circumstances, that where the accounts have been shown to be erroneous to a considerable extent, both in amount and in number of items, or where fiduciary relations exist and a less considerable number of errors are shown, or where the fiduciary relation exists and one or more fraudulent omissions or insertions in the account are shown, the court opens the account and does not merely surcharge and falsify.

However, it would seem that there must be something more than a breach of fiduciary obligation involved here. It needs to be shown that there were fraudulent (in the equitable sense) omissions or insertions in the accounts, so as to justify the re-opening of any of the accounts outside the limitation period. Otherwise, equity will follow the law and apply the legal limitation period.[71]

Just what post-dissolution profits are attributable to a partner's share of assets for the purposes of s 42 depends on the facts of each case and particularly how the partnership business was carried on in terms of those assets. In *Fry v Oddy*,[72] it was held that where a legal practice was carried on in partnership after dissolution making significant use of assets such as computer systems and other electronic technology rather than personal skill and endeavour of the continuing partners, all of the assets of the partnership contributed to the continuing profits by providing the apparatus which enabled the business to be carried on. Hence the outgoing partner was entitled to an equal share of the profits to reflect the equal share he retained in those assets.

70 (1877) 9 Ch D 529 at 533.
71 *Wheatley v Bower and Others* [2001] WASCA 293 (24 September).
72 [1998] VSCA 26.

20.3.3 Expulsion

Expulsion is a situation where one or more parties are legitimately excluded from the partnership such that the partnership is determined as regards the person so excluded. Partnership agreements commonly contain a provision permitting the expulsion of a partner by the others in the event of some specified types of wrongdoing or incapacity. Section 26 of the Fiji legislation requires that any power of expulsion be provided for expressly in the partnership agreement itself. There is, for example, no implicit power in a majority of partners to exclude one of their partners. Given this, it would not appear possible for the court to imply the existence of an expulsion clause.

Thus, the expulsion of one partner by another must take place pursuant to a clause in the agreement. Given this, the interpretation or construction of the expulsion clause in the agreement is a key element in such cases. On the one hand, there is the view that such clauses ought to be construed in light of decisions in other cases in order to produce some degree of consistency in commercial matters. The other predominant view is that an expulsion clause in any particular case is to be construed individually, according to its particular context. One may contrast the decision of Street J at first instance in *Bond v Hale*[73] relying on *In re A Solicitor's Arbitration*,[74] which reinforces the first approach. He said:

> In a field such as the construction of partnership agreements, where they appear in what has become a common form, there are strong reasons, based upon the pursuit of consistency in the law, for following and applying in this jurisdiction decisions of coordinate courts in other common-law jurisdictions.[75]

However, this approach was rejected by the majority on appeal.[76] It would appear that the latter approach prevails in that the question is one about the true construction of the expulsion clause in the particular partnership agreement that was before the court, which requires close consideration of the terms of the agreement in question.[77]

There still appears to be some scope to permit comparison in cases where standard or common forms are used. Much depends on the peculiarities of the agreement in question. In *Variety Video v Jones*,[78] Austin J of the New South Wales Supreme Court said:

---

73 (1969) 89 WN (Pt 1) (NSW) 404.
74 [1962] 1 WLR 353.
75 *Ibid.* at 408.
76 (1969) 72 SR (NSW) 201 at 208.
77 See also *Bond v Hale* supra and the decision of the Victoria Court of Appeal in *Hanlon v Brookes* (1997) 15 ACLC 1626.
78 [2001] NSWSC 5.

I draw from [the authorities] ... the principle that although consistency of inter-pretation of commercial agreements by courts is a desirable objective, the first task of any court is to construe the agreement before it. The question of consist-ency of interpretation arises only when one is satisfied that the instant agree-ment is indistinguishable from agreements previously construed by courts. This is most likely to occur when the agreements are in a standard or common form.

The expulsion clause in the present case is not, in its terms, significantly different from the expulsion clause in *Bond v Hale*. However, the partnership agreement in the present case is a poorly drafted document that cannot be regarded as a standard or common form agreement. The proper construction of the present agreement is influenced, in my view, by inadequacies of drafting that make it inappropriate for me to rely on decisions in other cases as direct precedents, and ensure that my decision cannot be seen as inconsistent with judicial decisions about the meaning of more carefully drawn instruments or instruments in common form.[79]

In *Greenaway v Greenaway*,[80] it was held that a physical assault by one partner upon another is at least capable of justifying expulsion, under a partnership clause which permits expulsion where a partner so conducts himself that the general interest of partners would be likely to suffer. But there might be circumstances in which an assault might be justified in particular cases.

Even if there was an unlawful expulsion, in the circumstances of this case, the only redress available to the wronged party would be an order for account and damages. It would not include a right to subsequently acquired property.[81] In most cases, expulsion by a resolution pursuant to the partnership agreement is with respect to one partner only. The authorities appear now to acknowledge that a single resolution might provide for a multiple exclusion of partners.[82]

Commonly, expulsion clauses permit exclusion on the ground of misconduct or serious misconduct of a party. In *Variety Video v Jones*, there was some con-tention that this notion was to be considered in light of the fiduciary duties that are owed by partners to each other. However, Austin J did not feel that it was necessary to decide this issue. He did, however, adopt the view that the question of serious misconduct, however vague it might be, was to be determined as a question of fact, and that "there is no serious misconduct if risk of loss or injury is very remote, or if any loss or injury (even if probable) would only be trivial in its nature and character".[83] Particular instances of conduct that might be trivial if

79 At paras 76 and 77.
80 (1940) 84 Sol J 43.
81 *Hall v Hall* supra at para 217.
82 *Hanlon v Brookes* (1997) 15 ACLC 1626.
83 [2001] NSWSC 5, paras 105 and 106.

considered in isolation might be part of a whole course of conduct which can be taken as either misconduct or serious misconduct.[84] Sometimes it is required by a particular agreement that the misconduct in question cause prejudice to the partnership business. Whether this requires proof of actual prejudice or likelihood of prejudice is a matter of construction of the clause in question. But even in a case where actual prejudice is required, this can be a matter of inference from a course of conduct undertaken by a partner. Reliable inference from individual occurrences is usually not sufficiently reliable.[85]

84 *Ibid.*, para 149.
85 *Ibid.*, para 152.

21
TERMINATION AND VARIATION OF TRUSTS

21.1 Variation of trusts

The court has no inherent power to vary a trust.[1] In those jurisdictions of the South Pacific where there remains some unresolved doubt about the applicability of the English legislation, and which do not have their own trustee legislation, it may be that the terms of the trust must remain as they are unless some mechanism is provided in the instrument for variation of the terms. That is so regardless of possibly disastrous consequences. It is to be noted, however, that there is inherent power on a court to grant additional powers to trustees in appropriate cases, and that of itself may assist in particular cases to achieve some extent of variation where it is needed. Variation might also be achieved with the assent of all the beneficiaries of a trust if they are of full age and capacity. Very often, however, this will not be the case, or it will be impractical to obtain their assent. A trust instrument may provide that under certain circumstances the terms of the trust may be varied. The trustee legislation also provides for a statutory power of variation by the court. The English Variation of Trusts Act 1958 was adopted by New Zealand[2] and therefore applies in jurisdictions such as the Cook Islands, Niue and other free association countries. Legislative provision for variation also applies in all states of Australia.

Section 86 of the Trustee Act of Fiji provides as follows:

86 (1) Without limiting any other powers of the Court, it is hereby declared that, where any property is held on trusts arising under any will, settlement

---

1 *Chapman v Chapman* [1954] AC 429.
2 See now s 64 Trustee Act 1956 (NZ).

DOI: 10.4324/9781003428060-26

or other disposition, or on the intestacy or partial intestacy of any person, or under any order of the Court, the Court may, if it thinks fit, by order approve, on behalf of–

(a) any person having, directly or indirectly, an interest, whether vested or contingent, under the trusts who, by reason of infancy or other incapacity, is incapable of assenting; or

(b) any person (whether ascertained or not) who may become entitled, directly or indirectly, to an interest under the trusts as being, at a future date or on the happening of a future event, a person of any specified description or a member of any specified class of persons; but this paragraph shall not include any person who would be of that description or a member of that class, if that date had fallen or that event had happened at the date of the application to the Court; or

(c) any unborn or unknown person; or

(d) any person, in respect of any discretionary interest of his under a protective trust, where the interest of the principal beneficiary has not failed or determined,

any arrangement (by whomsoever proposed, and whether or not there is any other person beneficially interested who is capable of assenting thereto) varying or revoking all or any of the trusts, or enlarging the powers of the trustees of managing or administering any of the property subject to the trusts.[3]

By sub-s (2), other than in relation to an arrangement on behalf of a person referred to in sub-s (1)(d), the court cannot approve an arrangement on behalf of any person if the arrangement is to that person's detriment. In determining the issue of detriment, the court is empowered to have regard to all of the benefits that may accrue to that person 'directly or indirectly in consequence of the arrangement, including the welfare and honour of the family to which he belongs'. Any rearrangement approved by the court is deemed to be binding on all persons on whose behalf it was so approved, and thereafter the trusts as so rearranged shall take effect accordingly.[4]

The legislation does not apply to trusts created by Act of Parliament. The power under s 86(1) may complement the existing powers of the court to grant further powers on a trustee. It has been said that the court's power should be broadly interpreted, although the courts have traditionally been reluctant to use the variation power to confer additional investment powers on trustees.[5] Variation for these purposes has been taken not to include resettlement of the property on entirely new trusts.[6] The sections also refer to 'revoking'. In this regard it has been said:

---

3 Section 41 Trustee Act (S).
4 *Ibid.*, s 86(3). *Singh v Devi* [2015] FJHC 883; HBC319.2014 (10 November 2015).
5 *Riddle v Riddle* (1952) 85 CLR 202.
6 *Re Ball's Settlement Trusts* [1968] 1 WLR 899; *Allen v Distillers Co* [1974] 2 WLR 481.

As to the meaning of the word 'revoking' the context in which it is used would appear to displace the primary meaning of the word which is to place the parties to the trust instrument where they were before the trust was executed. It would be rare for the court to order the trust fund to be returned to the settlor. The secondary meaning of the word would therefore appear to have been intended for most practical purposes, that is the termination of the trust by way of distribution of assets amongst beneficiaries on whose behalf the court has exercised its jurisdiction.[7]

With some exceptions set out in the legislation, it is also required that benefit be shown in order for the arrangement to be approved. This would include financial as well as nonfinancial benefit. The intention of the settlor may be taken into account, but it is not the sole consideration.[8] Applications to invoke the court's powers can be made by specified classes of beneficiary mentioned in the section. An order for variation so as to expand the powers of the trustee can be made even though the trustee might have a power of some such kind as that sought under the trust deed.[9]

The purpose of the section is to provide the court with a much wider power than was formerly available under its inherent jurisdiction. The relevant test appears to be that of expediency. In *Riddle v Riddle*, it was said:

I cannot see why it should be legally wrong or in any sense improper to make an order sufficiently general to enable the trustees to act at their own discretion in selecting, out of a list of shares named in the order, or out of a description of shares, defined in the order, particular shares from time to time for investment or for sale. I respectfully disagree with the view that the fact that all other trust estates with the same lack of power are affected in the same manner takes the case outside the section or affords a reason for refusing to make an order. The section contemplates the conferring of a power of investment outside the investments allowed by s 14 and, if it is 'expedient' to do this for reasons applicable only to the particular estate or a limited class of estates. I am unable to see why it is less expedient because the reasons are of general application. Nor am I able to assent to the view that the equivalent New South Wales provision in its application to powers to invest is confined to cases where a specific investment is found to be expedient so that the basis of the order must be the particular investment, though the authority given by the order may be a general power.[10]

---

7 Ford, HAJ and Lee, WA, *Principles of the Law of Trusts in Australia*, 1990, Sydney, Law Book Co, pp 669–70.
8 *Re Steed's Will Trusts* [1960] Ch 407.
9 *Degan v Lee* (1939) 39 SR (NSW) 234.
10 *Riddle v Riddle* (1951–52) 85 CLR 202 at 215.

In *Riddle v Riddle*, expediency was taken to mean 'expediency in the interests of the beneficiaries'. There would thus be no need for the trustees to prove the desirability of making a particular type of investment in order to obtain some special advantage or to avoid some special disadvantage. The High Court of Australia said further:

> the degree of proof that a proposed investment is expedient is no higher than the proof required that any sale, lease, mortgage, surrender, release, or disposition, or any purpose, investment, acquisition, expenditure, or transaction is expedient.[11]

There are some restrictions on the variation power, however. The variation power can only be employed for administrative purposes. In *Re Craven's Estate*,[12] it was said:

> the powers of the court under the section are purely administrative powers. There is equally no doubt that so long as the matter arises in the management or administration of the trust there is nothing which limits the power of the court under the section except the necessity that it should be exercised for the benefit of the particular trust as a whole.

Secondly, whilst expediency is the guiding issue to be considered by the court, this requires that the court determine that issue with reference to the interests of the beneficiaries as a whole and not just some of them.[13]

Under s 87 of the same Act, any trustee of any person beneficially interested under the trust can apply to the court for an order varying from time to time the amount of any payment, whether by way of annuity or otherwise, being made periodically to any beneficiary under the trust. The court may make such an order if it is of the opinion, having regard to all the circumstances of the case, that it is just and equitable that the amount be varied.

21.1.1 Termination of a trust

As we noted elsewhere, the idea that a trust should be rendered indestructible other than in cases of a charitable trust is contrary to established principles. A trust must in principle be capable of termination. There are a number of ways in which a trust might be terminated. Unlike corporations, however, where legislation provides elaborate procedures for the winding up of the corporation, no such machinery exists for trusts.

---

11 (1951–52) 85 CLR 202 at 221.
12 [1937] Ch 431.
13 See *In re Craven's Estate; Lloyd's Bank Ltd v Cockburn* (No 2) [1937] Ch 436.

First, a trust may be brought to an end on its own terms. It may be provided to be a trust to endure for a limited period only and so may expire by effluxion of time. Or it may be provided that the trust comes to an end on the happening of one or more specified events or the fulfilment of certain conditions. In this vein, a trust may be terminated by distribution of the trust estate to the beneficiaries entitled to it in terms of the trust. For example, in the case of a discretionary trust the trustee might exercise his or her discretion and allocate the whole of the property under the trust to one or more of the specified objects. That will mean that they no longer continue to hold their allocations as beneficiaries under the trust: it will bring the trust to an end and discharge the trustee from office. Similarly so in other circumstances where legitimate distribution takes place. The beneficiaries have a right to have the trust property transferred to them when their entitlement to it is fully established. This, of course, is subject to the right of the trustee to make a deduction for any liabilities due by the beneficiaries or charged on the trust assets, for example, in terms of the trustee's right of indemnity. A trustee is entitled under some circumstances, both by general law and by statute, to appropriate trust assets towards the satisfaction of the shares of individual beneficiaries on distribution. This would be so where the beneficiary is entitled to a legacy or to a share of residue, and presumably in other cases where the interest of the beneficiary is not, in itself, with respect to a specific asset in the trust. It is permissible where the trustee has a power of sale and therefore effectively sells the asset to the beneficiary in lieu of payment and sets the value off against the interest of the beneficiary. Valuation of the assets in question is required in order to bring the relevant amount to proper account. Like other trustee powers, this power is fiduciary and must not be exercised to prejudice the interests of the other beneficiaries.

Secondly, a trust may be terminated where there are express powers of termination or revocation of the trust contained in the trust instrument itself.[14] Sometimes such a power is implied, but this is rarely the case. The trust instrument may provide that these powers be exercised by the settlor, by the trustee or by some third person. Regardless of a provision in the trust instrument, a sole beneficiary who is also the settlor may terminate a trust and call on the trustee to transfer the property to him or her.[15] Whether the powers vested in the particular person concerned are in the nature of fiduciary powers to be exercised for the benefit of, say, the beneficiaries of the trust is a matter for the court to determine on normal fiduciary principles. In the case of a power vested in the trustee, this would almost always be the case. In some cases formal written notice may be required; in other cases not. However, the terms of the trust are taken as they were originally established and this will be accepted by the courts. There may be conditions imposed on the

---

14 See *Russell v Scott* (1936) HCA 34; 55 CLR 440; *Countess of Kenmore v IRC* [1958] AC 267; *Gosling v Gosling* [1859] Johns 265; *Re Smith* [1928] Ch 915.
15 *Beattie v Wein* (1908) 9 SR (NSW) 36.

exercise of the power. For example, the power may be exercisable on the occurrence of a particular event, on certain beneficiaries coming of age, on the settlor dying or otherwise.

The court may also terminate a trust pursuant to its power of variation discussed above. Alternatively, the trust may be terminated pursuant to the rule in *Saunders v Vautier*.[16] The rule states that where the beneficiary or beneficiaries are *sui juris* and their interests are fully vested (that is, in interest rather than in possession), then the beneficiary or the beneficiaries collectively may terminate the trust by calling on the trustee to transfer the trust property to him, her or them as the case may be. This is the case even though the express terms of the trust might anticipate a longer duration for the trust. The rule applies somewhat anomalously also to all the potential objects of a discretionary trust even though their interest cannot be said to be fully vested or proprietary in nature. Collectively those potential objects are treated as entitled to exercise the rule for their collective benefit. The existence of an unexercised power of appointment will not prevent the beneficiaries from invoking the rule even if it thereby prevents the exercise of the power to confer benefits on another. Nor, it would seem, would the existence of any other potential benefit to another person as a result of the nontermination of the trust.

The rule in *Saunders v Vautier* also applies even where the terms of the trust would seem, on the face of them, to prevent the beneficiary from taking an interest until a specific time. For example, if the trust required that income should be accumulated until the beneficiaries turned 40 years of age, the rule could still be invoked as and when all of the beneficiaries attained their majority. But the rule will only apply where all of the present and contingent beneficiaries are *sui juris* and consent to the termination of the trust.[17]

Sometimes, a trust estate may be in a situation of insolvency. There are provisions in the bankruptcy legislation which permit an insolvent trust estate to be administered in bankruptcy. The usual rules with respect to the suspension of creditors' recovery rights, the priorities for the payment of debts and the like will apply accordingly.

21.1.2 Distribution

On termination of the trust, the trustee is obliged to distribute the trust property to the beneficiaries in accordance with their entitlements under the trust instrument. It is normally said that the trustee has a duty to distribute the estate at the proper time regardless of whether or not the beneficiaries have demanded it. The proper

---

16 (1841) 41 ER 482; 4 Beav 115.

17 On the various tactics for circumventing application of the rule, for example by providing for a gift over to another beneficiary in the event that a contingency is not fulfilled, see Ford and Lee, *op cit* fn 7, p 687. See also *Michel v Equity Trustees Executors and Agency Co* [1964] VR 688.

time for distribution is a matter to be determined largely by reference to the trust instrument in question. However, when the beneficiaries' interests are fully vested and the beneficiaries are of full age and capacity, the duty to distribute arises immediately unless the trustee is directed by the beneficiaries to continue to hold the trust property for them under a bare trust.

This obligation to distribution places the trustee in a somewhat onerous position, as the trustee, in order to make a distribution, must not only ascertain the correct entitlements of the beneficiaries at law but calculate the shares to which they are entitled. It was once thought that a trustee who makes an incorrect distribution was only entitled to recover the amount of the wrong payment in the event that there had been a mistake of fact rather than a mistake of law. Most distributions tend perhaps to involve questions of law in so far as they are concerned with the calculation of legal entitlements, the interpretation of the trust deed and so on. At least there would usually be mixed questions of fact and law involved. In most cases, it is extremely difficult to ascertain which side of the line a particular issue falls and indeed the distinction tends to be rather artificial in its nature. The modern law of restitution tends to accept the fragility of this distinction and it now seems clear that a trustee may recover in either case on general restitutionary principles, particularly those relating to unjust enrichment. Nonetheless, the trustee may not always be able to recover and will be in breach of trust if he or she makes an incorrect distribution. Matters which raise doubts about questions of entitlement should therefore be clarified by the trustee seeking directions from the court.

The appropriate procedure for a trustee in any case where there is doubt about entitlements on distribution arising for example in respect of the interpretation of the trust deed or otherwise, or as to the right of a claimant to be considered, is to apply for directions from the court.[18] The trustee in distributing must also be involved necessarily in taking into account of the claims of outsiders against the trustee and for which the trustee in virtue of his or her position is personally liable.[19] This can occasion particular difficulty where the trustee is not in a good position to ascertain whether there are outstanding claims against him or her or claims to a share of the trust estate, either by potential creditors or by persons claiming a beneficial interest in the trust, which need to be taken into account. A trustee who failed to take steps in this regard would be exposed to personal liability, although the court has statutory power to relieve a trustee of personal liability.[20] Indeed, it is the duty of the trustee also to make diligent enquiries in relation to outstanding claims before distributing. A trustee can take measures to provide for liabilities or claims which are contingent or prospective by withholding property and therefore

---

18 The court has inherent power to give directions as well as statutory power: s 88 Trustee Act (F); s 43 Trustee Act (S).
19 On the indemnity rights of trustees and other special protections, see Chapter 9.
20 Section 71 Trustee Act (F); s 24 Trustee Act (S).

making merely an interim distribution. The administration in such a case would not be final until the claims were finally settled.

The trustee legislation establishes a procedure whereby the trustee can obtain immunity in relation to distribution subject to meeting only those claims of which he or she has notice. The legislation requires the publication of a notice to prospective claimants. Distribution subject only to those claims of which the trustee has notice will be regarded as in effect final and the trustee will be accorded immunity against those claims of which no notice was had at the time of distribution.[21] The legislation preserves the rights of claimants, if any, to follow trust assets into the hands of the persons receiving them.[22] The provisions apply to both testamentary trusts and trusts *inter vivos*. These provisions are modelled on s 27 of the UK Trustee Act 1925. Were it not for the legislative provision, the trustee could only protect himself or herself on distribution by retaining a sufficient amount of funds to meet contingent liabilities or by distributing pursuant to an administration order of the court.

A trustee is required to vest property in a beneficiary usually by the actual transfer of legal title to property to the beneficiary. In the case of personal representatives of deceased estates, it can be done by assent of the trustee, which is provided for in the wills legislation.[23] A trustee is also given power by the trustee legislation to appropriate specific assets to a beneficiary in satisfaction of which might otherwise be an entitlement to a legacy only.

21.1.3 Removal of trustees

As part of their inherent jurisdiction with respect to trustees, the courts may move a trustee in any given case.[24] The court will exercise this power only in appropriate cases. It is not enough that the beneficiaries would like the trustees removed or that they might have demanded it. The court is not compelled to do so even where the trustee has indicated a willingness to retire from office.[25] It is certainly not enough that the trustee is personally unpopular. Even the fact that the trustee is in a potential conflict situation or has committed a breach of trust is not a determining factor alone.[26] The court will, however, remove trustees who act obstructively or who have shown themselves opposed to the existence of the trust,[27] and certainly some breaches of trust, such as misappropriation of trust funds, will justify removal.[28]

---

21 Section 59 Trustee Act (F).
22 Section 90 Trustee Act (F).
23 A discussion of assents is best left to standard texts on succession law.
24 *Letterstedt v Broers* (1884) 9 App Cas 371; *Guazzini v Pateson* (1918) 18 SR (NSW) 275.
25 *Re Brockbank* [1948] Ch 206; *Shatfoon v Potts* [1948] NZLR 1214.
26 Ford and Lee, *op cit* fn 7, p 368.
27 See *Miller v Cameron* (1936) 54 CLR 572.
28 *Swanson v Dungey* [1892] SALR 87.

The absence of the trustee from the jurisdiction will justify removal on the basis partly that the trustee thereby impedes the administration of the trust,[29] but also this renders the trustee beyond the court's immediate supervisory jurisdiction. The trust instrument may provide a mechanism for removal of the trustee in certain circumstances, and this is something which the courts will enforce if the power is invoked. As we noted earlier, the courts will not generally interfere with the exercise of power or discretion by a trustee or the failure of a trustee to exercise a particular power or discretion either generally or in a particular way. Where, however, the trustee has refused to exercise a trust power which is obligatory in nature, there will be grounds for removal.

21.1.4 New and additional trustees

The court also has inherent power to appoint new trustees. This is complemented by provisions in the trustee legislation which provide for the appointment of new trustees in a number of particular cases. The standard provision is provided by s 73 of the Trustee Act of Fiji as follows:

> 73 (1) The Court may, whenever it is expedient to appoint a new trustee or new trustees, and it is found inexpedient, difficult or impractical to do so without the assistance of the Court, make an order appointing a new trustee or new trustees either in substitution for or in addition to any existing trustee or trustees, or although there is no existing trustee.[30]

By sub-s (2), the court may make an order appointing a new trustee where a trustee: (a) desires to be discharged; (b) has been held by the court to have misconducted himself or herself in the administration of the trust; (c) is convicted of any misdemeanour involving dishonesty, or of any felony; (d) is a person of unsound mind; (e) is bankrupt; or (f) is a corporation that has ceased to carry on business, is in liquidation or has been dissolved. These are particular cases which do not limit the generality of the court's power to appoint under sub-s (1). The court has power to make appropriate vesting orders in order to vest the trust property in newly appointed trustees.[31]

In *Re Tempest*,[32] three factors were indicated as those which should be taken into consideration by the court in respect of the application of s 73(1). These were, first, the wishes of the creator of the trust as expressed in the trust instrument. Secondly, the appointment should not favour the views of one class of benefi-

---

29 *Re Bignold's Settlement Trusts* (1872) 7 Ch App 223.
30 Section 29 Trustee Act (S).
31 Section 74 Trustee Act (F).
32 (1866) LR 1 Ch App 485.

ciaries as against another. Finally, consideration should be given to whether the appointment would advantage or restrict the administration and execution of the trust. On the latter ground, the courts would be unlikely, for example, to appoint a person who is outside the jurisdiction of the court. They will not appoint a person who is already a beneficiary or the spouse or other close associate, personal or business, of a beneficiary.

The trust instrument may contain provisions that allow for the appointment of new trustees in particular circumstances and might impose particular qualifications to be met in that regard. It might also provide for the appointment of additional trustees in particular cases, a right which is complemented by legislative provisions in some jurisdictions.[33]

21.1.5 Retirement of a trustee

The normal rule is that a trustee who has not disclaimed the office of trustee, where there is no compulsion to accept it in the first place, must remain in office during the continuance of the trust. A trustee may retire from office where the trust instrument provides for it. The court may allow a trustee to retire in certain circumstances as part of its supervisory jurisdiction but in practice, these matters are now dealt with under the legislation. The trustee legislation provides a power of retirement[34] and imposes a requirement that there be at least two trustees remaining in the event of the retirement. It is misleading to suggest that a trustee may retire with the consent of the beneficiaries, especially when what is usually meant is that the beneficiaries may terminate the trust. Retirement presumes the continuance of the trust. The mere retirement of a trustee will not necessarily relieve the trustee of all obligations to the trust. It may relieve him or her of obligations relating to administration. However, where the trustee retires simply in order to take up an opportunity that belongs to the trust, he or she might be subject to a constructive trust on general principles which relate to the misuse of property in breach of the trustee's fiduciary obligation earlier on discussed.

---

33 See s 2 of the Fiji legislation, whereby 'new trustee' includes 'additional trustee'.
34 Section 6 Trustee Act (F).

22

WINDING UP OF CORPORATE ENTITIES

22.1 What is winding up?

Winding up is sometimes called the liquidation of a company.[1] It is a specific process of external administration which is provided for in the relevant companies legislation of the region. This process eventually brings an end to the company's activities. From a legal point of view, the end product of the winding-up process is that the corporate personality of the company is terminated. In other words, the company closes down its operations both practically and legally.[2] It is to be distinguished from a receivership situation which might arise where, for example, a receiver is appointed by a secured creditor where a company has defaulted under a deed of charge or a mortgage against the assets of the company. Because it puts the company on a road to termination, it is also different from situations where a company is put into a scheme of arrangement or official management in an attempt to re-organise its affairs and pay its debts.

Winding up involves a process that needs to be undertaken in order to eventually close down the company. The winding-up process is commonly launched when a company finds itself in financial difficulty or insolvency. There is often no

---

1 See generally ss 8–27, 230 Insolvency Act 1986 (UK); s 122 ff Companies Act 1989 (UK); ss 213–365 Companies Act (F); ss 125–29 Companies Ordinance (K); ss 217–368 Companies Act (V); ss 210–394 Companies Act (NZ) (S); ss 36–67 Companies Act (T); ss 203–343 Companies Act (SI); ss 210–394 Companies Act (S). See generally Gower, LCB, *Gower's Principles of Modern Company Law*, 1992, 5th edn, London, Sweet & Maxwell pp 743–84.
2 For these reasons, the processes involved are similar to some extent to those involved in the administration of a deceased's estate or on the bankruptcy of an individual.

DOI: 10.4324/9781003428060-27

other way to effectively recover money owed by a defaulting company except to wind it up or at least threaten to wind it up.

There are, however, many other legal bases for winding up and we will examine these in due course. The business of the company might cease or there might be some other good reason why the shareholders or directors wish to wind up the company. Some types of winding up are forced on the company from outside, as for example in the debt recovery situation. These are generally known as involuntary winding-up procedures. Others are a result of decisions taken within the company itself. These are usually known as voluntary winding-up situations.

On a company going into winding up, whether it is pursuant to an order of the court or otherwise, it brings about a suspension of the powers of the directors, individually and collectively, to manage the affairs of the company. These affairs, and indeed total control of the company, are placed in the hands of a liquidator and the property of the company is vested in the liquidator. Normally, general meetings of the company are no longer held, although the court can, for example, require that they be held for particular purposes. Furthermore, the ability of the company itself to carry on its business is usually suspended, although the liquidator might permit it to continue to trade for limited purposes where he or she thinks that this is appropriate and in the interests of the company and its creditors. Dividends on shares can no longer be declared. Documents issued by the company thereafter have to contain the words 'in liquidation' after the name of the company.

The rights of creditors to recover moneys from the company are also suspended. One creditor cannot for example obtain payment of his or her debt because this would subvert the winding-up process and provide that creditor with an unfair advantage over other creditors. Even where a creditor has obtained a judgment against the company in respect of a debt or other liability, that judgment cannot be enforced against the company by way of execution or otherwise. Indeed, proceedings against a company which has been put into compulsory winding up by the court cannot be instituted by a creditor or other person except with leave of the court. At the same time, the ability of the company to pay its debts and meet its liabilities is suspended. The rights and liabilities of the company and the rights of the creditors are therefore overtaken by the liquidation process.

At the same time, the right of the company to dispose of any of its property is nullified by the winding up. The property technically remains vested in the company itself. There is no need for it to be vested in the liquidator. The company does not cease to exist with the making of a winding-up order. What takes place first is the process of liquidation for the final cessation of the existence of the corporate entity. Indeed, transactions to this effect made after the winding up has been made will be invalidated unless of course they are entered into by the liquidator for the purposes of the liquidation. As we will see in due course, there are special provisions in the legislation that deal with transactions by companies and their controllers which seek to avoid the consequences of winding up or which purport to confer advantages on particular creditors.

Normally, employees of the company are discharged by the entry into winding up.[3] The contract of service is effectively terminated. Some, or perhaps all, might be reemployed by the liquidator but there is no guarantee of this. Those who are owed salary or wages can of course prove their claims with the liquidator. Indeed, it would seem that under some circumstances employees might continue to have some provable claims against the company in respect of wrongful dismissal. The legislation gives some degree of priority to the payment of wage and salary claims, as will be seen below, but otherwise, they rank as ordinary creditors of the company who are all ranked in equal degree.

In other respects, contracts which were entered into by the company prior to winding up are not affected. It could be that a particular contract might provide otherwise where, for example, the contract contains a term to the effect that a winding-up order against the company will immediately terminate the contract. The court does have wide power to discharge or order the rescission of contracts with the company under some circumstances. As discussed below, the liquidator of the company is also entitled to disallow certain cumbersome transactions entered into by the company.

Transfers of shares in the company after an order for winding up has been made are usually treated as void. However, the court might sanction particular transfers in some cases. The company, through the liquidator, can still make calls on the unpaid share price of shareholders in the company. But, as we discussed earlier, the payment of the unpaid amount due in respect of shares held is the limit of the liabilities of a shareholder to contribute to the debts and liabilities of a limited liability company. Essentially, the winding up of the company cannot place any greater liability on the shareholders to contribute.

22.2 The role of the liquidator

It is the liquidator of the company who assumes control of the affairs of the company for the purposes of the winding-up process. A liquidator is effectively an officer of the court. The powers of the liquidator are generally established by statute and are not to be seen as something which is simply acquired by taking over the role of the directors of the company. It is the liquidator, however, who carries on the business of the company where that is deemed appropriate. It is the liquidator who brings any legal action in the name of the company.

A liquidator must take possession and control of the assets of the company so far as that is possible and as soon as it is possible. One of his/her primary functions is to realise those assets for the purposes of meeting claims against the company. A liquidator must also determine the validity of claims made by creditors and others against the company. This occurs through the proof of debt process, which we

---

3 See *Measures Brothers Ltd v Measures* [1910] 2 Ch 248; cf *Rebate v Union Manufacturing Co* [1918] 1 KB 592.

will discuss in due course. The liquidator, having made that determination, must then apply the assets of the company towards meeting the legitimate claims and also the costs of the liquidation. Where there is a surplus, the liquidator distributes that surplus to those who are entitled to it – usually the members of the company. The final task of the liquidator is to dissolve the company.

Liquidators have certain specific statutory duties in relation to the making and receiving of reports and the like. In the case of a compulsory winding up, a liquidator can be appointed provisionally as an interim step before a full hearing of the petition. This is not possible in the case of a voluntary winding up. The liquidator is regarded as in effect an agent of the company for most purposes. But it is also to be noted that the liquidator performs some duties which are quasi-judicial, such as in respect of determining the validity of claims against the company. A liquidator is regarded as a fiduciary in equity with all the trappings that this entails. The court in special cases might also impose particular standards. It has been conjectured from time to time whether liquidators are subject to special duties of fairness and high-principled action.[4] But this appears rather doubtful except in the context of acknowledging that the liquidator is often subject to special control by the court.[5]

22.2.1 Types of winding up

There are two types of winding-up process: involuntary (or compulsory) winding up, and voluntary winding up.[6] Compulsory winding up comes about by means of a court order to fold a company. There are various statutory grounds under which companies are compulsorily wound up. Action is brought by one or more parties, who could be creditors or even perhaps members of the company in some circumstances, to seek such an order. The company and other interested parties such as creditors can oppose the making of such an order. The court thus has to make a determination of the matter after a hearing.

Voluntary winding up is usually commenced at the instance of the company or the members of the company.[7] The matter does not involve disputed court

---

4 See *Ex p James* (1874) LR 9 Ch App 609; *Re Dominion Assurance Society Pty Ltd* (1962) 109 CLR 516.

5 *Hartogen Energy Ltd v Australian Gas Light Co* (1992) 36 FLR 557.

6 As to the general scheme, see *In re Dalgro (SI) Ltd* [1997] SBHC 43. Section 125(1) Companies Ordinance (K) provides a clear example of the types of winding up envisaged for companies operating in Kiribati. It states: "The winding up of a company may be either a voluntary winding up or an official winding up, and such winding up shall commence from the date on which the Registrar certifies that a copy of the special resolution to wind up has been delivered to him or, in the case of an official winding up, from the date on which the Court makes an order for official winding up". There is also a third strand of winding up conducted under the supervision of the court. See s 42 Companies Act (T), for example.

7 This can be further classified into members' and creditors' winding up. Note that under the statute a third type of winding up exists: winding up under the court's supervision.

proceedings but tends to be more an administrative process in most respects. The same difference exists in respect of proceedings for bankruptcy of a natural individual. Sometimes it is the creditor who seeks a bankruptcy order against the individual from the relevant court based, for example, on that individual having committed an act of bankruptcy.[8] However, an individual who is insolvent can also, in effect, put themselves into bankruptcy. In both cases, there are similarities with the winding-up process in respect of a company. The major difference is that on a company winding up, the company operation is first suspended whilst the company is in liquidation and in the end the entity ceases altogether. In bankruptcy, the individual's ability to pay and incur debts is suspended but eventually the individual is discharged from the bankruptcy and finally terminated, so to speak.

22.2.2 Winding up by the court

The instances under which a company can be wound up compulsorily have been clearly laid down by legislation in the region. Generally, this legislation adopts models found elsewhere, particularly those of the United Kingdom. In order for a person to seek a winding-up order from the court, he or she must apply, alleging and establishing the existence of one or perhaps more of these statutory grounds.

By way of example, s 220 of the Companies Act of Fiji provides:

A company may be wound up by the court, if–

(a) the company has, by special resolution, resolved that the company be wound up by the court;

(b) default is made in delivering the statutory report to the registrar or in holding the statutory meeting;

(c) the company does not commence its business within a year from its incorporation or suspends its business for a whole year;

(d) the number of members is reduced, in the case of a private company, below 2, or, in the case of any other company, below 7;

(e) the company is unable to pay its debts;[9]

(f) the court is of the opinion that it is just and equitable that the company should be wound up;

(g) in the case of a company incorporated outside Fiji and carrying on business in Fiji, winding-up proceedings have been commenced in respect of it in the country or territory of its incorporation or in any other country or territory in which it has established a place of business.

---

8 Failure to pay debts is in fact just one possible act of bankruptcy.

9 See s 221 (F) which provides the specified quantum of debts: FJ$100; in Vanuatu it is currently VT10,000: s 225 (V); and £750 in the case of the United Kingdom.

Equivalent provisions in the region are found in s 42 of the Companies Act of Tonga and s 210 of the Companies Act of the Solomon Islands. There are no direct provisions on this in Tuvalu except in connection with external companies.[10]

The inability of a company to pay debts cannot always be taken as an automatic basis for obtaining a winding-up order. Where the company substantially disputes the debt, the court will usually adopt a cautious approach in dealing with the winding-up position. The Court of Appeal of Fiji in *Offshore Oil NL v Investment Corp of Fiji Ltd* stated:

> The law is very clear that there is a discretion in a court seized of a winding up petition, to decline to hear the petition where the debt is contested on substantial grounds.[11]

A company which disputes a claim for a debt must, however, act promptly when it receives notice of the creditor's claim if it is to successfully resist the application for winding up. The dispute raised by the company must be *bona fide* in both a subjective sense (i.e. honestly) as well as objectively in the sense that it must be based on substantial or reasonable grounds.[12] Where the claim is disputed and there is widely conflicting evidence presented on both sides, it is inappropriate to deal with the matter by way of winding-up petition.[13] There must be something more than mere assertion on the company's part.[14] Where the company has admitted the debt or the creditor's claim is otherwise under dispute, the creditor will be entitled to an order on the petition.[15]

In the case of Kiribati, the two most important grounds for compulsorily winding up a company are the company's inability to pay its debts or where the court considers it just and equitable to wind up the company. What is also apparent from the situation in Kiribati is that there abound special grounds under which the Registrar could initiate the compulsory winding up of companies.[16] Furthermore, where an order is made for the official winding up of a company, the court shall appoint an official receiver. The official receiver is subject to the court's supervision.[17] This is not the case in the other South Pacific jurisdictions.

---

10 See s 230 (Tu).

11 *Offshore Oil NL v Investment Corporation of Fiji Ltd* [1984] FJLawRp 8; [1984] 30 FLR 90 (25 July 1984) at p 5; cf *President Hotel v Lami Town Council* 36 FLR 162; *In re Savusavu Hire Plant Services Ltd* [1998] FJHC 144; *In re Pacific Timber Development Ltd* [1999] FJHC 49; *Bateman Television Ltd v Coleridge Finance Co Ltd* (1971) NZLR 929.

12 *In re Savusavu Hire Plant Services Ltd* [1998] FJHC 144; *David Grant and Co Pty Ltd v Westpac Banking Corp* (1995) 184 CLR 265.

13 *In re Company No 00212 of 1998* [1995] TLR 186.

14 *Re Louisbridge Pty Ltd* (1994) 2 Qd R 144 at 145.

15 *In re Tweeds Garages Ltd* [1962] 1 Ch 407 at 408; *Cornhill Insurance plc v Improvement Services Ltd and Others* [1986] 1 WLR 114.

16 See ss 24, 120, 121 and 124 Companies Ordinance (K).

17 See s 129(2) and (3). Note that a body corporate cannot be eligible for appointment as an official receiver or liquidator of a company undergoing voluntary or compulsory liquidation; see s 322 Companies Act (V).

In Vanuatu, there are additional grounds for compulsory winding up which go beyond those in Fiji and Kiribati, as shown above. By s 224(g)—(i) of the Vanuatu legislation, a company can be wound up by the court if the company is in persistent breach of its duties or obligations under the Act, or if the company has failed to appoint a secretary or maintain the minimum number of directors or pay the annual company fees, or omits to keep its statutory books or engages in unlawful activities. In Tonga, the Privy Council, under s 42(g) of the Companies Act, is specifically empowered to order the compulsory winding up of any company.

It is to be noted under s 220 above that the company itself can initiate a petition for winding up by the court. The company must pass a special resolution as to winding up. In any case, including this one, a petition for winding up must be presented to the court and the application must be advertised in order to provide opportunities for interested parties such as creditors to join in the proceedings. The court, all other things being in order, makes an order as to winding up and for the appointment of a liquidator.[18] As noted above, a liquidator may be appointed on a provisional basis without certain of the procedural formalities or a full hearing. The appointment is interim only pending the final resolution of the petition. The function of the liquidator[19] is to see to the eventual closure of the company by receiving the assets of the company and by settling claims of creditors and shareholders where appropriate.[20]

If the winding-up process ensues for more than one year, the liquidator is expected to call a general meeting of the company where accounts for that period have to be submitted and stewardship is to be rendered. A gazettal notice is required for notices and resolutions prior to and after the general meeting.

The court can make an order compelling officers, employees and promoters to provide statements by means of affidavits. The court may on application order public examination of anyone connected with the company by the liquidator or official receiver.[21] A winding-up order operates retrospectively to the date of the presenting of the petition.[22] A winding-up order effectively terminates the powers of the company as a corporate legal entity to function on its own.[23]

---

18 See the powers of the liquidator as specified in s 242 Companies Act (F).

19 Where appropriate, an official receiver can also be appointed. See s 232 (F). Note that an official receiver, by virtue of his or her office, is generally considered as the provisional liquidator. See s 237(a) Companies Act (F).

20 See *Re Southard & Co Ltd* [1979] 1 WLR 1198 where the liquidator might face considerable difficulties in realising the assets in the course of distribution if the insolvent company operates within a network of group companies.

21 See ss 269, 270 Companies Act (V).

22 See s 46 Companies Act (T).

23 The following are the effects of a compulsory winding-up order by a court of competent jurisdiction: (1) The official receiver assumes the position of a liquidator provisionally. (2) Liquidations take effect from the presentation of petition. (3) Except with the leave of court, no disposition of the company's property is valid. (4) No new court proceedings against the company are to be

22.2.3 *The discretion of the court*

The courts have often stressed that there is considerable discretion reserved to them in respect of the making up of a winding-up order. They have also shied away from defining the scope of that discretion in particular terms. It remains open to the court to determine whether in the circumstances it would be appropriate to close down the company. Sometimes this is put in terms of a requirement that the courts should overall be satisfied that it is just and equitable to wind up the company. This is, of course, a separate ground of winding up *per se* that the court should form an opinion that it is just and equitable that the company be wound up as is provided in s 220(f) of the Fiji legislation above, just as it is in relation to the dissolution of a partnership. In respect of this ground, the courts can take account of a range of factors, including cases where the substratum of the company's operation has disappeared, where management is deadlocked, where its profit-making capacity has been substantially lost or where there is no longer an effective basis for the carrying on of the company's business in a reasonable way.[24]

However, as a general proposition in relation to consideration of the making of an order for winding up on any ground, the discretion vested in the court is apparently unlimited. The statutes themselves have not laid down the scope of what should constitute just and equitable circumstances, nor have they laid down the limits of the rule. The courts themselves have generally shied away from fettering the discretion that exists in relation to the grounds of winding up. The applicant is not entitled to an order as of right. It is therefore somewhat unclear whether a court should apply an objective or a subjective test. Courts are therefore free to imply what is just as well as equitable, taking into account peculiar circumstances. Across the region, a possible difficulty is the apparent dearth of jurisprudence expounding this principle of law. All that the courts in the region are left with are the judicial guidelines set by the English, Australian or New Zealand courts.[25]

One perhaps limited exception where a party applying for compulsory winding up appears to be entitled as of right to an order is where a creditor has standing to apply and cannot obtain payment from the company. Such a creditor is usually entitled to the winding-up order from the court. However, there are various grounds on which the company can resist the making of the order, such as where the company disputes the standing of the creditor or where it raises a substantial dispute as to the nature of the debt. Also, seeing that other creditors have an interest in obtaining payment from the company, they might resist the winding-up

---

instituted and those in progress are suspended until leave of court is obtained. (5) Employees of the company are deemed dismissed but may be re-engaged. See ICSA, *Company Law*, 1993, London, BPP Publishing, pp 331 ff.

24 See *Re Producer's Estate and Finance Co Ltd* [1936] VLR 235.
25 See *Ebrahimi v Westbourne Galleries Ltd* [1973] AC 360; *Re Yenidje Tobacco Co Ltd* [1916] 2 Ch 426.

order where they are of the view that the best course of action would be something other than winding up. The courts are entitled to have regard to the arguments of the other creditors and hence the discretion re-emerges in this context.[26]

22.2.4 Voluntary winding up

Voluntary folding or winding up can be effected by the actions of members or the company. By way of example, s 125(3) of the Companies Ordinance of Kiribati provides:

> A company may be voluntarily wound up if the company by special resolution resolves that the company may be wound up voluntarily and, prior to the date of such resolution, a declaration of solvency is made in accordance with sub-section (4) and delivered to the Registrar for registration prior to such date and particulars of such declaration are submitted to the meeting at which the said special resolution is passed, and a copy of such declaration is made available for inspection at the place of and prior to the said meeting.[27]

In voluntary winding up, members as well as creditors could engineer the petition to close down the company. Though both can be classified under the same subhead (as has been done by s 125) in Kiribati, in other jurisdictions in the region there are slight differences in the procedures governing their implementation. For this reason, we shall accord a brief treatment to each type separately.

22.2.5 Members' winding up

Through the passing of a special resolution, it is possible for members to bring about the winding up of the company.[28] But before such a company is eventually wound up, the directors of the company must in the first instance have presented a statutory declaration of solvency certifying the status of the current assets of the company.[29] Where this is done, the assets or property of the company can then be distributed accordingly to either the shareholders or the creditors or to both groups.

Generally speaking, a declaration of solvency is made by all the directors or a majority of them; it includes the company's assets and liabilities at the latest date

---

26 See *IOC Australia Pty Ltd v Mobil Oil Australia Ltd* (1975) 11 ALR 417.
27 Cf s 217 Companies Act (V).
28 See s 266 Companies Act (SI).
29 See s 125(5) Companies Ordinance (K), which provides that a statutory declaration of solvency is valid only when it has been made within five weeks immediately preceding the date of passing the resolution to wind up voluntarily and is delivered to the Registrar for registration before such date. See also s 265 Companies Act (SI).

prior to the declaration; it must be made before the members pass a resolution to wind up the company; and it must be delivered to the Registrar of Companies by the specified date.[30]

22.3 Creditors' winding up

This is used in situations where the directors realise that the company is insolvent but it is not willing to wind up itself. In this instance, a creditor or creditors petition the court to have it wound up.[31] Where directors failed to file a declaration of solvency,[32] any voluntary liquidation is presumed to be creditors' liquidation.[33]

The basic steps required to validate a creditors' winding up include the following: a general meeting of the company is to be held in order to pass an extraordinary resolution endorsing the winding up; thereafter a meeting of creditors is to be held for the creditors to satisfy themselves on matters concerning the winding up; and the company must comply with the statutory requirement for dispatch of notice of meeting to the creditors.[34]

22.3.1 Matters affecting liquidation[35]

As we mentioned above, the winding up of a company effectively suspends the right of creditors to recover moneys from the company itself. Their rights, as with creditors' rights on the bankruptcy of a natural individual, are converted into rights to prove their debts as part of the liquidation process. It might be the case in the end result that the creditors receive only a proportion of their actual debt. Much will depend on the realisable assets of the company, the extent of claims against the company and other factors of this nature.

There are two classes of creditor. There are those who have some form of security over the property of the company or some part of it. Hence, they are known as secured creditors. The security held could be by way of mortgage, debenture or charge of some kind. The purpose of having security of this nature is of course to provide the creditor with some special status as regards recovery of the debt or liability owed. Those who have no such security are known as unsecured creditors.

---

30 See also s 266 Cap 175 (SI) governing members' winding up.
31 See s 274 Companies Act (SI).
32 See s 123 Insolvency Act 1986 (UK) for the principles of the insolvency test.
33 See s 90 Insolvency Act 1986 (UK). There seem to be no equivalent provisions in the region.
34 See generally ss 8–27, 230 Insolvency Act 1986 (UK); s 122 ff Companies Act 1989 (UK); ss 213–365 Companies Act (F); ss 125–29 Companies Ordinance (K); ss 217–368 Companies Act (V); ss 210–394 Companies Act 1955 (NZ) (S); ss 36–67 Companies Act (T); ss 203–343 Companies Act (SI); ss 210–394 Companies Act (Samoa); see generally Gower, *op cit* fn 3, pp 743–84.
35 See generally ss 175, 212, 213, 215 Companies Act (UK); ss 310–18 Companies Act (F); ss 297–305 Companies Act (SI); ss 57–60 Companies Act (T); ss 306–14 Companies Act (V); ss 309–15 Companies Act (S).

The winding up of the company has no effect on the status of the security held by the secured creditor. The creditor continues to be entitled to enforce that security fully. The secured creditor can surrender the security and elect to prove as an unsecured creditor in the winding up, but this would generally produce some considerable disadvantage. As mentioned above, unsecured creditors are generally ranked equally, although particular types of debt are given some priority under the statutory order. They have the right to prove their debts in the liquidation process, which might, but often does not, yield a full payment of the debt concerned.

22.3.2 Proof of debts

The proof of debt procedure enables a liquidator to ascertain the genuineness or otherwise of claims put forward by creditors and other parties. As mentioned above, the rights of creditors against the company are suspended by the winding up. The procedure for proof of debt requires formal proof of the debts by means of evidence.[36] This is especially so because in trying to realise the assets of the company the liquidator will be dealing with not only a multiplicity of claims but also claimant-creditors, secured and unsecured, members and others who may have or have had dealings with the company.[37] Every proven debt is generally to be admitted by the company liquidator.[38] The liquidator is, however, excused from admitting liability on statute-barred debts.[39]

22.3.3 Disallowing cumbersome transactions

The liquidator may reject any transaction which s/he deems onerous or which is an undue burden on the assets of the company. The idea behind this principle of law is to enable a liquidator to operate freely without being encumbered by unnecessary and unprofitable transactions that add nothing but difficulties to the asset base of the company. In this context, s 312(1) of the Companies Act[40] of Samoa provides:

> Where any part of the property of a company which is being wound up consists of land or any tenure burdened with onerous covenants, of shares or stock in companies, of unprofitable contracts or of any other property that is unsalable, by reason of its binding the possessor thereof to the performance of any onerous act or to the payment of any sum of money, the liquidator of the company, notwithstanding that he had endeavoured to sell or has taken the possession

---

36 See s 260 Companies Act (F).
37 This may include past officers or directors of the company.
38 See s 310 Companies Act (F).
39 See various Statutes of Limitations operating in the region.
40 1955, New Zealand.

of the property or exercised any act of ownership in relationship thereto, may with the leave of the court and subject to the provisions of this section, by writing signed by him, any time within 12 months after the commencement of the winding up or such extended period as may be allowed by the court, disclaim the property.

There are equivalent provisions in s 316 of the Companies Act of Fiji and in s 302 of the Companies Act of the Solomon Islands. It is to be noted that the liquidator's powers to reject such transactions or contracts are not absolute for the following reasons. The exercise of power to disclaim any property, transaction or contract is subject to the court's confirmation. In addition, the liquidator can only exercise the right of disclaimer where such an event is made known to him or her within one month of the commencement of the winding up. Importantly, any aggrieved party can apply to the court for a rescission of a disclaimer order.[41] In spite of these limitations, however, one can assert that this principle of law affords the liquidator a good avenue through which transactions entered into by the company immediately prior to winding up could be properly scrutinised with a view to ascertaining their relevance or otherwise to the operations of the company.

22.3.4 Floating charges

As a general rule in the region, except in the case of Tonga,[42] a floating charge against the assets of the company is void if created within 12 months prior to liquidation.[43] The idea behind this principle is to avoid the use of a floating charge as a means of frustrating the claims of other creditors that are unaffected by the charge. This is more so in situations where the directors might want to wilfully pre-empt the distribution powers of the liquidator. Because a floating charge once created affects all the floating assets of the company until crystallisation, the directors seeking to avoid making payments to shareholders might opt for it. Once a petition for winding up is presented to the court, the floating charge crystallises into a fixed charge, thus ranking unsecured creditors (shareholders) at the bottom of the distribution scale.[44] The implication of this is that if there is nothing left to pay out of the assets of the company, the shareholders lose out completely. In this context, s 311 of the Companies Act of Vanuatu provides:

---

41 See s 316(2)–(6) Companies Act (F).
42 See s 60 Companies Act Cap 27 (formerly, now Cap 40.06) where the creation period is three months before the date of the winding up.
43 Section 245 Insolvency Act 1986 (UK); s 302 Companies Act (SI).
44 For a detailed discussion on floating charges, see Chapter 6.

Where a company is being wound up, a floating charge on the undertaking or property of the company created within 12 months of the commencement of the winding up shall, unless it is proved that the company immediately after the creation of the charge was solvent, be invalid, except to the amount of any cash paid to the company at the time of or subsequently to the creation of, and in consideration for, the charge, together with the interest on that amount at the rate of 10 per cent per annum or such other rate as may for the time being be prescribed by the Minister.

It is worthwhile to consider some implications arising from the foregoing section. First, it should be understood that while the charge itself is void, the money secured by the charge remains valid and is recoverable. Secondly, because the charge is void, the creditor automatically ranks as unsecured. The money can only be recovered as an ordinary debt. An unsecured creditor stands to lose out completely where there are insufficient funds to satisfy all the claims.

22.3.5 Priority of claims

Claims by creditors have to be dealt with during the course of the liquidation process. The priorities regarding claims have to be settled. This settlement is not always in accordance with the conventional pattern of settling priorities where secured creditors come first followed by unsecured creditors. In respect of the winding up of companies, statutes have altered the priority as between claimants. We have noted that in general all unsecured creditors are ranked equally. But as regards particular debts, the situation is altered to some extent by statute.

State taxes will have to be taken from the proceeds of liquidation first. Next come all state rents not more than one year in arrears; all wages or salaries of servants of the company other than directors; and relevant workmen company sums and superannuation funds if the company is not undergoing any restructuring processes.[45] It is only after the liquidator has satisfied these claims that other claims will be attended to in equal degree.[46]

22.3.6 Fraudulent preference

Closely related to priority of claims is the issue of fraudulent preference. The company statutes across the South Pacific region deny priority to any interest or charge created before six months of the date of winding up the company. Section 313 of the Companies Act of Fiji provides:

---

45 See s 312 Companies Act (F); s 57 Companies Act (T); s 299 Companies Act (SI).
46 Cf *Re MC Bacon* [1991] Ch 127.

(1) Any transfer, conveyance, mortgage, charge, delivery of goods, payment, execution or other act relating to property made or done by or against a company within 6 months before the commencement of its winding up which, had it been presented or done by or against an individual within 6 months before the presentation of the bankruptcy petition on which he is adjudged bankrupt, would be deemed in his bankruptcy a fraudulent preference shall, in the event of the company being wound up, be deemed a fraudulent preference of its creditors and void accordingly.

(2) Any transfer, conveyance or assignment by a company of all its property to trustees for the benefit of its creditors shall be void to all intents.[47]

It is to be noted, first of all, that the section is aimed at safeguarding creditors from being defrauded. The directors who are insiders know the internal financial situation of the company better than anyone else. They will be the first to know why and when the company is likely going to be wound up. Secondly, the provision is aimed at safeguarding the assets of the company from being wasted through careless or doubtful transactions by the directors of the company. Sometimes the directors might be acting with the clear intention of assisting the creditors, but the fact of the matter is that any such transactions executed by the directors within six months of the company's winding up would certainly raise a lot of doubtful questions.

Thirdly, by nullifying any such transactions conducted within six months of a company's winding up, the liquidator or official receiver would then be able to form a good picture of the company's asset base prior to the commencement of the winding up. Unnecessary and hurriedly executed encumbrances on the assets of the company have been done away with.

22.3.7 Preferential debts

As a general rule, creditors are treated equally. Payments may be made on a pro rata basis if there are insufficient funds to discharge them all at once.[48] This scenario has been replayed in the case of *Re Unit 2 Windows Ltd*.[49] Here the issue before the court was whether a creditor was entitled to set off an amount of money first against the proceeds of the company that was non-preferential. The court held that on the principle that equality was equity, the credit should also be set rateably between the preferential and non-preferential part of the debt.

---

47 Cf fraudulent trading under s 324 and offences that can be committed during winding up under s 321 (F). There are equivalent provisions in s 58 Companies Act (T); s 300 Companies Act (SI).

48 See s 175(2) Insolvency Act 1986 (UK); s 284 Companies Act (SI). It appears that there are no other equivalent provisions in the region.

49 [1985] 1 WLR 1383.

22.3.8 Fraudulent transactions

Transactions which are fraudulent in nature are not allowed to be carried out by the company after winding up has been initiated. The statutes specify what transactions are deemed fraudulent and hence prohibited.[50] The objective of such provisions is to safeguard the assets of the company and to preserve them for the benefit of claims of creditors and others.

---

50 See ss 319(1)(a)–(o), 321, 324 Cap 248 (F); ss 306, 310 Cap 175 (SI). However, it seems that no country in the region has provisions on prohibiting transactions in liquidations from being undervalued. On this point, see the rule in *Clayton's Case, Devaynes v Noble* (1876) 1 Merc 572. Cf *Re Yeovil Glove Ltd* [1965] Ch 148.

PART F

Foreign trade

Introduction

Global trends have indicated the need for caution in the way businesses are to be halted, closed down or liquidated. Some recent developments in the global commercial arena led to mass business failures in some of the most developed economies, notably due to the impact of the global COVID-19 pandemic, thus providing some justification for a detailed analysis of this aspect of the law in the South Pacific context. In this part, we examine the legal principles and procedures underpinning the processing of the winding up or termination of business entities as well as the dissolution of commercial activities and/or structures of these entities in the region.

DOI: 10.4324/9781003428060-28

23

THE WORLD TRADE ORGANISATION

23.1 The WTO

The World Trade Organisation (WTO) is a global trading arrangement with its foundation known as the GATT (the General Agreement on Tariff and Trade). The agreement is best described as a multilateral treaty regulating the conduct of trade and binding upon countries that have opted to be signatories to the agreement.

The formation of the GATT can be traced back to the Havana Charter of 1947. The Charter became operational in 1948 up until 1993, when the WTO came into being. The GATT is now under the auspices of the WTO – a body charged with the responsibility of administering the agreement. The agreement has itself undergone many revisions, with the latest version known as the GATT 1994.[1]

The main aim of the WTO is to achieve liberalisation of trade in goods and services at the global/international level by eliminating (totally or substantially) barriers that hinder effective trade between importers and exporters in different countries.

Over 128 countries are members of the WTO. Over 13 countries apply GATT rules but are not yet full members. There are also more than 35 countries with observer status in the WTO. China and Russia are not yet members of the WTO.[2] However, it is evident in the case of China that advanced steps to membership have already been negotiated.

The world is, and has always been, a place of diversity both in terms of climatic conditions and the resultant goods that are produced. This divergence is equally

1 Article XXIX GATT 1994.
2 See the Schedule to GATT 1994.

DOI: 10.4324/9781003428060-29

responsible for trade exchanges between peoples and nations. Enhanced technology has now added a new dimension to this diversity. This makes it necessary for trade between nations and people to take place so that surplus goods can find markets whilst customers in need of goods will also be able to source them.

This underlines the need for global trade exchanges and hence the evolution of the GATT and now the WTO. However, what is clear is that trading cannot take place without rules guiding its conduct or practice.

Thus, for some form of standardised trading exchanges to evolve (in the practice of buying and selling between countries), trading frameworks at both the global and regional levels need to be formulated and agreed upon. The Melanesian Spearhead Group (MSG), the South Pacific Regional Trade and Economic Cooperation Agreement (SPARTECA) and the Cotonou Agreement are instructive legal arrangements in the South Pacific which are responses to such trading difficulties. The global answer to problems of trade and the need for a unified system of trade is found in the GATT. This is now known as the WTO.

Operating within the framework of a global system like the WTO will not be trouble-free. In this trading relationship there will arise trade imbalances and disagreements between two unequal trading partners, whether at the regional or global level. The regional and global trading structures are therefore expected to offer some kind of legal platform for addressing these imbalances.

Opposing trading interests between members is the primary cause of disagreement in the global trading arena. In trying to protect their interests, countries sometimes adopt measures that are contrary to the spirit of the GATT dispute resolution system. These include some of the measures that will be discussed in this chapter. Countries also interpret the rules in different ways, often adopting an interpretation which might legitimise their actions. On numerous occasions, countries are deadlocked on trade disputes. Others tend to adopt unilateral retaliatory measures that are clearly outside the confines of the system.

What the dispute resolution mechanism under the GATT seeks to achieve is to provide a forum where through the process of negotiation, consultation and sometimes arbitration, disputes between members can be resolved amicably.

23.1.1 Most favoured nation principle

A key feature of the GATT system is that it is founded on the principle of equality of treatment. Member states must accord the same rights and benefits to each other. It is an important stipulation of the agreement that where a member grants certain advantages to another member in the conduct of trade, these same advantages are to be extended unconditionally to all other members of the WTO. These advantages can be in the form of reduced or zero-rated taxation and waiver of pre-shipment inspection. Others include customs formalities connected with importation and exemption from foreign exchange restrictions in repatriation of the profits arising from the import or export of the product.

Under Art I, certain conditions have to be fulfilled before a member is held accountable for its actions. The advantages given to one member should only be extended to other members of the WTO on 'like product'.

The product must have originated from the territory of a member of the WTO. Article I of the GATT cannot apply where the product is not a like product or where it originated from a third country that is not a member of the GATT. The GATT rules are unclear as to whether 'like product' is synonymous with 'same product' or 'comparable product'. It is also unclear whether the phrase refers to the generic kind of the product or its form or process.[3]

23.1.2 National treatment principle

National treatment underlines the idea that where the products of one member country are imported into the territory of another member country, whatever advantages are extended to the domestic product must be given to the comparable imported product within that national boundary. Products of a member country cannot be treated differently in another member country simply on account of the national origin of the imported products. Article III(4) of the GATT imposes a duty on the importing member country to apply the same rate of internal taxation and other charges to its domestic products as it does to like imported products.

23.1.3 Quantitative and non-quantitative restrictions

Trade is generally supposed to be conducted on equal terms or on an equal footing between countries. This is the ideal expectation, at least in theory. In practice, however, this is not always achievable. Thus, in the arena of international trade there is always a discernible gap between theory and practice.

Countries have different legal systems, with a variety of internal regimes of regulatory provisions dealing with domestic trade. Countries also operate parallel legal regimes for regulating international trade within their national boundaries. In so doing, such countries seek to protect local producers from the adverse effects of uncontrolled importation of products into the national economy. Some control measures imposed on imported products are directed at reducing the quantity, whilst others (in the form of tariff barriers) are aimed at making the price of imported products more expensive than comparable domestic products.

Both measures (whether of a quantitative nature or not) are aimed at curtailing imports into the territory of a member country. This might have adverse effects on exports from the exporting member country. Quantitative restrictions are prohibited by Art XI(1) of the GATT, though some general exceptions are found in Art XX.

---

3 See the case of *United States Nationals in Morocco* [1952] ICJR 192.

However, it is worth mentioning that when experiencing balance-of-payment problems, a country is legally permitted to apply restrictions on imports or exports so long as these are geared towards enhancing the country's foreign reserve position. An importing country should use these trade restrictions only as temporary measures.[4]

Furthermore, a member is permitted to veer from the rule regarding non-discriminatory imposition of quantitative restrictions, provided that its economy is in the doldrums and the country is implementing a monetary reform policy in line with what had been stipulated by the International Monetary Fund.[5]

23.1.4 Examples of quantitative restrictions

The following are a few examples of non-quantitative restrictions that are permitted under the WTO rules:

(a) Temporary export restraints to relieve shortages of foodstuffs or other products essential to the exporting country.[6]
(b) Import and export restrictions necessary to the application of standards or regulations for the classification, grading or marketing of commodities in international trade.[7]
(c) Import restrictions on any agricultural or fisheries product, etc.[8]
(d) Import quotas and import or export licences.[9]

As a general rule, quantitative restrictions must be applied in a non-discriminatory manner. Where the measures imposed by a member are directed at another member, all third countries must equally be affected by the same level of quantitative restrictions emanating from the first country. This is intended to ensure that all countries are treated equally in the WTO. Selective application of quantitative restrictions has the potential to trigger trade wars between member countries. This is what the rules aim to prevent.

Article XIII(1) is relevant in this regard. It provides:

No prohibition or restriction shall be applied by any member on the importation of any product of the territory of any other member or on the exportation of any product destined for the territory of any other member, unless the importation

---

4 This exception is found in Art XII(1).
5 This exception is found in Art XIV(1).
6 See Art XI(2)(a).
7 See Art XI(2)(b).
8 See Art XI(2)(c).
9 See Art XI(1).

of the like product of all third countries or the exportation of the like product to all third countries is similarly prohibited or restricted.

23.1.5 Exceptions

The principles of most favoured nation, national treatment and the prohibition of quantitative and non-quantitative restrictions can be done away with under the GATT/WTO rules where a customs union becomes operational. A customs union is therefore an exception. Other exceptions include a free trade area, waiver and developing countries.

23.1.6 Customs union

This is a combination of countries that are members of WTO whose territories are legally constituted into a single trading and economic bloc. All internal taxes and other restrictions to trade are minimised or substantially eliminated amongst them. The union will then have a common tariff policy in relation to its trading links with countries outside the customs union.

Article XXIV(8) of the GATT provides:

(a) A customs union shall be understood to mean a substitution of a single customs territory for two or more customs territories, so that
   (i) duties and other restrictive regulations of commerce ... are eliminated with respect to substantially all trade between the constituent territories of the union or at least with respect to substantially all trade in products originating in such territories.

In dealing with other countries that are not members of a customs union, a customs union is legally permitted to impose restrictions on imports from non-member countries. A customs union is also permitted to grant exclusive trading advantages to its members. These practices will not be regarded as being in breach of the most favoured nation or national treatment rules in the GATT/WTO. Where internal trade barriers of the constituent territories are eliminated, a harmonisation of the laws is usually achieved. This is one of the important features of a customs union. A complete harmonisation of the laws will allow for free movement of persons, goods and services within the customs union.

A very good example of a customs union is the European Union, founded by the Rome Treaty of 1957. The Pacific Community might explore this as a future model for a customs union in the South Pacific.

23.1.7 Free trade area

This is a group of customs unions or countries whereby between them most or all barriers to trade are eliminated. These barriers include import and export duties, internal taxes, import quota and import licences. In this regard, Art XXIV(8) provides:

(b) A free trade area shall be understood to mean a group of two or more customs territories in which the duties and other restrictive regulations of commerce ... are eliminated on substantially all the trade between the constituent territories in products originating in such territories.

Countries forming a free trade area still retain their distinct national boundaries. They do not have a common tariff policy. This is the feature that distinguishes it from a customs union.

23.2 Less developed members

Developing members of the WTO have been granted special privileges in view of their developing status. To this end, they are not expected to fully uphold or implement some provisions of the GATT 1994. By relying on Part IV, the least developed members are not obliged to grant equivalent concessions to the developed members. In this context, Art XXXVI(8) provides:

The developed contracting parties do not expect reciprocity for the commitments made by them in trade negotiations to reduce or remove tariffs and other barriers to the trade of less-developed contracting parties.

The general idea behind the stipulations in Part IV is to help the least developed member countries to diversify their economies and reduce, in the long term, their total reliance on the exports of primary products.

23.2.1 Waiver

The Council of the WTO can permit a member to deviate from implementing some provisions of the GATT 1994. Where a waiver is granted, the member would not be held responsible for not adhering to the waived provisions of the agreement. Australia had in the past been allowed to grant preferential access to imports from certain developing countries. Africa, Caribbean and Pacific (ACP) members of the Lomé Convention enjoy trading privileges from the European Union and the United States maintains a preferential trading regime in automotive goods with Canada.[10]

---

10 Wilde, KD and Islam, MR, *International Transaction: Trade and Investment, Law and Finance*, 1993, Sydney, Law Book Co, p 223.

23.2.2 Trade disruptions

Members of the WTO are generally expected to adhere to the principles of the system. Internal measures adopted by member states to advance their economies, increase their productive capacity or improve their competitive edge should be directed at enhancing rather than restricting trade. Measures adopted by one member state might have negative consequences on the economies of other member states. This can have the potential to trigger a trade war or escalate trading tensions in the WTO.

The dangers likely to arise from a potential disruption to trade have been recognised in Art III(1) and (2) of the GATT. The article provides:

> The members recognise that internal taxes and other internal charges, and law, regulations and requirements affecting internal sale, offering for sale, purchase, transportation, distribution or use of products, and internal quantitative regulations requiring the mixture, processing or use of products in specified amounts or proportions, should not be applied to imported or domestic products so as to afford protection to domestic production.
> The products of the territory of any member imported into the territory of any other member shall not be subject, directly or indirectly, to internal taxes or other internal charges of any kind in excess of those applied, directly or indirectly, to like domestic products. Moreover, no member shall otherwise apply internal taxes or other internal charges to imported or domestic products in a manner contrary to the principles set forth in paragraph 1.

The most important of such measures that can impede the free flow of goods or services between member countries are dumping and subsidy. We shall now consider these in turn.

23.3 Dumping of goods and anti-dumping levies

This is a process of circulating products in the economy or commerce of a member country by another member country as a result of which the price of the imported product is cheaper than comparable domestic product. The effect of dumping is to create a marketing stronghold for the imported product as against its domestic counterpart. If this trend is allowed to go on unabated by the host country, there is a risk of ruining its domestic market for that product. In this situation, it is only reasonable to expect the affected importing country to take countermeasures that would check or eliminate any adverse effects caused by the dumped product.

According to Art VI(1(a) and (b), dumping can be established where:

> A product is … introduced into the commerce of an importing country at less than its normal value, if the price of the product exported from one country to another

(a) is less than the comparable price, in the ordinary course of trade, for the like product when destined for consumption in the exporting country, or,

(b) in the absence of such domestic price, is less than either

   (i) the highest comparable price for the like product for export to any third country in the ordinary course of trade, or

   (ii) the cost of production of the product in the country of origin plus a reasonable addition for selling cost and profit.

The article also recognises the fact that a slight price differential between an imported and a like domestic product should not regarded as dumping, because of differences in taxation, production and transportation expenses in the exporting and importing countries. The question is, how can an importing country reasonably establish a case of dumping against an exporting country? Should it be in a position to actually establish such a case, what countermeasures are legally at the disposal of the importing country to adopt against the exporting country?

An importing country cannot at the whim of a policy statement allege that an exporting country has dumped goods in its territory. This has to be established against the background of legal criteria laid down by Art VI(1). The test is one which has to show that the imported product is causing or is likely to cause material injury to an established industry in the economy of the importing country. The test is one of disruption that can either be actual or potential. What are the verification measures that might ensure that there was such potential or actual risk of disruption to the importing economy? The crucial question here is, does the WTO have any monitoring scheme in place?

An importing country that establishes a case of dumping in its national economy is at liberty to take countermeasures against the exporting country by imposing a duty on the imported product. The amount of duty so imported is intended to offset the price differential between the dumped and the like domestic product.

An importing country cannot arbitrarily impose any amount as duty. It must be an amount equal to the difference between the price of the dumped imported and like domestic product. Article VI(2) provides:

> In order to offset or prevent dumping, a member may levy on any dumped product an anti dumping duty not greater in amount than the margin of dumping in respect of such product. For the purposes of this Article, the margin of dumping is the price difference determined in accordance with the provisions of paragraph 1.

The questions that remain to be answered are: should the levy or duty imposed on the imported products only affect the imported but unsold quantities, or should it be applied retroactively to already disposed-of dumped products? In which case, should the importer also be asked to refund the equivalent amount of duty to the host country on the goods already sold?

Subsidisation arises where the imported products have been supported with some financial or other fiscal incentives by the government of the exporting country in order to boost their sales or to make the products more competitive. Before an importing country is permitted to label an imported product as subsidised, the exporting country (and not private enterprises) must have financially supported the product. The Agreement on Subsidies and Countervailing Measures 1995[11] has identified and prohibited two forms of subsidy. These are export and local content subsidies. The two classes of subsidy are prohibited because of their adverse effects on trade or exporting capacity of other members.

The effect of subsidy on the importing economy would be similar to that of dumping, in that the comparable domestic products might be flushed out of the market. Subsidisation of products by an exporting country is prohibited by Art VI(3) of the GATT. The provision defines subsidy as: 'a special duty levied for the purpose of offsetting any bounty or subsidy bestowed, directly or indirectly, upon the manufacture, production or export of any merchandise'. Where imported products have been subsidised by the exporting country, the importing country is at liberty to impose a tax on such imports. This is referred to as countervailing duty. Article VI(3), dealing with countervailing duties, provides:

> No countervailing shall be levied on any product of the territory of a member imported into the territory of another member in excess of the amount equal to the estimated bounty or subsidy determined to have been granted.

By Art VI(6), the test for imposing a tax by an importing country on the products of an exporting country has to be looked at against the background of potential or actual disruption to the economy of the importing country.

Members who are signatories to the Agreement on Subsidies and Countervailing Measures 1995 are automatically empowered to apply countervailing measures on subsidised goods without having to satisfy the test of potential or actual injury to their economies. However, as a matter of practice and going by Art VI(5), a country cannot impose both anti-dumping and countervailing duties on one product. It has to elect that with the greater margin out of the two.

It is important to bear in mind that whilst the effects of dumping and subsidy are the same, the mechanisms for their implementation are different. Dumping is usually an act of private enterprises. They export and fix lower prices for the products than comparable domestic products. A subsidy is an act of the state. It is in most cases a deliberate government policy to promote or support local producers.

---

11 See www.wto.org./wto/goods/scm.

23.3.1 Processes of dispute resolution

It should be pointed out that private importers and exporters operating within a national territory cannot process trade complaints through the GATT channels. The treaty binds states and not private commercial entities. Any dispute on trade has to be taken up by the affected member state. It is equally important to point out that the WTO does not act *suo moto*. Aggrieved members must process their complaints through the channels provided, before the dispute resolution mechanism kicks in.[12]

The following processes provide avenues through which disputes between members are attended to: notification, consultation and arbitration. Others include panels/working parties through to the production of a report on the status of the dispute. These processes are outlined in Arts XIX, XXII and XIII of the GATT 1994.

Where a country faces the threat of potential or actual injury to its economy as a result of unchecked importation, the affected member is entitled to suspend or modify the concessions hitherto given to the exporting country in respect of that product. This practice will be consistent with the provisions of Art XIX.

By Art XIX(2) of the GATT 1994, before an importing country takes such action, the exporting country should be notified in writing. It states:

> Before any member shall take action ... it shall give notice in writing to the ... members having a substantial interest as exporters of the product concerned an opportunity to consult in respect of the proposed action.

The rationale behind the notification process is to ensure that the exporting country is not taken by surprise as a result of restrictions that might be imposed on its products by the importing country. This is certainly an initial step towards settling any potential problems that are likely to arise from such action.

The process of consultation is outlined in Art XXII of the GATT. It is also aimed at achieving some compromise in the early stages of the dispute. The article provides:

> Each member shall accord sympathetic consideration to, and shall afford adequate opportunity for consultation regarding, such representations as may be made by another member with respect to any matter affecting the operation of this Agreement.
> The GATT Secretariat may, at the request of a member, consult with any member or members in respect of any matter for which it has not been possible to find a satisfactory solution through consultation under paragraph 1.

---

12 Schmitthoff, C, *The Law and Practice of International Trade*, 2012, London, Sweet and Maxwell, p 1 et seq.

The establishment of a working party or panel (in the event of the failure of consultation) is not supported by any principal provision of the GATT.[13] It is a process often adopted as an additional method of settling the dispute between the members. This is especially so in instances where a party has complained of nullification of benefits of the GATT.[14] Article XXIII(2) provides the final actions that can be taken by the WTO against a defaulting member. Sub-paragraph (2) provides:

> If the GATT Secretariat considers that the circumstances are serious enough to justify such action, they may authorise a member or members to suspend the application to any other member or members of such concessions or other obligations under this Agreement as they determine to be appropriate in the circumstances. If the application to any member of any concession or other obligation is in fact suspended, that member shall then be free, not later than sixty days after such action is taken, give written notice to the Director General ... of its intention to withdraw from this Agreement

23.3.2 Dispute Settlement Board

The Dispute Settlement Board (DSB) is established by the Rules of Procedure made pursuant to the GATT 1994. Disputes arising from other related agreements to the GATT can also be dealt with by the DSB.[15] In resolving trade disputes between members, the DSB is expected to be governed by the provisions of the Understandings on Rules and Procedures Governing the Settlement of Disputes.[16] Article 2 of the Understanding establishes the DSB. It provides:

> 1 The Dispute Settlement Body is hereby established to administer these rules and procedures and, except as otherwise provided in a covered agreement, the consultation and dispute settlement provisions of the covered agreements. Accordingly, the DSB shall have the authority to establish panels, adopt panel and Appellate Body reports, maintain surveillance of implementation of rulings and recommendations and authorise suspension of concessions and other obligations under the covered agreements ... Where the DSB administers the dispute settlement provisions of a Pluri-lateral Trade Agreement, only those Members that are parties to that Agreement may participate in decisions or actions taken by the DSB with respect to that dispute.

---

13 It is to be found in the 1996 Procedures under Art XXIII; Wilde and Islam, *op cit* fn 10, p 215.

14 Schmitthoff, *op cit* fn 12, p 724.

15 Other agreements made pursuant to GATT 1994 include the following: Understanding on the Interpretation of Article II(1)(b); Understanding on the Interpretation of Article XVII; Understanding on Balance-of-Payment Provisions; Understanding in respect of Waivers of Obligations; and Understanding on the Interpretation of Article XXVIII.

16 See Annex 2 to the Marrakesh Agreement of April 1994 establishing the World Trade Organisation.

The ability of a country to be part of and benefit from the rules of the global trading system depends to a great extent on its internal fiscal and economic policies. These must in turn be anchored on sound legal foundations that not merely create, but equally facilitate an atmosphere for effective commercial interaction. The domestic market must be strengthened and its factors of production enhanced through rationalised use of resources in both the public and private sectors.

It is not enough for countries in or aspiring to be part of the global trading system to rush into the currents of trade liberalisation. They should be prepared to place themselves at a vantage point in order to benefit from the system in their areas of strength and be able to respond to challenges in their areas of weakness. This is the way towards improved trading relations with other countries.

It is interesting to observe here that the Cook Islands had taken the bold initiative of adopting the GATT as part of its domestic law by virtue of the provisions of the GATT Act No 1 of 1948. The Act is therefore considered as part of the Customs Act NZ (1913) by s 1.[17] South Pacific island states have a lot to gain from the global trading system and will have a lot to lose if they do not properly articulate their needs and aspirations in treaty negotiations prior to accession to the WTO. For those countries within the region that are already in the system, constant vigilance is needed in an effort to be prepared to critically review the performance of their economic indices with a view to moving forward. An understanding of the legal foundations of the global trading system and how it works might be a good beginning.

The WTO has deliberately opted for a more informal mechanism for settling trade disputes amongst its members. The reason for this approach might not be too far-fetched. States are independent entities governed by the rules of sovereignty.

States are therefore sensitive to any use of force to implement decisions against them. After all, a member can pull out of the WTO without any apparent reason. Where such a member does pull out, it can then impose whatever measures it wishes against other members without falling foul of any GATT rules. This would be disastrous for harmonious world trade.

The soft-handed approach might be the best possible means of resolving trade disputes between members if global trade is to be advanced. The interdependent nature of the global economy has made it an imperative of trade policies that it is in the best interest of all concerned to remain in agreement on major trade issues. An informal and persuasive way of resolving disputes is certainly a subtle and effective way of keeping the members of the WTO closely knit.

---

17 Section 619 Cook Islands Act 1915.

24

TRIPS

24.1 Nature of intellectual property rights

Intellectual property rights loosely represent a class of intangible rights which the
law protects in favour of a person who has exploited his/her talents, thus resulting
in the production of a commercially useable work. Where the law accords protection to such rights, it might be in the form of a patent, copyright or trade mark.
Generally speaking, therefore, we shall restrict ourselves to these three broad classifications of intellectual property rights.

24.1.1 Patent

This is defined as 'A statutory privilege granted by a government to investors for
a fixed period of years to exclude other persons from manufacturing, using or
selling patented product of process'.[1] Article 27(1) of Trade-Related Aspects of
Intellectual Property Rights (TRIPS) stipulates what should be covered by patent.
It provides:

> Subject to the provisions of paragraphs (2) and (3), patents shall be available for
> any inventions, whether products or processes, in all fields of technology, pro-
> vided that they are new, involve an inventive step and are capable of industrial
> application ... patents shall be available and patents rights enjoyable without

---

[1] See Technology Indicators and Developing Countries, UNCTAD/1/TP/TEC 19, p 16. For local
definitions, see Registration of UK Patent Act Cap 179 (SI); Registration of UK Patents 1977 Cap
87 (K); Patent Act Cap 239 (F).

DOI: 10.4324/9781003428060-30

discrimination as to the place of invention, field of technology and whether products are imported or locally produced.

Member countries can, however, refuse to grant patent protection to any invention on grounds of public morality, security, protection of life, health, etc.[2]

Article 28 confers exclusive rights on the owner of a patent as against the actions of third parties wanting to commercially exploit the invention without the permission of the patent holder. Full disclosure of an invention is to be made by the inventor before a member state can protect the invention. In this regard, Art 29(1) and (2) of TRIPS provide:

> Members shall require that an applicant for a patent shall disclose the invention in a manner sufficiently clear and complete for the invention to be carried out by a person skilled in the art and may require the applicant to indicate the best mode for carrying out the invention known to the inventor at the filing date or, where priority is claimed, the priority date of the application.
> Members may require an applicant to a patent to provide information concerning the applicant's corresponding foreign applications and grants.

The length of protection is normally 20 years from the date of filing the patent application.[3] Member states should also allow for recourse to judicial review processes, in the event that member states declare a patent as having been forfeited.[4]

We should also note that TRIPS mandates member states to extend the scope of protection to cover other patent-related areas, such as industrial designs and integrated circuits. The former are protected for ten years, whilst the latter may be protected for a period of up to 15 years if allowed by the laws of a member state.[5]

24.1.2 Copyright

This is the protection that is accorded the talents of a person that has been used in the creation or making of a work in literary, artistic, dramatic, musical, cinematographic and phonogramic fields.[6] As a significant step towards copyright protection by member states, the work so produced must exhibit a clear expression of an idea that had been expressed by the maker. Ideas *per se* are not protected under copyright. Article 9(2) provides: 'Copyright protection shall extend to expressions and not to ideas, procedures methods of operation or mathematical concepts as such'. Importantly, computer programs and compilations of data or

---

2 See Art 27(2) TRIPS.
3 *Ibid.*, Art 33.
4 *Ibid.*, Art 32.
5 *Ibid.*, Arts 25, 35–38.
6 See the Fiji case of *Crystal Clear Video Ltd v COP & AG* [1988] SPLR 130.

other topographic arrangements of published editions are also protected by copyright in the member states.

In this regard Art 10(1) and (2) are relevant. The article states:

Computer programs, whether in source or object code, shall be protected as literary works under the Berne Convention (1971).

Compilations of data or other material, whether in machine readable or other form, which by reason of the selection or arrangement of their contents constitute intellectual creations shall be protected as such. Such protection, which shall not extend to the data or material itself, shall without prejudice to any copyright subsisting in the data or material itself.

24.1.3 Length of protection

There is no uniform or standard term of protection for copyright. The length of protection for copyright varies with the nature of the property right. This is found in Arts 12 and 14(5) of the TRIPS Agreement 1994. The article provides:

Whenever the term of protection of a work, other than a photographic work or a work of applied art, is calculated on a basis other than the life of a natural person, such a term shall be no less than 50 years from the end of the calendar year of authorised publication, or, failing such authorised publication within 50 years from the making of the work, 50 years from the end of the calendar year of making.

In respect of broadcasts or phonograms, the length of protection is computed differently by the agreement. Article 14(5) provides:

The term of protection available under this Agreement to performers and producers of phonograms shall last at least until the end of a period of 50 years computed from the end of the calendar year in which the fixation was made or performance took place. The term of protection granted pursuant to paragraph 3 shall last for 20 years from the end of the calendar year in which the broadcast took place.

Paragraph (3) of Art 14 deals with re-transmission rights covering broadcast. This includes satellite and other wireless transmissions. Paragraph (3) grants rights only in respect of the first fixation or first broadcast. It does not seem to effectively cover breaches that might arise from downloading such a broadcast from the internet. There is now a direct legal relationship between the content of information on a domain server and copyright infringement, especially at the point of downloading information.[7] For this reason, Art 14 requires a further amendment to the TRIPS Agreement in order to incorporate this vital and emerging legal problem.

---

7 See *British Telecom plc v One in a Million Ltd* [1999] 1 WLR 903.

24.2 Trade mark

This is a sign or symbol that distinguishes one type of goods from other goods of the same class or make. Where the sign or symbol bears some distinctive characteristics as to make it different from another sign or symbol in respect of a similar kind of goods, then member states are obliged to accord it legal protection in order to guard against misuse or abuse. Article 15(1) provides:

> Any sign or combination of signs, capable of distinguishing the goods or services of one undertaking from those of other undertakings, shall be capable of constituting a trade mark. Such signs, in particular words including personal names, letters, numerals, figurative elements and combinations of colours as well as any combination of such signs, shall be eligible for registration as trademarks. Where signs are not inherently capable of distinguishing the relevant goods or services, Members may make registrability depend on distinctiveness acquired through use. Members may require, as a condition of registration, that signs are visually perceptible.

Article 16 further provides that a person who obtains a trade mark shall use the mark to the exclusion of all unauthorised third parties. By Art 18, a seven-year protection period is granted to the holder of the trade mark after registration. In addition to trade mark protection, trade marks also protect geographical indications pertaining to the origin of goods.

24.2.1 Application of national and most favoured nation principles

Just as in the GATT, by Arts 3 and 5 of TRIPS, member states are equally obligated to apply national and most favoured nation principles to the protection of intellectual property rights. The objective of the articles is to prevent arbitrary granting of advantages in intellectual property issues by one member to another, at the expense of all other members. Within a national boundary, all countries must enjoy the same level of protection. In dealings between countries, whatever advantages are granted by one member to another must also unconditionally be extended to all others.

The application of these principles may be excluded by Art 5 of the Treaty. In essence, this replicates the exclusions arising from the formation of a customs union under the WTO rules already considered.

24.2.2 Enforcement of intellectual property rights

Enforcement of intellectual property rights has been the area of most difficulties and disagreements between countries. The metropolitan economies that strongly pushed for the inclusion of TRIPS into the WTO Agreement (Uruguay Round) have always blamed developing countries for not doing enough to protect intellectual property rights within their countries. Developing countries on their part have argued that given their rate of economic and technological development, it would be asking too much from them to insist on the fact that they must adequately protect all aspects of intellectual property rights.

Both shades of opinion have their merits. However, it must be understood that for most developing countries, intellectual property right is just an emerging legal issue. Within the South Pacific for instance, except for Fiji, the Solomon Islands, Papua New Guinea and Samoa, other countries lack adequate institutional machinery for implementing TRIPS. Samoa and Fiji only passed their copyright laws in 1998 and 1999 respectively. Neither Vanuatu nor Nauru has copyright laws. For the others that have such laws,[8] they are still based on the outdated English models.

Most of the patent laws have not been reformed to catch up with current trends in the area. The only exception is probably in the area of trade mark.[9] It is the most widely used aspect of intellectual property rights in the South Pacific.

Against this background, it is not difficult to understand why the TRIPS Agreement sets out detailed guidelines that are expected to pilot the formulation of future intellectual property regimes in member states. In particular, Art 41(1) provides:

> Members shall ensure that enforcement procedures as specified in this part are available under their law so as to permit effective act against any act of infringement of intellectual property rights covered by this Agreement, including expeditious remedies to prevent infringements and remedies which constitute a deterrent to further infringements. These procedures shall be applied in such a manner as to avoid the creation of barriers to legitimate trade and to provide for safeguards against their abuse.

It is important to mention also that Arts 42–46 stipulate possible remedies that member states can include in their laws. These include injunction, damages, seizure and compensation. Article 61 provides for criminal penalties against offending persons.

Because of the TRIPS Agreement and its subsequent inclusion in the WTO Agreement of 1994, countries aspiring to be members of the WTO are now expected to amend their intellectual property law systems so as to be in conformity with TRIPS. The often-difficult question for most countries, but particularly for small South Pacific states, is how far they should go in order to be able to meet the demands of both TRIPS and the WTO.

---

8 See Copyright Ordinance Ch 16 1980 (K); Copyright Act Cap 121 (T); Copyright Act 1962 (CI); Copyright Act No 25 1998 (S); Copyright Right Act 1999 (F) as examples.
9 See Trade Marks Act Cap 120 (T); Trade Marks Act 1953 (CI); Trade Marks Act Cap 240 (F) as examples.

24.2.3 Impediments to TRIPS implementation by states

Vanuatu and quite a few other island countries are not yet part of the WTO. For these countries, it is difficult to immediately conceptualise the benefits that might accrue to them by acceding to TRIPS and the WTO. They are right. Apart from the psychological fact that they might also be part of a world trade body, direct economic benefits might take decades to trickle through to these nations. As a start, these countries need to develop the requisite technology if they are to effectively participate in TRIPS. However, in spite of these disadvantages, one would say that it is necessary for island countries to ultimately accede to TRIPS and subsequently the WTO.

Countries whose infrastructural arrangements are not so ready to fully implement the requirements of the TRIPS Agreement may, nonetheless, accede to the agreement but opt to utilise the safety valve being provided for developing countries. By relying on this opportunity, a country can be excused from immediately implementing some provisions of the agreement.

In this respect, Art 65(2) provides: "A Developing country Member is entitled to delay for a further four years of the date of application, as defined in paragraph 1, of the provisions of this Agreement other than Articles 3, 4 and 5". Furthermore, sub-para (5) provides: "A Member availing itself of a transitional period under paragraphs 1, 2, 3 or 4 shall ensure that any changes in its laws, regulations and practice made during that period do not result in a lesser degree of consistency with the provisions of this Agreement". These provisions are aimed at allowing leeway to countries intending to join the WTO, but which are not in a position to readily meet the requirements of TRIPS in the protection of intellectual property rights. These transitional provisions may be utilised by any existing or prospective developing member.

The agreement has further considered the case of least developed member countries, in that it appreciates their special position. This basically fits the needs of most South Pacific states. Transitional provisions are covered by Art 66(1) and (2):

> In view of the special needs and requirements of least developing country Members, their economic, financial and administrative constraints, and their need for flexibility to create a viable technological base, such Members shall not be required to apply the provisions of the Agreement, other than Arts 3, 4 and 5 for a period of 10 years from the date of application as defined under para 1 of Art 65. The Council of TRIPS shall, upon duly motivated request by a least-developed country Member, accord extensions of this period.
>
> Developed country Members shall provide incentives to enterprises and institutions in their territories for the purpose of promoting and encouraging technology transfer to least-developed country Members in order to enable them to create a sound and viable technological base.

The purport of Art 66 of TRIPS is clear. Countries falling within the purview of Art 66 are entitled to benefit from the transitory concessions under the agreement. What is unclear is the extent to which the transitional provisions can really go in order to provide the real foundation for a technological springboard in the least developed countries.

In the life of a nation, ten years is really only a short breathing space for any nation to fully brace itself and embrace the ideals of TRIPS and the WTO. It takes time to lay the technological and scientific foundations for the much-desired prosperity in global trade to flourish. A ten-year period is certainly too short for that. We must remember that most countries falling within Art 66 have only basic administrative, economic, technological and political infrastructures, which can barely cope with daily administrative matters. This is even leaving aside the need for sustained improvements in the existing human resource base of such countries. Article 66 would in our view be of little benefit to the so-called least developed member countries in their attempt to fully protect intellectual property rights. The period needs to be extended to 20 years or more.

The TRIPS Agreement is ambitious in its attempt to provide a globally acceptable framework for the protection of intellectual property rights. It encourages member countries to implement some common and uniform standards as the foundation for their protection system. Uniformity would in turn breed simplicity and compatibility in the enforcement of such property rights violations.

In spite of these likely advantages, it is important to remember that not all member countries have the same level of technological base. For most developing member countries, their production and export capacity is also limited. For these countries, the TRIPS Agreement is likely in the long run to be counter-productive to their developmental aspirations if they are to enforce the national and most favoured nation principles to protect intellectual property rights. These countries would be better off if the agreement had allowed them to pick and choose what technologies to fully or partially protect, after having taken into account their national development needs. As the TRIPS Agreement stands now, it may be plausible to argue that it represents a coercive instrument that has just been shoved down the throats of these nations. It seems that in this era of globalisation of trade, small and developing nation states have little room for any choices: they must either choke or attempt to swallow TRIPS. There is little wonder that the 1998 UN Development Report paints a very gloomy picture of the prosperity of the least developed countries. Its message was loud and clear. The globalisation of trade only benefited the developed nations. The disturbing aspect of the Report was that the gap between the developed and developing countries had widened in favour of the former.

The UN Report is now a call to developing countries to readjust their national development priorities. The question, then, is, should they go wholeheartedly into the WTO, or should a South-South parallel trading bloc be structured within the framework of UNCTAD?[10] This question should serve as food for thought for policy makers in developing countries. This position should also encourage the current developing members of the WTO to critically evaluate their standing in the global trading sphere. Perhaps the answer might be found in the formation of strong and effective regional trading blocs such as the SPARTECA, in the case of the South Pacific.

Intellectual property protection is a matter of great concern to island countries in the South Pacific. This is because of its direct or indirect effect on the culture, arts, music, custom ceremonies, traditional skills and knowledge and peoples' general way of life. For instance, the conventional method of copyright protection does not, as it stands today, protect customary and communal ownership of traditional carvings or customs dances as a collective art, or traditional or cultural performances of a community or people.[11]

Trade marks and patents do not extend their protective shields to the methods or processes of traditional herbs and shrubs, kava cultivation and storage and preservation. Thus, traditional knowledge and skills regarding medicinal herbs, shrubs and plants are left to exploitation by major pharmaceutical companies without any corresponding benefits flowing to the repositories of such knowledge. All these are matters that the WTO as well as the World Intellectual Property Organisation should look into. Global rules for the protection of intellectual property rights cannot be effective in areas where traditional knowledge and customary rights are not accorded some recognition.

10 This stands for 'United Nations Conference on Trade and Development'. It is an arm of the United Nations Organisation.
11 See Ahmadu, M, *External Trade and Investment Law*, 1999, Suva, IJALS, p 22.

25

THE MELANESIAN SPEARHEAD GROUP

25.1 Historical background

The MSG was instituted by its pioneering founders at a time of profound political, economic and social change in the region. Regional political developments arising from developments in Fiji, the Solomon Islands and Papua New Guinea and trade imbalances and low foreign reserves affecting most island countries will force a transformation in the future structure and effectiveness of the MSG. These developments will likely be complicated by the emergence of PICTA (Pacific Island Countries Trade Agreement) and PACER (Pacific Agreement on Closer Economic Relations), not necessarily at the theoretical but at the practical level.

The history of the MSG dates back to 1986, when the then Prime Ministers of Papua New Guinea and the Solomon Islands conceived the idea of forming the MSG at the Forum meeting in the Cook Islands. Fiji joined the MSG in 1996 and New Caledonia is the newest member. MSG meetings are held biannually. A preferential trade agreement was signed in 1994. The general idea behind the formation of the MSG and the subsequent signing of the trade agreement was to create a sort of free trade area encompassing the territories of the member states. It is expected that in time to come, other South Pacific island countries are likely to gradually be attracted into the MSG.[1] It is interesting to note that Vanuatu[2] has adopted it as part of domestic law, whilst the Solomon Islands has gazetted it to affect fisheries.

---

1 This paragraph has been developed out of a discussion with Mr M Roy, the Director of Trade of Vanuatu, on 19 August 1999.
2 MSG Vanuatu Extraordinary Gazette No. 2 [15 May 2008]; Solomon Islands Gazette Supplement No. 4 [8 March 2011].

DOI: 10.4324/9781003428060-31

25.1.1 The structure of the agreement

The basic structure of the MSG Trade Agreement replicates the standard text of international trade agreements. The objectives include the promotion and facilitation of a free flow of identified goods and services between member states in order to allow for fair competition, with the overall aim of fostering growth and development in member states.[3] The signatories to the agreement have also endorsed the most favoured nation principle as the basis of their trading relationship.[4] The agreement also mandates member states to gradually reduce customs duties with the eventual aim of eliminating restrictions to trade. Importantly, both quantitative (export and import) restrictions have been prohibited by the agreement.[5]

A key feature of the agreement (relevant to developing island states) is found in Art 11, which deals with the development of industry. The article provides:

A Party after consultation with the other Parties may for the purpose of encouraging new productive activities which contribute to economic development, whether by the establishment of a new industry or an extension of the range of commodities produced or manufactured by an existing industry suspend for a period of 3 years the application of the provisions of Article 6 of this Agreement and levy customs duties on goods contained in Schedule 1 to this Agreement which are imported from the territory of the other Parties and which are like, or competing with, goods produced by the new activities.

Duties shall not be levied under the provisions of paragraph 1 of this Article at a rate higher than the lowest rate applicable to import of similar goods from any third country.

In exceptional circumstances and after consultation and renegotiation with other Parties a Party may, for the purpose of establishing new industries or encouraging the expansion of established industries, withdraw items from Schedule 1 to this Agreement.

We shall make some comments on these provisions. First, Art 11 portrays a tacit recognition of the fact that trade in itself cannot fully engender genuine economic growth without a corresponding move to set up industries that process the traded goods. Secondly, by moving to develop or establish industries in their traditional areas of export, the member states are aiming at long-term benefits of improving their regional market share in the exports of intermediate and manufactured goods. This will help in the quest for hard-earned foreign currency and an improvement in their terms of trade. Thirdly, without a strong and sustainable industrial base, it is impossible to meaningfully advance the lives of people in the member states.

---

3 See Art 3.
4 See Art 5.
5 See Arts 7 and 8 respectively.

A sound industrial base, even if it is only meant to transform raw products into semi-finished goods, will greatly enhance a country's capacity to develop. Having an industrial base would also nurture the development of appropriate technology.

25.1.2 Derogation principle

Goods originating from the territory of a member state and destined for other member states enjoy preferential treatment provided they meet the rules of origin criteria and are those specified under the agreement.[6] Member states can derogate from their commitments under the agreement by utilising the exceptions found in Art 15. These include national security considerations, and the need to protect human, plant and animal life as well as the environment.

It is important to note that in spite of the fact that the agreement has been titled 'Melanesian Spearhead Group', any South Pacific island state that is a member of the South Pacific Forum is entitled to join. This is an open-door invitation to all countries within the Forum, except probably Australia and New Zealand.[7]

There is no doubt that the MSG Agreement is a novel attempt to foster trade and economic links between the parties to the agreement. Interestingly, with the exception of New Caledonia, all existing members are also members of the South Pacific Forum.

This raises the question of the status of the MSG countries as a free trade area in line with the requirements of Art XXIV of the WTO Agreement 1994 and now with PICTA, even though the latter allows for compatibility with prior existing agreements. As the Forum is also now moving towards the formation of a free trade area, some questions will need to be addressed one way or the other.[8] How can the MSG free trade area co-exist with the free trade area being proposed by the Forum, particularly in terms of products to be traded in? Should the MSG transform itself into a customs union in order to make it compatible with the free trade area being proposed by the Forum, or should it remain as it is? These are questions that are likely to occupy the minds of policy makers as the move towards the formation of a free trade area in the Forum eventuates into a formal agreement.

---

6 See Art 13.
7 See Art 16.
8 See *The Forum Magazine*, July/August 1999, p 1.

26

THE PACIFIC AGREEMENT ON CLOSER ECONOMIC RELATIONS

26.1 Structure of the agreement

The primary objectives of the agreement are anchored on the need to provide a sustainable trade and development mechanism for the 16 member states of the Forum. The agreement is to act as a platform for the gradual and continuous integration of the member states into the global economy. The Pacific Agreement on Closer Economic Relations (PACER) is not in itself a free trade area or a customs union, but is simply an arrangement that will hopefully lead to the evolution of either a customs union or a free trade area as contemplated by the Pacific Island Countries Trade Agreement (PICTA). We shall be discussing PICTA in the next chapter.

The main objectives of PACER are covered in Art 1(2). By way of example, it provides:

The objectives of this Agreement include the following:

(a) to provide a framework for cooperation leading over time to the development of a single regional market;

(b) to foster increased economic opportunities and competitiveness through more effective regional trade arrangements;

(c) to minimise any disruptive effects and adjustments costs to the economies of the Forum Island Countries, including through the provision of assistance and support for the Forum Island countries to undertake the necessary structural and economic adjustments for integration into the global economy;

DOI: 10.4324/9781003428060-32

(d) to provide economic and technical assistance to the Forum Island Countries in order to assist them in implementing trade liberalisation and economic integration and in securing the benefits from liberalisation and integration; and

(e) to be consistent with the obligations of any of the Parties under the Marrakesh Agreement Establishing the World Trade Organisation.

Whilst the objectives are ambitious and well-intentioned, there are no specific structures within the agreement that could truly support some of the objectives as presently outlined. There is a difference between mechanical integration into the global trading economy and actually being able to realise any tangible benefits from participating in it. The objectives have simply and naïvely assumed that by participating in the global trading economy, a country will automatically stand to reap the gains of such an involvement. We must realise that a number of the Forum countries would find it difficult even to diversify their economies because of the mono-cultural nature of their products. Most are also totally dependent on imported products and very often all produce identical products, whether it be fish or copra. It will be difficult in these circumstances to achieve comparative economies of scale. However, it should not be a distraction to the goals set out in the objectives of PACER. What may be needed to meet them is a truly functional and integrated approach towards implementing the agreement.

26.1.1 Economic integration

The guiding principles for Pacific economic integration assume a 'stepping stone' approach towards economic liberalisation and incorporation into the global economy. There is nothing particularly wrong about this approach. In fact, for small island states, this should be hailed as a pragmatic approach towards attaining the objectives of economic globalisation. The only perceived difficulty is the question of using the principality of a single regional market as a pedestal for stepping into the global economy.

A lot of work needs to be done in evolving a genuine and self-serving single regional market. Issues of size, similarity of products and limited internal markets are important considerations to bear in mind. We shall be exploring these and other factors in detail when discussing PICTA. Suffice to say here, a single regional market is not always synonymous with improved trading practices amongst member states. There is also no empirical evidence to suggest that it is actually a necessary condition towards global economic integration. Sometimes, the existence of a single regional market complicates effective integration into the international economy, whereas in this case, two developed countries are part of the agreement.

It is clear that PACER is not expected to serve as a customs union or free trade area in the South Pacific. Neither is it expected to serve as an interim arrangement or anything to that effect. In fact, Art 3(7) is very explicit on this matter when it states:

7 This Agreement is not intended to be:

(a) a customs union, an interim agreement leading to the formation of a customs union, a free trade area, or an interim agreement leading to the formation of a free trade area notifiable under Article XXIV of the General Agreement on Tariff and Trade;

(b) an agreement notifiable under Article V of the General Agreement on Trade in Services; or

(c) in derogation of any pre-existing arrangements, obligations or treaties.

A fundamental issue for concern here is that if PACER is what Art 3(7) says it is, then the text of the agreement is structurally flawed to the extent that its implementation is likely be predicated in a vacuum.[1] Article 4 mandates countries to commence trade liberalisation and economic integration amongst themselves first, of course taking into account their different priorities. However, there is no mention of the structural mechanisms through which this process is to be facilitated.

Australia, New Zealand, Fiji, the Solomon Islands and Papua New Guinea are members of the WTO. In this context, it is not clear how their existing obligations under the WTO may eventually either negatively or positively affect the other smaller, non-WTO island countries of the Forum. What safeguards are there for the smaller island countries to prevent their economies from being overwhelmed by the larger economies within the Forum, particularly the more advanced economies of Australia and New Zealand? We have to concede that in theory PACER has proposed a solution, but the reality has not actually been contemplated.

It is also not clear why, after only a relatively short period of the coming into force of PICTA, the island countries would be compelled to enter into negotiations towards establishing reciprocal free trade arrangements with Australia and New Zealand. When PICTA comes into force, would Australia and New Zealand enter into reciprocal free trade arrangements with island nations as a single trading bloc or on the basis of the individuality of countries?[2] The process of notification is mentioned, but there is no mention of the structural procedures by which this may be fully accomplished. In this regard, it is unclear to what extent Art 5(2) may be helpful in resolving this position.

Article 6 deals with consultations between Forum island countries and Australia and New Zealand relating to the negotiation of free trade arrangements. If a party

---

1 Cf Arts 5(2) and 6(3)(a), (b) PACER 2001.
2 Cf *ibid.*, Art 6(2).

enters into negotiations with any country that is not a member of the Forum, that party has an obligation to notify the Forum Secretariat, which shall then advise all the countries of the Forum.[3] Where a Forum country negotiates an agreement with a developed non-Forum member country, then that country shall open up consultations with Australia and New Zealand to commence negotiations for free trade arrangements.[4] Australia and New Zealand have corresponding obligations to enter into negotiations with a view to commencing free trade arrangements whether either or both of them commence formal negotiations with any country which is not a member of the Forum.[5] The significance of this provision lies in the fact that when complied with by both parties, a mutual atmosphere of tolerance and sincerity will prevail in their endeavour to foster good trading and economic relations.

In all situations involving negotiations under paras 3, 4 or 6 of PACER, the countries concerned must set out to negotiate arrangements that will be mutually beneficial by guaranteeing equal or better market access consistent with the principles of trade under the WTO.[6] It is difficult in practice to visualise how this provision might work, especially when not all island Forum countries are members of the WTO. Strictly speaking, this might amount to an imposition of very rigid standards of trade for nonparticipants in the WTO.

Australia and New Zealand are expected to maintain all existing arrangements covering market access in favour of Forum island countries at the time PACER becomes operative, or until such a time when a particular island country enters into agreements providing equal or better market access to other goods. The maintenance of existing obligations is excluded by para 10 of Art 6 of PACER. For purposes of clarity, we hereby reproduce the provisions of Art 6(10):

The obligations in paragraphs 3 and 4 do not apply to:

(a) the accession of any Pacific Island Country or Territory to the PICTA, provided that the PICTA rules of origin do not discriminate between Australia and New Zealand and other developed countries; or

(b) the negotiation of any bilateral or plurilateral free trade arrangements between or among countries each of which is a Forum Island Country, or a Pacific Island Country or Territory, or a least developed country, provided that the rules or origin of such bilateral or plurilateral free trade arrangements do not discriminate between Australia and New Zealand and other developed countries.

---

3 See *ibid.*, Art 6(2).
4 See *ibid.*, Art 6(3)(a).
5 See *ibid.*, Art 6(6).
6 See *ibid.*, Art 6(7).

To facilitate effective trade amongst parties to PACER, countries are to embark on voluntary tariff reduction.[7] Whilst this is a good provision, there is however no mechanism for evaluating the effect of this voluntary restraint mechanism.

Article 9 deals with the trade facilitation measures necessary to enhance regional trade amongst member countries. Member countries are expected to establish, in accordance with Annex 1, extensive programmes for the development and implementation of measures[8] which are expected to conform to other regional and international facilitation initiatives. The facilitation measures or initiatives sought shall take into account the special circumstances of the least developed countries and small island states.[9]

Article 10 mandates the application of the WTO's most favoured nation rule on sanitary and phytosanitary matters, customs procedures and standards and conformance. We have already considered the impact of Art 1 of the WTO rules dealing with the application of the most favoured nation rule in trade and services.[10]

Article 11 covers matters dealing with financial and technical assistance. It sanctions the development of a work programme through the infusion of additional resources in order to facilitate the implementation of PACER. Accordingly, all parties shall work together to develop a work programme as the basis for the grant of financial and technical assistance in the areas of trade facilitation and promotion, capacity building and structural adjustments including fiscal reform. The work programme will be administered by a unit operating from the Forum Secretariat. The work programme will be part and parcel of the Forum Secretariat's 'Budget Summary and Work Programme'. The work programme will be funded by Australia, New Zealand and other donors. The merits of having a work programme and a unit to coordinate this are not in doubt. However, the continued provision of aid by Australia and New Zealand is in the long run likely to create a dependency situation to the disadvantage of the island countries.

Article 12 deals with mutual assistance in the international trade and economic arenas, wherein member countries, especially members of WTO, are expected to offer incentives towards the attainment of the objectives of PACER. Implementation of special and differential provisions shall take into account the circumstances of individual countries regarding their stages of trade and economic development. To this end, Australia and New Zealand have undertaken to provide the necessary assistance to Forum island countries to augment their trade enhancement and liberalisation capacities.

---

7 See *ibid.*, Art 8.
8 See *ibid.*, Annex 1, Art 1(2). Every trade facilitation programme shall consist of: (a) a statement of objectives, (b) a statement of outcomes to be achieved, (c) a detailed plan of action and timeframe and (d) an annual budget sufficient to achieve the objectives of the programme, including the provision of technical assistance.
9 See *ibid.*, Art 9.
10 Refer to Chapter 18.

There are three notable advantages of this provision: First, it would allow members of the Forum who are also members of WTO to share their experiences with Forum countries who have little or no experience in trade and economic liberalisation matters when the current agreement is being implemented. Secondly, the built-in transitional arrangements will allow Forum island countries to adjust their national development objectives to meet the terms of the agreement. It will be very useful in cushioning any negative effects of the onerous provisions of the agreement. Thirdly, the two developed members of the Forum, by undertaking to provide assistance to Forum island countries in the implementation of the agreement, are willing to share their experiences at the regional level towards improving trade and commerce. The flip side is that there is no clear indication of how this assistance may be realised. This is something that needs to be explicitly laid out. Is such assistance needs-based, on demand or to be offered across the board?

In line with Art 11, the agreement should not be relied upon by any Forum member country as releasing it from obligations under any other international agreement. Membership of the agreement does not in any way vitiate the sovereign right of any Forum member country to conduct trade or enter into economic relations with other countries as it deems necessary. But by Art 14, parties to the agreement must notify the Forum Secretariat of any measures embarked upon by it that may affect the conduct of trade among Forum members. By way of example, it provides:

> The Parties shall keep each other informed of the implementation of, and the progress of, economic integration under all trade and economic integration arrangements operating among the Parties, including the arrangements established pursuant to part 2 of this Agreement.
>
> The Parties shall notify the Forum Secretariat of any substantive changes to their measures materially affecting trade relations between Parties, including the conclusion of economic integration arrangements with non-Forum countries.

Consultation between Forum countries on matters affecting the agreement are specified in Art 15, which provides that:

If a Party considers that:

(a) an obligation under this Agreement has not been, or is not being, fulfilled;
(b) any benefit conferred upon it by this Agreement is being, or may be, denied;
(c) the achievement of any objective of this Agreement is being, or may be, frustrated;
(d) a change in circumstances necessitates, or might necessitate, an amendment to this Agreement;

> it may notify any other Party, through the Forum Secretariat, of its wish to enter into consultations. The Party so requested shall enter into consultations in good faith and as soon as possible, with a view to seeking a mutually satisfactory solution.

The onus of seeking consultation is based on the affected party. There seems to be no corresponding obligation imposed on the potentially breaching party to inform the Forum Secretariat of its desired intention.

Article 16 provides for an annual review of the implementation and operation of the agreement and a general review three years from the date of the agreement coming into force. Except as otherwise indicated by the parties, the agreement will subsequently be subject to three-yearly reviews.

The purpose of the review process is outlined in Art 16(3). It provides:

3 The purpose of the reviews shall be to:

(a) make decisions, as required, on the opening and timetabling of negotiations for agreements or arrangements to provide for the broadening and deepening of economic integration of the Parties, and to monitor the progress of those negotiations;

(b) reach an agreement on actions necessary to harmonise and coordinate the trade and economic integration arrangements of the Parties;

(c) reach agreement, as required, to establish or modify trade facilitation programmes, review the implementation and success of established programmes, and make any decisions necessary for the development, establishment and implementation of trade facilitation programmes and specific trade facilitation measures;

(d) examine the implementation of the programme of work under Paragraph 2 of Article 11 and identify any issues which should be taken into account in subsequent development of the programme of work; and

(e) consider any other issue agreed to by the Parties.

Article 17 outlines the main functions of the Forum Secretariat in relation to the implementation of the agreement. The Secretariat is to provide all necessary secretariat services, which will include the following:

(a) the preparation and transmission of documentation including an annual report, required under this Agreement, including the transmission of communications between Parties;

(b) the provision of administrative support for meetings convened to review this Agreement or conduct negotiations or consultations under this Agreement;

(c) the provision of administrative support for meetings for the operation of financial and technical assistance under Article 11;

(d) liaising, as appropriate, between the Parties or with any other organisation;

(e) the provision of technical support to the Parties in the gathering and dissemination of information relevant to this Agreement;

(f) the provision of technical support to the Parties in the implementation of their obligations under this Agreement;

(g) the provision of other administrative or technical support, as determined by the parties, in respect of matters that relate to trade facilitation covered by this Agreement, including as required under Annex 1; and

(h) ensuring the smooth and orderly functioning of the Unit referred to in Article 11.

Article 18 deals with amendments to the text of the agreement. It provides to the effect that unanimity is to be achieved before any part of the agreement may be amended by the parties. Amendments shall become effective 30 days after they have been accepted by the members and communicated to the Secretary General of the Forum Secretariat. This is excellent in principle, in that decisions achieved through consensus show a bonding character in the decision-making process. But the difficulty is always that where members are divided over issues, thus preventing any consensus on particular issues, this will have the effect of undermining the efficient operation of the agreement.

Article 19 covers the processes of signature, ratification and accession by the parties to the agreement. For clarity, it provides:

This Agreement shall be opened for signature, subject to ratification, or accession by the Governments of Australia, the Cook Islands, Federated States of Micronesia, Fiji Islands, Kiribati, Republic of Marshall Islands, Nauru, New Zealand, Niue, Republic of Palau, Papua New Guinea, Samoa, Solomon Islands, Tonga, Tuvalu and Vanuatu.

This Agreement shall remain open for signature for one year from 18 August 2001 to 17 August 2002 at the Forum Secretariat in Suva.

Instruments of ratification or accession shall be deposited with the Secretary General.

Article 20 allows for accession by other countries or territories that are not current members of the Forum Secretariat, provided that this is unanimously agreed by all existing members of the Forum.

By Art 21, a country is at liberty to pull out of the agreement after notifying the Secretary General, who shall in turn inform other member countries. Withdrawal takes effect 180 days from the date of the notice. In the same vein, the entire agreement can be terminated by a unanimous decision of all members, 180 days from such a decision.

Article 22 deals with the entry into force of the agreement. By way of example, it provides:

This Agreement shall enter into force 30 days after the date of deposit of the seventh instrument of ratification or accession, and thereafter for each Party 30 days after the date of deposit of the instrument of acceptance, ratification or accession.

Subject to the terms of accession, a Pacific Island Country or Territory acceding pursuant to Article 20 shall become a Party to this Agreement 30 days after the date of deposit of an instrument of accession.

By Art 23, the Secretary General of the Forum Secretariat is the depository for PACER. To this end, the Secretary General is to register the agreement with the United Nations under Art 102 of the UN Charter; pass on certified copies of PACER to all parties; and inform all parties to the agreement of signatures, acceptances, ratifications, accessions to and withdrawals from PACER.

The general trend of PACER is good. If implemented to the letter, a potentially viable trading and economic environment might emerge within the South Pacific. However, in spite of this strength, we hasten to add that there are no indications of the negative implications of global trade.

PACER has started on the assumption that liberalisation of trade is always a good thing. This assertion contrasts with the UN Development Report, which has highlighted the negative impact of globalisation of trade on developing countries. In fact, what has been very clear so far is that the globalisation of trade has only benefited the developed economies.

PACER would need to do a lot of work to convince sceptics of its potentiality and viability. It is no doubt a worthy trade map to navigate.

27

PACIFIC ISLAND COUNTRIES TRADE AGREEMENT

27.1 Free trade area

According to Art 3, the primary focus of the agreement is the gradual establishment of a free trade area comprising all the island countries and Australia and New Zealand. In the process of the formation of such a free trade area, the peculiarities of the least developed countries and small island states will have to be taken into account. This is also expected to be consistent with the provisions of the General Agreement on Tariffs and Trade (GATT) Art XXIV of GATT/World Trade Organisation (WTO), discussed in Chapter 18. The agreement is expected to cover all aspects of trade in goods coming from one member country into the territory of another member country.[1]

27.1.1 Trade distortion measures

According to Art 9, parties to the agreement are to take all necessary measures to eliminate practices, rules or regulations that would severely affect free trade.[2] Parties should avoid the use of voluntary export restraints or orderly marketing arrangements in any trade covering originating goods. Such goods shall also not directly or indirectly be subjected to internal taxes or charges of any kind in excess of those applied to like or comparable domestic products. However, as an exception, an affected importing country might convert import restrictions into equivalent tariffs,

---

1 See Art 4.
2 These include all import or export provisions or restrictions on trade on originating goods, other than tariffs, custom duties and taxes, whether effected through quotas, import or export licences or similar measures.

DOI: 10.4324/9781003428060-33

but exporting countries have to be notified in advance of this. These restrictions do not apply to the payment of established subsidies or government procurement.

27.1.2 Emergency action

By Art 10, emergency action is directed at protecting domestic industries from the harmful effects of open competition and unguarded importation of goods. Before taking any emergency measures, an importing country shall establish serious injury or threat of serious injury to its domestic producers of like or comparable goods. A process of notification and consultation is necessary to ensure that rifts and unnecessary disagreements do not arise when an importing country decides to utilise any emergency measures outlined in the agreement. The period for such measures is restricted only to the actual period that would enable the importing country to ward off the harmful effects of the imports. The importing country seeking to apply emergency action must undertake periodic reviews if the measures are to be in place for more than three years.

27.1.3 Safeguard measures

Article 10 provides for the application of safeguard measures by an importing country affected or threatened by uncontrolled importation of products into its territory. The bottom line is that such importation must cause or threaten to cause serious injury to the domestic industry which produces like or directly competitive products. The decision by an importing country to apply any safeguard measure must be based on concrete and objective evidence showing a clear connection between the imports and effects on the domestic economy for comparable or like products. The safeguard measures must be provisional and must be imposed as tariffs, and should in the first instance be limited to a period of four years. In particular, Art 11(6), (7), (8) and (9) provides:

(6) No safeguard measure shall be applied to the import of product before the greater of:
  (a) two years; or
  (b) the total period of time, including any extension, during which the safeguard measure was applied,
  (c) has lapsed since a safeguard measure was in effect in relation to the same or like products.

(7) Notwithstanding the provisions of paragraph 6, a safeguard measure with a duration of 180 days or less may be applied again to the import of a product if:
  (a) at least one year has lapsed since the date of the introduction of a safeguard measure on the import of that product; and

      (b)   a safeguard measure has not been applied on the same product more than twice in the five year period immediately preceding the introduction of the measure.

(8) No Party shall apply for a safeguard measure to an import of a product until two years have lapsed following the completion or termination of measures taken to protect the domestic industry of that Party producing like or directly competitive goods under Article 14.

(9) No Party shall apply a safeguard measure to the import of a product listed in that Party's list of exempted imports or a product removed from a Party's list of exempted imports less than two years ago.

27.1.4 Dumped or subsidised goods

The definition of dumping is the same as that in Art VI of GATT and WTO, which we discussed in Chapter 18. It basically refers to the importation of goods into a country that are cheaper than comparative like products produced by the importing country that cause or threaten to cause a disruption of the domestic economy. Article 12 requires that an affected party should enter into negotiations with other parties with a view to determining how to reduce or prevent injury to the importing country. Where negotiations fail to avert the problem, an affected party may, after 60 days, be at liberty to impose anti-dumping or countervailing duties on the imports. Duties are reviewable every 12 months and thereafter determine the suitability of their continued imposition. The amount levied on the imports shall not exceed the rate of dumping or subsidisation found to exist at the time of the review.

Importantly, Art 12(7) provides:

> The parties agree to eliminate any subsidies that cause of threaten to cause serious injury to a domestic industry producing like or directly competitive goods, or to materially retard the establishment of a domestic industry to produce like or directly competitive goods, in another Party. Such parties shall enter into consultations, in accordance with Article 21, with a view to agreeing on measures or reduce or prevent injury or retardation which is consistent with the objectives of this Agreement.

27.1.5 Balance of payments

In the event of established material injury or where serious threats to the domestic economy are foreseeable, and these have resulted in an impairment of the importing country's foreign reserves or seriously affected its monetary and financial stability, an affected party is permitted to impose or increase tariffs for the minimum period necessary to ameliorate or redress the serious decline in reserves or to enable it to stabilise its reserves. However, the imposition of corrective measures is not to be arbitrarily imposed. In this context, Art 13(3) and (4) is relevant. It provides:

(3) In applying restrictions under this Article, Parties shall:
   (a) avoid unnecessary change to the commercial and economic interests of any other Party;
   (b) not prevent unreasonably the importing of any goods in minimum commercial quantities, the exclusion of which would impair regular channels of trade; and
   (c) not prevent the importing of commercial samples or prevent compliance with patent, trade mark, copyright, or similar procedures.
(4) If there is a persistent and widespread application of restrictions under this Article, including the existence of a general disequilibrium which is restricting international trade, the Parties shall review the Agreement to consider whether other measures might be taken to remove the underlying causes of the disequilibrium.

27.1.6 Protection of developing industries

Whilst free and unhindered trade is one of the guiding principles of PICTA, it is still necessary to protect domestic and developing industries from the harmful effects of unrestricted importation. This is one of the only ways to eventually achieve successful free trade in the region. To this end, Art 14 contemplates the imposition of measures necessary to avert the destruction of developing industries. Where goods are imported into the domestic economy in such quantities as to cause harm to the developing industries, the affected country may raise tariffs in order to check the harmful effects of the imports.

However, as a general rule, tariff should not be raised further than is necessary to prevent the material retardation caused by the imports. The period of tariff imposition will go beyond five years, but small island states or least developing countries may make it 10 years. Where the initial period is more than one year, a two-yearly review process must be instituted by the party imposing the tariff. No tariff will be imposed on imports before the developing domestic industry commences production.

As an underlying consideration, Art 14(6) provides:

The Parties shall, in accordance with Article 23, periodically review the operation of this Article and the time limits provided therein, with a view to preventing unjustifiable restrictions on trade between the Parties and ensuring that the objectives of this Agreement on fair competition in trade between the Parties are achieved.

27.2 Government procurement

Government is a very large consumer of goods and services. As such, it wields enormous trading powers when it contracts or sources goods from the public. To that extent, it is possible in some cases for an economy to experience trade distortions where the overwhelming economic power of the government is not used in a fair and balanced way.

Article 15 aims to commit the parties to the objective of liberalising trade purchases made by government. To achieve this objective, the parties to PICTA have agreed to a number of measures outlined in Art 15(2) of the agreement. It provides:

In order to achieve this objective, the Parties agree:

(a) to identify existing measures and practices which prohibit or restrict the achievement of the objective set out in Paragraph 1;

(b) to adopt transparent measures and practices in respect of contract valuations, technical specifications, qualification and performance requirements, tendering procedures, and invitation, selection and challenge processes;

(c) that each party shall, as soon as possible, take appropriate measures needed to minimise and remove the measures and practices identified in Paragraph 2(a);

(d) within two years of the entry into force of this Agreement, to conclude arrangements for detailed rules on government procurement. Those rules shall be included as a protocol to this Agreement;

(e) in accordance with Article 23, to periodically review progress made in liberalising government procurement and shall endeavour to resolve any problems arising in respect of the implementation of this Article.

27.2.1 General exceptions

Strict application of Arts 1–15 of PICTA would surely go a long way in fostering free and closer trading relationships between the parties to the agreement. However, it is possible for problems to arise even if the agreement is implemented with the best of intentions. This is why Art 16 has outlined a range of exceptions that would apply as and when circumstances permit. The aim of liberalising trade is to facilitate the rapid and efficient flow of goods and services within nations and not to create conditions that will be inimical to harmonious trade.

By way of example, we refer to the full contents of Art 16, which provides as follows:

(1) Provided that such measures are not used as a means of arbitrary or unjustifiable discrimination between Parties, or as disguised restriction on trade

between the parties, nothing in this Agreement shall prevent the adoption or reinforcement of measures:

(a)   necessary to protect public morals;

(b)   necessary to protect human, animal or plant life or health;

(c)   relating to trade in gold and silver;

(d)   necessary to secure compliance with laws and regulations which are not inconsistent with the provisions of this Agreement;

(e)   necessary to secure compliance with laws and regulations which are not inconsistent with the provisions of this Agreement relating to the protection of patents, trade marks and copyrights, and the prevention of deceptive practices;

(f)   necessary for the prevention of disorder and crime;

(g)   relating to products of prison labour;

(h)   imposed for the protection of national treasures of artistic, historical, anthropological, palaeontological archaeological or other cultural or scientific value;

(i)   necessary to reserve for approved purposes the use of Royal Arms or national, state, provincial and territorial arms, flags, crests and seals;

(j)   necessary to protect indigenous flora or fauna;

(k)   undertaken in pursuance of its rights and obligations under a multilateral international commodity agreement;

(l)   necessary to prevent or relieve shortages of foodstuffs or other essential goods; or

(m) relating to the conservation of exhaustible natural resources if such measures are made effective in conjunction with restrictions on domestic production or consumption.

(2) Nothing in this Agreement shall prevent the adoption and enforcement by a Party of measures:

(a)   necessary to protect its essential interests or implement international obligations or national policies:

(i)   relating to the non-proliferation of biological and chemical weapons, nuclear weapons or other nuclear devices;

(ii) relating to the traffic in arms, ammunitions and implements of war, and to such traffic in other goods, materials and services as is carried on directly or indirectly for the purpose of supplying a military establishment; or

(iii) in time of war or other serious international tension.

(b)   to prevent any Party from taking action in pursuance of its obligations under the United Nations Charter for the maintenance of peace and security.

27.2.2 Other provisions

There are a number of provisions covering other issues that are fundamental to the agreement. These include: the degree of transparent practices expected of parties to the agreement (Art 17); measures aimed at facilitating trade amongst them (Art 18); means of evolving relationships with the aim of widening and deepening such relationships (Art 19); notification procedures to parties and the Forum Secretariat on matters concerning the agreement (Art 20); consultations (Art 21); processes for the settlement of disputes (Art 22); review of the agreement primarily through the Forum Trade Ministers' Meeting or through other appropriate channels (Art 23); amendments (Art 25); signature, ratification and accession (Art 26); duration, withdrawal and termination (Art 28); entry into force of the agreement (Art 29); functions of the Forum Secretariat (Art 30); and depositary issues (Art 31).

It does not seem apparent, at least in theory, that PICTA is on a collision course with the South Pacific Regional Trade and Economic Cooperation Agreement (SPARTECA), the WTO or the Melanesian Spearhead Group (MSG). The general intendment is for all these agreements to perfectly co-exist in facilitating both regional and global trade.

PICTA does not prevent parties from entering into any agreements relating to the establishment of customs union, free trade or other trading concessions, but this is the case only where they are consistent with PICTA. This might raise conceptual problems because as it stands, members of PICTA are made up of both WTO and non-WTO members. There are also member states which are intent on being part of PICTA but still maintain and would want to continue maintaining their compact agreement with the United States. This is something that the Forum Secretariat needs to pay careful attention to.

The dominant role of Australia, New Zealand and, to an extent, Fiji will in the near future be a source of concern to smaller island states which are not in a position to compete at arm's length with the two developed partners of the Forum. Businesses in Samoa and a few other countries have already expressed serious reservations about the practicality of PICTA.

There is no doubt that PICTA will eventually succeed in opening up free trade across the region, but this will be at an enormous cost. There will be redundancies as businesses shape up to compete efficiently with other regional producers. This will lead to unemployment and other attendant social problems. Amongst island countries producing identical primary products, it is doubtful whether PICTA will be able to foster any free trade between them. This is an issue that will be debated for some time to come.

28

THE COTONOU AGREEMENT

28.1 Main objectives of the agreement

The Cotonou Agreement was signed on 23 June 2000 by ACP (African, Caribbean and Pacific) states and the European Union and aimed to reduce and possibly eradicate poverty in ACP states. It is also meant to facilitate the entry of the ACP states into the global economy through a sustainable development process. The agreement is considered as the basis of a new partnership predicated on a new cooperative arrangement set to promote economic, social and cultural development of the ACP states. This is in turn expected to usher in a new era of peace, security and progressive democratic culture. Historically speaking, the precursor to the Cotonou Agreement was the Lomé Convention, which expired on 29 February 2000. We shall be referring to the Lomé Convention after this discussion in order to illustrate its significance and the extent to which it has assisted the ACP countries, especially in the area of preferential trade practices. In this chapter, the articles being referred to are not those of the Cotonou Agreement itself, but are those of the Summary Document provided by the European Union.[1]

28.1.1 Membership

The current membership of the Cotonou Agreement had its roots in the defunct Lomé Convention, which was first signed on 28 February 1975 in Lomé, Togo Republic. There are now over 70 countries (part of the ACP states) affected by the Convention. Eight of these are in the South Pacific. These are Fiji, Kiribati,

---

1 See OJ L 317 of 15 December 2000.

DOI: 10.4324/9781003428060-34

Papua New Guinea, the Solomon Islands, Tonga, Tuvalu, Vanuatu and Samoa.[2] This would constitute the same membership for the Cotonou Agreement.

28.1.2 Comprehensive approach

The Cotonou Agreement is multi-dimensional in approach. It provides an integrated framework aimed at strengthening politics, trade and development in a combined fashion. This contrasts with the Lomé Convention, which basically centred on the granting of nonreciprocal trading privileges to goods originating from ACP states and entering the European Union. On the basis of this integrated approach, the Cotonou Convention is to last for 20 years with the possibility of revision every five years.

28.1.3 Pillars of partnership

The Cotonou Agreement places emphasis on five interrelated approaches as the basis for a successful and enduring relationship between the ACP states on one hand and the European Union on the other. According to Art 4, these include the following:

- a comprehensive political dimension;
- promotion of participatory approaches;
- development strategies and priority for the objective of poverty reduction;
- the establishment of a new framework for economic and trade cooperation; and
- reform of financial cooperation.

28.1.4 Thematic and cross-cutting issues

A number of issues have been identified by the Cotonou Agreement as being fundamental to this new cooperation. For clarity, we refer to Art 10, which provides:

> The Comprehensive framework for development strategies also provides for systematic consideration of three cross-cutting issues in all fields of cooperation:
>
> [a] gender equality;
> [b] sustainable management of the environment;
> [c] institutional development and capacity building.

The question of integrating sustainable management of the environment covers several subjects, for example, tropical forests, water resources, desertification, the use of renewable energy sources and so on.

---

2 *Island Business*, July 1997.

28.2 New trade arrangements

Negotiating trade liberalisation is the cornerstone of the agreement, thus bringing to an end the system of nonreciprocal trade preferences. However, the ACP states will continue to benefit from nonreciprocity up to 2008. Negotiations for the new trading arrangements occurred in 2002. In the context of these negotiations, it is clear that the European Union will take into account political, economic and social constraints of ACP states. To this end, 39 ACP states have been designated by the Cotonou Agreement as being least developed countries.

The new trading arrangement between the ACP states and the European Union will not only cover conventional trading but also will now extend to trade-related issues such as the protection of intellectual property rights, trade and labour standards and services.

28.2.1 Reform of financial cooperation

The Cotonou Convention contemplates an elaborate process of reform in the way the European Union is to grant financial assistance to the ACP states. It is now going to be need-based instead of being based on free outright grants. It will no longer be automatic, but will depend upon the circumstances of each situation. By way of example, Art 10 provides:

> The guiding principle of financial cooperation reflects the comprehensive approach of the partnership: consistency, flexibility and efficiency; ensuring by specific rolling programming for each country or region accompanied by regular reviews; change in the nature of assistance with a move towards budgetary and sectoral support programmes; indicative financial allocations rather than established rights; comprehensive approach: participation of nonstate actors; dialogue at the local level, timetables and coordination from the bottom up.

Under the Cotonou Agreement, European Development Fund (EDF) resources will be made available to the ACP states by means of grant and investment facilities. It is apparent that under this new arrangement, responsibility is placed on recipient ACP states for the proper and efficient management of the programmes funded through EDF resources. All ACP states are expected to produce results in respect of all such funded programmes. An annual review process is now an in-built monitoring mechanism in all EDF projects, and programmes must exhibit a clear indication of the level of participation of local actors. This should be consistent with the principle of decentralisation enunciated by the European Union.

The European Union will continue to support the prices of agricultural and mineral products from ACP states, but not under the Stabex and Sysmin systems as formerly operated under the Lomé Convention.

28.2.2 Financial resources

At the current rate, a substantial amount of resources is to be committed by the European Union towards the ninth EDF. By way of example, Art 11 provides:

> The financial resources are as follows:
>
> Ninth European Development Fund (EDF): 13.5 billion
> Long term envelope: 10 billion
> Regional envelope: 1.3 billion
> Investment Facility: 2.2 billion
>
> Unexpended balance from previous EDFs: + 9.9 billion
> Own resources of the European Investment Bank (EIB): 1.7 billion
> The financial protocols are concluded for a period of five years.

The implementing authorities for all EDF programmes are the Chief Authorising Officer, the National Authorising Officer and the Head of Delegation. The Head of Delegation has the administrative and financial responsibilities for the EDF and is invested with competent authority to disburse funds up to a certain amount.

28.2.3 Institutional provisions

In this regard, the organisational structures of the Lomé Convention have been retained under the Cotonou Agreement. These are: the Council of Ministers; the Committee of Ambassadors; and the Joint Parliamentary Assembly. The Council of Ministers is the overall policy-making unit of the Convention. It also helps in determining actions that are likely to impede trade between member states. The Committee of Ambassadors is entrusted with the responsibility of supervising the implementation of the Convention. It can also carry out any functions assigned to it by the Council of Ministers. The Joint Assembly is a consultative body that seeks to promote cooperation and trade through dialogue. It complements the activities of the Council of Ministers and the Committee of Ambassadors.

28.2.4 Humanitarian aid and emergency aid

These are now specifically covered under the Cotonou Convention. By way of example, Art 14 provides:

> These are short term measures aimed at responding to exceptional serious social and economic difficulties resulting from natural disasters or man-made crises, such as war. They involve humanitarian aid measures including aid for

refugees, the development of mechanisms for the prevention of natural disasters and disaster preparedness, etc. This aid is financed by the indicative programme of the ACP state concerned and by the Community budget.

28.3 Violation of essential elements of the agreement

In this context, substantive Art 96 of the Cotonou Agreement covers the possibility of taking appropriate actions against violations by parties to the agreement, primarily to uphold human rights, democratic principles and the rule of law. Consultation processes are mandated for dispute resolution and last resort measures such as suspension of the agreement may be invoked in appropriate cases.

28.3.1 The defunct Lomé Convention[3]

The Lomé Convention expired in 2000, thus ushering in the Cotonou Convention. We have decided to discuss the Lomé Convention briefly in order to highlight the weaknesses that brought about the evolution of the present Cotonou Agreement. This will help us to appreciate the necessity for the new partnership under the Cotonou Agreement, unlike the dependency situation created by the nonreciprocal system of trade privileges under the defunct Lomé Convention.

The Lomé Convention was to be seen in the context of having formalised a trading, economic and legal arrangement binding the ACP countries on one hand and the European Union on the other.

28.3.2 Aims of the defunct Lomé Convention

The Convention sought to foster trade, economic cooperation and social and cultural development between members, particularly of the ACP states. By way of example, Article 1 states:

> The Community and its Member States ... and the ACP States ... hereby conclude this cooperation Convention in order to promote and expedite the economic, cultural and social development of the ACP States and to consolidate and diversify their relations in a spirit of solidarity and mutual interest ... the Contracting parties hereby express their resolve to intensify efforts to create, with a view to a more just and balanced international economic order, a model for relations between developed and developing states and to work together to affirm in the international context the principles underlying their cooperation.

---

3 This section is a revised extract from the publication Ahmadu, ML, *External Trade and Investment Law in the South Pacific*, 2000, Suva, IJALS.

Other objectives of the Convention were found in Arts 2–7. Of these, Arts 5 and 6 stand out. Article 5(3) states:

> At the request of the ACP States, financial resources may be allocated, in accordance with the rules governing development finance cooperation, to the promotion of human rights in the ACP States and to measures aimed at democratisation, a strengthening of the rule of law and good governance.

Article 6(1) and (2) provides:

> With a view to attaining more balanced and self reliant economic development in the ACP States, special efforts shall be made under this Convention to promote rural development, food security for the people, rational management of resources, and the preservation, revival and strengthening of agricultural production in the ACP States.
>
> The Contracting Parties recognize that priority must be given to environmental protection and the conservation of natural resources, which are essential conditions for sustainable and balanced development from both the economic and human viewpoints. They recognize the importance of promoting, in the ACP States, an environment favourable to the development of market economy and the private sector.

The principles of cooperation outlined in the Convention also took cognisance of the difficulties faced by landlocked or island countries. A stated objective of the Convention in this regard was to help such countries overcome the difficulties posed by geography.[4]

Importantly, the parties also realised that the objectives of the Convention would remain unfulfilled unless the ACP states were willing to put in place legal, economic and social structures within their territories that would complement the implementation of the stated objectives.[5]

28.3.3 Nonreciprocity principle

The underlying principle that governed the application of the defunct Lomé Convention was based on the concept of nonreciprocity of preferences. This is unlike the General Agreement on Tariffs and Trade (GATT) system, which is based on the most favoured nation rule. The principle of nonreciprocity implied that trade concessions or benefits given to a member were not automatically extended to other members. It therefore meant that such trade preferences could

4 Article 8.
5 Articles 9, 10.

be selectively granted. The recipient state was not under any obligation to give equivalent concessions or benefits to the granting state. Article 25 states:

> The aim of the general trading arrangements … shall be based on the principle of free access to the Community market for products originating in the ACP States, with special provisions for agricultural products … the arrangements shall not comprise any element of reciprocity for those States as regards free access.

For a number of reasons, the principle of nonreciprocity was made the cardinal aspect of the Convention. Though these reasons cannot be found in the Convention itself, it is not difficult to work them out. The very nature of the trading arrangement showed that agricultural products are the basic commodities of sale from the ACP states to the European Union. Most of the ACP countries are traditionally situated in the tropics. Because of this climatic factor, they have to sell products that cannot be commercially cultivated in the European Union because of its climate.

This therefore means that the European Union cannot competitively export such like products to the ACP states. Bearing this in mind, it would have been pointless to anchor the Convention on the principle of reciprocity. This would, in a legal sense, have defeated the purpose of the trading arrangement.

28.3.4 Trading arrangements

Trading arrangements were basically directed at raw materials originating from the agricultural sectors of the ACP states. These products were granted preferential access into the European Union. The basic intention[6] was to facilitate trade between the member states.

The article provides:

(1) In the field of trade cooperation, the object of the Convention is to promote trade between the ACP States and the Community …
(2) In pursuit of this objective, particular regard shall be had to securing effective additional advantages for ACP States' trade with the Community, and, to improving the conditions of access for their products to the market in order to accelerate the growth of their trade and, in particular, of the flow of their exports to the Community and to ensure a better balance in the trade of the Contracting Parties and thus accelerate exports to regional and international markets.

---

6 See Art 167(1), (2) Lomé Convention.

The above objective would not have been achieved without a concrete legal stipulation in the Convention itself. Unless specific concessions were granted to the products of the ACP states by the European Union, it would have been extremely difficult for the former to compete with other more efficient producers from other regions of the world who are not members of the Convention. It was for this reason that Art 168 of the defunct Lomé Convention set out schedules that covered a range of products which enjoyed preferential access into the European Union.

Importantly, Art 168 did categorically exempt such scheduled products from customs duties and other forms of charge having equivalent effects. Furthermore, Art 169 barred the European Community from imposing quantitative restrictions (such as import quotas) on products from the ACP states.

General exceptions to Arts 168 and 169 were to be found in Art 170. Where Art 170 was to be utilised, the European Union must be governed by the most favoured nation rule in relation to other members of the European Community.

The combined effect of Arts 168 and 169 was to grant preferential access to products originating from the ACP states at zero-rated duty. This partly explained why the European Union had committed itself to importing reasonable quantities of sugar and bananas from ACP states at a competitive and guaranteed price during the currency of the now defunct Convention.

However, in spite of these concessions, each South Pacific member was still free to levy the rate of duty allowed by its tax laws on imports from the European Union. It was also possible, therefore, to maintain different rates of duty on the same product being imported into the countries of the South Pacific from the European Union.

28.3.5 Stabex

This is an acronym that stands for 'stabilisation of export prices'. The agenda for setting up the Stabex was to be found in Art 28 of the Lomé Convention. The article provides, *inter alia*, that: 'The Contracting Parties agree to confirm the importance of the system for the stabilization of export earnings … which aim to stabilize agricultural commodities markets'.

The stabilisation mechanism was established by Art 186. The intention of the mechanism was to redress the harmful effects of the instability of earnings affecting primary products from the ACP states. Article 187 lists the products that benefit from the price stabilisation process. For the price of any product to benefit from this stabilisation system, the affected country would have to make a formal request for stabilisation assistance to the Council of Ministers.

The Stabex system therefore provided some form of financial assistance to the affected ACP state in order to support the price of the commodity concerned. This was in turn expected to boost the exports of such agricultural products from the ACP state to the community.

28.3.6 Sysmin

Whilst the Stabex was aimed at stabilising the prices of agricultural products, the Sysmin was aimed at doing the same thing but for hard minerals. Just as for agricultural products, minerals are also subject to fluctuations in price, demand and supply. Article 214 sets up the Sysmin system under the defunct Lomé Convention. The Sysmin was a special financing facility set up for those ACP states whose mining sectors occupied an important place in their economies and were facing difficulties that were already perceived or foreseeable in the near future. According to Art 214(2), the main function of the system was to contribute towards a more solid and wider basis for the development of the ACP states.

Article 215(a) stated that for a member to benefit from the Sysmin, the enterprises in a particular mining sector must have been adversely affected by unforeseen problems beyond the control of the affected ACP state, whether of a political, economic or technical nature. A formal request for assistance was required to be forwarded to the European Union before an affected ACP state could be allowed to draw from the Sysmin fund.

The Sysmin system was therefore aimed at offering financial relief to the affected ACP state in order to support the price of the export mineral concerned. This in turn is expected to boost the export of such minerals from the ACP state to the European Union.

However, it should be noted that the financing facility under the Sysmin came in the form of soft loans. Unlike the Stabex system, the loans were to be repaid when the price had been stabilised.[7] Perhaps this was why the grant under Sysmin has been described as an aid.[8]

The significance of the defunct Lomé Convention as a trading bloc cannot be totally ignored. It has served the relationship between the European Union and the ACP states since 1964 (Yaoundé Convention). The principle of nonreciprocity gave it a special legal character, in that unlike a conventional trading arrangement, ACP states were not obligated to reciprocate any trading privileges to the European Union.

Legally speaking, there was nothing inherently objectionable in this arrangement. However, practically speaking, it made the ACP states over-dependent on the European Union. This had consequences for developing ACP states because it completely maintained their status as exporter of primary products. This dependency relationship had retarded their technological and industrial development.

Given the above developments, it is not surprising that the Cotonou Agreement portrays itself as a partnership rather than an aid arrangement. Nonreciprocal trading privileges will gradually be phased out in order to make the ACP states more responsive to the global forces of demand and supply.

---

7 Article 240.
8 Article 219(5).

29

THE SOUTH PACIFIC REGIONAL TRADE AND ECONOMIC COOPERATION AGREEMENT

29.1 Fundamentals

The South Pacific Regional Trade and Economic Cooperation Agreement (SPARTECA) is a multilateral agreement signed between Australia and New Zealand and the island countries of the Forum Secretariat. These include Fiji, Kiribati, Nauru, Niue, Papua New Guinea, the Solomon Islands, Tonga, Tuvalu and Samoa. Australia and New Zealand represent the developed members of the Forum Secretariat. It is aimed at facilitating closer trading links between island countries on one hand and Australia and New Zealand on the other. The globalisation of trade is now forcing countries to reassess their trading priorities. Most countries have realised that they can no longer go it alone if they take into account fluctuations in world prices of commodities and currencies.

The preamble to the agreement succinctly recites the need for such a special trading arrangement between the members of the Pacific Community. It provides:

> RECOGNISING the need to foster trade in products currently produced in the region as well as trade in new products, primary, processed and manufactured; and
> MINDFUL of the differing economic potential of Forum Island Countries and the special development problems of smaller Forum Island Countries

The preamble to the agreement thus outlines the basic concept of SPARTECA.

DOI: 10.4324/9781003428060-35

29.1.1 *Free access*

Goods or products originating from any of the Forum island countries (FICS) can enter Australia and New Zealand at minimal duty or at zero-rated duty. For goods on which tax is payable, there will, over a period of time, be a gradual relaxation of the duty. The intention is therefore to admit such imported goods on a level of preferential treatment that may not be granted to other goods originating from the territories of non-Forum members.

Article II(a) and (c) provide:

The objectives of the Agreement are:

(a) To achieve progressively in favour of Forum Island Countries duty free and unrestricted access to markets of Australia and New Zealand over a wide range of products as possible...

(c) To promote and facilitate this expansion and diversification through the elimination of trade barriers...

SPARTECA does not operate in isolation to grant preferential access to goods from the Forum island countries into Australia and New Zealand. The agreement has to be read in the context of particularly ss 4 and 153A–153S of the Australian Customs Act 1901 and the Customs Regulations 107A and 107B made pursuant to the principal Act. By the same token, the equivalent provisions in the case of New Zealand are ss 148–51J of the Customs Act 1966 and Customs Regulations 72C–72CG made pursuant to the same Act.

29.1.2 *Conditions for access*

Goods originating from the Forum island countries do not have automatic free access into Australia or New Zealand. Such goods not only have to meet certain entry criteria, but must also fully comply with the rules regarding their marks of origin.

In the case of Australia, imported goods from the Forum island countries are rated duty-free except for sugar.[1] The reason for exempting sugar has a lot to do with the fact that the sugar originating from the South Pacific members of the Cotonou Agreement[2] enjoys preferential access into the European Union. Australia is also a producer of sugar. In the case of New Zealand, all goods originating from the territories of the Forum island countries enjoy free and unrestricted access into New Zealand, including sugar. This is the general purport of Art III(1) and (2) of SPARTECA.

---

1 SPARTECA Handbook, 1996, p 5.
2 Formerly Lomé Convention.

Goods that enjoy preferential access must meet the requirements of origin as set out in Art V. Without satisfying these legal requirements, such imported goods will be denied free access and hence be subject to the prevailing duty rates.

To satisfy the rules of origin test, the goods must be primary agricultural products. In the case of manufactured goods, the last process of manufacturing must have been done in the exporting Forum island country and where at least 50% of the cost of production in value of labour or materials is embodied in such goods. By Art V(1), labour and materials used in the goods must have been from one or more of the Forum island countries and/or Australia or New Zealand.

It is important also to bear in mind that the application of Art V(1) is further dependent upon sub-para (2), which provides:

Before the provisions of sub paragraph (b)(ii)(d) or sub paragraph (b)(ii)(e) of paragraph 1 of this Article can be applied, the following additional requirements must be complied with:

(a) not less than 25 per cent of the factory or works costs of the goods is represented by the value of labour or materials, or both, of one or more Forum Island Countries; and
(b) the products of New Zealand origin included in the goods consist of products traded free of duty and quantitative and other restrictions between Australia and New Zealand at the time of importation.

There are a number of noticeable implications that flow from this provision. First, it seems that the rules of origin under SPARTECA place too much emphasis on the content and make-up of the imported product. The origin of the product is given second priority. This is more so when examined in the context of the 50% content requirements. Fifty per cent is too high as a value-added threshold for the Forum island countries. If the whole intention of SPARTECA were to encourage trade and development in the Forum island countries, one would reasonably have expected the content requirement (regarding marks of origin) to be somewhere within the range of about 25–30%, but certainly not 50%.

Secondly, by specifying a content requirement of up to 50% before goods can qualify as originating from the FICS, smaller and aspiring economies have been denied the advantage of acting as trans-shipment ports for entrée-port trade. Entrée-port trade is likely also to attract the establishment of value-added industries by firms in the electronics and related sectors in order to take advantage of cheaper labour costs and proximity to larger markets in Australia, New Zealand and the USA. This in turn will lead to increased gross national product, employment opportunities and manpower development in the FICS.

In this regard, it would have been better if SPARTECA had taken a cue from the mark of origin rules in Art IX(2), (5) and (6) of the General Agreement on Tariffs and Trade (GATT)/World Trade Organisation (WTO).

29.1.3 Refusal of free access

Australia and New Zealand are, by the agreement, entitled to refuse unrestricted access to goods from the Forum island countries, provided the refusal is aimed at safeguarding their national, economic or industrial security. These are listed as general exceptions in Art VI of SPARTECA. An important feature of these exceptions is that where the imported products from the Forum island countries are being dumped or subsidised, Australia or New Zealand, as the case may be, is allowed to impose anti-dumping or countervailing duties on such imports. The objective would be to offset any margin of advantage that would be enjoyed by the imported product, thus setting it at a competitive price level with like domestic products.

However, para (4) outlines the procedures to satisfy before Australia or New Zealand may levy anti-dumping or countervailing duty. Article VI(4) states:

(b) Before the Government of Australia or New Zealand takes action in accordance with sub-paragraph (a) of this paragraph it shall notify in writing, and if requested consult with, the Party or Parties from whose territory the goods are being exported ...

(c) If mutually satisfactory solution of the matter is not reached within 60 days from the commencement of the consultations ... the Party into the territory of which goods are being imported may, after giving notice to the Party from the territory of which the goods are being exported, levy dumping or countervailing duties on the goods.

Australia and New Zealand can override these procedures under para (d) of Art VI. Furthermore, going by the provisions of Art VII the two countries are even at liberty to vary or suspend the terms of the agreement. In this connection, Art VII(3) provides:

Notwithstanding the provisions of paragraphs 1 and 2 of this Article, the Government of Australia may suspend its obligations in the manner referred to in paragraph 1 of this Article, without prior consultation where, in its opinion, the circumstances are so critical that delay would cause severe difficulty before consultations provided for in sub paragraph 2(b) of this Article could be held. In taking provisional action under this paragraph, the Government of Australia shall provide urgent written advice of the action to the [Secretary General] who shall notify the other parties. Articles VI and VII make the Agreement very much a one sided affair. The two developed countries of the Forum will certainly be justified in taking measures that would protect their national, economic or industrial security. This is a right given to any sovereign state by International law. However, what is lacking in SPARTECA is a monitoring mechanism that can independently determine the propriety of actions undertaken by member states especially, where such measures are likely to affect the dependent party to the Agreement. The Regional Committee on Trade established by Article XI cannot effectively deal with monitoring issues. It has no such powers. The Committee is more or less a consultative body that takes decisions on the basis of consensus.[3]

29.1.4 Non-reciprocity principle

This is one of the most important features of the agreement. The Forum island countries are not obliged to reciprocate the preferences they enjoy under SPARTECA. Legally speaking, there is nothing in the agreement preventing any of the FICS from levying duties on goods originating from Australia and New Zealand.[4] The non-reciprocity principle in SPARTECA is akin to what obtains under the former Lomé Convention. This principle will continue to be the cornerstone of SPARTECA because the developed members of the South Pacific Forum need the markets of Pacific island countries.

SPARTECA is no doubt a novel attempt at bringing together some of the South Pacific island countries to form a unified trading system. The developed members of the Forum have taken the initiative to grant preferential access to goods from the FICS. If the FICS take advantage of these concessions, they could boost their export capacity in primary products. This would set a good foundation for an ultimate drive to export diversification.

There are, however, some snags to SPARTECA. It is clear that the level of access given and the quantity of goods that are permitted into the territories of the developed members are regulated not by SPARTECA but by the domestic customs legislation in these two countries. This might create room for long-term uncertainties as future changes in governments in Australia and New Zealand might result in domestic policy shifts and changes in the domestic customs legislation. Where this happens, the FICS are without any remedy. SPARTECA cannot be of any help here. This brings into focus one of its main limitations. A regional trading agreement should not be tied to any domestic law. It should be the other way round.

Except for the duty exemption, there seems to be no articulated industrial development policy counterpart to trade promotion. The emphasis seems to be only on export trade and the granting of assistance to the FICS on a bilateral basis. If SPARTECA is to truly serve as a regional model for trade and development cooperation, a common fund should be set whereby FICS can directly draw from it relative to their needs for technical assistance, subject to the agreement of all

---

3 See Art V(4)(a), which gives Australia or New Zealand unilateral power to assess the level of expenditure on factory or work costs.
4 In the case of New Zealand, Art V(3)(a) lists the goods.

members. This would by far be a better model for regional cooperation than the present system of bilateral aid arrangements.

To widen the scope and the future potential for trade and development within the region, the Pacific Community could start looking towards establishing a customs union or free trade area. This would have far more advantages than SPARTECA could currently provide. A look at the CARICOM[5] might be a good start.

---

5 This stands for Caribbean Common Market, a group of small island states having similar characteristics to the South Pacific island states.

30

ELECTRONIC COMMERCE

30.1 Background

The South Pacific rim is generally a little-known part of the global economy, especially by those living outside the region.[1] Improvement in communications is gradually exposing this region as a haven for tax-free financial transactions, an exotic tourism destination and a place of abundant natural pearls.[2] Whilst this conjured image of the region is partly correct, the ecological and environmental characteristics, including geographical factors, provide a contrast. For this reason, it is necessary to begin by briefly outlining the context upon which e-commerce will be analysed.[3]

In whatever way globalisation is defined, whether as a multifarious process involving political, technological and social forces or in the narrower perspective of economic progress, it is not a new phenomenon.[4] What is new though in this globalising process is the advent of digital technology as a revolutionising force in

1 In the context of this paper, the phrase 'South Pacific' refers generally to the 12 countries comprising the University of the South Pacific region. The term is rather amorphous and used in different ways by different writers and agencies. See for instance Lal, B (ed) *The Pacific Islands: An Encyclopaedia* (2000); and Crocombe, R, *The South Pacific* (2000) 16–19.
2 Cf Krugman, P, 'Technology and Changing Comparative Advantage in Pacific Region' in Soesatro, H *et al.* (eds) *Technological Challenge in the Asia-Pacific Economy* (1990) 25.
3 Campbell, IC, 'Constructing General Histories in Pacific Islands History' in Lal, B (ed) *The Journal of Pacific History* (1994) 46.
4 See generally, Mazrui, A, 'Pretender to Universalism: Western Culture in a Globalizing Age' (2001) 21(1) *Journal of Muslim Minority Affairs*, 11–24; Nichols, P, 'Regulating Transnational Bribery in Times of Globalization and Fragmentation' (1999) 24 *Yale Journal of International Law*, 257–306; and cf Rimmer, P, 'Introduction: Integration and Globalisation of the Asia-Pacific Economy' in Rimmer, P (ed) *Pacific Rim Development* (1997) 1.

DOI: 10.4324/9781003428060-36

the way societies are organised and managed, changing both the level and depth of human and material interactions. Their relative isolation, limited population and susceptibility to natural and environmental factors can easily be converted into strengths by embracing the digital age and by wisely choosing from the beneficial aspects of globalisation. What they lack in terms of land area and solid mineral resources is compensated by exotic cultures, expansive Exclusive Economic Zones and abundant marine, fisheries and plant life.

Together, Pacific islands cover approximately 30 million square kilometres of ocean and are made up of 22 sovereign and dependent states. For many years, these nations have based their unique development strategies in terms of their geographical isolation, comparatively small land area, cultural and ethnic diversity and vulnerability to nature and foreign influences.[5] The geography of the South Pacific region, consisting of numerous islands, can complicate logistics and transportation. Efficient delivery systems may be lacking, affecting the supply chain. The issues of information communication, technology, development[6] and the role of culture[7] in these countries are to be looked at as intertwined issues.[8] According to Beddis, the many factors leading to differences in economic and social development do not operate in isolation, but converge at a point. To that extent, government policies also have a tremendous impact on the process of development.[9] Most of the countries in the region are sovereign states and imbibe democratic principles.[10] They are all developing and modern to some degree.[11] At the same time, they are also influenced by cultural traditions.[12] Contrary to popular view, the South Pacific is not a monolithic entity. It is made of people of diverse ethnic origin, language and culture.[13] This diversity is noticeable even within the same country.[14]

---

5 *Pacific Social and Human Development Issues*, South Pacific Commission (SPC) Noumea, 2.
6 Uphoff, N and Ilchman, W (eds), *The Political Economy of Development* (1972) ix, 88; and *Roundtable Proceedings on Socio-Cultural Issues and Economic Development in PIS* 11 (1997) Asian Development Bank 50.
7 Mayo, M, *Cultures, Community and Identity* (2000).
8 Lindstrom, L, 'Cultural Tourism in the Pacific' (1997) 18(1) *South Pacific Study* 36–45.
9 Beddis, R, *The Third World: Development and Interdependence* (1993) 111.
10 Levi, W, *Contemporary International Law* (2nd edn, 1991) 80–81; cf Berad, C, 'The Teutonic Organs of Representative Government' 26 *Am. Pol. Sci. Rev.* 28.
11 LiPuma, E, 'The Formation of Nation-States and National Cultures in Oceania' in Foster, R (ed) *Making Emergent Identities in Postcolonial Melanesia* (1997) 43–44; McLennan, G, Held, D and Hall, S, *The Idea of the Modern State* (1997) 1–241; cf Wood, EM, 'Modernity, Post modernity or Capitalism?' (1997) 4(3) *Review of International Political Economy* 539–60.
12 Linnekin, J, 'The Politics of Culture in the Pacific' in Linnekin, J and Poyer, L (eds), *Cultural Identity and Ethnicity in the Pacific* (1990) 149.
13 Linnekin, J, 'The Politics of Culture' in Linnekin, J and Poyer, L (eds), *Cultural Identity and Ethnicity in the Pacific* (1990) 149.
14 Paterson, D, 'South Pacific Customary Law and Common Law: Their Interrelationship' (1995) *Commonwealth Law Bulletin*, 661–71; and LiPuma, E, 'The Formation of Nation-States and National Cultures' in Oceania in Foster, R (ed) *Making Emergent Identities in Postcolonial Melanesia* (1997) 33.

In spite of their general distinctiveness, they are collectively characterised by some similarities. These range from smallness in size and isolation to environmental degradation. As will be seen later, these limitations can be offset by the use of information and communications technology to open up trade and investment in the region.

30.1.1 Regulatory framework for e-commerce[15]

Unclear or restrictive regulations can pose challenges to businesses. Developing a conducive regulatory environment is crucial for the growth of e-commerce. The regulatory landscape varies across the South Pacific region, but efforts have been made to address e-commerce. Countries may have their own regulations, and there may be regional agreements in place. The Pacific Islands Forum has been actively discussing e-commerce policies and strategies to foster growth in the digital economy. Given the above background, it is also necessary to now present a profile of the existing structures for e-commerce in selected island countries in the region, namely, Kiribati, Fiji, Samoa, Tonga and Vanuatu.[16] The idea is to paint a rough picture of what is currently obtainable and the challenges that lie ahead.[17] It will also augment the general contextual background for discussing some of the issues affecting e-commerce in the region. A comparative schema is presented as follows (Figure 30.1).

A cursory glance at the table sends some ominous signals. What is apparent from the profile is that a number of steps need to be taken by countries in the region to upgrade the structures and laws for e-commerce. Except perhaps for Vanuatu, even the basic legislative framework to support the efficient practice of e-commerce is lacking. The possible ways out will be discussed later in the chapter.

30.2 Trade and economic issues

30.2.1 WTO

The World Trade Organisation (WTO) is a global and multilateral trading institution whose profound aim, at least theoretically, is to foster trade liberalisation by

---

15 The tables are adapted from: Ahmadu, ML, 'Capacity Building Needs of the Legal Profession for Harmonized Development of E-Commerce Legal and Regulatory Systems in Asia-Pacific', A Paper for the UN-ESCAP Regional Office, Thailand, July 2004. Information reproduced here was based on field research conducted by the author in Fiji, Kiribati, Vanuatu and Samoa in 2001 and 2002. It is possible that some of the information may now have been updated.

16 Kiribati is Micronesian; Tonga and Samoa are Polynesian; Vanuatu is Melanesian; and Fiji is a hybrid between the three.

17 Cf, Kesan, J and Gallo, A, 'Optimizing Regulation of Electronic Commerce' (2004) 72 *University of Cincinnati Law Review* 1497–593.

FIJI
Fiji's has a National ICT Policy and National Broadband Policy 2011. The issue with both is that they do not address critical issues for e-commerce businesses, while broadband service demand and supply need to be improved. The Electronic Transaction Act 2008 is in place, however, Fiji has no comprehensive policy or strategy promoting e-commerce. There have been numerous e-commerce initiatives including the introduction of mobile money in 2010 via Vodafone and Digicel. For Fiji's legal and regulatory environment to address critical areas of e-commerce readiness it needs to focus more on cybercrime as well as data protection and privacy.

KIRIBATI
E-commerce laws in Kiribati are relatively limited due to its smaller size and less developed digital infrastructure compared to larger countries. Kiribati has an e-commerce law, Electronic Transactions Act 2021 in line with the United Nations Commission on International Trade Law (UNCITRAL) Model law on Electronic Commerce 1996. There is also a Copyright Act 2018 which does offer protection to computer software or programmes.

SAMOA
Samoa is in the process of developing an e-commerce legal framework. Samoa has an Information and Communication Technology Sector Plan (ICTSP) FY2022/23 – 2026/27 which supports the implementation of the Key Priority Areas in the Pathway for the Development of Samoa (PDS) FY2021/22 - FY2025/26. While there is no one legislation encompassing the full protection for e-commerce, there are legislations offering protection in the e-commerce space: Broadcasting Act 2010, Companies Act 2001, Copyright Act 1998, Crimes Act 2013, Electronic Transactions Act 2008, Intellectual Property Act of 2011, Money Laundering Prevention Act 2007, National Payment System Act 2014 and Telecommunications Act 2005.

TONGA
The *Tonga Digital Government Strategic Framework* 2019-2024 (TDGSF) and the *Tonga E-commerce Strategy and Roadmap* 2021, focusses on accelerating digitisation of the Micro, Small, and Medium Enterprises sector, to enable enterprises to digitise more of their transactions, while forming market linkages with their stakeholders. Tonga's Data Residency law, encourages the use of localised secure cloud-based data services, supported by a Broadband Policy enabling competition in the telecommunication sector. The TDGSF promotes an environment which enables fair access to ICT and data channels, further enabling all providers access to ICT services such as Unstructured Supplementary Service Data (USSD). The Communications Act 2015, Computer Crimes Act 2003 and Radiocommunication Act 2003 relate to e-commerce while Tonga's National ICT Policy 2008 and National ICT Strategy 2009 are supported in the 2015-25 Tonga Strategic Development Framework.

VANUATU
Vanuatu has a National ICT Policy. However, e-commerce in Vanuatu is focussed on seven policy priority areas outlined in the Vanuatu E-Commerce Strategy and Roadmap 2022 supporting the achievement of the strategic outputs of the Vanuatu Government's National Sustainable Development Plan (NSDP), TPFU 2019 – 2025 as well as the objectives of Vanuatu's updated ICT Policy. The e-commerce law, Electronic Transactions Act 2000 will need to be amended to meet the UNCITRAL Model law on e -commerce alongside other relevant laws, including the development of a Consumer Protection Act which encompasses all transactions within the e-commerce context, a Data Protection Act and Privacy Act to ensure confidence and trust in the use of e-commerce.

FIGURE 30.1   E-commerce legal and regulatory systems in case study nations of the South Pacific.

eliminating all barriers to trade between countries. South Pacific countries, as members of the WTO, engage in discussions related to trade liberalisation and dispute resolution. Issues such as tariff reductions, agricultural subsidies and market access are pertinent. The emerging prominence of the WTO[18] is to be seen in the context of the current dynamics of the international economy which are driven by a number of globalising forces, particularly information and communications technology.

The Organisation is founded on the most favoured nation rule. The principle enjoins member states to accord the same rights, privileges and benefits to each other without any discrimination.[19] The main exception to this rule relates to the formation of a customs union,[20] where the granting of exclusive privileges to designated members is permissible.[21]

At the practical level, both the objectives of this multilateral institution and the way it is governed portray a culture of dominance exhibited by the major metropolitan powers over the vast majority of its members which are developing countries. According to Bhaja, for example:

> The global trading system is dominated by a few a hegemonic trading powers … This minority tends to be far more interested in gaining market access to, or shutting imports out from, developing countries than in promoting export-oriented growth in those countries. The powers preach free trade until they come to the negotiating table with developing countries when they become mercantilists.[22]

Whilst trade liberalisation can be credited with the expansion of the global economy, it is also evident that the gap between the rich industrialised countries and the predominantly capital-importing countries is widening in favour of the former.[23] The insistence by the major trading powers on incorporating TRIPS (Trade-Related Aspects of Intellectual Property Rights) into all forms of trading arrangements,[24] granting agricultural subsidies to their farmers and arbitrarily applying tariff and nontariff restrictions to imports from developing countries

---

18 The predecessor being the General Agreement on Tariffs and Trade (GATT) 1948.
19 See Article I of the WTO Agreement 1994.
20 See Article XXIV(8) of the WTO Agreement 1994.
21 Other exceptions are the formation of free trade area (Article XXIV(8)); concessions to less developed member countries (Article XXXVI(8)); and waiver from complying with some provisions of the WTO Agreement.
22 See Bhaja, R, 'Challenges of Poverty and Islam Facing American Trade Law', (2003) 17 *Saint John's Journal of Legal Commentary* 471–93.
23 In the context of the South Pacific, see Hildebrand, S, 'WTO, EU and the Pacific', *Pacific Islands Monthly* (1999) 30.
24 Cho, S, 'A Bridge Too Far: The Fall of the Fifth WTO Ministerial Conference in Cancun and the Future of Trade Constitution' (2004) 7 *Journal of International Economic Law* 219–32.

raise the prospects for questioning the relevance of the Organisation to the economic aspiration of small Pacific island countries.

However, given the current global trading climate, it is inconceivable that these countries have any real alternative but to take steps to gradually integrate into the global economy.[25] A few such countries are already members of the WTO whilst the vast majority are not. For these countries, participating in regional trading arrangements is expected to prepare them for the rigours of WTO negotiations and subsequent accession.

30.3 Economic integration

30.3.1 SPARTECA[26]

At the sub-regional level, the process of integration began with their accession to a number of multilateral trading arrangements. Economic integration within the region is pursued through various agreements. The Pacific Island Countries Trade Agreement (PICTA) and the Pacific Agreement on Closer Economic Relations (PACER) are examples. These agreements aim to enhance economic cooperation, facilitate trade and promote regional integration. The primordial legal instrument in this regard was the SPARTECA. It is a multilateral agreement signed between Australia and New Zealand on the one hand, and island countries of the Forum Secretariat on the other.[27]

Goods or primary products originating from any of the Forum island countries can enter Australia or New Zealand at minimal duty or at zero-rated duty. Over time a gradual reduction of duty on all other imports will be achieved. The main premise for free access is based on a 50% local content requirement. Thus, all goods or primary products covered by the agreement must satisfy the conditions in Article 5 on the rules of origin. The entire agreement is based on the principle of nonreciprocity. The main drawbacks relate to the unilateral power of Australia or New Zealand to refuse access and to impose anti-dumping or countervailing duty. The other significant concern is the 50% local content threshold, which most Pacific island countries consider excessive.[28] It is not surprising that Forum island countries have now shifted their emphasis to PICTA and PACER.[29]

---

25 Cf Maduro, MP, 'The Constitution of the Global Market' in Snyder, F (ed), *Regional and Global Regulation of International Trade* (2002) Chapter 2; and Tan, LH, 'Will ASEAN Economic Integration Progress Beyond a Free Trade Area?' (2004) 53 *International and Comparative Law Quarterly*, 935–62.

26 The acronym stands for the South Pacific Regional Trade and Economic Cooperation Agreement.

27 These include Fiji, Kiribati, Nauru, Niue, Papua New Guinea, Solomon Islands, Tonga, Tuvalu and Samoa.

28 Ahmadu, ML, *External Trade and Investment Law in the South Pacific* (2000) Chapter 5.

29 See Yavala, P, 'SPARTECA's Last Stand', *Pacific Islands Monthly* (June 1998).

Since its inception as a special sub-regional trading arrangement, except for a limited expansion of textiles export or primary products,[30] it is difficult to point to convincing and demonstrable benefits in the development of the industrial capacity of these countries. The failures of SPARTECA may perhaps have informed the Forum Secretariat to consider alternative but WTO-compliant trading arrangements, such as PACER and PICTA.

30.3.2 PACER Plus[31]

PACER Plus is a trade and economic integration agreement among Pacific island countries and Australia and New Zealand. It aims to promote regional cooperation, economic development and trade liberalisation. The primary objectives of the agreement centre on the need to provide a sustainable trade and development mechanism for the 16 member states of the Forum.[32] The agreement is to act as a platform for the gradual and continuous integration of the member states into the global economy. PACER Plus is not in itself a free trade area or a customs union, but is simply an arrangement that would hopefully lead to the evolution of either a customs union or a free trade area as contemplated by PICTA.[33] Whilst the objectives are ambitious and well-intentioned, there are no specific structures within the agreement which can effectively support the realisation of these objectives. There is a difference between mechanical integration into global trading and being actually able to garner tangible benefits from it. The objectives have simply and naïvely assumed that by participating in the global trading economy, a country will automatically reap the gains of such an involvement. It is to be realised that a number of the Forum countries are finding it difficult even to diversify their economies because of the mono-cultural nature of their products. Many island countries are also totally dependent on imported products and very often all produce identical products, whether it is fish or copra. It will be difficult in these circumstances to achieve comparative economies of scale. That however should not be seen as a distraction to the attainment of the goals set out in the objectives of PACER Plus. What may be needed is a functional and integrated approach towards implementing the agreement.[34] That requires strong political will.

---

30 See generally Bora, B and Findlay, C (eds), *Regional Integration and the Asia-Pacific* (1998) 2.
31 PACER stands for the phrase 'Pacific Agreement on Closer Economic Cooperation'. The Agreement was formalised in Nauru on 18 August 2001.
32 The main objectives of PACER are covered in Article 1 (2).
33 The 24-article agreement will only come into force if endorsed by at least seven countries of the Forum.
34 Ahmadu, ML and Hughes, R, *Commercial Law and Practice in the South Pacific* (Forthcoming) Cavendish Publishing, London, Chapter 22.

30.3.3 PICTA[35]

PICTA is another regional trade agreement among Pacific island countries. It seeks to reduce barriers to trade in goods and services among member countries. The agreement is aimed at strengthening, expanding and diversifying trade between the island countries of the South Pacific, including Australia and New Zealand. The agreement hopes to facilitate trade diversification, harmonisation and the gradual elimination of tariffs in an integrated way, by covering a range of products with the goal of eventually creating a single regional market and a free trade area. In a way, this development is also expected to contribute to the expansion of both regional and global trade. In evolving a free trade area, the peculiarities of the least developed countries and small island countries will have to be taken into account.[36] It is expected that PICTA will eventually succeed in opening up free trade across the region, but this will be at enormous costs. There will be redundancies as businesses shape up to compete with other efficient regional producers. This will lead to unemployment and other attendant social problems. Amongst island countries having identical primary products, it is doubtful whether PICTA will be able to enhance free trade between them. This is an issue which will be debated for some time to come.[37]

Given the current economic and investment climate prevailing in most island countries in the Pacific, the effect of these trading arrangements remains to be seen. The geographic, fiscal and economic limitations already alluded to can easily be overcome by a strategic decision to incorporate e-commerce as a facilitative and complimentary vehicle for fostering trade and investments, both regionally and internationally. E-commerce structures have the potential of raising not only the capacity but also the international trading profile of small island countries. This may assist in turning their economies from being import-dependent to export-driven. Their economic capacity is constrained, except where information technology is used as a strategic development tool. The South Pacific region faces challenges in developing e-commerce, with issues ranging from infrastructure to regulatory environments. The regulatory framework varies, and trade and economic issues are addressed through regional agreements like PACER and PICTA, as well as through participation in international organisations such as the WTO.

Two queries that will persistently be raised regarding the region's attempt to integrate into the global economy will not necessarily be financial or technological. These will relate more to the extent of their absorptive capacity and whether in practice, economic globalisation is necessarily good for small island countries.

---

35 The acronym stands for 'Pacific Islands Countries Trade Agreement', which was concluded on the 18th of August 2001 in Nauru.

36 See Article 3.

37 Ahmadu, ML and Hughes, R, *Commercial Law and Practice in the South Pacific, 2006,* Cavendish Publishing, London, Chapter 23.

It is against this scenario that the techno-legal mechanics of e-commerce and its relevance to the region will be discussed.

30.4 Structural aspects of e-commerce[38]

30.4.1 Definition of e-commerce

As with other concepts, it is difficult to have one acceptable definition of the process of e-commerce because it may mean different things to different people, depending on the perspective it is approached from and by whom. However, it can still simply be referred to as an electronic process of transacting between buyers and sellers using the instrumentality of the internet.[39] The products marketed through e-commerce are not restricted to physical commodities but also include digitised goods and services.

30.4.2 Internet profile

An outline of the important characteristics of analogue and digital technologies and how this impacts the transmission of information through the internet[40] is essential in highlighting the legal implications to e-commerce. To begin with, the internet has been defined as a network of computers linked together and working in a coordinated fashion.[41] Many South Pacific countries face challenges related to internet infrastructure and connectivity. Limited access to high-speed internet can hinder the growth of e-commerce.[42] It is the primary technological platform for the transmission of digital and analogue data. Because e-commerce is heavily reliant on internet technology, a brief discussion of how it works is important in underscoring the interconnection between law and technology and the facilitative role this plays in commerce.

As the architecture of the internet shows, data sent from one computer to another is conveyed at random by many servers and using the most efficient routing until it finally reaches its intended destination. In the course of transmission, data is broken into 'packets'. This is reassembled into its original form at the point

---

38 See generally Swindells, C and Henderson, K, 'Legal Regulation of Electronic Commerce' (1998) 3 *The Journal of Information, Law and Technology*; and the UNCITRAL Model Law on Electronic Commerce 1996.

39 See UNCITRAL Model Law on Electronic Commerce 1996.

40 Historically, what we know as the internet today began as the ARPAnet in 1969 (Advanced Research Project Agency) as a military internet-work. It was later used as a scientific academic research internet-work. Today, it is an open commercial internet-work.

41 Jackson-Carter, M, 'International Shoe and Cyberspace: The Shoe Doesn't Fit When It Comes to the Intricacies and Nuances of Cyberworld' (1998) 20 *Whittier Law Review*, 217–40.

42 Crichton, B and Seve, F, 'Telecommunications reform in Samoa: The introduction of Competition law – Preliminary findings from the Telecommunications Project' (2018) 8 *International Journal of Advances in Computer Science and Its Applications* 31.

of receipt. Transporting data through the network would require the use of a pro- tocol, the most essential being the Transport Control Protocol (TCP).[43] For onward or continuous transmission of data, the internet protocol (IP) determines what server is to receive the 'packet of information'. Accessing a website on the inter- net[44] would require the user to input the correct Uniform Resource Locator (URL).

The architecture of the internet raises a number of conceptual problems for e-commerce. These, at a practical level, are important in appreciating the extent to which Pacific island countries could achieve effective integration into the global economy. The first deals with the difficulties created by digital technology; the second relates to online contracts; and the third addresses the problems of tax- ing e-businesses. For a proper and successful e-commerce structure to develop in the region,[45] these are to be looked at in an integrated manner and not as isolated issues.

30.4.3 Digital and analogue technologies

A basic characteristic of digital technology is that data is transmitted in perfect quality, without loss or interruption to any of its constituent parts. Digital trans- mission eliminates the quality-reducing elements of the data. According to Yang et al., digital technology allows the making and transmission of perfect copies which are identical.[46] The digitalisation process and the resultant effect on the quality of data transmitted is shown in Figure 30.2.

In contrast, analogue transmission results in a reduction in the quality of the data conveyed. The nature of the technology accounts for the difference in the quality of the transmission.[47] As shown in Figure 30.2, digital technology trans- mits by breaking down the data into small packets which are then reassembled at the point of receipt. Analogue technology transmits the whole information at once, hence forcing a reduction in the quality of the data[48] (Figure 30.3).

One of the legal problems afflicting digital technology lies in the way it facili- tates easy copying or content reproduction.[49] In effect, this overstretches the

---

43 See Braden, R, 'Requirements for Internet Hosts – Communication Layers' in Reed, C, *Internet Law: Text and Material* (2000) 12, where he says: "The TCP controls the exchange of packets between hosts; it sets outs the mechanisms for checking whether the packet has arrived, for check- ing to ensure that it has not been corrupted in transit, and for resending it if transmission fails".
44 The protocol defining the content of information is the Hypertext Transfer Protocol (HTTP).
45 See Gray, G, 'Electronic Trading Made for our Region', *Island Business* (January 1999) 47.
46 Yang, M and Gorman, F, 'What's Yours is Mine: Protection and Security in a Digital World' (2003, Dec) 36 *Maryland Bar Journal* 24–36.
47 Jensen, C, 'The More Things Change, The More They Stay the Same: Copyright, Digital Technology and Social Norms' (2003) 56 *Stanford Law Review* 531–70.
48 Yu, P, 'The Copyright Divide' (2003) 25 *Cardozo Law Review* 331–447.
49 Cf Bainbridge, D, 'Trademark Infringement, the Internet and Jurisdiction' (2003) 1 *Journal of Information, Law and Technology*.

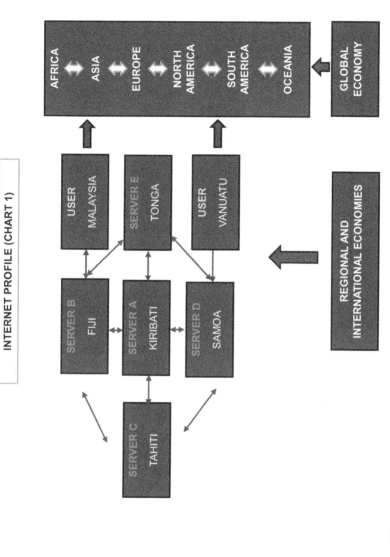

FIGURE 30.2 Illustrates a basic profile of the internet.

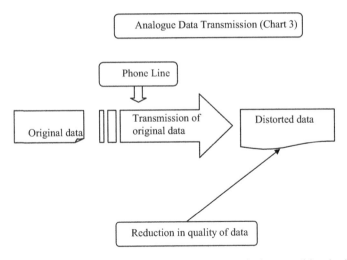

FIGURE 30.3 Portrays the net process of analogue transmission, resulting in deterioration in the quality of the data.

boundaries of conventional copyright rules.[50] According to Short, 'unlike in the taking of real property that deprives another of its use altogether, digitised information can be copied outside of the owner's knowledge'.[51] This has led to calls for the development of a new principle of copyright to specifically protect digitised products.[52] Whilst in theory the use of encryption technology in works holding copyright may help to reduce unauthorised copying, this is not always effective because of the relative ease with which codes are deciphered.[53]

---

50 Jensen, C, 'The More Things Change, the More They Stay the Same: Copyright, Digital Technology and Social Norms' (2003) 56 *Stanford Law Review* 531–70; Yu, P, 'The Copyright Divide' (2003) *Cardozo Law Review* 331–447; and Wade, C, 'The Quest for Access in the Digital Era: Copyright and the Internet' (2001) 1 *Journal of Information, Law and Technology.*

51 See Short, J, 'An Economic Analysis of the Law Surrounding Data Aggregation in Cyberspace' (2004) 56 *Maine Law Review* 61–106, who is against the development of new property rights to cover data aggregation.

52 Roemer, R, 'Trusted Computing, Digital Rights Management, and the Fight for Copyright Control on Your Computer' (Fall, 2003) *UCLA Journal of Law and Technology* 8–45. Digital rights management may include technologies restricting the use of digital files in order to safeguard the copyright of authors or makers of such works; cf Short, J, 'An Economic Analysis of the Law Surrounding Data Aggregation in Cyberspace' (2004) 56 *Maine Law Review* 61–106, who is against the development of new property rights to cover data aggregation.

53 Roemer, R, 'Trusted computing, Digital Rights Management, and the Fight for Copyright Control on Your Computer' (2003) *UCLA Journal of Law and Technology* 8–45; see also Lipton, J, 'Information Property: Rights and Responsibilities' (2004) 56 *Florida Law Review* 135–190; and Lloyd, I, *Information Technology Law* (3rd edn, 2000) 108–44.

The use of digital technology as an integral part of e-commerce in performing tasks or making decisions which may be susceptible to legal disputes creates problems for the judiciary in understanding how the information was derived, processed and presented and in weighing the probative value of the information against its potential to confuse.[54] Limited digital literacy among the population can hinder the adoption of e-commerce. Education and training programmes may be needed to enhance digital skills. To assist the judiciary in this regard, laws relating to computer misuse, computer crimes, digital signatures, digital telecommunications, multimedia and tele-medicine are to be passed, when necessary.

30.4.4 Online contracts

The usual rules of contract on offer, acceptance, consideration and intention to create legal relations do not present problems when it comes to determining the validity of conventional transactions. Whilst this is also partly the case with online contracts, the use of digital technology and the architecture of the internet raise some issues worthy of consideration.[55] The lack of widely adopted and secure online payment systems poses a challenge. E-commerce development often relies on efficient and trustworthy payment gateways. The problems of user identification,[56] security of payment systems,[57] the question of authenticating digital signatures[58] and encryption[59] and the liability of the internet service provider[60] for copyright violations or defamation will no doubt continue to interdict the effectiveness of e-commerce.[61]

---

54 See, Hugenholtz, PB, *Copyright and Electronic Commerce: An Introduction* (2000) 1; and cf Markowitz, K, 'Legal Challenges and the Market Rewards to the Use and Acceptance of Remote Sensing and Digital Information as Evidence' (2002) 12 *Duke Environmental Law and Policy Forum* 219–55.

55 See generally Trompenaars, B, 'Legal Support for Online Contracts' in Hugenholtz, PB (ed), *Copyright and Electronic Commerce* (2000) 367; Ong, R, 'Consumer Based Electronic Commerce: A Comparative Analysis of the Position in Malaysia and Hong Kong' (2004) 12 *International Journal of Law and Information Technology* 101–20; and cf Knoll, A, 'Any Which Way But Loose: Nations Regulate the Internet' (1996) 4 *Tulane Journal of International and Comparative Law* 275–98.

56 Ford, M, 'Identity Authentication and E-Commerce' (1998) 3 *Journal of Information, Law and Technology.*

57 See generally Berkowitz, L, 'Computer Security and Privacy: The Third Wave of Property Law' (2004) 33 *Colorado Lawyer* 57–62.

58 See Reed, C, 'What is a Signature' (2000) 3 *Journal of Information, Law and Technology.*

59 McCullagh, A *et al.*, 'Signature Stripping: A Digital Dilemma' (2001) 1 *Journal of Information, Law and Technology.*

60 See generally Deturbide, M, 'Liability of Internet Service Providers for Defamation in the US and Britain: Same Competing Interest, Different Responses' (2000) 3 *Journal of Information, Law and Technology.*

61 For a more detailed discussion on the legal scope of online contracts, see Ahmadu, ML, 'E-Procurement as Development Imperative for Small Island States in the South Pacific' (2004) 10 *James Cook University Law Review* 51–70.

The need to develop a clear online dispute resolution mechanism for e-businesses also needs to be looked into.[62] The question of the proper e-forum and choice of law will continue to pose additional legal dilemmas for e-commerce.[63] For small island countries, the impact of these issues on the development of their e-commerce structures is fundamental, taking into account their limited technical and financial limitations. As has already been pointed out, a cooperative regional approach provides a better way of dealing with these issues.

30.4.5 Taxation of e-businesses

The internet has no physical territory in the conventional geographical sense.[64] To that extent, the physical determinants for apportioning tax incidence, such as the residence rule, are hardly a satisfactory sign-post for levying tax.[65] The problem is further compounded when e-commerce is carried out through several servers located in different locations around the globe.[66] It is difficult to see how the conventional tax principle governing withholding tax or tax credit may satisfactorily apply.[67] Given the rather amorphous nature of the internet, it remains to be seen how national tax authorities will deal with the incomes of non-resident internet-based trading entities. The challenge will be to develop a tax system that is not only relevant[68] but is also appropriate to the conduct of e-transactions, even if the present tax regime is to be modified to address new and emerging issues.[69] The need for a satisfactory resolution of these issues cannot be overemphasised in the case of small countries in the region, whose conventional tax base is likely to be eroded by the improper regulation of e-commerce.

62 See Wahab, M, 'Globalisation and ODR: Dynamics of Change in E-Commerce Dispute Settlement' (2004) 12 *International Journal of Law and IT* 123.
63 See generally Wolpert, I, 'Overcoming Presumptive Validity of Forum-Selection Clause' (2004) 37 Oct *Maryland Bar Journal* 55–58.
64 See Morgan, M, 'The Department of Revenue Perspective' (2004) 88 *Marquette Law Review* 11–16.
65 See generally Thorpe, K, 'International Taxation of Electronic Commerce: Is the Concept of Permanent Establishment Obsolete?' (1997) 11 *Emory International Law Review* 633–77; and Basu, S, 'To Tax or Not to Tax? That is the Question? Overview of Options in Consumption Taxation in E-Commerce' (2004) 1 *Journal of Information, Technology and Law*.
66 Cockfield, AJ, 'Jurisdiction to Tax: A Law and Technology Perspective' (2003) 38 *Georgia Law Review* 85–109.
67 See generally Picciotto, S, *International Business Taxation: A study in the Internationalization of Business Regulation* (1992).
68 Cf Cockfield, AJ, 'Balancing National Interests in the Taxation of Electronic Commerce Business Profits' (1999) 74 *Tulane Law Review* 133–207.
69 Cf Sawyer, A, 'Electronic Commerce: International Policy Implications for Revenue Authorities and Governments' (1999) 19 *Virginia Tax Review* 73–102.

30.5 Challenges to e-commerce

It is not totally out of place to say that unless proactive measures are taken by both the public and private sectors in Pacific island countries, the sub-region will be hindered in its development efforts by a technological deficit. A number of issues will be examined as ways of overcoming these challenges.

30.5.1 Technical infrastructure

The combination of the high cost of telecommunication services, limited band-width and structural inaccessibility in rural settings[70] is by far one of the greatest challenges to e-commerce in the region. According to Verzola, internet technol-ogy is good, but accessibility is at a considerable cost and is restricted to a small percentage of people, especially in developing countries.[71] There is an absence of a coherent government policy on information and communication technology (ICT) to address these problems. This limitation has a flow-on effect on the capacity of the private sector to effectively utilise e-commerce as a means of venturing into the international product and service markets.

The absence of a regional facility to certify digital signatures to validate online transactions is a major institutional drawback. Their comparatively smaller sizes, remoteness, limited financial resources and paucity of highly skilled technical manpower have also exacerbated this problem.

A possible way out is the adoption of a regional and collective approach to the provision of communication facilities, technical expertise, cooperative exchange of information and the establishment of jointly owned and administered facil-ities such as certification authorities. This may even include the adoption of a region-wide standard relating to encryption technology. Whilst to larger and more developed economies these issues may seem easy to handle, the peculiarities of small island countries mean that only a collective approach is feasible in both the medium and long term.

Pacific island countries have the potential to greatly benefit from upgrading their present commodity-based trading systems to knowledge-based economies. One of the starting points is the effective use of intellectual property rights to protect and market their products and the subsequent digitisation and sale of these rights. Their strengths lie in the vast reserves of marine, fisheries and plant varie-ties within their territories. This issue will be considered later.

---

70 See Toland, J and Purcell, F, 'Information and Communication Technology in the South Pacific: Shrinking the Barriers of Distance' December 2002, *Development Bulletin* 92.
71 Versola, R, 'The Internet: Towards a Deeper Critique', www.inomy.com, visited on 7 June 2002.

30.5.2 E-government structure

The prevailing reality in the region suggests that for e-commerce to galvanise the private sector, strong and interventionist e-government policies are also needed.[72] This will supplement the private sector-led development of e-commerce. At present, e-government structures are limited to portals hosting basic information on the functions of state organs.[73] Except in very limited instances in Vanuatu for example, there are as yet no integrated online systems for filing of transactions, lodgement of forms or processing of permits in most of the region. The opportunities offered by the internet need to be fully tapped by the public sector in the region. According to Toland and Purcell:

> South Pacific governments can use the Internet to assist with public sector operations. For example, ICT can provide governments with an increased capacity to collect revenue from fishing, agriculture and tourism. An intranet can allow different government departments to share information without having to make it available to the general public.[74]

The benefit of improved revenue collection and widely accessible public sector information will ensure transparency, minimise corruption and enhance the operations of government structures.[75] The net result will be a minimisation of bureaucratic red tape. However, the question of confidentiality and privacy of information derived from private sources, resulting from people's interaction with the government will have to be addressed. Privacy and access to public information laws have to be passed in several countries in the region.

30.5.3 Endowments and intellectual property rights

Operating in a knowledge-based global economy will be one of the promising possibilities for opening up the marine and plant resource potentials of Pacific island countries. To do this, however, a clear articulation of how the present intellectual property regime will benefit communally owned rights is necessary.[76] The

---

72 See generally *E-Government Handbook for Developing Countries* (2002) InfoDev-World Bank and Centre for Democracy and Technology (November 2002).
73 Cf *Internet Infrastructure and e-Government in Pacific Island Countries: A Survey on the Development and Use of the Internet*, UNESCO (March 2002).
74 See Toland, J and Purcell, F, 'Information and Communication Technology in the South Pacific: Shrinking the Barriers of Distance', December 2002 *Development Bulletin* 91.
75 Cf Saidi, N *et al.*, 'e-government: Technology for Good Governance, Development and Democracy in the MENA Countries', www.ictdar.org, visited on 8 December 2002.
76 Cf Shim, Y-G, 'Intellectual Property Protection of Biotechnology and Sustainable Development in International Law' (2003) 29 *North Carolina Journal of International Law and Commercial Regulation* 157–225.

conventional system for the protection of intellectual property is mainly geared towards private property rights, which in most cases is unsuited to the specific requirements of customary-based societies.

By way of example, the basic aim of the TRIPS Agreement is to protect private intellectual property rights embodied in products sold within member countries. This protection is afforded in respect of copyright, patent or trade mark. The idea behind such a protection system is to ensure that trade in technology-based products is not unnecessarily hindered through the production and sale of counterfeit goods or the provision of low-grade services.[77]

Whilst in general many aspects of property rights in small island countries can be protected through this system, it is also becoming clear that community-based rights over marine resources, folklore, songs, dances and other culturally driven performances will not.[78] The diverse marine, fisheries and plant life in these countries needs to be exploited in a sustainable way[79] and utilised for the benefit of the local communities, the expansion of global trade and the enhancement of indigenous industrial capacity to participate in and enlarge international trade.[80] Certainly, this will require all the stakeholders to address two issues: evolving a suitable way of marketing the intellectual property attributes of these commodities as digitised products;[81] and instituting an appropriate protection standard for safeguarding the rights of indigenous resource owners, where this is collectively owned.[82]

The abundance of untapped varieties of fisheries,[83] marine and plant life provides promising areas of investment, research and development in pharmacology and biogenetic engineering.[84] It is a fact today that there are in the region gene patents held by bioengineering transnational corporations over the blood group

---

77 See generally Ahmadu, ML, *External Trade and Investment Law in the South Pacific* (2000) Ch 3.

78 Cf Segal, G, 'Computer Databases: Domestic Protection and International Trade' (1998) 13 *Intellectual Property Law Journal* 305–35.

79 See e.g., Chang, H, 'Toward a Greener GATT: Environmental Trade Measures and Shrimp-Turtle Case' (2000) 74 *Southern California Law Review* 31–45; and cf Syme-Buchanan, F, 'Black Days for Pearl Farming' *Pacific Islands Monthly* (October 1998) 12.

80 Bluemel, EB, 'Substance without Process: Analyzing TRIPS Participatory Guarantees in Light of Protected Indigenous Rights' (2004) 86 *Journal of Patent and Trademark Office Society* 671–709.

81 Cf Vaver, D, 'Recreating a Fair Intellectual Property System for the 21st Century' 15 *Intellectual Property Law Journal* 123–41.

82 See generally, 'Panel II: The Law and Policy of Protecting Folklore, Traditional Knowledge, and Genetic Resources' (2002) 12 *Fordham Intellectual Property, Media and Entertainment Law Journal* 753–88; and Carpenter, M, 'Intellectual Property Law and Indigenous Peoples: Adapting Copyright Law to the Needs of a Global Community' (2004) 7 *Yale Human Rights and Development Law Journal* 51–76.

83 See generally 'Fortunes to be Made in the Deep Sea', *Pacific Islands Monthly* (October 1986).

84 See Rohini Acharya, 'Patenting of Biotechnology-GATT and the Erosion of the World's Biodiversity' (1991) 25(6) *Journal of World Trade Law* 71; Marin, PLC, *Providing Protection for Plant Genetic Resources* (2002); and cf Tutangata, T, 'Genetic Engineering: The Right to Say No' May 1999, *Islands Business* 42.

of indigenous people. Recently, clinical tests have revealed the potential curative powers of a plant variety to cure AIDS. Exotic strands of coral, reef and aquatic life keep finding their way to markets in Europe and the United States. These developments present commercial prospects which should delight island countries. One of the most far-reaching and low-cost mechanisms for marketing these products will be the internet. Furthermore, being one of the geographical locations of the world that has the highest density of languages per population,[85] their rich traditional folklore, songs, dances and even custom ceremonies[86] can support a viable online entertainment industry.

Lastly, the introduction of new and even the most efficient technology is not without costs. Digital technology is not an exception. However, for small island countries, the internet holds great potential for their economic advancement. The challenge will be to inaugurate a techno-legal framework that is not only appropriate to their needs and circumstances but is also cost-effective and easy to administer. This will require a coherent public-private sector partnership. It is neither to be left solely to the rigidity of public policy or to the unguarded and exploitative nature of market forces.

There exist opportunities for online transactions in respect of both conventional commodities as well as digitised products in the region. The internet will provide a window for the region's resources to global investments and markets. The initial transition might be arduous, but the long-term benefits of having a properly structured and deregulated digitised economy operating in conjunction with the commodity-based system, will by far outweigh the disadvantages.

---

85 Motluk, A, 'You Are What You Speak', New Scientist (Nov 30, 2002) 34–38 – with Asia having 33 % of all world's languages. This is followed by Africa having 30% and with the Pacific in third place, having 1,302 (19%).

86 See Rasmussen, TR, 'Leap of Faith', *Pacific Islands Monthly*, (July 1991) 29. A traditional land-diving ceremony has been practised from time immemorial on the island of Pentecost in Vanuatu. Whilst this has not been protected by intellectual property, the recently introduced bungy jumping has.

INDEX

Printed and bound by CPI Group (UK) Ltd, Croydon, CR0 4YY

05/09/2024

01032209-0016